# Domestic Violence and Child Abuse
## SOURCEBOOK

## Health Reference Series

### *First Edition*

# Domestic Violence and Child Abuse
## SOURCEBOOK

*Basic Consumer Health Information about Spousal/Partner, Child, Sibling, Parent, and Elder Abuse, Covering Physical, Emotional, and Sexual Abuse, Teen Dating Violence, and Stalking; Includes Information about Hotlines, Safe Houses, Safety Plans, and Other Resources for Support and Assistance, Community Initiatives, and Reports on Current Directions in Research and Treatment*

*Along with a Glossary, Sources for Further Reading, and Governmental and Non-Governmental Organizations Contact Information*

### *Edited by*
### *Helene Henderson*

## Omnigraphics

615 Griswold Street • Detroit, MI 48226

# BIBLIOGRAPHIC NOTE

Because this page cannot legibly accommodate all the copyright notices, the Bibliographic Note portion of the Preface constitutes an extension of the copyright notice.

## Edited by Helene Henderson

Joan Margeson, Barry Puckett, Jenifer Swanson, *Research Associates*
Dawn Matthews, *Verification Assistant*
Margaret Mary Missar, *Research Coordinator*

## Omnigraphics, Inc.

Matthew P. Barbour, *Vice President, Operations*
Laurie Lanzen Harris, *Vice President, Editorial Director*
Kevin Hayes, *Production Coordinator*
Thomas J. Murphy, *Vice President, Finance and Comptroller*
Peter E. Ruffner, *Senior Vice President*
Jane J. Steele, *Marketing Coordinator*

Frederick G. Ruffner, Jr., *Publisher*
Copyright © 2000 Omnigraphics, Inc.

**Library of Congress Cataloging-in-Publication Data**

Domestic violence & child abuse sourcebook: basic consumer health information about spousal/partner, child, sibling, parent, and elder abuse, covering physical, emotional, and sexual abuse, teen dating violence, and stalking; includes information about hotlines, safe houses, safety plans, and other resources for support and assistance, community initiatives, and reports on current directions in research and treatment: along with a glossary, sources for further reading, and governmental and non-governmental organizations contact information/ edited by Helene Henderson.— 1st ed.

   p. cm. — (Health reference series)
Includes bibliographical references and index.
ISBN 0-7808-0235-7 (lib. binding: alk. paper)
1. Family violence—United States. 2. Child abuse—United States. 3. Family violence—United States—Prevention. I. Title: Domestic violence and child abuse sourcebook. II. Henderson, Helene, 1963– III. Series.

HV6626.2 .D66 2000
362.82'927'0973—dc21

00-058436

∞

This book is printed on acid-free paper meeting the ANSI Z39.48 Standard. The infinity symbol that appears above indicates that the paper in this book meets that standard.

Printed in the United States

# Contents

## Part III—Child Abuse

## Part IV—Sibling Abuse and Parent Abuse

## Part V—Elder Abuse

## Part VI—Prevention and Treatment Strategies for Individuals, Communities, and Government

## Part VII—Research

## Part VIII—Additional Help and Information

# *Preface*

## *About This Book*

Domestic violence, including partner violence, child abuse, elder abuse, and sibling and parent abuse, affects millions of Americans each year. According to Richard J. Gelles of the University of Rhode Island Family Violence Research Program and co-author of three national surveys of the incidence of domestic violence, two million women are beaten by their husbands each year. He speculates that the number could be as high as four million if ex-husbands and boyfriends were counted. This number doesn't include emotional abuse or lesser physical violence, such as pushing or slapping. According to the FBI, approximately 1,500 women are killed each year by husbands or boyfriends. State child protective services report about three million children were abused in 1996, representing reported cases only. Very little research has been done on sibling abuse, but its foremost expert, Vernon Wiehe, professor of social work at the University of Kentucky, speculates that it occurs more frequently than partner violence and child abuse. Gelles reports that various surveys on adolescent to parent violence show it occurs at a rate between 5% and 12%. In 1998 the National Elder Abuse Incidence Study, conducted by the National Center on Elder Abuse, found that approximately 551,000 elders suffered in 1996 from abuse or from self-neglect. Rosemary Chalk, study director of the National Research Council Committee on the Assessment of Family Violence Interventions, and Patricia A. King, professor of law, medicine, ethics, and public policy at the Georgetown University Law Center, in their article reproduced in Chapter 27, point out that "family violence also contributes to the development of other social problems such as alcoholism, drug abuse, delinquency, crime, teenage pregnancy, and homelessness." This *Sourcebook* was designed to help people in abusive relationships and those who care about them to identify the different forms of domestic violence and provide suggestions for staying safe and finding help.

The *Domestic Violence and Child Abuse Sourcebook* is unique to the *Health Reference Series* in that it is caused not by bacteria or viruses or other elements that fall within the realm of physical medicine, but by human beings. This fact has a critical impact on the level of scientific knowledge about domestic violence at this time. Psychology is notoriously less exact than other health-related sciences. When the perpetrators are human beings, rather than microscopic ones, and the causes of those human behaviors necessarily deviate from absolutes into shades of gray, educated and well-meaning people expert in various fields disagree about why some people behave violently toward others. Like diseases and physiological conditions covered in other *Health Reference Series* volumes, however, domestic violence results in the death of some of its victims, physical damage in many more, and emotional suffering in just about everyone it touches.

Professionals in many fields—psychology and psychiatry, social work, sociology, and criminology as well as medicine—devote themselves to understanding interpersonal violence and finding ways to prevent it and treat both its survivors and perpetrators. However, as Rosemary Chalk and Patricia A. King write, "the state of research knowledge about family violence and the effectiveness of interventions is not well developed" and "serious gaps in our understanding of the origins and causes of family violence still exist." "Critical tools," they observe, "that provide the foundation of solid evaluation studies in other fields—strong theory, large longitudinal and follow-up studies, reliable measures, and consistent definitions and diagnostic criteria—are only beginning to develop in the field of family violence studies." Coupled with the fact that the field of inquiry has been open to so many approaches, it is not surprising that controversies abound. Prominent among these are the heated debates between those who locate the origins of domestic violence in Western society's traditionally patriarchal organization and those who search the complexities and pathologies of the individual personality and family systems. This book attempts to present some competing viewpoints to survey the field, but its primary mission is to provide the most helpful possible information for people affected by family violence.

## How to Use This Book

This book is divided into parts, chapters, and sections. Parts focus on broad areas of interest. Chapters are devoted to single topics within a part. Sections cover various aspects of a particular topic.

*Part I: Historical Background and Social and Political Dimensions of Domestic Violence* presents a historical overview of domestic violence in its various forms and also introduces social and political controversies surrounding it.

*Part II: Spousal and Partner Abuse* covers issues related to spousal and partner violence, including issues relevant to immigrant and refugee women, disabled women, gay men, lesbian women, and women in rural areas. It also covers stalking, teen dating violence, and the relationship of domestic violence to alcohol and drug abuse, poverty, and HIV/AIDS. It also contains information on strategies for staying safe and helpful information about dealing with the justice system.

*Part III: Child Abuse* presents information on all forms of child abuse, including physical, emotional, and sexual abuse and shaken baby syndrome. It also contains articles on the relationship between child abuse and spousal/partner abuse, the repressed memory controversy, and prevention and treatment efforts.

*Part IV: Sibling Abuse and Parent Abuse* describes these less well-known forms of domestic violence, their aftereffects, intervention, and treatment.

*Part V: Elder Abuse* explains the forms of elder abuse and discusses prevention and treatment strategies.

*Part VI. Prevention and Treatment Initiatives for Individuals, Communities, and Government* presents steps individuals and society can take to help end domestic violence, as well as justice system initiatives and legislative action.

*Part VIII: Research* offers some of the most current research efforts to understand, prevent and treat spousal/partner violence and child abuse, to measure the economic costs of domestic violence, and to reduce family and other violence in American society.

*Part IX: Additional Help and Information* provides a glossary of important terms and a listing of spousal/partner abuse, child abuse, and elder abuse hotlines, as well as government agencies, national, state, and local organizations devoted to spousal/partner, child, and elder abuse. This section closes with a bibliography for further reading.

## Bibliographic Note

This volume contains documents and excerpts from publications issued by the following government agencies: Administration of Aging, U.S. Department of Health and Human Services; National Center for Injury Prevention and Control, Centers for Disease Control and Prevention; National Clearinghouse for Alcohol and Drug Information, U.S. Department of Health and Human Services; National Clearinghouse on Child Abuse and Neglect, U.S. Department of Health and Human Services; National Institute of Justice, U.S. Department of Justice; Office of Justice Programs, U.S. Department of Justice; Office for Victims of Crime, U.S. Department of Justice; Social Security Administration; U.S. Department of Health and Human Services; U.S. Department of Justice; Violence Against Women Office, U.S. Department of Justice; U.S. General Accounting Office.

In addition, this volume contains copyrighted articles from the following organizations: American Bar Association Commission on Domestic Violence; American Federation of State, County, and Municipal Employees (AFSCME); American Humane Association, Children's Division; American Psychological Association; Beach Center on Families and Disabilities, University of Kansas, Lawrence; Brazos County Rape Crisis Center, Bryan, Tex.; Bureau for At-Risk Youth; Center on Crime, Communities & Culture, Open Society Institute; Domestic Abuse Intervention Project, Duluth, Minn.; Domestic Violence Project, Inc./SAFE House, Ann Arbor, Mich.; Family Violence Prevention Fund; Institute for Women's Policy Research; Mid-Valley Women's Crisis Center, Salem, Ore.; Minnesota Coalition for Battered Women; National Center on Elder Abuse; National Center for Missing & Exploited Children; National Center for Victims of Crime; National Center on Women and Family Law; National Coalition for the Homeless; Na-

xvi

tional Coalition of Anti-Violence Programs; National Domestic Violence Hotline; National Network to End Domestic Violence Fund; National Network for Child Care; National Organization of Women Legal Defense and Education Fund; National Resource Center on Domestic Violence; New York City Gay and Lesbian Anti-Violence Project; Northwest Network of Bisexual, Trans & Lesbian Survivors of Abuse, Seattle, Wash.; Pennsylvania Coalition Against Domestic Violence, Harrisburg; Prevent Child Abuse America (formerly National Committee to Prevent Child Abuse); Privacy Rights Clearinghouse; Spokane County Domestic Violence Consortium, Spokane, Wash.; Support Network for Battered Women, Mountain View, Calif.; Texas Council on Family Violence, Austin; VAWnet Resources (The National Electronic Network on Violence Against Women), a project of the National Resource Center on Domestic Violence. Copyrighted articles from the following publications are reprinted with permission: *Issue Note* (Welfare Information Network), *Issues in Science and Technology* (University of Texas at Dallas), *Mother Jones* magazine (Foundation for National Progress), *The Women's Quarterly* (Independent Women's Forum). Selections from the following books are reprinted with permission: Barnett, Ola W., Cindy L. Miller-Perrin, and Robin D. Perrin. "The Repressed Memory Controversy," pp. 97-98, and excerpts from "Marital Violence: Batterers," pp. 237-38, 238-45, 246-49. In their *Family Violence Across the Lifespan: An Introduction*. Thousand Oaks, Calif.: Sage Publications, 1997; Bergen, Raquel Kennedy. "Violence in Gay and Lesbian Relationships," pp. 114-16. In her *Issues in Intimate Violence*. Thousand Oaks, Calif.: Sage Publications, 1998; Center on Crime, Communities & Culture. Excerpts from "Health Care" (http://www.soros.org/crime/DVDir-Health.html) and "Social Services" (http://www.soros.org/crime/DVDir-Soc.htm). *Domestic Violence: National Directory of Professional Services*. New York: Open Society Institute, 1999; Gelles, Richard J. "Violence between Intimates: Historical Legacy—Contemporary Approval," pp. 19-38, excerpt from "Prevention and Treatment: Society's Response and Responsibility," pp. 165-67, and excerpt from "Hidden Victims: Siblings, Adolescents, Parents, Elders, and Gay and Lesbian Couples," pp. 108-13. In his *Intimate Violence in Families*. Third edition. Thousand Oaks, Calif.: Sage Publications, 1997; Wiehe, Vernon R. "Sibling Abuse," pp. 167-218. In his *Understanding Family Violence: Treating and Preventing Partner, Child, Sibling, and Elder Abuse*. Thousand Oaks, Calif.: Sage Publications, 1998.

Full citation information is provided on the first page of each chapter or section. Every effort has been made to secure all necessary rights to reprint the copyrighted material. If any omissions have been made, please contact Omnigraphics to make corrections for future editions.

## Acknowledgments

In addition to the organizations listed above, special thanks must go to the following people who went out of their way to provide up-to-date material, answer questions, and/or ease the permissions process: Robyn Alsop, American Humane Association; Karen Zentner Bacig, Minnesota Center Against Violence and Abuse; Danica Bornstein, Northwest Network of Bisexual, Trans & Lesbian Survivors of Abuse; Sandi McLeod, National Clearinghouse on Child Abuse & Neglect Information; Lara Murray, National Center for Victims of Crime; Anna Rockett, Institute for Women's Policy Research; Samantha Snell, National Resource Center on Domestic Violence; and Grace Terzian, *The Women's Quarterly*. I am also indebted to Joan Margeson, Margaret Mary Missar, Barry Puckett, and Jenifer Swanson for their extraordinary research assistance, permissions specialist Maria Franklin for her expertise, Dawn Matthews for speedy fact-checking, and Dan Harris for somehow not only keeping afloat in the flood of material I sent his way, but superbly typesetting it as well.

During the process of compiling this book, my family was suddenly added to the long list of families who have suffered the tragic effects of domestic violence. The pain and the memories never do go away completely, but strengths can arise to assuage them, from reaching out and supporting each other to discovering the motivation to serve in shelters and related programs to help others.

This book is dedicated to the memory of Mary G. Hill (1941-1999).

## Note from the Editor

This book is part of Omnigraphics' *Health Reference Series*. The *Series* provides basic information about a broad range of medical concerns. It is not intended to serve as a tool for diagnosing illness, in prescribing treatments, or as a substitute for the physician-patient or psychologist-patient relationship. All persons concerned about medical symptoms or the possibility of disease are encouraged to seek professional care from an appropriate health care provider.

## Our Advisory Board

The *Health Reference Series* is reviewed by an Advisory Board comprised of librarians from public, academic, and medical libraries. We would like to thank the following board members for providing guidance to the development of the series:

## Health Reference Series Update Policy

The inaugural book in the *Health Reference Series* was the first edition of *Cancer Sourcebook* published in 1992. Since then, the *Series* has been enthusiastically received by librarians and in the medical community. In order to maintain the standard of providing high-quality health information for the lay person, the editorial staff at Omnigraphics felt it was necessary to implement a policy of updating volumes when warranted.

Medical researchers have been making tremendous strides, and the challenge to stay current with the most recent advances is one our editors take seriously. Each decision to update a volume will be made on an individual basis. Some of the considerations will include how much new information is available and the feedback we receive from people who use the books. If there's a topic you would like to see added to the update list, or an area of medical concern you feel has not been adequately addressed, please write to:

Editor, *Health Reference Series*
Omnigraphics, Inc.
615 Griswold
Detroit, MI 48226

The commitment to providing on-going coverage of important medical developments has also led to some technical changes in the Health Reference Series. Beginning with books published in 1999, each new volume will be individually titled and called a "First Edition." Subsequent updates will carry sequential edition numbers. To help avoid confusion and to provide maximum flexibility in our ability to respond to informational needs, the practice of consecutively numbering each volume has been discontinued.

# Part One

# Historical Background and Social and Political Dimensions of Domestic Violence

# Chapter 1

# Violence Between Intimates

## Historical Legacy—Contemporary Approval

*Richard J. Gelles*

Violence between intimates is not new. The Bible begins with sibling violence—Cain killing Abel (Gen. 4:8). Similarly, there are other biblical descriptions of family violence. Genesis also describes God's commandment that Abraham sacrifice his son Isaac. Later, in the New Testament, Jesus was presumably saved from Herod's "slaughter of the innocents."

If family and intimate violence is not new, perhaps it is more common today than decades or centuries earlier. Many social commentators and some social scientists, noting the apparent increase in reports of family violence and abuse, propose that rising rates of family violence are yet another sign of the disintegration of both the modern family and society in general.

The question of whether we are more violent now than during previous times in history is difficult to answer. The selective inattention to the problem of intimate violence meant that official records of family violence were not kept until the past three decades. Similarly, until the past few decades, researchers were reluctant to conduct surveys and ask questions about violence or abuse. Until the 1980s, there had been no research conducted that attempted to measure the changing rates of violence toward children or between spouses.

The first section of this chapter examines the historical legacy of family violence. Modern Americans are neither the first to use violence on loved ones nor are we the only society in the world to be violent toward those we love. The next section explores the social transformation of violence and traces the evolution of the issue of family violence from selective inattention, when nearly all that was written on violence in the home appeared on the front page of the *National Enquirer*, to the present, when violence between intimates is discussed and analyzed on television and radio talk shows, on television dramas, in national magazines, in legislative bodies, and by presidential task forces. The chapter concludes with a discussion of contemporary attitudes about intimate violence.

## The Historical Legacy of Family and Intimate Violence

We take for granted that today's children have the right to live and grow to achieve their full developmental potential. Women have fought for centuries for equal rights with men. We have begun to take for granted that women have a right to equal treatment. What we take for granted has not always been the case, and the history of the subordination of women and children is closely connected to the history and causes of violence and abuse in the family.

### Infanticide and the Abuse of Children

The history of Western society is one in which children have been subjected to unspeakable cruelties. The historian Samuel Radbill (1987) reports that in ancient times, infants had no rights until the right to live was ritually bestowed on them by their fathers. If the right to live was withheld by fathers, infants were abandoned or left to die. Although we do not know how often children were killed or abandoned, we do know that infanticide was widely accepted among ancient and prehistoric cultures. Infants could be put to death because they cried too much, because they were sickly or deformed, or because they had some perceived imperfection. Girls, twins, and the children of unmarried women were the special targets of infanticide (Robin, 1982).

Many societies also subjected their offspring to rituals or survival tests. Some North American Indians threw their newborns into pools of water and rescued them only if they rose to the surface and cried. The Greeks exposed their children to the natural elements as a survival test.

Lloyd DeMause (1974) has examined the history of childhood and graphically explains that by 1526 the latrines of Rome were said to "resound with the cries of children who had been plunged into them" (p. 29). Infanticide continued through the 18th and 19th centuries. Illegitimate children continue to run the greatest risk of infanticide even today. A few years ago, an old steamer trunk was opened in a mill town in southern New Hampshire. Inside the trunk were a number of small skeletons, alleged to have been illegitimate children killed at birth.

Killing children was not the only form of abuse inflicted by generations of parents. From prehistoric times right through colonial America, children were mutilated, beaten, and maltreated. Such treatment was not only condoned, it was often mandated as the most appropriate child-rearing method (Greven, 1990; Miller, 1983; Straus, 1994). Children were hit with rods, canes, and switches. Boys have been castrated to produce eunuchs. Our forefathers in colonial America were implored to "beat the devil" out of their children (Greven, 1990; Straus, 1994). Stubborn-child laws were passed that permitted parents to put to death unruly children, although it is not clear whether children were actually ever killed.

## Women: The "Appropriate" Victims

The subordinate status of women in America and in most of the world's societies is well documented. Because physical force and violence are the ultimate resources that can be used to keep subordinate groups in their place, the history of women throughout the world has been one in which women have been victims of physical assault.

The sociologists Rebecca Dobash and Russell Dobash (1979) explain that to understand wife beating in contemporary society, one must understand and recognize the century-old legacy of women as the "appropriate" victims of family violence.

Roman husbands and fathers not only had control over their children but over their wives as well. A Roman husband could chastise, divorce, or kill his wife. Not only that, but the behaviors for which these punishments were appropriate—adultery, public drunkenness, and attending public games—were the very same behaviors that Roman men engaged in daily (Dobash & Dobash, 1979)!

As with children, women's victimization goes as far back as biblical times. Eve is blamed for eating the forbidden fruit. For Eve's transgression, the Bible tells us that all women are to be punished by having to bear children. The very same passage in Genesis that multiplies women's sorrow and calls for them to bear children also sanctions the husband's rule over women (Gen. 3:16).

Although legend has it that Blackstone's codification of English common law in 1768 asserted that a husband had the right to "physically chastise" an errant wife provided that the stick was no thicker than his thumb—and thus the "rule of thumb" was born—such a passage cannot be found in Blackstone (Sommers, 1994). Actually, there have been laws prohibiting wife beating in the United States since the time of the Revolution (Pleck, 1987). However, although the laws existed, they were often indifferently enforced. Furthermore, although the laws outlawed assault and battery and prescribed punishments such as fines and whippings as punishment, courts often allowed a certain amount of chastisement or correction of so-called errant wives "within legal bounds." In 1824, a Mississippi court allowed corporal punishment of wives by husbands. The right to chastise wives was finally overturned by courts in Alabama and Massachusetts in 1871.

## *Intimate Violence Around the World*

Not only does conventional wisdom err when it argues that family violence is a modern phenomenon, it also errs when it asserts that private violence is unique to American families or, if not unique, that the problem is greater in the United States than in other societies.

The anthropologist David Levinson (1981) has examined the records of the Human Relations Area Files at Yale University. These records contain descriptive and statistical information on a wide range of societies over time and around the world. Levinson reports that wife beating is the most common and frequent form of family violence, thus confirming the theory that woman are generally considered the most appropriate victims of intimate violence (see Table 1).

Gathering information on family violence in other societies has been difficult. Only the United States, Canada, and Australia have specific legislation that requires the reporting of child abuse and neglect; thus, there are no official report data on child or spouse abuse available in other nations. There are, however, an increasing number of local, regional, or national surveys conducted on family violence in other countries.

## *Table 1. Relationship Between Physical Punishment and Wife Beating*

| Wife Beating | Physical Punishment | | | |
| --- | --- | --- | --- | --- |
| | **Rare** | **Infrequent** | **Frequent** | **Common** |
| Rare | Andamans<br>Copper<br>  Eskimo<br>Ifuago<br>Iroquois<br>Ona<br>Thailand | Rural Irish<br>Hopi<br><br>Trobrianders | | |
| Infrequent | Kanuri<br>Lapps<br>Lau<br>Mataco<br>Tucano | Klamath<br>Masai<br>Ojibwa<br>Pygmies<br>Santal<br>Taiwan<br>Tikopia<br>Tzeltal | Ashanti<br>Cagaba<br>Garo<br>Pawnee<br>Wolof | |
| Frequent | Bororo<br>Iban<br>Tarahumara | Kapauku<br>Korea<br>Kurd<br>Toradja | Azande<br>Dogon<br>Somali | Amhara |
| Common | Chuckchee<br>Tlingit<br>Yanoama | Aymara<br>Hausa | Ganda<br>Truk | Serbs |

Source: Levinson (1981); reprinted with permission from *Child Abuse & Neglect*, 5(2), David Levinson, "Physical Punishment of Children and Wifebeating in Cross-Cultural Perspective." Copyright © 1981, Pergamon Press, Ltd.

7

In 1993, Statistics Canada conducted the first national survey of violence against women in Canada. A telephone survey was conducted with a nationally representative sample of 12,300 women age 18 or older. Of the currently or previously married women, 3 in 10 reported experiencing at least one incident of physical or sexual violence at the hands of a marital partner. Three percent of the women were assaulted by a partner in the year prior to the survey (Rodgers, 1994).

Two national surveys on violence toward women were conducted in New Zealand in 1994. The first study was a survey of a nationally representative sample of 2,000 men, and the second was a follow-up survey of 200 of the 2,000 men. Twenty-one percent of the men surveyed reported committing one act of physical violence against a partner in the previous year, and 53% reported committing an act of emotional abuse. Thirty-five percent of the men reported ever using an act of physical violence, and 62% reported ever using emotional abuse toward a partner (Leibrich, Paulin, & Ransom, 1995).

In addition to these two national surveys, there are other studies that examine the incidence and prevalence of violence against women around the world (United Nations, 1994). The World Bank Discussion Papers, *Violence Against Women: The Hidden Health Burden* (Heise, 1994), describe numerous studies of violence against women. A 1993 study in Chile found that 60% of Chilean women involved in a relationship for 2 or more years had been abused by their male partners (Larrain, 1993). A 1992 study in Ecuador reported that 60% of low-income women had been beaten by a partner. In Japan, 59% of the 769 women surveyed said they were physically abused by a partner (Domestic Violence Research Group, 1993). A Korean study found 38% of Korean women had been battered by a spouse in the past year (Kim & Cho, 1992). Of course, these studies are not really comparable because of varying definitions of violence, abuse, battering, and beating, various survey methodologies, and differing methods of measuring violence. However, collectively the research certainly points out the existence of violence against women in many and varied cultures and societies.

Other research and anecdotal accounts uncover some unique types of violence against women. India, for example, has a problem of dowry-related violence, whereby husbands attack or often burn their wives as a means of extorting more dowry from their wives' families (Prasad, 1994).

There are fewer national surveys of child abuse or child maltreatment. This is because of the great difficulty that occurs when researchers attempt to develop a cross-cultural definition of child maltreatment (Finkelhor & Korbin, 1988; Gelles & Cornell, 1983; Korbin, 1981). Korbin (1981) points out that because there is no universal standard for optimal child rearing, there can be no universal standard for what constitutes child abuse and neglect. Finkelhor and Korbin (1988) explain that a definition of child abuse that could be used internationally should accomplish at least two objectives: (a) It should distinguish child abuse clearly from other social, economic, and health problems of international concern; and (b) it should be sufficiently flexible to apply to a range of situations in a variety of social and cultural contexts. They note that some of what is talked about as child abuse in Western societies has very little meaning in other societies. Finkelhor and Korbin (1988) propose the following definition of child abuse for cross-cultural research: "Child abuse is the portion of harm to children that results from human action that is proscribed (negatively valued), proximate (the action is close to the actual harm—thus, deforesting land that results in child malnutrition does not fit this definition), and preventable (the action could have been avoided)" (p. 4). However, because such a definition has not yet been adopted by researchers or put to use in cross-national studies of the extent and patterns of child maltreatment, we have few true cross-cultural studies of child abuse and neglect and must rely on more anecdotal information.

The People's Republic of China has been frequently described as a society with little or no child or wife abuse. However, case examples of severe child abuse in China made their way into the American press in recent years. In the closing months of 1992, three Chinese children were killed by their parents, and their deaths caused an unusual public discussion in China about a problem barely acknowledged in China before ("3 Deaths Trigger Debate," 1992, p. C-3). Although many observers in China viewed these deaths as barbaric, there is the lingering Confucian notion that children must be absolutely obedient to their parents. This, combined with the single-child policy in China and parents' high ambitions placed on the one child, has raised concern about possible increases in the problem of physical abuse.

Similarly, Israel is a country where it is thought there is little physical abuse of children. Hanita Zimrin (personal communication, September 17, 1991) notes that considerable attention was paid to physical abuse in Israel after a child was beaten to death by a parent on a kibbutz. Zimrin explains, with some irony, that such a case challenged the notion of the "perfect society" and the "perfect child-rearing setting"—the kibbutz.

Scandinavian countries are also described as having few problems with child abuse. This is generally thought to be due to social conditions being good, the widespread use of contraceptives limiting the number of unwanted children, free abortions, and the fact that working mothers can leave their children at day care institutions (Vesterdal, 1977)

My colleague Åke Edfeldt and I tested the notion that Scandinavian countries have few problems with child abuse (Gelles & Edfeldt, 1986). Åke Edfeldt, Professor of Education at the University of Stockholm, replicated our national survey of family violence (Straus, Gelles, & Steinmetz, 1980). He translated the Conflict Tactics Scales (Straus, 1979) into Swedish and conducted interviews with a nationally representative sample of 1,168 respondents who had children at home 3 to 17 years of age (this was essentially the same sampling approach we used in our 1976 National Family Violence Survey; Straus et al., 1980).

The results of the comparison between the United States and Sweden were mixed. In general, the Swedish parents reported using less overall violence than did parents in the United States. However, when we confined our analysis to only the most severe and abusive forms of violence, there was no significant difference between the two countries. Whereas differing social conditions may have played a role in limiting spankings, slaps, and other so-called minor acts of violence, parents in both countries are about equally likely to beat, kick, and punch their children.

Students of family violence around the world have tried to synthesize the various data that are available and come up with a general statement that explains why violence toward children is common in some societies and rare in others. The anthropologist Jill Korbin (1981) concludes that if children are valued for economic, spiritual, or psychological qualities, they are less likely to be maltreated. Certain children who are perceived to have undesirable qualities are at greatest risk of abuse. Thus, illegitimate children, orphans, stepchildren, females, or retarded or deformed children are often at greatest risk of abuse. Some students of the new "one child" policy in the People's Republic of China note that an unintended consequence of the law to limit families to one child has been a rather dramatic increase in female infanticide (Korbin, 1981).

Dobash and Dobash (1979) also find that cultural values about women play a role in the risk of wife abuse. The more women are viewed as property of their mates, the greater the risk of abuse.

# The Social Transformation of Intimate Violence

The problems of child abuse and wife abuse are not new nor are other forms of family violence—sibling violence and violence toward parents. Perhaps the only new form of family violence is the abuse of elderly persons. This is essentially due to the increase in life expectancy: 50 or 100 years ago, most people simply did not live long enough to become vulnerable to abuse at the hands of their middle-aged children.

Yet although we find cases of family violence throughout recorded history, viewing family violence as a social issue and a social problem is a relatively new phenomenon. For most of the time there has been violence between loved ones, it has literally and figuratively occurred behind closed doors. It gradually became both a social issue, that is, a condition that captures public attention and generates concern, controversy, and in some cases collective action, and a social problem, that is, a condition found to be harmful to individual and societal well-being.

It is tempting to look for some dramatic change that took place 30 years ago that propelled family violence out from behind closed doors into the public spotlight. That, however, would be naive. Rather, violence in the home came to public attention gradually. The fortress doors of the private family did not swing open, they moved inch by inch over the decades.

## Discovering Childhood and Children

The historical treatment of children is not entirely bleak. Children's rights were recognized, but slowly. Six thousand years ago, children in Mesopotamia had a patron goddess to look after them. The Greeks and Romans had orphan homes. Some historical accounts also mention the existence of foster care for children. Samuel Radbill (1987) reports that child protection laws were legislated as long ago as 450 B.C. At the same time, the father's complete control over his children was modified. Anthropologists have noted that nearly every society has laws and rules regarding sexual access to children.

The social historian Phillipe Aries, in his book *Centuries of Childhood* (1962), claims that the concept of childhood as a distinct stage emerged after the Middle Ages (from about 400 A.D. to 1000 A.D.). Before then, childhood as a stage ended when an infant was weaned. Children were seen as miniature adults and were portrayed as such in the artwork of the Middle Ages. Paintings and sculptures of chil-

11

dren pictured them with little heads and miniature adult bodies, dressed in adult clothing. Renaissance art was the first time children were portrayed as children.

Michael Robin (1982) has traced the roots of child protection. He found that the Renaissance, a 300-year period spanning 1300 to 1600, was the beginning of a new morality regarding children. Children were seen as a dependent class in need of the protection of society. This was also a time when the family was looked to for teaching children the proper rules of behavior. At the same time, the power of the father increased dramatically.

Although society paid more attention to children, this was not without some dire consequences. Puritan parents in colonial America were instructed by leaders such as Cotton Mather that strict discipline of children could not begin too early (Greven, 1990).

The Enlightenment of the 18th century brought children increased attention and services. The London Foundling Hospital was founded during this period. The hospital not only provided pediatric care but, as Robin (1982) recounts, was also the center of the moral reform movement on behalf of children.

In the United States, the case of Mary Ellen Wilson is almost always singled out as the turning point in concern for children's welfare. In 1874, 8-year-old Mary Ellen lived in the home of Francis and Mary Connolly but was not the blood relative of either. Mary Ellen was the illegitimate daughter of Mary Connolly's first husband. A neighbor noticed the plight of Mary Ellen, who was beaten with a leather thong and allowed to go ill clothed in bad weather. The neighbor reported the case to Etta Wheeler, a "friendly visitor" who worked for St. Luke's Methodist Mission. In the mid-1800s, child welfare was church based rather than government based. Wheeler turned to the police and the New York City Department of Charities for help for Mary Ellen Wilson and was turned down—first by the police, who said there was no proof of a crime, and second by the charity agency, who said they did not have custody of Mary Ellen. The legend goes on to note that Henry Bergh, founder of the Society for the Prevention of Cruelty to Animals, intervened on behalf of Mary Ellen, and the courts accepted the case because Mary Ellen was a member of the animal kingdom. In reality, the court reviewed the case because the child needed protection. The case was argued not by Henry Berge, but by his colleague, Elbridge Gerry.

Mary Ellen Wilson was removed from her foster home and initially placed in an orphanage. Her foster mother was imprisoned for a year, and the case received detailed press coverage for months. In December 1874, the New York Society for the Prevention of Cruelty to Children was founded.

Protective societies rose and fell during the next 80 years. The political scientist Barbara Nelson (1984) notes that by the 1950s public interest in abuse and neglect was practically nonexistent. Technology helped to pave the way for the rediscovery of child abuse. In 1946, the radiologist John Caffey (1946) reported on a number of cases of children who had multiple long-bone fractures and subdural hematomas. Caffey used X-rays to identify the fractures, although he did not speculate about the causes. In 1953, P. V. Woolley and W. A. Evans (1955) did speculate that the injuries might have been inflicted by the children's parents. Caffey (1957) looked again at his X-ray data and speculated that such injuries could have been inflicted by parents or caretakers. By 1962, the physician C. Henry Kempe and his colleagues at the University of Colorado Medical Center (Kempe et al., 1962) were quite certain that many of the injuries they were seeing and the healed fractures that appeared on X-rays were intentionally inflicted by parents.

Kempe's article became the benchmark of the public and professional rediscovery of child abuse. Kempe's article and a strong editorial that accompanied the article created considerable public and professional concern. *Time, Newsweek*, the *Saturday Evening Post*, and *Life* followed up the Kempe article with news or feature stories. Barbara Nelson (1984) has traced the record of professional and mass media articles on child abuse and neglect. Prior to 1962, it was unusual that a single mass media article on abuse would be published in a year. After Kempe's article, there was a tenfold increase in popular articles that discussed child abuse. Today, a year does not go by without each major periodical publishing at least one cover story on child abuse. Kempe founded his own professional journal, *Child Abuse & Neglect: The International Journal*, and thousands of professional articles are published annually in medical, sociology, psychology, social work, and other scholarly journals. There are now nearly a dozen scientific journals devoted to family and intimate violence in general, or some aspect of family violence such as sexual or emotional abuse.

That public and professional media coverage of child abuse grew rapidly and in tandem was not a coincidence. Each professional journal article produced additional fodder for the mass media (many scholars and scholarly journals issue press releases to accompany publication of a new article). Each popular article added legitimacy to the public concern for abuse and stimulated a new round of research and scholarly publication.

The symbiotic relationship between scholarly and popular media was not without some problems. The translation of scientific writing into popular presentation often leveled, sharpened, or distorted the scientific findings and statements. For instance, the editorial that accompanied Kempe's article in the *Journal of the American Medical Association* said that "it is likely that [the battered child syndrome] will be found to be a more frequent cause of death than such well recognized and thoroughly studied diseases as leukemia, cystic fibrosis and muscular dystrophy and might rank well above automobile accidents" ("The Battered-Child Syndrome," 1962, p. 42). By the time the statement in the editorial had found its way to the public press, it had been slightly changed to state that child abuse was one of the five leading causes of death of children, even though at the time there were no actual data to support such an assertion. Similarly, estimates of the incidence of child abuse and the possible causes were stated and restated so often that they took on lives of their own apart from the initial speculative presentations in scholarly journals.

Two other forces worked to move child abuse out from behind closed doors during the 1960s. The first was the passage of child abuse reporting laws, and the second was the effort in the federal government to focus concern on the plight of abused children.

One of the concrete consequences of the rediscovery of child abuse after the publication of Kempe's 1962 article on the battered child syndrome was the passage of child abuse reporting laws in each of the 50 states between 1963 and 1967. Reporting laws were the quickest, most concrete measure states could take to demonstrate that they wanted to "do something" about the abuse of children. The underlying theme of many of the popular and professional publications on child abuse from the time of Mary Ellen Wilson was the fact that abused children were "missing persons" in social and criminal justice agencies. Many abused children came to public attention only at the point of death. Logic seemed to dictate that if society were to help abused children, it would have to identify those in need of help. Not coincidentally, child abuse reporting laws were often viewed as a no- or low-cost means for state legislators to do something about abuse. Few legislators who jumped on the reporting law bandwagon could foresee that reporting laws would lead to uncovering millions of children who required state-funded protective services. The myth that family violence was rare had such a strong hold that most legislators assumed that the laws they passed would lead to uncovering only a handful of abused and neglected children in their state.

The Children's Bureau, first an agency in the Department of Labor, then an agency of the Department of Health, Education, and Welfare, and finally located within the Department of Health and Human Services, was the first federal focal point of discussion and concern for abused children. The Children's Bureau was active in the cause of abused children as far back as the 1950s. The bureau was founded in 1912 by an act of Congress with the mandate of disseminating information on child development. The bureau also acquired the budget and mandate to conduct research on issues concerning child development. The Children's Bureau engaged in a variety of activities regarding child abuse and neglect. The agency participated in one of the earliest national meetings on child abuse sponsored by the Children's Division of the American Humane Association. After the publication of Kempe's 1962 article, the bureau convened a meeting to draft a model child abuse reporting law. The model law was drafted in 1963. Finally, the bureau funded a variety of research projects, including David Gil's first national survey of officially reported cases of child abuse. In 1974, Congress enacted the Child Abuse Prevention and Treatment Act and located the National Center on Child Abuse and Neglect in the Children's Bureau.

Congressional interest in child abuse prior to 1973 was limited to the passage of a reporting law for the District of Columbia and some attempts to pass national reporting laws. In 1973, then Senator Walter Mondale introduced the Child Abuse Prevention and Treatment Act (42 U.S.C. 5101). The act, enacted in 1974, defined child abuse and neglect, established the National Center on Child Abuse and Neglect, set forth a budget for research and demonstration projects, and called for a national survey of the incidence of child abuse and neglect.

Child abuse appeared to be a "safe" congressional issue. Again, the myth that abuse was rare and confined to the mentally disturbed seemed to limit the scope of the problem and the need for large, federal spending. Who could disagree, after seeing slides of horribly abused children, that such children did not need care and protection? Mondale needed a safe issue. He had seen his Comprehensive Child Development Act vetoed by then President Nixon. Even Nixon, Mondale would say, could not be in favor of child abuse.

Child abuse was not as safe an issue as it first seemed. Although one witness at Mondale's Senate hearings on the Child Abuse Prevention and Treatment Act, Jolly K., a former child abuser and founder of Parents Anonymous, captured media and congressional attention with her testimony recounting her abuse of her child, another witness, the social welfare expert David Gil, showed the "unsafe" side of the issue when he insisted on linking abuse to poverty. Moreover, Gil went beyond the narrow scope of the public stereotype of child abuse and introduced the issue of corporal punishment and spanking into his testimony. Finally, Gil concluded that the bill as written was too narrow to identify, treat, and prevent the real problem.

The Child Abuse Prevention and Treatment Act passed. It was never clear whether President Nixon could be against child abuse—he signed the bill in the midst of mounting public clamor over Watergate. The final amount of money made available for research and demonstration projects was relatively small, $85 million. Many child abuse experts who realized how extensive the problem was and how difficult it would be to treat suggested that such a trifling amount was but a rounding error at the Pentagon. Yet despite concern over the scope of the legislation and the narrowness of the mandate of the law, the passage of the Child Abuse Prevention and Treatment Act succeeded in creating a federal presence and a federal bureaucracy that could serve as a focal point of public and professional awareness of child abuse and neglect.

### Discovering Wife Abuse

There was no Mary Ellen for battered women, no technological breakthroughs such as pediatric radiology to uncover years of broken jaws and broken bones. No medical champion would capture public and professional attention in the way Kempe had for battered children. There was no "Women's Bureau" in the federal government. And initially, there was no powerful senator who used a congressional committee chairmanship as a bully pulpit to bring attention to the plight of battered women.

The discovery of wife abuse was a traditional grassroots effort. Attention to the problem of wife battering came from women themselves. A women's center in the Chiswick section of London founded by Erin Pizzey became a refuge for victims of battering. Pizzey wrote the first book on wife abuse, *Scream Quietly or the Neighbors Will Hear* (1974), and produced a documentary movie of the same name. Both captured the attention of women in Europe and the United States. Women's groups began to organize safe houses or battered wife shelters as early as 1972 in the United States. The National Organization for Women created a task force to examine wife battering in 1975.

The results of research on wife abuse in the United States began to be published in 1973. The data on the extent of the problem, the patterns of violence, factors associated with wife abuse, and other analyses were quickly seized on by those who believed that the abuse of women deserved the same place on the public agenda that child abuse had attained. As with child abuse, the scholarly publications fed media articles and the media articles fed public interest, which led to more research and professional attention.

Still, by the early 1980s, public and professional interest in wife battering had lagged far behind interest in child abuse. There were some congressional hearings on wife abuse and then Congresswoman Barbara Milkulski introduced legislation for a National Domestic Violence Prevention and Treatment Act. A federal Office of Domestic Violence was established in 1979 only to be closed in 1981.

Some progress was made in the mid-1980s. The National Domestic Violence Prevention and Treatment Act (42 U.S.C. 13701) was passed into law, although spending from this legislation was but a trickle. The U.S. Attorney General's Task Force on Family Violence held hearings across the country in 1984 and published the final report in September 1984.

The year 1994 was a watershed year for the issue of violence against women. Perhaps not coincidentally, this was the year that Nicole Brown Simpson and Ron Goldman were murdered and Brown Simpson's ex-husband, O. J. Simpson, was charged with the murder. At about the same time the murders took place, Congress was completing the 1994 Violent Crime Control and Law Enforcement Act, which included Title IV, the Violence Against Women Act (VAWA). This crime bill, with the VAWA, was passed by Congress in August 1994 and was signed into law by President Clinton on September 13, 1994. The VAWA appropriated $1.5 billion to fight violence against women, including $3 million over 3 years to reestablish a national hot line to help victims and survivors of domestic violence. An additional $26 million was appropriated for state grants that would encourage states to take more creative, innovative, and effective approaches in law enforcement and prosecutor training; development and expansion of law enforcement and prosecution, such as special domestic violence units; improved data collection and communication strategies; improved victim service programs; and improved programs concerning stalking. The VAWA also included various provisions to increase protec-

17

tion of battered women, including a civil rights title that declared "all persons in the United States shall have the right to be free from crimes of violence motivated by gender." Last, an office on domestic violence was established within the U.S. Department of Justice.

At about the same time the VAWA was passed, the Family Violence Prevention Fund, along with the Advertising Council, began a national public awareness campaign titled "No Excuse for Domestic Violence." Public service announcements that were designed to educate the public about domestic violence and promote prevention and intervention appeared on television and in newspapers.

Legal reforms also occurred at the state level. States enacted legislation designed to establish domestic violence prosecution units, to criminalize sexual assault of wives by their husbands or ex-husbands, to improve protection for victims of stalking, and to develop more effective legal sanctions for domestic violence offenders.

## *A Concern for Private Violence*

It is tempting to give credit for the discovery of a social problem to a single great person or a single tragic event. The field of child abuse and neglect certainly owes much to the late C. Henry Kempe. Walter Mondale was thought a hero by those concerned for child protection, and Senator Joseph Biden was instrumental in passing the Violence Against Women Act.

Another point of view is that no single person, journal article, or piece of legislation propels a problem from obscurity onto the public agenda. Rather, an issue slowly and gradually becomes a public issue.

The "great man" and the slow social movement explanations of the social transformation of family violence are inadequate. Rather, a variety of social movements and social concerns combined in the late 1960s to create a climate where people were ready and willing to listen to those concerned with the victimization of women and children.

The assassinations of John F. Kennedy, Robert Kennedy, and Martin Luther King, Jr. focused public concern on violence. The focus led to the establishment of the President's Commission on the Causes and Prevention of Violence. The commission's national survey on attitudes and experience with violence produced invaluable data for researchers in the field of family violence.

The 1960s were also a period of violent social protest and race riots, again focusing public concern on violence. The baby boomers of the 1950s were teenagers in the 1960s, and as is the case for those

18 to 24 years of age, they engaged in innumerable acts of delinquency and violence, pushing up the national homicide, assault, and rape rates. The public believed that we were in the midst of an epidemic of violence. Fear of violent crime began to paralyze American society. The Figgie Report, published in 1980, found that 4 out of 10 Americans were afraid of being assaulted, robbed, raped, or murdered in their homes or on the streets where they lived and worked.

Concern for violence would not have meant much had it not occurred at the same time as we were undergoing a resurgence of both the women's and the children's movements. These existing social movements provided the forum, the workers, and the energy to collect, organize, and present information on private victimization. Existing national groups who lobbied on behalf of women and children made it easier to lobby for national and regional attention to the problems of the abuse of women and children.

A final necessary and sufficient piece that made the puzzle into a portrait of a problem was the research being carried out by social and behavioral scientists. Until there could be scientific data that shattered the myths of abuse, it was impossible to convince the public and legislators that family violence was a legitimate problem deserving a continued place on the national agenda.

## Contemporary Attitudes

Violence between family members has a historical tradition that goes back centuries and cuts across continents. It should come as no surprise that contemporary social scientists have proposed that in the United States and many other countries, "the marriage license is a hitting license" (Straus et al., 1980). Numerous surveys and situations emphasize the point that today in the United States some people still believe that under certain circumstances, it is perfectly appropriate for a husband to hit his wife. The parents who fail to hit their children are considered to be deviant, not the parents who hit.

At the end of the 1960s, the U.S. Commission on the Causes and Prevention of Violence carried out a study of violence in the United States. The primary purpose of the study was to try to understand the causes of the tragic rash of assassinations and riots that plagued the country between 1963 and 1968. Along with the questions on public violence, the commission asked a number of questions about private violence. Among the conclusions was that about one quarter of all adult men, and one in six adult women, said they could think of circumstances in which it would be all right for a husband to hit his wife or for the wife to hit her husband. Overall, about one in five (21%) of those surveyed approved of a husband slapping his wife (Stark & McEvoy, 1970). The same survey found that 86% of those surveyed agreed that young people needed "strong" discipline. Of the sample, 70% thought that it was important for a boy to have a few fist fights while he was growing up.

Fifteen years after the U.S. Commission on the Causes and Prevention of Violence conducted their research, my colleagues Murray Straus and Suzanne Steinmetz and I carried out the first national survey on family violence. Our questions of people's attitudes toward violence in the home confirmed the findings from earlier research. Just under one in four wives and one in three husbands thought that a couple slapping one another was at least somewhat necessary, normal, and good (Straus et al., 1980, p. 47). More than 70% of those questioned thought that slapping a 12-year-old child was either necessary, normal, or good.

Anecdotal accounts further underscore the widespread cultural approval of private violence. In 1964, a young woman named Kitty Genovese was returning home to her apartment in the Queens section of New York City. She was accosted and repeatedly stabbed by a man, and although a number of her neighbors heard her screams for help and watched the assault from windows, no one called the police. The young woman's death led many people to conclude that American society was corrupt, because bystanders seemed too apathetic or unwilling to get involved in a homicide. However, on closer examination, it was suggested that the apathy of Kitty Genovese's neighbors was not the result of their lack of concern, or the fact that they were immune to violence after years of watching television. Rather, many of the witnesses thought that they were seeing a man beating his wife, and that, after all, is a family matter.

In Worcester, Massachusetts, a district court judge sat on the bench and tried an occasional wife abuse case despite the fact that he was a wife beater who misrepresented his behavior under oath during a divorce trial (D'Agostino, 1983).

Millions laughed (and still laugh) when Jackie Gleason would rant, "Alice, [you're going] to the moon" while shaking an angry fist at his television wife in the popular program "The Honeymooners."

Fairy tales, folklore, and nursery rhymes are full of violence against children. Hansel and Gretel, before they were lured into the gingerbread house, had been abandoned by their parents to starve in the forest because money was scarce. Snow White was taken in the woods to be killed by the huntsman on the order of the wicked queen, who was her stepmother. Mother Goose's "Old Woman Who Lived in a Shoe" beat her children soundly and sent them to bed. "Humpty Dumpty" is a thinly disguised metaphor for the fragility of children, and "Rock-a-Bye Baby," with the cradle falling from the tree, is not even thinly disguised.

## Changing Attitudes

There is evidence from surveys that attitudes regarding family violence are changing. Murray Straus and I repeated our National Family Violence Survey in 1985. Approval for a husband slapping his wife and a wife slapping her husband declined from 1975. In 1985, only 13% of those surveyed could approve of a husband slapping his wife in some situations. The level of approval of a husband slapping his wife declined to 12% in 1992 and further declined to 10% in 1994. Approval for a wife slapping her husband stayed relatively unchanged between 1968 and 1994 with about one in five respondents approving of a wife slapping her husband in some situations (Gelles & Straus, 1988; Straus, Kaufman Kantor, & Moore, 1994).

Other surveys also find decreasing public tolerance for violence against women. Surveys conducted for the Family Violence Prevention Fund found that four in five surveyed consider domestic violence an extremely important social issue, ranking it more important than teen alcoholism and pregnancy and about as important as the environment. An increasing number of Americans believe outside intervention is needed if a man hits his wife (87% agreed in 1995 compared with 80% in 1994). In the 1995 survey, 57% of men agreed that abusers should be arrested compared with 49% agreement in 1994 (Family Violence Prevention Fund, 1995).

The trend of contemporary attitudes regarding violence against children is more mixed. There has been a steady increase in the proportion of the public who disapprove of child abuse and neglect. The National Committee to Prevent Child Abuse has conducted annual public opinion polls since 1987 to measure the extent to which the public perceives child abuse to be a serious social problem, as well as the extent to which the public is committed to preventing the abuse of children. Each survey found that the majority of the public viewed physical punishment and repeated yelling and swearing as harmful to children's well-being. In 1995, only 22% of the public felt that physical punishment never leads to injury and only 6% believed repeated yelling and swearing never leads to long-term emotional harm (Daro, 1995; Daro & Gelles, 1992).

Paradoxically, although the general public appears more willing to view physical punishment and yelling and swearing as harmful, the public still endorses spanking. The National Opinion Research Center's General Social Survey found that in 1991, 73% of adults agree that it is sometimes necessary to discipline a child with a good hard spanking. This is down from 83% for the period 1983-1987 (National Opinion Research Center, 1991).

## *Prevention*

Treatment is necessary to protect the lives and welfare of the victims or potential victims of intimate violence. But even the implementation of effective and efficient treatment programs will not break the cycle of cultural norms and values that contribute to the violent nature of the family and intimate relationships. Nor do treatment programs alone alter the characteristics of society and the family that increase the risk that certain relationships will be violent and abusive.

The central goal of programs and policies aimed at intimate violence is to prevent violence. The findings presented in *Intimate Violence in Families* (third edition, 1997) clearly point to the fact that some fundamental changes in values and beliefs will have to occur before we see a real decrease in the level of violence in intimate relationships. Looking toward the future, there are a number of policy steps that could help prevent intimate violence.

1.  *Eliminate the norms that legitimize and glorify violence in the society and the family.* The elimination of spanking as a child-rearing technique; gun control, to get deadly weapons out of the home; elimination of corporal punishment in school; elimination of the death penalty; and an elimination of media violence that glorifies and legitimizes violence are all necessary steps. In short, we need to cancel the hitting license in society.

2.  *Reduce violence-provoking stress created by society.* Reducing poverty, inequality, and unemployment and providing for adequate housing, feeding, medical and dental care, and educational opportunities are steps that could reduce stress in families.

3. *Integrate families into a network of kin and community.* Reducing social isolation would be a significant step that would help reduce stress and increase the abilities of families to manage stress.

4. *Change the sexist character of society.* Sexual inequality makes violence possible in homes. The elimination of men's work and women's work would be a major step toward equality in and out of the home.

5. *Break the cycle of violence in the family.* This step repeats the message of Step 1—violence cannot be prevented as long as we are taught that it is appropriate to hit the people we love. Physical punishment of children is perhaps the most effective means of teaching violence, and eliminating it would be an important step in violence prevention.

Such steps require long-term changes in the fabric of society. These proposals call for such fundamental change in families and family life that many people resist them and argue that they could not work or would ruin the family. The alternative, of course, is that not making such changes continues the harmful and deadly tradition of intimate violence.

## References

Aries, P. *Centuries of Childhood*. New York: Knopf, 1962.

"The Battered Child Syndrome." *Journal of the American Medical Association* 181 (1962): 42.

Caffey, J. "Multiple Fractures in the Long Bones of Infants Suffering from Chronic Subdural Hematoma." *American Journal of Roentgenology, Radium Therapy, and Nuclear Medicine* 58 (1946): 163–73.

D'Agostino, S. "Finally, Judgment." *Worcester Magazine* (August 17, 1983): 11–13.

Daro, D. *Public Opinion and Behaviors Regarding Child Abuse Prevention: The Results of NCPCA's 1995 Public Opinion Poll*. Chicago: National Committee to Prevent Child Abuse, 1995.

Daro, D., and R. J. Gelles. "Public Attitudes and Behaviors with Respect to Child Abuse Prevention." *Journal of Interpersonal Violence* 7 (1992): 517–31.

De Mause, L., ed. *The History of Childhood*. New York: Psychohistory Press, 1974.

Dobash, R., and R. Dobash. *Violence Against Wives*. New York: Free Press, 1979.

Domestic Violence Research Group. *A Study of Violence Precipitated by Husbands (Boyfriends) in Japan: Preliminary Findings*. Paper presented at the NGO parallel activities at the United Nations World Conference on Human Rights, Vienna, Austria, June 1993.

Family Violence Prevention Fund. "Poll Finds Rising Concern about Abuse." *Speaking Up* 1 (1995): 1ff.

Finkelhor, D. and J. Korbin. "Child Abuse as an International Issue." *Child Abuse & Neglect: The International Journal* 12 (1988): 3–23.

Gelles, R. J., and C. Cornell, eds. *International Perspectives on Family Violence*. Lexington, Mass.: Lexington Books, 1983.

Gelles, R. J., and Ä. Edfeldt. "Violence toward Children in the United States and Sweden." *Child Abuse & Neglect: The International Journal* 10 (1986): 501–10.

Gelles, R. J., and M. A. Straus. *Intimate Violence*. New York: Simon & Schuster, 1988.

Greven, P. *Spare the Child: The Religious Roots of Punishment and the Psychological Impact of Physical Abuse*. New York: Knopf, 1990.

Heise, L. L. *Violence Against Women: The Hidden Health Burden*. World Bank Discussion Papers No. 255. Washington, D.C.: World Bank, 1994.

Kempe, C. H., F. N. Silverman, B. F. Steele, W. Droegemueller, and H. K. Silver. "The Battered Child Syndrome." *Journal of the American Medical Association* 181 (1962): 107–12.

Kim, K., and Y. Cho. "Epidemiological Survey of Spousal Abuse in Korea," 277-82. In E. Viano, ed. *Intimate Violence: Interdisciplinary Perspectives*. Washington, D.C.: Hemisphere, 1992.

Korbin, J., ed. *Child Abuse and Neglect: Cross-Cultural Perspectives*. Berkeley, Calif.: University of California Press, 1981.

Larrain, S. *Estudio de frequencia de la violencia intrafamiliar y la condicion de la mujer en Chile* [Study of the Frequency of Intrafamiliar Violence and the Condition of Women in Chile]. Santiago, Chile: Pan-American Health Organization, 1993.

Leibrich, J., J. Paulin, and R. Ransom. *Hitting Home: Men Speak about Abuse Toward Women Partners.* Wellington, New Zealand: Department of Justice in association with AGB McNair, 1995.

Levinson, D. "Physical Punishment of Children and Wifebeating in Cross-Cultural Perspective." *Child Abuse & Neglect: The International Journal* 5 (1981): 193–96.

Miller, A. *For Your Own Good: Hidden Cruelty in Child-Rearing and the Roots of Violence.* New York: Farrar, Straus, and Giroux, 1983.

National Opinion Research Center. *General Social Surveys, 1972–1991 Cumulative Codebook.* Storrs, Conn.: Roper Center for Public Opinion Research, 1991.

Nelson, B. J. *Making an Issue of Child Abuse: Political Agenda Setting for Social Problems.* Chicago: University of Chicago Press, 1984.

Pleck, E. *Domestic Tyranny: The Making of American Social Policy Against Family Violence from Colonial Times to the Present.* New York: Oxford University Press, 1987.

Prasad, D. "Dowry-Related Violence: A Content Analysis of News in Selected Newspapers." *Journal of Comparative Family Studies* 25 (1994): 71–89.

Radbill, S. "Children in a World of Violence: A History of Child Abuse," 3–20. In R. Helfer and R. Kempe, eds. *The Battered Child.* Fourth edition. Chicago: University of Chicago Press, 1987.

Robin, M. "Historical Introduction: Sheltering Arms: The Roots of Child Protection," 1-41. In E. H. Newberger, ed. *Child Abuse.* Boston: Little, Brown, 1982.

Rodgers, K. "Wife Assault: The Findings of a National Survey." *Juristate Service Bulletin* 14 (1994): 1–22.

Sommers, C. H. *Who Stole Feminism? How Women Have Betrayed Women.* New York: Simon & Schuster, 1994.

Stark, R., and J. McEvoy. "Middle Class Violence." *Psychology Today* 4 (1970): 52–65.

Straus, M. A. *Beating the Devil Out of Them: Corporal Punishment in American Families.* New York: Lexington Books, 1994.

Straus, M. A. "Measuring Intrafamily Conflict and Aggression: The Conflict Tactics Scale (CT)." *Journal of Marriage and the Family* 41 (1979): 75–88.

Straus, M. A., R. J. Gelles, and S. K. Steinmetz. *Behind Closed Doors: Violence in the American Family*. Garden City, N.Y.: Anchor, 1980.

Straus, M. A., G. Kaufman Kantor, and D. Moore. *Change in Cultural Norms Approving Marital Violence*. Paper presented at the annual meetings of the American Sociological Association, Los Angeles, August 1994.

"3 Deaths Trigger Debate over Child Abuse in China." *Providence Journal* (December 26, 1992), p. C-3.

United Nations. *Violence Against Women in the Family*. New York: United Nations, 1994.

Vesterdal, J. "Handling of Child Abuse in Denmark." *Child Abuse & Neglect: The International Journal* 1 (1977): 193–98.

Woolley, P., and W. Evans. "Significance of Skeletal Lesions Resembling Those of Traumatic Origin." *Journal of the American Medical Association* 158 (1955): 539–43.

# Chapter 2

# *Hitting the Wall*

*Nancy Updike*

After 20 years of domestic violence research, scientists can't avoid hard facts. A surprising fact has turned up in the grimly familiar world of domestic violence: Women report using violence in their relationships more often than men. This is not a crack by some antifeminist cad; the information will soon be published by the Justice Department in a report summarizing the results of in-depth, face-to-face interviews with a representative sample of 860 men and women whom researchers have been following since birth. Conducted in New Zealand by Terrie Moffitt, a University of Wisconsin psychology professor, the study supports data published in 1980 indicating that wives hit their husbands at least as often as husbands hit their wives [*see* Chapter 28 for the results published in *Findings about Partner Violence from the Dunedin Multidisciplinary Health and Development Study*].

When the 1980 study was released, it was so controversial that some of the researchers received death threats. Advocates for battered women were outraged because the data seemed to suggest that the risk of injury from domestic violence is as high for men as it is for women, which isn't true. Whether or not women are violent themselves, they are much more likely to be severely injured or killed by domestic violence, so activists dismissed the findings as meaningless.

---

But Moffitt's research emerges in a very different context—namely, that of a movement that is older, wiser, and ready to begin making sense of uncomfortable truths. Twenty years ago, "domestic violence" meant men hitting women. Period. That was the only way to understand it or to talk about it. But today, after decades of research and activism predicated on that assumption, the number of women killed each year in domestic violence incidents remains distressingly high: a sobering 1,326 in 1996, compared with 1,600 two decades earlier. In light of the persistence of domestic violence, researchers are beginning to consider a broader range of data, including the possible significance of women's violence. This willingness to pay attention to what was once considered reactionary nonsense signals a fundamental conceptual shift in how domestic violence is being studied.

Violence in the home has never been easy to research. Even the way we measure it reflects the kind of murky data that has plagued the field. For instance, one could argue that the number of fatalities resulting from domestic violence is not the best measure of the problem, as not all acts of brutality end in death. It is, however, one of the few reliable statistics in a field where concrete numbers are difficult to come by. Many nonlethal domestic violence incidents go unreported or are categorized as something else—aggravated assault, simple assault—when they are reported. But another reason we haven't been able to effectively measure domestic violence is that we don't understand it, and, because we don't understand it, we haven't been able to stop it. Money and ideology are at the heart of the problem.

For years, domestic violence research was underfunded and conducted piecemeal, sometimes by researchers with more zeal for the cause of battered women than training in research methodology. The results were often ideology-driven "statistics," such as the notorious (and false) claim that more men beat their wives on Super Bowl Sunday, which dramatized the cause of domestic violence victims but further confused an already intricate issue. In 1994, Congress asked the National Research Council, an independent Washington, D.C., think tank, to evaluate the state of knowledge about domestic abuse. The NRC report concluded that "this field of research is characterized by the absence of clear conceptual models, large-scale databases, longitudinal research, and reliable instrumentation." [*See also* Chapter 27.]

Moffitt is part of a new wave of domestic violence researchers who are bringing expertise from other areas of study, and her work is symbolic of the way scientists are changing their conception of the roots of domestic violence.

"[She] is taking domestic violence out of its standard intellectual confines and putting it into a much larger context, that of violence in general," says Daniel Nagin, a crime researcher and the Theresa and H. John Heinz III Professor of Public Policy at Carnegie Mellon University.

Moffitt is a developmental psychologist who has spent most of her career studying juvenile delinquency, which was the original focus of her research. She started interviewing her subjects about violence in their relationships after 20 years of research into other, seemingly unrelated aspects of their lives: sex and drug-use habits, criminal activities, social networks and family ties, and signs of mental illness.

"I had looked at other studies of juvenile delinquency," Moffitt says, "and saw that people in their 20s were dropping out of street crime, and I wondered, 'Are all of these miraculous recoveries where they're just reforming and giving up crime? Or are they getting out of their parents' home and moving in with a girlfriend and finding victims who are more easily accessible?' So I decided we'd better not just ask them about street violence, but also about violence within the home, with a partner."

What she found was that the women in her study who were in violent relationships were more like their partners, in many ways, than they were like the other women in the study. Both the victims and the aggressors in violent relationships, Moffitt found, were more likely to be unemployed and less educated than couples in nonviolent relationships. Moffitt also found that "female perpetrators of partner violence differed from nonviolent women with respect to factors that could not be solely the result of being in a violent relationship." Her research disputes a long-held belief about the nature of domestic violence: If a woman hits, it's only in response to her partner's attacks. The study suggests that some women may simply be prone to violence—by nature or circumstance—just as some men may be.

Moffitt's findings don't change the fact that women are much more at risk in domestic violence, but they do suggest new ways to search for the origins of violence in the home. And once we know which early experiences can lead to domestic violence, we can start to find ways to intervene before the problem begins.

Prevention is a controversial goal, however, because it often calls for changes in the behavior of the victim as well as the batterer, and for decades activists have been promoting the seemingly opposite view. And even though it is possible to talk about prevention without blaming victims or excusing abusers, the issue is a minefield of preconceived ideas about gender, violence, and relationships, and new approaches may seem too scary to contemplate.

In domestic violence research, it seems, the meaning of any new data is predetermined by ideological agendas set a long time ago, and the fear that new information can be misinterpreted can lead to a rejection of the information itself. In preparing this column, I called a well-known women's research organization and asked scientists there about new FBI statistics indicating a substantial recent increase in violent crime committed by girls ages 12 to 18. The media contact told me the organization had decided not to collect any information about those statistics and that it didn't think it was a fruitful area of research, because girls are still much more likely to be victims of violence than perpetrators.

It's impossible to know yet whether such numbers are useful, whether they're a statistical blip or a trend, or whether the girls committing violent crimes now are more likely to end up in violent relationships. But to ignore them on principle—as activists and researchers ignored the data about women's violence years ago—is to give up on determining the roots of violence, which seem to be much more complicated than whether a person is born with a Y chromosome.

What's clear is that women's and girls' violence is not meaningless, either for researchers or for the women themselves. It turns out that teenage girls who commit violent crimes "are two times more likely than juvenile male offenders to become victims themselves in the course of the offending incident," according to an FBI report. I'd like to hear more about that, please, not less. Moffitt's findings about women's violence and the FBI statistics are invitations to further research—not in spite of the fact that so many women are being beaten and killed every year, but because of it.

# Chapter 3

# *It's Always His Fault*

*Sally L. Satel*

## *The Feminist Zeal to Condemn Men May Be Endangering the Lives of Battered Women*

Let's call him "Joe Six Pack." Every Saturday night, he drinks way too much, cranks up the rock 'n roll way too loud, and smacks his girlfriend for acting just a bit too lippy. Or let's call him "Mr. Pillar of the Community." He's got the perfect wife, the perfect kids. But he's also got one little problem: every time he argues with his wife, he loses control. In the past year, she's been sent to the emergency ward twice. Or let's say they're the Tenants from Hell. They're always yelling at each other. Finally a neighbor calls the police.

Here is the question. Are the men in these scenarios: a) in need of help; b) in need of being locked up; or c) upholders of the patriarchy?

Most people would likely say a) or b) or perhaps both. In fact, however, c) is the answer that more and more of the agencies that deal with domestic violence—including the courts, social workers, and therapists—now give. Increasingly, public officials are buying into Gloria Steinem's assertion that "the patriarchy requires violence or the subliminal threat of violence in order to maintain itself." They are deciding that the perpetrators of domestic violence don't so much need

Reprinted from *The Women's Quarterly*, a publication of the Independent Women's Forum (www.iwf.org), Summer 1997, pp. 4–10.

to be punished, or even really counseled, but instead indoctrinated in what are called "profeminist" treatment programs. And they are spending tax dollars to pay for these programs.

A portion of the money for the re-education of batterers comes from Washington, courtesy of the 1994 Violence Against Women Act (VAWA). To obtain passage of VAWA, feminist organizations like the National Organization for Women and even secretary of Health and Human Services Donna Shalala, pelted legislators with facts and fig-ures: "The leading cause of birth defects is battery during pregnancy." "In emergency rooms, twenty to thirty percent of women arrive be-cause of physical abuse by their partner." "Family violence has killed more women in the last five years than Americans killed in the Viet Nam War." Happily, these alarming factoids aren't true. But the femi-nist advocacy groups were able to create new bogus statistics faster than the experts were able to shoot the old ones down. And some of the untruths—like the fiction that wife-beating soars on Super Bowl Sunday—have become American myths as durable as the story of young George Washington chopping down the cherry tree.

Still, the problem of domestic violence, even if grossly exaggerated, is horrific enough. So Congress generously authorized $1.6 billion to fund VAWA. Few taxpayers would begrudge this outlay if it actually resulted in the protection of women. But instead there is increasing evidence that the money is being used to further an ideological war against men—one that puts many women at even greater risk.

The feminist theory of domestic abuse, like the feminist theory of rape, holds that all men have the same innate propensity to violence against women: your brother and my boyfriend are deep down every bit as bad as Joel Steinberg.* Men who abuse their mates, the theory goes, act violently not because they as individuals can't control their impulses, and not because they are thugs or drunks or particularly troubled people. Domestic abuse, in feminist eyes, is an essential ele-ment of the vast male conspiracy to suppress and subordinate women. In other words, the real culprit in a case of domestic violence is not a violent individual man, it is the patriarchy. To stop a man from abus-ing women, he must be taught to see the errors of the patriarchy and to renounce them.

Thus, a position paper by the Chicago Metropolitan Battered Women's Network explains: "Battering is a fulfillment of a cultural

---

[*Ed. note: Joel Steinberg beat his never-adopted daughter, Lisa, age 6, to death in 1987, and battered his live-in companion, Hedda Nussbaum for about ten years.]

32

expectation, not a deviant or sick behavior." Thus, too, the Seattle-based psychologist Laura Brown, a prominent feminist practitioner, argues that feminist psychotherapy is an "opportunity to help patients see the relationship between their behavior and the patriarchal society in which we are all embedded."

As well, feminists have stretched the definition of abuse to include acts of lying, humiliation, withholding information, and refusing help with child care or housework, under the term "psychological battery." A checklist from a brochure of the Westchester Coalition of Family Violence agencies tells women if their partner behaves in one or more of the following ways, including "an overprotective manner," "turns minor incidents into major arguments," or "insults you," then "you might be abused."

With money provided by VAWA, this view has come to pervade the bureaucracies created to combat domestic violence. In at least a dozen states, including Massachusetts, Colorado, Florida, Washington, and Texas, state guidelines effectively preclude any treatment other than feminist therapy for domestic batterers. Another dozen states, among them Maine and Illinois, are now drafting similar guidelines. These guidelines explicitly prohibit social workers and clinicians from offering therapies that attempt to deal with domestic abuse as a problem between a couple unless the man has undergone profeminist treatment first. Profeminists emphatically reject joint counseling, the traditional approach to marital conflict. Joint counseling and other couples-based treatments violate the feminist certainty that it is men who are always and solely responsible for domestic violence: any attempt to involve the batterer's mate in treatment amounts to "blaming the victim."

The dogma that women never provoke, incite, or aggravate domestic conflict, further, has led to some startling departures in domestic law. Hundreds of jurisdictions have adopted what are called "must-arrest" policies: that is, when local police are called to a scene of reported domestic abuse, they must arrest one partner (almost always the man) even if, by the time the authorities arrive, the incident has cooled off and there is no sign of violence, and even if (as is often the case) the woman doesn't want the man arrested. Many of these same jurisdictions have also enacted "no-drop" policies—meaning that if a woman does press charges, she will not be permitted to change her mind and drop them later. Under VAWA, $33 million will be spent this year [1997] on the "Grants to Encourage Arrest" program, which uses federal money to induce localities to adopt must-arrest policies. Next year [1998], the budget of the "Grants to Encourage Arrest" program will jump to $59 million.

Of course, it's hard to feel sorry for men charged with abuse. And there is a satisfying, frontier-justice aspect to the feminist treatment programs: what better punishment for a loutish man than to make him endure hours of feminist lecturing? The trouble is, domestic violence—as these same feminists constantly remind us—is no joke. And there are virtually no convincing data that this feminist approach to male violence is effective.

Indeed, the paternalistic intrusiveness that characterizes so much of feminist domestic violence policy frequently has the unintended consequence of harming the very women it was meant to protect. Judge William S. Cannon, who has handled thousands of domestic violence cases through South Bay (San Diego) Family Court, finds that "about eighty percent of the couples we see in court end up staying together." Nonetheless, the California legislature has made it mandatory for judges to issue a restraining order separating the parties in all domestic violence cases. "It's ridiculous," the judge says of this mandatory separation, "each situation is different." Sometimes a woman doesn't want the separation, particularly if the threat from her husband is mild. "If the woman feels relatively safe, she might well rather have her kids' father home with the family," Judge Cannon says. In California, however, this option is no longer open to women. As Judge Cannon says, "We treat women as brainless individuals who are unable to make choices. If a woman wants a restraining order, she can ask us for it."

Persuading victims of domestic violence that they need no psychological help or are never to blame can also backfire, because it pushes many women away from seeking counseling that they plainly need. A prosecutor from southern California, who preferred not to be identified, told me that many of the women he refers to treatment reject his advice. "They're influenced by the prevailing view in the advocate community that tells them they don't need help. Meanwhile, I'm accused of blaming the victim," the prosecutor says. Some of these women return to husbands who injure or even kill them, when a therapist might have helped them find the strength to stay away. Others end up doing the killing themselves, a tragedy that has happened "more than once on my watch," the prosecutor said. The defense attorneys then claim that the wife is "a victim of battered woman syndrome. They'll say the system failed her because she was never referred for professional help."

34

It is likewise far from clear that must-arrest policies help victims of domestic abuse. Several studies—including one by Lawrence W. Sherman of the University of Maryland, whose early study on mandatory arrest in a single midwestern city actually gave rise to the program's popularity—suggest that mandatory arrest can escalate spousal violence in some men by further enraging them, and causing them to seek revenge on their lovers once they are released from jail.

But the implicit goal of feminist treatment and legal responses is to separate women from their abusive partners—no matter what the circumstances, and no matter how fervently the women wish otherwise. Many shelter counselors interviewed by Kimberle Crenshaw of the UCLA School of Law believe that a batterer is incapable of breaking the cycle of abuse and the woman's only hope of safety is to leave the relationship. In a *New York Times Magazine* story about spousal abuse, writer Jan Hoffman summed up the advice of Ellen Pence, founder of the much-replicated Duluth Abuse Intervention Program and a staunch believer that all batterers are gripped by a hatred of women: "Ellen Pence's advice to women in battering relationships is simply this: Leave. Leave because even the best of programs, even Duluth's, cannot ensure that a violent man will change his ways."

Not very encouraging words from a nationally regarded expert. Perhaps if feminist treatment of domestic violence recognized some cold truths about women and intimate violence, success rates might improve.

For example, contrary to the prevailing view of battered women as weak, helpless, and confused, professor Jacquelyn Campbell reported in 1994 in the *Journal of Family Violence* that the majority of battered women do take steps to end the abuse in their relationships. In truth, the average abused woman is not Hedda Nussbaum (the obsessed lover of psychopath Joel Steinberg). The sad facts, as discussed by Christine Littleton in the 1993 book *Family Matters: Readings on Family Lives and the Law*, are that many "women who stay in battering relationships accurately perceive the risks of remaining, accurately perceive the risks of leaving, and choose to stay either because the risks of leaving outweigh those of staying or because they are trying to rescue something beyond themselves"—such as their family.

And here is the cruelest failure of profeminist therapy. Since many victims of domestic abuse do want to hold their families together, and since they are trying to weigh the risks of staying with an abusive mate, it does them an enormous disservice to put a dangerous man through a program that cannot fulfill its promise to cure him. "The woman thinks to herself, 'Well, now he's changed,' so she goes back to him and drops her guard. Sometimes with devastating effects," says Dr. Richard J. Gelles of the University of Rhode Island's Family Violence Research Program, a pioneer researcher in domestic violence. Professor Richard M. McFall, an expert on marital violence with Indiana University, observes that "typically, the man comes out of a useless mandated treatment program no less violent than when he went in, but now he's got a clean bill of psychological health."

Furthermore, the woman herself can be swept into the vortex of misguided efforts prescribed by feminists. While her partner is being reprogrammed to challenge his sexist assumptions, the wives are often sent to feminist support groups. Valerie T., a patient of Dr. Virginia Goldner, a couples therapist at New York's Ackerman Institute for the Family, attended such a group. "Valerie came back and told me she'd felt worse about herself ever since joining the group because 'everyone was supposed to hate the men and want to leave them'," said Goldner. Cathy Young, author of the forthcoming book, *Beyond the Gender Wars,** says, "Oftentimes the sole qualification to work with battered women is to be one yourself and, of course, to have an abiding hatred of men." In the course of her research, she said, "I remember Renee Ward, director of a Minneapolis shelter, telling me how the advocates' own unresolved anger at men made it very difficult for them to be helpful to the clients, most of whom very much wanted to be in relationships. But it was unthinkable to ever discuss this tension."

Many advocates are also apparently so blinded by ideology that they are unable to draw distinctions between types of abusers. Some men, for example, are first-time offenders, others are brutal recidivists, others attack rarely but harshly, others frequently but less severely, and many are alcoholics. Such a heterogeneous population cannot be treated with a one-size-fits-all approach. Amy Holtzworth-Munroe, an associate professor of psychology at Indiana University, says, "states are basing rigid treatment policy on rhetoric and ideology, not data."

Take the case of "Don," a senior administrator at a southern university. Arrested once for slapping his wife (they are still together), Don was required to attend a Duluth-model program. About fifteen men sat for three hours on ten consecutive Wednesday nights in a classroom headed by two counselors. "The message was clear," Don told me, "whatever she does to you is your fault, whatever you do to her is your fault. It would have been a lot more helpful if they taught

[Ed. note: *This book was published under the title *Ceasefire! Why Women and Men Must Join Forces to Achieve True Equality*, by The Free Press in 1999.]

us to recognize when we felt ourselves being driven into positions where we lash out. The message should have been 'recognize it, deal with it, and quit hitting.' But all they gave us to work with was guilt." According to Don, "bathroom and cigarette breaks were filled with comments about the whole thing being stupid. In the sessions, group discussions among participants were not allowed to develop—maybe the leaders were afraid we'd unite and challenge their propaganda." Rather than improve their relationships, Don felt the therapy only helped to increase polarization between men and women. "Wives went to support groups and we went to our groups."

Complementing these biases was an equally great omission: the role of alcohol in domestic violence. Though studies show a persistent correlation between intoxication and aggression in families, Don's group leaders were adamant that alcohol was never a cause of violence. Don claimed, however, that "every man in the room had been drinking when he was arrested." Booze, of course, is never an acceptable excuse for bad behavior, but there's no question that alcohol pushes some people into violence. Feminist theory downplays the relevance of alcohol abuse, and as a particularly foolish result in Don's program, failed to make sobriety a condition of the treatment for domestic batterers.

Glenna Auxiera, a divorce resolution counselor in Gainesville, Florida, attended a training course on male batterers sponsored by the Duluth Abuse Intervention Program. She reports being "stunned" by what she heard. "The course leaders were fixated on male-bashing," Auxiera says. "I was a battered woman, too, and I see the part I played in the drama of my relationship. Hitting is wrong. Period. But a relationship is a dynamic interaction and if both want to change, counselors should work with them."

But this, of course, is precisely what state guidelines in nearly half the country now or will soon prohibit as the first course of treatment. They would outlaw, for instance, the kind of help that saved the decade-long marriage of a midwestern couple we'll call "Steve and Lois M." Mr. and Mrs. M. were regarded by their community as a model couple. Mr. M. was in fact a high-profile businessman. But two or three times a year, he turned violent. After their last fight, in which he gave Mrs. M. a fractured arm, she gave him an ultimatum: unless he went with her to marriage therapy, she would take their nine-year-old son and leave. He agreed, and the couple saw Eve Lipchik, a Milwaukee, Wisconsin, expert in family therapy. "One can still deplore the aggression and be an advocate for the relationship when two people want to stay together and are motivated to make changes in the relationship," says Lipchik. "It's too easy to stuff people into boxes labeled villains and victims."

Mrs. M. did not feel "blamed" when she and her husband saw Lipchik together for four months with follow-up sessions at six and eighteen months. She got what she most wanted: her marriage saved and the violence ended. Of course, the happy ending of the story of Mr. and Mrs. M. does not necessarily await every combative couple: spousal assault is a difficult behavior to change. But with a good therapist, difficult change is not impossible. Richard Heyman, of the State University of New York at Stony Brook, found that group conjoint therapy (several couples treated together) produced a significant reduction in both psychological and physical aggression immediately following treatment and one year later. This applied when the couple was intact, the degree of violence not severe, and the couple acknowledged that aggression was a problem, and often a mutual one.

Of course, joint-therapy is not for everyone. It may even be outright dangerous when the man causes frequent injury or when the woman is afraid of him. Not only will the woman be hesitant to tell the truth in counseling sessions, but her husband might well retaliate for disclosures she makes to the counselor. A woman in such a situation is at real risk and must protect herself though she may find it hard—psychologically and physically—to pull away. For her, writes Dr. Virginia Goldner, "the ideological purity and righteous indignation of the battered woman's movement is all that protects her from being pulled back into the swamp of abuse." Maybe so, but more often the violence is less intense and, as psychologist Judith Shervin writes, "men and women are bound in their dance of mutual destructiveness....Women must share responsibility for their behavior and contributions to domestic violence."

These contributions are far bigger than feminists are willing to admit. According to the landmark 1980 book, *Behind Closed Doors: Violence in the American Family* by Murray A. Straus, Richard J. Gelles, and Suzanne K. Steinmetz, about twelve percent of couples engage in physical aggression. Severe violence such as punching, biting, kicking, or using a weapon is as likely to be committed by wives as husbands—at a rate of about one in twenty for both sexes. Rates of less severe assault such as pushing and grabbing are also comparable, about one in thirteen for both men and women.

At first glance, these data don't seem consistent with those of the Department of Justice's statistics. Its 1994 National Crime Victimization Survey stated that "women were about six times more likely than men to experience violence by an intimate." But this merely reflects the fact that women, unlike men, are rarely violent outside the home. Sometimes their aggression is in self-defense. A 1995 DOJ report showed that wives committed forty-one percent of all spousal murders in 1988 (the year covered in the report). However, eighty-one percent of the accused wives, compared to ninety-four percent of the accused husbands, were convicted of homicide. The lower conviction rate for wives, the report said, reflected the fact that they were more likely to have killed in self-defense. Even so, the sentences varied dramatically: wives received average prison sentences of six years, husbands sixteen and a half years.

But self-defense doesn't explain all female-on-male aggression. The National Family Violence Survey, developed by Straus and Gelles and funded by the National Institute of Mental Health, is a widely respected assessment that taps a representative sample of married and cohabiting couples. The researchers interviewed thousands of couples in 1975, 1985, and 1992. Extrapolating from their 1985 survey of more than six thousand couples, the authors estimate that 1.8 million females are the victims of severe domestic violence each year (with injuries suffered by one in ten), but so were about 2.1 million men. The rates of male-on-female aggression declined between 1975 and 1992 while female-on-male stayed constant. The surveys also revealed that women suffered actual injury at about seven times the rate of men but that they used weapons such as baseball bats, boiling water, and knives (among other things) to make up for their physical disadvantage. Many of these women freely admitted on the survey that their use of weapons was not in self-defense.

Actually, when it comes to the murder of intimates, as criminologist Coramae Richey Mann documented in her 1996 study of female killers, *When Women Kill*, murderesses are seldom helpless angels: seventy-eight percent of the women in Mann's study had prior arrest records and fifty-five percent a history of violence. Lately, Straus has been revising his views. "I [once] explained the high rate of attacks by wives largely as a response to or as a defense against assault by the partner. However, new evidence raises questions about that interpretation," he wrote in his contribution to the 1996 book, *Domestic Violence*.

After reviewing the available research, Straus concludes that twenty-five to thirty percent of violent married and cohabiting couples are violent solely because of attacks by the wife. About twenty-five percent of violence between couples is initiated by men. The remaining half is classified as mutual. This is true whether the analysis is based on all assaults or only potentially injurious and life-threatening ones. (These findings are corroborated by other studies, including the 1991 Los Angeles Epidemiology Catchment Area study, and the 1990 National Survey of Households and Families.)

In fact, among America's rapidly growing population of elderly couples, violence by women appears more common than violence by men. A well-regarded 1988 Boston survey by Karl Pillemer and David Finkelhor found that wives were more than twice as likely to assault an elderly husband as vice versa.

Anyone still inclined to blame domestic violence on the patriarchy and male aggression ought to take a look at the statistics on violence against children. A just-released report from the Department of Health and Human Services, "Child Maltreatment in the United States," finds that women aged twenty to forty-nine are almost twice as likely as males to be "perpetrators of child maltreatment." According to a 1994 Department of Justice report, mothers are responsible in fifty-five percent of cases in which children are killed by their parents. The National Center on Child Abuse Prevention attributes fifty percent of the child abuse fatalities that occurred between 1986 and 1993 to the natural mother, twenty-three percent to the natural father, and twenty-seven percent to boyfriends and others.

Finally, consider domestic aggression within lesbian couples. If feminists are right, shouldn't these matches be exempt from the sex-driven power struggles that plague heterosexual couples? Instead, according to Jeanie Morrow, director of the Lesbian Domestic Violence Program at W.O.M.A.N., Inc. in San Francisco, physical abuse between lesbian partners is at least as serious a problem as it is among heterosexuals. The Battered Women's Justice Project in Minneapolis, a clearinghouse for statistics, confirms this. "Most evidence suggests that lesbians and heterosexuals are comparably aggressive in their relationships," said spokeswoman Susan Gibel.

Some survey studies have actually suggested a higher incidence of violence among lesbian partners, but it's impossible to know for certain since there's no reliable baseline count of lesbian couples in the population at large. According to Morrow, the lesbian community has been reluctant to acknowledge intimate violence within its ranks—after all, this would endanger the all-purpose, battering-as-a-consequence-of-male-privilege explanation. Morrow's program treats about three hundred women a year but she wonders how many more need help. Because they are "doubly closeted," as Morrow puts it, women who are both gay and abused may be especially reluctant to use services or report assaults to the police.

Like so many projects of the feminist agenda, the battered women's movement has outlived its useful beginnings, which was to help women leave violent relationships and persuade the legal system to take domestic abuse more seriously. Now they have brought us to a point at which a single complaint touches off an irreversible cascade of useless and often destructive legal and therapeutic events. This could well have a chilling effect upon victims of real violence, who may be reluctant to file police reports or to seek help if it subjects them to further battery from the authorities. And it certainly won't help violent men if they emerge from so-called treatment programs no more enlightened but certainly more angry, more resentful, and as dangerous as ever.

Aggression is a deeply personal and complex behavior, not a social defect expressed through the actions of men. Yet to feminists, it can only be the sound of one hand slapping: the man's. So long as this view prevails, we won't be helping the real victims; indeed, we will only be exposing them to more danger.

*Sally L. Satel, M.D., is a psychiatrist and lecturer at the Yale School of Medicine. She also serves on the National Advisory Board of the Independent Women's Forum.*

# Part Two

# Spousal and Partner Abuse

# Chapter 4

# *Definitions and Incidence*

## *Chapter Contents*

## 4.1

# *Domestic Violence...What Is It?*

U.S. Department of Justice, Violence Against Women Office, July, 1996.

As domestic violence awareness has increased, it has become evident that abuse can occur within a number of relationships. The laws in many states cover incidents of violence occurring between married couples, as well as abuse of elders by family members, abuse between roommates, dating couples and those in lesbian and gay relationships.

In an abusive relationship, the abuser may use a number of tactics other than physical violence in order to maintain power and control over his or her partner.

**Emotional and verbal abuse:** Survivors of domestic violence recount stories of put-downs, public humiliation, name-calling, mind games and manipulations by their partners. Many say that the emotional abuse they have suffered has left the deepest scars.

**Isolation:** It is common for an abuser to be extremely jealous, and insist that the victim not see her friends or family members. The resulting feeling of isolation may then be increased for the victim if she loses her job as a result of absenteeism or decreased productivity (which are often associated with people who are experiencing domestic violence).

**Threats and intimidation:** Threats—including threats of violence, suicide, or of taking away the children—are a very common tactic employed by the batterer.

The existence of emotional and verbal abuse, attempts to isolate, and threats and intimidation within a relationship may be an indication that physical abuse is to follow. Even if they are not accompanied by physical abuse, the effect of these incidents must not be minimized.

## Section 4.2

# *Domestic Violence*

- An estimated six million women are assaulted by a male partner each year and of these, 1.8 million are severely assaulted. (*Straus, 1993.*)

- In 1995, twenty-six percent (26%) of all female murder victims were slain by their husbands or boyfriends. (*Federal Bureau of Investigation, 1996.*)

- In 1994, sixty-two percent (62%) of the victimizations of females (2,981,419 victimizations) were committed by persons they knew while sixty-three percent (63%) of the victimizations of males (3,949,285) were by strangers. (*Craven, 1997.*)

- Of the National Women's Study sample of 4,008 adult women, 1.2 percent (1.2%), or an estimated 1,155,600 adult American women, were forcibly raped one or more times by their husbands. (*National Victim Center & Crime Victims Research and Treatment Center, 1992.*)

## *Definition*

The lack of a single accepted definition for domestic violence exemplifies the misconceptions and conflicting ideas that exist. In relation to laws pertaining to domestic violence, current definitions include assault, battery, homicide, weapon use, kidnaping, unlawful imprisonment and trespassing (National Victim Center, Legislative Database). From a clinical perspective, domestic violence can be defined as assaultive behavior involving persons in a dating and/or intimate, sexual, theoretically peer and often co-habitating relationship (Goolkasian, 1986).

According to the American Medical Association, the U.S. home is "more dangerous to women than city streets" (American Medical Association, 1991, p. 5). Domestic violence is a common presenting complaint among women seeking emergency medical attention although most of women who are either abused or at risk for abuse are not detected by physicians (Abbott, Johnson, Koziol-McLain & Lowenstein, 1996). Approximately 17% of the 4.4 million people treated in hospital emergency rooms for violence-related injuries were injured by intimates (Rand, 1997). With the identification of domestic violence as a "national epidemic" by physicians, public health experts and public policy leaders, recommendations have come from the American Medical Association, the American College of Emergency Physicians, the Emergency Nurses Association, and the American College of Obstetricians and Gynecologists to improve methods of detection, counseling, and referral for domestic violence in emergency treatment settings (Marwick, 1994).

While domestic violence, including threats, physical assaults and homicide, continues to be one of the most frequent crimes in our nation, it remains one of the most under-reported. Too often in the past, when the victim did report, the incident was not thoroughly investigated because a determination was made that it was a "family" or "personal" matter and, thus, did not warrant the urgency of other crimes (Goolkasian, 1986). Law enforcement has greatly improved its response to domestic violence over the past decade, taking a pro-active approach to the arrest of the batterer and the protection of the victim in many jurisdictions. Yet, improvements still need to be made not only by law enforcement, but by the entire criminal justice system, as such deficiencies may often deter victims from reporting incidents and filing criminal charges.

## The Victim and Abuser

The violent behavior of the batterer has often been explained by the characteristics of the victim. Many studies have been done on battered women's personalities, mental health, and self-esteem, questioning "What makes a woman susceptible to abuse?" and "Why are some women abused?" These questions in and of themselves place a certain amount of blame on the woman, giving her responsibility for what has happened to her. It would be better to focus on the characteristics of the abuser.

Male batterers, while exhibiting many different personalities, do share some characteristics. Many batterers show a higher level of dependence on their wives than non-battering men. Their dependence conflicts with a fear of intimacy and loss of control. Batterers also exhibit higher levels of suspicion and paranoia, according to the Minnesota Multiphasic Personality Inventory (MMPI). Batterers often will isolate their wives and are jealous to the point of suspicion of any interactions with other men, thus creating suspicions of infidelity. In addition, batterers have been observed to have an excessive need for control in the relationship. High levels of hostility, depression and anxiety have also been noted. Batterers tend to deny responsibility for their actions, blaming the victim for provoking them, or ignoring the violent incident altogether (Vaselle-Augenstein & Ehrlich, 1992) [see also Chapters 9 and 28].

While many factors may contribute to abuse, it is difficult to attribute a direct causal relationship to any one factor. Some batterers lack the ability to control their actions and do not know how to react appropriately and nonviolently to stress and dissatisfaction. A need for power and control, an abusive family background, feelings of isolation, inadequacy, and stress may all contribute to the abusive behavior.

## *Why Victims Stay*

Often the beginnings of abuse are subtle. It may start with verbal put-downs and anger directed at objects—breaking and throwing things. As it builds in severity and frequency, the victim is gradually conditioned to the situation.

In most cultures, women are brought up being taught that dependence on a male and affiliation with a family is the expected, preferred and most rewarding way of life for them. Once in an abusive relationship, a woman may not leave because she hopes or believes that the abuser will change. Many women will return to an abusive relationship as soon as their partner starts counseling, without waiting for a change in behavior patterns. Then when the abuser gradually stops counseling and the abuse continues, the woman finds herself in the same situation as before she left, and perhaps even worse off.

Other reasons that domestic violence victims may stay in abusive relationships include:

- A belief in commitment;
- A desire not to hurt their partner;
- Their fear of being seen as a quitter;
- The need to protect children and parents;
- Financial considerations; and/or
- Religious convictions.

Religious convictions are often an important factor in many victims' decisions to stay or leave the relationship. One research study showed that clergy were the second most often sought source for help—after the police—following the first battering incident. However, this study also found that of the women who contacted the clergy, most later identified women's groups and social services as the most helpful, and none identified the clergy as most helpful. Another study claims that while the church is the institution most often contacted by battered women, clergy also had the highest negative influence compared to women's groups, psychologists, police, relatives, lawyers, and friends (Barnett and LaViolette, 1993).

Battered women are tied to their husbands by more than just emotional and moral obligations; many are economically dependent upon their husbands as well. Leaving their husbands/partners and trying to support both themselves and their children can prove to be too intimidating a prospect for many victims. With no way to support themselves, battered women are reluctant to leave their situation.

Another factor in the decision to leave is the severity of the abuse. As reviewed in Barnett and LaViolette (1993), studies indicate that the more severe the abuse, the longer the battered woman took to decide to leave the relationship, but once she had left, she was less likely to return. Women in relationships of minor violence were likely to leave, but also likely to return to the relationship.

## The Pattern of Violence

Battering is usually not an isolated incident, but rather it tends to be a cycle that increases in frequency and severity over time. This cycle of violence is usually broken down into three phases. The first phase is a tension-building phase where anger builds and minor incidences of violence occur. It may include verbal abuse towards the victim, threats, and breaking things. This phase lasts indefinitely, but eventually builds to an acute battering incident—the phase in which the actual violence occurs.

The level of violence of a particular battering depends upon many variables, including the level of violence previously evident in the relationship, the level of substance abuse, the state of mind of the abuser and other factors. Usually the batterer will blame the use of force on the victim. Regardless of the level of force actually used, the use of violence in the context of an intimate relationship is always frightening.

The acute battering incident is followed by a third phase, usually referred to as the honeymoon phase, where the batterer is remorseful or fearful of losing his partner, begging forgiveness and trying to make amends. Some abusers, however, may show little or no remorse during this phase. Often the honeymoon is only a short-lived period of no violence.

The victim may often become very protective of her batterer during the honeymoon phase—believing that she has overreacted to his violence—and she begins to have hope that their relationship will be restored and the abuse will never happen again. The cycle gradually returns to the tension-building phase, however, as the batterer places all the blame for his actions on others and the victim internalizes all the blame on herself.

These different phases and types of violence and reactions combine to create what is known as the "cycle of violence." This cyclical theory was first set forth by domestic violence expert Lenore Walker (1979) to describe the battered woman's syndrome, which occurs as a response to a series of severe and frequent assaults and encompasses the victim's severe stress reactions and the fear, anxiety, depression, guilt, confusion, passivity and low self-esteem that accompany it. Most battered women are blamed over and over by their batterers for the abuse; gradually, the battered woman begins to take responsibility for the beatings and learns that she is unable to stop or avoid them. This results in frustration, confusion and a reduction in her ability to effectively solve her problems.

Her situation and resulting mental attitude causes her to become more able to survive in the relationship and less able to escape. Much like the war victim or prisoner of war who is under constant stress and subjected to arbitrary and intermittent violence, the battered woman learns to feel that she is helpless and that the violence is unavoidable. She loses the ability to learn new avoidance techniques, thus making her situation more dangerous and more difficult to leave.

Domestic violence affects every member of the family—even if they are not the ones being directly abused. Research has provided evidence that children who observe domestic violence may grow to accept it as a natural part of adult, especially intimate, relationships and may grow up to become offenders or victims themselves. Children who witness violence learn that violence is an acceptable way of coping with anger and frustration.

Additional findings indicate that children of battered women may sustain some developmental delays as a result of observing abuse and battering (Widom, 1992). They also suffer feelings of loss, anger, fear, sadness, confusion, and guilt as a result of witnessing violence at home, disruption of normal coping patterns, difficult living conditions, and the emotional unavailability of their mother (Peled & Edleson, 1994).

## Trying to Leave

Leaving an abusive relationship is not always the safest solution for the victim. Many domestic assaults occur either as or after the victim tries to leave the relationship. A person who is being abused should consider the options available and work to find a way to end the violence as safely as possible. This may mean waiting to end the relationship, or it may mean getting out as quickly as possible. Only the abused person can truly judge what will be the safest and best option for them.

Once a person has decided to leave an abusive relationship, a detailed safety plan should be made. The person should know where to go, how to leave, and how and if their children will leave with them. Before leaving it is good to pack a suitcase of necessities and put it in a safe place that is not in the home, but is readily available for quick pick up. Include in this emergency suitcase:

- A change of clothes;
- Money—whatever is available;
- Identification;
- Copies of essential legal papers;
- Important medication;
- Phone numbers; and
- Other important personal items.

A trusted neighbor or friend should be told about the situation, and a separate plan should be made with them in the event that the abused person needs assistance (i.e., decide on a visual signal to indicate that the neighbor should call the police immediately).

[*If you are currently in an abusive relationship, see* Chapter 12, Section 12.3: INFOLINK, No. 14A, "Suggested Safety Plan Guidelines for Victims of Domestic Violence" *for more information and suggestions. Also see* Section 12.6 *for a blank personalized safety plan.*]

Support networks exist in many communities. There are hotlines, counseling services, support groups, legal resources, and shelters which provide support, advice, financial assistance, counseling and legal help. There are also batterers' programs in almost every community which assist abusive partners in learning how to control themselves. Referrals for these programs can be obtained through each county's Family Court Division or Adult Probation Office, and are often a court-mandated condition of sentences when batterers are convicted on domestic violence charges.

## Restraining Orders

Restraining order application forms can be obtained from the local police department, county Family Court Division and/or local domestic violence programs or shelters. There are several forms of restraining orders. Some states have an emergency restraining order that a police officer can issue when responding to a domestic violence call. This is usually good until the end of the next business day, and allows the victim time to apply for a more permanent order. Other restraining orders last from 30 days to a few years and can be indefinitely renewed. Each jurisdiction and community may differ in the types of restraining orders available and the process for application and issuance of orders.

The realities of restraining orders, however, are that they are not always effective. They are not always enforced, and it is sometimes difficult to catch a person in the process of breaking the order—which is a requirement in many jurisdictions before the police can enforce the order.

A person with a restraining order should keep a copy in a safe place and file another copy with their local law enforcement. Neighbors should also be alerted of the situation and informed of the abuser's identity. If it becomes necessary to call the police, the restraining order should be shown to the officers immediately upon their arrival.

[*For more information regarding restraining orders in your jurisdiction, please contact your local law enforcement, your county Family Court Division, your local domestic violence programs, or the victim assistance program in your local county or city prosecutor's office. See also* Chapter 36.]

## What Can I Do about This Problem?

If you know someone who is being abused, support them in their efforts to end the violence. Don't blame them for the abuse. Give them the strength and emotional support to leave if they need it, but do not try to force them to leave. Support them in their decision to stay or leave.

Teach young people that violence is not acceptable. Support your local program for battered women, sharing time and resources. Encourage training in non-violent conflict resolution in the schools—at every grade-level—and curricula in social studies classes on domestic violence.

Victims of domestic violence, as well as batterers, need help and supportive services. An understanding of the violence in American homes and an acknowledgment of the severity and criminality of these offenses by local and national law enforcement, medical service providers and social service agencies may provide a foundation for breaking the vicious cycle of domestic violence [see Chapters 12, 20, and 36].

## References

Abbott, Jean, Robin Johnson, Jane Koziol-McLain, and Steven Lowenstein. (1995). "Domestic Violence Against Women: Incidence and Prevalence in an Emergency Department Population." *Journal of the American Medical Association* 273, 22: 1763–67.

American Medical Association. (1991). "Domestic Violence: No Longer a Family Secret." *Five Issues in American Health*. Chicago, Ill.: American Medical Association.

Attorney General's Family Violence Task Force, Pennsylvania. (1989). *Domestic Violence: A Model Protocol for Police Response*. Harrisburg, Pa.

Barnett, Ola, and Alyce LaViolette. (1993). *It Could Happen to Anyone: Why Battered Women Stay*. Newbury Park, Calif: Sage.

Craven, Diane. (1997). *Sex Differences in Violent Victimization, 1994*. Washington, D.C.: Bureau of Justice Statistics, U.S. Department of Justice.

Federal Bureau of Investigation. (1996). *Crime in the United States, 1995*. Washington, D.C.: USGPO.

Goolkasian, Gail. (1986). *Confronting Domestic Violence: A Guide for Criminal Justice Agencies*. Washington, D.C.: U.S. Department of Justice, National Institute of Justice.

National Victim Center. (1995). "Domestic Violence and the Law," *INFOLINK* No. 58. Arlington, Va.: National Victim Center.

National Victim Center. (1995). "Suggested Safety Plan Guidelines for Domestic Violence Victims," *INFOLINK* No. 14. Arlington, Va.: National Victim Center.

National Victim Center and Crime Victims Research and Treatment Center. (1992). *Rape in America: A Report to the Nation.* Arlington, Va.: National Victim Center and Crime Victims Research and Treatment Center.

Peled, Einat, and Jeffrey Edleson. (1994). "Process and Outcome in Small Groups for Children of Battered Women." In Einat Peled, Peter Jaffe, and Jeffrey Edleson, eds. *Ending the Cycle of Violence.* Newbury Park, Calif.: Sage.

Rand, Michael. (1997). *Violence-Related Injuries Treated in Hospital Emergency Departments.* Washington, D.C.: Bureau of Justice Statistics, U.S. Department of Justice.

Straus, Murray. (1993). "Physical Assaults by Wives: A Major Social Problem." In Richard Gelles and Donileen Loseke, eds. *Current Controversies on Family Violence.* Newbury Park, Calif.: Sage.

Vaselle-Augenstein, Renata, and Annette Ehrlich. (1993). "Male Batterers: Evidence for Psychopathology." In Emilio Viano, ed. *Intimate Violence: Interdisciplinary Perspectives.* Washington, D.C.: Hemisphere Publishing Corporation.

Walker, Lenore. (1979). *The Battered Woman.* New York: Harper & Row.

Widom, Cathy Spatz. (1989). *The Cycle of Violence.* Washington, D.C.: U.S. Department of Justice, National Institute of Justice.

# Section 4.3

# *Intimate Partner Violence Fact Sheet*

National Center for Injury Prevention and Control, Centers for Disease
Control and Prevention, 1998.

## *Problem Definition*

Intimate partner violence (IPV) is a substantial public health problem for Americans that has serious consequences and costs for individuals, families, communities, and society.[1,2] Recent efforts have been
made to increase resources to address gaps in knowledge and to improve services for victims, perpetrators, and child witnesses.[3,4,5]

IPV is actual or threatened physical or sexual violence, or psycho-
logical/emotional abuse. Some of the common terms that are used to
describe intimate partner violence are domestic abuse, spouse abuse,
domestic violence, courtship violence, battering, marital rape, and date
rape. Intimate partners include current or former spouses, boyfriends,
or girlfriends (including heterosexual or same-sex partners). Readers
should consult the references cited here for their exact definitions of
IPV, which may vary from that described above.

Many experts consider the following figures to be underestimates
of IPV, because victims may underreport IPV on surveys and because
data sources may lack information identifying victim-perpetrator relationships.[1,4] Further, definitions and research methods vary across
studies, leading to different estimates of IPV.[3]

## *Recent Findings*[21]

**Non-lethal intimate violence:** Data from a household survey on
criminal victimization, the National Crime Victimization Survey, between 1992 and 1996 indicate:

- Nearly 1 million incidents of non-lethal IPV occurred each year
from 1992 to 1996; 85% of victims were women.[2]

- On average each year from 1992 to 1996, approximately 8 in
1,000 women and 1 in 1,000 men age 12 or older experienced a

violent victimization perpetrated by a current or former spouse, boyfriend, or girlfriend.[2]

- On average each year between 1992 and 1996, approximately 12 per 1,000 black women experienced violence by an intimate partner, compared with about 8 per 1,000 white women. These rates are not adjusted for socioeconomic status, which may account for the higher rates in black women.[2]

- The number of violent victimizations by an intimate partner has been declining for women. In 1996, women reported 840,000 violent victimizations by an intimate partner, down from 1.1 million in 1993.[2]

- For years 1992–1993, 92% of rapes of women were committed by known assailants. About half of all rapes and sexual assaults against women are committed by friends or acquaintances; 26% are by intimate partners.[2]

**Lethal intimate violence:** Data from FBI Uniform Crime Reports between 1992 and 1996 indicate:

- For men and for blacks, murders by intimate partners have decreased.[2]

- In 1996 about 2,000 murders were attributed to intimate partners, down from 3,000 two decades earlier.[2]

- In 1996, 30% of all female murders were perpetrated by husbands, ex-husbands, or boyfriends. Three percent of all male murder victims were killed by wives, ex-wives, or girlfriends.[6]

**Pregnancy:** A 1996 review of the literature indicated that estimated proportions of women experiencing IPV during pregnancy ranged between 0.9% and 20.1%. The proportion of pregnant women who had experienced IPV at any time in the past ranged between 9.7% and 29.7%.[7]

**Stalking:** A term that generally refers to repeated harassing or threatening behavior, stalking is more prevalent in the U.S. than previously thought. In a national study in which the definition of stalking required the victim to report a high level of fear, an estimated 1 million women and 370,000 men were stalked annually. Most victims were women (78%) and most perpetrators were men (87%).[8] [*See also* Chapter 10.]

## Health Effects

Studies of emergency department (ED) visits by women have found:

- Women accounted for nearly 40% of all ED visits for violent victimization in 1994.[9]

- In 36% of all ED visits by women for violent victimizations, intimate partners were identified as the perpetrators.[9]

- Women account for 84% of those treated for injuries by intimate partners, which includes spouses, ex-spouses, boyfriends, girlfriends.[9]

- In one study of ED visits by women, over half of all women in the study had experienced IPV at some time in their lives, while 11% of those with current husbands or boyfriends gave IPV as the reason for the visit.[10]

As a consequence of severe intimate partner violence, female victims are more likely than male victims to need medical attention, take time off from work, spend more days in bed, and suffer more from stress and depression. [11]

Psychological consequences for victims of intimate partner violence can include depression, suicidal thoughts and attempts, lowered self-esteem, alcohol and other drug abuse, and post-traumatic stress disorder.[3]

## Risk Factors

**Income:** Women in families with incomes below $10,000 are more likely than other women to be victims of violence by an intimate partner.[1]

**Age:** Women age 19 to 29 are more likely than other women to be victims of violence by an intimate partner.[1]

**Children:**
- Women whose children have been abused by a parent or other caretaker are at increased risk for IPV.[12]

- Increased frequency of violence toward a spouse is associated with increased risk of the violent spouse (particularly a husband) also being abusive to the child.[13]

- Each year more than ten million American children witness IPV within their families.[14]
- Witnessing violence is stressful and it is a risk factor for long-term physical and mental health problems such as alcohol and substance abuse, child abuse and IPV.[14]

**Alcohol and other drugs:** Data from the National Crime Victimization Survey indicate an association between IPV and alcohol or other drug use. Among IPV victims who were able to describe alcohol or drug use by the perpetrator, 75% reported offender alcohol or other drug use at the time of the crime.[15] [*See also* Chapter 6.]

- The nature of the relationship between IPV and substance abuse is not yet clear. Many assaults against intimate partners do not occur in the context of substance abuse, and many substance abusers are not violent with their intimate partners.[3]

**Stalking and other forms of violence:** Data from the National Violence Against Women Survey of 1995-96 indicate a strong association between stalking and other forms of violence in intimate relationships: 81% of women who were stalked by a current or former husband or cohabiting partner were also physically assaulted by that partner; 31% were also sexually assaulted by that partner.[7]

## Costs

Data from the National Crime Victimization Survey between 1992 and 1996 indicate:[2]

- Non-lethal intimate violence results in financial losses to women victims that are conservatively estimated to be $150 million per year.
- Medical expenses accounted for at least 40% of these costs, property losses for another 44%, and lost pay for the remainder.

[*See* Chapter 35 *for more information.*]

## Prevention and Intervention

Increasing access to services for victims and perpetrators of IPV and their children is a priority. [16]

59

One promising strategy, the use of coordinated community initiatives, may strengthen safety networks for high-risk individuals and families.[17]

School-based prevention programs for IPV have focused both on teen dating violence and on IPV among adult partners. Topics addressed have included exploration of gender roles and expectations, personal safety, legal statutes, and social norms that tolerate violence.[18]

Home visitation services and interventions with child witnesses to violence have shown some promise in prevention of IPV among high-risk families.[18]

Practice guidelines for health care providers include recommendations to ask all women patients if they have experienced IPV.[19,20] Health care providers may also provide information to women at risk for IPV about community resources, such as shelters for battered women and legal resources.

## *Selected Bibliography*

1.  Bachman R., and L. E. Saltzman. *Violence Against Women: Estimates from the Redesigned Survey, Bureau of Justice Statistics, Special Report*. Washington, D.C.: U.S. Department of Justice, August 1995.

2.  Greenfield L., et al., eds. *Violence by Intimates: Analysis of Data on Crimes by Current or Former Spouses, Boyfriends, and Girlfriends*. Bureau of Justice Statistics Factbook. Washington, D.C.: U.S. Department of Justice, March 1998. NCJ-167237.

3.  National Research Council. *Understanding Violence Against Women*. Washington, D.C.: National Academy Press, 1996: 79–80.

4.  Straus, M. A., and R. J. Gelles. *Physical Violence in American Families: Risk Factors and Adaptations to Violence in 8,145 Families*. New Brunswick, N.J.: Transaction, 1990.

5.  Schechter, S. *Women and Male Violence: The Visions and Struggles of the Battered Women's Movement*. Boston: South End Press, 1982.

6. FBI. *Crime in the United States—1996*. Uniform Crime Reports: 1996. p. 17.

7. Gazmararian, J. A., S. Lazorick, A.M. Spitz, et al. "Prevalence of Violence Against Pregnant Women." *Journal of the American Medical Association* 275 (1996): 1915–20.

8. NIJ/CDC Research in Brief. *Stalking in America: Findings from the National Violence Against Women Survey*. April 1998.

9. Rand, M. R. *Violence-Related Injuries Treated in Hospital Emergency Departments*. Bureau of Justice Statistics, Special Report. Washington, D.C.: U.S. Department of Justice, August 1997.

10. Abbott, J.R. Johnson, J. Koziol-McLain, et al. "Domestic Violence Against Women: Incidence and Prevalence in an Emergency Department Population." *Journal of the American Medical Association* 273 (1995): 1763–67.

11. Stets, J. E., and M. A. Straus. "Gender Differences in Reporting Marital Violence and Its Consequences," 151–65. In M. A. Straus and R. J. Gelles, eds. *Physical Violence in American Families: Risk Factors and Adaptations to Violence in 8,145 Families*. New Brunswick, N.J.: Transaction, 1990.

12. McKibben L., E. DeVos, and E. Newberger. "Victimization of Mothers of Abused Children: A Controlled Study." *Pediatrics* 84 (1989): 531–35.

13. Ross, S. "Risk of Physical Abuse to Children of Spouse-Abusing Parents." *Child Abuse and Neglect* 20 (1996): 589–98.

14. Straus, M. A. "Children as Witnesses to Marital Violence: A Risk Factor for Lifelong Problems among a Nationally Representative Sample of American Men and Women," 98–104. In D. F. Schwartz, ed. *Children and Violence: Report of the Twenty-third Ross Roundtable on Critical Approaches to Common Pediatric Problems*. Columbus, Ohio: Ross Laboratories, 1992.

15. Greenfield, L., ed. *Alcohol and Crime: An Analysis of National Data on the Prevalence of Alcohol Involvement in Crime*. Pre-

pared for the Assistant Attorney General's National Symposium on Alcohol and Crime. Washington, D.C., April 1998.
NCJ-168632.

16.  Rosenberg, M. L., and M. A. Fenley. *Violence in America: A Public
     Health Approach*. New York: Oxford University Press, 1991.

17.  American Medical Association. *Family Violence: Building a
     Coordinated Community Response, A Guide for Communities*.
     Chicago: American Medical Association, 1996.

18.  National Research Council/Institute of Medicine. *Violence in
     Families: Assessing Prevention and Treatment Programs*.
     Washington, D.C.: National Academy Press, 1998.

19.  American Medical Association. *Diagnostic and Treatment
     Guidelines on Domestic Violence*. Chicago: American Medical
     Association, March 1992.

20.  Osattin, A., and L. Short. *Intimate Partner Violence and
     Sexual Assault: A Guide to Training Materials and Programs
     for Health Care Providers*. Atlanta, Ga.: National Center for
     Injury Prevention and Control, Centers for Disease Control
     and Prevention, 1998.

21.  According to *Intimate Partner Violence,* a Bureau of Justice
     Statistics Special Report that was published too late to be in-
     cluded in this volume, in 1998 the overall figure of intimate
     partner violence remained the same as in 1996: about 1 mil-
     lion violent crimes were committed against persons by their
     current or former spouses, boyfriends, or girlfriends. However,
     women experienced intimate partner violence at lower rates
     in 1998 (7.7 per 1,000 women) than in 1993 (9.8 per 1,000
     women). For more information, see Rennison, Callie Marie,
     and Sarah Welchans, *Intimate Partner Violence*, Bureau of
     Justice Statistics Special Report, U.S. Department of Justice,
     May 2000 (NCJ 178247).

## Section 4.4

# *The Impact of Domestic Violence on Victims*

Excerpted from *Understanding Domestic Violence: A Handbook for Victims and Professionals.* U.S. Department of Justice, undated.

## *Post-Traumatic Stress Disorder*

Humans respond similarly to threats such as natural disasters, war, captivity, personal attack, and battering. When faced with danger, most victims focus on self-protection and survival, or the survival of a loved one. Victims experience initial feelings of shock, denial, disbelief, and fear. The most terrifying fear is one of serious injury or death.

Women's reactions to violence by a partner have been compared to reactions of survivors of other traumatic events. For example, prisoners of war who are emotionally abused with the threat of physical violence and are isolated, and who are given irregular praise and punishment while sometimes fearing for their lives become crippled, unable to act and dependant. Prisoners of war often adapt by becoming numb, by complying to the demands made, and by agreeing with the abuser's actions and points of view. When the victims are extremely helpless, as in concentration camps, there is a surprising lack of anger expressed towards their captors. In domestic violence, the abuse may be ongoing and the victim may not ever be able to escape the stress.[1]

In the hands of the one they love, battered victims are repeatedly exposed to threats, intimidation, and violence. Battering affects victims' thinking, their feelings, their relationships with others, the way they act and their bodies. The following are statements made by victims of domestic violence.

> At the time of the assault, I was horrified and upset. I felt hopeless and **helpless about escaping.** Once in the bedroom, I thought a lot about dying...**I was sure that I was going to die.** I have never felt that helpless before...I felt alone and afraid. I always thought I would die peacefully and of old age.

---

[1]Taken from Mary P. Koss, Lisa A. Goodman, Angela Browne, Louise F. Fitzgerald, Gwendolyn P. Keita, Nancy F. Russo, *No Safe Haven: Male Violence Against Women at Home, at Work, and in the Community*, American Psychological Association, Washington DC, 1994.

*Many of my thoughts were on how I could survive this frightening, terrifying night.*

*While in the hospital, I was also very solemn and depressed. I couldn't understand how it happened or why it happened to me. I felt very afraid too. I tried to help him, and I couldn't understand how a person could treat someone who helps them so badly. I felt hurt that someone I loved did this to me. It made me question everything. I questioned myself and blamed myself. I just kept **reliving that night over and over** again. I had **nightmares** and would wake up in my sleep screaming and crying. One time, an intern came in the room at night while I was sleeping to draw blood. As I was waking up I thought it was my abuser and started screaming, "Get away! Help!"*

*After the assault, I didn't want to talk to anyone. I felt embarrassed and **ashamed** and didn't want to be **judged by people.** At one point **I used to be an optimistic and fun-loving individual, but now I'm very cold.** I stay secluded and I am **quick to anger** (especially towards men). I'm sad all of the time because I'm constantly remembering the good things before that night versus the bad things that are a result of that night. I don't want it to ever happen again. **I'm not sure what to do to protect myself.***

***It has really changed how I am with men.** At this point, I almost need a social security number before I'm willing to go out with them. I don't trust men at all. I'm worried that this could happen again. I have so much anger towards men that I eat to distract my thoughts from the possibility of it happening again.*

*Last week, on my way home one night, while staying at the Shelter for battered women, I was hurrying to make the curfew when I heard footsteps behind me. I thought to myself, Oh my God, my abuser's people found me. When the counselor opened the door, I stormed in so fast that I ran into her and hurt her knee. **I jumped up, slammed the door, and began screaming, "they found me, they got a gun!"** I remember thinking **I'm dead.** A knock came to the door, a counselor answered, it was another resident. Everyone sighed with relief. It took me the rest of the night to calm down.*

# Indicators of Trauma in Domestic Violence Victims

**Fear/Terror**—The more severe the violence and the more difficult it is to escape the violence, the more likely you will experience an extreme form of fear/terror. If you have experienced domestic violence, you may become fearful of anything that reminds you of the violence.

**Nightmares/flashbacks and sleeping problems**—These and other intrusive symptoms may make victims experience frightening events related to the abuse. Your abuser may recognize that certain things remind you of the violence and may use these things to control you.

**Avoidance**—Some traumatized victims cope with extreme violence by detaching themselves, withdrawing, and by blocking feelings. They may forget, minimize the violence, or become "numb."

**Anxiety**—Generalized fear of anything that reminds victims of past abuse becomes a trigger for their fears. Anxiety can take the form of panic attacks (e.g., unsteady feelings, trembling or shaking, being hyper, sweating, fear of going crazy or losing control) or nervousness.

**Difficulty concentrating**—Difficulty concentrating may cause some victims to have problems at work, at school, or elsewhere.

**Hyper vigilance, suspiciousness**—Traumatized victims may feel unable to relax or let down their guard.

**Psychological reactivity**—Research has found that victimization causes problems with our bodies' ability to regulate emotional and physical reactions to stress. This causes victims to react (e.g., become afraid or angry) to new stressors like they were the old ones, even when they are much less severe.

**Anger/rage**—A traumatized victim's anger or rage at the abuse can be directly expressed to the abuser or taken out on a safer target (e.g., children, co-workers, family, friends). It may be kept inside and result in headaches or other physical symptoms.

**Grief/depression/suicide**—Traumatized victims may experience feelings of loss or sadness resulting from the loss of friends and family supports. They are unable to do the things that are enjoyable and rewarding. Many women who attempt suicide say that battering fueled their attempts.

**Lower self-esteem/shame/embarrassment**—Many battered women devalue themselves and believe they don't deserve better treatment. They may feel bad, like they are damaged goods.

**Health and physical complaints**—Victims may experience health and physical problems such as headaches, lower back pain, gastrointestinal problems (e.g., stomach aches, nausea), heart disease, and cancer.

**Addictive behaviors**—Drugs or alcohol may be used by some victims to self-medicate their distress. These substances may be used to reduce anxiety, increase feeling "numb," block the pain and distress mentioned already.

**Impaired functioning**—Battered victims often report that they are not able to be with friends because they feel too depressed or angry, and they may be preoccupied with the abuse or the decisions they have to make.

**Changes in beliefs**—Some traumatized victims may come to feel that the world is no longer a safe place. They may lose the view that the world is meaningful and may feel helpless to effect change, to escape, or to protect themselves. They may blame themselves for causing the violence, for not stopping the violence, or for not being able to tolerate violence. They may believe that they cannot trust their own perceptions and judgments any more.

**Attachment and dependency**—Common responses to trauma. For some victims, the decreased sense of self-worth and increased isolation results in a greater dependency upon the abuser (known as "traumatic bonding"). The victim may protect the abuser from harm (e.g., calling the police), from embarrassment (e.g., telling family or friends).

**Difficulty with trust**—Victims have difficulty believing that they will not be physically or emotionally abused. Victims often respond to new partners with anger or fear as though they were the old partners.

# Chapter 5

# *Special Populations*

## *Chapter Contents*

## Section 5.1

# *The Facts: The Needs of Underserved Communities*

National Network to End Domestic Violence Fund, Copyright © 1997.
Used with permission.

According to the American Psychological Association, family violence is ongoing violence that occurs within a relationship that is expected to be caring, loving, and nurturing. Thus the bond between the victim and the abuser is often a strong one.

Domestic violence is prevalent in the United States and yet it is still underreported. It is particularly underreported in situations where the victim faces additional barriers to coming forward. For example, she may be disabled, elderly, or an immigrant battered woman. She may be unable to speak for herself, be incapacitated, or face a multitude of language, cultural, and economic barriers. In some instances, the victim may rely on the abuser to accomplish daily living tasks. For African American, Asian/Pacific Islanders, Latin Americans, Native Americans and other women of diverse backgrounds, cultural issues may affect their ability to seek help for services or through the justice system. Lesbian battered women may find it difficult to identify an ally and support from within the mainstream.

However, as much as these women are different, they face many of the same challenges. They too may live in fear: Fear for their lives and safety for their children. And, yet, the issues that these women who are underserved by traditional battered women services and systems face are complex and range from language barriers, gender and class oppression, and housing and employment discrimination to name a few.

- [An African American woman] is more likely to feel protective of [her batterer] because of discrimination and "hard times" he has faced, and obligated to support and assist [him] emotionally to preserve some sense of family.

- African American women of lower socioeconomic status who have been battered are more likely than middle class white women to need extensive services and support.

Edward W. Gondolf, *Assessing Women Battering in Mental Health Services* (Sage Publications, 1998).

- Asian Pacific teenagers' allegiance to their families and maintaining their families' respectability may cause feelings of shame and reluctance to seek help.

Mieko Yoshihama et al., "Dating Violence in Asian/Pacific Communities," *Dating Violence: Young Women in Danger* (Barrie Levy, ed., Seal Press, 1991).

- Battered Latina women in shelters are likely to have experienced a longer duration of abuse, be married at a younger age, have larger families, and stay in relationships longer.

Edward W. Gondolf, et al., "Racial Differences Among Shelter Residences: A Comparison of Anglo, Black, and Hispanic Battered Women." *Black Family Violence: Current Research and Theory* (R. L. Hampton, ed., Sage Publications, 1991).

- Asian women, especially Asian immigrant women, may be hesitant to disclose battering or abuse because of their cultural views about privacy, perseverance, and self-restraint or their fears about their immigration status.
- It may be difficult for battered immigrant women to speak out against abuse because many cultures value family loyalty. Therefore, it may go against what battered immigrant women consider important.

Christine K. Ho, "An Analysis of Domestic Violence in Asian American Communities: A Multicultural Approach to Counseling," *Diversity and Complexity in Feminist Therapy* (L. S. Brown and M. P. P. Root, eds., Haworth, 1990).

- In order to maintain control over their immigrant wives, men may threaten to take her children away from the United States, fail to file papers to legalize her immigration status, or threaten to report her to INS [Immigration and Naturalization Service] to get her deported.

Leti Volpp, Family Violence Prevention Fund, *Working with Battered Immigrant Women: A Handbook to Make Services Accessible* (1995).

- Native American womens' sense of tribal sovereignty and loyalty may conflict with making a police report about her husband who assaults her.
- In 1994 there were about 241,000 reports of domestic elder abuse.
- A family member is involved in nearly a third of all murders of people aged 60 or older.
- Men are more often the perpetrators of <u>physical</u> elder abuse, and elders are more likely to be abused by someone with whom they live.

American Psychological Association, *Violence and the Family: Report of the American Psychological Association Presidential Task Force on Violence and the Family* (1996).

A survey conducted of 100 lesbians illustrates the dynamics of lesbian battering. While this survey may not be representative of the lesbian population as a whole, it was found that women may stay with abusive women for the same reasons that women may stay with abusive men.

Of the 100 women surveyed:

- 8% were living with their abuser.
- 14% were still involved with their abuser.
- 65% reported that they were involved in the relationship for 1-5 years.
- 20% reported that they were involved in the relationship less than a year.
- 14% reported that they were involved in the relationship for more than 5 years.
- 77% of the abuse occurred less than 6 months after the relationship began.
- 71% reported that the abuse grew worse over time.
- 11% reported psychological abuse.
- 87% reported physical abuse and psychological abuse.
- 19% sought help of the police, with 0 reporting it was very helpful.
- 13% sought shelter services, with 3 reporting it was very helpful.

Claire Renzetti, *Violent Betrayal: Partner Abuse in Lesbian Relationships* (Sage Publications, 1992).

In order for shelters, services, and programs to meet the needs of underserved communities, they need to hire and train multilingual, multicultural counselors and interpreters. Service providers need to be patient, may need to speak slowly, listen carefully, assess safety and needs of the victim, and validate the victim's feelings. It is also important for the service provider not to make assumptions based on known stereotypes.

## Suggested Readings

American Psychological Association. *Violence and the Family: Report of the American Psychological Association Presidential Task Force on Violence and the Family*. Washington, D.C., 1996.

Anetzberger, Georgia J. "Elderly Adult Survivors of Family Violence: Implications for Clinical Practice." *Violence Against Women* (October 1997): 499–515.

Gondolf, Edward W. *Assessing Women Battering in Mental Health Services*. Sage Publications, 1998.

Loke, Tien-Li. "Trapped in Domestic Violence: The Impact of United States Immigration Laws on Battered Immigrant Women." *Boston University Public Interest Law Journal* 6 (1997): 589.

Quinn, M. *Elder Abuse and Neglect: Causes, Diagnosis, and Intervention Strategies*. Second edition. Springer Publications, 1997.

Renzetti, Claire. *Violent Betrayal: Partner Abuse in Lesbian Relationships*. Sage Publications, 1992.

Richie, Beth. *Compelled to Crime: The Gender Entrapment of Battered Black Women*. Routledge, 1996.

Sev'er, Aysan, ed. *A Cross-Cultural Exploration of Wife Abuse: Problems and Prospects*. Edwin Mellen Press, 1997.

Strong, Marlene F., and Ann Cupolo Freeman. *Caregiver Abuse and Domestic Violence in the Lives of Women with Disabilities*. Berkeley Planning Associates, 1997.

Wang, Karin. "Battered Asian American Women: Community Responses from the Battered Women's Movement and the Asian American Community." *Asian Law Journal* 3 (1996): 151.

## Section 5.2

# *Questions & Answers for Immigrant and Refugee Women*

Family Violence Prevention Fund, Copyright © 1996. Used with permission.

## *You have a right to be free from violence in your own home*

The Family Violence Prevention Fund has made this helpful brochure available in English, Spanish, Arabic, Chinese, Tagalog, Vietnamese, Russian, and Korean.

### *What is "domestic violence"?*

Is your partner (husband, boyfriend, or "ex") extremely jealous and does he discourage you from speaking to friends or family? Does he prevent you from getting a job or learning English? Has your partner ever threatened to take away your children? Has he told you that he will have you deported?

Have you ever been hit by your partner? Has he forced you to have sex when you did not want to? Has he ever threatened to harm you with weapons like guns, knives or other objects?

Does your partner claim that his violence is your fault? Has he ever told you his violence is not serious? Does he blame drugs or alcohol for his violent behavior? Does he make you feel like you are crazy? Does he call you names that are hurtful and shameful to you?

*If you answered yes to any of these questions, you are not alone. Many other women like you are in the same situation. Your partner's behavior is not your fault. Help is available to you.*

Domestic violence tends to get worse over time. It does not go away on its own. We will outline some things you can do to protect yourself and your children from continuing violence.

We will refer to the abuser as "he." Some women are abused by other women, and some men are abused by women. While not all the legal remedies will apply to lesbian relationships, we will still provide some basic information about things you can do to make yourself safe. We will use the term "partner" to refer to a husband, boyfriend, or "ex" who may be abusing you.

## *What can I do?*

There are a variety of <u>services available</u> to assist you to stop the violence in your home: shelters, hospitals, police, legal aid and other community services.

## *Should I leave my home if I am in danger?*

YES. Go to a friend's house or a battered women's shelter. Shelters are usually free and often will have information about other services available in your community. If you stay with a friend or a family member, keep your location secret if possible. *You have the right to keep your immigration status private.*

If you leave your home, make every effort to take your children with you. It is also helpful if you can bring documents, such as:

- driver's license
- identification
- passports
- visas for yourself and your children
- birth certificates
- documents from any public assistance programs
- rental agreements
- checkbooks
- credit cards
- paycheck stubs
- marriage license
- copies of tax returns for yourself and your partner.

Information about your husband also can be helpful. If you cannot get a copy of his resident alien card or certificate of naturalization, copy down the information from those documents on a piece of paper. If you think you may need to leave in the future, pack these items in a bag so you can find them quickly as you leave or take them to a friend's home.

## *Should I call the police?*

YES. Domestic violence is against the law. The police can escort you and your children out of the house if you want to leave and often can take you to a safe place. Officers may arrest your partner if they believe a crime has been committed. If the police officer does not speak your language, find someone other than your child or abuser to interpret for you.

Always ask the police to complete a report about the incident and get an incident report number so you can get a copy of the report. Also ask for and write down the name and badge number of the officer making the report. The police generally will not turn in a woman reporting domestic violence to the Immigration and Naturalization Service (INS).

If your partner is taken into custody, he may be released in as soon as two hours. Use this time to find a safe place to go.

## *I have heard of protection orders. What do they do?*

A protection order can keep the abuser from coming near you, attacking, sexually assaulting or contacting you, your children, or other family members.

Along with this protection order, in most states you also can ask for custody of your children and child support. In most states, you also can ask that the batterer be removed from your home and that the batterer not interfere with your immigration status.

You do not need to be a citizen or legal resident to get a protection order. For a protection order to be effective, you must be willing to call the police to enforce the order.

## *Can I get protection even if I am not a U.S. citizen?*

YES. You do not need to be a citizen or legal permanent resident to get a protection order. A lawyer may be helpful, but it is not necessary to have one in order to get a protection order.

Applications are generally available at courthouses, women's shelters, legal services offices, and some police stations. A court generally will not ask about your immigration status when you ask for a protection order, a child custody order, or a dissolution. Ask a legal services attorney (i.e., attorneys who provide free legal services to low-income individuals) or an immigrant advocacy group in your area about the policy in your court.

## How can I get lawful permanent residency without my husband's help?

A law passed by the U.S. government called the Violence Against Women Act (VAWA) creates two ways for women who are married to U.S. citizens or lawful permanent residents to get their residency.

The first is called "self-petitioning." Instead of depending upon your husband to apply for your residency with INS, *you can apply on your own for yourself and your children. Your husband plays no role in the process and does not have to know you are applying for residency.*

*However, because the law is complicated, you should not go to the INS without first consulting a shelter worker, immigration attorney, or a domestic violence or immigration agency for assistance.*

Because you must be married to self-petition, immediately contact an attorney if you receive divorce or annulment papers from your husband.

The second way to obtain residency is called "cancellation of removal." This is available to you only if you are in, or can be placed into, deportation proceedings. If you qualify for cancellation, the court may waive your deportation and grant you residency. However, because you must be in deportation proceedings before you can apply, be certain to see an immigration attorney before proceeding.

## My husband is threatening to take my children away if I leave him. What can I do?

If your partner is threatening to take your children away or take them to his home country, you should:

1. Immediately get a custody order. This order can include an order to prohibit your husband/intimate partner from removing the children from the country in which you live.

2. If the children are U.S. citizens, send a copy of this order to the embassy of your partner's home country and a copy to the U.S. Department of State to prevent the issuance of passports and visas for the children.

3. Give a copy of the order to the children's schools and tell the schools not to release the children to anyone but yourself.

4. Make sure that you have recent photos, passports and birth certificates for the children. Keep a list of addresses and

phone numbers of your husband's/intimate partner's friends and relatives in his home country.

## *How can I support myself and my children if I leave my husband?*

The law requires that the father of your children support them, even if you are living apart, even if you were never married to him, and without regard to immigration status. You should contact a family lawyer or a domestic violence advocate to find out how to obtain child support in your state. Some married women also may be eligible to receive spousal support or alimony.

Lawful permanent residents may use their "green cards" or resident alien cards to demonstrate their eligibility to work. Refugees and other immigrants must apply for authorization to work. An immigration attorney will be able to tell you whether you are eligible for work authorization. It is very important that you do not use false papers to work or make false claims of United States citizenship.

## *I am a legal permanent resident. Am I eligible to receive welfare and Medicaid?*

Some legal permanent residents are eligible for Food Stamps, although most legal permanent residents are not. Eligibility for Medicaid, Temporary Aid to Needy Families, and general assistance by legal permanent residents varies from state to state. You should consult an immigration or domestic violence advocate in your area.

## *I am a refugee. Can I receive welfare and Medicaid?*

In the first five years after they arrive in the United States, refugees are eligible for Food Stamps, Temporary Aid to Needy Families, Medicaid, and other public benefit programs to the same extent as U.S. citizens.

Most refugees who have been in the United States for five years or more will no longer be eligible for Food Stamps. Eligibility for Medicaid, Temporary Aid to Needy Families, and general assistance by refugees who have been in the United States for five years or more varies from state to state. You should consult an immigration or domestic violence advocate in your area.

## *I am undocumented. Can I receive welfare and Medicaid?*

If you are a battered undocumented woman whose husband has applied for legal permanent residency on your behalf, or if you have applied for legal permanent residency under the Violence Against Women Act, you are eligible for the same benefits as a legal permanent resident. (See above.)

If you are not eligible to apply for legal permanent residency, you will be ineligible for most forms of welfare. However, you are still eligible for emergency Medicaid. Contact an immigration or domestic violence advocate to help you find "safe" hospitals that will not report your undocumented status. You also are eligible for services from community groups, such as food distribution by churches, and assistance from domestic violence shelters.

## *Are my U.S. citizen children eligible for public benefits and Medicaid?*

YES. Even if you are undocumented, your U.S. citizen children are eligible for public benefits just as other citizen children are. However, if you are undocumented, DO NOT reveal your immigration status when applying for benefits on behalf of your children, *even if you are asked.* The welfare office does not need to know what your status is in order to give benefits to your citizen children.

## *Will I be deported if I take any of the above actions?*

If you are now a U.S. citizen, or you are a lawful permanent resident, or you possess a valid visa, you cannot be deported unless you entered the United States on fraudulent documents, violated conditions of your visa, or have committed certain crimes.

If you are undocumented or are unsure about your immigration status, you should seek the assistance of an immigration attorney to see if you can legalize your status. Until then, you should do what you need to do to make yourself safe.

Even if your husband/intimate partner were to report you to the INS, deportation may not follow, would not be immediate, and, in most cases, you would have the opportunity to present your case to a judge.

## Will my husband/intimate partner be deported if I take action?

NO. If you seek assistance from a shelter or lawyer, it is extremely unlikely to result in the deportation of your partner.

If you contact the police and your partner is convicted of a crime, he may be deported, depending on his immigration status and the seriousness of the crime.

*It is important to remember that you must keep yourself and your children safe. It is your partner that has put himself at risk by his actions.*

## Do I need to see an immigration attorney even if I cannot afford one?

*Do not go to the INS without a lawyer or consulting with a lawyer.* Your conversation with the attorney will be confidential, and he or she cannot report you to the INS. If you cannot afford to pay an attorney, contact the nearest legal services office or an immigration organization.

For more in-depth coverage of these issues, consult the manual *Domestic Violence in Immigrant and Refugee Communities: Asserting the Rights of Battered Women,* produced by the Family Violence Prevention Fund.

# Section 5.3

# *Violence in Gay and Lesbian Relationships*

*Raquel Kennedy Bergen*

Of all the types of intimate violence addressed in *Issues in Intimate Violence*, violence in gay and lesbian couples is the subject most overlooked. As Renzetti (1997) and Merrill (*Issues in Intimate Violence*, Chap. 8) argue, this form of intimate violence has been virtually ignored by researchers. Two reasons are the rampant heterosexism among social scientists and the commonly shared belief that violence is confined to heterosexual couples (Renzetti, 1997). As Gelles (1997) notes, the term *family violence* has historically referred to violence in traditional, heterosexual couples. Violence in same-sex couples was not mentioned within the early literature on domestic violence. Even when "violence among intimates" was discussed, the focus was still on heterosexual couples. Another significant factor is that studies of violence between intimates did not originally include lesbian couples because of the common belief that men batter women but women do not batter other women (Renzetti, 1997). Similarly, it was not believed that domestic violence occurred in relationships between gay men, that any physical violence between men was perceived as a "fair fight" (Merrill, *Issues in Intimate Violence*, Chap. 8). Thus, programs were created to assist women victims of male violence, including battered women's shelters and support groups for abused wives. Women and men who have been battered by their same-sex partners have been largely invisible to those who study violence between intimate partners (Gelles, 1997; Renzetti, 1997).

The few studies that have examined violence in gay and lesbian couples indicate that violence is far from uncommon in homosexual relationships. It is estimated that between 11% and 20% of gay men are abused by their partners each year (Bourg & Stock, 1994; Island & Letellier, 1991). Rates of violence between lesbian partners range from 11% to 73% (Renzetti, 1992; *Issues in Intimate Violence*, Chap. 7). As Renzetti (*Issues in Intimate Violence*, Chap. 7) cautions, these estimates should be interpreted with great caution because, to date, studies of violence in gay and lesbian couples have been based on small nonprobability samples. This is in contrast with the large random samples that have generated prevalence rates of heterosexual battering.

Studies have indicated not only that violence commonly occurs in many gay and lesbian relationships but also that this violence is not normatively a one-time occurrence. For example, Renzetti (1992) found that 54% of women in her sample had been abused more than 10 times during their relationships. The most common form of violence experienced was psychological abuse. Research on gay men (Kelly & Warshafsky, 1987) indicates that gay men are more likely than lesbians to use physical aggression with their partners (Renzetti, 1992). A variety of other forms of violence, however, are common in abusive gay and lesbian relationships. For example, in her research, Renzetti found that battered lesbians commonly experience physical, psychological, sexual, and emotional abuse and destruction of property and pets. She quotes that (*Issues in Intimate Violence*, Chap. 7) lesbian battering is best defined as

> a pattern of violent [or] coercive behaviors whereby a lesbian seeks to control the thoughts, beliefs, or conduct of her intimate partner or to punish the intimate for resisting the perpetrator's control. (Hart, 1986, p. 173)

A similar definition could be used for gay battering. Importantly, this definition indicates that violence in homosexual couples is in many ways similar to violence in heterosexual couples: Both types of abusers are attempting to control their partners through manipulation, punishment, coercion, and so on (see Renzetti, *Issues in Intimate Violence*, Chap. 7).

As Renzetti (1992) argues, however, violence in homosexual couples is different from violence in heterosexual couples in some ways. Importantly, a common form of emotional abuse in same-sex couples is the threat of "outing." This is when the abuser threatens to reveal to others that his or her partner is a homosexual. Given the extreme homophobia in this society, outing is a powerful form of control because gays and lesbians often face severe discrimination as a result of their sexual identity (Renzetti, 1992; *Issues in Intimate Violence*, Chap. 7). Another differentiating factor, as Merrill (*Issues in Intimate Violence*, Chap. 8) argues, is that violent gay partnerships are often characterized by high rates of substance abuse and AIDS.

Research on violence in gay and lesbian relationships has traditionally relied on models of heterosexual violence for explanatory value. This is problematic, as Renzetti (1992; *Issues in Intimate Vio-*

*lence*, Chap. 7) argues, because the dynamics of relationships differ in terms of race, social class, ethnicity, and sexual orientation of the persons involved. In analyses of violence in homosexual relationships, it has been generally believed that the violence reflects the partners' roles in the relationship. In brief, it is assumed that the abuser is playing the masculine or "butch" role and that the victim is the feminine or "femme" partner. Researchers (Letellier, 1994; Renzetti, 1992) have found, however, that these roles have little correlation with violence, in that the partner who is more "masculine" in terms of physical size, strength, and mannerisms is not necessarily the abuser. Furthermore, there is a great deal of diversity and role differentiation in gay and lesbian couples, and these stereotypical images of homosexual couples perpetuate misunderstandings and homophobia (Renzetti, *Issues in Intimate Violence*, Chap. 7).

Some researchers have examined the role that drugs and alcohol play in gay and lesbian violence (Kelly & Warshafsky, 1987). Others have hypothesized that the intergenerational transmission of violence is the best explanation for violence in same-sex relationships (Lie, Schilit, Bush, Montague, & Reyes, 1991). To date, the most credence has been given to theories that explore power and power inequality as the key to understanding violence in intimate couples (Gelles, 1997). As Merrill notes (*Issues in Intimate Violence*, Chap. 8), these theoretical explanations are inadequate in explaining why the partner with seemingly less power in a relationship (e.g., financial power, physical strength, social status) is often the abuser. In her work, Renzetti (1997; *Issues in Intimate Violence*, Chap. 7) has argued that a multidimensional explanation is needed to adequately explain violence in gay and lesbian relationships. Thus, she considers not only power inequality but also internalized homophobia and dependency as factors essential to understanding this form of intimate violence.

## References

Bourg, S., & Stock, H.V. (1994) "A Review of Domestic Violence Arrest Statistics in a Police Department Using a Pro-Arrest Policy: Are Pro-Arrest Policies Enough?" *Journal of Family Violence*, 9, 177–192.

Gelles, R. (1997). *Intimate Violence in Families* (3rd ed.). Thousand Oaks, CA: Sage.

Hart, B. (1986). "Lesbian Battering: An Examination." In K. Lobel (Ed.), *Naming the Violence* (pp. 173–189). Seattle: Seal.

Island, D., & Letellier, P. (1991). *Men Who Beat the Men Who Love Them.* New York: Harrington Park.

Kelly, E. E., & L. Warshafsky, (1987, July). *Partner Abuse in Gay Male and Lesbian Couples.* Paper presented at the Third National Conference for Family Violence Researchers, Durham, NH.

Letellier, P. (1994). "Gay and Lesbian Male Domestic Violence Victimization: Challenges to Feminist Theory and Responses to Violence." *Violence and Victims,* 9, 95–106.

Lie, G-Y., R. Schilit, J. Bush, M. Montague, & L. Reyes. (1991). "Lesbians in Currently Aggressive Relationships: How Frequently Do They Report Aggressive Past Relationships?" *Violence and Victims,* 6, 121–135.

Renzetti, C. (1992). *Violent Betrayal: Partner Abuse in Lesbian Relationships.* Newbury Park, CA: Sage.

Renzetti, C. (1997). "Violence and Abuse among Same-Sex Couples." In A. P. Cardarelli (Ed.), *Violence between Intimate Partners: Patterns, Causes, and Effects* (pp. 70–89). Boston: University of Massachusetts.

# Section 5.4

# *Abuse and Women with Disabilities*

*By Margaret A. Nosek, Ph.D. and Carol A. Howland, M.P.H.\**
*(\*Candidate working on thesis, all other requirements completed)*

## *Defining Disability and Abuse*

For the purpose of this paper, the term disability will encompass the following impairments: disability that can increase vulnerability to abuse may result from physical, sensory, or mental impairments, or a combination of impairments; physical disability resulting from injury (e.g., spinal cord injury, amputation), chronic disease (e.g., multiple sclerosis, rheumatoid arthritis), or congenital conditions (e.g., cerebral palsy, muscular dystrophy); sensory impairments consisting of hearing or visual impairments; and mental impairments comprising developmental conditions (e.g., mental retardation), cognitive impairment (e.g., traumatic brain injury), or mental illness.

Emotional abuse is being threatened, terrorized, severely rejected, isolated, ignored, or verbally attacked. Physical abuse is any form of violence against one's body, such as being hit, kicked, restrained, or deprived of food or water. Sexual abuse is being forced, threatened, or deceived into sexual activities ranging from looking or touching to intercourse or rape.

## *Prevalence of Violence Against Women with Disabilities*

The prevalence of abuse among women in general has been fairly well documented, yet only a few North American studies (review by Sobsey, Wells, Lucardie, & Mansell, 1995), primarily from Canada, have examined the prevalence among women with disabilities.

The DisAbled Women's Network of Canada (Ridington, 1989) surveyed 245 women with disabilities and found that 40% had experienced abuse; 12% had been raped. Perpetrators of the abuse were primarily spouses and ex-spouses (37%) and strangers (28%), followed by parents (15%), service providers (10%), and dates (7%). Less than half these experiences were reported, due mostly to fear and dependency. Ten percent of the women had used shelters or other services, 15% reported that no services were available or they were unsuccessful in their attempts to obtain services, and 55% had not tried to get services.

Sobsey and Doe (1991) conducted a study of 166 abuse cases handled by the University of Alberta's Sexual Abuse and Disability Project. The sample was 82% women and 70% persons with intellectual impairments, and covered a very wide age range (18 months to 57 years). In 96% of the cases, the perpetrator was known to the victim; 44% of the perpetrators were service providers. Seventy-nine percent of the individuals were victimized more than once. Treatment services were either inadequate or not offered in 73% of the cases.

The Ontario Ministry of Community and Social Services (*Toronto Star,* April 1, 1987) surveyed 62 women and found that more of the women with disabilities had been battered as adults compared to the women without disabilities (33% versus 22%), but fewer had been sexually assaulted as adults (23% versus 31%).

An extensive assessment of the sexuality of noninstitutionalized women with disabilities, which included comprehensive assessment of emotional, physical, and sexual abuse, was conducted by the Center for Research on Women with Disabilities (CROWD) through a grant from the U.S. National Institutes of Health. This study also covered other areas that may be associated with abuse, such as sexual functioning, reproductive health care, dating, marriage, parenting issues, and the woman's sense of self as a sexual person. The design of the study consisted of (1) qualitative interviews with 31 women with disabilities, and (2) a national survey of 946 women, 504 of whom had physical disabilities and 442 who did not have disabilities. Disabilities reported most frequently included spinal cord injury, cerebral palsy, muscular dystrophy, multiple sclerosis, and joint and connective tissue diseases.

Abuse issues emerged as a major theme among the 31 women interviewed in the first phase of this study. An analysis of reports of abuse in those interviews was described by Nosek (1996). Twenty-five of the 31 women reported being abused in some way. Of 55 separate abusive experiences, 15 were reported as sexual abuse, 17 were physical (nonsexual) abuse, and 23 were emotional abuse.

The findings from the qualitative study were used to develop items for the national survey. Two pages of the 51-page survey were devoted to abuse issues, encompassing more than 80 variables, including type of abuse by perpetrator and age when abuse began and ended, plus two open-ended questions. Analyses of these data (Young, Nosek, Howland, Chanpong, & Rintala, 1997) have revealed that abuse prevalence (including emotional, physical and sexual abuse) was the same (62%) for women with and without disabilities. There were no significant differences between percentages of women with and without disabilities who reported experiencing emotional abuse (52% versus 48%), physical abuse (36% in both groups), or sexual abuse (40% versus 37%). The most common perpetrators of emotional and physical abuse for both groups were husbands, followed by mothers, then fathers. Emotional abuse by husbands was reported by 26% of all women in both groups; physical abuse by husbands was reported by 17% of all women with disabilities and 19% of all women without disabilities. The most common perpetrator of sexual abuse was a stranger, as reported by 11% of women with disabilities and 12% of women without disabilities. Women with disabilities were significantly more likely to experience emotional and sexual abuse by attendants and health care workers. Women with disabilities reported significantly longer durations of physical or sexual abuse compared to women without disabilities (3.9 years versus 2.5 years). In an analysis of sexual functioning, abuse was found to be a significant predictor of lower levels of satisfaction with sex life among women with disabilities (Nosek, Rintala, Young, Howland, Foley, Rossi, & Chanpong, 1995).

Others have reported a history of sexual abuse among 25% of adolescent girls with mental retardation (Chamberlain, Rauh, Passer, McGrath, & Burket, 1984), 31% of those with congenital physical disabilities (Brown, 1988), 36% of multihandicapped children admitted to a psychiatric hospital (Ammerman, Van Hasselt, Hersen, McGonigle, & Lubetsky, 1989), and 50% of women blind from birth (Welbourne, Lipschitz, Selvin, & Green, 1983). In spite of these high percentages, few women receive treatment from victim services specialists (Andrews & Veronen, 1993).

## *Abuse Interventions for Women with Disabilities*

There have been virtually no studies that examine the existence, feasibility, or effectiveness of abuse interventions for women with disabilities. In both the disability rights movement and the battered women's movement, it is generally acknowledged that programs to assist abused women are often architecturally inaccessible, lack interpreter services for deaf women, and are not able to accommodate women who need assistance with daily self-care or medications (Nosek, Howland, & Young, 1998). Merkin and Smith (1995), in discussing the needs of deaf women, state that counseling is more effective when sensitive to deaf culture issues and appropriate communication techniques.

Crisis interventions typically include escaping temporarily to a woman's shelter, having an escape plan ready in the event of imminent violence if the woman chooses to remain with the perpetrator, and escaping permanently from the abuser. These options may be problematic for the woman with a disability if the shelter is inaccessible or unable to meet her needs for personal assistance with activities of daily living, if the shelter staff are unable to communicate with a deaf or speech-impaired woman, if she depends primarily on the abuser for assistance with personal needs and has no family or friends to stay with, or if she is physically incapable of executing the tasks necessary to implement an escape plan such as packing necessities, hiding money, and driving or arranging transportation to a shelter or friend's home.

Andrews and Veronen (1993) list four requirements for effective victim services for women with disabilities. First, service providers need to provide adequate assessment of survivors, including questions about disability-related issues. Second, abuse service providers should be trained to recognize and effectively respond to needs related to the disability, and disability service providers should be trained in recognizing and responding to physical and sexual trauma. Third, barriers to services should be eliminated by providing barrier-free information and referral services, by ensuring physical accessibility to facilities, by providing 24-hour access to transportation, to interpreters, and to communication assistance, and by providing trained personnel to monitor risks and respond to victims receiving services through disability programs. Finally, persons with disabilities who are dependent on caregivers, either at home or in institutions, may need special legal protection against abuse.

The National Domestic Violence Hotline keeps a database of battered women's shelters throughout the country, with indications of their architectural accessibility and the availability of interpreter services. Although the hotline is equipped with telecommunication devices for persons who are deaf, it is rarely used. The National Coalition Against Domestic Violence has issued a manual that gives specific guidelines for battered women's programs on implementing accessibility modifications according to the requirements of the Americans with Disabilities Act and increasing sensitivity and responsiveness among program staff to the needs of abused women with disabilities (National Coalition Against Domestic Violence, 1996).

## Critique of Studies on Abuse and Disability

Until recently, the problem of abuse among people with disabilities has received very little attention. Early studies suffered from many methodological weaknesses. Essential constructs and variables important to statistical analysis were rarely defined. There was a particular lack of distinction among emotional, physical, and sexual abuse. The studies used unstandardized measurement instruments and techniques. Global references were made to the type of abuse, for example, emotional versus sexual; however, there was little attempt to document or categorize specific incidents by perpetrator. Samples in these studies were generally quite heterogeneous in terms of disability type, gender, and age. There was also the use of convenience sampling, such as using clients of intervention programs or police reports, as opposed to representative or random sampling. Statistical analyses rarely go beyond frequencies and measures of central tendency. Due to the heterogeneity of the samples, analyzing specific experiences of individuals with specific characteristics (such as sexual abuse among adult women with mental illness) would result in subsamples too small to allow the use of more sophisticated analytic procedures.

The recent study by the Center for Research on Women with Disabilities addressed a number of these issues. It had clearly defined variables; assessed types of abuse, perpetrator, and duration of abuse; sampled a broad range of women nationwide, including an able-bodied comparison group; and was restricted to a defined sample of adult women with physical disability. The issue of designing and implementing appropriate intervention studies for women with disabilities has received no attention beyond observation and speculation.

## Conclusion

There is no question that abuse of women with disabilities is a problem of epidemic proportions that is only beginning to attract the attention of researchers, service providers, and funding agencies. The gaps in the literature are enormous. For each disability type, different dynamics of abuse come into play. For women with physical disabilities, limitations in physically escaping violent situations are in sharp contrast to women with hearing impairments, who may be able to escape but face communication barriers in most settings designed to help battered women. Certain commonalities exist across disability groups, such as economic dependence, social isolation, and the whittling away of self-esteem on the basis of disability as a precursor to abuse. Research that employs methodologic rigor must be conducted with women who have disabilities such as blindness, deafness, mental illness, and mental retardation. Particular attention must be paid to identifying vulnerability factors that are disability-related as opposed to those factors experienced by all women.

We must know more about interventions that are effective for women with disabilities. Considerable work has been done in this area for women in general; however, many of the recommended strategies are not feasible for women with disabilities. Few of the strategies listed in classic safety plans are possible for women who must depend on their abuser to get them out of bed in the morning, dress them, and feed them. There are only a handful of programs across the country that specifically address the needs of abused women with disabilities, making controlled intervention studies very difficult.

Much more work must be done to increase the awareness of providers of disability-related services so that they can recognize abuse among their clients and make appropriate referrals to battered women's programs. Correspondingly, much more work must be done to increase the capacity of battered women's programs to serve women with all types of disabilities.

## References

Ammerman, R. T., V. B. Van Hasselt, M. Hersen, J. J. McGonigle, & M. J. Lubetsky (1989). "Abuse and Neglect in Psychiatrically Hospitalized Multihandicapped Children." *Child Abuse & Neglect* 13, 335–343.

Andrews, A. B., & L. J. Veronen (1993). "Sexual Assault and People with Disabilities." Special issue: Sexuality and disabilities: A guide for human service practitioners. *Journal of Social Work and Human Sexuality* 8(2), 137–59.

Asch, A., & M. Fine (1988). "Introduction: Beyond Pedestals." In: M. Fine & A. Asch, (eds.) *Women with Disabilities: Essays in Psy-*

*chology, Culture, and Politics.* Philadelphia, PA: Temple University Press.

Brown, D. E. (1988). "FActors Affecting Psychosexual Development of Adults with Congenital Physical Disabilities." *Physical and Occupational Therapy in Pediatrics* 8(2–3), 43–58.

Chamberlain, A., J. Rauh, A. Passer, M. McGrath, & R. Burket (1984). "Issues in Fertility Control for Mentally Retarded Female Adolescents I: Sexual Activity, Sexual Abuse, and Contraception." *Pediatrics* 73, 445–450.

Merkin, L., & M. J. Smith (1995). "A Community Based Model Providing Services for Deaf and Deaf-blind Victims of Sexual Assault and Domestic Violence." *Sexuality and Disability* 13(2), 97–106.

National Coalition Against Domestic Violence. (1996*). Open Minds, Open Doors: Technical Assistance Manual Assisting Domestic Violence Service Providers to Become Physically and Attitudinally Accessible to Women with Disabilities.* Denver, CO: National Coalition Against Domestic Violence.

Nosek, M. A. (1996). "Sexual Abuse of Women with Physical Disabilities." In D. M. Krotoski, M. A. Nosek, & M. A. Turk (Eds.), *Women with Physical Disabilities: Achieving and Maintaining Health and Well-Being.* (pp. 153–173). Baltimore, MD: Paul H. Brookes.

Nosek, M. A. (1996). "Wellness among Women with Physical Disabilities." In D. M. Krotoski, M. A. Nosek, & M. A. Turk (Eds.), *Women with Physical Disabilities: Achieving and Maintaining Health and Well-Being.* (pp. 17–33). Baltimore, MD: Paul H. Brookes.

Nosek, M. A., C. A. Howland, & M. E. Young (1998). "Abuse of Women with Disabilities: Policy Implications." *Journal of Disability Policy Studies* 8 (1,2), 158–175.

Nosek, M. A., D. H. Rintala, M. E. Young, C.A. Howland, C. C. Foley, C. D. Rossi, & G. Chanpong (1995). "Sexual Functioning among Women with Physical Disabilities." *Archives of Physical Medicine and Rehabilitation* 77, (2), 107–115.

Ontario Ministry of Community and Social Services. (1987). "Disabled Women More Likely to Be Battered, Survey Suggests." *The Toronto Star,* April 1, F9.

Ridington, J. (1989*). Beating the "Odds": Violence and Women with Disabilities* (Position Paper 2). Vancouver: DisAbled Women's Network: Canada.

Sobsey, D., D. Wells, R. Lucardie, & S. Mansell, (Eds.) (1995). *Violence and Disability: An Annotated Bibliography.* Baltimore, MD: Paul H. Brookes.

Sobsey, D., & T. Doe (1991). "Patterns of Sexual Abuse and Assault." *Sexuality and Disability* 9(3), 243–260.

Welbourne, A., S. Lipschitz, H. Selvin, & R. Green (1983). "A Comparison of the Sexual Learning Experiences of Visually Impaired and Sighted Women." *Journal of Visual Impairment and Blindness* 77, 256–259.

Young, M. E., M. A. Nosek, C. A. Howland, G. Chanpong, D. H. Rintala (1997) "Prevalence of Abuse of Women with Physical Disabilities." *Archives of Physical Medicine and Rehabilitation Special Issue* 78 (12, Suppl. 5) S34–S38.

## Section 5.5

# *Sexual Violence Against People With Disabilities*

National Center for Injury Prevention and Control, Centers for Disease Control and Prevention, 1998.

## *Definitions*

### *Sexual Violence*

Researchers who study sexual violence against people with disabilities use a wide variety of definitions for sexual abuse, sexual assault, and rape. In this fact sheet where we summarize the findings of many such studies, we include all of those definitions in the term sexual violence.

Studies of sexual violence in the general population usually distinguish between abuse during childhood and assaults or rape during adulthood. However, many acts of violence against people with disabilities are labeled abuse regardless of the victims' age or the specific offenses committed against them.

## *Disability*

This term also has a wide variety of definitions. In this summary, we define disability as limitations in physical or mental function, caused by one or more health conditions, in carrying out socially defined tasks and roles that individuals generally are expected to be able to do.[6]

## *Magnitude of the Problem*

Comparing the percentages of sexual violence victims who have disabilities with the percentages of sexual violence victims who do not have disabilities is difficult because of the differences in the terminology and methods used to determine these rates. However, most data appear to indicate that people with disabilities are at higher risk for sexual violence than are people without disabilities.[1, 3, 5, 7, 10, 11, 14, 16, 18]

Sexual violence has been investigated more widely among people with disabilities related to cognitive impairments (including mental retardation and learning disabilities) than among people with other types of disabilities. For adults with cognitive impairments, reported rates for lifetime experience of sexual violence range from 25% to 67%.[2, 10, 15]

Among women with disabilities, reported rates of sexual violence range from 51% to 79%.[9, 15]

Among adolescent boys with disabilities, reported rates of sexual violence range from 4% to 6%; for adolescent girls reported rates are around 24%.[3, 16]

## *Study Parameters*

For the most part, this summary does not include findings from studies that exclusively address sexual violence against people with disabilities who are institutionalized, mentally impaired, younger than 14 years old, or older than 65 years old. We need further research to address the special issues of these groups.

## Characteristics of Victims

From 72% to 82% of people with disabilities who have been sexually victimized are female.[4, 8, 12, 13, 17]

Among adult victims whose level of cognitive impairment is known, 52% to 76% had a mild to moderate impairment, whereas 24% to 48% had a severe to profound impairment.[2, 4, 8, 13]

## Characteristics of Perpetrators

Most perpetrators are male (88% to 98%) and are known to the victim. [4, 8, 12, 13] Perpetrators include family members, acquaintances, other people with disabilities, and health care providers.[4, 12, 13, 17]

## Where Sexual Violence Occurs

Residences, particularly the victim's home, are the most common place for episodes of sexual violence.[4, 12, 17] Other places include vehicles, places of employment, public areas, schools, and day or leisure facilities.[3, 4, 12, 17]

## Description of the Sexual Violence

Published data that describe the type of violence perpetrated suggest that most cases involve multiple episodes of sexual contact. About 95% of sexual violence episodes involve sexual contact (e.g. intercourse, fondling, or masturbation).[2, 17] Only 19% to 23% of all sexual violence cases were limited to one episode [2, 8, 12, 13]

## Recommendations

- Conduct scientific studies to determine the magnitude of violence against people with disabilities.

- Research the causes and risk factors associated with this public health problem.

- Use the findings from these studies to develop prevention programs for at-risk populations.

- Improve the availability, accessibility, and timeliness of sex education and self-protection training for people with disabilities.

- Make services for victims of sexual violence accessible to people with disabilities, and inform people with disabilities of the availability of such services.

- Train people who serve victims of violence (including law enforcement personnel, health care professionals, and advocates) in how to communicate with and respond to the special issues of people with disabilities who have experienced sexual violence.

## *References*

1. Bachman, R., and L. Saltzman. *Violence against Women: Estimates from the Redesigned Survey. Bureau of Justice Statistics: Special Report*; Washington, D.C.: U.S. Department of Justice, Aug. 1995; NCJ-154348.

2. Beail, N., and S. Warden. "Sexual Abuse of Adults with Learning Disabilities." *Journal of Intellectual Disability Research* 39, 5 (1995): 382-87.

3. Chamberlain, A., J. Rauh, A. Passer, M. McGrath, and R. Burket. "Issues in Fertility Control for Mentally Retarded Female Adolescents: Part I. Sexual Activity, Sexual Abuse, and Contraception." *Pediatrics* 73, 4 (1984): 445–50.

4. Furey, E. M. "Sexual Abuse of Adults with Mental Retardation: Who and Where." *Mental Retardation* 32, 3 (June 1994): 173–80.

5. Hall, E. R., and P. J. Flannery. "Prevalence and Correlates of Sexual Assault Experiences in Adolescents." *Victimology* 9, 3-4 (1984): 398–406.

6. Institute of Medicine. *Disability in America: Toward a National Agenda for Prevention*. Washington, DC: National Academy Press, 1991: 35.

7. Koss, M. P. "Detecting the Scope of Rape: A Review of Prevalence Research Methods." *Journal of Interpersonal Violence* 8, 2 (1993): 198–222.

8. Mansell, S., D. Sobsey, and P. Calder. "Sexual Abuse Treatment for Persons with Developmental Disabilities." *Professional Psychology—Research & Practice* 23, 5 (1992): 404–09.

9. Masuda, S. *Don't Tell Me To Take a Hot Bath: Resource Manual for Crisis Workers.* Vancouver, BC: DAWN Canada (DisAbled Women's Network Canada), 1995.

10. McCabe, M. P., R. A. Cummins, and S. B. Reid. "An Empirical Study of the Sexual Abuse of People with Intellectual Disability." *Sexuality & Disability* 12, 4 (1994): 297–306.

11. Rodgers, K. "Wife Assault: The Findings of a National Survey." *Juristat Service Bulletin* 14, 9 (1994): 1–11. Ottowa: Canadian Centre for Justice Statistics.

12. Sobsey, D., and T. Doe. "Patterns of Sexual Abuse and Assault." *Sexuality & Disability* 9, 3 (1991): 243–59.

13. Sobsey, D., and S. Mansell. "An International Perspective on Patterns of Sexual Assault and Abuse of People with Disabilities." *International Journal of Adolescent Medicine & Health* 7, 2 (1994): 153–78.

14. Sorenson, S. B., J. A. Stein, J. M. Siegel, J. M. Golding, and M. A. Burnam. "The Prevalence of Adult Sexual Assault: The Los Angeles Epidemiologic Catchment Area Project." *American Journal of Epidemiology* 126, 6 (1987): 1154–64.

15. Stromsness, M. M. "Sexually Abused Women with Mental Retardation: Hidden Victims, Absent Resources." *Women & Therapy* 14, 3-4 (1993): 139–52.

16. Suris, J. C., M. D. Resnick, N. Cassuto, and R. W. Blum. "Sexual Behavior of Adolescents with Chronic Disease and Disability." *Journal of Adolescent Health* 19, 2 (1996): 124-31.

17. Turk, V., and H. Brown. "The Sexual Abuse of Adults with Learning Disabilities: Results of a Two-Year Incidence Survey." *Mental Handicap Research* 6, 3 (1993): 193–216.

18. Wilson, C., and N. Brewer. "The Incidence of Criminal Victimisation of Individuals with an Intellectual Disability." *Australian Psychologist* 27, 2 (1992): 114–17.

# Section 5.6

# *American Indian/Alaska Natives and Intimate Partner Violence*

National Center for Injury Prevention and Control, Centers for
Disease Control and Prevention, 1997.

## *Background*

- There are 556 federally recognized American Indian and Alaska
  Native (AI/AN) tribes (330 American Indian tribes and 226
  Alaska Native villages). Twenty-three tribes have state recognition only; numerous others have neither federal nor state recognition.[1] The total estimated AI/AN population is about 2 million
  persons.[2]

- In 1995 approximately 209 North American Indian languages
  were still spoken, roughly half the number that existed 500
  years earlier. Nearly 80% of these languages face extinction
  within a single lifetime because they are spoken by only a few of
  the oldest persons in the community. [3]

- A 1977 joint resolution by the National Congress of American
  Indians and the National Tribal Chairmen's Association designated that people indigenous to North America be referred to as
  American Indian/Alaska Natives except when specific tribal
  designations are appropriate. [2]

- One-third of AI/ANs live on federal Indian reservations, the remainder in off-reservation rural areas/cities. Significant migration occurs between reservation and non-reservation settings.[2]

- To date, the problem of intimate partner violence (IPV) among
  AI/ANs has received little attention in the literature.[4] Association of IPV with child abuse, alcohol use, suicide, and homicide
  has been suggested.[5-11] Further research is needed to determine
  the statistical significance of these associations [8, 12, 13]

95

## *Culture, History and Ethnography: Risk and Protective Factors*

- Traditional family structures, social and religious practices, greater balance of power between men and women, and the role of women central to family organization in pre-reservation AI/AN societies likely served as protective factors for IPV in AI/AN communities.[7, 14-17]

- Community and family destruction brought on by forced change, changes in traditional marriage systems and social controls, and constant economic and subsistence deprivation likely were and are risk factors for IPV among AI/ANs.[16, 18-20]

## *Homicide Among American Indian and Alaska Native Women*

- Approximately 75% of female AI/AN homicide victims are killed by someone they know; almost one-third are killed by family members. Among all U.S. female homicide victims, 65% are killed by someone they know.[21]

## *Incidence/Prevalence of IPV Among AI/AN Populations*

- No reliable data exist on the incidence/prevalence of IPV among AI/AN populations. The 1985 National Family Violence Resurvey determined one-year prevalence rates in the general population. 15.5% of 204 American Indian couples sampled reported violence in their relationship and 7.2% of Indian couples reported severe violence compared to 14.8% and 5.3%, respectively, among American White counterparts.[12]

- The survey did not collect data on tribal affiliation or residence. Data were analyzed on AI/AN married/cohabiting couples only. "Violence" was limited to a range of physical behaviors. There was no representation of persons who did not have telephones, 12 persons in remote areas with no access to telephones, or non-English speakers.[13]

## Intervention/Prevention Programs

- IPV prevention in "Indian Country" is primarily a grass roots effort which began in 1977 with the formation of the White Buffalo Calf Woman Society, Rosebud Reservation, South Dakota. There are approximately 15 Indian-specific shelters, which are primarily reservation-based. [2, 13]

- Community-based AI/AN IPV intervention/prevention programs are based on the philosophy that IPV was not a traditional or common occurrence prior to European contact 500 years ago and subsequent colonization of North and South America. [17, 22-27]

- In 1995 the Department of Justice (DOJ) began funding STOP Violence Against Women Grants in AI/AN communities. A total of 98 AI/AN IPV programs will have been funded in FY98 [Fiscal Year 1998].

## American Indian/Alaska Native IPV Prevention Programs and Curricula

**Mending the Sacred Hoop,** Violence Against Indian Women Technical Assistance Project. 4032 Chicago Ave. South, Minneapolis, MN 55407. TEL 1-800-903-0111, ext. 1. Eileen Hudon and Loretta Rivera, Coordinators. This program is part of the Minnesota Program Development, Inc., Duluth, MN. In Duluth, MN, TEL (218) 722-2781. Don Chapin, Coordinator.

**Family Violence Prevention Program,** Indian Health Service. 5300 Homestead Road, NE, Albuquerque, New Mexico 87110. TEL (505) 248-4245. Beverly Wilkins, Coordinator.

**Cangleska, Inc. (Medicine Wheel),** Oglala Lakota Nation, P.O. Box 260, Porcupine, South Dakota 57772. TEL (605) 867-1035. Marlin Mousseau, Coordinator.

## References

1.  "Indian Entities Recognized and Eligible to Receive Services From the United States Bureau of Indian Affairs." *Federal Register* 61; 220. 58211-58216. November 13, 1996.

2.  Norton, I. M., and S. M. Manson, "A Silent Minority: Battered American Indian Women." *Journal of Family Violence* 10 (1995): 307–17.

3.  Goddard, I., ed. *Handbook of North American Indians*. Volume 17. Languages. Washington, D.C.: Smithsonian Institution, 1996.

4.  Crowell, N. A., and A. W. Burgess, *Understanding Violence Against Women*. Washington, D.C.: National Academy Press, 1996.

5.  Arbuckle, J., L. Olson, M. Howard, J. Brillman, C. Anctil, and D. Sklar. "Safe at Home? Domestic Violence and Other Homicides Among Women in New Mexico." *Annals of Emergency Medicine* 27 (1996): 210–15.

6.  Bohn, D.O. "Nursing Care of Native American Battered Women." *OHIOANS Clinical Issues in Perinatal and Women's Health Nursing* 4 (1993): 424–36.

7.  Chapin, D. "Peace on Earth Begins in the Home." *The Circle* 14 (1990): 1.

8.  DeBruyn, L. M, C. C. Lujan, and P. A. May. "A Comparative Study of Abused and Neglected American Indian Children in the Southwest." *Social Science Medicine* 35 (1992): 305–15.

9.  Durst, D. "Conjugal Violence: Changing Attitudes in Two Northern Native Communities." *Community Mental Health Journal* 27 (1991): 359–73.

10. Herman, J. L. *Trauma and Recovery: The Aftermath of Violence—From Domestic Abuse to Political Terror.* New York: Basic Books, 1992.

11. Shkilnyk, A. *A Poison Stronger Than Love: The Destruction of an Ojibwa Community.* New Haven: Yale University Press, 1985.

12. Bachman, R. *Death and Violence on the Reservation: Homicide, Family Violence, and Suicide in American Indian Populations.* New York: Auburn House, 1992.

13. Chester, B., R. W. Robin, M. P. Koss, J. Lopez, and D. Goldman. "Grandmother Dishonored: Violence Against Women by Male Partners in American Indian Communities." *Violence and Victims* 9 (1994): 249–58.

14. Allen, P. G. "Violence and the American Indian Woman." *Working Together to Prevent Sexual and Domestic Violence* 5 (1985): 3–7. Seattle: Center for the Prevention of Sexual and Domestic Violence.

15. Allen, P.G. *The Sacred Hoop: Recovering the Feminine in American Indian Traditions.* Boston: Beacon Press, 1989.

16. DeBruyn, L. M., B. J. Wilkins, and K. Artichoker. *"It's Not Cultural": Violence Against Native American Women.* 89th American Anthropological Association Meeting. New Orleans, Louisiana, 1990.

17. Family Violence Prevention Team, Indian Health Service. *A Model for the Prevention of Family Violence in Native American Communities.* Mental Health/Social Services Programs Branch. Albuquerque, New Mexico, 1994.

18. Stannard, D. E. *American Holocaust: Columbus and the Conquest of the New World.* New York: Oxford University Press, 1992.

19. Thornton, R. *American Indian Holocaust and Survival: A Population History Since 1492.* Norman: University of Oklahoma, 1987.

20. Wolk, L. E. *Minnesota's American Indian Battered Women: The Cycle of Oppression: A Cultural Awareness Training Manual for Non-Indian Professionals.* St. Paul, MN: St. Paul Indian Center, 1982.

21. Wallace, L. D. J., A. D. Calhoun, K. E. Powell, J. O'Neil, and S. P. James. *Homicide and Suicide Among Native Americans, 1979–1992.* Atlanta, GA: Centers for Disease Control and Prevention, National Center for Injury Prevention and Control, 1996. Violence Surveillance Summary Series, No. 2.

22. Fleming, C. M., and S. M. Manson. "Native American Women," 143–48. In R. C. Engs, ed. *Women, Alcohol and Other Drugs.* Iowa: Kendall/Hunt Publishing, 1990.

23. Klein, L. F., and L. A. Ackerman. *Women and Power in Native North America.* Norman: University of Oklahoma Press, 1995.

24. McIntyre, M. "Societal Barriers Faced by American Indian Battered Women." *Women of Nations Newsletter* (Summer 1988).

25. Neithammer, C. *Daughters of the Earth: The Lives and Legends of American Indian Women.* New York: Macmillan, 1977.

26. Powers, M. N. "Hard Times," 173–78. In M.N. Powers, ed. *Oglala Women: Myth, Ritual, and Reality.* Chicago: University of Chicago Press, 1988.

27. Shinkwin, A. D., and M. C. Pete. *Homes in Disruption: Spouse Abuse in Yupik Eskimo Society.* University of Alaska, Fairbanks. Unpublished manuscript, 1983.

## Section 5.7

## *Rural Battered Women*

Minnesota Coalition for Battered Women's "Hands Are Not for Hitting" campaign, 1995.

Battered women living in rural areas have many of the same experiences as battered women everywhere. But rural battered women have certain experiences and face certain barriers which are unique to rural settings.

Rural batterers frequently isolate their partners as one tactic of maintaining power and control over their victims. They also commonly:

- Refuse access to family vehicles or prevent a woman from getting a driver's license.

- Ridicule her in front of friends and family so she's reluctant to reinvite them.

- Accuse her of flirting or having affairs, and because of this suspicion beating her for even limited contact with another person.

- Remove the telephone when leaving the home or calling her every hour to monitor her whereabouts.

- Threaten or beat her when she returns from outings with women friends.

- Keep her bruised so she is ashamed to be seen in public.

- Threaten to kill her if she tells anyone.

A woman isolated in these ways has a difficult time escaping from a violent partner. She fears leaving. She fears calling someone for help. Battered women everywhere experience some form of isolation as controlled by their partners, but for rural battered women the isolation becomes magnified by geographical isolation. Other rural factors can greatly impact a rural battered woman's isolation and chances of reaching safe shelter. Consider that:

- A rural battered woman may not have phone service.

- Usually no public transportation exists, so if she leaves she must take a family vehicle.

- Police and medical response to a call for help may take a long time.

- Rural areas have fewer resources for women—jobs, childcare, housing and health care, or easy access to them is limited by distance.

- Extreme weather often exaggerates isolation—cold, snow, and mud regularly affect life in rural areas and may extend periods of isolation with an abuser.

- Poor roads thwart transportation.

- Seasonal work may mean months of unemployment on a regular basis and result in women being trapped with an abuser for long periods.

- Hunting weapons are common to rural homes and everyday tools like axes, chains, pitchforks, and mauls are potential weapons.

- Alcohol use, which often increases in winter months when rural people are unemployed and isolated in their homes, usually affects the frequency and severity of abuse.

- Travelling to a "big city" (perhaps 20,000) can be intimidating to rural battered women and city attitudes may seem strange and unaccepting.

- A woman's bruises may fade or heal before she sees neighbors, and working with farm tools and equipment can provide an easy explanation for injuries.

- Farm families are often one-income families and a woman frequently has no money of her own to support herself and her children.

- A family's finances are often tied up in land and equipment, so a woman thinking of ending a relationship faces an agonizing reality that she and her partner may lose the family farm or her partner will be left with no means of income.

- Court orders restraining an abuser from having contact with a woman are less viable for rural women because their partners cannot be kept away from the farm if it is their only source of income.

- Rural women frequently have strong emotional ties to the land and to farm animals, and if she has an attachment to her animals she fears they may be neglected or harmed.

- Rural woman are usually an integral part of a family farm business, so if she leaves the business may fail.

Rural battered women have some unique problems, but alternatives to living with abuse do exist. A battered women's program can provide personal support, safety planning for you and your children, information about options available to you, transportation, legal information, safe shelter, and referrals to financial assistance, job training, and education options.

# Chapter 6

# *Domestic Violence & Alcohol and Other Drugs*

"Alcohol is associated with a substantial proportion of human violence, and perpetrators are often under the influence of alcohol."
*Eighth Special Report to the U.S. Congress on Alcohol and Health (Secretary of Health and Human Services, September 1993)*

Studies of domestic violence frequently document high rates of alcohol and other drug (AOD) involvement, and AOD use is known to impair judgment, reduce inhibition, and increase aggression. Alcoholism and child abuse, including incest, seem tightly intertwined as well. The connection between child abuse and alcohol abuse "may take the form of alcohol abuse in parents or alcohol intoxication at the time of the abuse incident."[1] Not only do abusers tend to be heavy drinkers, but those who have been abused stand a higher probability of abusing alcohol and other drugs over the course of their lifetime.

Alcohol consistently "emerges as a significant predictor of marital violence."[2] Alcoholic women have been found to be significantly more likely to have experienced negative verbal conflict with spouses than were nonalcoholic women. They were also significantly more likely to have experienced a range of moderate and severe physical violence.

Studies have shown a significant association between battering incidents and alcohol abuse. Further, a dual problem with alcohol and

National Clearinghouse for Alcohol and Drug Information, Publication No. ML001, Spring 1995.

103

other drugs is even more likely to be associated with the more severe battering incidents than is alcohol abuse by itself. The need for preventing alcohol and other drug problems is clear when the following statistics are examined:

- In 1987, 64 percent of all reported child abuse and neglect cases in New York City were associated with parental AOD abuse.[3]

- A study of 472 women by the Research Institute on Addictions in Buffalo, NY, found that 87 percent of alcoholic women had been physically or sexually abused as children, compared to 59 percent of the nonalcoholic women surveyed (Miller and Downs, 1993).[4]

- A 1993 study of more than 2,000 American couples found rates of domestic violence were almost 15 times higher in households where husbands were described as often drunk as opposed to never drunk.[5]

- Battered women are at increased risk of attempting suicide, abusing alcohol and other drugs, depression, and abusing their own children.[6]

- Alcohol is present in more than 50 percent of all incidents of domestic violence.[5]

While alcohol and other drug use is neither an excuse for nor a direct cause of family violence, several theories might explain the relationship. For example, women who are abused often live with men who drink heavily, which places the women in an environment where their potential exposure to violence is higher.

A second possible explanation is that women using alcohol and other drugs may not recognize assault cues and even if they do, may not know how to respond appropriately. Third, alcohol and other drug abuse by either parent could contribute to family violence by exacerbating financial problems, child-care difficulties, or other family stressers.

Finally, the experience of being a victim of parental abuse could contribute to future alcohol and other drug abuse.

To reduce the incidence of these problems in the future, prevention of alcohol and other drug abuse must be a top priority. For more information, call the National Clearinghouse for Alcohol and Drug Information at 1-800-729-6686.

## References

All statistics cited in this *Making the Link* fact sheet come from the following sources:

1.  Widom, Cathy Spatz. "Child Abuse and Alcohol Use." *Research Monograph 24: Alcohol and Interpersonal Violence: Fostering Multidisciplinary Perspectives.* Rockville, MD: National Institute on Alcohol Abuse and Alcoholism, 1993.

2.  Kantor, Glenda Kaufman. "Refining the Brushstrokes in Portraits of Alcohol and Wife Assaults." *Research Monograph 24: Alcohol and Interpersonal Violence: Fostering Multidisciplinary Perspectives.* Rockville, MD: National Institute on Alcohol Abuse and Alcoholism, 1993.

3.  Chasnoff, I. J. *Drugs, Alcohol, Pregnancy and Parenting.* Northwestern University Medical School, Departments of Pediatrics and Psychiatry and Behavioral Sciences, Hingham, MA, Klawer Academic Publishers, 1988.

4.  Miller, Brenda A., and William R. Downs. "The Impact of Family Violence on the Use of Alcohol by Women." *Alcohol Health and Research World* 17, 2, (1993): 137–43. U.S. Department of Health and Human Services, National Institute on Alcohol Abuse and Alcoholism.

5. Collins, J. J., and M. A. Messerschmidt. "Epidemology of Alcohol-Related Violence." *Alcohol Health and Research World* 17, 2 (1993): 93–100. U.S. Department of Health and Human Services, National Institute on Alcohol Abuse and Alcoholism, 1993.

6.  *Fact Sheet on Physical and Sexual Abuse.* Substance Abuse and Mental Health Services Administration, April 1994.

Chapter 7

# Domestic Violence and Poverty

## Chapter Contents

# Section 7.1

# *Domestic Violence and Homelessness*

National Coalition for the Homeless, *NCH Fact Sheet #8,* April 1999.
Used with permission.

## *Background*

When a woman leaves an abusive relationship, she often has no-where to go. This is particularly true of women with few resources. Lack of affordable housing and long waiting lists for assisted hous-ing mean that many women and their children are forced to choose between abuse at home or the streets. Moreover, shelters are fre-quently filled to capacity and must turn away battered women and their children. An estimated 32% of requests for shelter by homeless families were denied in 1998 due to lack of resources (U.S. Conference of Mayors, 1998).

## *Domestic Violence as a Contributing Factor to Homelessness*

Many studies demonstrate the contribution of domestic violence to homelessness, particularly among families with children. A 1990 Ford Foundation study found that 50% of homeless women and chil-dren were fleeing abuse (Zorza, 1991). More recently, in a study of 777 homeless parents (the majority of whom were mothers) in ten U.S. cities, 22% said they had left their last place of residence because of domestic violence (Homes for the Homeless, 1998). In addition, 46% of cities surveyed by the U.S. Conference of Mayors identified domes-tic violence as a primary cause of homelessness (U.S. Conference of Mayors, 1998). State and local studies also demonstrate the impact of domestic violence on homelessness:

- In Minnesota, the most common reason for women to enter a shelter is domestic violence. Approximately one in five women (19%) surveyed indicated that one of the main reasons for leav-ing housing was to flee abuse; 24% of women surveyed were homeless, at least in part, because of a previous abuse experi-ence (Wilder Research Center, 1998).

- In Missouri, 18% of the sheltered homeless population are victims of domestic violence (De Simone et al., 1998).

- A 1995 survey of homeless adults in Michigan found that physical abuse/being afraid of someone was most frequently cited as the main cause of homelessness (Douglass, 1995).

- Shelter providers in Virginia report that 35% of their clients are homeless because of family violence (Virginia Coalition for the Homeless, 1995). This same survey found that more than 2,000 women seeking shelter from domestic violence facilities were turned away.

## Policy Issues

Shelters provide immediate safety to battered women and their children and help women gain control over their lives. The provision of safe emergency shelter is thus a necessary first step in meeting the needs of women fleeing domestic violence.

A sizable portion of the welfare population experiences domestic violence at any given time; thus, without significant housing support, many welfare recipients are at risk of homelessness or continued violence. In states that have looked at domestic violence and welfare receipt, most report that approximately 50–60% of current recipients say that they have experienced violence from a current or former male partner (Institute for Women's Policy Research, 1997). In the absence of cash assistance, women who experience domestic violence may be at increased risk of homelessness or compelled to live with a former or current abuser in order to prevent homelessness. Welfare programs must make every effort to assist victims of domestic violence and to recognize the tremendous barrier to employment that domestic violence presents.

Long-term efforts to address homelessness must include increasing the supply of affordable housing, ensuring adequate wages and income supports, and providing necessary supportive services.

## References

DeSimone, Peter, et al. *Homelessness in Missouri: Eye of the Storm?*, 1998. Available for $6.00 from the Missouri Association for Social Welfare, 308 E. High St., Jefferson City, MO 65101; (573)-634-2901.

Douglass, Richard. *The State of Homelessness in Michigan: A Research Study,* 1995. Available, free, from the Michigan Interagency Committee on Homelessness, c/o Michigan State Housing Development Authority, P.O. Box 30044, Lansing, MI 48909; (517)-373-6026.

Homes for the Homeless. *Ten Cities 1997–1998: A Snapshot of Family Homelessness Across America.* Available from Homes for the Homeless & the Institute for Children and Poverty, 36 Cooper Square, 6th Floor, New York, NY 10003; (212)-529-5252.

Institute for Women's Policy Research. "Domestic Violence and Welfare Receipt," 1997. *IWPR Welfare Reform Network News,* Issue No. 4. April. Available from Institute for Women's Policy Research, 1707 L. Street, N.W., Suite 750, Washington, DC 20036; (202)-785-5100.

Mullins, Gretchen. "The Battered Woman and Homelessness," in *Journal of Law and Policy,* 3, (1994)1:237–55. Entire issue available for $30.00 from William S. Hein & Co., Inc., 1285 Main St., Buffalo, NY 14209; (800)-828-7571.

Owen, Greg, et al. *Minnesota Statewide Survey of Persons Without Permanent Shelter; Volume I: Adults and Their Children,* 1998. Available for $20.00 from the Wilder Research Center, 1295 Bandana Blvd., North, Suite 210, St. Paul, MN 55108-5197; (612)-647-4600.

U.S. Conference of Mayors. *A Status Report on Hunger and Homelessness in America's Cities: 1998.* Available for $15.00 from the U.S. Conference of Mayors, 1620 Eye St., NW, 4th Floor, Washington, DC 20006-4005; (202)-293-7330.

Virginia Coalition for the Homeless. *1995 Shelter Provider Survey,* 1995. Out of print. Virginia Coalition for the Homeless, P.O. Box 12247, Richmond, VA 23241; (804)-644-5527.

Zorza, Joan. "Woman Battering: A Major Cause of Homelessness," in *Clearinghouse Review,* vol. 25, no. 4, 1991. Available for $6.00 from the National Clearinghouse for Legal Services, 205 W. Monroe St., 2nd Floor, Chicago, IL 60606-5013; (800)-621-3256.

# Section 7.2

# *The Facts: Battered Women and Economics*

National Network to End Domestic Violence Fund, 1997.

One of the many problems that women who are battered may face is their inability to provide basic necessities for themselves and their children. In 1996, Congress passed the Personal Responsibility and Work Opportunity Reconciliation Act (Welfare Reform) (Pub. L. No. 104-193), which brought about sweeping changes to state and federal law aimed to move women off of welfare into work. Essentially, the new law grants states more autonomy to decide who receives aid and who does not. Unlike the Aid to Families with Dependent Children (AFDC) benefit program that existed for more than 60 years, Temporary Aid to Needy Families (TANF) is a fixed block grant to the states for which states must meet certain requirements. The new federal law provides that one would be eligible to receive assistance for a maximum of 60 months—five years—over one's lifetime. Some states provide even shorter time limits than the federal law. States must ensure that 90 percent of two-parent families receiving aid are working by 1999.

The two criterion that have the greatest impact on women who are battered is the 60-month lifetime time limit for receiving benefits and the requirement that recipients work in order to receive aid.

Beginning in July of 1997 each state must have submitted its plan for implementation to the federal government. States are permitted a hardship exemption to be given to persons who cannot meet the restrictions. The total of these persons must not exceed 20 percent of its TANF caseload or the state faces severe financial penalties. For example, persons with disabilities, the elderly, and persons with long-term incapacitation may fall under the 20 percent hardship exemption.

Another component of the new law is the Family Violence option (FVO). Designed to assist states in better meeting the needs of domestic violence victims, the FVO permits states to screen and identify women who are battered, refer them to counseling and/or support services, and waive program requirements. As of November 25, 1997, twenty-nine states plus Puerto Rico and Guam have adopted or enacted the FVO provisions in their state welfare plans. Seventeen states plus the District of Columbia and the Virgin Islands have not adopted the FVO provisions, but have incorporated domestic violence language in their welfare plans.

Four states have neither adopted the FVO provisions nor incorporated domestic violence language in their state plans.

The arguments for providing safeguards for battered women in moving women from welfare to work are compelling. Therefore, five years may not be enough time for a woman who is battered to be safe, self-sufficient and provide for her family, simultaneously. Such sweeping restrictions do not account for the complexities of violence a woman may experience. For instance, her partner may sabotage every effort on the part of a woman to improve herself. He may threaten or terrorize her at work, causing her to lose her job. He may destroy her books so that she can not study. He may beat her so badly that she is physically unable to go to work or school. A woman who is battered may also have invisible scars. She may need to rebuild her self-confidence and her self-esteem. It may have taken her many years to leave her partner, but the new welfare-to-work time restrictions envision that she must become financially stable in only five.

Every battered woman is different; her circumstances may pose challenges that cannot be met in the boilerplate formula offered by federal and state welfare laws. The following statistics demonstrate some of these complexities.

## Women, Family, and Work

- In 1996, poverty threshold for a family of three was $12,516.

Daniel H. Weinberg, Press briefing on *1996 Income, Poverty, and Health Insurance Estimates* (Sept. 29, 1997).

- In 1997, full-time working women earned only 74.9% ($429.00) of median earnings for men.

Bureau of Labor Statistics, U. S. Dept. of Labor, *Usual Weekly Earnings of Wage and Salary Workers: Third Quarter 1997* (Oct. 22, 1997).

- 1 year after divorce women's incomes average only 67% of their pre-divorce incomes, compared to 90% for men.

American Psychological Association, *Violence and the Family: Report of the American Psychological Association Presidential Task Force on Violence and the Family* (1996) citing National Commission on Children.

- In 1992, 12 million families were maintained by women in the United States.
- In 1991, 39% of households maintained by women were below the poverty level.

Women's Bureau, U.S. Dept. of Labor, *Women Who Maintain Families* (June 1993).

- In 1995, the average weekly earning for women in a non-supervisory position working in a video tape rental store was $135.00, and $200.00 for women working in a variety store.

Bureau of Labor Statistics, U.S. Dept. of Labor, *Employment, Hours, and Earnings United States, 1988–96* (1996).

- The first year after leaving AFDC, 30% of mothers earn more than $9,000, while 59% earn less than $6,000.
- Even with the earned income tax credit (EITC), 55% of single mothers working full time would not be able to escape poverty due to child care costs and payroll taxes.

Barbara Leyser et al., Center on Social Welfare Policy and Law, *Welfare Myths: Fact or Fiction: Exploring the Truth About Welfare* (1996).

- It costs an average of $74/week for child care, or 8% of monthly family income.
- In 1993, poor families who paid for child care spent 18% of their income on child care.

Lynne M. Casper, U.S. Census Bureau, *What Does It Cost to Mind Our Preschoolers?* (Visited Dec. 5, 1997 < http://blue.census.gov/population/www/socdemo/child/p7052.html >

## Women and Welfare

- In 1994, the average monthly welfare check for a family of three was $366/month or $4,392/year.
- In 1993, 6% of 1,408.2 billion dollars of the **federal budget** was spent on **all** programs aiding poor families with children.

Barbara Leyser et al., Center on Social Welfare Policy and Law, *Welfare Myths: Fact or Fiction: Exploring the Truth About Welfare* (1996).

- In 1992 welfare caseload consisted of 9.2 million children and 4.4 million adults (the majority of them women).
- If welfare was combined with food stamps and housing assistance, only 1 in 5 families would be above the poverty line.
- 1/4 of AFDC families receive added assistance to pay for housing.

House Committee on Ways and Means, U.S. Congress, 104th Cong., *Overview of Entitlement Programs, 1994 Green Book* (U.S. Government Printing Office, 1994).

- Most AFDC households are able to provide shelter, clothing, transportation, household necessities on an annual average income of $8,000 for a family of three when combined with AFDC and food stamps.

Sharon Parrott, Center on Budget and Policy Priorities, *How Much Do We Spend on 'Welfare'?* (Mar. 1995).

## Women, Work, and Domestic Violence

- Homicide is the most frequent manner in which women workers are fatally injured at work. From 1992-94, 17 percent of their alleged attackers were current or former husbands or boyfriends.

Bureau of Labor Statistics, U.S. Department of Labor, Report 908, *Fewer Women Than Men Die of Work-Related Injuries, Data Show, in Fatal Workplace Injuries in 1994: A Collection of Data and Analysis* (1996).

- In a small non-random study of domestic violence victims, 96 percent of those who were employed had some type of problem in the workplace as a direct result of their abuse or abuser. These included being late (more than 60%), missing work (more than 50%), having difficulty performing one's job (70%), being reprimanded for problems associated with the abuse (60%), or losing a job (30%).

Women's Bureau, U.S. Department of Labor, No. 96-3, *Domestic Violence: A Workplace Issue* (1996), citing Domestic Violence Intervention Services, Inc., *Domestic Violence: An Occupational Impact Study* (July 27, 1992).

- Violence against women is often exacerbated as women seek to gain economic independence, and often increases when women attend school training programs, and batterers often prevent women from attending such programs, and often sabotage their efforts at self-improvement.

S. Con. Res. 66 104th Cong. (1996).—Relative to Welfare Reform Submitted by Senator Wellstone, et al. to the Committee on Finance.

- In a 1995 study of 846 AFDC recipients in a welfare-to-work program, some of the women were experiencing physical domestic violence (14.6%), and said that their partners did not encourage their attempts at education and training.

Jody Raphael & Richard M. Tolman, Taylor Institute, *Trapped by Poverty, Trapped by Abuse: New Evidence Documenting the Relationship Between Domestic Violence and Welfare* (1997).

- Abusive partners harass 74% of employed battered women at work, either in person or over the telephone, which results in their being late for work, missing work altogether, and eventually, 20% lose their jobs.

Joan Zorza, "Women Battering: A Major Cause of Homelessness," *Clearinghouse Review* 1991.

- In 1993, approximately 26% of the women killed in the workplace were murdered by their husbands or boyfriends, current or former.

Guy Toscano and William Weber, "Violence in the Workplace." *Compensation and Working Conditions* 47, 4 (Apr. 1995): 1–8.

- Victims of family violence are at increased risk for poor or impaired job performance, whether or not they work inside or outside the home.

American Psychological Association., *Violence and the Family: Report of the American Psychological Association Presidential Task Force on Violence and the Family* (1996).

## Suggested Readings

Bassuk, Ellen L., et al. *Single Mothers and Welfare.* Scientific American, Inc., 1996.

Goldscheid, Julie, and Pamela Coukos. "Violence Against Women Affects the Workplace: Legal Remedies for Women and Advocates." *Clearinghouse Review* Special Issue (1996).

Leyser, Barbara et al. *Welfare Myths: Fact or Fiction: Exploring the Truth About Welfare.* Center on Social Welfare Policy and Law, 1996.

Institute for Women's Policy Research. *Measuring the Cost of Domestic Violence Against Women and the Cost-Effectiveness of Interventions,* 1997.

Pollack, Wendy, and Martha F. Davis. "The Family Violence Option of the Personal Responsibility and Work Opportunity Reconciliations Act of 1996: Interpretation and Implementation." *Clearinghouse Review* (Mar.–Apr. 1997).

## Section 7.3

# *Domestic Violence as a Barrier to Women's Economic Self-Sufficiency*

*Heidi Sachs*

## *Background*

While domestic violence affects women from all sectors of society, many studies demonstrate that the percentage of welfare recipients who are victims of domestic violence is much higher than among the general population. Recognition of this phenomenon and realization that many victims would not be able to fulfill the strict work requirements necessitated under PRWORA [the Personal Responsibility and Work Opportunity Reconciliation Act], led Congress to adopt the Wellstone/Murray Amendment as part of the new welfare law (P.L. 104–193).

The Wellstone/Murray amendment gives states the option to adopt the Family Violence Option (FVO), which allows states to waive work requirements and time limits, and increase services to victims of domestic violence and their families without being penalized financially. The temporary waivers under the FVO are intended to allow victims of domestic violence the time needed for a successful transition off of welfare by allowing flexibility in complying with work and job training requirements. The waivers also allow victims to receive TANF [Temporary Aid to Needy Families] benefits, without having to identify the father of their children or supply child support enforcement agencies with other pertinent information. Such actions can endanger a battered woman since violence may increase when child support action is taken against an abuser. States choosing to adopt the

116

Family Violence Option are required to screen applicants for domestic violence while maintaining confidentiality, refer victims to counseling and other supportive services, and provide "good-cause waivers" from TANF program requirements where meeting those requirements might endanger victims.

While 39 states have adopted the Family Violence Option to date, it is important to note that it is not a panacea for domestic violence. In some states that have adopted the FVO, programs and policies around family violence are not being implemented in local welfare offices. Furthermore, several states that have not adopted the FVO have effective practices in place, which address domestic violence. For more information on the domestic violence provisions of PRWORA, refer to NOW Legal Defense and Education Fund's "The Family Violence Option in the New Welfare Law" *http://www.nowldef.org/html/policy/fvo.htm* or call 212-925-6635.

In addition to state human service offices, employers can play an important role in assisting victims of domestic violence in their efforts at self-sufficiency. While the FVO and similar provisions temporarily exempt some victims of domestic violence from work requirements, it is important to keep in mind that many victims are already in the workplace and in most cases, those who are not currently working will eventually have to take part in work activities. Therefore, employers should be aware of strategies they can employ to mitigate the effects of domestic violence in the workplace. [*See also* Chapter 23.]

## Policy Issues

### Are state human service offices effectively serving victims of domestic violence?

Parallel to the larger welfare bill, states and counties have a great amount of flexibility in designing and implementing policies and programs around family violence. While some states are undoubtedly serving battered women in ways that are effective, other states' programs and policies are weak at best. Anecdotal evidence as well as several studies demonstrate that many human service caseworkers simply are not trained to work with victims of family violence. This phenomenon has far-reaching implications. Failure to possess information about the needs of battered women can further endanger this population and put them at greater risk of long-term poverty. Also, when caseworkers are unaware of domestic violence and are not

117

trained in how to handle it, they cannot effectively prepare their clients for work. Furthermore, without help from caseworkers, there is an unnecessary disconnect between human service agencies and employers. For example, employers who have workers transitioning off of welfare may want to know whether their employees are receiving necessary support services.

A recent article in the *Seattle-Post Intelligencer* documents this lack of education and training among caseworkers. In Washington State, domestic violence advocates found that many caseworkers do not even know about the Family Violence Option. Only one four-hour training on domestic violence has been offered to welfare workers in the past two years. Furthermore, caseworkers are failing to screen for abuse, and victims who make the disclosure on their own are often held to job search requirements, in violation of the FVO. For more information on this article, contact Ruth Teichroeb at 206-448-8175 or *ruthteichroeb@seattle-pi.com*

A report by the Taylor Institute (Raphael and Haennicke, 1999a) documents similar findings. This recent study of the implementation of states' family violence policies found that 20 states have notice and assessment processes that appear largely inadequate. If a victim does not understand that she may disclose the abusive situation and why it may be in her interest to do so, she cannot make an informed choice whether or not to disclose.

### How can TANF agencies better help victims of family violence find and maintain employment?

The first step in the process of helping victims of domestic violence is notice and assessment. Several barriers to disclosure (i.e., clients' distrust of the caseworker, denial of abuse, fear that children will be taken away, fear that the abusive partner will discover the disclosure, and lack of training on the part of the caseworker) make it unlikely that victims will admit to abuse. With this in mind, it is essential that women applying for and receiving TANF are informed of the waivers and kinds of support services that may be available to them as victims of domestic violence. Thus, states and localities may want to consider how they communicate with clients about their work requirements and the special provisions that may be available if working would put clients in danger of increased abuse.

A recent report by the Taylor Institute (Raphael and Haennicke, 1999a) provides a comprehensive overview of states' assessment practices. Some of the "best practices" highlighted by the report have a notification process, in which the term "domestic violence" is excluded. This may be preferable because many victims of domestic violence do not identify themselves with this label. The report also highlights state assessments that are informative, such as cases where caseworkers inform clients that they may be able to be temporarily excused from work or work activities if participation would put them in danger of abuse. For example, Rhode Island's notice states, "If working, looking for a job or going to school may put you or your children in danger of physical, emotional or sexual abuse, we may be able to excuse you from these activities until the situation is resolved." Also, the state's FVO notice form informs TANF recipients that their child support obligations can be waived due to danger of abuse.

In order to best help a victim who has disclosed abuse, TANF agencies should offer employment-related services in combination with various supportive services to assist clients as they move from welfare to work. These services may combine case management services and domestic violence support with employment-related services, such as literacy training, job readiness training, and job placement services.

### With whom can TANF agencies and employers work to help victims of domestic violence become self-sufficient?

Coordination between welfare agencies, domestic violence service providers, battered women's shelters, law enforcement, child welfare, health care providers, schools, child care providers, child support enforcement, and education and training providers is tantamount to a victim's safety as well as her efforts to become economically self-sufficient. Several states and counties have had a great deal of success when contracting with community-based domestic violence service providers. Having a trained domestic violence worker on staff at the TANF agency not only provides victims with immediate services, but also allows for the training of TANF personnel. Victims are best served in situations where there is a strong safety net in place, comprised of several supportive entities.

### What are the funding sources for programs and services that address the needs of victims of domestic violence?

The funding for domestic violence services for welfare recipients comes primarily from TANF. States may use TANF funds for a broad array of services, including but not limited to education and training of caseworkers, contracting with domestic violence providers, and transporting women from domestic shelters to their place of work.

Additional resources are available through several other federal agencies: The U.S. Department of Labor Employment and Training Administration provides grants to model programs that target clients with multiple barriers to employment. Approximately 20 grants were given in 1999 to projects that work with victims of domestic violence. The states that received these grants included Arkansas, California, Connecticut, Illinois, Maine, Maryland, New Hampshire, New York, North Carolina, Oregon, Tennessee, Texas, Virginia, and Washington. More information on the Welfare-to-Work grantees can be found at *http://wtw.doleta.gov/competitive/default.htm*

The U.S. Department of Health and Human Services [HHS] also provides money to prevent violence against women. The Fiscal Year (FY) 1999 budget included $156 million for HHS programs to prevent violence against women, including $1.2 million for the National Domestic Violence Hotline. For HHS programs under the Violence Against Women Act, the Department received $88.8 million for grants to states for battered women's shelters, $15 million for programs to reduce sexual abuse among runaway, homeless and street youth, $45 million for grants to states for rape prevention and education programs, and $6 million for coordinated community responses. In addition, $7 million from the Preventive Health and Health Services Block Grant was earmarked for rape prevention programs. The President's FY 2000 budget includes an additional $27.9 million to fund a Department-wide initiative to prevent violence against women from occurring and to provide services for its victims. In addition, this past August, an additional $1.25 million in new grants to help communities address domestic violence were awarded. These 14 new grants went to state domestic violence coalitions, community-based organizations, universities and a tribal council. The 3 grants to universities will help train researchers, scholars, and practitioners working on domestic violence in underserved communities. *http://waisgate.hhs.gov/*

The United States Department of Justice also funds programs around domestic violence. In FY 1999, Congress appropriated $23 million for STOP Violence Against Women grants, specifically designated for civil legal assistance programs for victims of domestic violence. The Office of Justice Programs' Violence Against Women Office (VAWO) is the administering agency. VAWO encourages applicants to develop programs that reach diverse and traditionally underserved populations. Grants are also targeted towards collaborative efforts between domestic violence advocacy organizations, local agencies (such as police, prosecutors, or courts), local services and businesses (such as public housing agencies, hospitals, community and other health clinics, public schools, and public libraries) to provide on-site legal advocacy and/or legal assistance information in places battered women are likely to access. *http://www.ojp.usdoj.gov/ocpa/NewAct/vawo.htm*

## Research

Several studies have shown the impact of domestic violence on the workplace. According to a recent study done by the Institute for Wisconsin's Future (Moore and Sekowe, 1999), finding and keeping a job is extremely difficult for women when their lives are continually interrupted by violence. In the W-2 study, approximately 30% of respondents reported that they had been fired or lost a job because of domestic abuse and 35% reported that the abuse hurt their education and training efforts. More than half (57.8%) of women surveyed indicated that they had been threatened to the point where they were afraid to go to school or work. Surveys completed by 274 domestic violence victims from around the state also document that abused women are consistently overlooked under Wisconsin Works (W-2), due to a lack of effective screening methods for identifying victims, insufficient caseworker training, and the frequent failure of caseworkers to provide victims with information on available support services and program options. For more information on this study, call IWF at 414-384-9094.

In 1997, the Institute for Poverty Research completed a study on the effects of abuse on female labor force participation (Lloyd 1997). Through a random survey of low-income women in the Humboldt Park area of Chicago, researchers found that roughly 40% of the women had at some point experienced male aggression directed at them, and 28.4% reported having experienced severe aggression. The women who were the target of physical or severe aggression (ever or in the past 12 months) were significantly more likely to have received AFDC, food stamps and Medicaid. For additional information, contact Susan Lloyd at *slloyd@macfdn.org*

The New Chance Study, a national research and demonstration program that operated between 1989 and 1992, documents similar findings. Welfare-to-Work program staff reported that some women were unwilling to attend training classes due to fear of provoking their partners' "anger and further assaults." For more information, contact the Manpower Demonstration Research Corporation at 212-532-3200. Additional research can be found at *http://www.welfareinfo.org/domestic.htm*

## *Additional Research Underway:*

The Family Violence Prevention Fund (FVPF) is launching a four-year Economic Independence Project to demonstrate how communities across the country can develop programs and policies to assist abused women transition successfully into the workforce and achieve economic independence. In collaboration with Wider Opportunities for Women, the FVPF will partner with a range of experts and advocates representing the broad spectrum of issues that affect abused women's struggle for economic independence. The project will work to identify existing services and supports, educate caseworkers, assist employers in domestic violence awareness and build on resources that are available. For more information, contact the FVPF at 415-252-8900.

The NOW Legal Defense and Education Fund is in the first phase of a long-term project, called The Advocacy Project, the goal of which is to assess and influence the impact of state-level welfare changes on women. One of the 4 key issues the project will focus on is domestic violence. The initial focus is on seven states—California, Illinois, Massachusetts, New Jersey, New York, Texas, and Washington. For more information, call NOW LDEF at 212-925-6635 or 202-544-4470.

The Taylor Institute/University of Michigan School of Social Work has a collaborative Project for Research on Welfare, Work and Domestic Violence, which is putting together a compilation of approximately 10 studies on domestic violence. A description of each program is to be posted on their web-site (http://www.ssw.umich.edu/trapped/) Some of the major studies to be listed on this site include:

- The Effects of Male Violence on Female Employment, Joint Center for Poverty Research and Institute for Policy Research

- Domestic Violence in the Lives of Welfare Recipients: Implications for the Family Violence Option, University of Michigan Poverty Research and Training Center

- Good Cause Temporary Waivers and Modifications for TANF Clients Who Are Also Victims of Domestic Violence, The Center for Social Work Research (CSWR), University of Texas at Austin School of Social Work
- New Approaches to Self-Sufficiency and Safety in Public Assistance and Child Support Agencies: Preliminary Findings from Three Demonstration Projects, Center for Policy Research

## Innovative Practices

### *Colorado:*

As part of a federal research effort, the Colorado Division of Child Support Enforcement developed and implemented a standardized training plan and screening and assessment tools for intake workers in three county welfare and child support enforcement offices. Welfare agency caseworkers (from the Office of Social Services) used a one-page form to screen all public assistance applicants for domestic violence. Afterward, and if appropriate, clients were given information on community resources and referred to the Child Support Enforcement Office for a good cause evaluation. At this point, child support intake workers used a more detailed assessment tool to probe the nature of the domestic violence in clients' lives and to offer needy clients the opportunity to apply for good cause exemptions. The Denver Office of Social Services has dropped this screening approach, but is now working with community domestic violence service providers to sponsor two paid staff in the Office of Social Services. It is intended that these staff will provide domestic violence support services to clients (for instance, help in gaining access to temporary shelter or obtaining a restraining order). Contact Jessica Pearson, Esther Griswold, Center for Policy Research, 303-837-1555.

El Paso County has also hired staff from women's shelters to work in the county Department of Human Services offices. These staff members provide training in domestic violence to caseworkers, as well as services to clients. For more information, contact Levetta Love, Family Independence Program, El Paso County Department of Human Services, 719-444-8153.

## *Illinois:*

Chicago State University and several other partners have formed the Chicago State University Works Program. It will target individuals in the far south and southeast sections of the city who are facing barriers to their successful transition from welfare to work as a result of problems associated with domestic violence. One of the partners is Family Rescue, an Illinois domestic violence provider agency (the largest provider in the target areas). The agency will work with clients and provide education and training to the other partner agencies involved in the project. Welfare recipients will partake in several job readiness and retention activities. Support services, such as child care, substance abuse treatment, psychological counseling, transportation, emergency or transitional housing, and books and supplies are available to participants. For more information, contact Carolyn Moore-Assem, Chicago State University, 773-995-2383.

## *Maine:*

The Training & Development Corporation program will work in tandem with the current formula grant activities to provide additional services to victims of domestic violence. Such services include: domestic violence counseling, classes in parenting and literacy, legal advocacy, housing, child care, and transportation. All participants will attend a job readiness program, "Success @ Work," which also provides information on the impact of domestic violence on a woman's ability to find and keep a job. As part of the program, job mentors will provide post-employment (subsidized and unsubsidized) assistance and support services. Staff will receive domestic violence training in the dynamics of domestic abuse and its impact on victims and their children. Additionally, an employer education and support program will help employers understand domestic violence and its effects on their workers and workplaces. The program will serve welfare recipients in Penobscot, Hancock and Piscataquis counties. For more information, contact Charles G. Tetro, 207-469-6385.

The Richmond Area Rural Health Center in central Maine has a battered woman's advocate from the Maine Coalition to End Domestic Violence on staff. Funded through a grant from the Department of Justice, the advocate has trained the entire staff (including receptionist, maintenance personnel, and medical records clerk) in domestic violence issues. She has worked with a staff committee to develop a screening tool for use during all pre-natal and well-women visits and a logging system to record assessments and referrals. For more information, contact Polly Campbell, Muskie School of Public Service, Institute for Public Sector Innovation, 207-780-5864 or Tracy Cooley, Maine Coalition to End Domestic Violence, 207-941-1194.

## *Maryland:*

In the fall of 1996, the Anne Arundel County Department of Social Services' Domestic Violence Awareness Training and Service Planning Agency received a grant from the U.S. Department of Health and Human Services (DHHS) to develop and pilot-test a domestic violence training curriculum for administrative and frontline social services staff. The training model, which was developed in collaboration with the YWCA of Annapolis and Anne Arundel County, is intended to better equip staff to identify and serve clients of TANF and other public assistance programs who may be victims of domestic violence, and provide general education to the public about domestic violence. The county implemented the three-day training program in 1997 and the Maryland Department of Human Resources is now implementing the program statewide. The model draws on the one used by the Domestic Abuse Intervention Project in Duluth, Minnesota. Videotapes are incorporated into the training and are used as instructional devices. For more information, contact Vesta Kimble, Deputy Director, Anne Arundel County Department of Social Services, 410-269-4603.

## *New Hampshire:*

Administered by North Harris Montgomery Community College, the PATHWAYS program provides participating welfare recipients with post-employment multi-track, multi-level educational options, life skills, communication, and cultural diversity training. One of the many components of the program works to "break the cycle" of domestic violence by offering preventative programs for participants' children. For more information, contact Dr. Lindy McDaniel, 409-273-7310, *lindymc@nhmccd.edu*

## *New York:*

Victim Services in New York City works with area corporations to develop sensitive domestic violence policies in the workplace. The organization provides consultations with supervisors, security staff, and human resources personnel on domestic violence awareness. Victim Services also provides training on how to recognize and respond to employees coping with abuse, educate employees on how to prevent or deal with violence, establish a corporate policy around the issue, set up risk-management teams to respond to potentially threatening situations in the workplace, and stay informed about employer liability. Contact Victim Services, 212-577-5080.

### Oregon:

The Office of Adult and Family Services (AFS) within the Oregon Department of Human Resources recently developed and implemented a domestic violence service plan that includes comprehensive staff training and domestic violence services for needy clients. Each AFS district office appoints a domestic violence contact person to coordinate training and services. All welfare agency staff receive training (both initial and ongoing) on how to identify and refer victims of domestic violence. The training model includes the use of a screening and assessment tool to help identify victims. The model was developed by AFS with input from the Oregon Coalition Against Domestic and Sexual Violence. Contact Shirley Iverson, Field Services Manager, 503-945-6902, or Carol Krager, Domestic-Violence Lead, 503-945-5931.

### Rhode Island:

Welfare workers give every TANF applicant written information about both work waivers and counseling resources. When a woman asks for help, welfare workers page a local domestic violence advocate who immediately comes to the DSHS office to provide assistance. For more information, contact the Taylor Institute at 312-342-5510.

### Tennessee:

Centerstone Community Mental Health Services, Inc. will provide employment and support services to victims of domestic violence. Case managers will be placed in each participating domestic violence shelter to refer individuals to the WtW/ Family First (TANF) programs for job placement, and to follow up with job retention and life skills training. For more information, contact David Gouth, 615-463-6600.

### Washington State:

In an effort to determine how many abused women need services, the state began tracking the number of welfare recipients identified as domestic violence victims in the fall of 1999. Domestic violence advocates have also been invited to participate in an advisory committee for the Economic Services Division of DHHS. A pilot project that will fund on-site domestic violence counselors for 10-15 welfare offices around the state is also in the planning stages.

The Spokane Works Project will coordinate existing services, so that an effective package is created to mitigate barriers to employment for eligible recipients. For more information, contact Daniel O. Jordan, 509-456-7111 ext. 215.

### Nationwide:

The Family Violence Prevention Fund (FVPF) has compiled a list of 28 companies, trade organizations, and labor unions, which have implemented policies in the workplace that address domestic violence. For a comprehensive list of model workplace practices and participating corporations, go to *http://www.fvpf.org/workplace/index.html* or contact FVPF at *fund@fvpf.org* or 415-252-8900.

The United States Office of Personnel Management: In 1998, President Clinton directed the U.S. Office of Personnel Management (OPM) to prepare a handbook on domestic violence for federal employees and supervisors. The booklet, called *Responding to Domestic Violence: Where Federal Employees Can Find Help*, provides concrete advice for employees who are victims and guides supervisors through an array of resources and management tools that can be used to assist federal employees in abusive relationships. The entire handbook can be viewed online at *http://www.opm.gov/workplac/html/domestic.html-ssi*

Levi Strauss and Co's. Red Tab Foundation: The company's foundation has a Domestic Abuse Pilot Program, based at the sewing facility in Tennessee, which provides employees with education, resources, counseling and emergency funds to address domestic abuse in their lives. Nearly 1,000 employees and managers received extensive training about warning signs of domestic abuse, how to talk to someone who is being abused, and where to go for help in the workplace and the community. Additionally, managers and those in supervisory roles have actively created an atmosphere that supports employees in their efforts to break free from the cycle of abuse. The Red Tab Foundation has expanded the Domestic Abuse Pilot Program to other LS&CO. facilities.

## Resource Contacts

Center for Law and Social Policy. Contact Vicky Turetsky, 202-328-5140, *http://www.clasp.org*

Center for Policy Research. Contact Jessica Pearson, 303-837-1555.

Family Violence Prevention Fund, San Francisco, CA. Contact Ester Solar, 415-252-8900, *http://www.fvpf.org*

Institute for Women's Policy Research, Washington, DC. Contact Jackie Chu, 202-785-1921, *http://www.iwpr.org/*

National Center on Poverty Law, *WomanView*, Chicago, IL. Contact Wendy Pollack, 312-263-3830 x238, *http://www.povertylaw.org/womanview/womanvw.htm*

National Coalition Against Domestic Violence, 303-839-1852, *http://www.ncadv.org/*

National Employment Project, 212-764-2204.

National Network to End Domestic Violence, *http://www.nnedv.org/*

National Resource Center on Domestic Violence, Harrisburg, PA. Contact Anne Menard, 800-537-2238.

NOW Legal Defense and Education Fund, Washington, DC. 202-544-4470, *http://www.nowldef.org/html/policy/violence.htm*

The Project for Research on Welfare, Work and Domestic Violence at The University of Michigan School of Social Work, 734-998-8511, *http://www.ssw.umich.edu/trapped/*

Taylor Institute. Contact Jody Raphael, 312-342-5510.

Aron, Laudan, and Krista Olson. "Efforts by Child Welfare Agencies to Address Domestic Violence in Public Welfare." American Public Human Services Association. Summer 1997. 202-628-0100. *http://aspe.os.dhhs.gov/hsp/cyp/dv/intro.htm*

The Institute for Wisconsin's Future. "Domestic Violence and W-2 Results of 150 Interviews." Contact Vicky Selkowe for more information, 414-384-9094, *http://www.execpc.com/~iwf/research.htm#welfare*

Jons, Pamela. "Monitoring Domestic Violence Policy and Practice in State Welfare Programs: The Role of Community-Based Groups and Providers—A How-to-Guide." The Project for Research on Welfare, Work, and Domestic Violence at the University of Michigan School of Social Work. March 1999. *http://www.ssw.umich.edu/trapped/pubs_monitor.pdf*

State Temporary Assistance for Needy Families (TANF) Programs." Taylor Institute. September 1999a. *http://www.ssw.umich.edu/trapped/pubs_fvo1999.pdf*

Raphael, Jody, and Richard Tolman. "Trapped By Poverty/Trapped By Abuse: New Evidence Documenting the Relationship Between Welfare and Domestic Violence." The Project for Research on Welfare, Work, and Domestic Violence at the University of Michigan School of Social Work. April 1997. *http://www.ssw.umich.edu/trapped/pubs_trapped.pdf*

Turetsky, Vicki. "Implementing the Family Violence Option—Lessons from Child Support 'Good Cause' Policies." Center for Law and Social Policy. November 1997. 202-328-5140. *http://www.clasp.org/pubs/childenforce/fvo.htm*

U.S. Department of Labor Education and Training Administration. "Features of the Grants Awarded in Round One of Welfare-to-Work Competitive Grants-Projects focusing on: Domestic Violence." *http://wtw.doleta.gov/intrestweb.htm#domestic*

U.S. General Accounting Office. "Domestic Violence: Prevalence and Implications for Employment Among Welfare Recipients." November 1998. *http://www.gao.gov/AIndexFY99/abstracts/he99012.htm*

Women's Programs Office of the American Psychological Association. "Making 'Welfare to Work' Really Work: Poor Women Are Often Battered Women." *http://www.apa.org/pi/wpo/domestic.html*

Section 7.4

# *Domestic Violence and Insurance Discrimination*

Excerpted from Center on Crime, Communities & Culture, (1999). *Domestic Violence: National Directory of Professional Services.* New York, NY: Open Society Institute. Used with permission.

## *Payment*

The financial survival of a voluntary insurance system such as we have in the United States depends on its beneficiaries' obtaining coverage before they need it. To keep costs managable, insurers use "pre-existing conditions" to deselect certain individuals from insurance coverage when they may otherwise require extensive, costly health care services.[1] One pre-existing condition that has been used to deny women insurance is injury resulting from domestic violence. Some victims of domestic violence have been excluded from receiving coverage based on behavior, i.e., their decision to stay in a violent relationship has been deemed a lifestyle choice.[2]

In 1993, members of the House Judiciary Committee conducted an informal survey of the 16 largest insurance companies in America to determine what criteria the companies were using to make coverage determinations for women seeking health, life, disability, home, and auto insurance.[3] When analyzing the reasons for coverage denial, the Committee found that half of the companies studied use domestic violence as a criterion to deny insurance coverage or to raise premiums. State surveys found that 24 percent of all insurance companies admitted discriminating against women who reported being victims of domestic violence.

Contrary to the informal findings described above, the American Council of Life Insurance, which represents 557 indemnity firms, publicly states that life insurance is widely available to women victims of domestic violence.[4] Their own figures show that 96 percent of women survivors of domestic abuse who apply for insurance are approved. One member, State Farm Insurance, has formed the group Corporate Alliance to End Partner Abuse. The Alliance works to encourage corporate America to recognize domestic violence as a public health crisis and to fund violence prevention programs. Other member firms support such efforts as crisis intervention projects, workshops, counseling, and treatment programs.

The National Association of Insurance Commissioners (NAIC), the oldest association of state public officials in the country, has formed a Discriminatory Practices Working Group charged with studying and evaluating the extent of discrimination against victims of domestic violence who seek insurance coverage. In 1995, the Group began to craft a model state law addressing insurance discrimination against victims of domestic violence. Among the provisions of the model law are sections prohibiting insurers from "breaching the confidentiality of an abuse victim's medical, police, court, credit, employment, or insurance records" without prior authorization from the victim.[5] Insurers are also required to disclose their reasons for taking adverse insurance action against any victim of domestic violence. Publicity surrounding recently proposed federal legislation such as the Victims of Abuse Access to Health Insurance Act and the Domestic Violence Victims Insurance Protection Act may be a catalyst toward changing conservative policymaking decisions in all areas of insurance. Passage of federal legislation would guarantee that battered women could receive health care even if they were to relocate out of state to flee abuse.

## *References*

1. Health Coverage Availability and Affordability Act of 1996: Committee Reports, House of Representatives, 104th Congress, 2nd Sess. 497 (1996, March 25).

2. Congressional Testimony of Sen. Nancy Kassebaum before the Senate Labor and Human Resources Committee of the U.S. Senate, Insurance for Victims of Domestic Violence, H.R. Rep. No. 1201, 103rd Congress, 2nd Sess. (1995, July 28).

3. Congressional Testimony of Nancy Durborow before the Labor and Human Resources Committee of the U.S. Senate, H.R. Rep. No. 497, 104th Congress, 2nd Sess. (1995) p. 12.

4. Legislation would bar insurance firms from discriminating against victims, (1997). Silver Spring, MD: CD Publications.

5. Congressional Testimony of Deborah Senn before the Labor and Human Resources Committee of the U.S. Senate, H.R. Rep. No. 497, 104th Congress, 2nd Sess. (1995), p. 7.

Chapter 8

# The HIV/AIDS Connection to Domestic Violence

*Barbara A. Nissley*
*Mary Allen, Contributor*

*I can't believe this is happening to me. This happens to other people, not to me or even anyone I know. I can't tell anyone. I'm too ashamed. If I tell, they'll blame me for being in this situation and say it's my fault. If people find out at work, they'll be afraid. I don't know if I could be fired for this or not. Not being able to talk to anyone makes me feel so isolated and alone. I don't know anyone else who is going through this. Nobody I know even talks about it. I know there are hotlines and places I could go for help, but I just can't. I'm just too afraid. I tried to get help once, but I wasn't treated very well. It seemed like the people who were supposed to help me kept jumping to these strange conclusions about me, before they even knew me and my situation.*

*I go to the doctor or the emergency room when it gets really bad, but they just treat the symptoms. They don't ask me if anything else is going on. Sometimes my body just hurts everywhere and I feel tired and I ache. I feel just awful. I have no control over*

This material was reprinted from the publication entitled *Drugs, Alcohol and Addiction: A Resource Manual for Advocates Working to End Domestic Violence,* produced by the Pennsylvania Coalition Against Domestic Violence. Written by Barbara J. Hart and Frank Jans.

*what's happening. One of these days I'll be dead from this, I just know it. The dreams I had for my life, where have they gone?*

*I hope I don't get pregnant. It would be too much to handle all this and a pregnancy at the same time. And who knows what could happen to the baby.*

*I never imagined I'd be in this predicament. I don't see any way out. This is my life and it probably won't change until this kills me.*

Is this the voice of a battered woman or a woman struggling with HIV disease? Perhaps she is dealing with both. These epidemics—domestic violence and HIV/AIDS—have much in common:

- isolation
- fear
- victim-blaming
- discrimination
- health problems
- pregnancy concerns
- widespread misconceptions
- a fundamental lack of control
- possible death

Domestic violence and HIV/AIDS are both compounded by society's lack of concern for those affected and rooted in society's ills such as sexism, racism, classism, and heterosexism. Additionally, in both cases, alcohol and drug use and abuse can play a devastating role—contributing to the on-going danger for the survivor of battering and for the person with HIV.

There are a range of issues, related to violence against women, HIV disease, and drug abuse, that as a society we simply do not wish to confront. These include:

- sexuality, including sexual abuse, sexual practices and sexual identity
- the cause, prevention and treatment of drug and alcohol abuse
- violence in all its myriad forms
- prostitution or the sex industry
- illness and physical health problems
- dying and death

All of these have ties to the issues that confront battered women. The connections between HIV, domestic violence, and substance abuse are complex and present great challenges to those who work with survivors of battering. Of course, very little about domestic violence is simple; HIV is but one additional complication to understand in order to best serve battered women.

This essay addresses a few basic concepts about the intersection of battering, HIV infection, and alcohol and drug abuse. The goal is not to become an HIV/AIDS expert, but rather to be more comfortable providing advocacy and support to battered women, who are also HIV-infected, by understanding the issues that they face.

## HIV Infection Does Not Cause Battering

To attribute domestic violence to any outside cause or force excuses the violence and blurs a batterer's responsibility for its occurrence. For example, alcohol or other drug abuse does not cause battering, nor does job stress, poverty, anger, an abusive childhood or having a bad day. HIV/AIDS also does not cause the abuse of women.

HIV/AIDS and the illnesses associated with it can create horrifying experiences in the lives of people living with the virus and their caregiving partners. Indeed, AIDS is an extraordinarily stressful disease; it is unpredictable, its symptoms are difficult to manage, and it produces disabling and disfiguring effects. Nonetheless, HIV/AIDS does not produce, cause, or in any way justify abuse and violence— even though batterers may attempt to justify their violence by attributing it to their HIV status and related problems. Battered women may also attribute the violence they are experiencing to their partner's stress as a result of health problems related to HIV that one or both are suffering. This is true regardless of gender and/or sexual identity.

When working with battered women, it is important not to label HIV as the culprit responsible for the violence. Accurate information about the dynamics of power and control related to domestic violence can help survivors see the abuse as part of a larger dynamic rather than a specific response to a health problem. Survivors can be reminded that the vast majority of individuals with HIV are not abusive to their partners, and that no matter how stressful it can be, domestic violence is not an appropriate coping strategy.

## *HIV as a Weapon of Control*

Perpetrators of domestic violence employ a wide variety of tactics of abuse to control their partners, including physical, sexual, psychological and economic abuse. Most batterers display a terrifying ingenuity in their selection of violent tactics, frequently tailoring the abuse to the specific vulnerabilities of their partner. As a means of control, HIV can be a very powerful weapon. Advocates working with battered women who have HIV/AIDS, or whose partners do, need to understand the facts about the disease, its transmission and what constitutes safer sex. (See Appendix B, Fact Sheet on HIV/AIDS in *Drugs, Alcohol and Addiction*). It is also important to be aware of the magnitude of HIV/AIDS discrimination in this country in order to help address the fears battered women may face.

All individuals in domestic violence situations are at risk for HIV infection. If the abuser is HIV-infected, the odds are great that the partner will become infected through sexual transmission. Rape and sexual assault are often an integral part of a perpetrator's violence, and there is little reason to believe that a batterer who will rape will use a condom. Conversations about safer sex or insistence on using a condom may actually trigger violence that may include sexual assault.

Perhaps even more insidious are perpetrators who deliberately infect their partners with HIV to keep them from leaving. The perpetrator may reason that infecting the partner will make her less desirable to others and more dependent on the relationship, telling his partner, "No one else will want you; you have to stay with me."

Threats related to HIV are also powerful mechanisms of control. To create an atmosphere of intimidation and fear that can immobilize their partners, batterers threaten to:

- infect a partner with HIV
- withhold medication
- not allow a person who is HIV-infected to seek medical attention
- reveal someone's HIV status

Threats against an individual with HIV/AIDS can be particularly effective in maintaining a batterer's control, since revealing HIV status and sexual identity in the case of lesbians and gay men could result in job loss and the subsequent loss of health insurance, custody battles, housing problems and other forms of HIV discrimination.

136

Batterers may also use their partner's HIV status as an excuse for violence. Additionally, if the target of the violence is HIV-infected, asymptomatic HIV, symptomatic HIV or AIDS diagnosed, the physical and emotional toll of battering can be devastating to that person's already impaired immune system. The result can accelerate the progression of the disease.

The abuser also often controls access to financial resources, healthcare, and support systems. As the disease progresses, the battered woman becomes less able to care for herself and more dependent on the batterer for shelter, food, medication, access to health care, and care of their children. Thus, the battered partner may become increasingly trapped in the abusive relationship.

## Difficulties in Leaving an Abusive Partner

HIV infection can have a tremendous impact on a survivor's motivation and ability to leave the violent partner. For example, some survivors of battering report that their HIV-infected partners will fake illness in order to convince them not to leave or to entice them back once they have left. For some, leaving a batterer who has HIV may mean leaving a person who may be ill or dying to fend for themselves without a primary caregiver. A battered woman may feel guilty and believe that she is betraying her partner, her partner's family, and even the community by not staying and providing care.

For battered women who are HIV-infected, leaving may raise an array of concerns about caregiving, failing health and the stigma of having HIV/AIDS. Many may believe that their only hope for a relationship is to stay with their current partner no matter how abusive the relationship may be. For individuals with an AIDS diagnosis, leaving may not seem possible. These women may be on disability or another fixed income and, therefore, financially dependent on their partners for money to survive and pay for the costly drugs and treatments often necessary in the treatment of HIV/AIDS. A battered woman with children may be particularly reluctant to leave if she is ill, for fear of not being able to take care of herself or her kids. In lesbian and gay male relationships, even very sick individuals may be unable to return to their family of origin for support or care because of homophobia and AIDS-phobia in this culture.

## *The Connections to Substance Use and Abuse*

There is a well-documented and direct connection between HIV and substance abuse. The three easiest ways of transmitting HIV are:

- sharing needles and drug works, such as cotton and the water or cooker
- not using new works when injecting drugs
- not cleaning works with bleach between episodes of use

Indeed, it is estimated that approximately 70% of women who are HIV-infected are injection or intravenous drug users themselves, or are the partners of injection or intravenous drug users. This means that a battered woman with HIV may be abused by a partner who has HIV, with one or both having a substance abuse problem. HIV infection is therefore a red flag for battered women's advocates to be mindful of substance abuse issues, even when general indicators of substance use are not immediately apparent.

Additionally, the use of alcohol, crack, heroin, speed or virtually any other drug has been shown to impair decision-making abilities regarding sexual partners as well as safer sex practices. It is not safe to assume that battered women know what constitutes safer sex practices. Survivors of battering are likely to be isolated in their communities and unable to obtain accurate information. They may have relied on their abusive partner's claims about what constitutes safer sex and may have distorted ideas about HIV transmission.

Battered women seeking domestic violence services, as well as their abusers, may have drug and alcohol problems that place them at risk for becoming HIV-infected. Advocates need to be prepared to deal with issues and problems that arise within programs and shelters related not to just drug and alcohol use or abuse, but also to the connected reality of HIV infection and AIDS.

Accurate, current information is the foundation for providing quality services to persons with HIV infection and those at risk. Advocates should examine their own values and attitudes about this disease and the persons affected and infected as they acquire information and develop the skills necessary to provide effective advocacy and alternatives that are empowering.

Chapter 9

# *Identifying Spousal and Partner Abuse*

## *Chapter Contents*

## Section 9.1

## *Have You Been Abused?*

SAFE House, Ann Arbor, Mich., 1996. Used with permission.

*This is a series of questions designed to help you think about whether you have been abused.*

- Have you been hit? Choked? Slapped? Pushed? Bit? Burned? Grabbed?
- Has your partner used a weapon against you? Gun? Knife?
- Has your partner used an object to hit you with? Iron? Telephone? Belt?
- Have you had bruises from being hit, held or squeezed?
- Have you had a black eye, cut lip or broken tooth from being attacked?
- Have you had to see a doctor because of an injury?
- Has he threatened to have sex with the children or beat them unless you do what he says?
- Has he forced you to have sex? Oral sex? Anal sex?
- Has he forced you to have sex in front of the children?
- Has he forced you to have sex with other men or women?
- Has he put objects into you against your will?
- Has he forced you to have sex with an animal?
- Has he stopped you from taking classes?
- Has he stopped you from getting a job?
- Has he stopped you from going to work, or shown up at work and abused or threatened you there?
- Has he caused you to be late, or to miss work?
- Does he keep/take your paycheck and give you a little bit back, or make you ask or beg for money you need?
- Does he keep all the money under his control?
- Does he not let you go places—church, visit friends, see family?
- Does he not let you use the car? Does he take your keys or disable your car?

140

- Does he not pay the bills?
- Does he fight with, or call names, or make it awful for your friends and family to visit you?
- Does he make you tell him where you've been every minute?
- Does he make you write down what you've done all day?
- Does he call you names? Does he tell you that you are ugly, fat, stupid, a bitch, a slut or a whore?
- Does he say that no one would ever want you if you left him? Does he threaten to cut you so bad that no man would ever want to look at you?
- Does he tell you you're not a real woman?
- Does he accuse you of having sex with every man you meet, or smile, or talk to?
- Do you change what you want to do or plan to do because you're scared of his temper?
- Does he tell others that you are hysterical and crazy and that he is forced to restrain you?
- Do you feel like you're walking on eggshells?
- Are you afraid that if you left him he would kill you?
- Are you afraid that if you left him he would kill himself?
- Has he hurt or killed a pet?
- Has he made you do things that you're ashamed of?
- Has he made you commit a crime?
- Does he encourage you to drink too much?
- Does he make or force you to use drugs?
- If you are addicted to alcohol or other drugs, does he buy you liquor or drugs? Does he stop you from going to meetings?
- After he has hit you, does he act sweet and loving?
- Does he say he's sorry, buy you presents, cry and say he'll never do it again?
- Does he want to have sex after he's beaten you?
- Does he act like two totally different people? (Dr. Jekyll and Mr. Hyde?)

- Does he tell you that if you try to leave he will take the children and that you will never see them again? Does he tell you that he will get custody and you will never see the children?

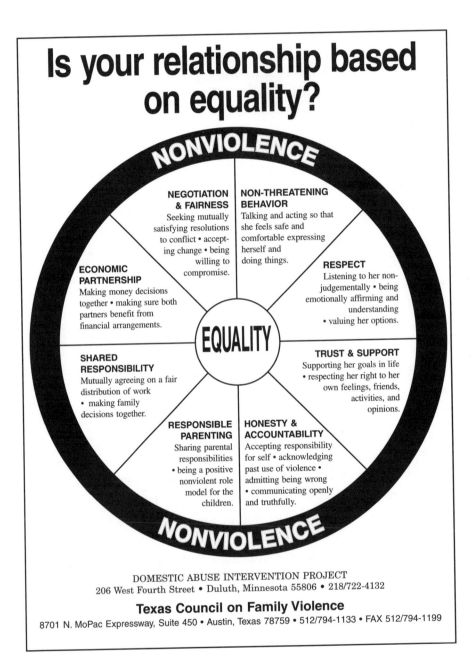

# Is your relationship based on equality?

## NONVIOLENCE

### EQUALITY

**NEGOTIATION & FAIRNESS**
Seeking mutually satisfying resolutions to conflict • accepting change • being willing to compromise.

**NON-THREATENING BEHAVIOR**
Talking and acting so that she feels safe and comfortable expressing herself and doing things.

**ECONOMIC PARTNERSHIP**
Making money decisions together • making sure both partners benefit from financial arrangements.

**RESPECT**
Listening to her non-judgementally • being emotionally affirming and understanding • valuing her options.

**SHARED RESPONSIBILITY**
Mutually agreeing on a fair distribution of work • making family decisions together.

**TRUST & SUPPORT**
Supporting her goals in life • respecting her right to her own feelings, friends, activities, and opinions.

**RESPONSIBLE PARENTING**
Sharing parental responsibilities • being a positive nonviolent role model for the children.

**HONESTY & ACCOUNTABILITY**
Accepting responsibility for self • acknowledging past use of violence • admitting being wrong • communicating openly and truthfully.

## NONVIOLENCE

DOMESTIC ABUSE INTERVENTION PROJECT
206 West Fourth Street • Duluth, Minnesota 55806 • 218/722-4132

## Texas Council on Family Violence
8701 N. MoPac Expressway, Suite 450 • Austin, Texas 78759 • 512/794-1133 • FAX 512/794-1199

# Or, is your relationship based on power and control?

Physical and sexual assaults, or threats to commit them, are the most apparent forms of domestic violence and are usually the actions that allow others to become aware of the problem. However, regular use of other abusive behaviors by the batterer, when reinforced by one or more acts of physical violence, make up a larger system of abuse. Although physical assaults may occur only once or occasionally, they instill threat of future violent attacks and allow the abuser to take control of the woman's life and circumstances.

The Power & Control diagram is a particularly helpful tool in understanding the overall pattern of abusive and violent behaviors, which are used by a batterer to establish and maintain control over his partner. Very often, one or more violent incidents are accompanied by an array of these other types of abuse. They are less easily identified, yet firmly establish a pattern of intimidation and control in the relationship.

## PHYSICAL VIOLENCE — SEXUAL

**COERCION & THREATS**
Making and/or carrying out threats to do something to hurt her • threatening to leave her, to commit suicide, or to report her to welfare • making her drop charges • making her do illegal things.

**INTIMIDATION**
Making her afraid by using looks, actions, and gestures • smashing things • destroying her property • abusing pets • displaying weapons.

**MALE PRIVILEGE**
Treating her like a servant • making all the big decisions • acting like the "master of the castle" • being the one to define men's and women's roles.

**EMOTIONAL ABUSE**
Putting her down • making her feel bad about herself • calling her names • making her think she's crazy • playing mind games • humiliating her • making her feel guilty.

## POWER & CONTROL

**ECONOMIC ABUSE**
Preventing her from getting or keeping a job • making her ask for money • giving her an allowance • taking her money • not letting her know about or have access to family income.

**ISOLATION**
Contolling what she does, who she sees and talks to, what she reads, and where she goes • limiting her outside involvement • using jealousy to justify actions.

**USING CHILDREN**
Making her feel guilty about the children • using the children to relay messages • using visitation to harass her • threatening to take the children away.

**MINIMIZING, DENYING & BLAMING**
Making light of the abuse and not taking her concerns about it seriously • saying the abuse didn't happen • shifting responsibility for abusive behavior • saying she caused it.

## PHYSICAL VIOLENCE — SEXUAL

143

**Note:** "He" is used for the assailant because men are assailants in the majority of the cases. Battering **does** occur in lesbian and gay relationships and there are rare occasions when a woman is physically assaulting her male partner.

## *For family and friends...*

- Does she appear anxious, depressed, withdrawn, and reluctant to talk?

- Does her partner criticize her in front of you, making remarks that make you feel uncomfortable when you're around the two of them?

- Do you see or hear about repeated bruises, broken bones, or other injuries that reportedly result from "accidents"?

- Have there been suicide or homicide attempts in this family?

- Does her partner try to control her every move, make her account for her time, and accuse her of having affairs?

- Is there alcohol or drug abuse in the family?

- Is she often late or absent from work, has she quit a job altogether, or does she leave social engagements early because her partner is waiting for her?

## Section 9.2

# *Are You in a Relationship with an Abusive Partner?*

Emotional abuse in same-sex or queer relationships can be subtle and confusing. The following list is adapted from an article entitled "Lesbian Violence, Lesbian Victims: How to Identify Battering in Relationships," written by Lee Evans and Shelly Banister. The article appeared in *Lesbian Ethics*, Vol. 4, #1. This list may be helpful in identifying emotional abuse.

### *Here are some good questions to ask yourself:*

- Do I withhold information from my partner about my social interactions for fear of what she may do or say?
- Do I have the feeling that it is somehow "bad" if I want to be emotionally intimate with someone other than my partner?
- Does this relationship prevent me from feeling that I am part of a community, or from maintaining a support system?
- When I am around my partner and other friends or family, am I nervous about what she might say or do to embarrass or humiliate me?
- Does my partner seem to "take over" my friendships?
- Do I ever find myself making excuses for my partner's behavior when we are out in public?
- Do I feel like I am isolated from my friends and family, or feel like I have to stop spending time with my acquaintances and can only be involved with her circle of friends?
- When I catch my lover in lies and then question her, does she then make me feel like I've done something wrong, or make me question my own sense of reality?

- Do I have feelings of being controlled, isolated, intimidated, or exhausted? Do I experience shame or guilt in my relationship with my partner?

## Here are a few examples of coercive behaviors that occur in same-sex or queer relationships:

### Isolation

- Your partner is so jealous that you limit your contact with other people so that you won't have to put up with her jealous remarks or rage.
- Your partner finds fault with all your friends. For example, she may criticize them for being too political and radical, or insufficiently political and radical.
- Your partner decides she wants you to stay in the closet or go back into the closet for her/your career's sake, or for her/your emotional well-being, or because she knows what's best for you.
- Your partner is always in the midst of a crisis so that you can never leave her alone.
- Your partner becomes sick, needy or angry when you try to spend time away from her, or with friends and family.
- Your partner creates embarrassing scenes in front of your friends or family so that none of them feel comfortable visiting you anymore.
- Your partner always seems to know what's best for you, how to dress, how to be a lesbian, who you should talk to, creating a you-and-me scenario.
- Your partner tries to convince you that it's you and her against the world and that no one else can or will understand your relationship.

### Monopolization of Perceptions

- You feel like it is easier to go along with your partner than to fight for your own decision.

- Your partner's explanations always seem to make more sense than yours do, her politics are always more correct, her opinions more important.
- You watch what you say so that it meets with her approval.
- Her very presence overwhelms everything else that is happening.
- She's been out longer than you, therefore she tells you how and what you need to be doing in your life to be queer.
- She ridicules or belittles your identity as bisexual, trans, femme, butch, etc.

## Inducement of Debility and Exhaustion

- Your partner wakes you up to fight in the middle of the night or keeps you from sleeping until she is ready to quit fighting.
- Your partner criticizes you around a disability you have, belittling it or denying its existence or harmful effects.
- Your partner tries to convince you if you'd just change your attitude (or something else about your lifestyle, like the food you eat or how much you sleep), you could cure yourself.
- Your partner controls your access to food and sleep.

## Threats

- Your partner threatens to come out for you to your family or to your job.
- Your partner threatens to slander you in your community.
- Your partner threatens to break or destroy things that you love.
- Your partner silences you with a look or an expression when you are in public.
- Your partner threatens to physically hurt you or others.
- Your partner threatens to destroy your car, hide your keys, or otherwise prevent you from leaving the house.

## Demonstrating Power

- Your partner always claims to be politically correct and know the right way to do things.
- Your partner always claims to know what you are thinking and what you are planning.
- Your partner always seems to know more about you than you know about yourself.
- Your partner claims to have friends who report back to her on your activities.

## Degradation

- Your partner puts you down in a way that makes you think there is something essentially wrong with you.
- Your partner talks you into doing sexual things which are embarrassing to you or that feel bad.
- Your partner "jokingly" makes fun of you in front of others.
- Your partner interrogates you about past lovers or lovers she THINKS you have currently, or that you do have currently.

## Enforcing Trivial Demands

- Your partner demands detailed reports from you when you get back from errands or work.
- Your partner has rigidly defined ways of doing things that you must adhere to, from the way you clean the house, to making beds, washing dishes, driving the car, doing laundry, or your appearance, etc.
- Your partner is  super critical of your way of doing things.

## Crazy-Making Behavior

- Your partner lies to you and then denies it.

- Your partner contradicts herself in the same conversation and then denies making the contradictory statement.
- Your partner changes the rules of the relationship without warning or explanation, leaving you constantly confused about what just happened.
- When you refer to an agreement you previously made, she says she does not remember it, or tells you it did not happen.
- She tells you that you are irrational or crazy.
- She convinces you that you are at fault for everything that goes wrong.

### *Occasional Indulgences*

- Your partner surprises you with presents when you least expect it.
- You learn to believe that your partner is the only person that can make you really feel better about yourself, and when she's being nice to you, you really feel good about yourself and your abilities.
- Your lovemaking is sometimes sweet, tender and wonderful.
- Your partner occasionally apologizes for being hurtful or demanding, but the pattern doesn't seem to change.

Section 9.3

# *Domestic Violence in Gay Relationships*

New York City Gay and Lesbian Anti-Violence Project, copyright © 1997.
Used with permission.

## *Is This Happening to You?*

*"I feel so confused? Why did I let myself get into this? Something must be wrong with me, 'cause I feel like going back to my lover, even after he hit me."*

If your lover has been abusive towards you, it is **not** your fault. It may be difficult to separate the affection you feel for your lover from his violence problem. But remember: your lover, and only your lover, is responsible for his abusive behavior.

*"My situation is different. It's true that my lover controls who I see, what I wear, and how I spend my time, but he never hits me!"*

Physical violence is only one kind of abuse that can occur in a relationship. Even if your lover has never hit you—if he controls your finances, or the way you spend your time, or your contacts with friends and/or family—the situation might be domestic violence.

*"When I told my best friend about the violence, he said: 'You must be exaggerating. You're a man, you can defend yourself!'"*

Violence in gay relationships occurs at the same rate as in heterosexual relationships—as many as one in every three gay relationships includes some form of domestic violence. It is a myth that battering cannot exist in a gay couple because men can defend themselves. This ignores the fact that in an abusive relationship, the batterer is a person with a violence problem.

*"If only my lover stopped drinking and taking drugs, everything would be OK. My lover only gets aggressive when he is drunk or high."*

If your lover is abusive to you when he uses drugs or alcohol, this means that your lover has two serious problems: a substance abuse problem **and** a violence problem. Even if your lover recovers from a substance abuse problem, he still needs to resolve his violence problem.

### Domestic Violence Includes but Is Not Limited to:

**Physical Abuse**—hitting, choking, slapping, burning, shoving, using a weapon, neglecting, locking up in a room.

**Isolation: Restricting Freedom**—controlling personal/social contacts, access to information and participation in groups or organizations.

**Psychological & Emotional Abuse**—criticizing constantly, ridiculing, degrading, lying.

**Threats & Intimidation**—threatening children, family or friends; threatening harm or to make reports to authorities endangering relationships to children, immigration or legal status.

**Heterosexist Control**—threatening to reveal gay identity to family, neighbors, employers, ex-spouses or city, state, and/or federal authorities.

**Economic Abuse**—controlling resources, fostering dependency, stealing money or goods, running up debts.

**Sexual Abuse**—forcing sex or specific sexual acts, assaulting "sexual parts", criticizing performance.

**Property Destruction**—destroying mementoes, breaking furniture or windows, throwing or smashing objects, threatening or hurting pets, trashing clothes.

## *What You Should Know*

### *Facts About Domestic Violence*

- Domestic violence cases account for almost 30% of all cases reported to the NYC Gay and Lesbian Anti-Violence Project.

- Domestic violence can happen in a gay relationship. In fact, it occurs at the same rate as in straight couples.

- Domestic violence happens in all parts of our community, regardless of race, class, ethnicity, age, ability, education, politics, or religion.

- Domestic violence has nothing to do with sex roles or physical appearance. A batterer can be a top or a bottom, large or small, tall or short.

- Domestic violence is a crime. Batterers can be prosecuted through criminal court. Survivors may be entitled to an order of protection, a court order that prohibits a batterer from talking to or approaching the victim.

- The police are required to treat cases of gay domestic violence the same way as they do heterosexual domestic violence, including mandatory arrest of the batterer in certain situations.

## *What You Can Do About It*

### *If You Are a Victim of Domestic Violence*

- Remember, it is not your fault. You are not responsible for the violent acts of another person.

- Be aware that violence in a relationship almost always gets worse, not better.

- Create your own survival plan. Think about how you would get out if you must leave quickly. 1) Have a bag ready and easily accessible with essential documents, such as identification, money and anything else you might need. 2) Tell someone about the abuse. Think about telling a friend, someone you could stay with in an emergency, someone who could give you keys to her/his apartment. 3) Call the Anti-Violence Project (AVP).

The Domestic Violence Program at AVP provides counseling, advocacy with the police and criminal justice system, and support groups to help you become a **survivor**.

## How You Can Help

### *If You Are Not a Victim of Domestic Violence*

- Then you probably know someone who is. You can help him become a **survivor**.

- Break the silence around domestic violence in gay relationships. Share the information in this article with your friends. Call AVP to arrange for a workshop/presentation on domestic violence to your community organization.

- Support a friend who is a victim of domestic violence: let him know that he can call you for help; give him keys to your house; tell him about AVP services.

- Don't give up, and don't criticize him or turn him away even if he doesn't leave the batterer right away. Remember: it is **never** easy to leave a lover, even when he is abusive. Let your friend know that, whatever decision he makes, he can always call you.

# Section 9.4

# *Male Batterers Fact Sheet*

National Center for Injury Prevention and Control, Centers for Disease
Control and Prevention, 1998.

## *Incidence*

Estimates from survey research conducted in 1985 indicate that
at least three out of every 100, or 1.8 million, men severely assaulted
their female partner or cohabitant during the preceding 12 months.[1]
These assaults included punching, kicking, choking, threats with a
knife or gun, or use of a knife or gun.

## *Characteristics Associated With Batterers*

Witnessing intimate partner violence (IPV) as a child or adolescent, or experiencing violence from caregivers as a child are the risk
factors which have been most consistently identified with the perpetration of IPV.[2]

Men who are physically violent towards their partners are also
likely to be sexually violent towards their partners, and are likely to
use violence towards children.[2]

Chronic alcohol abuse by the male batterer may be more strongly
associated with IPV than acute intoxication.[3]

High levels of marital conflict and lower socioeconomic status [SES]
have been consistently associated with the occurrence and persistence
of IPV.[4, 5, 6, 7] However, findings from studies with representative
samples indicate that IPV is not exclusive to those with lower SES.[8]

Perpetrators of IPV may have interpersonal skills deficits (such as
lack of communication skills, poor spouse-specific assertion) in comparison with nonviolent men, particularly in the context of problematic marital situations.[9]

Research findings are mixed on the association between anger and
the perpetration of IPV. Some research reports that men who perpetrate violence towards their partners have higher levels of general
anger/hostility than the men who are non-violent.[10] Others report that
anger and hostility felt towards a partner is associated with perpe-

tration of violence, while generalized feelings of anger and aggression are not.[11]

A high proportion of batterers identified through court-ordered or other clinical populations have been found to have traits consistent with diagnoses of personality disorders, such as schizoidal/borderline, personality, antisocial or narcissistic, passive dependent/compulsive disorders.[12, 13] As these data come from clinical populations, however, it is not clear that psychopathology causes battering.

*Comment: Further theory-driven consensus on the variables which may distinguish batterers from nonbatterers would be helpful for guiding future research.*

## Batterer Types

A number of researchers have suggested that batters are a heterogenous group. Clarification of the variables which distinguish violent from non-violent men, or type-specific treatment effectiveness might be explored if different types of batterers could reliably be identified.[14, 15] A review of typology research on batterers suggest that three types can be distinguished on the basis of: severity of IPV perpetrated, generality of the violence (toward the woman and toward others), and psychopathology/personality disorders.[16] The three types proposed are:

**The family-only batterer:** may perpetrate less severe violence, use relatively little psychological or sexual abuse, and display few or no symptoms of psychopathology.

**The dysphoric/borderline batterer:** may perpetrate moderate to severe violence, mostly confined to the family, and be generally distressed, dysphoric [unhappy], or emotionally volatile.

**The generally violent/antisocial batterer:** may engage in moderate to severe IPV, the most extrafamilial violence, and have the most extensive history of criminal involvement, alcohol and drug abuse, and antisocial personality disorder or psychopathology.

Further research is necessary to: 1) replicate and establish the validity of these proposed types, 2) to develop simple and efficient assessment tools which can reliably distinguish among batterer types, 3) determine how these subtypes differ from nonviolent men, and 4) identify the developmental and situational factors associated with individuals and society which may contribute to the development of different batterer types.

## References

1. Straus, M. A., and R. J. Gelles. (1990). "How Violent are American Families? Estimates from the National Family Violence Resurvey and Other Studies." In: Straus, M. A. and R. J. Gelles, (editors). *Physical Violence in American Families: Risk Factors and Adaptations to Violence in 8,145 Families* (pp. 95–112). New Brunswick, N.J.: Transaction Publishers.

2. Hotaling, G. T., and D. B. Sugarman. (1986). "An Analysis of Risk Markers in Husband to Wife Violence: The Current State of Knowledge." *Violence and Victims* 1, 101–24.

3. Tolman, R. M., and L. W. Bennett. (1990). "A Review of Quantitative Research on Men Who Batter." *Journal of Interpersonal Violence* 5 (1), 87–118.

4. Sugarman, D. B., and S. L. Frankel. (1996). "Patriarchal Ideology and Wife-Assault: A Meta-Analytic Review." *Journal of Family Violence* 11 (1): 13–40.

5. Aldarondo, E., and D. B. Sugarman. (1996). "Risk Marker Analysis of the Cessation and Persistence of Wife Assault." *Journal of Consulting and Clinical Psychology* 64 (5), 1010–19.

6. Hotaling, G. T., and D. B. Sugarman. (1990). "A Risk Marker Analysis of Assaulted Wives." *Journal of Family Violence* 5 (1), 1–13.

7. Sugarman D. B., and Hotaling G. T. (1989). "Violent Men in Intimate Relationships: An Analysis of Risk Markers." *Journal of Applied Social Psychology.* 19: 1034–48.

8. Straus, M. A., R. J. Gelles, and S. K. Steinmetz. (1980). *Behind Closed Doors: Violence in the American Family*. New York: Anchor/Doubleday.

9. Holtzworth-Munroe, A. (1992). "Social Skill Deficits in Martially Violent Men: Interpreting the Data Using a Social Infor-

mation Processing Model." *Clinical Psychology Review* 12: 605–17.

10. Holtzworth-Monroe, A, L. Bates, N. Smutzler, and E. Sandin. (1997). "A Brief Review of the Research on Husband Violence. Part 1: Maritally Violent versus Non Violent Men." *Aggression and Violent Behavior* 2, 65–99.

11. Boyle, D. J., and D. Vivian. (1996). "Generalized Versus Spouse-Specific Anger/Hostility and Men's Violence against Intimates." *Violence and Victims* 11: 293–317.

12. Hamberger, K. L., and J. E. Hastings. (1988). "Characteristics of Male Spouse Abusers Consistent with Personality Disorders." *Hospital and Community Psychiatry* 39, 763–70.

13. Hamberger, K. L., and J. E. Hastings. (1986). "Personality Correlates of Men Who Abuse Their Partners: A Cross-Validation Study." *Journal of Family Violence* 1 (4), 323–41.

14. Gondolf, E. W. (1988). "Who Are Those Guys? Toward a Behavioral Typology of Batters." *Violence and Victims* 3, 187–203.

15. Saunders, D. G. (1992). "A Typology of Men Who Batter Women: Three Types Derived From Cluster Analysis." *American Orthopsychiatry* 62, 264–75.

16. Holtzworth-Monroe, A., and G. L. Stuart. (1994). "Typologies of Male Batterers: Three Subtypes and the Differences among Them." *Psychological Bulletin* 116 (3), 476–97.

# Section 9.5

# *Signs to Look for in a Battering Personality*

National Domestic Violence Hotline, Texas Council on Family Violence, May, 1996. Adapted courtesy of "Project for Victims of Family Violence," Fayetteville, Arkansas. Reprinted with permission.

Many people are interested in ways that they can predict whether they are about to become involved with someone who will be physically abusive. Usually battering occurs between a man and woman, but same-sex battering occurs as well. Below is a list of behaviors that are seen in people who beat their partners; the last four signs listed **are battering**, but many don't realize this is the beginning of physical abuse. If the person has several of the other behaviors **(three or more)** there is a strong **potential** for physical violence—the more signs a person has, the more likely that person is a batterer. In some cases, a batterer may have only a couple of behaviors that can be recognized, but they are very exaggerated (e.g., will try to explain behavior as signs of love and concern, and a partner may be flattered at first). As time goes on, the behaviors become more severe and serve to dominate and control the partner.

1.  **Jealousy:** At the beginning of a relationship, an abuser will always say that jealousy is a sign of love. Jealousy has nothing to do with love; it's a sign of possessiveness and lack of trust. The batterer will question the wo/man about who s/he talks to, accuse her of flirting, or be jealous of time spent with family, friends or children. As the jealousy progresses, the batterer may call frequently during the day or drop by unexpectedly. The batterer may refuse to let her work for fear s/he'll meet someone else, or even exhibit strange behaviors such as checking car mileage or asking friends to watch her.

2.  **Controlling Behavior:** At first, the batterer will say this behavior is because s/he's concerned for the wo/man's safety, her need to use her time well, or her need to make good decisions. The batterer will be angry if the partner is "late" coming back from the store or an appointment, the batterer will question her closely about where s/he went, who s/he talked to. As this behavior gets worse, the batterer may not let the wo/man make personal decisions about the house, personal clothing,

going to church; the batterer may keep all the money or even make her ask permission to leave the house or room.

3. **Quick Involvement:** Many battered wo/men dated or knew the abuser for less than six months before they were married, engaged or living together. The batterer comes on like a whirlwind, claiming, "You're the only person I could ever talk to," "I've never felt loved like this by anyone." The batterer will pressure the wo/man to commit to the relationship in such a way that later s/he may feel very guilty or that s/he's "letting him/her down" if s/he wants to slow down involvement or break-off.

4. **Unrealistic Expectations:** Abusive people will expect a partner to meet all their needs; the batterer expects her to be the perfect wife, mother, lover, friend. The batterer will say things like, "If you love me, I'm all you need—you're all I need." S/he is supposed to take care of everything for him/her emotionally as well as in the home.

5. **Isolation:** The abusive person tries to cut the partner off from all resources. If s/he has men friends, s/he's a "whore"; if s/he has wo/men friends, s/he's a "gay"; if s/he's close to family, s/he's "tied to the apron strings." The batterer accuses people who form her support network of "causing trouble." The batterer may want to live in the country without a phone, the batterer may not let her use a car (or have one that is reliable), or the batterer may try to keep the wo/man from working or going to school.

6. **Blames Others for Problems:** If the batterer is chronically unemployed, someone is always "doing him wrong; out to get him." The batterer may make mistakes and then blame the wo/man for upsetting him and keeping him from concentrating on work. The batterer will tell the partner that s/he is at fault for anything that goes wrong.

7. **Blames Others for Feelings:** The batterer will tell the wo/man, "You make me mad." "You're hurting me by not doing what I want you to do," "I can't help being angry." The batterer will use feelings to manipulate the wo/man. Harder to identify are claims that "You make me happy," "You control how I feel."

8. **Hypersensitivity:** An abuser is easily insulted, and may claim that his feelings are "hurt" when really he is very mad or he takes the slightest setbacks as personal attacks. The batterer will "rant and rave" about the injustice of things that have happened—things that are really just part of living like being asked to work overtime, getting a traffic ticket, being told some behavior is annoying, being asked to help with chores.

9. **Cruelty to Animals or Children:** This is a person who punishes animals brutally or is insensitive to their pain or suffering. The batterer may expect children to be capable of doing things beyond their ability (whips a two year old for wetting a diaper) or the batterer may tease children or younger brothers and sisters until they cry. The batterer may not want children to eat at the table or expect to keep them in their room all evening while the batterer is home.

10. **"Playful" Use of Force in Sex:** This kind of person may like to throw the wo/man down and hold her down during sex. The batterer may want to act out fantasies during sex where the partner is helpless. The batterer's letting her know that the idea of rape is exciting. He may show little concern about whether the wo/man wants to have sex and uses sulking or anger to manipulate her into compliance. The batterer may start having sex with the wo/man while s/he is sleeping or demand sex when s/he is ill or tired.

11. **Verbal Abuse:** In addition to saying things that are meant to be cruel and hurtful, this can be seen when the abuser degrades the partner, cursing him/her, running down her accomplishments. The abuser will tell the partner that s/he's stupid and unable to function without him/her. This may involve waking the wo/man up to verbally abuse him/her or not letting him/her go to sleep.

12. **Rigid Sex Roles:** The abuser expects a wo/man to serve; the batterer may say the wo/man must stay at home, that s/he must obey in all things—even things that are criminal in nature. The abuser will see wo/men as inferior to men, responsible for menial tasks, stupid, and unable to be a whole person without a relationship.

13. **Dr. Jekyll and Mr./Ms. Hyde:** Many wo/men are confused by the abuser's "sudden" change in mood—they may think the abuser has some special mental problem because one minute the batterer's nice and the next the batterer's exploding. Explosiveness and moodiness are typical of people who beat their partners, and these behaviors are related to other characteristics like hypersensitivity.

14. **\*\*\*Past Battering:** The batterer has hit wo/men in the past, but, "They made me do it." The wo/man may hear from relatives or ex-spouses/girlfriends that the person is abusive. A batterer will beat **any** partner if s/he stays long enough for the violence to begin; **situational circumstances do not make a person resort to violence**.

15. **\*\*\*Threats of Violence:** This could include any threat of physical force meant to control the partner: "I'll slap your mouth off." "I'll kill you." "I'll break your neck." Most people do not threaten their mates, but a batterer will try to excuse threats by saying "everybody talks like that."

16. **\*\*\*Breaking or Striking Objects:** This behavior (breaking loved possessions) is used as a punishment, but is really designed to terrorize the wo/man into submission. The abuser may beat on the table with a clenched fist, or throw objects around and near the wo/man. Again, this is very remarkable behavior—not only is this a sign of extreme emotional immaturity, but there's great danger when someone thinks they have the "right" to punish or frighten their partner.

17. **\*\*\*Any Force During an Argument:** [Kicking, punching, slapping, hair-pulling, pinching, biting, stomping, poking, and spitting are all forms of physical violence.] This may involve holding a wo/man down or physically restraining her from leaving the room. The batterer may hold the wo/man against the wall and say, "You're going to listen to me!" Weapons (knives, guns, baseball bats, tools) are often involved as well.

## Section 9.6

# *Animal Cruelty and Intimate Partner (Domestic) Violence*

### *A child that hurts an animal is an adult that hurts their partner.*

Spokane County Domestic Violence Consortium, Spokane, Wash.
Copyright © October 1998.

### *What Is Animal Cruelty?*

Animal cruelty is behavior that intentionally causes unnecessary pain, suffering, distress and/or death of an animal. It includes:

- Physical harm, bodily injury or assault

- Sexual Assault

- Neglect

Specific cruel behaviors include depriving an animal of food, water, and/or shelter, beating, throwing kicking, drowning, burning, torturing or killing an animal.

Cruelty to animals is one of the symptoms of conduct disorder in children and adolescents.

It is a crime in all 50 states and may be a felony offense.

### *Why Is It a Concern?*

Animal cruelty is a predictor for past, present and future violence, both inside and outside of the home.

Children who hurt animals need help themselves.

### *What Is the Connection Between Animal Cruelty and Intimate Partner Violence?*

Children who commit violent acts against animals are more likely to abuse their intimate partners as adults.

They use cruel acts to gain power and control, which is the driving force behind perpetrators of intimate partner violence.

In fact, studies have shown that many violent adult offenders have childhood histories of repeated and serious animal cruelty.

## *Why Is a Child Cruel to Animals?*

Many children who hurt animals are from violent homes in which they are victims of child abuse and/or witnesses to violence between their parents. It has been well documented that adults who abuse their partners often commit cruel acts against family pets to frighten and control their partners and children, to serve as a threat of potential attacks, and as punishment.

The children may be copying things that they have seen or had done to them. The violence in their home leaves them feeling powerless and they seek control by acting out against others, including their pets.

## *How Do I Know If a Child Has Been a Witness to, or a Perpetrator of, Cruelty to Animals?*

A child who has witnessed animal cruelty may talk about the violence. They may also act out with other children, animals and/or adults at school or while playing.

A child who has been cruel to animals may brag about their violence to other children and/or adults.

## *What Can I Do?*

Without intervention and accountability, children who harm animals are more likely to commit violent acts against loved ones as they become adults.

Animal cruelty must be taken seriously.

## *You Can Make a Difference...*

**Keep your eyes open** and learn to recognize animal cruelty.

**Report** suspected cases of animal cruelty to local animal control agencies.

**Break the silence.** Speak out about the relationship between animal cruelty and intimate partner violence.

**Stop the violence.** Make yourself aware of treatment services available to children who are cruel to animals. Breaking the cycle early is the key.

You will be helping the animal and you may be saving a human life.

# Chapter 10

# *Stalking*

## *Chapter Contents*

# Section 10.1

# *Background*[1]

Excerpted from the U.S. Department of Justice, *Stalking and Domestic Violence: The Third Annual Report to Congress under the Violence Against Women Act*, July 1998.

The passage of the Violence Against Women Act [VAWA, 1994], notwithstanding, domestic violence and stalking continue to be significant problems facing our society. As reported in the first and second annual reports to Congress, because these social problems have gone unacknowledged for so long in this country, until recently there has been a dearth of reliable information about addressing or preventing domestic violence and stalking effectively. This knowledge deficit is particularly acute for stalking.

Although there is greater interest in this issue as a result of the passage of VAWA, research in this field is still in its infancy. Some of the earliest research focused on stalkers who had come to the attention of the criminal justice system. This nonrandom sample underrepresented stalkers who had a prior intimate relationship with their victims, in part because of the legal system's inclination to arrest and prosecute higher profile cases involving strangers and a general hesitance to prosecute cases involving domestic violence.[2] This systemic bias, combined with the enormous media attention accorded cases involving celebrities, created an impression that stalking is largely a crime involving strangers, generally with a public figure as the victim. Subsequent national surveys have revealed, however, that stalking most often occurs in an intimate-partner context.[3] Therefore, to develop appropriate responses and prevention strategies, this crime must be examined and understood in all its contexts.

Throughout this decade, behaviors generally associated with stalking—obsessive, repeated following and harassment—have received considerable attention from public policymakers and have led to the enactment of laws in every state. This in turn has generated considerable interest in learning more about all aspects of stalking, including the identity and motivation of perpetrators. While there are now many more variations as research increases, generally stalkers are classified in one of three broad categories based on their relationship with the victim:

- **Intimate or former intimate stalking:** The stalker and victim may be married or divorced, current or former cohabitants, serious or casual sexual partners, or former sexual partners. A history of domestic violence may exist.

- **Acquaintance stalking:** The stalker and victim may know each other casually, either through formal or informal contact. For example, they may be co-workers or neighbors, or they may have dated once or twice but were not sexual partners.

- **Stranger stalking:** The stalker and victim do not know each other at all. Cases involving celebrities and other public figures generally fall into this category.[4]

Some researchers have established classification systems that are based on the motivations and mental capacity of stalkers.[5] None of these classifications, however, provides a reliable indicator of a stalker's capacity for potential violence against the victim. It is estimated that stalkers are violent toward their victims between 25 and 35 percent of the time, and the group most likely to be violent is composed of those who have had an intimate relationship with the victim.[6] Nearly one-third of all women killed in this country die at the hands of a current or former intimate.[7] Although no national figures are available, it is estimated that between 29 and 54 percent of female murder victims are battered women.[8] A significant number of these murders and attempted murders of women are believed to be preceded by stalking.[9]

Further, very little information is available on who will or won't become a stalker, particularly in cases involving strangers or acquaintances. In instances of stalking involving intimates, researchers at the University of Washington found that batterers who are insecure and fearful of abandonment are more likely to become obsessed and stalk their victims upon separation than other types of batterers.[10] Numerous studies indicate that separation is the most dangerous period for victims of domestic violence.[11] Fearing loss of control over their victims, batterers often escalate their abuse when their victims seek to escape.[12]

In the National Violence Against Women (NVAW) Survey, discussed in Section 10.2, victims cited the stalkers' desire to control them as the most frequent reason for the stalking behavior. Only a small percentage of the victims surveyed cited mental illness or substance abuse as the reason for the stalking. The survey corroborated what domestic violence victim advocates had long suspected—there is a strong link between stalking and abusive behavior in intimate relationships. Moreover, stalking by intimates or former intimates lasts significantly longer than stalking involving non-intimates.

The NVAW Survey also provided evidence of the positive impact of state antistalking laws: More victims are coming forward and reporting these crimes; however, the laws do not appear to have made a significant impact on law enforcement's response to these crimes. The number of arrests remained about the same before and after enactment of these state laws. Overall, the percentage of stalking cases prosecuted was quite small, but in nearly half the prosecuted cases, the perpetrator was convicted, and two-thirds of these convictions resulted in a jail or prison term.

An OJP-commissioned anecdotal survey of criminal justice practitioners found that stalkers continue to be charged and sentenced under harassment, intimidation, or other related laws instead of under a state's antistalking statute. This survey, as well as the NVAW Survey, found that criminal justice officials still do not fully understand—and, therefore, continue to underestimate—the potential dangerousness of stalkers to their victims. The results of both surveys underscore the need to provide comprehensive training to judges, prosecutors, law enforcement officers, probation and parole officers, and others in the criminal justice system who are involved in managing stalking cases. It is critical that all components of the system coordinate their efforts both within and among each other to ensure that victims are kept safe and offenders are held accountable.

## References

1.  Stalkers and batterers can be either men or women; however, for consistency in style, this report [Sections 10.1 and 10.2] refers to stalkers and batterers as men and victims as women.

2.  J. Reid Meloy, "Stalking (Obsessional Following): A Review of Some Preliminary Studies." *Aggression and Violent Behavior* 1 (1996): 149–50.

3.  Patricia Tjaden and Nancy Thoennes, "Stalking in America: Findings from the National Violence Against Women Survey." National Institute of Justice and Centers for Disease Control and Prevention, April 1998, Grant No. 93-IJ-CX-0012. Doris M. Hall, "Outside Looking in: Stalkers and Their Victims," un-

published dissertation, 1997. Her findings are based on a non-random sample of 145 self-defined stalking victims across the country.

4. "Domestic Violence, Stalking, and Antistalking Legislation," Attorney General's First Annual Report to Congress under the Violence Against Women Act, *National Institute of Justice Research Report* (Washington, DC: U.S. Department of Justice, National Institute of Justice, April 1996): 5.

5. See, for instance, J. Reid Meloy, "Stalking (Obsessional Following): A Review of Some Preliminary Studies," p. 149. See also Ronnie B. Harmon, Richard Rosner, and Howard Owens, "Obsessional Harassment and Erotomania in a Criminal Court Population," *Journal of Forensic Sciences* 40 (March 1995): 189–91; Vernon Geberth, "Stalkers," *Law and Order* 40 (October 1992): 138–40; Harvey Wallace, *Family Violence: Legal, Medical, and Social Perspectives* (New York: Simon & Schuster, 1996): 280–83.

6. J. Reid Meloy, ed., *The Psychology of Stalking: Clinical and Forensic Perspectives* (San Diego, CA: Academic Press, 1998): 8.

7. Lawrence Greenfield, Michael Rand, et al., "Violence by Intimates: Analysis of Data on Crimes by Current or Former Spouses, Boyfriends, and Girlfriends," *Bureau of Justice Statistics Factbook*, NCJ-167237, March 1998.

8. Neil Jacobson and John M. Gottman, *When Men Batter Women: New Insights into Ending Abusive Relationships* (New York: Simon & Schuster, 1998): 239.

9. Raoul Felder and Barbara Victor, *Getting Away with Murder: Weapons for the War Against Domestic Violence* (New York: Touchstone, 1997): 214.

10. Jacobson and Gottman, p. 253. They conducted a 10-year study of 200 couples involved in violent relationships and categorized the batterers into two distinct groups, based on several factors, including their emotional and physiological reactions preceding and during the aggression. They found that one type of batterer, which they labeled as "cobras," are much less likely to stalk the victim after she leaves because

they are more independent and "not interested in deep emotional commitments."

11. Jacobson and Gottman, p. 239. See also Martha R. Mahoney, "Legal Images of Battered Women: Redefining the Issue of Separation," *Michigan Law Review* 90 (October 1991): 65.

12. Barbara J. Hart, "The Legal Road to Freedom," in M. Hansen and M. Harway, eds. *Battering and Family Therapy: A Feminist Perspective* (Newbury Park, CA: Sage Publications, 1993): 2.

## Section 10.2

# *Stalking and Domestic Violence in America*[1]

U.S. Department of Justice, *Stalking and Domestic Violence: The Third Annual Report to Congress under the Violence Against Women Act*, July 1998.

Unprecedented interest in stalking over the past decade has produced media accounts of stalking victims,[2] passage of antistalking laws in all 50 states and the District of Columbia,[3] and development of a model antistalking code.[4] Despite this interest, research on stalking has been limited to studies of small, unrepresentative, or clinical samples of known stalkers;[5] law journal reviews of the constitutionality and effectiveness of specific antistalking statutes;[6] and case studies of individual stalkers.[7] Thus, empirical data have been lacking on such fundamental questions about stalking as:

- How much stalking is there in the United States?
- Who stalks whom?
- How often do stalkers overtly threaten their victims?
- How often is stalking reported to the police?
- What are the psychological and social consequences of stalking?

This chapter presents data from the first-ever national study on stalking and addresses these and related questions. The data are from the National Violence Against Women (NVAW) Survey, a nationally representative telephone survey of 8,000 U.S. women and 8,000 U.S. men. The survey, which asked detailed questions about respondents' experiences with violence, including stalking, was sponsored jointly by the National Institute of Justice (NIJ) and the Centers for Disease Control and Prevention (CDC) through a grant to the Center for Policy Research.

## What Is Stalking?

Stalking generally refers to harassing or threatening behavior that an individual engages in repeatedly, such as following a person, appearing at a person's home or place of business, making harassing phone calls, leaving written messages or objects, or vandalizing a person's property. These actions may or may not be accompanied by a credible threat of serious harm, and they may or may not be precursors to an assault or murder.[8]

Legal definitions of stalking vary widely from state to state. Though most states define stalking as the willful, malicious, and repeated following and harassing of another person, some states include in their definition such activities as lying-in-wait, surveillance, nonconsensual communication, telephone harassment, and vandalism.[9] While most states require that the alleged stalker engage in a course of conduct showing that the crime was not an isolated event, some states specify how many acts (usually two or more) must occur before the conduct can be considered stalking.[10] State stalking laws also vary in their threat and fear requirements. Most stalking laws require that the perpetrator, to qualify as a stalker, make a credible threat of violence against the victim; others include in their requirements threats against the victim's immediate family; and still others require only that the alleged stalker's course of conduct constitute an implied threat.[11]

The definition of stalking used in the NVAW Survey closely resembles the definition of stalking used in the *Model Antistalking Code for States* developed by NIJ.[12] The survey defines stalking as "a course of conduct directed at a specific person that involves repeated visual or physical proximity, nonconsensual communication, or verbal, written or implied threats, or a combination thereof, that would cause a reasonable person fear," with repeated meaning on two or more occasions. The model antistalking code does not require stalkers to make a credible threat of violence against victims, but it does require victims to feel a high level of fear ("fear of bodily harm"). Similarly, the

171

definition of stalking used in the NVAW Survey does not require stalkers to make a credible threat against victims, but it does require victims to feel a high level of fear.

## How Much Stalking Is There?

In the NVAW Survey, stalking victimization was measured in terms of lifetime prevalence and annual prevalence. Lifetime prevalence refers to the percentage of persons within a demographic group (*e.g.*, male or female) who were stalked sometime in their lifetime. Annual prevalence refers to the percentage of persons within a demographic group who were stalked sometime in the 12 months preceding the survey.

Using a definition of stalking that requires victims to feel a high level of fear, the NVAW Survey found that 8 percent of women and 2 percent of men in the United States have been stalked at some time in their life.[13]

Based on U.S. Census estimates of the number of women and men in the country, 1 out of every 12 U.S. women (8.2 million) has been stalked at some time in her life, and 1 out of every 45 U.S. men (2 million) has been stalked at some time in his life (see exhibit 1).[14]

Ninety percent of the stalking victims identified by the survey were stalked by just one person during their life. Nine percent of female victims and 8 percent of male victims were stalked by two different persons, and 1 percent of female victims and 2 percent of male victims were stalked by three different persons.

The survey also found that 1 percent of all women surveyed and 0.4 percent of all men surveyed were stalked during the 12 months

## Exhibit 1: Percentage and Estimated Number of Men and Women Stalked in Lifetime

| Group | Persons Stalked in Lifetime | |
| --- | --- | --- |
| | Percentage* | Estimated Number** |
| Men (N = 8,000) | 2.2 | 2,040,460 |
| Women (N = 8,000) | 8.1 | 8,156,460 |

*Differences between men and women are significant at ≤.001.

**Based on estimates of men and women aged 18 years and older, U.S. Bureau of the Census, Current Population Survey, 1995.

preceding the survey. These findings equate to an estimated 1,006,970 women and an estimated 370,990 men who are stalked annually in the United States (see exhibit 2).

The average annual estimates of stalking victimization generated by the survey are relatively high compared to the average lifetime estimates. Two factors account for this finding. The first has to do with the age of the population most at risk of being stalked. The survey found that 74 percent of stalking victims are between 18 and 39 years old. Since men and women between 18 and 39 years comprise nearly half (47 percent) the adult population from which the sample was drawn, a large proportion of men and women in the survey sample were at risk of being stalked in the 12 months preceding the interview. As the proportion of the U.S. population aged 18–39 years declines, so should the number of persons stalked annually. However, the lifetime estimates of stalking victimization should remain relatively constant.

Another reason annual estimates of stalking victimization are relatively high compared to lifetime rates is that stalking, by definition, involves repeated and ongoing victimization. Thus, some men and women are stalked for months or years on end. Because some men and women are stalked from one year to the next, the average annual estimates of stalking victimization cannot be added to produce an estimate of the total number of men and women who will be stalked in two, three, or more years. Thus, average annual rates of stalking victimization will appear higher than expected when compared to lifetime rates of stalking victimization.

---

### Exhibit 2: Percentage and Estimated Number of Men and Women Stalked in Previous 12 Months

| Group | Persons Stalked in Previous 12 Months | |
|---|---|---|
| | Percentage* | Estimated Number** |
| Men (N = 8,000) | 0.4 | 370,990 |
| Women (N = 8,000) | 1.0 | 1,006,970 |

*Differences between men and women are significant at $\leq$.001.

**Based on estimates of men and women aged 18 years and older, U.S. Bureau of the Census, Current Population Survey, 1995.

## Comparison with Previous Stalking Estimates

Prior to this study, information on stalking prevalence was limited to guesses provided by mental health professionals based on their work with known stalkers. The most frequently cited "guesstimates" of stalking prevalence were made by forensic psychiatrist Park Dietz, who in 1992 reported that 5 percent of U.S. women are stalked at some time in their life and approximately 200,000 U.S. women are stalked each year.[15] Thus, the NVAW Survey's estimate that 8 percent of U.S. women have been stalked at some time in their life is 1.6 times greater than Dietz's guesstimate, and the survey's estimate that 1,006,970 U.S. women are stalked annually is 5 times greater than Dietz's guesstimate.

How prevalent is stalking compared to other forms of violence against women in the United States? The NVAW Survey found that 0.3 percent of all women surveyed experienced a completed or attempted rape in the 12 months preceding the survey, and 1.9 percent experienced a physical assault in the 12 months preceding the survey (see exhibit 3). Thus, in a 1-year period, women are three times more likely to be stalked than raped, but they are two times as likely to be physically assaulted than stalked.

If a less stringent definition of stalking is used—one requiring victims to feel only somewhat frightened or a little frightened by their assailant's behavior—stalking prevalence rates rise dramatically. Specifically, the lifetime stalking prevalence rate increases from 8 percent to 12 percent for women and from 2 percent to 4 percent for men; and the annual stalking prevalence rate increases from 1 per-

### Exhibit 3: Percentage of Men and Women Victimized in Previous 12 Months, by Type of Violence

| Type of Violence | Persons Victimized in Previous 12 Months (%) | |
|---|---|---|
| | Men (N = 8,000) | Women (N = 8,000) |
| Rape | <0.1* | 0.3 |
| Physical Assault | 3.4 | 1.9 |
| Stalking | 0.4 | 1.0 |
| Any of the Above | 3.9 | 3.0 |

*Based on five or fewer cases.

cent to 6 percent for women and from 0.4 percent to 1.5 percent for men. Based on these higher prevalence rates, an estimated 12.1 million U.S. women and 3.7 million U.S. men are stalked at some time in their life; and 6 million women and 1.4 million men are stalked annually in the United States. These results show how stalking prevalence varies with the level of fear included in the definition. A higher standard of fear produces lower prevalence rates, and a lower standard of fear produces higher prevalence rates.

## Stalking Risk for Racial and Ethnic Minorities

Information from the NVAW Survey presents a complex picture of stalking, race, and ethnicity. When data on African-American, American Indian/Alaska Native, Asian/Pacific Islander, and mixed-race women are combined, there is no difference in stalking prevalence between white women and minority women: 8.2 percent of white women (see exhibit 4) and 8.2 percent of nonwhite women (not shown) reported ever being stalked in their lifetime. However, a comparison of stalking prevalence across specific racial and ethnic groupings shows that American Indian/Alaska Native women report significantly more stalking victimization than women of other racial and ethnic backgrounds (see exhibit 4). This finding should be viewed with caution, however, given the small number of American Indian/Alaska Native women in the sample. This finding also underscores the need for specificity when comparing prevalence rates among women of different racial or ethnic backgrounds.

*Exhibit 4: Percentage of Men and Women Stalked in Lifetime, by Race and Ethnicity of Victim*

| | | | **Persons Stalked in Lifetime (%)** | | | |
|---|---|---|---|---|---|---|
| **Group** | **Total** | **White** | **African-American** | **Asian/Pacific Islander** | **American Indian/Alaska Native** | **Mixed Race** |
| Men | (N = 7,759) | (N = 6,424) | (N = 659) | (N = 165) | (N = 105) | (N = 406) |
| | 2.3 | 2.1 | 2.4 | 1.8* | 4.8 | 3.9 |
| Women** | (N = 7,850) | (N = 6,452) | (N = 780) | (N = 133) | (N = 88) | (N = 397) |
| | 8.2 | 8.2 | 6.5 | 4.5 | 17.0 | 10.6 |

*Based on five or fewer cases.

**Differences between racial and ethnic groups are significant at ≤.05.

175

Indian/Alaska Native women in the sample. This finding also underscores the need for specificity when comparing prevalence rates among women of different racial or ethnic backgrounds.

Since information on violence against American Indian and Alaska Native women is limited, it is difficult to explain why they report more stalking victimization. A previous study found that the overall homicide rates for Native Americans were about two times greater than U.S. national rates.[16] Thus, there is some evidence that Native Americans are at significantly greater risk of violence—fatal and nonfatal—than other Americans. How much of the variance in stalking prevalence may be explained by demographic, social, and environmental factors remains unclear and requires further study. Moreover, there may be significant differences in stalking prevalence among women of diverse American Indian tribes and Alaska Native communities that cannot be determined from the survey, since data on all Native Americans were combined.

There is some evidence that Asian and Pacific Islander women are at significantly less risk of being stalked than women of other racial and ethnic backgrounds (see exhibit 4). Again, however, given the small number of Asian/Pacific Islander women in the sample, this finding must be viewed with caution. It has been suggested that traditional Asian values emphasizing close family ties and harmony may discourage Asian women from disclosing physical and emotional abuse by intimate partners.[17] Thus, the smaller stalking prevalence rate found among Asian/Pacific Islander women may be, at least in part, an artifact of underreporting. There may also be a significant difference in stalking prevalence between Asian women and Pacific Islander women that cannot be determined from the survey, since data on these two groups were combined.

The survey found no significant difference in stalking prevalence among men of different racial and ethnic backgrounds. This finding must also be viewed with caution, given the sample's small number of male victims falling into specific racial and ethnic groupings. A larger sample of male stalking victims is needed to produce more reliable information on the relative risk of stalking among men of different racial and ethnic backgrounds.

The survey found no significant difference in stalking prevalence among men and women of Hispanic and non-Hispanic origin (see exhibit 5). Since previous studies comparing the prevalence of violence among Hispanic and non-Hispanic women have produced contradictory conclusions,[18] these findings neither confirm nor contradict earlier findings.

### Exhibit 5: Percentage of Men and Women Stalked in Life-time, by Hispanic/Non-Hispanic Origin of Victim

| Group | Persons Stalked in Lifetime (%) | | |
|---|---|---|---|
| | Total | Hispanic* | Non-Hispanic |
| Men | (N = 7,916)<br>2.2 | (N = 581)<br>3.3 | (N = 7,335)<br>2.1 |
| Women | (N = 7,945)<br>8.1 | (N = 628)<br>7.6 | (N = 7,317)<br>8.2 |

*Persons of Hispanic origin may be of any race.

## Who Stalks Whom?

Though stalking is a gender-neutral crime, women are the primary victims of stalking and men are the primary perpetrators. Seventy-eight percent of the stalking victims identified by the survey were women, and 22 percent were men. Thus, four out of five stalking victims are women. By comparison, 94 percent of the stalkers identified by female victims and 60 percent of the stalkers identified by male victims were male. Overall, 87 percent of the stalkers identified by victims were male.

Young adults are also the primary targets of stalkers. Fifty-two percent of the stalking victims were 18–29 years old and 22 percent were 30–39 years old when the stalking started (see exhibit 6). On average, victims were 28 years old when the stalking started.

The survey confirms previous reports that most victims know their stalker.[19] Only 23 percent of female victims and 36 percent of male victims were stalked by strangers. The survey also indicates that women tend to be stalked by intimate partners, defined as current or former spouses, current or former cohabitants (of the same or opposite sex), or current or former boyfriends or girlfriends. Thirty-eight percent of female stalking victims were stalked by current or former husbands, 10 percent by current or former cohabiting partners, and 14 percent by current or former dates or boyfriends. Overall, 59 percent of female victims, compared with 30 percent of male victims, were stalked by some type of intimate partner (see exhibit 7).

It has been reported previously that when women are stalked by intimate partners, the stalking typically occurs after the woman attempts to leave the relationship.[20] To test this assumption, the NVAW Survey

## Exhibit 6: Victim's Age When First Stalked*

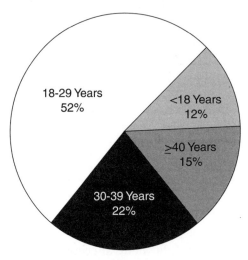

*N = 797 male and female victims. Percentages do not total 100 due to rounding.

## Exhibit 7: Relationship between Victim and Offender

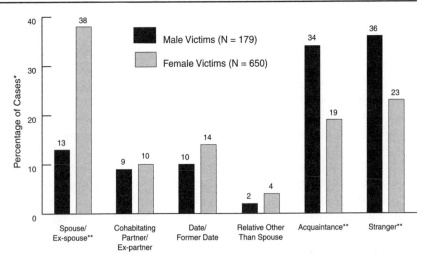

\* Percentages exceed 100% because some victims had more than one stalker.
\*\* Differences between males and females are significant at ≤.05.

asked women who had been stalked by former husbands or partners when in the relationship the stalking occurred. Twenty-one percent of these victims said the stalking occurred before the relationship ended, 43 percent said it occurred after the relationship ended, and 36 percent said it occurred both before and after the relationship ended (see exhibit 8). Thus, contrary to popular opinion, women are often stalked by intimate partners while the relationship is still intact.

The survey found that men tend to be stalked by strangers and acquaintances (see exhibit 7), 90 percent of whom are male. It is unclear from the survey data why men are stalked by male strangers and male acquaintances. There is some evidence that homosexual men are at greater risk of being stalked than heterosexual men: Stalking prevalence was significantly greater among men who had ever lived with a man as a couple compared with men who had never lived with a man as a couple (see exhibit 9). Thus, in some stalking cases involving male victims and stranger or acquaintance perpetrators, the perpetrator may be motivated by hatred toward homosexuals, while in others the perpetrator may be motivated by sexual attraction. It is also possible that some men are stalked by male strangers and male acquaintances in the context of inter- or intragroup gang rivalries. Clearly, more research is needed to determine under what circumstances men are stalked by male strangers and male acquaintances.

*Exhibit 8: Point in Intimate Relationship When Stalking of Women\* Occurs*

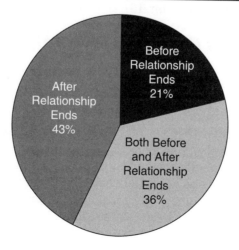

\* N = 263 female victims.

179

**Exhibit 9: Percentage of Men Stalked in Lifetime, by Whether They Ever Cohabited with a Man**

| Men Stalked/ Not Stalked in Lifetime* | Cohabitation Experience | |
|---|---|---|
| | Cohabited with a Man (N = 65) % | Never Cohabited with a Man (N = 7,935) % |
| Stalked | 7.7** | 2.2 |
| Not Stalked | 92.3 | 97.8 |

\* Differences between men who "cohabited" and "never cohabited" are significant at <.01.
\*\* Based on five or fewer cases.

Although men tend to be stalked by strangers and acquaintances, women are at significantly greater risk of being stalked by strangers and acquaintances than men. A comparison of stalking prevalence among women and men by victim-offender relationship shows that 1.8 percent of all U.S. women, compared with 0.8 percent of all U.S. men, have been stalked by strangers; and 1.6 percent of all U.S. women, compared with 0.8 percent of all U.S. men, have been stalked by acquaintances (see exhibit 10).

## How Do Stalkers Harass and Terrorize?

When asked to describe specific activities their stalkers engaged in to harass and terrorize them, women were significantly more likely than men to report that their stalkers followed them, spied on them, or stood outside their home or place of work or recreation (see exhibit 11). Women were also significantly more likely to report that their stalkers made unsolicited phone calls. About equal percentages of female and male victims reported that their stalkers sent them unwanted letters or items, vandalized their property, or killed or threatened to kill a family pet (see exhibit 11).

## Exhibit 10: Percentage of Men and Women Stalked in Lifetime, by Victim-Offender Relationship

|  | Persons Stalked in Lifetime (%) | |
| --- | --- | --- |
| Victim-Offender Relationship | Men (N = 8,000) | Women (N = 8,000) |
| Intimate* | 0.6 | 4.8 |
| Relative | 0.1** | 0.3 |
| Acquaintance* | 0.8 | 1.6 |
| Stranger* | 0.8 | 1.8 |

\* Differences between men and women are significant at ≤.05.
\*\* Based on five or fewer cases.

## Exhibit 11: Stalking Activities Engaged in by Stalkers

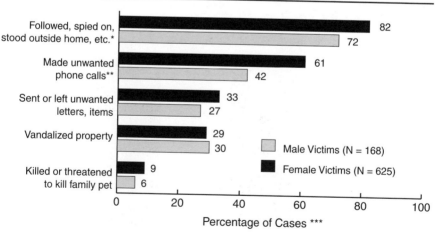

\* Differences between males and females are significant at ≤.05.
\*\* Differences between males and females are significant at ≤.001.
\*\*\* Percentages exceed 100% because the question had multiple responses.

181

## How Often Do Stalkers Threaten Overtly?

Many state antistalking laws include in their definition of stalking a requirement that stalkers make an overt threat of violence against their victim.[21] Survey findings suggest that this requirement may be ill-advised. By definition, stalking victims in this survey were either very frightened of their assailant's behavior or feared their assailant would seriously harm or kill them or someone close to them. Despite the high level of fear required, the survey found that less than half the victims—both male and female—were directly threatened by their stalker (see exhibit 12). This finding shows that stalkers do not always threaten their victim verbally or in writing; more often they engage in a course of conduct that, taken in context, causes a reasonable person to feel fearful. The *Model Antistalking Code* reflects this reality by not including in its definition of stalking a requirement that the stalker make a credible threat of violence against the victim.[22]

## Why Stalkers Stalk Their Victims

To generate information on motivations for stalking, the survey asked victims why they thought they had been stalked. Since stalk-

*Exhibit 12: Percentage of Victims Who Were Overtly Threatened by Their Stalkers*

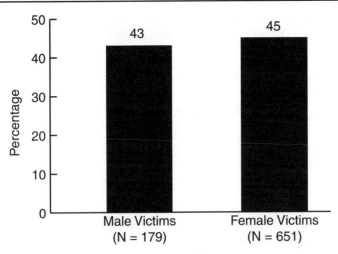

ing occurs in a variety of situations and between people who have various relationships, it is not surprising that responses to this question varied. Based on victims' perceptions of why they were stalked, it appears that much stalking is motivated by stalkers' desire to control, or instill fear in, their victim (see exhibit 13). The survey results dispel the myth that most stalkers are psychotic or delusional. Only 7 percent of the victims said they were stalked because their stalkers were mentally ill or abusing drugs or alcohol.

## Relationship between Stalking and Other Forms of Violence

The NVAW Survey provides compelling evidence of the link between stalking and other forms of violence in intimate relationships. Eighty-one percent of the women who were stalked by a current or former husband or cohabiting partner were also physically assaulted by the same partner, and 31 percent of the women who were stalked by a current or former husband or cohabiting partner were also sexually assaulted by the same partner. By comparison, 20 percent of the

*Exhibit 13: Victims' Perceptions of Why They Were Stalked\**

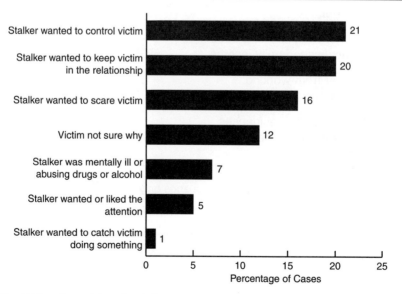

* N = 624 male and female victims.

*Exhibit 14: Percentage of Ex-Husbands Who Engaged in Emotionally Abusive or Controlling Behavior, by Whether They Stalked\**

| Types of Emotionally Abusive/ Controlling Behavior** | Ex-Husbands Who Stalked (%) (N = 166) | Ex-Husbands Who Did Not Stalk (%) (N = 2,645) |
|---|---|---|
| Had a hard time seeing things from her point of view | 87.7 | 57.8 |
| Was jealous or possessive | 83.7 | 46.3 |
| Tried to provoke arguments | 90.3 | 45.3 |
| Tried to limit her contact with family and friends | 77.1 | 32.3 |
| Insisted on knowing where she was at all times | 80.7 | 34.4 |
| Made her feel inadequate | 85.5 | 40.9 |
| Shouted or swore at her | 88.0 | 44.5 |
| Frightened her | 92.2 | 33.1 |
| Prevented her from knowing about or having access to family income | 59.6 | 20.8 |
| Prevented her from working outside the home | 30.7 | 13.0 |
| Insisted on changing residences even when she didn't need or want to | 33.9 | 11.9 |

\* Based on responses for first ex-husbands only

\*\* Differences between ex-husbands who stalked and ex-husbands who did not stalk are significant at ≤.001.

women who were ever married or ever lived with a man were physically assaulted by a current or former husband or partner, and 5 percent of women who were ever married or ever lived with a man were sexually assaulted by a current or former husband or partner. Thus, husbands or partners who stalk their partners are four times more likely than husbands or partners in the general population to physically assault their partners, and they are six times more likely than husbands and partners in the general population to sexually assault their partners.

The survey also provides compelling evidence of the link between stalking and controlling and emotionally abusive behavior in intimate relationships. To provide a context for violence occurring between intimate partners, respondents to the survey were asked a series of questions about controlling and emotionally abusive behavior they experienced at the hands of their current or former spouses or cohabiting partners. The survey found that ex-husbands who stalked (either before or after the relationship ended) were significantly more likely than ex-husbands who did not stalk to engage in emotionally abusive and controlling behavior toward their wife (see exhibit 14 for details).

## How Often Is Stalking Reported to Police?

Fifty-five percent of female victims and 48 percent of male victims said their stalking was reported to the police. In most of these cases, the victims made the report (see exhibit 15). The percentage of women reporting stalking is identical to the percentage of female victims reporting lone-offender violent crimes to police during 1987–89, as measured by the National Crime Victimization Survey.[23]

Police responses to stalking cases involving male victims and female victims were virtually identical, with two notable exceptions: Police were significantly more likely to arrest or detain a suspect in cases involving female victims, and they were significantly more likely to refer female victims to services (see exhibit 15).

There is some evidence that stalking reports to the police by victims have increased since passage of antistalking laws. According to information from the survey, stalking cases occurring before 1990—the year California passed the nation's first antistalking law—were significantly less likely to be reported to the police than stalking cases occurring after 1995, the year by which all 50 states and the District of Columbia had laws proscribing stalking. There was no significant difference, however, in the number of arrests made in stalking cases that occurred before 1990 and those that occurred after 1995. When asked why they chose not to report their stalking to the police, victims were most likely to state that their stalking was not a police matter, they thought the police would not be able to do anything, or they feared reprisals from their stalkers (see exhibit 16).

Overall, stalking victims gave police a 50/50 approval rating (see exhibit 17). Respondents who said their stalkers were arrested were

**Exhibit 15: Percentage and Characteristics of Stalking Cases Reported to the Police, by Sex of Victim**

| Reported to Police/Response | Stalking Victims (%) | | |
|---|---|---|---|
| | **Male** | **Female** | **Total** |
| Was case reported to the police? | (N = 178) | (N = 641) | (N = 819) |
| Yes | 47.7 | 54.6 | 53.1 |
| No | 52.3 | 45.4 | 46.9 |
| Who reported the case?* | (N = 84) | (N = 350) | (N = 434) |
| Victim | 75.0 | 84.0 | 82.3 |
| Other | 25.0 | 16.0 | 17.7 |
| Police Response*** | (N = 84) | (N = 350) | (N = 434) |
| Took report | 66.7 | 68.6 | 68.0 |
| Arrested or detained perpetrator*** | 16.7 | 25.1 | 23.5 |
| Referred to prosecutor or court | 19.0 | 24.3 | 23.3 |
| Referred to victim services* | 8.3 | 15.1 | 13.8 |
| Gave advice on self-protective measures | 29.8 | 34.0 | 33.2 |
| Did nothing | 16.7 | 19.4 | 18.9 |

  * Based on responses from victims whose stalking was reported to the police.
 ** Percentages exceed 100 percent because of multiple responses.
*** Differences between males and females are significant at $\leq$.05.

## Exhibit 16: Victims' Reasons for Not Reporting Stalking to Police*

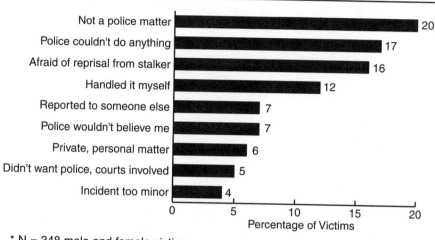

* N = 348 male and female victims.

## Exhibit 17: Victims' Satisfaction with the Police*

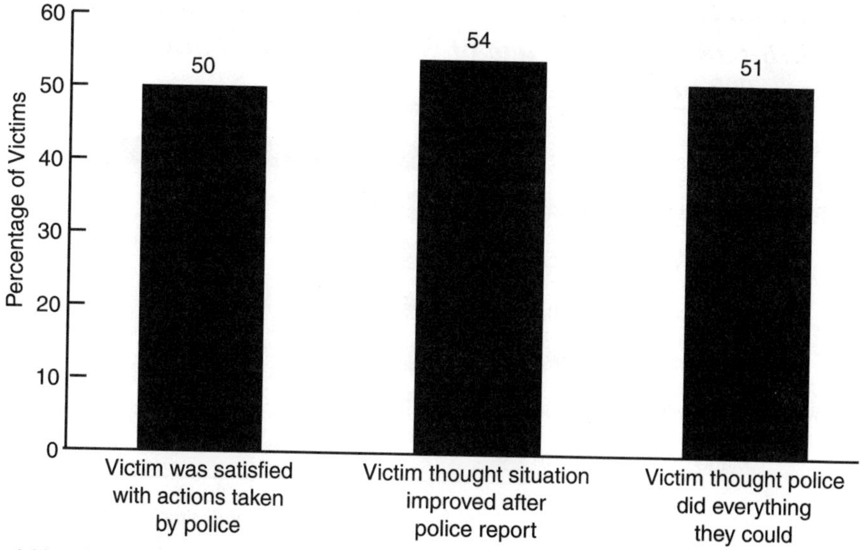

* N = 435 male and female victims.

significantly more likely to be satisfied with the way the police handled their case than respondents who said their stalkers were not arrested (76 percent versus 42 percent).

Victims who thought the police "should have done more" in their cases were asked to describe what specific actions they thought the police should have taken. Forty-two percent thought the police should have put the assailant in jail, 20 percent said the police should have taken the situation more seriously, and 16 percent said the police should have done more to protect them (see exhibit 18).

## How Often Are Stalkers Criminally Prosecuted?

Overall, 13 percent of female victims and 9 percent of male victims reported that their stalkers were criminally prosecuted (see exhibit 19). These figures increase to 24 percent and 19 percent, respectively, when only those cases with police reports are considered. The stalkers were charged with a wide variety of crimes, including stalking, harassment, menacing or threatening, vandalism, trespassing, breaking and entering, robbery, disorderly conduct, intimidation, and simple and aggravated assault. Survey participants reported that about half the stalkers (54 percent) who had criminal charges filed against them were convicted

*Exhibit 18: Victims' View of Other Actions Police Should Have Taken\**

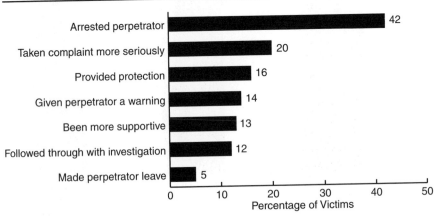

\* N = 201 male and female victims who thought police should have done more.

188

## Exhibit 19: Percentage and Outcomes of Criminal Prosecutions in Stalking Cases, by Sex of Victim

| Outcome | Stalking Victims (%) | | |
| --- | --- | --- | --- |
| | Male | Female | Total |
| Was perpetrator prosecuted? | (N = 178) | (N = 645) | (N = 823) |
| Yes | 9.0 | 13.1 | 12.1 |
| No | 91.0 | 86.9 | 87.9 |
| Was perpetrator convicted?* | (N = 15) | (N = 72) | (N = 87) |
| Yes | 60.0 | 52.8 | 54.0 |
| No | 40.0 | 47.2 | 46.0 |
| Was perpetrator sentenced to jail or prison?** | (N = 9) | (N = 37) | (N = 46) |
| Yes | 77.8 | 59.5 | 63.0 |
| No | 22.2*** | 40.5 | 37.0 |

* Based on responses from victims whose perpetrator was prosecuted.
** Based on responses from victims whose perpetrator was convicted.
*** Based on five or fewer sample cases.

of a crime. Of those convicted, nearly two-thirds (63 percent) were believed to have been sent to jail or prison.

## *Obtaining Protective or Restraining Orders Against Stalkers*

Results from the survey also indicate that female victims were significantly more likely than male victims (28 percent and 10 percent) to obtain a protective or restraining order against a stalker (see exhibit 20). This finding is expected, since women are significantly more likely than men to be stalked by intimate partners who have a history of being violent toward them. Of those who obtained restraining orders, 69 percent of the women and 81 percent of the men said the stalker violated the order.

**Exhibit 20: Percentage and Outcomes of Protective Orders in Stalking Cases, by Sex of Victim**

| Outcome | Stalking Victims (%) | | |
| --- | --- | --- | --- |
| | Male | Female | Total |
| Did victim obtain a protective or restraining order?* | (N = 175) | (N = 597) | (N = 772) |
| Yes | 9.7 | 28.0 | 23.8 |
| No | 90.3 | 72.0 | 76.2 |
| Was the order violated?** | (N = 16) | (N = 166) | (N = 182) |
| Yes | 81.3 | 68.7 | 69.8 |
| No | 18.7 | 31.3 | 30.2 |

\* Differences between males and females are significant at $\leq$.05.
\*\* Based on responses from victims who obtained a restraining order.

## What Are the Psychological and Social Consequences of Stalking?

The survey produced strong confirmation of the negative mental health impact of stalking. About a third of the women (30 percent) and a fifth of the men (20 percent) said they sought psychological counseling as a result of the stalking victimization. In addition, stalking victims were significantly more likely than non-stalking victims to be very concerned about their personal safety and about being stalked, to carry something on their person to defend themselves, and to think personal safety for men and women had gotten worse in recent years (see exhibit 21).

Over a quarter (26 percent) of the stalking victims said the victimization caused them to lose time from work. While the survey did not query victims about why they lost time from work, it can be assumed they missed work for a variety of reasons—to attend court hearings, to meet with a psychologist or other mental health professional, to avoid contact with the assailant, and to consult with an attorney. When asked how many days of work they lost, 7 percent of these victims said they never returned to work. On average, however, victims who lost time from and returned to work missed 11 days.

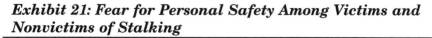

**Exhibit 21: Fear for Personal Safety Among Victims and Nonvictims of Stalking**

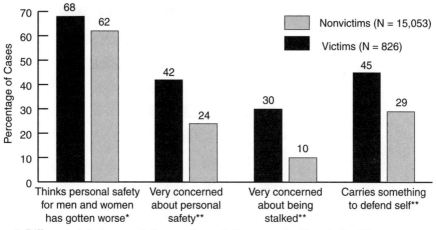

\* Differences between victims and nonvictims are significant at ≤.01.
\*\* Differences between victims and nonvictims are significant at ≤.001.

Stalking victims were asked whether they took any measures (other than reporting their victimization to the police or obtaining a protective order) to protect themselves from the stalker. Fifty-six percent of the women and 51 percent of the men reported taking some type of self-protective measure (see exhibit 22).

## When and Why Does Stalking Stop?

At the time of the interview, 92 percent of the victims were no longer being stalked. Based on information provided by these victims, about two-thirds of all stalking cases last a year or less, about a quarter last 2–5 years, and about a tenth last more than 5 years (see exhibit 23). On average, stalking cases last 1.8 years. However, stalking cases involving intimates or former intimates last, on average, significantly longer than stalking cases involving nonintimates (2.2 years and 1.1 years, respectively).

Victims who were no longer being stalked at the time of the interview were asked why they thought the stalking had ceased; 19 percent said the stalking stopped because they (the victims) moved away (see exhibit 24). These findings suggest that address confidentiality programs may be an effective means of combating stalking. Such pro-

### Exhibit 22: Self-Protective Measures Undertaken by Stalking Victims*

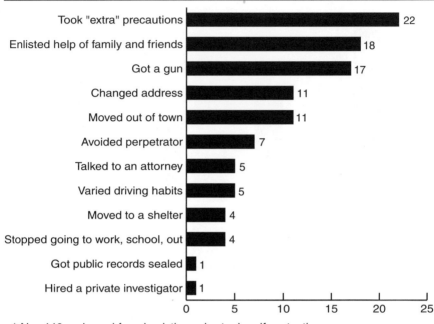

* N = 440 male and female victims who took self-protective measures.

grams encourage victims who face continued pursuit and unusual safety risks to develop a personal safety plan that includes relocating as far from the stalker as possible and securing a confidential mailing address that provides mail-forwarding service but does not reveal the victim's new location.[24]

Some stalking cases are resolved when the perpetrator gets a new love interest. Eighteen percent of the victims said the stalking stopped because the assailant got a new spouse, partner, or boyfriend/girlfriend.

It has been reported previously that informal law enforcement interventions, such as detective contacts, can be an effective means of deterring stalkers, particularly in cases where the victim and the suspect had some prior relationship and where the stalker is not suffering from mental illness.[25] Findings from the NVAW Survey provide some support for this theory. Victims were more likely to credit informal, rather than formal, justice system interventions for the cessation of the stalking. For example, 15 percent of victims said the stalking stopped after their assailants received a warning from the police. By comparison, only 9 percent of victims said the stalking ceased because the

## Exhibit 23: Distribution of Cases by Number of Years Stalking Lasted*

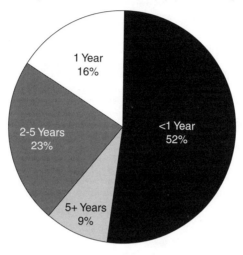

1 Year
16%

2-5 Years
23%

<1 Year
52%

5+ Years
9%

\* N = 759 cases.

stalker was arrested, 1 percent said the stalking stopped because the stalker was convicted of a crime, and less than 1 percent said the stalking stopped because they obtained a restraining order against the stalker. The fact that so few victims credited formal justice system interventions is not surprising, given the paucity of arrests, criminal prosecutions, and restraining orders in stalking cases.

## Conclusion

The results of the NVAW Survey clearly indicate that stalking is much more prevalent than previously thought and should be treated as a significant problem. An estimated 8 percent of women and 2 percent of men in the U.S. have been stalked at some point during their lifetime. While stalkers can be men or women, an overwhelming majority are male. Moreover, women are significantly more likely than men to be stalked by an intimate, such as a husband, cohabiting partner, or date. The survey also revealed a strong link between stalking and domestic violence. Intimates who stalk their partners are also more likely to physically and sexually assault their victims prior to the termination of the relationship. What's more, stalking cases in-

## Exhibit 24: Victim's Perception of Why Stalking Stopped*

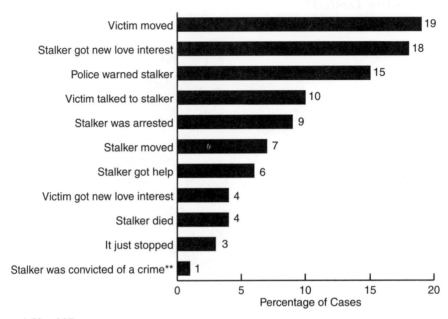

| | Percentage of Cases |
|---|---|
| Victim moved | 19 |
| Stalker got new love interest | 18 |
| Police warned stalker | 15 |
| Victim talked to stalker | 10 |
| Stalker was arrested | 9 |
| Stalker moved | 7 |
| Stalker got help | 6 |
| Victim got new love interest | 4 |
| Stalker died | 4 |
| It just stopped | 3 |
| Stalker was convicted of a crime** | 1 |

\* N = 665 cases.
\*\* Based on 5 or fewer cases.

volving current or former intimates last longer than those involving nonintimates.

Stalkers employed a variety of activities to harass and terrorize their victims, but less than half the victims were overtly threatened, underscoring the need to eliminate the requirement in many state antistalking statutes that the stalker issue a credible threat of violence against the victim. This absence of overt threats complicates effective management of stalking cases by the criminal justice system and contributes significantly to the victim's sense of frustration at the system's inability to respond appropriately. The survey found that the state antistalking statutes are having a positive impact on the number of cases reported to authorities. However, victims were divided on police response, with half of them expressing dissatisfaction with the way their cases were handled by police. Overall, a very small percentage of the stalking cases were prosecuted, highlighting the critical need for criminal justice professionals to receive comprehensive training to process and manage these cases to enhance victim safety and hold offenders accountable.

## *Violence Among Intimates in America*

A report* produced by the Justice Department's Bureau of Justice Statistics (BJS) indicated that women make up the vast majority of victims in crimes involving intimate** violence. This report, which is a compilation of data from the National Crime Victimization Survey and the FBI's Uniform Crime Reporting Program, revealed the following:

• Women were more likely than men to have been murdered by an intimate. In 1996, nearly 2,000 murders were committed by intimates, and in almost 3 out of 4 of these killings, the victim was a woman.

• Each year, approximately 30 percent of all women killed in this country die at the hands of a current or former intimate, compared to 6 percent of men. The intimate murder rate for men has been sharply decreasing, dropping from 1,357 in 1976 to 516 in 1996.

• In 1996, women were victimized by intimates in about 840,000 incidents of rape, sexual assault, robbery aggravated assault, and simple assault. By contrast, men were victims of about 150,000 violent crimes committed by an intimate. (On average, about a million women are victimized by an intimate each year.)

• The highest per capita rates of intimate violence were among women aged 16–24, paralleling the findings of the NVAW Survey, which revealed that more younger women were victims of stalking.

• Approximately half the incidents of intimate violence against women were reported to the police. These figures are similar to the findings of the NVAW Survey in which roughly half the stalking victims reported the crime to the authorities.

• The three most common reasons offered for not reporting the crime were that the incident was considered a private or personal matter, fear of offender reprisals, and a perception that law enforcement would not or could not assist. Again, these explanations virtually mirror the findings of the NVAW Survey.

*Copies of this report, "Violence by Intimates," can be obtained from the BJS Internet website: http://www.ojp.usdoj.gov/bjs/ or by calling (800) 732-3277 and requesting publication NCJ #167237.

**Intimates can be spouses, ex-spouses, boyfriends, girlfriends, ex-boyfriends, and ex-girlfriends.

## References

1. This section was prepared by Dr. Patricia Tjaden and Dr. Nancy Thoennes of the Center for Policy Research as a "Research in Brief" and is based on findings of the National Violence Against Women Survey. The survey was jointly funded by NIJ and CDC under NIJ Grant No. 93-IJ-CX-0012. The opinions and conclusions expressed in this section are solely those of the authors and do not necessarily reflect the views of the Department of Justice or the agencies that funded the research.

2. See, for example, John Ellement, "Police Arrest Boston Man, 18, for Violating State Stalking Law," *Boston Globe*, May 28, 1992; Kristin N. Sullivan, "Woman's Case Illustrates Need for State Stalking Law, Some Say," *Houston Chronicle*, April 19, 1992; Josh Meyer, "Man Held in Stalking of Pop Singer Janet Jackson," *Los Angeles Times*, June 25, 1992; George Lardner, "The Stalking of Kristin: The Law Made It Easy for My Daughter's Killer," *Washington Post*, November 22, 1992; Maria Puente, "Legislators Tackling the Terror of Stalking: But Some Experts Say Measures Are Vague," *USA Today*, July 21, 1992; Mike Tharp, "In the Mind of a Stalker," *U.S. News and World Report*, February 17, 1992.

3. Donna Hunzeker, "Stalking Laws," *State Legislative Report*, Denver, Colo.: National Conference of State Legislatures, 17, 19 (October 1992): 1–6.

4. National Criminal Justice Association, *Project to Develop a Model Anti-Stalking Code for States* (Washington, DC: U.S. Department of Justice, National Institute of Justice, October 1993).

5. See, for example, Park Dietz and Daniell Martell, "Threatening and Otherwise Inappropriate Letters to Members of the United States Congress," *Journal of Forensic Sciences* 36(5), 1991; Ronald Holmes, "Stalking in America: Types and Methods of Criminal Stalkers," *Journal of Contemporary Criminal Justice* 9(4), December 1993; M. A. Zona et al., "Comparative Study of Erotomaniac and Obsessional Subjects in a Forensic Sample," *Journal of Forensic Sciences* 38(4), July 1993; M. Rudden et al., "Diagnosis and Clinical Course of Erotomania and Other Delusional Patients," *American Journal of Psychiatry* 147, 5 (1990): 625–28.

6.  See, for example, Susan E. Bernstein, "Living Under Siege: Do Stalking Laws Protect Domestic Violence Victims?" *Cardoza Law Review* 15 (1993): 525–29; Katherine M. Boychuk, "Are Stalking Laws Unconstitutionally Vague or Overbroad?" *Northwestern University Law Review* 88, 2 (1994): 769–802; Robert A. Guy, Jr., "Nature and Constitutionality of Stalking Laws," *Vanderbilt Law Review* 46, 4 (1993): 991–1029; Mattlaw Gilligan, "Stalking the Stalker: Developing New Laws to Thwart Those Who Terrorize Others," *Georgia Law Review* 27 (1992): 285–342; Brenda K. Harmon, "Illinois' Newly Amended Stalking Law: Are All the Problems Solved?" *Southern Illinois University Law Journal* 19 (1994): 165–98; Richard A. Lingg, "Stopping Stalkers: A Critical Examination of Anti-Stalking Legislation," *Saint John's Law Review* 67, 2 (1993): 347–81; Kathleen G. McAnaney et al., "From Impudence to Crime: Anti-Stalking Laws," *Notre Dame Law Review* 68 (1993): 819-909; K. S. Morin, "The Phenomenon of Stalking: Do Existing State Statutes Provide Adequate Protection?" *San Diego Justice Journal* 1, 1 (1993): 123-62; Ellen Sohn, "Antistalking Statutes: Do They Actually Protect Victims?" *Criminal Law Bulletin* 30, 3 (1994): 203–41; Silvija Strikis, "Stopping Stalking," Note, *Georgetown Law Journal* 81 (1993): 2772–2813; Kenneth R. Thomas, "How to Stop the Stalker: State Anti-Stalking Laws," *Criminal Law Bulletin* 29, 2 (1992): 124–36; Julie Miles Walker, "Anti-Stalking Legislation: Does it Protect the Victim without Violating the Rights of the Accused?" *University of Denver Law Review* 71, 2 (1993): 273–302.

7.  George Lardner, *The Stalking of Kristin: A Father Investigates the Murder of His Daughter* (New York: Atlantic Monthly Press, 1995); Doreen Orion, *I Know You Really Love Me: A Psychiatrist's Journal of Erotomania, Stalking, and Obsessive Love* (New York: Macmillan, 1997).

8.  Thomas, "How to Stop the Stalker: State Anti-Stalking Laws" (see note 6).

9.  Hunzeker, "Stalking Laws" (see note 3).

10. "Domestic Violence, Stalking, and Antistalking Legislation," Attorney General's First Annual Report to Congress under the Violence Against Women Act, *National Institute of Justice Research Report* (Washington, DC: U.S. Department of Justice, National Institute of Justice, April 1996).

11. Ibid.

12. National Criminal Justice Association, *Project to Develop a Model Antistalking Code for States* (Washington, DC: U.S. Department of Justice, National Institute of Justice, October 1993).

13. The findings of the survey, as in any sample survey, are subject to sample fluctuations or sampling error. Using the sampling methods described in this report (see "Survey Methodology"), the maximum sampling error at the 95 confidence level for a sample of 8,000 is plus or minus 1.1 percentage points if the response distribution on a categorical variable is a 50/50 split.

14. According to the U.S. Bureau of the Census estimates, there were 100,697,000 women and 92,648,000 men aged 18 and older residing in the United States in 1995.

15. While testimony provided at a September 29, 1992, Senate Judiciary Committee Hearing on S.B. 2922 (Violence Against Women) is generally cited as the source for these estimates, the figures first appeared in a *USA Today* article on stalking (see Puente in note 2). The statistics contained in the article were attributed to "guesses" provided by Park Dietz, a Los Angeles-based forensic psychiatrist, presumably on the basis of his research on a nonrepresentative sample of known celebrity stalkers (see Dietz in note 5).

16. L. J. D. Wallace, A. D. Calhoun, K. E. Powell, J. O'Neill, and S. P. James, "Homicide and Suicide Among Native Americans, 1979-1992," Violence Surveillance Series, No. 2, Atlanta, GA: Centers for Disease Control and Prevention, National Center for Injury Prevention and Control, 1996.

17. National Research Council, *Understanding Violence Against Women* (Washington, DC: National Academy Press, 1996): 40–41.

18. S. B. Sorenson, J. A. Stein, J. M. Siegel, J. M. Golding, and M. A. Burnam, "The Prevalence of Adult Sexual Assault: The Los Angeles Epidemiologic Catchment Area Project," *American Journal of Epidemiology* 126 (1987): 1154-64; S. B. Sorenson and C. A. Tells, "Self-Reports of Spousal Violence in a Mexican American and a Non-Hispanic White Population," *Violence and Victims* 6 (1991): 3–16.

19. A survey of 90 Florida law enforcement agencies reported that in most stalking cases, the victim knew the offender. See J. T. Tucker, "The Effectiveness of Florida Stalking Statutes Section 784,048," *Florida Law Review* 45, 4 (1993): 609–707.

20. See National Institute of Justice. "Domestic Violence, Stalking, and Antistalking Legislation" (see note 10).

21. Ibid.

22. See National Criminal Justice Association, *Project to Develop a Model Anti-Stalking Code for States* (see note 4).

23. Ronet Bachman, "Violence Against Women: A National Crime Victimization Survey Report," Washington, DC: U.S. Department of Justice, Bureau of Justice Statistics, January 1993.

24. See, for example, the Address Confidentiality Program, Post Office Box 69, Olympia, Washington 98507-0069, (360) 753–2971.

25. W. L. Williams, J. C. D. Lane, and M. A. Zona, "Stalking: Successful Intervention Strategies," *The Police Chief* (February 1996): 24–26; and M. A. Zona, K. K. Sharma, and J. C. Lane, "A Comparative Study of Erotomanic and Obsessional Subjects in a Forensic Sample," *Journal of Forensic Sciences* 38, 4 (July 1993): 894–903.

# Chapter 11

# *Teen Dating Violence*

## Chapter Contents

Section 11.1

# Dating Violence: Youth at Risk

*Joan G. Sculli*

## What Is Dating Violence?

Dating violence can be described as a pattern of repeated threats or acts of physical, sexual or emotional abuse by a member of an unmarried, noncohabitating couple.

This inappropriate and dangerous behavior may take a physical or emotional form. Physical abuse is any attempt to injure or constrain another individual. It includes assault, use of force, abandonment in a dangerous place, unwanted or uncomfortable touching, persistent sexual advances, forced sex, even hurting playfully during sex.

Emotional abuse includes a variety of behaviors which makes an individual fearful, anxious or uncomfortable. This includes threats, intimidation, humiliation, name-calling, the silent treatment, withholding affection and/or sex, vicious criticizing, destroying or defacing valued objects, sabotaging successes or advancement, and/or demeaning one's achievements.

These behaviors are unnecessary, inappropriate, and sometimes illegal. As time passes, they will destroy the quality of the relationship and kill any idea of happiness and satisfaction within it.

Dating violence is most often part of a pattern of behavior that begins with verbal and emotional abuse and eventually escalates into physical battering.

## Why Are Teens At Risk?

Dating is a part of growing up that allows young people to discover facts about themselves and how they relate to others. In trying to achieve independence, they experiment and take risks. They are afraid that asking for advice or help, especially from parents or other concerned adults, will demonstrate that they cannot handle the problems themselves.

Ideas of male and female roles can be rigid and extreme during adolescence. Young women's behavior may be defined as passive and emphasize caretaking, dependence, and the responsibility to make the relationship work. Being male may be defined as taking charge, making all the decisions, and being sexually aggressive.

Adolescents may have difficulty managing the complex feelings and conflicts that arise in relationships because they are generally inexperienced, are less aware of the long-term consequences, and lack practice in making complex decisions. By thinking romantically, they may accept many distorted images, especially those presented in the media, that interpret jealousy, possessiveness, and abuse as signs of love. To further complicate the picture, being involved with the "wrong person" can create doubts about one's self-worth, making it more difficult to go through the scary process of evaluating the relationship.

## Advice to Parents

Being informed about the nature of dating violence and recognizing that it can occur in any cultural, religious or socioeconomic group is important. Learning to be a good observer and listening carefully to how your children describe their interactions with their boy or girl friends in order to identify "warning signs" are the first steps to helping.

- Don't be afraid to talk to your children about relationships.
- Use opportunities to comment about TV dramas, news events, or other people to open conversations about behavior.
- Ask simple, direct questions in a comfortable way, with good eye contact and body language expressing sincere concern.
- Listen to responses calmly; don't judge.
- Questions beginning with the word "Why" should be avoided but questions like "What happens when you fight? How does he express anger? Have you ever been frightened during an argument?" are appropriate.

Even if the youth does not respond, you have shown that you care and are informed, and that you know abuse can enter any relationship.

It is always important to take adolescents seriously. Never minimize what is going on by thinking that kids like to dramatize their situations. Never underestimate the amount of bonding that takes place in the relationship and expect a child to quickly and easily break it off.

Reassure the youth that your discussions are private and that you will not share what you are told without permission. The hardest thing may be not rushing to speak to the abusive partner. Listen closely and let the victim guide the action to be taken. Know where you can get good professional help.

The strongest influence in a youth's choice of partner comes from the way children see people interact at home. Be a good model. If you're having problems yourself, get help!

## How to Help

It is natural for loving adults to try to rush in and save their children from pain and hardship. Unfortunately, in dating situations, it is usually the youth who must decide which actions to take. Providing a supportive role rather than a commanding one can be difficult but that is often what is necessary for parents.

The best place for information and help is your local domestic violence program. You can find its location by calling Information (411) and asking for the Coalition Against Domestic Violence nearest you.

Many programs offer 24 hour, 7 day a week hotlines where victims, abusers, parents or friends can get information, seek safety or get telephone counseling. Hotlines offer free information without taking risks. Callers don't have to confide who they are or where they are calling from. No action will be put in motion until the caller is ready.

Courts in many states provide Orders of Protection or Restraining Orders to help protect victims. In many places, these are only available in criminal court after charges against the abuser have been formally made with the district attorney. Some communities allow Family Court Orders, which are private proceedings, not criminal.

Orders of Protection are an important source of help when appropriate. They are not the best solution to the problem in every case and in some cases can increase the danger to the victim. Because of this, it is suggested that the victim get expert advice before going to court in order to understand the procedures involved and whether the court order will help or make the situation more dangerous. Local battered women's programs are usually the best place for this information.

*Don't hesitate to ask for information or help. A life is at stake!*

# Section 11.2

# *Fact Sheet on Dating Violence*

National Center for Injury Prevention and Control, Centers for Disease Control and Prevention, February 1999.

Dating violence may be defined as the perpetration or threat of an act of violence by at least one member of an unmarried couple on the other member within the context of dating or courtship.[1] This violence encompasses any form of sexual assault, physical violence, and verbal or emotional abuse.

## *Scope of the Problem*

Violent behavior that takes place in a context of dating or courtship is not a rare event. Estimates vary because studies and surveys use different methods and definitions of the problem.

- A review of dating violence research found that prevalence rates of nonsexual, courtship violence range from 9% to 65%, depending on whether threats and emotional or verbal aggression were included in the definition.[1]

- Data from a study of 8th and 9th grade male and female students indicated that 25% had been victims of nonsexual dating violence and 8% had been victims of sexual dating violence.[2]

- Summarizing many studies, the average prevalence rate for nonsexual dating violence is 22% among male and female high school students and 32% among college students. Females are somewhat more likely than males to report being victims of violence.[1]

- In a national study of college students, 27.5% of the women surveyed said that they had suffered rape or attempted rape at least once since age 14.[3] Only 5% of those experiences were reported to the police.[3] The term "hidden rape" has emerged because this survey and many other studies found that sexual assaults are seldom reported to the police.[3, 4, 5, 6, 7]

- Over half of a representative sample of more than 1,000 female students at a large urban university had experienced some form of unwanted sex. Twelve percent of these acts were perpetrated by casual dates and 43% by steady dating partners.[8]

- Studies of college students[9, 10] and high school students[11] suggest that both males and females inflict and receive dating violence in equal proportion, but the motivation for violence by women is more often for defensive purposes.[10, 12] Other studies have found that women and girls were victims of dating violence twice as often as men and boys,[12 13] and that females suffer significantly more injuries than males.[12, 13]

- A recent National Crime Victimization survey found that women were 6 times more likely than men to experience violence at the hands of an intimate partner.[14] Intimate partners include current or former spouses, boyfriends, girlfriends, dating partners, regardless of whether they are cohabiting or not.

- Nearly half of the 500,000 rapes and sexual assaults reported to the police by women of all ages were committed by friends or acquaintances.[14] From 80% to 95% of the rapes that occur on college campuses are committed by someone known to the victim.[8, 15]

## Risk Factors

### *Characteristics of Victims*

- Young women aged 12-18 who are victims of violence are more likely than older women to report that their offenders were acquaintances, friends, or intimate partners.[14]

- The likelihood of becoming a victim of dating violence is associated with having female peers who have been sexually victimized,[16] lower church attendance,[17] greater number of past dating partners,[11] acceptance of dating violence,[11] and personally having experienced a previous sexual assault.[18]

### *Characteristics of Perpetrators*

- Studies have found the following to be associated with sexual assault perpetration: the male having sexually aggressive peers;[18, 19, 20, 21, 22] heavy alcohol or drug use;[23, 24] and the man's acceptance of dating violence,[11] the male's assumption of key roles in dating such as initiating the date, being the driver, and paying dating expenses; miscommunication about sex; previous sexual intimacy with the victim; interpersonal violence, traditional sex roles, adversarial attitudes about relationships, and rape myths.[23, 24]

- Men who have a family history of observing or experiencing abuse are more likely to inflict abuse, violence, and sexual aggression.[16]

- As the consumption of alcohol by either the victim or perpetrator increases, the rate of serious injuries associated with dating violence also increases.[25]

## *References*

1. Sugarman, D. B., and G. T. Hotaling, "Dating Violence: Prevalence, Context and Risk Markers," 3–32. In M. A. Pirog-Good and J. E. Stets, eds. *Violence in Dating Relationships*. New York: Praeger, 1989.

2. Foshee, V. A., G. F. Linder, K. E. Bauman, S. A. Langwick, X. B. Arriaga, J. L. Heath, P. M. McMahon, and S. Bangdiwala. "The Safe Dates Project: Theoretical Basis, Evaluation Design, and Selected Baseline Findings. Youth Violence Prevention: Description and Baseline Data From 13 Evaluation Projects." *American Journal of Preventive Medicine. Supplement* (K. Powell; D. Hawkins, Eds.) 12, 5 (1996): 39–47.

3. Koss, M. P., C. A. Gidycz, and N. Wisniewski. "The Scope of Rape: Incidence and Prevalence of Sexual Aggression and Victimization in a National Sample of Higher Education Students." *Journal of Consulting and Clinical Psychology* 55 (1987): 162–70.

4. Koss, M. P. "The Hidden Rape Victim: Personality, Attitudinal and Situational Characteristics." *Psychology of Women Quarterly* 9 (1985): 193–212.

5. Koss, M. P. "Defending Date Rape." *Journal of Interpersonal Violence* 7, 1 (1992): 121-26.

6. Kilpatrick, D. G., C. L. Best, L. J. Veronen, A. E. Amick, L. A. Villeponteaux, and G. A. Ruff. "Mental Health Correlates of Criminal Victimization: A Random Community Survey." *Journal of Consulting and Clinical Psychology* 53 (1985): 866–73.

7. Russell, D. E. H. *Sexual Exploitation: Rape, Child Sexual Abuse and Workplace Harassment.* Beverly Hills, CA: Sage Publications, 1984.

8. Abbey, A., L. T. Ross, D. Mcduffie, and P. Mcauslan. "Alcohol and Dating Risk Factors for Sexual Assault among College Women." *Psychology of Women Quarterly* 20, 1 (1996): 147–69.

9. Arias, I., M. Samios, and K. Daniel O'Leary. "Prevalence and Correlates of Physical Aggression during Courtship." *Journal of Interpersonal Violence* 2, 1 (March 1987): 82–90.

10. White, J. W., and M. P. Koss. "Courtship Violence: Incidence in a National Sample of Higher Education Students." *Violence and Victims* 6, 4 (1991): 247–56.

11. Gray, H. M., and V. Foshee. "Adolescent Dating Violence: Differences between One-Sided and Mutually Violent Profiles." *Journal of Interpersonal Violence* 12, 1 (1997): 126–41.

12. Makepeace, J. M. "Gender Differences in Courtship Violence Victimization." *Family Relations* 35 (1986): 383–88.

13. Makepeace, J. M. "Life Events, Stress and Courtship Violence." *Family Relations* 32 (1983): 101–09.

14. Bachman, R., and L. E. Saltzman. *Violence Against Women: Estimates from the Redesigned Survey, Bureau of Justice Statistics, Special Report*, U.S. Department of Justice, August 1995.

15. Abbey, A. "Acquaintance Rape and Alcohol Consumption on College Campuses: How Are They Linked?" *College Health* 39 (January 1991): 165–69.

16. Gwartney-Gibbs, P. A., J. Stockard, and S. Bohmer. "Learning Courtship Aggression: The Influence of Parents, Peers and Personal Experiences." *Family Relations* 36 (1987): 276–82.

17. Makepeace, J. M. "Social Factor and Victim-Offender Differences in Courtship Violence." *Family Relations* 36 (1987): 87–91.

18. Ageton, S. *Sexual Assault among Adolescents*. Lexington, MA: Heath, 1983.

19. Adler, C. "An Exploration of Self-Reported Sexually Aggressive Behavior." *Crime and Delinquency* 31 (1985): 301–31.

20. DeKeseredy, W. S. *Woman Abuse in Dating Relationships.* Toronto, CA: Canadian Scholars' Press, 1988.

21. Gwartney-Gibbs, P., and J. Stockard. "Courtship Aggression and Mixed-Sex Peer Groups," 185–204. In M. A. Pirog-Good and J. E. Stets, eds. *Violence in Dating Relationships.* New York, NY: Praeger, 1989.

22. Kanin, E. J. "Date Rapists: Differential Sexual Socialization and Relative Deprivation." *Archives of Sexual Behavior* 14 (1985): 219–31.

23. Kanin, E. J. "Date Rape: Unofficial Criminals and Victims." *Victimology: An International Journal* 9, 1 (1984): 95–108.

24. Muehlenhard, C. L., and M. A. Linton. "Date Rape and Sexual Aggression in Dating Situations: Incidence and Risk Factors." *Journal of Counseling Psychology* 34 (1987): 186–96.

25. Makepeace, J. M. "The Severity of Courtship Violence and the Effectiveness of Individual Precautions. Family Abuse and Its Consequences," 297–311. In Gerald T. Hotaling, David Finkelhor, John T. Kirkpatrick, and Murray A. Straus, eds. *Family Abuse and Its Consequences: New Directions in Research.* Newbury Park, CA: Sage Publications, 1988.

Section 11.3

# *Date Rape*

Brazos County Rape Crisis Center, Inc. Copyright © 1996 Cybercom Corp.
Used by permission.

**Legal definition of sexual assault** says a person commits sexual assault "if that person causes the penetration of the anus, vagina, or mouth of another person with a sexual organ or object, without that person's consent OR causes another person to contact or penetrate the mouth, anus, or sexual organ of another person without their consent."

**Date rape follows the same motivation as rape by a stranger.** It is an expression of anger, power, dominance and control; not sexual frustration. Some rapists prefer to know their victims. They are able to get closer to them or trap them in a vulnerable position without arousing alarm. They may also have access to certain information about them—whether they live alone, when they're alone, and their routines. The rapist gains the confidence and trust of his intended victim and manipulates it to isolate and violate her. The advantages of this type of assault for the offender include: her trust, reluctance on her part to practice caution for fear of offending him, and the information he possesses. All of these make the attack easier. One added disadvantage for the victim is that she is often unable to identify the extent of the danger until she is past a safety point.

During the intrusion stage by an acquaintance rapist, he may use unwanted touches, uncomfortable looks or very personal conversation. At this stage, he is not usually threatening. He is testing the waters. During the desensitization stage, he senses that she is used to his intrusions, has dropped her guard, and has accepted his behavior as natural for him. She tries to push aside the sensation of uneasiness. At the point of the isolation stage, he has her alone. She may have been raised to be polite and accept the preferences of her date. She may not want to hurt his feelings. Suppression of her feelings and true fears may be something she has learned to do. Women who might otherwise react assertively to the same situation with a stranger may be quite passive with a date.

**Some danger signals to watch for:** A man who doesn't listen or chooses to ignore your limits is not sensitive to your needs. This is a sign of a man for whom consent is not important in physical intimacy. If anger is a typical response when limits are set and is repeated, this may be a man who cannot allow women to counter him. The man may be a power tripper.

Other signs include:

- Jealousy
- Blames others for his problems/feelings
- Possessiveness
- Cruelty to animals or children
- Verbal abuse
- Sudden mood changes
- Threats of violence
- Breaking objects
- Unrealistic expectations of himself and others
- Isolation of victim from resources
- Any force used during an argument.

## Date Rape Myths Vs. Realities

**Myth:** It's not as bad if she knows him.

**Reality:** It is no less traumatic, threatening or dangerous if she knows her attacker. It may cause deeper and longer lasting emotional and psychological effects due to the betrayal of trust and manipulation.

**Myth:** If she doesn't report the attack, it isn't rape.

**Reality:** Most victims of date rape don't report it since he most likely used coercion and manipulation rather than physical violence. She may have no outward signs of the abuse. She fears she will not be believed.

**Myth:** If she didn't resist, it wasn't rape.

**Reality:** She may not physically resist for a number of reasons—he catches her by surprise, she fears for her life or serious injury, or he is a friend and she doesn't want to hurt him. Texas law recognizes psychological coercion as a weapon and does not require resistance if she believes he can carry out his threats and she "earnestly resists" the attack.

**Myth:** When she says "NO", she really means yes or maybe.

**Reality:** She means "NO". This myth underlies the societal attitudes that perpetuates an atmosphere that allows and even encourages date rape.

**Myth:** If he paid for dinner and a show, she owes him something in return.

**Reality:** Rigid sex role stereotyping that still exists in dating situations puts unnecessary stress and rules for behavior on both the male and female. There is no excuse for forced sex.

**Myth:** It's not rape if she is too drunk to give consent.

**Reality:** In fact, because the legal definition of rape deals with "consent", sexual contact with someone too drunk to be capable of giving permission is technically a crime.

## Who Can Date Rape Happen to?

Our teenaged children, college women, men, or a woman who dates or socializes with male friends—*anyone!*

## Where Can It Happen?

At school, at home, in the car, at a party—*anywhere!*

The victims of date rape have been much overlooked and misrepresented by the system.

The victim of an acquaintance rape suffers as much, if not more, trauma than the individual victimized by a stranger. Due to societal attitudes, the victim of acquaintance rape usually does not report the crime or seek help. Victims tend to feel ashamed, guilty, depressed, and angry at themselves. The trust and integrity of a relationship has been shattered. They feel betrayed by their own judgment. Victims may find themselves in the position of having to face their assailant again, particularly in school and work settings.

*Let someone assist you through the stages of recovery.*

## *Here Are Some Dating Tips to Remember:*

- Find out as much as possible about your date, particularly if he is a blind date or someone you do not know well.

- Consider double-dating the first few times you go out with a male with whom you are not well acquainted.

- Know beforehand the exact plans for the evening, and make sure a parent or a friend knows these plans and what time to expect you home.

- Be aware of your decreased ability to react under the influence of alcohol or drugs.

- Think carefully about leaving a party or gathering with a man you may not know well. If you do leave with someone, make sure you tell another person you are leaving and with whom.

- Avoid out-of-the-way or secluded areas.

- Trust your instincts! If the situation makes you uncomfortable, try to be calm and think of ways to remove yourself from the situation.

- Examine how you behave with men, especially those behaviors that could be misinterpreted.

- Assert yourself when necessary. Be firm and straightforward in your relationships with men. When you say *NO*, say it loudly and clearly and make sure he understands your resistance.

# Section 11.4

# *Date Rape Drugs*

Brazos County Rape Crisis Center, Inc. Copyright © 1996 Cybercom Corp.
Used by permission.

Recently there have been a number of reports of sexual assault in which drugs and/or other substances have been slipped into people's beverages. For centuries, rapists have used alcohol to sedate their victims. Today, they can use a wide variety of substances to commit crimes of assault.

Clearly, substance-related rape poses unique difficulties for both survivors and for those trying to reduce their risk of assault. Rape crisis counselors and others involved with helping survivors of sexual assault need to be armed with information that may help survivors and also reduce the risk of this crime. The general advice provided here applies to sexual assault involving any substance. It is important to recognize, however, that different substances, when misused in this way, can produce very different health risks.

## *Emotional Effects of Substance-Related Rape*

Rape survivors assaulted under the influence of a sedating substance will have additional issues that are likely to affect their recovery—issues oftentimes involving their inability to recall the incident.

Because survivors will have been heavily sedated, they may not have complete recall of the assault. It is likely that they will be uncertain about exactly what happened and who was involved. The "unknowns" may create tremendous anxiety as survivors are left to fill in the gaps with their imagination. This dynamic exacerbates the loss of control that most survivors feel and that they must overcome in their healing process.

Survivors may not know the identity of their assailants, so added to their concerns is the question: "Whom should they fear?" While most survivors have fears regarding their perpetrator, someone assaulted under the influence of a sedating substance will have more generalized fear. They may find themselves looking at men in various settings wondering, "Is he the one...?"

214

Eventually, survivors must come to terms with the fact that they likely will never be able to fill in those missing pieces. The questions may remain unanswered. Coming to this resolution is not unlike the process experienced by adult survivors of childhood sexual abuse who have only partial recall of repressed memories.

Additionally, the inability to recall important facts makes prosecution of these crimes extremely difficult. While law enforcement personnel are becoming more aware of the misuse of sedating substances and their effects on victims, there may continue to be some skepticism on the part of those unfamiliar, or inexperienced, in dealing with these types of crimes.

## Reducing the Risk of Substance-Related Rape

People can take a number of precautions to reduce their risks:

1. Do not leave beverages unattended.

2. Do not take any beverages, including alcohol, from someone you do not know well and trust.

3. At a bar or club, accept drinks only from the bartender, waiter or waitress.

4. At parties, do not accept open container drinks from anyone.

5. Be alert to the behavior of friends. Anyone appearing disproportionately inebriated in relation to the amount of alcohol they have consumed may be in danger.

6. Anyone who believes they have consumed a sedative-like substance should be driven to a hospital emergency room or should call 911 for an ambulance. Try to keep a sample of the beverage for analysis.

## Actions to Take if Someone Has Been Drugged

Someone who experiences dizziness, confusion or other sudden and unexplained symptoms after drinking a beverage should call a family member, friend, the police, a doctor, or 911 for help in getting them to a hospital emergency room.

If someone believes they have been raped or sexually assaulted, they should:

1.  Get to a safe place and call a rape crisis center if they want information or support. For a toll-free rape crisis hotline, survivors can call 1-800-656-4673.

2.  Determine whether or not they want to report to the police. If there is any chance they want to report the assault, they should not shower, bathe, douche, change clothes, or straighten up the area until the medical and legal evidence has been collected.

3.  If they choose to report, they should first call the police and then go to the hospital to have the medical evidence collection (rape kit exam) done.

4.  Go to a hospital, clinic, or private doctor for treatment of external and/or internal injuries, tests for pregnancy and sexually transmitted diseases, and support services.

5.  Request a urine test for the presence of sedating substances as soon as possible. The screening should test for Gamma Hydroxybutyrate (GHB), flunitrazepam (Rohypnol) and other drugs. Every hour matters. Chances of getting proof are best when the sample is obtained soon after the substance has been ingested.

## Sedating Substances

For years, rape crisis centers have been dealing with substance-related rape, particularly those involving alcohol. But recent media coverage has focused largely on two sedating substances: Gamma Hydroxybutyrate (GHB), a central nervous system depressant that has been investigated as an anesthetic and for treatment of narcolepsy and alcoholism, and Rohypnol (flunitrazepam), a prescription sleeping medication available outside the United States.

Although there has been considerable media attention on these two substances, it is important to recognize that many other substances can be misused to commit these crimes as well. In investigating any case of sexual assault, there is a need to fully explore the possibility that any number of substances may have been used.

## Physical Effects of Sedating Substances

There are several telltale signs that an individual has been drugged. If an individual appears disproportionately inebriated in relation to the amount of alcohol they have consumed, they may have unknowingly ingested one of any number of substances. Sedating substances can temporarily inhibit a person's ability to remain awake and conscious. Someone who has been sedated may experience sudden and unexplained drowsiness and have trouble with motor coordination. Other possible effects include impaired judgment, disinhibition, dizziness, and confusion.

Brief periods of impaired memory also may result from the misuse of sedating substances. This means the person who has been raped may not remember the details of what happened while under the drug's influence. Depending on the drug and the presence of other substances in the person's system, more dangerous side effects may occur.

Even marginally increased doses of GHB have been reported to result in severe adverse effects. These include slowed heart beat, decreased respiratory effort, unconsciousness, seizure-like activity, and coma. Such effects can appear within fifteen minutes of oral ingestion of the drug, and acute symptoms appear to decrease after three to four hours. As with most substances, health risks increase sharply when GHB is mixed with other drugs and/or alcohol. (G.P. Galloway, et al. "Gamma-hydroxybutyrate." *CSAM News: Newsletter of the California Society of Addiction Medicine*, 23, 1 [Summer 1996]: 1.)

## Facts on Rohypnol

Rohypnol is a medication that is prescribed by physicians in more than 64 countries for people with severe and debilitating sleep disorders. It also is used in a number of countries as a preanesthetic before surgery or other medical procedures. Rohypnol is manufactured in Europe, Asia Pacific, and Latin America by the Swiss-based pharmaceutical company F. Hoffmann-La Roche Ltd. for medical use in those countries where it has been approved. Hoffmann La Roche never sought U.S. Food and Drug Administration approval for Rohypnol in the United States. The medication therefore is not marketed in this country. Drug traffickers, however, are illegally smuggling Rohypnol into the United States from Mexico and South America and are selling it as a "street drug." Common street names for Rohypnol include Roofies, Roachies, La Rocha, the forget pill, and the date rape drug.

On March 5, 1996, the U.S. Customs Service announced a ban on the importation of Rohypnol into the United States, which has begun to have a significant impact on reducing the illegal importation. As efforts to end the diversion of Rohypnol are being implemented, however, there have been reports that other substances, such as GHB, are being used similarly in sexual assault situations.

As a sleeping medication, Rohypnol produces a sedating effect. This property can be enhanced by the dosage, the individual's sensitivity to the medication, and the presence of alcohol. Generally, Rohypnol's effects begin within 20 to 30 minutes of ingestion. The medication's strongest effects occur within one to two hours. Rohypnol's overall sedating effects usually last six to eight hours following a 2 mg. dose. Impaired ability to remember details of events is more likely to occur with larger doses, and particularly when ingested with alcohol and/or other drugs or central nervous system depressants.

As with many other drugs, Rohypnol becomes extremely dangerous when mixed with alcohol, narcotic drugs, and/or other central nervous system depressants. This combination is potentially life-threatening and can be fatal.

## Proving a Substance-Related Rape

Anyone who thinks they have been drugged should ask the rape crisis center, the hospital emergency room, or the police to run a urine test as soon as possible. Most substances can be detected through appropriate drug testing. The findings of such tests can provide valuable evidence in a court of law if the rape survivor chooses to prosecute the case.

Hoffman-La Roche has made available a drug testing service for cases of sexual assault in which Rohypnol is believed to be involved. The testing service is free of charge, and the urine sample is handled by an independent, National Institute on Drug Abuse (NIDA)-approved laboratory that follows appropriate chain-of-custody procedures so the findings can be used by the rape survivor in court. Tests show that Rohypnol can be found in the urine for 72 hours after ingestion, and may be present even longer, depending on the person's metabolism and dose.

Because the test results are returned by the laboratory to the rape crisis center, hospital or police department that submitted the sample, the strict confidentiality of the rape survivor's identity can be maintained. Rape survivors should be informed that the urine test for flunitrazepam also tests for the presence of other benzodiazepines (the family of compounds to which flunitrazepam belongs), as well as for marijuana, cocaine, and some opiates and barbiturates.

To access the testing service, rape crisis centers, medical or police personnel can call Hoffmann-La Roche at 1-800-608-6540.

# Chapter 12

# *Safety Strategies*

## *Chapter Contents*

Section 12.1

# How Survivors Cope

Mid-Valley Women's Crisis Center, Salem, Ore. Copyright © 1996.
Used with permission.

Women and children who survive domestic violence have talked about the various ways they developed to cope until they found safety. The coping strategies they worked out enabled them to survive.

Some of the most common coping strategies are:

**Denial.** The survivor tells herself, in effect, that the abuse isn't really happening. A survivor in denial will say, "This bruise? Oh, it's nothing" or "He doesn't really hurt me." Denial helps the survivor avoid feelings of terror and humiliation.

**Minimization.** This is a form of denial. The survivor minimizes when she says, "This isn't really abuse. Abuse is more serious" or "Well, he only hit me once with his fist."

**Nightmares.** These help the survivor experience some strong feelings such as fear, anger, panic, and shame which she cannot safely share with anyone at the time.

**Shock and dissociation.** These two reactions can numb the survivor's mind and body while the assault takes place and for a time afterward. The reactions help her avoid dealing with immediate feelings until she has found safety.

Even after the survivor finds safety and supportive people, she may continue to use these coping strategies until she realizes they are neither necessary nor helpful any more. At that point, the survivor may be interested in receiving counseling or other support services.

## The Separation Cycle

When a woman leaves her abuser, the abuser goes through a process of emotions and behaviors that is quite predictable. This is the separation process:

**Indifference.** At first, the batterer says such things as, "Go ahead and leave. I don't care. I've got lots of women after me. I don't need you."

**Manipulative anger.** Now the batterer shows his "anger." Anger is a tool batterers use to gain and maintain control. If there are children in the family, for instance, he may say his anger is because the survivor is keeping the children from him, and "I have a right to see my kids."

**Manipulative Courting.** The abuser tries to hook the victim back into the relationship—and succeeds in more than a few cases. The abuser begins to court the survivor again, perhaps with a trip down memory lane: "Remember when we met?" "Remember when the baby was born?" He also promises to change: "I'll quit drinking." "I'll get counseling." He won't discuss the abuse; he will talk only about past good times and the promise of good times to come. He says he wants her back.

**Defaming the survivor.** He tells lies about the survivor to everyone who knows her. The goal is to isolate her socially and to wipe out any support she might have among friends and family. Many times, the woman does not know about the lies. One of the most common lies is that the woman was having an affair, a lie that he can use to justify his violent behavior.

**Renewed manipulative anger.** Once he recognizes the survivor is not coming back to him, he renews his manipulative anger. *The victim is in danger.* The abuser is likely to carry out threats he made during the relationship and earlier in the separation cycle.

# Section 12.2

# *Getting Help: Finding Shelter*

Excerpted from Center on Crime, Communities & Culture. (1999). *Domestic Violence: National Directory of Professional Services.* New York, NY: Open Society Institute. Used with permission.

Battered women who decide to leave their abusers can turn to friends, family, or women's shelters for refuge. Every state has a domestic violence coalition office that serves as a resource for local shelters, heightens public awareness of the issue, and makes referrals for women in crisis. Local shelters may be large or small buildings within the community that may or may not offer a range of services to women and their children depending on outside funding. Privacy and confidentiality are maintained and strict rules are enforced in order to guarantee the residents' safety.

## How to Get Help for Victims

The following is a general description of the steps a battered woman must follow in order to be placed in a shelter. First, she must get away from her abuser long enough to be able to call the hotline, state coalition, or local service provider for a referral to a shelter. This step alone can be upsetting or frustrating, as she will most likely be asked a series of very personal questions about her life in order for the shelter to determine her suitability for placement.* She may be referred to several other agencies before making contact with someone who can address her particular needs. When she is successful in getting through to a shelter, the woman is given an intake interview either over the phone or in person which can take up to an hour. At this point, she will be referred to a shelter that has a bed or she may be told to try again in the future.

---

* Some of the questions she is most likely to be asked are: What was the nature of her relationship to her abuser? Is she safe right now? Is she receiving public assistance or does she have any source of income? If she has children, she will be asked if they have been abused and, if so, physically or sexually? The shelter will ask these and other similar questions on intake, including, Is she on any medications or using narcotics?

If she is successful in being placed in a shelter, the woman is then reinterviewed at the shelter where 'house rules' are explained—such as what time the doors are locked and whether or not clients must vacate the premises during the day. Other issues that come into play are: whether or not the shelter can accommodate children, what types of counseling may be arranged for her, and whether or not the state in which the shelter is located will agree to accept a resident from out-of-state who is welfare-dependent and taking up a bed that could otherwise be occupied by an in-state resident on welfare. A woman who is able to work while she is in the shelter will be informed of the amount she will be expected to pay to cover expenses. This can range from $25 to $75 per night.

If a client has stayed in the shelter for the maximum time allotted (usually 90 days), a new complexity is added to the situation. She will then have to decide to either return to her place of residence where her abuser is most likely still living, or she has to make financial arrangements to provide for herself and any children she has with her. Women who are being abused often conclude that they have no option but to return home to face a difficult but known situation instead of going into society on their own with little or no way to provide for themselves or their children. A third option is for women to take on a whole new identity, including obtaining a new social security number. [*See* Sections 12.9 and 12.10.] This can be a complicated process but may afford some protection for those women whose abusers are misusing a social security number for the purpose of continuing to harass or cause harm.

# Section 12.3

# *Domestic Violence: Safety Plan Guidelines*

National Center for Victims of Crime, *INFOLINK* Publication No. 15.
Copyright © 1997. Used with permission.

These safety suggestions have been compiled from safety plans distributed by state domestic violence coalitions from around the country. Following these suggestions is **not a guarantee** of safety, but could help to improve your safety situation.

## *Personal Safety with an Abuser*

1.  Identify your partner's use and level of force so that you can assess danger to you and your children before it occurs. If an abusive situation seems likely, try to diffuse your partner's anger. Swallow your pride, if necessary, and agree with your partner to avoid an episode of violence.

2.  Try to avoid an abusive situation by leaving. Go for a walk, and let your partner cool down.

3.  Identify safe areas of the house where there are no weapons and there are always ways of escape. If arguments occur, try to move to those areas.

4.  Don't run to where the children are as your partner may hurt them as well.

5.  If violence is unavoidable, make yourself a small target; dive into a corner and curl up into a ball with your face protected and arms around each side of your head, fingers entwined.

6.  If possible, have a phone accessible at all times and know the numbers to call for help. Know where the nearest pay phone is located. Know your local battered women's shelter number. Don't be afraid to call the police.

7. Let trusted friends and neighbors know of your situation and develop a plan and visual signal [or code word] for when you need help.

8. Teach your children how to get help. Instruct them not to get involved in the violence between you and your partner. Plan a code word to signal to them that they should get help.

9. Tell your children that violence is never right, even when someone they love is being violent. Tell them that neither you nor they are at fault or cause the violence, and that when your partner is being violent it is important to keep yourselves safe.

10. Practice how to get out safely. Practice with your children.

11. Plan for what you will do if your children tell your partner of your plan or if your partner otherwise finds out about your plan.

12. Keep weapons like guns and knives locked up and as inaccessible as possible.

13. Make a habit of backing the car into the driveway and keep it fueled. Keep the driver's door unlocked and others locked—for a quick escape.

14. Develop the habit of not wearing scarves or long jewelry that could be used to strangle you.

15. Have several plausible reasons for leaving the house at different times of the day or night.

## Getting Ready to Leave

1. Keep any evidence of physical abuse, such as pictures, etc.

2. Know where you can go to get help; tell someone what is happening to you.

3. If you are injured, go to a doctor or an emergency room and report what happened to you. Ask that they document your visit.

4. Plan with your children and identify a safe place for them (for example, a room with a lock or a friend's house where they

can go for help). Reassure them that their job is to stay safe, not to protect you.

5. Contact your local battered women's shelter and find out about laws and other resources available to you before you have to use them during a crisis.

6. Keep a journal of all violent incidences.

7. Acquire job skills as you can, such as learning to type or taking courses at a community college.

## General Guidelines for Leaving an Abusive Relationship

1. You may request a police stand-by or escort while you leave.

2. If you need to sneak away, be prepared:
   - Make a plan for how and where you will escape;
   - Plan for a quick escape;
   - Put aside emergency money as you can;
   - Hide an extra set of car keys; and
   - Pack an extra set of clothes for yourself and your children and store them at a trusted friend or neighbor's house. Try to avoid using next-door neighbors, close family members and mutual friends.

3. Take with you important phone numbers of friends, relatives, doctors, schools, etc., as well as other important items, including:
   - Driver's license;
   - Regularly needed medication;
   - List of credit cards held by self or jointly, or the credit cards themselves if you have access to them;
   - Pay stubs; and
   - Checkbooks and information about bank accounts and other assets.

   If time is available, also take:
   - Citizenship documents (such as your passport, greencard, etc.);

- Titles, deeds and other property information;
- Medical records;
- Children's school records and immunization records;
- Insurance information;
- Copy of marriage license, birth certificates, will and other legal documents;
- Verification of social security numbers;
- Welfare identification; and
- Valued pictures, jewelry, or personal possessions.

4. Create a false trail. Call motels, real estate agencies, schools in a town at least six hours away from where you actually are located. Ask questions that require a call back to your house in order to leave phone numbers on record.

## *After Leaving the Abusive Relationship*

1. If getting a restraining order and the offender is leaving:
   - Change locks and phone number;
   - Change work hours and route taken to work;
   - Change route taken to take kids to school;
   - Keep restraining order in a safe place;
   - Inform friend, neighbor and employers that you have a restraining order in effect; and
   - Call police to enforce the order.

2. If you leave:
   - Consider renting a post office box for your mail or using the address of a friend;
   - Be aware that addresses are on restraining orders and police reports;
   - Be careful to whom you give your new address and phone number; and
   - Change your work hours if possible.

3. Alert school authorities of situation.

4. Consider changing your children's schools.

5.  Reschedule appointments that offender is aware of when you leave.

6.  Use different stores and frequent different social spots.

7.  Alert neighbors and request that they call the police if they feel you may be in danger.

8.  Talk to trusted people about the violence.

9.  Replace wooden doors with steel or metal doors. Install security systems if possible.

10. Install a lighting system that lights up when a person is coming close to the house (motion-sensitive lights).

11. Tell people you work with about the situation and get your calls screened.

12. Tell people who take care of your children who is allowed to pick up the children and that your partner is not allowed to do so.

13. Call telephone company about caller ID. Ask that your phone be blocked so that if you call, neither your partner nor anyone else will be able to get your new, unlisted phone number.

## Section 12.4

# *More Safety Planning Tips, Plus Documenting Evidence*

Excerpted from *Understanding Domestic Violence: A Handbook for Victims and Professionals*. U.S. Department of Justice, n.d.

### Safety During a Violent Incident

- If an argument seems unavoidable, try to have it in a place without any weapons (e.g., especially those in the kitchen) and where you will have a way to leave.

- Use the signal or code word you trained your children or neighbors to respond to!

- Be aware of any different or strange behavior of the abuser during and after arguments/fights. Write everything down when you are safe.

- Use your own instincts and judgment. Do what you have to do to avoid injury and report the assault when you are safe. If necessary you can pretend to faint or pass out. If friends and family have repeatedly told you that the abuser may kill you some day, you may have become numb to the dangers of the violence. You should take extra precautions even when you don't really seem to be worried about being seriously injured.

- Always remember—You don't deserve to be hit or threatened!

## Safety When Preparing to Leave—Especially if You Are Being Stalked

Victims of domestic violence frequently leave the residence they share with the battering partner. Leaving must be done carefully in order to increase safety. Abusers often strike back when they believe that a victim is leaving a relationship. Frequently, there is a critical period after the relationship has been ended in which it becomes clear whether or not the abuser is going to continue pursuing or stalking the victim.

- Consider staying with friends/relatives temporarily until it is clear that the abuser is not going to try to stalk you. If the abuser does stalk you, try to be with someone as much as possible—especially when leaving from your house, your work, or places where the abuser knows your routine. If you must be alone, report to a friend/family about where you are, when you are leaving and when you should be back.

- Change the locks (preferably use double key dead bolts) as soon as possible. Buy additional locks and safety devices to secure your windows and doors.

- Consider if any/all of the following will increase your security: alarm system; dog; bars on your windows; the alarm that hearing impaired people sometimes use.

- Go to the nearest police district or precinct to apply for SPE-CIAL ATTENTION. This tells the police that they should watch your house more closely and alerts them that you feel threatened by the abuser. You can also ask them to come through your neighborhood at specified times (e.g., when you are leaving home or returning home from work).

- Be aware of your surroundings. Before leaving your home or work, look outside to ensure that abuser is not there. If you are entering your home, ask someone else to enter with you and check to see if the abuser has somehow gotten inside.

- Make sure a carefully thought out safety plan has been rehearsed and worked out with your children. Make sure that this plan does not put the children in danger.

- Find someone in the criminal justice system who seems to know the system well who can help inform you of steps to take for your safety. If you find a particularly good police officer, advocate, prosecutor to help you, keep them informed about what is happening. If you are being stalked, it is critical that you follow instructions for collecting evidence so that the police can respond in the most effective manner.

- Write down all harassment in a journal with names, dates, type of harassment and time, State the nature of the harassment. (See the section entitled "Documenting Evidence" on the next page.) Writing everything down is critical in cases where the abuser is really persistent and is clever about the law.

- Go to the police station and give them copies of all police reports——make any relevant law enforcement officials aware of what is going on.

- Take a self-defense class.

## What to Do if Your Abuser Is Extremely Dangerous, Resourceful, and Persistent

- Consider leaving when the abuser least expects you to (when everything has calmed down). Never give the abuser any clue that you are getting ready to leave.

- Consider that you may be putting friends/family into danger by staying with them if the abuser knows where to find you.

- If you can, go to a shelter for battered women in your neighborhood or in a different neighborhood.
- Go to friends/relatives out of town that abuser doesn't know about.
- Change your housing location.
- Contact your housing development authorities and ask to be transferred.
- Move to another apartment—don't list your phone number.
- In situations where you are working closely with a prosecutor, you could ask the prosecutor if you are eligible for witness protection.
- Look for an apartment to live in that has the following:
  - Underground parking.
  - Security system.
  - Security staff.
  - High rise so that abuser can't get in the windows.
  - Allows you to have a watch dog.
  - Deadbolt locks.

## Documenting Evidence

It is extremely important to keep track of evidence. Evidence may consist of photographs of injuries, past court documents such as protection or restraining orders, or prior arrest warrants or any medical records. Evidence helps the prosecuting attorney convict the defendant.

- Have a voice-activated microcassette tape recorder. If you think there is a chance of any verbal abuse, threats, or assaults, make sure you have the tape recorder with you. If possible, record such conversations.
- Keep a journal—with dates giving information about what happened and who witnessed it.
- Take photographs of injuries, and put your name and the date on the photographs.
- When receiving medical treatment for injuries sustained from domestic violence, make sure to tell the doctor to write down what happened using the name of the abuser.
- Keep copies of all court-related documents.

- Whenever you talk to the police, ask officers/detectives/officials for their cards, get their names, phone numbers, police district/precinct, police report numbers, and copies of reports. Try to make sure you understand what they are doing and whether or not you need to follow up with anything. During an incident, make sure you know whether or not they have filed a report. If you find someone particularly helpful, try to work more closely with them.

- Screen your phone calls and save messages where the abuser is harassing or threatening you.

- Buy a microphone with a suction cup that goes on your phone which will enable you to tape record any phone conversations. If you are tape recording a call, try to get the abuser to state their name and facts about past criminal incidents if you are being harassed by phone.

- Phone safety

  — Make sure your phone number is unlisted.

  — If possible obtain caller ID, so you can prepare for or avoid harassing phone calls.

  — When you receive threatening or harassing mail from the batterer, don't throw it away. Make a copy of the envelope and the letter and give the original to the police.

## Safety and Substance Abuse

- Substance abuse by either the batterer or the victim increases the risk of severe or deadly injuries. If you are using drugs or alcohol, you may not be aware of the danger you or your children may be in. You may not be able to protect your children from the violence and may expose them to harmful situations. We recommend getting help for yourself if you are abusing drugs.

- If both you and your abuser are addicted to drugs, your children are in danger of being seriously harmed. Consider having a relative take care of them. You may need to have them placed in foster care until you can address the problem.

- If the abuser is high on drugs or alcohol, we recommend leaving the area or having another person who can protect you present. Remember only the batterer can decide to get help for him/herself—you are not responsible for making sure s/he recovers. Besides, taking responsibility for the batterer may backfire. The abuser may start to feel protected from the consequences of his or her actions rather than seek help.

- Read up on the problems related to the drug the abuser is using. Particularly dangerous substances that often lead to excessive violence are crack/cocaine, PCP, and chronic alcohol abuse.

## Section 12.5

# *Safety Planning for Children Exposed to Domestic Abuse*

Excerpted from *Understanding Domestic Violence: A Handbook for Victims and Professionals.* U.S. Department of Justice, n.d.

As a parent or caretaker, you can talk about safety with your child. Here are some suggestions.

- **Help your child understand signals or cues that the abuser may become violent.** Help child identify ways you and your partner were acting prior to fights. Child may remember drugs/alcohol were involved or notice patterns (e.g., time of day/week, topics associated with fights). Factors related to the onset of violence are warning signs.

- **Identification of the child's response and outcome of this action.** Help child in identifying how they reacted in the past, such as yelling at abusive parent, running away, attempting to protect their mother, withdrawing, calling the police, etc. Consider the outcome of these actions. Was the child injured while attempting to protect their parent/family member?

- **Formulation of options and a plan of action.** Based on the previously gathered information help children identify immediate steps to protect themselves. Plan could include having the child call the police or person who is available 24 hours a day. Younger children can be encouraged to hide someplace safe in the home, or run next door and tell someone they trust. The child can identify a password or signal to use with the nonabusive parent or supportive persons outside of the home to alert them of trouble. If the child wants to have the plan written down, the child should be asked to identify a place where the plan can be kept and where the abusive parent is unlikely to discover it.

## Teach Your Children to Follow the Rules in This "Children's Safety Plan."

- Call 911 if you feel someone in your family might get hurt. Even if you only dial 911 and hang up, the police will have to call back or come and check on your family.

- Find a safe place to go (not the kitchen or bathroom) like a bedroom or a neighbor's or friend's home.

- Do not get in the middle of a physical fight. This may cause the violence or anger to increase or turns towards you. You could get hurt.

- Help yourself by finding someone you can trust and talk about your problems with, such as a teacher, minister, babysitter, counselor at school, etc. Talking about your feelings can make you feel better.

- Do not blame or attack either parent, because doing so may call attention to you and you may get hurt.

# Section 12.6

## *Personalized Safety Plan*

Barbara J. Hart and Jane Stuehling, Pennsylvania Coalition Against Domestic Violence, copyright © 1992. Used with permission.

*The following steps represent my plan for increasing my safety and preparing in advance for the possibility for further violence. Although I do not have control over my partner's violence, I do have a choice about **how** to respond to him / her and how to best get myself and my children to safety.*

Name: _____

Date: _____

Review dates: _____

_____

_____

**Step 1: Safety during a violent incident.** Women cannot always avoid violent incidents. In order to increase safety, battered women may use a variety of strategies.

I can use some or all of the following strategies:

A. If I decide to leave, I will _____.
(Practice how to get out safely. What doors, windows, elevators, stairwells or fire escapes would you use?)

B. I can keep my purse and car keys ready and put them (place) _____ in order to leave quickly.

C. I can tell_____ about the violence and request they call the police if they hear suspicious noises coming from my house.

I can also tell _____ about the violence and request they call the police if they hear suspicious noises coming from my house.

D. I can teach my children how to use the telephone to contact the police and the fire department.

E. I will use _____ as my code word with my children or my friends so they can call for help.

F. If I have to leave my home, I will go _____ (Decide this even if you don't think there will be a next time.)

If I cannot go to the location above, then I can go to
_____ or _____.

G. I can also teach some of these strategies to some/all of my children.

H. When I expect we are going to have an argument, I will try to move to a space that is lowest risk, such as _____. (Try to avoid arguments in the bathroom, garage, kitchens, near weapons or in rooms without access to an outside door.)

I. I will use my judgment and intuition. If the situation is very serious, I can give my partner what he/she wants to calm him/her down. I have to protect myself until I/we are out of danger.

**Step 2: Safety when preparing to leave.** Battered women frequently leave the residence they share with the battering partner. Leaving must be done with a careful plan in order to increase safety. Batterers often strike back when they believe that a battered woman is leaving a relationship.

I can use some or all of the following safety strategies:

A. I will leave money and an extra set of keys with _____ _____ so I can leave quickly.

B. I will keep copies of important documents or keys at _____ _____.

C. I will open a savings account by _____, to increase my independence.

D. Other things I can do to increase my independence include:

_____

_____

_____

_____

E. The domestic violence program's hotline number is
_____. I can seek shelter by calling this hotline.

F. I can keep change for phone calls on me at all times. I understand that if I use my telephone credit card, the following month the telephone bill will tell my batterer those numbers that I called after I left. To keep my telephone communications confidential, I must either use coins or I might get a friend to permit me to use their telephone credit card for a limited time when I first leave.

G. I will check with _____and _____
_____to see who would be able to let me stay with them or lend me some money.

H. I can leave extra clothes with _____.

I. I will sit down and review my safety plan every _____
_____ in order to plan the safest way to leave the residence. _____(domestic violence advocate or friend) has agreed to help me review this plan.

J. I will rehearse my escape plan and, as appropriate, practice it with my children.

**Step 3: Safety in my own residence.** There are many things that a woman can do to increase her safety in her own residence. It may be impossible to do everything at once, but safety measures can be added step by step.

Safety measures I can use include:

A. I can change the locks on my doors and windows as soon as possible.

B. I can replace wooden doors with steel/metal doors.

C. I can install security systems including additional locks, window bars, poles to wedge against doors, an electronic system, etc.

D. I can purchase rope ladders to be used for escape from second floor windows.

E. I can install smoke detectors and purchase fire extinguishers for each floor in my house/apartment.

F.  I can install an outside lighting system that lights up when a person is coming close to my house.

G.  I will teach my children how to use the telephone to make a collect call to me and to _____ (friend/ minister/other) in the event that my partner takes the children.

H.  I will tell people who take care of my children which people have permission to pick up my children and that my partner is not permitted to do so. The people I will inform about pick-up permission include:

_____ (school),

_____ (day care staff),

_____ (babysitter),

_____ (Sunday school teacher),

_____ (teacher),

and _____

_____ (others).

I.  I can inform _____ (neighbor),

_____ (pastor), and

_____ (friend) that my partner no longer resides with me and they should call the police if he is observed near my residence.

**Step 4. Safety with a protection order.** Many batterers obey protection orders, but one can never be sure which violent partner will obey and which will violate protection orders. I recognize that I may need to ask the police and the courts to enforce my protection order.

The following are some steps that I can take to help the enforcement of my protection order:

A.  I will keep my protection orders (location). (Always keep it on or near your person. If you change purses, that's the first thing that should go in.)

B. I will give my protection order to police departments in the community where I work, in those communities where I usually visit family or friends, and in the community where I live.

C. There should be a county registry of protection orders that all police departments can call to confirm a protection order. I can check to make sure that my order is in the registry. The telephone number for the county registry of protection orders is: _____.

D. For further safety, if I often visit other counties, I might file my protection order with the court in those counties. I will register my protection order in the following counties: _____ and _____.

E. I can call the local domestic violence program if I am not sure about B., C., or D. above or if I have some problem with my protection order.

F. I will inform my employer, my minister, my closest friend and _____and _____ that I have a protection order in effect.

G. If my partner destroys my protection order, I can get another copy from the courthouse by going to the Office of the Prothonotary located at _____.

H. If my partner violates the protection order, I can call the police and report a violation, contact my attorney, call my advocate, and/or advise the court of the violation.

I. If the police do not help, I can contact my advocate or attorney and will file a complaint with the chief of the police department.

J. I can also file a private criminal complaint with the district justice in the jurisdiction where the violation occurred or with the district attorney. I can charge my battering partner with a violation of the protection order and all the crimes that he commits in violating the order. I can call the domestic violence advocate to help me with this.

**Step 5: Safety on the job and in public.** Each battered woman must decide if and when she will tell others that her partner has battered her and that she may be at continued risk. Friends, family and co-workers can help to protect women. Each woman should consider carefully which people to invite to help secure her safety.

I might do any or all of the following:

A.  I can inform my boss, the security supervisor and _____ _____at work of my situation.

B.  I can ask _____to help screen my telephone calls at work.

C.  When leaving work, I can _____ _____.

D.  When driving home if problems occur, I can_____ _____.

E.  If I use public transit, I can _____ _____.

F.  I can use different grocery stores and shopping malls to conduct my business and shop at hours that are different than those when residing with my battering partner.

G.  I can use a different bank and take care of my banking at hours different from those I used when residing with my battering partner.

H.  I can also _____.

**Step 6: Safety and drug or alcohol use.** Most people in this culture use alcohol. Many use mood-altering drugs. Much of this use is legal and some is not. The legal outcomes of using illegal drugs can be very hard on a battered woman, may hurt her relationship with her children and put her at a disadvantage in other legal actions with her battering partner. Therefore, women should carefully consider the potential cost of the use of illegal drugs. But beyond this, the use of any alcohol or other drugs can reduce a woman's awareness and ability to act quickly to protect herself from her battering partner. Furthermore, the use of alcohol or other drugs by the batterer may give him/

her an excuse to use violence. Therefore, in the context of drug or alcohol use, a woman needs to make specific safety plans.

If drug or alcohol use has occurred in my relationship with the battering partner, I can enhance my safety by some or all of the following:

A. If I am going to use, I can do so in a safe place and with people who understand the risk of violence and are committed to my safety.

B. I can also _____.

C. If my partner is using, I can _____.

D. I might also _____.

E. To safeguard my children, I might _____ and _____.

**Step 7. Safety and my emotional health.** The experience of being battered and verbally degraded by partners is usually exhausting and emotionally draining. The process of building a new life for myself takes much courage and incredible energy.

To conserve my emotional energy and resources and to avoid hard emotional times, I can do some of the following:

A. If I feel down and ready to return to a potentially abusive situation, I can _____.

B. When I have to communicate with my partner in person or by telephone, I can _____

_____.

C. I can try to use "I can..." statements with myself and to be assertive with others.

D. I can tell myself—"_____ " —whenever I feel others are trying to control or abuse me.

E. I can read _____ to help me feel stronger.

F. I can call _____, _____, and _____as other resources to be of support to me.

243

G.  Other things I can do to help me feel stronger are _____
    _____, _____
    and _____.

H.  I can attend workshops and support groups at the domestic
    violence program or _____, _____
    _____, or _____to gain
    support and strengthen my relationships with other people.

**Step 8: Items to take when leaving.** When women leave partners,
it is important to take certain items with them. Beyond this, women
sometimes give an extra copy of papers and an extra set of clothing
to a friend just in case they have to leave quickly.

Items with asterisks on the following list are the most important to
take. If there is time, the other items might be taken, or stored outside the home.

These items might best be placed in one location, so that if we have
to leave in a hurry, I can grab them quickly.

When I leave, I should take:
- Identification for myself*
- Children's birth certificates*
- My birth certificate*
- Social Security cards*
- School and vaccination records*
- Money*
- Checkbook, ATM (Automatic Teller Machine) card*
- Credit cards*
- Keys—house/car/office*
- Driver's license and registration*
- Medications*
- Welfare identification*
- Work permits*
- Green card*
- Passport(s)*

- Divorce papers*
- Medical records—for all family members*
- Lease/rental agreement, house deed, mortgage payment book*
- Bank books*
- Insurance papers*
- Small saleable objects
- Address book
- Pictures
- Jewelry
- Children's favorite toys and/or blankets
- Items of special sentimental value

**Telephone numbers I need to know:**

Police department—home _____

Police department —school _____

Police department—work _____

Battered women's program _____

County registry of protection orders _____

Work number _____

Supervisor's home number _____

Minister _____

Other _____

_____

Section 12.7

# *Is He Really Going to Change this Time?*

## *A Guide for Women Whose Partners Are in a Battering Intervention and Prevention Program*

Texas Council on Family Violence, copyright © 1995.
Used with permission.

If your partner has entered an intervention program for batterers, you're probably relieved that he's getting help. It's important to know that there are no miracle cures for his violence—he is the only one that can make the decision to change. This article will tell you what you need to know about a good program, what signs to watch for in your partner, and what to do if you think you may still be in danger of being abused.

### *How Do You Know If the Program Will Work?*

There are no guarantees that any program will work; a lot depends on your partner's motivation and capacity for change. But some programs work better than others. The ones that work well use the following standards:

- *Your safety is the first priority.* Programs should always assess your safety when communicating with you. A program should never disclose information that you have given them without your permission. A program should not misrepresent its ability to change his behavior. A program's definition of success is the quality of your and your children's lives, starting with safety.

- *Lasts long enough.* Change takes time. Programs should last at least 18 weeks and require at least 36 hours of participation during that time—in addition to any individual sessions that may be scheduled for orientation or evaluation. The longer the program, the better the chances are that he will change. A year or more in a program is preferable, although that is not always possible.

- *Holds him accountable.* The first step of accountability is that he takes responsibility for choosing to use violence in the relationship. A program should recognize that his behavior is the problem and will not allow him to use your behavior as an excuse. His violence is the problem, not you. Programs should hold him accountable for attendance, participation, and complying with the group's rules. (You can get a copy of the rules by calling the program.)

- *The curriculum gets to the root of his problem.* The content of the program is set up to challenge his underlying belief system that he has the right to control and dominate you. Programs that only address his anger, communication skills, and stress do not get to the root of his problem.

- *Make no demands on you to participate.* You're not the one with the problem. Some programs offer groups for partners of batterers. *Your participation is entirely optional.* Don't let anyone lead you to believe that his progress is dependent upon your participation.

- *Is open to your input.* If you initiate contact with the program to ask questions or give input you think may be useful, a program should welcome your participation. This is different from requiring you to participate. Sometimes, a program may initiate contact with you to discuss your partner's behavior outside the program. You should not feel obligated to share information, especially if you feel it might create a risk of violence against you.

- *Encourages follow-up support.* Completing a program does not guarantee he will be nonviolent. Staying nonviolent can be a lifelong challenge. A program should promote self-help and social support beyond the duration of the program, in the form of activities such as community service or participation in self-help programs.

## How Do You Know If He's Really Changing?

Positive signs include:
- He has stopped being violent or threatening to you or others.
- He acknowledges that his abusive behavior is wrong.
- He understands that he does not have the right to control and dominate you.
- You don't feel afraid when you are with him.

- He does not coerce you into having sex when you don't want to.
- You can express anger toward him without feeling intimidated.
- He does not make you feel responsible for his anger or frustration.
- He respects your opinion even if he doesn't agree with it.
- He respects your right to say "no."
- You can negotiate without being humiliated and belittled by him.
- You don't have to ask his permission to go out, go to school, get a job, or take other independent actions.
- He listens to you and respects what you have to say.
- He communicates honestly and does not try to manipulate you.
- He recognizes that he is not "cured" and that changing his behavior, attitudes, and beliefs is a lifelong process.
- He no longer does _____ (fill in the blank with any behavior that used to precede his violence, manipulation, or emotional abuse).

## How Do You Know You're Safe?

If you feel that you will be safer away from your partner while he is in an intervention program, you have every right to leave. Even if you leave, you must understand that his participation in the program is no guarantee that he will not be a threat to you. The risk that he may be violent toward you can even increase when you leave. For your own safety and the safety of your children, watch for these signs of a problem in the way he behaves toward you while he is in the program.

- *Tries to find you if you've left.* He may try to get information from your family and friends about your whereabouts, either by threatening them or trying to get their sympathy.
- *Tries to get you to come back to him.* He may do anything to get you to come back—if promising to change and being charming or contrite don't work, his efforts could then escalate to threats and violence.
- *Tries to take away the children.* He may try to kidnap the children as a way of forcing you to stay with him.
- *Stalks you.* If you always seem to run into him when you are on your way to work, running errands, or out with friends, or if you receive lots of mysterious phone calls, he could be stalking you.

248

## Warning Signs "Venting" Is Not OK

Techniques and therapies like pillow-punching or primal scream-ing are NOT appropriate for batterers. They tend to reinforce, rather than discourage, violent behavior. These techniques should not be a part of any intervention program.

## Manipulation

Old habits die hard. Your partner's abusive behavior is rooted in a desire to control the relationship, and that pattern isn't going to change overnight. He may no longer be violent, but he may still try to exert control by manipulating you into doing what he wants. Here are some common manipulative behaviors:

- Tries to invoke sympathy from you or family and friends.
- Is overly charming; reminds you of all the good times you've had together.
- Tries to buy you back with romantic gifts, dinners, flowers, etc.
- Tries to seduce you when you're vulnerable.
- Uses veiled threats—to take the kids away, to quit attending the program, to cut off financial support.
- His promises to change don't match his behavior.

You may be so hopeful for change that you want to believe him, even if things don't feel any different. But trust your instincts. If you don't feel safe, then chances are, you're not.

## The Six Big Lies

If you hear your partner making statements like these while he is in a program, you should understand that he is lying to himself—and to you.

1. "I'm not the only one who needs counseling."
2. "I'm not as bad as a lot of the other guys in there."
3. "As soon as I'm done with this program, I'll be cured."
4. "We need to stay together to work this out."

249

5. "If I weren't under so much stress, I wouldn't have such a short fuse."

6. "Now that I'm in this program, you have to be more understanding."

These statements have one thing in common: they let him off the hook for his abusive behavior. Remember, he needs to be willing to accept responsibility for his violence in order to change.

## What Do They Do In There, Anyway?

In Texas, we have guidelines developed by battered women's advocates that battering intervention programs should follow. If you're not sure whether the program your partner is in follows these standards, make it a point to find out.

### 1. Education on the Nature of Domestic Violence

Many batterers do not understand that abuse includes not only physical battering, but also things like emotional and verbal assaults, destroying property, stalking, and other behaviors which can terrify or intimidate victims and their families. Batterers need to learn that there is no excuse for any abusive behavior—and that it is never the victim's fault.

### 2. Changing Attitudes and Beliefs

Batterers have beliefs and attitudes that lead to violence, such as: men are superior; women are possessions of men; and aggression is an acceptable way to resolve conflicts. The program should work to establish new, non-aggressive attitudes, such as: women are worthy of respect; violent behavior is the batterer's responsibility; and there are ways to express emotion effectively without being violent.

### 3. Achieving Equality in Relationships

The program should help batterers come up with long-term strategies for achieving the mutual respect, trust, and support that is necessary to maintain a non-abusive relationship. It should also help them develop long-term plans for sharing responsibility with their partners in areas such as family finances and parenting.

### 4. Community Participation

It is important that the program help the batterer understand that he has committed a crime against the community. He can acknowledge his violence by discussing his efforts to change with friends or co-workers, referring other abusive men to the program, participating in community service projects (under supervision) that promote programs for the victims of domestic violence, and making meaningful amends for past offenses (such as replacing destroyed or stolen property).

Throughout the program, batterers should become aware of their own patterns of violent behavior. The program should offer them techniques for maintaining nonviolent behavior, including "time outs" that keep potentially violent situations from escalating, along with ways of helping to maintain nonviolence, such as "buddy" phone calls, support groups, relaxation, and exercise.

## Steps You Can Take to Keep Yourself Safe.

If you have any reason to believe you may be at risk for abuse while your partner is in a program, there are several things you can do to protect yourself.

1.  Contact a local battered women's shelter or battered women's support program for assistance.

2.  Contact a legal advocate if you feel you need help in dealing with threats to take your children; your local battered women's program can provide referrals.

3.  If you feel comfortable doing so, contact the program he is in to let them know about any threatening or potentially threatening behavior.

4.  If you have left him, tell as few family members and friends as possible where you are. If they don't know how to find you, they can't be frightened or manipulated into telling him.

## Warning Signs: A Call From the Program

A battering intervention program should alert you if it is clear from your partner's behavior in the program that you are in danger. While most programs have confidentiality policies that prevent them from telling you specifically what he has discussed in group meetings, they are obligated to warn you if they believe any immediate danger exists. If you get a call from them about this, take it seriously.

## Couples Counseling Won't Stop the Violence

Your partner may try to get you to go to couples counseling, telling you that you both have a problem and should work on it together. Couples counseling does have its place in working out problems, but his abuse is not something it can help with. That's his problem, and he needs to work on it in the program. If you think the two of you would benefit from joint counseling, then by all means, go—*after* he completes the program and is no longer violent.

*Look in the yellow pages of your telephone directory under "Crisis Intervention Services," "Abuse," or "Women's Shelters" for the telephone number of the nearest battering intervention program, battered women's shelter, or other family violence service. For immediate help with a domestic assault in progress, call 911 or your local police or sheriff's department.* [See also Chapter 39—Hotlines and Organizations.]

## Section 12.8

# *How an Abuser Can Discover Your Internet Activities*

American Bar Association, Commission on Domestic Violence, n.d. Copyright © American Bar Association. All rights reserved.
Reprinted by permission.

### *Email*

If an abuser has access to your email account, he or she may be able to read your incoming and outgoing mail. If you believe your account is secure, make sure you choose a password he or she will not be able to guess.

If an abuser sends you threatening or harassing email messages, they may be printed and saved as evidence of this abuse. Additionally, the messages may constitute a federal offense. For more information on this issue, contact your local United States Attorney's Office.

### *History / Cache File*

If an abuser knows how to read your computer's history or cache file (automatically saved web pages and graphics), he or she may be able to see information you have viewed recently on the internet.

You can clear your history or empty your cache file in your browser's settings.*

- **Netscape:** Pulldown Edit menu, select Preferences. Click on Navigator and choose "Clear History." Click on Advanced then select Cache. Click on "Clear Disk Cache".

  On older versions of Netcape: Pulldown Options menu. Select Network Options, select Cache. Click on "Clear Disk Cache".

- **Internet Explorer:** Pulldown View menu, select Internet Options. On General page, under Temporary Internet Files, click on "Delete Files." Under History, click on "Clear History."

- **AOL:** Pulldown Members menu, select Preferences. Click on WWW icon. Then select Advanced. Purge Cache.

---

* This information may not completely hide your tracks. Many browser types have features that display recently visited sites. The safest way to find information on the internet would be at a local library, a friend's house, or at work.

# Section 12.9

# *Changing a Battered Woman's Name and Social Security Number*

## *Change of Name*

It should be legal, under the common law, to just change a name by using another one (except if this would be for fraudulent reasons). However, the welfare department, Social Security Administration and the Immigration and Naturalization Service (INS) usually only recognize name changes granted by courts. State statutes for change of name usually require publication, in order to notify law enforcement officials, creditors and others who have a right to know of a change of name.

In order to prevent the batterer from learning of the name change, a motion can be made to the court for the woman to notify each creditor, the probation office, the INS (if an alien), the military (if ever a member) and other interested parties (if necessary) directly, without publication, to preserve her safety. The woman can testify or file an affidavit that she has only certain creditors, naming them, and that she will notify each of them directly. This would obviate the need for publication. She must also ask the court to keep the records confidential, or to sequester or impound the file or any papers with the confidential information, including not listing anything on the docket sheet which would reveal her address (if unknown to the batterer) and new name. The woman should explain that she can keep this information away from the batterer only if it is completely inaccessible to everyone. And she should explain how endangered she is.

In the alternative, the woman can request that she be allowed publication of a notice that simply says that the woman is changing her name, without saying what her new name will be, and indicating that anyone with questions can contact her lawyer (if she has one) or the court. Again, ask the court to keep anything confidential.

If the woman is divorced or was never married to her abuser and she has children who are also the children of the batterer, changing their names is much more difficult. Basically the same procedure is followed, except that their father must be notified that their names are being changed so that he has an opportunity to argue against their name changes if he wishes. Ask the court that on his copy of the papers their new name(s) not be listed.

## Change of Social Security Number

The battered woman must go to the Social Security Administration office and explain why she needs the change of social security number along with the change of name—to protect herself against the batterer's locating her (and/or her children).

The woman must promise Social Security never again to use or reveal her old Social Security number until the first time that she claims any benefits from the Social Security Administration. They will then cross-reference the old Social Security number to the new one so that she can get her full benefits.

A change of Social Security number will not fully protect the woman, particularly if she does not also change her name, and vice versa. Anything that links her to her past may give her batterer a way to find her. For example, continuing to use the same credit cards, having her mail forwarded, forwarding of school or medical records, telephone contact with relatives or other persons from her past, or having money transferred from an old bank account to a new one could be used to track her down.

Women can sometimes get assistance in making these changes from Victims Services programs or the Travellers Aid Society. They will be more likely to help her if she has a custody order for any children and the children's father has no visitation rights. [*See* Section 12.10.]

## Section 12.10

# *Social Security Administration (SSA) Provides Assistance to Victims of Domestic Violence*

Social Security Administration, n.d.

The SSA joins with other federal agencies to provide greater assistance to victims of domestic violence. Some victims seeking to elude their abuser and reduce the risk of further violence choose to establish a new identity. As part of that effort, it may be helpful to obtain a new Social Security number (SSN).

### *How to Apply for a New Social Security Number*

- Apply in person at any Social Security Office;
- Take evidence of your age, identity, and U.S. citizenship or lawful alien status;
- If you have changed your name as the Department of Justice recommends, take evidence identifying you by both your old and new names;
- If new SSNs are being requested for children, take evidence showing you have custody; and
- Take any evidence you may have documenting the harassment or abuse. The Social Security Administration will assist you in obtaining any additional corroborating evidence, if needed. The best evidence comes from third parties, such as police, medical facilities or doctors and describes the nature and extent of the domestic violence. Other evidence might include court restraining orders, letters from shelters, letters from family members, friends, counselors, or others with knowledge of the domestic violence.

### *Protective Actions Recommended by the Department of Justice*

A new SSN alone cannot protect you, particularly if your original SSN did not play a role in the domestic violence. There are other important steps you need to take for personal protection. In addition to changing your name, you should consider getting an unlisted telephone number, changing jobs, and moving to a new area/state.

Victims of domestic violence also are encouraged to contact the National Domestic Violence Hotline toll-free number, 1-800-799-SAFE. People who are deaf or hard of hearing may call the toll-free "TTY" number, 1-800-787-3224.

## Protecting Your New SSN

SSA's records are confidential. SSA does not furnish your SSN to third parties. Therefore, you should be careful about sharing your SSN unnecessarily with third parties who may not need it to provide you with a benefit or service.

## Questions and Answers Regarding Domestic Violence Policy Change

*Question 1: What will SSA do differently in processing requests for a new number?*

Answer: Previously SSA required the individual to establish that the abuser had either misused the individual's SSN or could be expected to misuse it to locate the individual. Only in cases of extremely severe abuse or endangerment of the person's life did SSA assume misuse. Now SSA will presume SSN misuse is possible in all abuse cases.

*Question 2: Should a person change his/her name before contacting SSA for a new number?*

Answer: Changing one's name is one of the important steps a domestic violence victim needs to take for personal protection. Since SSA assigns an SSN based on the name shown on the identity document submitted with the application for a number, it is best that the applicant have a document showing his/her new name.

## Section 12.11

# *Are You Being Stalked? Tips for Protection*

Excerpted from Privacy Rights Clearinghouse *Fact Sheet # 14*, © June 1994, revised August, 1997. Utility Consumers' Action Network. Used by permission.

## *Stalking Prevention Tips*

These tips will help you guard your personal information and lessen the chance that it will get into the hands of a stalker or harasser. However, some of these tips are extreme and should only be used if you are indeed being stalked. Harassment can take many forms, so this information may not be appropriate in every situation and may not resolve serious stalking problems. (See also the Supplement following this fact sheet, "Security Recommendations for Stalking Victims," provided by the Los Angeles Police Department's Threat Management Unit.)

1.  **Use a private post office box.** Residential addresses of post office box holders are generally confidential. However, the U.S. Postal Service will release a residential address to any government agency, or to persons serving court papers. The Post Office only requires verification from an attorney that a case is pending. This information is easily counterfeited. Private companies, such as Mail Boxes Etc., are more strict and will require that the person making the request have an original copy of a subpoena. Use your private post office box address for all of your correspondence. Print it on your checks instead of your residential address. Instead of recording the address as "Box 123," use "Apartment 123."

2.  **File a change-of-address card with the U.S. Postal Service** giving the private mail box address. Send personal letters to friends, relatives and businesses giving them the new private mailbox address. Give true residential address only to the most trusted friends. Ask that they do not store this address in rolodexes or address books which could be stolen.

3. **Make sure you have an unpublished and unlisted phone number.** The phone company lists names and numbers in directory assistance (411) and publishes them in the phone book. Make sure you delete your information from both places. Don't print your phone number on your checks. Give out a work number when asked.

4. **If your state has Caller ID, order Complete Blocking** (called "Per Line" Blocking in some states). This ensures that your phone number is not disclosed when you make calls from your home. (See PRC fact sheet 19 on Caller ID.)

5. **Avoid calling 800, 888 and 900 number services.** Your phone number could be "captured" by a service called Automatic Number Identification. It will also appear on the called party's bill at the end of the month. If you do call 800 numbers, use a pay phone.

6. **Have your name removed from any "reverse directories."** The entries in these directories are in numerical order by phone number or by address. These books allow anyone who has just one piece of information, such as a phone number, to find where you live. Reverse directories are published by phone companies and direct marketers. (See PRC fact sheet no. 4 on "junk mail.")

7. **Let people know that information about you should be held in confidence.** Tell your employer, co-workers, friends, family and neighbors of your situation. Alert them to be suspicious of people inquiring about your whereabouts or schedule.

8. **Do not use your home address when you subscribe to magazines.** In general, don't use your residential address for anything that is mailed or shipped to you.

9. **Avoid using your middle initial.** Middle initials are often used to differentiate people with common names. For example, someone searching public records or credit report files might find several people with the name, Jane Doe. If you have a common name and want to blend in with the crowd, don't add a middle initial.

10. **When conducting business with a government agency,** only fill in the required pieces of information. Certain govern-

ment agency records are public record. Anyone can access the information you disclose to the agency within that record. Public records such as county assessor, county recorder, DMV and business licenses are especially valuable finding tools. **Ask the agency if it allows address information to be confidential in certain situations.** If possible, use a post office box and do not provide your middle initial, phone number or your Social Security number. If you own property or a car, you may want to consider alternative forms of ownership, such as a trust. This would shield your personal address from the public record. (For more information on "government records and privacy," see PRC fact sheet number 11.)

11.  **Put your post office box on your driver's license.** Don't show your license to just anyone. Your license has a lot of valuable information to a stalker.

12.  **Don't put your name on the list of tenants** on the front of your apartment building. Use a variation of your name that only your friends and family would recognize.

13.  **Be very protective of your Social Security number.** It is the key to much of your personal information. Don't pre-print the SSN on anything such as your checks. Only give it out if required to do so and ask why the requester needs it. The Social Security Administration may be willing to change your SSN. Contact the SSA for details. (See PRC fact sheet number 10 on "SSNs" and Section 12.10 in this volume)

14.  **Alert the three credit bureaus**—TRW, Equifax and Trans Union—to your situation. Ask them to "flag" your record to avoid fraudulent access. (See PRC fact sheet number 6 on "credit reporting" for addresses and phone numbers. See also fact sheet number 17 on "identity theft.")

15.  **If you are having a problem with harassing phone calls,** put a beep tone on your line so callers think you are taping your calls. Use an answering machine to screen your calls, and put a "bluff message" on your machine to warn callers of possible taping or monitoring. Be aware of the legal restrictions on taping of conversations. (See PRC fact sheet number 3 on "harassing phone calls." See also fact sheet number 9 on "wiretapping and eavesdropping.")

16. **If you use electronic mail and other online computer services,** change your e-mail address if necessary. Do not enter any personal information into online directories. (See PRC fact sheet number 18 on "privacy in cyberspace.")

17. **Keep a log** of every stalking incident, plus names, dates and times of your contacts with law enforcement and others. Save phone message tapes and items sent in the mail.

18. **Consider getting professional counseling** and/or seeking help from a victims support group. They can help you deal with fear, anxiety and depression associated with being stalked.

19. **Make a police report. Consider getting a restraining order** if you have been physically threatened or feel that you are in danger. When filed with the court, a restraining order legally compels the harasser to stay away from you, or he/she can be arrested. Be aware that papers filed for a restraining order or police report may become public record. Put minimal amounts of information and only provide a post office box address. You should contact an attorney or legal aid office if a restraining order becomes necessary. (Note: Some security experts warn that restraining orders sometimes lead to violence. Before obtaining a restraining order, consider your options carefully.)

20. **And these final tips** from someone who was stalked for over three years: For your own protection, carry pepper spray. Get a car phone and/or a beeper. Carry a Polaroid or video camera. Never verify anything, like your home address, over the phone.

## *Security Recommendations For Stalking Victims*

### Supplement to Privacy Rights Clearinghouse *Fact Sheet No. 14.*

*The following is reprinted with the permission of the Los Angeles Police Department, Threat Management Unit, Detective Headquarters, 150 N. Los Angeles St., Los Angeles, CA 90012.*

### Residence Security

1. Be alert for any suspicious persons.

2. Positively identify callers before opening doors. Install a wide angle viewer in all primary doors.

3. Install a porch light at a height which would discourage removal.

4. Install dead bolts on all outside doors. If you cannot account for all keys, change door locks. Secure spare keys. Place a dowel in sliding glass doors and all sliding windows.

5. Keep garage doors locked at all times. Use an electric garage door opener.

6. Install adequate outside lighting.

7. Trim shrubbery. Install locks on fence gates.

8. Keep fuse box locked. Have battery lanterns in residence.

9. Install a loud exterior alarm bell that can be manually activated in more than one location.

10. Maintain an unlisted phone number. Alert household members to unusual and wrong number calls. If such activity continues, notify local law enforcement agency.

11. Any written or telephone threat should be treated as legitimate and must be checked out. Notify the appropriate law enforcement agency.

12. All adult members of the household should be trained in the use of any firearm kept for protection. It should be stored out of reach of children.

13. Household staff should have a security check prior to employment and should be thoroughly briefed on security precautions. Strictly en-

force a policy of the staff not discussing family matters or movement with anyone.

14. Be alert for any unusual packages, boxes, or devices on the premises. Do not disturb such objects.

15. Maintain all-purpose fire extinguishers in the residence and in the garage. Install a smoke detector system.

16. Tape emergency numbers on all phones.

17. When away from the residence for an evening, place lights and radio on a timer. For extended absences, arrange to have deliveries suspended.

18. Intruders will attempt to enter unlocked doors or windows without causing a disturbance. Keep doors and windows locked.

19. Prepare an evacuation plan. Brief household members on plan procedures. Provide ladders or rope for two-story residences.

20. A family dog is one of the least expensive but most effective alarm systems.

21. Know the whereabouts of all family members at all times.

22. Children should be accompanied to school or bus stops.

23. Routes taken and time spent walking should be varied.

24. Require identification of all repair & sales people prior to permitting entry into residence.

25. Always park in a secured garage if available.

26. Inform trusted neighbor regarding situation. Provide neighbor with photo or description of suspect and any possible vehicles.

27. Inform trusted neighbors of any anticipated extended vacations, business trips, etc.

28. During vacations, etc., have neighbors pick up mail and newspapers.

29. If residing in an apartment with on-site manager, provide the manager with a picture of the suspect. If in a secured condominium, provide information to the doorman or valet.

## Office Security

1. Central reception should handle visitors and packages.

2. Office staff should be alert for suspicious people, parcels, and packages that do not belong in the area.

3. Establish key and lock control. If keys possessed by terminated employees are not retrieved, change the locks.

4. Park in secured area if at all possible.

5. Have your name removed from any reserved parking area.

6. If there is an on-site security director, make him/her aware of the situation. Provide him/her with suspect information.

7. Have secretary or co-worker screen calls if necessary.

8. Have a secretary or security personnel screen all incoming mail (personal) or fan letters.

9. Be alert to anyone possibly following you from work.

10. Do not accept any package unless you personally ordered an item.

## Personal Security

1. Remove home address on personal checks and business cards.

2. Place real property in a trust, and list utilities under the name of the trust.

3. Utilize a private mail box service to receive all personal mail.

4. File for confidential voter status or register to vote utilizing mail box address.

5. Destroy discarded mail.

6. Phone lines can be installed in a location other than the person's residence and call-forwarded to the residence.

7. Place residence rental agreements in another person's name.

8. The person's name should not appear on service or delivery orders to the residence.

9. Do not obtain a mail box with the United States Post Office.

10. Mail box address now becomes the person's official address on all

records and in all rolodexes. It may be necessary or more convenient to list the mail box as "Suite 123" or "Apartment #123" rather than "Box 123".

11. File a change of address card with the Post Office giving the mail box address as the person's new address. Send postcards [rather than U.S. Post Change of Address cards] to friends, businesses, etc., giving the mail box address and requesting that they remove the old address from their files and rolodexes.

12. All current creditors should be given a change of address card to the mail box address. (Some credit reporting agencies will remove past addresses from credit histories if a request is made. We recommend this be done.)

13. File a change of address with the DMV to reflect the person's new mail box address. Get a new driver's license with the new address on it.

**Vehicle Security**

1. Park vehicles in well-lit areas. Do not patronize parking lots where car doors must be left unlocked and keys surrendered; otherwise surrender only the ignition key. Allow items to be placed in or removed from the trunk only in your presence.

2. When parked in the residence garage, turn the garage light on and lock the vehicle and garage door.

3. Equip the gas tank with a locking gas cap. The hood locking device must be controlled from inside the vehicle.

4. Visually check the front and rear passenger compartments before entering the vehicle.

5. Select a reliable service station for vehicle service.

6. Keep doors locked while vehicle is in use.

7. Be alert for vehicles that appear to be following you.

8. When traveling by vehicle, plan ahead. Know the locations of police stations, fire departments, and busy shopping centers.

9. Use a different schedule and route of travel each day. If followed, drive to a police station, fire department, or busy shopping center. Sound the horn to attract attention.

10. Do not stop to assist stranded motorist. (Phone in.)

## Section 12.12

# *What to Do When You Are Attacked*

There are no set rules because every situation and every person is different. Here are some alternatives to consider.

- **Talk**—say anything that may allow you to escape (i.e. "I'm pregnant"; "I have VD"; "I have AIDS"; etc.)

- **Fight**—aim for sensitive parts of the body: groin, eyes, windpipe, kneecap. The first blow is very important and must be accurate. You may not have a second chance.

- **Submit**—submitting is not the same as consenting, and it may be the only way to save your life; however, do not allow the rapist to tie you up. At that point, you will lose all your options to escape and may not be able to get the situation back under control.

- **Run**—your main objective is to get away. Look for crowds, houses with lights on, a busy street, etc.

- **Remember**—Violence is seldom far from the surface of a rapist's mixed-up mind. Rape is a crime of violence using sex as the weapon. If persuasion and resistance do not work, concentrate on identity: age, height, hair color, eye color, scars or birthmarks, clothes, car and license number. Personal protection articles carried in your purse are not easily accessible and can be used against you. Mace should not be used outdoors because the wind can cause it to blow into your face, not the face of the attacker.

- **What If**—consider circumstances and places that someone may try to attack you and play the "What if" game (i.e., what could you do to avoid an attack at the mall, in your home, in your car).

Surprise and fear are two tactics rapists use to their advantage. By being aware at all times (not paranoid), you can eliminate these and remain in control when someone approaches you. Keeping your wits about you is the key during the first three minutes of an attack. Concentrate on the situation. If you scream, can anyone hear you? If you run, is there anywhere to hide?

### *After a Rape...*

- *Don't* destroy evidence by bathing, douching, washing hands, brushing teeth, changing clothes or linens, eating or drinking.

- *Do* notify someone immediately. It may help you if a friend or neighbor goes with you to the hospital and police.

- *Do* seek medical attention in the ER of a local hospital. You need to have a rape exam even if you decide not to press charges. The exam is used to collect evidence (which will be needed if you later decide to prosecute) as well as assure you that you did not sustain injuries which may not be visible yet (i.e., internal injuries, bruises).

- *Do* call police as soon as possible. Even if you don't want to file any charges, you can file an informational report that may help police locate your attacker and protect others. Most rapists are repeat offenders!

- *Do* take a change of clothes with you to the hospital.

- *Do* write down the details about the rapist and the circumstances of the rape as soon as possible.

- *Do* call a rape crisis center if you need someone to talk to or answer questions or if you want someone from the center to accompany you to the hospital, police station, or courthouse.

### *Reactions to Rape...*

Rape can affect a victim in many ways. All of the following reactions are normal. Some of them should be expected.

- Anger–Shock–Disbelief–Suppression
- Fear of being alone
- Fear of crowds
- Fear of the return of the attacker
- Obsession with assault
- Fear of men
- Fear of husband/friends/family finding out
- Embarrassment/Guilt
- Disruption of normal sex life

## Section 12.13

# *The Availability of Domestic Violence Protection Orders to Victims of Same-Sex Violence*

Excerpted from *1997 Report on Lesbian, Gay, Bisexual & Transgender Domestic Violence*, The New York City Gay and Lesbian Anti-Violence Project (AVP) and the National Coalition of Anti-Violence Programs (NCAVP), October, 1998. Used with permission.

## *Introduction*

In this section, we will explore the question of whether or not legal remedies are as available to lesbian, gay, bisexual, and transgender victims as they are to their heterosexual counterparts.

Domestic violence laws were originally passed in response to awareness of a problem often referred to as "wife battering." Women's groups and others called for legislation designed to protect women victims of male abuse. This view of domestic violence framed the responses of lawmakers and was perpetuated through the resulting legislation. Even if the laws were written (or later revised) in a gender-neutral framework, the gendered conception of domestic violence became further entrenched in the application of the laws by police, court personnel, attorneys, and judges. Simply removing personal pronouns from a law does not ensure that it will be enforced beyond the gendered frame of reference within which the law was created.

Every state and the District of Columbia has enacted some form of legislation designed to address domestic violence. Orders of protection for victims of domestic abuse are available in all fifty-one jurisdictions. Typically, statutes allow "family and household members" to petition for protective orders, but each state defines that term differently. Relationships of affinity (by marriage, including in-law relationships) and consanguinity (by blood) are generally protected. Other "household" relationships may or may not include persons in romantic or sexual relationships, persons engaged in dating relationships, or persons residing in the same household. Often, cohabitation is required, which may be interpreted in a number of ways, including living together with or without a sexual relationship, or living as spouses.

The availability of orders of protection—also called restraining orders, no-contact orders, stay-away orders, and TROs (temporary restraining orders)—depends on two things. First, laws must grant courts the authority to issue such orders. Second, once laws are passed, police officers, judges, and others must interpret, implement and enforce those laws. Our findings are confined to the first necessary element: do laws exist which allow courts to issue restraining orders in domestic violence situations where both the abuser and the abused are of the same sex?

## Domestic Violence Orders Provide Important Protections

Domestic violence protective orders are perhaps the most significant legal remedy available to victims of abuse. Designed specifically to address violence in family relationships, domestic abuse statutes grant judges broad authority to restrain or direct the behavior of the abuser, regardless of whether criminal charges have been filed. At their simplest, domestic violence orders direct the abuser to refrain from abusing the victim, and usually to stay away from the victim's home, school, or place of employment. Most laws allow judges to go far beyond these simple steps.

A domestic violence restraining order may evict the abuser from the shared household, often without regard to whose name is on the lease. The order may restrict use of jointly owned property, such as cars, checkbooks, or keys. It may require that the abuser pay temporary monetary support as well as child support. The order may require that the abuser pay damages, such as medical, dental, or counseling expenses, loss of earnings, cost of repair or replacement of real property, moving expenses, and attorney fees. The abuser may be prohibited from transferring, selling, or concealing property. He or she may also be required to relinquish guns or other weapons. One significant protection of a restraining order is that it usually authorizes or requires police to arrest the abuser on the spot, without a warrant, for committing any of the acts prohibited by the order. In most states, violating a protective order is a criminal offense.

The process for obtaining a domestic violence order is simpler than filing other court actions. Often, a state will provide domestic violence advocates at the courthouse or the district attorney's office will assist the victim throughout the legal process. Clerks may be directed to provide assistance with paperwork, and fill-in-the-blank forms are frequently available. Significantly, filing fees are commonly waived for low-income victims, and often there are no fees at all to petition for a domestic violence protective order.

For a victim of abuse by a partner of the same sex, these protections may not be available. Laws written to address domestic violence from a heterosexual perspective make it more difficult for a battered lesbian, gay man, bisexual or transgender person to escape the cycle of abuse which is characteristic of domestic violence. In order to leave a violent same-sex relationship, a person may be forced to leave his or her home, give up access to jointly owned property, absorb staggering financial losses, and terminate relationships with children. Without a restraining order, a victim of same-sex abuse may be unable to sustain employment or educational efforts if the abuser repeatedly contacts the victim at school or work. The victim may also be wrongly arrested if the police cannot rely on a protective order to determine the aggressor in a violent situation. Without access to the support provided by protective orders, a victim of same-sex abuse may feel compelled to remain in the abusive relationship, thus prolonging the violence and risk to the victim's life.

## *Domestic Violence Protective Orders Are Clearly Unavailable for Victims of Same-Sex Abuse in Seven States*

The laws in seven states which allow a victim to petition the court for an order of protection are generally written to define eligible petitioners as members of opposite-sex couples. These states include: Arizona, Delaware, Louisiana, Montana, New York, South Carolina, and Virginia.

In South Carolina, for example, the law protects family and household members, but defines those terms to include marital and blood relationships, persons who have a child in common, and "a male and female who are cohabiting or formerly have cohabited." In New York state, domestic violence orders are issued by family courts, which have jurisdiction in family offense proceedings only over persons related by consanguinity or affinity, persons legally married, persons formerly married, or persons who have a child in common—all categories which legally exclude same-sex relationships. Montana protects "partners" but defines that term to include only relationships between persons of the opposite sex. In Virginia, the domestic violence statute protects persons who cohabit or who cohabited in the last twelve months, but a 1994 Attorney General opinion defines "cohabit" as persons living together as husband and wife, specifically excluding roommates and members of lesbian and gay relationships from the class of persons protected by the law.

## Protective Orders Are <u>*Arguably Unavailable*</u> *for Victims of Same-Sex Abuse in Three States*

The domestic violence statutes in three states are written so that a court could easily interpret them to limit protection to heterosexuals, or to require acknowledgment of an illegal sexual relationship when petitioning for protection. These states include: Florida, Maryland, and Mississippi.

For example, Florida's statute protects persons "residing as a family" and Mississippi protects persons "living as spouses." But sodomy laws in both states criminalize homosexual acts and both states ban same-sex marriage—legal policies which would support an argument that domestic violence orders were not intended to protect same-sex couples. Maryland's statute protects cohabitants, but defines cohabitant as "a person who has had a sexual relationship with the respondent in the home" for a specific period of time. Unfortunately, acknowledging a same-sex sexual relationship in Maryland could leave the victim of abuse vulnerable to prosecution under the state prohibition of "unnatural or perverted sex practices" commonly known as a sodomy law.

## Domestic Violence Protective Orders are <u>*Neutrally Available*</u> *to Victims of Same-Sex Abuse in Thirty-Seven Jurisdictions*

In about two-thirds of the states (and in the District of Columbia), a victim of same-sex abuse should be able to obtain an order of protection because the laws in these jurisdictions are written in gender-neutral language. These jurisdictions include: Alabama, Alaska, Arkansas, California, Colorado, Connecticut, District of Columbia, Georgia, Idaho, Indiana, Iowa, Kansas, Maine, Massachusetts, Michigan, Minnesota, Missouri, Nebraska, Nevada, New Hampshire, New Jersey, New Mexico, North Carolina, North Dakota, Oklahoma, Oregon, Pennsylvania, Rhode Island, South Dakota, Tennessee, Texas, Utah, Vermont, Washington, West Virginia, Wisconsin, and Wyoming.

In Colorado, for example, the law protects parties who have been involved in an "intimate relationship" as well as parties who live or have lived together. The District of Columbia protects those who share or have shared a residence and persons who maintain or maintained a "romantic relationship not necessarily including a sexual relationship." Idaho domestic violence restraining orders are available to persons who reside or have resided together, and the statute further provides that the law be "construed liberally." Minnesota domestic violence laws apply to persons residing together, or persons who are or have been in a "substantive dating or engagement relationship" as determined by factors such as the duration and type of relationship. North Dakota's law is one of the most liberal, allowing an action for protection by any person "if the court determines that the relationship between that person and the alleged abusing person is sufficient to warrant the issuance of a domestic violence order." Texas protects current and former household members, defining household as "a unit composed of persons living together in the same dwelling, without regard to whether they are related to each other." Similarly, Wyoming protects "adults sharing common living quarters." In December of 1997, North Carolina law was broadened to include "former and current household members" which should allow access to protective orders for at least some same-sex victims; however, the statute also warns that such an order may not be used as a defense for persons charged with the "crime against nature" prohibited by the North Carolina sodomy law.

In any of these states, the availability of a protective order for an individual victim of same-sex abuse will depend on a variety of factors particular to the state and to the victim. Some states may protect roommates; others do not. Some states protect persons who are dating; other states require that the parties live together. Sexual relationships may define the protected class, or a sexual relationship may be expressly irrelevant. However, the laws in these states should be accessible by victims of same-sex abuse in the same manner that they are available to victims of opposite-sex domestic violence.

## Domestic Violence Protective Orders Are <u>Affirmatively Available</u> for Victims of Same-Sex Abuse in Four States

Only four states affirmatively make protective orders available to victims of same-sex domestic violence. These states include: Hawaii, Illinois, Kentucky, and Ohio.

Of these four states, only Hawaii law specifically addresses same-sex relationships, providing access to protective orders for "reciprocal beneficiaries." By registering for reciprocal beneficiary status, same-sex couples are granted many of the rights and obligations of legally married heterosexual couples—including protection under Hawaii domestic violence laws.

Laws in the other three states—Illinois, Kentucky, and Ohio—are actually written in gender-neutral terms, but courts in those states have interpreted the statutes to apply to same-sex relationships. One Kentucky court has ruled that the statutory term "unmarried couples" included same-sex couples. Similarly, an Illinois court upheld one man's protective order against his male abuser. In Ohio, at least three courts have found that a member of a same-sex couple is a "person living as a spouse" for purposes of the domestic violence laws.

## Other Remedies May Be Available for Victims of Same-Sex Abuse

In addition to domestic violence protective orders, some state laws provide other civil protection orders which apply to specific crimes such as harassment and stalking. These orders may be limited in scope to ordering the restrained person to stay away from the victim. The court probably will not be able to evict an abuser from his or her home, or require an abuser to pay damages or refrain from selling jointly owned property, and the victim may be required to pay filing fees. Secondly, individuals may be able to obtain protective orders if they pursue criminal charges against their abuser which many victims are reluctant to do. Finally, although cumbersome and difficult to obtain, injunctions may be sought which can order the abuser to refrain from abuse.

Because of the complex interplay of the laws, a victim of domestic abuse should consult a local attorney or domestic violence program for legal advice and for current, accurate interpretations of local laws.

Chapter 13

# Law Enforcement and Judicial Interventions

## Chapter Contents

# Section 13.1

# *Criminal Justice Interventions*

Excerpted from "Male Batterers Fact Sheet," National Center for Injury Prevention and Control, Centers for Disease Control and Prevention, 1998.

## Arrest

Research findings are mixed regarding the effectiveness of police arrest policies as a deterrent to intimate partner violence (IPV). Some studies have reported deterrence effects from arrest policies when compared with strategies such as counseling or short separation.[1] Other studies, however, have failed to replicate these findings.[2, 3] Additional studies have suggested that the deterrent effects of arrest may vary depending on factors such as length of time in police custody and the characteristics of the individual arrested.[4]

*Comment: While arrest in and of itself may not act as a deterrent to the perpetration of IPV for all individuals, it is important that arrest policies and practices be evaluated in the context of an integrated criminal justice response, in which arrest for IPV is followed by the laying of charges, and the appropriate administration of sanctions by other criminal justice agencies.*

## Prosecution Policies

To date, there has been little investigation of the deterrent effects of prosecution for IPV. One study, which compared reassault rates for prosecution versus alternative interventions (police only or social service contacts) reported that prosecution led to no overall preventive effects on reassault.[5] Later analyses suggested that criminal justice interventions may be most effective at reducing chances of reassault by perpetrators with a history of less severe violence.[6]

Another study assessed rates of reassault for men randomly assigned to one of three court outcomes (pretrial diversion to counseling for perpetrators of IPV, prosecution to conviction with a recommendation of counseling as a condition of probation, or prosecution to conviction with presumptive sentencing). Findings indicated that all conditions showed a drop in the rates of reassault in the six months following arrest. Under conditions of victim-initiated complaints, permitting victims to drop charges significantly reduced their risk of future violence. This reduced risk was attributed to the increased empowerment which the victim may have gained by having the criminal justice system in alliance to maintain her safety, although actually dropping the charges may not have increased the woman's safety.[7]

## *Batterer Intervention Programs*

Batterer intervention programs, which seek to educate or rehabilitate known perpetrators of IPV to be nonviolent, have proliferated since the 1980s, under the auspices of both the criminal justice system and mental health system. Three theoretical approaches to the conduct of these programs have been consistently documented.[8] These theories influence the content and delivery of interventions:

**Society and culture:** attributes battering to social and cultural norms and values that endorse or tolerate the use of violence by men against their women partners. The feminist model of intervention educates men concerning the impact of these social norms and values, and attempts to resocialize men through education, emphasizing nonviolence and equality in relationships.

**The Family:** family-based theories of IPV focus on the structure and social isolation of families. The family systems model of intervention focuses on communication skills, with the goal of family preservation and may use couples counseling/conjoint therapy.

**The Individual:** psychological theories attribute perpetration of IPV to personality disorders, the batterer's social environment during childhood or biological predispositions. Psychotherapeutic interventions target individual problems and/or build cognitive skills to help the batterer control violent behaviors.

Many programs adopt components of each approach. Currently there is little evidence to suggest the effectiveness of one approach over another, or of the differential effectiveness of different programs with different "types" of batterers, although one study has suggested that process-psychodynamic groups may function better for men with dependent personalities, while cognitive-behavioral groups may be more effective for those with antisocial traits.[9]

The most widely evaluated intervention model for men who batter are group interventions using cognitive-behavioral techniques, often in combination with feminist content. One review of these studies reported that percentages of successful outcomes (i.e., reduced or no reassault) from these programs varied from 53% to 85%.[10] However, other reviews have pointed out that methodological problems in the studies limit conclusions about the effectiveness of such programs.[11]

*Comment: At present, several large evaluation studies of batterer intervention programs are underway which compare a variety of treatment modalities.[12, 13] These studies may clarify our understanding of the effectiveness of these programs.*

## Attrition

The majority of intervention or education groups for men who batter report high attrition rates,[14] with as many as 50%–75% of men failing to complete the mandated program.[15] Factors which have been found to be associated with attrition include: lifestyle instability (e.g., youth, low education, unstable work histories) and incongruence between the batterer's self-identified problems and the treatment provided.

Evidence of the efficacy of court-mandating men to treatment as a means of increasing program completion are mixed. Some studies report increased completion, while others suggest reduced completion.[15]

*Comment: Further research on the interaction effects between the characteristics of the offender, the treatment program, and the criminal justice system in relation to treatment completion is needed.*

## Standards

Despite the limited evidence for the effectiveness of batterer intervention programs, many states have or are in the process of developing standards for the conduct of these programs. At the present time, 25 states have county and/or state standards; five states have drafted standards and 13 states and the District of Columbia are developing standards. These standards vary in how they are implemented, and may be voluntary or mandatory. However, the majority support the use of programs based on cognitive-behavioral principals, some to the exclusion of other approaches.[16]

**Comment:** *It is possible that the legislation of standards at this time may restrict necessary enquiry into alternative approaches.*

[*See also* Chapter 30]

## References

1.  Sherman, L. W., and R. A. Berk. (1984). "The Specific Deterrent Effects of Arrest for Domestic Assault." *American Sociological Review* 49, 261–72.

2.  Dunford, F. W., D. Huizinga, and D. S. Elliott. (1990). "The Role of Arrest in Domestic Assault: The Omaha Police Experiment." *Criminology* 28: 183–206.

3.  Hirschel, J. L., I. W. Hutchinson, and C. W. Dean. (1992). "The Failure of Arrest to Deter Spouse Abuse." *Journal of Research in Crime and Delinquency* 20, 7–33.

4.  Sherman, L. W., J. D. Schmidt, D. P. Rogan, P. R. Gartin, K. G. Cohen, D. J. Collins, and A. R. Bacich. (1991). "From Initial Deterrence to Longterm Escalation: Short Custody Arrest for Poverty Ghetto Domestic Violence." *Criminology* 29: 821–50.

5.  Fagan, J., E. Friedman, S. Wexler, and V. L. Lewis. (1984). *National Family Violence Evaluation: Final Report: Vol 1. Analytic Findings.* San Francisco: URSA Institute.

6.  Fagan, J. (1989). "Cessation of Family Violence: Deterrence and Dissuasion." In L. Ohlin & M. Tonry, eds., *Family Violence* (pp. 377–426). Chicago: University of Chicago Press.

7.  Ford, D. A., and M. J. Regoli. (1993). "The Criminal Prosecution of Wife Assaulters: Process, Problems and Effects." In N. Z. Hilton ed., *Legal Responses to Wife Assault: Current Trends And Evaluation* (pp. 127–63). Newbury Park: Sage.

8.  Healey, K., C. Smith, and C. O'Sullivan. (1997). "Batterer Intervention: Program Approaches and Criminal Justice Strategies." Paper presented at Meeting the Challenges of Crime and Justice: The Annual Conference of Criminal Justice Research and Evaluation. Washington DC, July 20–23.

9.  Saunders, D. G. (1996). "Feminist-Cognitive-Behavioral and Process-Psychodynamic Treatments for Men Who Batter: Interaction of Abuser Traits and Treatment Models." *Violence and Victims* 11: 393–414.

10. Tolman, R. M., and L. W. Bennett. (1990). "A Review of Quantitative Research on Men Who Batter." *Journal of Interpersonal Violence* 5: 87–118.

11. Hamberger, L. K., and J. E. Hastings. (1993). "Court-Mandated Treatment of Men Who Assault Their Partners: Issues, Controversies, and Outcomes." In N. Z. Hilton, ed. *Legal Responses to Wife Assault: Current Trends and Evaluation* (pp. 188–229). Newbury Park, CA: Sage.

12. Gondolf, E. W. (1997). *A Multi-Site Evaluation of Batterer Intervention Systems: A Summary of Preliminary Findings.* Indiana, PA: Mid-Atlantic Addiction Training Institute.

13. Dunford, F. W. (1997). *History of the San Diego Project and Baseline Data, the San Diego Navy Project.* Working draft, the University of Colorado.

14. Gondolf, E. W, and R. A. Foster. (1991). "Pre-Program Attrition in Batterer Programs." *Journal of Family Violence* 6, 337–49.

15. Cadsky, O., R. K. Hanson, M. Crawford, and C. Lalonde. (1996). "Attrition from a Male Batterer Treatment Program: Client-Treatment Congruence and Lifestyle Instability." *Violence and Victims* 11 (1), 51–64.

16. Austin, J., and J. Dankwort. (1997). *A Review of Standards for Batterer Intervention Programs.* Harrisburg, PA: National Resource Center on Domestic Violence—VAWnet.

Section 13.2

# What You Need to Know about the Judicial System

Excerpted from *National Handbook on Teen Dating Violence and the Law*. Copyright © 1996 National Center on Women and Family Law, and NOW Legal Defense and Education Fund. Reprinted with permission.

## Civil Laws and Criminal Laws

There are two systems of laws which you need to know about — the civil laws and the criminal laws.

Civil law includes rules about how we go about our lives and handle the problems that come up: accidents, divorces, credit cards, apartment leases, parking violations, constitutional rights, and dog bites are examples of civil law matters. The civil law is often set up so that people can work out their problems and compromise in reaching solutions. Sometimes in a civil law case, a person agrees to do or not to do something, or he or she pays a sum of money to settle the other person's claims. If people involved in a civil law case cannot agree on a settlement, a judge will decide the case for them.

The criminal law is somewhat different; we can say that its purpose is punishment. Society has decided certain acts are so bad that the people who commit them must be severely punished and perhaps put in jail. In other instances, judges decide to monitor an offender's behavior, to fine that person, or to direct that the offender go through a counseling and/or substance abuse program.

Sometimes, you can sue someone in civil court and also bring criminal charges against that person. For example, in the case of a car accident, the victim can sue the driver in civil court to recover money for medical bills. In addition, the prosecutor may charge the driver with a crime because of drunkenness, and after a trial in criminal court, the driver can be put in jail.

Most state laws have similarities when it comes to domestic abuse, although these laws differ as to who can be a victim protected by a specific state's laws. In many states, you can decide to file for a civil order of protection and to request that the abuser be prosecuted in criminal court as well. Therefore, if you do not qualify as a civil domestic abuse victim in your state because of your age or relationship to the abuser, you should consider attempting to obtain protection from abuse by using the criminal laws in your state.

In certain states (such as New York), you can protect yourself legally through the special domestic abuse criminal laws. Usually there are the same restrictions on who can use the law and the type of abuse that is covered. In criminal law there are strict requirements for proving your case. You also have to cooperate with the prosecutor who will take over your case and present it to the judge.

## Getting Advice

It's a good idea to get advice before going to the courthouse. You may know a lawyer, or there may be a legal services office in your area which you can call or visit. Legal services lawyers usually do not charge if you qualify. If you want to hire a lawyer, you can call the county or city bar association for the name of an attorney experienced in abuse cases. Lawyers will usually talk with you briefly about your case, but most charge for legal representation. You should ask if there will be a fee.

If you don't think you would be comfortable telling a lawyer what is happening to you and why you are afraid, first try calling the domestic abuse expert in your state. They are trained to assist people like you and to understand your situation. In addition, they should be able to help you contact a battered women's shelter near you so you can find out about more help close to where you are. You should be able to call these places anonymously if you are embarrassed or ashamed to give your name.

If you are comfortable talking to a school counselor or there is another adult you know and also would feel comfortable talking to, ask that person to get information for you.

## The Courthouse

A courthouse can seem like a difficult place in which to feel comfortable. Usually there will be a security guard at the door or a clerk at a desk who can answer your questions and tell you where to go. If not, check the list of offices—which should be posted on the wall—and look for the Court Clerk's room. A friend or relative can go with you. It's important to dress carefully, be polite, and to know what you want to say in advance. Although a clerk may be able to help you, it will be easier if you are organized, are able to tell exactly what happened and the dates it happened, have names and addresses handy, and bring any photographs, witnesses, hospital records or other evidence you may have about the abuse or threats.

You may be able to see a judge immediately, or you may be told to come back on another date. Keep track of your court dates and times; if you do not come back, your case may be dismissed.

You may get a protection order that first time in court. Ask the judge any questions you have about it; make sure you know what to do with it, whether you have to give a copy to the abuser, whether the police will get a copy, what you should do if the abuser does not obey the order, and when you have to go back to court.

### How can I get reimbursed for medical expenses and other losses?

Sometimes a victim is so severely injured by the batterer that he or she requires substantial medical treatment, hospital confinement, or both. In some cases the injuries also require the victim to miss a lot of time from school or work, or the victim has other major problems because of his or her injuries. A victim of domestic violence who receives serious injuries may be able to sue the abuser for money damages to compensate for the pain, injuries, and other losses suffered. You should consult an attorney who specializes in personal injury work if you think you have this type of claim against your abuser.

Victims of domestic violence may also be able to seek restitution from the abuser or from a state's violent crime compensation fund for financial losses caused by the violence. You should ask the prosecutor or District Attorney for information and assistance if you want to make this type of claim.

## What Else Do I Need to Know?

### Protection when you travel

There is a federal law which provides that an order of protection a victim receives from a state court in one state will be recognized and enforced by the courts of any other state in the country under most circumstances. [*See also* Section 24.2.] For example, if a college student in Maryland obtains an order of protection against a batterer in the Maryland courts but the student lives in Missouri, law enforcement personnel in Missouri and the Missouri courts are required to enforce the Maryland order of protection in the same manner in which an order actually issued by Missouri courts would be enforced. This interstate protection is available to any victim of domestic violence who has an order of protection from one state's courts and travels to another state for any purpose, if the initial order was granted properly by the first court.

## Crossing state lines

If the abuser crosses state lines with the purpose of hurting you and does commit an act of domestic violence against you or violates your order of protection, he or she can be sentenced to a prison term of up to 20 years if convicted under federal law. In a situation where the abuser forces you to cross state lines and commits an act of violence against you, that person can also receive a prison term of up to 20 years.

When two or more states are involved, the victim of domestic violence will be notified prior to the court's release of the abuser before trial, and the victim will have a chance to tell the court why he or she will be in danger if the abuser is released.

## Guns

Violent incidents between boyfriends and girlfriends which involve guns are twelve times more likely to result in death than those involving other weapons.[1] Some states have reacted to this problem by passing laws to remove guns from the possession and residence of an alleged or convicted abuser when an order of protection is granted. In certain states these laws can also require law enforcement to remove guns from your home if one of your parents has abused you or your other parent.

No one has the right to threaten you and make you afraid for your safety. Since violent people are much more dangerous when they have guns, these laws are important so guns can be removed from the home or the possession of an abuser before someone is killed.

---

1. Salzman, Linda, Ph.D., James A. Marcy, Ph.D., Patrick W. O'Carroll, M.D., M.P.H., Mark L. Rosenberg, M.D., M.P.P., Philip H. Rhodes, M.S. "Weapon Involvement and Injury Outcomes in Family and Intimate Assaults." *Journal of the American Medical Association* 267, 22 (June 10, 1992).

# Part Three

# Child Abuse

# Chapter 14

# *Definitions and Incidence*

## *Chapter Contents*

# Section 14.1

# *What Is Child Maltreatment?*

National Clearinghouse on Child Abuse and Neglect, 1996.

Child abuse and neglect are defined in both federal and state legislation. The federal legislation provides a foundation for states by identifying a minimum set of acts or behaviors that characterize maltreatment. This legislation also defines what acts are considered physical abuse, neglect, and sexual abuse.

## *How Do We Define Child Abuse and Neglect?*

**The Child Abuse Prevention and Treatment Act (CAPTA),** as amended and reauthorized in October 1996 (Public Law 104-235, Section 111; 42 U.S.C. 5106g) provides the following definitions.

*Child* is a person who has not attained the lesser of:

- The age of 18
- Except in cases of sexual abuse, the age specified by the child protection law of the state in which the child resides.

*Child abuse and neglect* is, at a minimum:

- Any recent act or failure to act on the part of a parent or caretaker which results in death, serious physical or emotional harm, sexual abuse or exploitation
- An act or failure to act which presents an imminent risk of serious harm.

*Sexual abuse* is:

- The employment, use, persuasion, inducement, enticement, or coercion of any child to engage in, or assist any other person to engage in, any sexually explicit conduct or simulation of such conduct for the purpose of producing a visual depiction of such conduct

- The rape, and in cases of caretaker or inter-familial relationships, statutory rape, molestation, prostitution, or other form of sexual exploitation of children, or incest with children.

***Withholding of medically indicated treatment*** is: The failure to respond to the infant's life-threatening conditions by providing treatment (including appropriate nutrition, hydration, and medication) that in the treating physician's or physicians' reasonable medical judgment, will be most likely to be effective in ameliorating or correcting all such conditions.

But, the term does not include the failure to provide treatment (other than appropriate nutrition, hydration, and medication) to an infant when, in the treating physician's or physicians' reasonable medical judgment:

- The infant is chronically and irreversibly comatose
- The provision of such treatment would
  - — Merely prolong dying
  - — Not be effective in ameliorating or correcting all of the infant's life-threatening conditions
  - — Otherwise be futile in terms of the survival of the infant
- The provision of such treatment would be virtually futile in terms of the survival of the infant and the treatment itself under such circumstances would be inhumane.

***Each state is responsible for providing its own definitions of child abuse and neglect*** within the civil and criminal context. Civil laws, or statutes, describe the circumstances and conditions that obligate mandated reporters to report known or suspected cases of abuse, and they provide definitions necessary for juvenile/family courts to take custody of a child alleged to have been maltreated. Criminal statutes specify the forms of maltreatment that are criminally punishable. (The State Statutes Series from the National Clearinghouse on Child Abuse and Neglect Information and the American Prosecutors Research Institute summarizes nearly 40 civil and criminal state statutes pertaining to child maltreatment.)

# *What Are the Main Types of Maltreatment?*

There are four major types of maltreatment: physical abuse, neglect, sexual abuse, and emotional abuse. While state definitions may vary, operational definitions include the following:

**Physical Abuse** is characterized by the infliction of physical injury as a result of punching, beating, kicking, biting, burning, shaking or otherwise harming a child. The parent or caretaker may not have intended to hurt the child, rather the injury may have resulted from over-discipline or physical punishment.

**Child Neglect** is characterized by failure to provide for the child's basic needs. Neglect can be physical, educational, or emotional. Physical neglect includes refusal of or delay in seeking health care, abandonment, expulsion from the home or refusal to allow a runaway to return home, and inadequate supervision. Educational neglect includes the allowance of chronic truancy, failure to enroll a child of mandatory school age in school, and failure to attend to a special educational need. Emotional neglect includes such actions as marked inattention to the child's needs for affection, refusal of or failure to provide needed psychological care, spouse abuse in the child's presence, and permission of drug or alcohol use by the child. The assessment of child neglect requires consideration of cultural values and standards of care as well as recognition that the failure to provide the necessities of life may be related to poverty.

**Sexual Abuse** includes fondling a child's genitals, intercourse, incest, rape, sodomy, exhibitionism, and commercial exploitation through prostitution or the production of pornographic materials. Many experts believe that sexual abuse is the most under-reported form of child maltreatment because of the secrecy or "conspiracy of silence" that so often characterizes these cases.

**Emotional Abuse** (psychological/verbal abuse/mental injury) includes acts or omissions by the parents or other caregivers that have caused, or could cause, serious behavioral, cognitive, emotional, or mental disorders. In some cases of emotional abuse, the acts of parents or other caregivers alone, without any harm evident in the child's behavior or condition, are sufficient to warrant child protective services (CPS) intervention. For example, the parents/caregivers may use extreme or bizarre forms of punishment, such as confinement of a child in a dark closet. Less severe acts, such as habitual scapegoating, belittling, or rejecting treatment, are often difficult to prove and, therefore, CPS may not be able to intervene without evidence of harm to the child.

Although any of the forms of child maltreatment may be found separately, they often occur in combination. Emotional abuse is almost always present when other forms are identified. For more information, contact the Clearinghouse.

# Section 14.2

## *Child Abuse*

National Center for Victims of Crime, INFOLINK Publication No. 5., copyright ©1997. Used by permission.

- The National Committee for Prevention of Child Abuse estimated 3,126,000 reported child abuse victims in 1996, as compared to 1,919,000 in 1985. This does not include cases of abuse that were not reported (Wang & Daro, 1997).

- In 1996, an estimated 1,046 children died from abuse and neglect. In other words, almost three children died daily in the U.S. as a result of maltreatment. This signifies a 20% increase from 1985 (Wang & Daro, 1997).

- Most sexual abuse offenders are not strangers, but persons that the abused child knows and trusts (La Fontaine, 1990)

## *History*

In 1874, the abuse of a child by her parents was brought to the attention of Henry Bergh, the founder and president of the Society for the Prevention of Cruelty to Animals (S.P.C.A.). Without any statutes pertaining to child abuse, Mr. Bergh could only acquire a lawyer and pursue the case on the grounds that "children ought to be deemed just as worthy of protection from abuse as dogs and cats" (Weller, S., 57). The case, named after the abused child, became known as the "Little Mary Ellen Case" and went to court on April 10, 1874, providing for the establishment of the Society for the Prevention of Cruelty to Children (S.P.C.C.) in 1875. A year later, the S.P.C.A. and the S.P.C.C. merged, forming the American Humane Association (A.H.A.) which has pioneered standards for the protection of children and animals since its formation.

*The Child Abuse Prevention and Treatment Act of 1974* has further served the needs of abused children throughout the U.S. in many ways including: providing financial assistance to child abuse prevention and treatment programs; establishing a National Center on Child Abuse; and providing resources for research to prevent child abuse.

## Overview

Child abuse does not discriminate. It spans all racial, gender, socio-economic and demographic boundaries. While it may be more likely to be reported and thus reflected in greater numbers of cases involving lower income families, it is by no means a problem limited to members of one economic or racial group.

In recent years, public awareness of child abuse has been heightened by highly publicized cases such as the brutal beating death of Lisa Steinberg in New York City by her adoptive father, attorney Joel Steinberg. Yet many cases of child abuse continue to go unreported and many signs of abuse remain undetected.

Child abuse rarely occurs as a single incidence. Abuse usually manifests itself as a pattern of events which can start as early as infancy and as late as adolescence. Often abused children don't realize that there is anything abnormal or wrong in their family. As they are brought up not knowing anything different, what they experience they assume to be what everyone else experiences (Ackerman and Graham, 1990).

Abuse can produce low self-esteem, aggressive behavior, acting out, suicidal tendencies, running away, wariness of adults, withdrawal, inhibition, and school and social adjustment problems. As symptoms combine, they can develop into codependancy. Abused teens learn to cope. Coping mechanisms include caretaking—growing up quickly and taking care of the house, keeping it running smoothly and trying to be "good." They can also withdraw and isolate themselves, trying not to be noticed. Sometimes teens will equate their abuse with love, when the only attention they receive is abuse, some teens will provoke it, searching for the attention they receive as a result (Ackerman and Graham, 1990).

Very often children and teens will not talk about their abuse. They will protect their abuser, making excuses for their injuries. For this reason, it is often hard to uncover abuse. Detection of abuse takes careful observation over a period of time. Just as unreported and un-disclosed abuse is unjust, so is the unfounded and inaccurate report-ing. A false report is devastating and lasting, the stigma stays long after the report has been cleared. Therefore it is important that careful investigation is done before accusations are made.

There is, sometimes, a fine line between what distinguishes be-tween abuse and harsh, if appropriate, punishment. This confusion about what constitutes abuse may influence the high level of under-reporting. Abuse of children can be divided into four categories:

## Physical Abuse

Physical abuse is often the most recognizable form of abuse, as visible physical indications may be evident. It can be defined as "an injury or a pattern of injuries to a child that is non-accidental." In-cluded in this definition may be the following physical signs:

- welts;
- burns;
- bites;
- strangulation;
- broken bones;
- internal injuries;
- cigarette burns;
- immersion burns; and/or
- dry burns (La Fontaine, 1990).

Physical abuse can be as emotionally traumatizing as it is physically traumatizing. The betrayal that the child will associate with a trusted parental figure hurting them can be devastating. It is also usually ac-companied by emotional abuse, the physical assaults being interspersed with verbal insults and unreasonable expectations. Physical abuse can lead to delayed development, learning disorders, motor disorders, men-tal retardation, hearing loss or poor physical growth.

## Emotional Abuse

Perhaps one of the more difficult forms of abuse to identify, emotional abuse can be described as the "willful destruction of significant impairment of a child's competence" (La Fontaine, 1990). Emotional abuse can include: name-calling, ridicule, degradation, exacerbating a fear, destroying personal possessions, torture or destruction of a pet, excessive criticism, inappropriate, excessive demands, withholding of communications, or routine labeling or humiliation.

The victim may react by separating him or herself from the abuser, or internalizing the abusive message. In the case of sibling emotional abuse, the child may also redirect the abuse and abuse another sibling, or fight back by insulting and degrading the abuser (Wiehe, 1990). [*See also* Chapter 18.] Since emotional abuse involves a failure to meet the emotional needs of the child, most of the consequences are due to the psychological component of abuse. Emotional abuse often results in abnormal or disrupted attachment development and a tendency for the victim to blame him or herself for the abuse, leading to a learned helplessness, emotional numbing and overly passive behavior. Psychological abuse is often combined with other forms of abuse (Starr, MacLean, and Keating, 1991).

## Physical/Emotional Neglect

Physical and emotional neglect may accompany other forms of abuse, and may result in long-term devastating consequences. Physical neglect includes a "pervasive" situation where parents or guardians do not or can not provide the necessary food, shelter, medical care, supervision, and education for children under 18 years old (La Fontaine, 1990). Emotional neglect may also include deprivation of love, stimulation and security.

Although it is often forgotten or overlooked, the majority of fatalities due to child maltreatment are attributed to neglect. However, there are other factors involved. Often neglect is correlated with poverty and it is difficult to distinguish between what is immediately due to the neglect and what is a result of the poverty. For example, undernourishment may simply be an inability to afford the proper food, or it may be a lack of effort on the part of the parent. Medical neglect is also difficult to study since more than one factor affects medical compliance. It is sometimes unclear if it is the parent who is not attentive to the child's needs, or if it is the child's unwillingness to co-operate that is the cause of the medical neglect (Dubowitz, 1991).

## Sexual Abuse

Exploitation of a child for the sexual gratification of an adult en-compasses the terms child sexual abuse, assault and exploitation (La Fontaine, 1990). This definition also applies to the abuse of a child by those not legally considered adults. It may include one or more of the following:

- obscene language;
- pornography;
- exposure;
- fondling;
- molesting;
- oral sex;
- intercourse; and
- sodomy.

Contrary to popular belief, the perpetrator of sexual abuse is not the stranger and "dirty old man" of myths; he is usually someone that is known to the child. All too common, its occurrence has been estimated between 6% and 45%. Effects are numerous and can be long-term. They range from depression and low self-esteem to posttraumatic stress disorder, and multiple personality and borderline syndromes.

Frequency and duration have been identified to mediate the effects of the abuse; longer duration and higher frequency have been corre-lated with greater trauma (Wyatt, Newcomb and Riederle, 1990).

## All Abuse

Some important signs to look for in identifying all types of child abuse are:

- unexplained injuries;
- poor hygiene;
- inadequate nutrition;
- failure to thrive;

- lack of supervision, or abandonment;
- destructive behavior;
- sleep or speech disorders;
- difficulty walking or sitting;
- pain or bleeding in the genital area; and
- venereal disease.

It has been found that the vast majority of maltreated infants form insecure attachment relationships with their caregivers which, through development, tend to become anxious avoidant patterns of attachment. The style of attachment has been linked to later adaptation and development. Likewise, the development of an autonomous self esteem is found to be low or unresolved, and children in abusive environments are more "aggressive, frustrated, and noncompliant" than normal. They are also slow in developing external awareness and differentiation of inanimate and animate objects, and their social skills are immature or dysfunctional (Wolfe and McGree, 1991). This indicates that beyond the immediate abuse, there are short- and long-term effects of the abuse that affect the general development and emotional health of the abused child.

## The Cycle of Abuse

It is important to note that a parent or guardian is at a substantially greater risk of abusing a child if he or she was abused. Increased substance abuse has also been attributed to the incessant rise in cases of child abuse.

Identification and reporting to proper officials—such as the police and local social services—are among the components essential to breaking the cycle of abuse that continues to plague America's children.

## References

Ackerman, Robert J., and Dee Graham. (1990). *Too Old to Cry: Abused Teens in Today's America*. Blue Ridge Summit, PA: HIS and TAB Books.

Dubowitz, Howard. (1991). "The Impact of Child Maltreatment on Health." *The Effects of Child Abuse and Neglect*. Raymond H. Starr, Jr. and David A. Wolfe, eds. New York, NY: The Guilford Press.

La Fontaine, J. S. (1990). *Child Sexual Abuse*. Cambridge, England: Polity Press: 109–10.

Starr, Raymond H., Darla J. MacLean, and Daniel P. Keating. (1991). "Life-Span Development of Child Maltreatment." *The Effects of Child Abuse and Neglect*. Raymond H. Starr, Jr. and David A. Wolfe, eds. New York, NY: The Guilford Press.

Wang, Ching-Tun, and Deborah Daro. (1997) *Current Trends in Child Abuse Reporting and Fatalities: The Results of the 1996 Annual Fifty State Survey*. Chicago, IL: National Center on Child Abuse Prevention Research, National Committee to Prevent Child Abuse.

Weller, Sheila. "Battered Children: How Can We Save Them?" *McCall's* 115 (June 1988): 57.

Wiehe, Vernon R. (1990). *Sibling Abuse: Hidden Physical, Emotional and Sexual Trauma*. Lexington, MA: Lexington Books.

Wolfe, David A., and Robin McGree. (1991). "Assessment of Emotional Status Among Maltreated Children." *The Effects of Child Abuse and Neglect*. Raymond H. Starr, Jr. and David A. Wolfe, eds. New York, NY: The Guilford Press.

Wyatt, Gail Elizabeth, Michael D. Newcomb, and Monika H. Riederle. (1990). *Sexual Abuse and Consensual Sex*. Newberry Park, CA: Sage Publications, Inc.

## Section 14.3

# In Fact...Frequently Asked Questions on Child Abuse and Neglect

National Clearinghouse on Child Abuse and Neglect, 1999.

To answer frequently asked questions on child abuse and neglect, this fact sheet synthesizes information from several federally supported sources. Much of the data comes from the National Child Abuse and Neglect Data System (NCANDS) and the National Incidence Study (NIS) of Child Abuse and Neglect, both sponsored by the U.S. Department of Health and Human Services. The NCANDS annually collects and analyzes information on child maltreatment provided by state child protective services (CPS) agencies. These CPS agencies are public social service organizations with the primary responsibility for receiving and responding to reports of alleged maltreatment. The NIS periodically surveys community professionals who come into contact with children (5,600 professionals in 1993) to estimate the incidence of child maltreatment, including cases both reported and not reported to CPS.

### 1. How many children are reported and investigated for abuse or neglect?

In 1997, CPS agencies investigated an estimated 2 million reports that involved the alleged maltreatment of approximately 3 million children.

### 2. How many children are victims of maltreatment?

In 1997, CPS agencies determined just under 1 million children were victims of substantiated or indicated child abuse and neglect. The term "substantiated" means that an allegation of maltreatment was confirmed according to the level of evidence required by state law or state policy. The term "indicated" is an investigation finding used by some states when there is insufficient evidence to substantiate a case under state law or policy, but there is reason to suspect that maltreatment occurred or that there is risk of future maltreatment.

Several studies suggest that more children suffer from abuse or neglect than are evident in official statistics from state CPS agencies. Based on reports received and investigated by CPS, about 13.9 children per 1,000 younger than 18 in the general population were victims of abuse or neglect. In comparison, the NIS-3 estimated that 42 children per 1,000 in the population were harmed or endangered by maltreatment.

### 3. Is the number of abused and neglected children increasing?

Nationally, the number of victims of substantiated or indicated maltreatment decreased between 1996 and 1997, from slightly over one million (1,030,751) to just under one million (984,000). Previously, the rate of maltreatment had been on the increase between 1990 and 1996, with an overall increase for that period of 18 percent.

The 1996 NIS reported a dramatic increase in maltreatment between 1986 (NIS-2) and 1993 (NIS-3). According to the NIS, the estimated number of children who experienced harm from abuse and neglect increased 67 percent between the two studies (from 931,000 children to 1,553,800). In particular, the estimated number of seriously injured children quadrupled from 141,700 in 1986 to 565,000 in 1993.

### 4. What are the most common types of maltreatment?

Neglect is the most common form of child maltreatment. CPS investigations determined that 54 percent of victims in 1997 suffered neglect; 24 percent, physical abuse; 13 percent, sexual abuse; 6 percent, emotional maltreatment; and 2 percent, medical neglect. Many children suffer more than one type of maltreatment.

### 5. Who are the child victims?

Child abuse and neglect affects children of all ages. Among children confirmed as victims by CPS agencies in 1997, more than half were 7 years old or younger, and one-quarter were younger than 4 years old. Approximately 22 percent of victims were children ages 8 to 11; another 25 percent were youth ages 12 to 18. A greater proportion of neglect and medical neglect victims were children younger than 8, while a greater proportion of physical, sexual, and emotional abuse victims were children age 8 or older.

In 1997, approximately 52 percent of victims of maltreatment were female, and 47 percent were male. Available data suggest that some differences exist in the types of maltreatment experienced by male and female children. A review of data showed that 77 percent of sexual abuse victims were girls and 23 percent boys. Victims of emotional maltreatment also were somewhat more likely to be female (51%) than male (49%).

Conversely, a slightly greater proportion of victims of other types of maltreatment were male, with males comprising approximately 51 percent of neglect victims and 52 percent of both physical abuse and medical neglect victims.

Two-thirds (67%) of all victims were white, while 27 percent were African American. Hispanic children were about 13 percent of victims, American Indian/Alaska Native children about 2.5 percent of victims, and Asian/Pacific Islander children about 1 percent of victims.

While children of families in all income levels suffer maltreatment, research suggests that family income is strongly related to incidence rates. The NIS-3 found that children from families with annual incomes below $15,000 per year were more than 25 times more likely than children from families with annual income above $30,000 to have been harmed or endangered by abuse or neglect.

## 6. How many children die from abuse or neglect?

Based on data reported by CPS agencies in 1997, it is estimated that nationwide, 1,196 children died as a result of abuse or neglect. Children age 3 and under accounted for more than three-quarters of these child fatalities. The actual number of deaths may be higher, as not all child maltreatment fatalities are known to CPS.

## 7. Who abuses and neglects children?

In 1997, the majority of perpetrators of child maltreatment (75%) were parents, and another 10 percent were other relatives of the victim. People who were in other caretaking relationships to the victim (e.g., child care providers, foster parents, and facility staff) accounted for only 2 percent of perpetrators. About 13 percent of all perpetrators were classified as noncaretakers or unknown. (In many states, perpetrators of child maltreatment by definition must be in a caretaking role.)

Over 80 percent of all perpetrators were under age 40. Overall, approximately 62 percent of perpetrators were female, although perpetrator gender differed by type of maltreatment. Neglect and medi-cal neglect were most often attributed to female perpetrators, while sexual abuse was most often attributed to male perpetrators.

## 8. Who reports child maltreatment?

In 1997, more than half (81%) of all reports alleging maltreatment and referred for investigation came from professionals, including edu-cators, law enforcement and justice officials, social services workers, and medical and mental health personnel. About 18 percent of reports were received from parents, other relatives of the child or the victims themselves, 8.5 percent from friends and neighbors, 12 percent from anonymous sources, and 8 percent from other sources. An estimated two-thirds of substantiated or indicated reports were from profes-sional sources.

## 9. Are victims of child abuse more likely to engage in criminality later in life?

According to a 1992 study sponsored by the National Institute of Justice (NIJ), maltreatment in childhood increases the likelihood of arrest as a juvenile by 53 percent, as an adult by 38 percent, and for a violent crime by 38 percent. Being abused or neglected in childhood increases the likelihood of arrest for females by 77 percent. A related 1995 NIJ report indicated that children who were sexually abused were 28 times more likely than a control group of non-abused chil-dren to be arrested for prostitution as an adult. [See also Chapter 32.]

## 10. Is there any evidence linking alcohol or other drug use to child maltreatment?

A 1999 study by the National Center on Addiction and Substance Abuse found that children of substance-abusing parents were almost 3 times likelier to be abused and more than 4 times likelier to be ne-glected than children of parents who are not substance abusers. Other studies suggest that an estimated 50 percent to 80 percent of all child abuse cases substantiated by CPS involve some degree of substance abuse by the child's parents.

# References

Child Welfare League of America. (1989). *Highlights of Questions from the Working Paper on Chemical Dependency.* Washington, DC: Author.

Reid, J., P. Macchetto, and S. Foster. (1999). *No Safe Haven: Children of Substance-Abusing Parents.* The National Center on Addiction and substance Abuse at Columbia University, New York, NY.

U.S. Advisory Board on Child Abuse and Neglect. (1995). *A Nation's Shame: Fatal Child Abuse and Neglect in the United States.* Washington, DC: Department of Health and Human Services, Administration for Children and Families.

U.S. Department of Health and Human Services, National Center on Child Abuse and Neglect. (1999). *Child Maltreatment 1997: Reports from the States to the National Child Abuse and Neglect Data System.* Washington, DC: GPO.

U.S. Department of Health and Human Services, National Center on Child Abuse and Neglect. (1991). *National Incidence and Prevalence of Child Abuse and Neglect: The 1988 Revised Report* (NIS-2). Washington, DC: GPO.

U.S. Department of Health and Human Services, National Center on Child Abuse and Neglect. (1996). *Third National Incidence Study of Child Abuse and Neglect: Final Report* (NIS-3). Washington, DC: GPO.

Widom, C.S. (1992). *The Cycle of Violence.* Washington, DC: National Institute of Justice.

Widom, C.S., & Ames, M.A. (1994). Criminal Consequences of Child Sexual Victimization. *Child Abuse and Neglect, 18,* 303–18.

# Section 14.4

## *Shaken Baby Syndrome*

American Humane Association *Fact Sheet,* November 1997.
Used with permission.

Shaken baby syndrome is the medical term used to describe the violent shaking and resulting injuries sustained from shaking. Often, there are no obvious outward signs of injury to a baby or young child's body, but there is injury inside, particularly in the head or behind the eyes. These injuries can include:

- Brain swelling and damage;
- Subdural hemorrhage;
- Mental retardation, developmental delays;
- Blindness, hearing loss, paralysis, and speech and learning difficulties; and
- Death.

The term was first discussed in medical literature in 1972 but knowledge about the syndrome continues to develop. Shaken baby syndrome can occur when children are violently shaken either as part of a pattern of abuse or simply because an adult—or young caretaker—has momentarily succumbed to the frustration of responding to a crying baby.

Violent shaking is especially dangerous to infants and young children because their neck muscles are undeveloped and their brain tissue is exceptionally fragile. Their small size further adds to the risk of injury. Vigorous shaking repeatedly pitches the brain in different directions.

Those sudden motions can cause some parts of the brain to pull away, tearing brain cells and blood vessels in the process. When a child is shaken in anger and frustration, the force is multiplied 5 or 10 times more than it would be if the child had simply tripped and fallen. That force is repeated many times in succession while the child is being shaken.

Shaken baby syndrome can have disastrous consequences for the family, the victim, and society. If the child survives, medical bills can be enormous. The victim may require lifelong medical care for brain damage injuries such as mental retardation or cerebral palsy. The child may even require institutionalization or other types of long-term care.

According to the California Medical Association, for many years doctors failed to recognize the cause of brain bleeding in small children who were actually victims of shaken baby syndrome because the children usually do not exhibit any external signs of injury. Doctors saw only the results, most frequently convulsions and brain damage and sometimes death. Often, the injuries were attributed to other causes.

Until recently, some medical programs, designed to treat infants who are prone to sleep apnea, supported the use of "tactile stimulation" as first-aid treatment when the infant stopped breathing. Parents were instructed to "shake gently, then vigorously." Since parents of infants who are at high risk for sleep apnea are usually very stressed and frequently exhausted, thereby increasing the risk for physical abuse, educational materials from the California Medical Association specifically advise parents not to shake babies for apnea or for any other reason.

Most of the time, shaken baby syndrome occurs because a parent or caretaker is frustrated or angry with a child. Other times, children become victims when a parent or caretaker, not realizing how seriously this behavior can harm, throws a small child into the air vigorously, plays too roughly, or hits an infant too hard on the back. Anyone who takes care of a baby or small child—parents, older siblings, babysitters, child care professionals, and others—should be reminded to never shake babies or small children.

There are organizations in local communities that can provide help to parents whose patience has been strained by the burden of caring for an infant who cries continually or who might need more help with parenting and coping skills.

There are also some nonviolent ways to stop a baby from crying. These might include:

- Running a vacuum cleaner within hearing range of the infant,

- Giving the baby a pacifier after checking to make sure that he/she is not hungry or wet,

- Putting the baby in a safe carrier on top of a clothes dryer while it is operating (not leaving the baby unattended), or

- Simply hugging and cuddling the child gently. Very young infants can be carried around in a "Snugli" or other type of carrier that holds the infant close to the body.

If these suggestions do not work, you do not think the baby is ill, and you cannot take the crying and stress anymore, put the baby on his/her side in a safe place, such as a crib. Take a short break, and, if possible, call someone to take care of the baby for a while. (*Crying: What Should I Do?* by Jacy Showers, Ed.D., SBS Prevention Plus.)

Information about shaken baby syndrome is not intended to make parents afraid to touch their children. It is intended to remind parents that special care must be taken when handling children, especially in the infant to 3-year age range and that **children must never be shaken for any reason.** Dr. Jacy Showers, a national expert on shaken baby syndrome, suggests that as long as a child is smaller than you are, it is never "safe" to shake them and better to err on the side of the child's safety than take risks.

Specific questions on the subject of shaken baby syndrome should be directed to your physician or pediatrician. Check with your local hospital for additional information on this, as well as for information on support groups for parents with infants.

## Section 14.5

# *Child Fatalities Fact Sheet*

National Clearinghouse on Child Abuse and Neglect, 1999.

Children are one of the most vulnerable groups in our society. Child fatalities due to maltreatment represent the worst case scenario in attempts to protect children. Despite the efforts of the child protection system, child fatalities remain a serious problem. Although the untimely deaths of children due to illness and accidents have been closely monitored, the same cannot be said of children who have died as the result of physical assault or severe neglect. Intervention strategies targeted at resolving this problem face complex challenges.

### *Child Fatalities Due to Maltreatment Are Increasing*

Although child deaths caused by abuse and/or neglect are relatively infrequent, the rate of child maltreatment fatalities, confirmed by Child Protective Services (CPS) to have been the result of child maltreatment, has steadily increased over the last decade. The National Child Abuse and Neglect Data System (NCANDS) reported that in 1997 there were an estimated 1,196 child fatalities, or 1.7 children per 100,000 in the general population. (This estimate was based on reports from 41 states that reported a total of 967 fatalities.) The U.S. Advisory Board on Child Abuse and Neglect in *A Nation's Shame: Fatal Child Abuse and Neglect in the United States,* reported that a more realistic estimate of annual child deaths as a result of abuse and neglect, both known and unknown to CPS agencies, is about 2,000, or approximately five children per day. Experts such as Ryan Rainey from the National Center for Prosecution of Child Abuse believe that the number of child deaths from maltreatment per year may be as high as 5,000.

### *The Actual Number of Child Fatalities May Be Underreported*

Determining the actual numbers of children who die annually from abuse is complex. Many researchers and practitioners believe that child fatalities are underreported because some deaths labeled as accidents, child homicides, and/or Sudden Infant Death Syndrome (SIDS) might be attributed to child maltreatment if more comprehensive investigations were conducted. It is difficult to distinguish a child who has been suffocated from a child who has died as a result of SIDS, or a child who was dropped, pushed, or thrown from a child who dies from a legitimate fall. Some researchers and practitioners have gone so far as to estimate that there may be twice the number of deaths as a result of abuse and/or neglect as are reported by NCANDS if cases unknown to CPS agencies are included.

### There Is a Lack of Standard Terminology for Child Fatalities

To further complicate the issue, different terminology is used to discuss child fatalities, sometimes interchangeably. NCANDS defines "child fatality" as a child dying from abuse or neglect, because either (a) the injury from the abuse or neglect was the cause of death, or (b) the abuse and/or neglect was a contributing factor to the cause of death. Researchers such as Finkelhor and Christoffel use the term "child abuse homicide" to define a childhood death resulting from maltreatment (either assault or neglect) by a responsible caretaker. Law enforcement and criminal justice agencies also use the term "child abuse homicide," but their definition, while including the caretaker as perpetrator, also includes the "criminal act of homicide by non-care-takers" (death at the hands of another, felony child endangerment, and criminal neglect). More specifically, the term "infanticide" is increasingly used to define the murdering of children younger than 6 or 12 months by their parents.

### Young Children Are the Most Vulnerable

Research supports that very young children (age 5 and younger) are the most frequent victims of child fatalities. NCANDS data for 1997 from a subset of states demonstrated that children 3 or younger accounted for 77 percent of fatalities. This population is the most vulnerable for many reasons including their small size and inability to defend themselves. The fatal abuse usually occurs in one of two ways: repeated abuse and/or neglect over a period of time (battered child syndrome) or in a single, impulsive incident of assault (drowning, suffocating, or shaking the baby, for example).

307

## *Primary Caretakers Are the Most Frequent Perpetrators*

No matter how the fatal abuse occurs, one fact of great concern is that most of the perpetrators are, by definition, primary caretakers such as parents and other relatives.

Though there is no single profile for the perpetrator of fatal child abuse, there are consistent characteristics that reappear in studies. Frequently the perpetrator is a young adult in his/her mid-20s without a high school diploma, living at or below the poverty level, depressed, and who may have difficulty coping with stressful situations. In many instances, the perpetrator has experienced violence first-hand.

## *The Response to Fatal Child Abuse or Neglect Is Complex*

The response to the problem is often hampered by inconsistencies:

- The inaccurate reporting of the number of children who die each year as a result of abuse and neglect
- The lack of national standards for child autopsies or death investigations
- The different roles that CPS agencies play in the investigation process
- The use in many states of an elected coroner who is not required to have any medical or child abuse and neglect training rather than a medical examiner.

## *Child Fatality Review Teams*

To address some of these inconsistencies, multidisciplinary/ multiagency Child Fatality Review Teams have emerged in many states to provide a coordinated approach to the investigation of child deaths. These teams are comprised of prosecutors, coroners or medical examiners, law enforcement personnel, CPS workers, public health care providers, and others.

The teams review cases of child deaths and facilitate appropriate follow-up. The follow-up may include assuring that services are provided for surviving family members, providing information to assist in the prosecution of perpetrators, and developing recommendations to improve child protection and community support systems. In addition, teams can assist in determining avenues for prevention efforts and improving training for front-line workers. Well-designed, properly organized Child Fatality Review Teams appear to offer the greatest hope for defining the underlying nature and scope of fatalities due to child abuse and neglect and for offering solutions.

### *Prevention Services Are Key*

When addressing the issue of child maltreatment, and especially child fatalities, prevention is a recurring theme. In 1995, the U.S. Advisory Board on Child Abuse and Neglect recommended a universal approach to the prevention of child fatalities that would reach out to all families through the implementation of several key strategies. These efforts would begin by providing services such as home visitation by trained professionals or paraprofessionals, hospital-linked outreach to parents of infants and toddlers, community-based programs designed for the specific needs of neighborhoods, and effective public education campaigns.

## *References*

Christoffel, K. K. (1992). "Child Abuse Fatalities." In S. Ludwig, & A.E. Kornberg, eds. *Child Abuse. A Medical Reference* (2nd ed.). New York: Churchill Livingstone, Inc.

Department of Justice. Office of Juvenile Justice and Delinquency Programs. (1994, February 16–17). *Child Fatality Review Teams: A Multi-agency Approach.* (Participant Guide). National Training Teleconference.

Finkelhor, D. (1997). In G. Kaufman Kantor and J. Jasinski eds. *Out of the Darkness: Contemporary Perspectives on Family Violence.* Thousand Oaks, CA: Sage Publications.

Kaplan, S. R. (1996). *Child Fatalities and Child Fatality Review Teams.* Washington, DC: ABA Center on Children and the Law.

Lewit, E. M. (1994). "Reported Child Abuse and Neglect." In *The Future of Children (Sexual Abuse of Children),*(4)2.

National Center on Child Abuse and Neglect. (1992). *National Child Abuse and Neglect Data System: 1990 Summary Data Component, Working Paper* 1. Washington, DC: U.S. Department of Health and Human Services.

U.S. Advisory Board on Child Abuse and Neglect. (1995). *A Nation's Shame: Fatal Child Abuse and Neglect in the United States.* Washington, DC: U.S. Department of Health and Human Services.

U.S. Department of Health and Human Services, Children's Bureau. (1999). *Child Maltreatment 1997: Reports from the States to the National Child Abuse and Neglect Data System.* Washington, DC: U.S. Government Printing Office.

Walsh, B. (1994). "Section II: Criminal Investigation of Physical Abuse and Neglect." In J. Briere, L. Berliner, J. A. Bulkley, C. Jenny, and T. Reid eds. *The APSAC Handbook on Child Maltreatment.* Chicago, IL: American Professional Society on the Abuse of Children (APSAC).

Wang, C. T., and D. Daro. (1998). *Current Trends in Child Abuse Reporting and Fatalities: The Results of the 1997 Annual Fifty State Survey.* Chicago, IL: National Committee to Prevent Child Abuse.

## Section 14.6

## *Child Sexual Abuse*

National Center for Victims of Crime, INFOLINK Publication No. 6, copyright @ 1997. Used with permission.

### *At a Glance*

• Twenty-nine percent of female rape victims in America were younger than eleven when they were raped (National Victim Center and Crime Victims Research and Treatment Center, 1992).

• According to the National Committee to Prevent Child Abuse's annual survey, state child protective agencies received 218,820 reports of child sexual abuse in 1996 (Wang and Daro, 1997).[1]

• In the United States, at least 20% of women and 5% to 10% of men were sexually abused as children (Finkelhor, 1994).

### *Overview*

Child sexual abuse has been at the center of unprecedented public attention during the last decade. All fifty states and the District of Columbia have enacted statutes identifying child sexual abuse as criminal behavior (Whitcomb, 1986). This crime encompasses different types of sexual activity, including voyeurism, sexual dialogue, fondling, touching of the genitals, vaginal, anal, or oral rape and forcing children to participate in pornography or prostitution.

## Child Sexual Abusers

Perpetrators of child sexual abuse come from different age groups, genders, races and socio-economic backgrounds. Women sexually abuse children, although not as frequently as men, and juvenile perpetrators comprise as many as one-third of the offenders (Finkelhor, 1994). One common denominator is that victims frequently know and trust their abusers.

Child abusers coerce children by offering attention or gifts, manipulating or threatening their victims, using aggression or employing a combination of these tactics. "[D]ata indicate that child molesters are frequently aggressive. Of 250 child victims studied by DeFrancis, 50% experienced physical force, such as being held down, struck, or shaken violently" (Becker, 1994).

## Child Sexual Abuse Victims

Studies have not found differences in the prevalence of child sexual abuse among different social classes or races. However, parental inadequacy, unavailability, conflict and a poor parent-child relationship are among the characteristics that distinguish children at risk of being sexually abused (Finkelhor, 1994). According to the Third National Incidence Study, girls are sexually abused three times more often than boys, whereas boys are more likely to die or be seriously injured from their abuse (Sedlak & Broadhurst, 1996). Both boys and girls are most vulnerable to abuse between the ages of 7 and 13 (Finkelhor, 1994).

## Incest

Incest traditionally describes sexual abuse in which the perpetrator and victim are related by blood. However, incest can also refer to cases where the perpetrator and victim are emotionally connected (Crnich and Crnich, 1992). "[I]ntrafamily perpetrators constitute from one-third to one-half of all perpetrators against girls and only about

311

one-tenth to one-fifth of all perpetrators against boys. There is no question that intrafamily abuse is more likely to go on over a longer period of time and in some of its forms, particularly parent-child abuse, has been shown to have more serious consequences" (Finkelhor, 1994).

## Symptoms of Child Sexual Abuse

Many sexually abused children exhibit physical, behavioral and emotional symptoms. Some physical signs are pain or irritation to the genital area, vaginal or penile discharge and difficulty with urination. Victims of known assailants may experience less physical trauma because such injuries might attract suspicion (Hammerschlag, 1996).

Behavioral changes often precede physical symptoms as the first indicators of sexual abuse (American Humane Association Children's Division, 1993). Behavioral signs include nervous or aggressive behavior toward adults, sexual provocativeness before an appropriate age and the use of alcohol and other drugs. Boys "are more likely than girls to act out in aggressive and antisocial ways as a result of abuse" (Finkelhor, 1994). Children may say such things as, "My mother's boyfriend does things to me when she's not there," or "I'm afraid to go home tonight."

## Consequences of Child Sexual Abuse

Consequences of child sexual abuse range "from chronic depression to low self-esteem to sexual dysfunction to multiple personalities. A fifth of all victims develop serious long-term psychological problems, according to the American Medical Association. These may include dissociative responses and other signs of post-traumatic-stress syndrome [*sic*], chronic states of arousal, nightmares, flashbacks, venereal disease and anxiety over sex or exposure of the body during medical exams" (American Humane Association Children's Division, 1993).

## Cycle of Violence

Children who are abused or neglected are more likely to become criminal offenders as adults. A National Institute of Justice study found "that childhood abuse increased the odds of future delinquency and adult criminality overall by 40 percent" (Widom, 1992). Child sexual abuse victims are also at risk of becoming ensnared in this cycle of violence. One expert estimates that forty percent of sexual abusers were sexually abused as children (Vanderbilt, 1992). In addition, victims of child sexual abuse are 27.7 times more likely to be arrested for prostitution as adults than non-victims (Widom, 1995). Some victims become sexual abusers or prostitutes because they have a difficult time relating to others except on sexual terms.

## Stopping the Cycle of Violence

With early detection and appropriate treatment, society can prevent some victimized children from becoming adult perpetrators. In order to intervene early in abuse, parents should educate their children about appropriate sexual behavior and how to feel comfortable saying no (American Humane Association Children's Division, 1993).

Although about 40% of untreated nonincest offenders recidivate, studies have found that treatment can successfully decrease recidivism rates (Becker, 1994). Depo-Provera and other pharmacological treatments can decrease sexual thoughts, urges or drives by lowering male sexual offenders' testosterone levels. This method is sometimes referred to as chemical castration. Offenders' inappropriate attraction to children can be diminished by behavioral modification techniques, such as aversive conditioning, masturbatory satiation, and covert sensitization. Psychological treatment such as psychotherapy and counseling can help offenders understand their behavior and identify its origins (Groth and Oliveri, 1989).

Steps must be taken to ensure that perpetrators do not attack again once the criminal justice system's punitive measures have taken their course. All states and the federal government have enacted versions of Megan's Law that require community notification and sex offender registration. Under these laws, authorities are required to notify communities when sex offenders move in. In some cases, law enforcement agencies make the notification while the offender is responsible in others. Registration laws require offenders to provide information such as name and address to a law enforcement agency. The FBI maintains a nationwide sex offender registry (Walsh, 1997).

## Child Sexual Abuse Reporting

Children may resist reporting sexual abuse because they are afraid of angering the offender, blame themselves for the abuse or feel guilty and ashamed. In order to increase reporting, parents and adults who

313

interact with children, such as school personnel, teachers, counselors, child care workers, Boy and Girl Scout troop leaders, and coaches, should be educated about the behavioral and physical symptoms of child sexual abuse (American Humane Association Children's Division, 1995). Children are more likely to reveal sexual abuse when talking to someone who appears to 'already know' and is not judgmental, critical or threatening. They also tend to disclose when they believe continuation of the abuse will be unbearable; they are physically injured; or they receive sexual abuse prevention information. Other reasons may be to protect another child or if pregnancy is a threat ("Child Sexual Abuse..." 1993).

## Recovery from Child Sexual Abuse

Once a child discloses the abuse, an appropriate response is extremely important to the child's healing process. The adult being confided in should encourage the victim to talk freely, reassure the child that he or she is not to blame and seek medical and psychological assistance. Family members may also benefit from mental health services (American Academy of Child and Adolescent Psychiatry, 1992).

## Legal Action

Suspicions of child sexual abuse should be reported to a child protective services agency or law enforcement agency. Local child protection agencies investigate intrafamilial abuse and the police investigate extrafamilial abuse. The law requires professionals who work with children to report suspected neglect or abuse.

In addition to reporting child sexual abuse to the authorities, victims can sue their abusers in civil court to recover monetary damages or win other remedies (Crnich and Crnich, 1992). Many states have extended their criminal and civil statutes of limitation for child sexual abuse cases (National Victim Center, 1995). In addition, the delayed discovery rule suspends the statutes of limitation if the victim had repressed all memory of the abuse or was unaware that the abuse caused current problems (Crnich and Crnich, 1992).

## Adult Survivors of Child Sexual Abuse

Survivors of child sexual abuse use coping mechanisms to deal with the horror of the abuse. One such mechanism, protective denial, entails repressing some or all of the abuse. This may cause significant memory gaps that can last months or even years. Victims also use dissociative coping mechanisms, such as becoming numb, to distance themselves from the psychological and physiological responses to the abuse. They may also turn to substance abuse, self-mutilation and eating disorders. In order to recover, adult survivors must adopt positive coping behaviors, forgive themselves, and relinquish their identities as survivors (Sgroi, 1989). The healing process can begin when the survivor acknowledges the abuse. When working with adult survivors of child sexual abuse, therapists should consider the survivor's feeling of security and the personal and professional ramifications of disclosure.

Societal influences play a big role in the recovery process. Although males are raised to shoulder responsibility for what happens to them, male victims need to understand that the victimization was not their fault. Only then can they begin to accept that they were not responsible for the abuse ("Male Survivors of Childhood Sexual Abuse," 1990).

## End Notes

1. Calculated by multiplying the estimated number of reported child victims (3,126,000) by the percentage of sexual abuse cases (7%).

## Works Cited

American Academy of Child and Adolescent Psychiatry. (1992). *Child Sexual Abuse*. Washington, D.C.: American Academy of Child and Adolescent Psychiatry.

American Humane Association Children's Division. (1993). *Child Sexual Abuse: AHA Fact Sheet #4*. Englewood, CO: American Humane Association.

American Humane Association Children's Division. (1995). *Guidelines to Help Children Who Have Been Reported for Suspected Abuse or Neglect: AHA Fact Sheet #14*. Englewood, CO: American Humane Association.

Becker, Judith. (1994). "Offenders: Characteristics and Treatment." *The Future of Children* 4(2): 179, 186.

"Child Sexual Abuse: Does the Nation Face an Epidemic—or a Wave of Hysteria?" (1993). *CQ Researcher* 3(2): 27–28.

Crnich, Joseph, and Kimberly Crnich. (1992). *Shifting the Burden of Truth: Suing Child Sexual Abusers—A Legal Guide for Survivors and Their Supporters*. Lake Oswego, OR: Recollex Publishing.

Finkelhor, David. (1994). "Current Information on the Scope and Nature of Child Sexual Abuse." *The Future of Children* 4(2): 31, 46–48.

Groth, Nicholas, and Frank Oliveri. (1989). "Understanding Sexual Offense Behavior and Differentiating among Sexual Abusers: Basic Conceptual Issues." *Vulnerable Populations: Sexual Abuse Treatment for Children, Adult Survivors, Offenders, and Persons with Mental Retardation Volume 2*, Suzanne Sgroi, ed. Lexington, MA: Lexington Books.

Hammerschlag, Margaret. (1996). *Sexually Transmitted Diseases and Child Sexual Abuse*. Washington, D.C.: Office of Juvenile Justice and Delinquency Prevention, U.S. Department of Justice.

"Male Survivors of Childhood Sexual Abuse." (1990). *Virginia Child Protection Newsletter* 31: 1–12.

National Victim Center. (1995). "Extensions of the Criminal and Civil Statutes of Limitation in Child Sexual Abuse Cases." *INFOLINK*, No. 57. Arlington, VA: National Victim Center.

National Victim Center and Crime Victims Research and Treatment Center. (1992). *Rape in America: A Report to the Nation*. Arlington, VA: National Victim Center and Crime Victims Research and Treatment Center.

Sedlak, Andrea, and Diane Broadhurst. (1996). *Executive Summary of the Third National Incidence Study of Child Abuse and Neglect*. Washington, D.C.: National Center on Child Abuse and Neglect, U.S. Department of Health and Human Services.

Sgroi, Suzanne. (1989). "Stages of Recovery for Adult Survivors of Child Sexual Abuse." *Vulnerable Populations: Sexual Abuse Treatment for Children, Adult Survivors, Offenders, and Persons with Mental Retardation Volume 2*, Suzanne Sgroi, ed. Lexington, MA: Lexington Books.

Walsh, Elizabeth Rahmberg. (1997). "Megan's Laws—Sex Offender Registration and Notification Statutes and Constitutional Challenges." *The Sex Offender: New Insights, Treatment Innovations and Legal Developments*, Barbara Schwartz and Henry Cellini, eds. Kingston, NJ: Civic Research Institute.

Wang, Ching-Tung, and Deborah Daro. (1997). *Current Trends in Child Abuse: The Results of the 1996 Annual Fifty State Survey.* Chicago, IL: The National Center on Child Abuse Prevention Research, The National Committee to Prevent Child Abuse.

Whitcomb, Debra. (1986). *Prosecuting Child Sexual Abuse: New Approaches*. Washington, D.C.: National Institute of Justice, U.S. Department of Justice.

Widom, Cathy Spatz. (1992). *The Cycle of Violence*. Washington, D.C.: National Institute of Justice, U.S. Department of Justice.

Widom, Cathy Spatz. (1995). *Victims of Childhood Sexual Abuse— Later Criminal Consequences*. Washington, D.C.: National Institute of Justice, U.S. Department of Justice.

# Chapter 15

# *Spousal/Partner Abuse and Child Abuse*

## *Chapter Contents*

## Section 15.1

# *The Relationship Between Domestic Violence and Child Abuse*

Researchers have long been aware of the link between domestic violence and child abuse. Even if children are witnesses to acts of violence and not the intended targets, they can be affected in the same way as children who are physically and sexually abused.[1] Since domestic violence is a pattern of behavior, not a single event, episodes may become more severe and more frequent over time, resulting in an increased likelihood that the children eventually become victims.

### *What is domestic violence?*

Domestic violence is a pattern of assaultive and coercive behaviors, including physical, sexual, and psychological attacks, as well as economic coercion, that adults or adolescents use against their intimate partners. The U.S. Department of Justice estimates that 95% of reported assaults on spouses or ex-spouses are committed by men against women.[2]

### *What is child abuse?*

Prevent Child Abuse America defines child abuse as a nonaccidental injury or pattern of injuries to a child. Child abuse is damage to a child for which there is no "reasonable" explanation. Child abuse includes nonaccidental physical injury, neglect, sexual molestation, and emotional abuse.

### *How common are these problems?*

Domestic violence is a widespread problem with long-term consequences to the victim and all family members as well as to the abuser. Recent surveys indicate that increased public awareness about domestic violence, along with a more understanding attitude toward victims, has encouraged women to come forward.[3] In a survey conducted in early 1995, 31 percent of women said they had personally faced abuse, while in a similar survey conducted in July 1994 only 24 percent they had been abused.[3]

Child abuse has become a national epidemic. More than one million children are confirmed each year as victims of child abuse and neglect by state departments of child protective services.[4] And every day a minimum of three children die as a result.[4] Violence in the home has been listed as a major factor contributing to the growth of reports of child abuse and neglect.[4]

### *How does domestic violence affect children?*

Domestic violence often includes child abuse. Children may be victimized and threatened as a way of punishing and controlling the adult victim of domestic violence. Or they may be injured unintentionally when acts of violence occur in their presence. Often episodes of domestic violence expand to include attacks on children. However, even when children are not directly attacked, they can experience serious emotional damage as a result of living in a violent household. Children living in this environment come to believe that this behavior is acceptable.

The estimated overlap between domestic violence and child physical or sexual abuse ranges from 30 to 50 percent.[5,6] Some shelters report that the first reason many battered women give for fleeing the home is that the perpetrator was also attacking the children.[7] Victims report multiple concerns about the effects of spousal abuse on children.[8]

### *Are there similarities between families involved in domestic violence and families involved in child abuse?*

The two populations share several similarities as well as some important differences. Both forms of abuse cross all boundaries of economic level, race, ethnic heritage, and religious faith. Neither child abuse nor domestic violence is a phenomenon of the twentieth century. Children have been physically traumatized, deprived of the necessities of life, and molested sexually by adults since the dawn of human history.[9] Traditionally, parents claimed ownership of their children and society hesitated to interfere with the family unit. Similarly, society in the past has sanctioned the belief that men have the right to use whatever force is necessary to control the behavior of women. Those in intimate relationships as well as those who abuse children often are repeating learned behaviors transmitted inter-generationally. Both forms of abuse are identified by patterns. Neither domestic violence nor child abuse is an isolated event. Both occur with some regularity, often increasing and becoming more serious. Adults who were abused as children have an increased risk of abusing their children, and adults who grew up in a violent home are more likely to become perpetrators or victims of domestic violence. For a number of reasons including shame, secrecy, and isolation, both types of abuse are underreported.

Domestic violence and child abuse also differ in some significant ways. Parental stress is an important factor in instances of child abuse, but this link has not been established in cases of domestic violence. Reported perpetrators of child maltreatment are equally men and women, but the majority of perpetrators of domestic violence are men.

## How can we prevent these problems?

Domestic violence and child abuse proliferate in an environment that accepts the lesser status of women and children. Shrouding the violence in secrecy allows this behavior to continue. Educating the public about the extent of the problem establishes a foundation that permits victims to come forward.

Prevention efforts that reach parents before or soon after the birth of their baby, and provide intensive services on a moderately long-term basis can greatly reduce the incidence of child abuse as well as identify other problems such as domestic violence. Home visitors using a comprehensive approach can tailor their services to match a family's needs [see Section 17.3]. After establishing a trusting relationship with the family, the home visitor will be able to identify problems. While the home visitor may not be able to offer intervention services, he or she can provide resources and ensure the safety of the children.

Other prevention efforts include the following:

- Educate health and child welfare agencies about the prevalence of domestic violence and its effect on children.

- Involve the community in a multidisciplinary approach to provide intervention and prevention services to those families in need.

- Educate the public about domestic violence and child abuse and the long-term costs to society.

- Provide access to self-help groups and other supportive services for all perpetrators, victims, and survivors of abuse.
- Educate all who work with children and families, including teachers, service providers, and health care professionals about the interplay between domestic violence and child abuse.

## *Notes*

1.  Goodman, G., and M. Rosenberg. 1987. "The Child Witness to Family Violence: Clinical and Legal Considerations." *Domestic Violence on Trial: Psychological and Legal Dimensions of Family Violence,* edited by D. Sonkin. New York: Springer.

2.  Douglas, H. 1991. "Assessing Violent Couples." *Families in Society* 72(9): 525–35.

3.  Lieberman Research Inc. 1996. *Domestic Violence Advertising Campaign Tracking Survey,* Wave 3, November 1995. San Francisco, CA: Family Violence Prevention Fund and The Advertising Council.

4.  Lung, C. T., and D. Daro. 1996. *Current Trends in Child Abuse Reporting and Fatalities: The Results of the 1995 Annual Fifty State Survey.* Chicago, IL: Prevent Child Abuse America.

5.  Jaffe, P., D. Wolfe, and S. Wilson. 1990. *Children of Battered Women.* Newbury Park, CA: Sage Publications.

6.  Straus, M. A., and R. Gelles. 1990. *Physical Violence in American Families.* New Brunswick, NJ: Transaction.

7.  New Beginnings. 1990. *A Survey of Battered Women Seeking Shelter at New Beginnings, A Shelter for Battered Women in Seattle, Washington.*

8.  Hilton, N. Z. 1992. "Battered Women's Concerns about Their Children Witnessing Wife Assault." *Journal of Interpersonal Violence* 7: 77–86.

9.  Prevent Child Abuse America. 1993. *Think You Know Something about Child Abuse?* Chicago, IL: Prevent Child Abuse America.

Section 15.2

# The Co-occurrence of Intimate Partner Violence Against Mothers and Abuse of Children

National Center for Injury Prevention and Control, Centers for Disease Control and Prevention. Domestice Violence Prevention Fact Sheet, April, 1998.

Violence against mothers by their intimate partners is a serious risk factor for child abuse.[1] Conversely, mothers of abused children are at higher risk of being abused than mothers of non-abused children.[2] Co-occurrence of violence against mothers and their children by intimate partners of women is critical for community advocates, child protection workers, educators and maternal and child health care providers and others to address the safety of mothers and their children.[3,4]

## Scope of the Problem:

The concurrence "rate" of child abuse and intimate partner violence against mothers is defined as the proportion of families in the population or sample in which a woman and her child are both victims of violence by an intimate. In the mother's case, the intimate is her partner: the child may be abused by the mother's intimate partner or the battered mother. Concurrence rates vary widely in the literature; however, the quality of these studies, their data sources and their definitions of abuse also vary considerably. Approximately 20 studies exist with original data on concurrence rates.

The four most rigorous studies describe concurrence rates of approximately 50%. These four studies utilized samples representative of the U.S. population, multivariate analyses or control samples.[2,5,6,7] Selected results are presented below.

McKibben and colleagues,[2] the only study to use a control population, found that 40-60% of mothers of 32 abused children were also victimized compared to 13% of mothers of 32 matched children with no record of abuse in an urban public hospital. A fifth study supports the results of the smaller, controlled study. Stark and Flitcraft (n=116;

concurrence rate=32–45%) used a retrospective hospital record review and a similar data classification method.[8]

Ross' analysis[7] of 3,363 American parents interviewed for the 1985 National Family Violence Survey[6] indicates that each additional act of violence toward a spouse increases the probability of the violent spouse also being abusive to the child, particularly for fathers. Women who were the most chronically violent to their spouse had a 38% probability of also physically abusing a male child, the gender most often physically abused. However, the most chronically violent husbands had a nearly 100% probability of also physically abusing their male children.

The Ross[7] results suggest that measurement of concurrence rates will vary significantly by gender of the abusive partner as well as the child, and by intensity of the abuse. Future studies should include these risk factors in the analyses.

## *Promising Strategies:*

Traditionally services for battered women and their abused children have not been coordinated and are often in conflict regarding the goals of their interventions.

The AWAKE Project at Boston Children's Hospital began in 1986 to address the safety of child abuse victims and their mothers victimized by intimate partners. It is cited in "Best Practices: Innovative Domestic Violence Programs in Health Care Settings," a resource from the Family Violence Prevention Fund.[9] AWAKE's chief innovation is the "pairing of battered women and their abused children with an advocate experienced with family violence" to devise and update safety plans to keep mothers and children together. Case management input is sought from the hospital's Child Protection Team, the District Attorney, the Department of Social Services, and outside agencies. Long-term support is also offered to these families.[9]

There are a number of programs in other settings that may provide "dual advocacy" and counseling services to women and children, such as some state child protection agencies,[10] battered women's shelters with children's programs, some child/family advocacy centers (primarily for child sexual abuse evaluation), some court settings, and certain child visitation centers (which provide supervised visitation for batterers and other services.)

## Selected Bibliography

1.  Stark, E., and A. Flitcraft. "Spouse Abuse" (p. 142) in *Violence in America: A Public Health Approach* Edited by Rosenberg and Fenley: Oxford University Press, 1991.

2.  McKibben, L., E. DeVos, and E. Newberger. "Victimization of Mothers of Abused Children: A Controlled Study." *Pediatrics* 84 (1989): 531–35.

3.  Wright, R. J., R. O. Wright, and N. E. Isaac. "Response to Battered Mothers in the Pediatric Emergency Department: A Call for an Interdisciplinary Approach to Family Violence." *Pediatrics* 99 (1997): 186–92.

4.  Peled, E. "The Battered Women's Movement Response to Children of Battered Women: A Critical Analysis." *Violence Against Women* 3 (1997): 424–46.

5.  Straus, M., R. J. Gelles, and S. K. Steinmetz. 1980. *Behind Closed Doors: Violence in the American Family*. New York: Doubleday/Anchor.

6.  Straus, M., R. J. Gelles. 1990. *Physical Violence in American Families: Risk Factors and Adaptations to Violence in 8,145 Families.* New Brunswick, NJ: Transaction Publishers.

7.  Ross, S. "Risk of Physical Abuse to Children of Spouse Abusing Parents." *Child Abuse and Neglect* 20 (1996): 589–98.

8.  Stark, E., and A. H. Flitcraft. "Women and Children At Risk: A Feminist Perspective on Child Abuse." *International Journal of Health Service* 18 (1988): 97–118.

9.  Nudelman, J., N. Durborow, M. Gramb, and P. Letellier. *Best Practices: Innovative Domestic Violence Programs in Health Care Settings.* The Family Violence Prevention Fund, 1997.(Ph: (415) 252-8900; Website: http://www.fvpf.org/health/)

10. Hangen, E. (1994) *DSS (Dept. of Social Services) Interagency Domestic Violence Team Pilot Project: Program Data Evaluation.* Boston: Massachusetts Department of Social Services.

Section 15.3

# *The Facts: Children and Domestic Violence*

National Network to End Domestic Violence Fund, copyright © 1997. Used with permission.

For more than 20 years, battered women's advocates have supported services and public policy that protects children by protecting their mothers. Likewise, the effect of domestic violence on children has been researched for nearly 20 years. Studies indicate that children who witness violence in the home can suffer the same degree of trauma as children who are abused physically. The American Psychological Association confirms that violence is a learned behavior and that most of the learning takes place in the home. Since domestic violence is not a single event, but rather a pattern of abuse that escalates in severity over time, it is easy to understand why children who witness abuse of a parent may be more susceptible to anxiety and trauma. The following statistics demonstrate the prevalence of children exposed to domestic violence.

- Over 3 million children annually observe violence within their homes.[1]

- In a national survey of over 6,000 families, 50% of the men who frequently assaulted their wives also frequently abused their children.[2]

- Child abuse is 15 times more likely to occur in families where domestic violence is present.[3]

- Two-thirds of abused children are being parented by battered women.[4]

- Children from homes where domestic violence occurs are physically abused and/or seriously neglected at a rate of fifteen times the national average.[4]

## *Direct and Indirect Effects*

There are many direct and indirect effects associated with children who witness domestic violence. Children who witness domestic violence may suffer from behavioral, cognitive and physical problems that can be detected from infancy through adolescence. These children often live in fear that their mother will be killed, and live with guilt that they could not do anything to stop the abuse. Boys may be very aggressive toward their mother and toward other children, and may act out in school. Girls may withdraw and become depressed. As they get older, studies have shown that girls may experiment with alcohol, drugs, and engage in sex.

- Children who witness violence at home display emotional and behavioral disturbances as diverse as withdrawal, low self-esteem, nightmares, self-blame and aggression against peers, family members, and property.[5]

- Children who are exposed to abuse tend to be more aggressive toward their own children (as adults).[6]

- Children often display the following indirect symptoms from witnessing domestic violence: sleep disorders, headaches, stomachaches, diarrhea, ulcers, asthma, enuresis [bedwetting], depression, truancy, and learning problems.[7]

- A comparison of delinquent and non-delinquent youth found that a history of family violence or abuse is the most significant difference between the two groups.[8]

- Children exposed to domestic violence often have problems with school and social adjustment, problems with substance abuse, and higher rates of suicide attempts.[9]

## Teens and Dating Violence

As teens, the cycle of abuse may continue. The lessons they learned as children often carry over into new relationships. Boys may be abusive towards their girlfriends, and girls may remain in abusive relationships. Some boys may have learned that violence in relationships is acceptable. Similarly, some girls may mistake abuse and control for love. Research has also indicated that teens may have a higher tolerance level for accepting abuse. Therefore, they believe that some abuse is a normal part of their relationship.

- 10 million teenagers may be exposed to parental violence each year.[2]

- High school students whose parents had been in violent relationships had a statistically higher rate of violence in their own relationships.[10]

- 1 in 10 teen dating couples experience physical violence.[11]
- One-third of high school and college-aged students experience violence with an intimate.[11]
- Men who have witnessed their parents' domestic violence are three times more likely to abuse their own wives than children of non-violent parents.[12]
- Boys who witness parental abuse during their childhood are at a higher risk of being physically aggressive in dating and marital relationships.[13]
- Girls who witness maternal abuse may tolerate abuse as adults more than girls who do not.[14]

Children who witness domestic violence are the forgotten victims of abuse. They may not have visible bruises that eventually heal, but rather deep-rooted internal bruises that shape who these children will become. Children learn by example. They mimic what they see, and believe that what they experience is normal. Without proper intervention, the cycle may continue.

## Notes

1.  Carlson, B. E. *Children's Observations of Interpersonal Violence. Battered Women and Their Families,* 60. New York: Springer, 1984.

2.  Straus, M. A., and R. J. Gelles, eds. *Physical Violence in American Families.* New Brunswick, NJ: Transaction Publishers, 1990.

3.  Stacy, W., and A. Shupe. *The Family Secret.* Boston, MA: Beacon Press, 1983.

4.  McKay, M. *The Link Between Domestic Violence and Child Abuse: Assessment and Treatment Considerations,* 29–39. Child Welfare League of America, 1994.

5.  Peled, Inat, Peter G. Jaffe, and Jeffrey L. Edleson, eds. *Ending the Cycle of Domestic Violence: Community Responses to Children of Battered Women.* Thousand Oaks, CA: Sage Publications, 1995.

6.  Steele, B. F. "The Psychology of Child Abuse." *Family Advocacy* 17, 3 (1995): 19–23.

7.  Davidson, Howard. *The Impact of Domestic Violence on Children: A Report to the President of the American Bar Association.* Chicago: American Bar Association, 1994.

8.  Miller, G. "Violence By and Against America's Children." *Juvenile Justice Journal* XVII, 12 (June 21, 1989): 4.

9.  Clarke, C. Office of the United States Attorney, District of Columbia, U.S. Dept. of Justice. *Understanding Domestic Violence: A Handbook for Victims and Professionals.*

10. O'Keefe, et al. "Teen Dating Violence." *Social Work* (November/ December 1986): 466.

11. Levy, B., ed. *Dating Violence: Young Women in Danger* 73. Seattle, WA: Seal Press, 1991.

12. Straus, M. A., R. J. Gelles, and S. K. Steinmetz. *Behind Closed Doors: Violence in the American Family.* Doubleday, Anchor, 1980.

13. Rosenbaum, A., and K. D. O'Leary. "Children: The Unintended Victims of Marital Violence." *American Journal of Orthopsychiatry* (1981): 692–99.

14. Hotaling, G. T., and D. B. Sugarman. "An Analysis of Risk Markers in Husband and Wife Violence: The Current State of Knowledge." *Violence and Victims* 1 (1986): 101–24.

## Suggested Readings

Cappell, C., and R. B. Heiner. "The Intergenerational Transmission of Family Aggression." *Journal of Family Violence* 5 (1990): 135.

Carlson, Bonnie E. "Adolescent Observers of Marital Violence." *Journal of Family Violence* 5 (1990): 285.

Henning, K., et al. "Long-Term Psychological and Social Impact of Witnessing Physical Conflict between Parents." *Journal of Interpersonal Violence* 11 (1996): 35.

Jaffe, Peter G., et al. *Children of Battered Women.* Sage Publications, 1990.

Kashani, Javad H. *The Impact of Family Violence on Children and Adolescents.* Sage Publications, 1997.

Levy, Barrie, ed. *Dating Violence: Young Women in Danger.* Seal Press, 1991.

Levy, Barrie, ed. *In Love and in Danger: A Teen's Guide to Breaking Free of Abusive Relationships.* Seal Press, 1993.

## Section 15.4

# The Relationship Between Parental Alcohol or Other Drug Problems and Child Maltreatment

Prevent Child Abuse America (formerly National Committee to Prevent Child Abuse), Fact Sheet No. 14, copyright ©1996. Used by permission.

The relationship between parental alcohol or other drug problems and child maltreatment is becoming increasingly evident. And the risk to the child increases in a single parent household where there is no supporting adult to diffuse parental stress and protect the child from the effects of the parent's problem. The following is a summary of what we know.

### What is the scope of the problem?

Both alcohol and drug problems are widespread in this country. Almost 14 million adult Americans abuse alcohol.[1] The number of illicit drug users exceeds 12 million.[2] Illicit drugs include marijuana, cocaine, inhalants, hallucinogens, heroin, and non-medical use of psychotherapeutics.[2] With more than 6.6 million children under the age of 18 living in alcoholic households,[3] and an additional number of children living in households where parents have problems with illicit drugs, a significant number of children in this country are being raised by addicted parents.

Child maltreatment has become a national epidemic. More than one million children are confirmed each year as victims of child abuse and neglect by state child protective service agencies.[4] Every day at least three children die as a result of abuse and neglect.[4] State child

331

welfare records indicate that substance abuse is one of the top two problems exhibited by families in 81% of the reported cases.

### Do parental alcohol or other drug problems cause child maltreatment?

Recent research on the connection between these problems and child maltreatment clearly indicates a connection between the two behaviors. Among confirmed cases of child maltreatment, 40% involve the use of alcohol or other drugs.[5] This suggests that of the 1.2 million confirmed victims of child maltreatment, an estimated 480,000 children are mistreated each year by a caretaker with alcohol or other drug problems.[5] Additionally, research suggests that alcohol and other drug problems are factors in a majority of cases of emotional abuse and neglect. In fact, neglect is the major reason that children are removed from a home in which parents have alcohol or other drug problems. Children in these homes suffer from a variety of physical, mental, and emotional health problems at a greater rate than children in the general population.[6] Children of alcoholics suffer more injuries and poisonings than children in the general population. Alcohol and other substances may act as disinhibitors, lessening impulse control and allowing parents to behave abusively. Children in this environment often demonstrate behavioral problems and are diagnosed as having conduct disorders.[7] This may result in provocative behavior. Increased stress resulting from preoccupation with drugs on the part of the parent combined with behavioral problems exhibited by the child adds to the likelihood of maltreatment.

### What characteristics do parents with alcohol and other drug problems and parents involved in child maltreatment share?

Histories of these parents reveal that typically both were reared with a lack of parental nurturing and appropriate modeling and often grew up in disruptive homes.[8] Family life in these households also have similarities. The children in them often lack guidance, positive role modeling, and live in isolation. Frequently, they suffer from depression, anxiety, and low self-esteem. They live in an atmosphere of stress and family conflict. Children raised in both households are more likely to have problems with alcohol and other drugs themselves.[9]

### Does the use of alcohol or other drugs by pregnant women affect their infants?

Pregnant women who use alcohol may bear children suffering from fetal alcohol syndrome (FAS). FAS is the leading known environmental cause of mental retardation in the Western world.[10] Each year 4,000 to 12,000 babies are born with the physical signs and intellectual disabilities associated with FAS, and thousands more experience the somewhat lesser disabilities of fetal alcohol effects.[11]

### How does a parent's alcohol or other drug problem affect children?

Children of alcoholics are more likely than children in the general population to suffer a variety of physical, mental, and emotional health problems.[12] Similar to maltreatment victims who believe that the abuse is their fault, children of alcoholics feel guilty and responsible for their parent's drinking problem.[13] Both groups of children often have feelings of low self-esteem and failure and suffer from depression and anxiety. It is thought that exposure to violence in both alcohol-abusing and child-maltreating households increases the likelihood that the children will commit and be recipients of acts of violence. Additionally, the effects of child maltreatment and parental alcohol abuse don't end when the children reach adulthood. Both groups of children are likely to have difficulty with coping and establishing healthy relationships as adults. In addition to suffering from all the effects of living in a household where alcohol or child maltreatment problems exist, children whose parents abuse illicit drugs live with the knowledge that their parents' actions are illegal. While research is in its infancy, clinical evidence shows that children of parents who have problems with illicit drug use may suffer from an inability to trust legitimate authority because of fear of discovery of a parent's illegal habits.

### Are these patterns passed on from one generation to the next?

Some individuals can and do break the cycle of abuse. These resilient children share some characteristics that lead to their successful coping skills such as ability to obtain positive attention from other people, adequate communication skills, average intelligence, a caring attitude, a desire to achieve, a belief in self-help.[14] Additionally, the involvement of a caring adult can help children develop resiliency and break the cycle of abuse. However, a significant number of individuals fall victim to the same patterns exhibited by their parents. Those who have been severely physically abused often have symptoms of post-traumatic disorder and dissociation.[15] Individuals suffering from mental health disorders may use alcohol and illicit drugs to decrease or mitigate their psychological distress.[16] Research suggests that adults who were abused as children may be more likely to abuse their own children than adults who were not abused as children.[17]

## Why are these patterns so hard to break?

One explanation for the continuing cycle is the secrecy, denial, and stigma involved in both problems. Many child maltreatment cases do not get reported and many children of alcoholics go unidentified. Within both populations, victims often are afraid to speak up because they do not think anyone will believe them. Often they do not realize that what seems to be normal behavior is indeed maltreatment, and learn to repeat these behaviors unconsciously. The lack of positive parental role modeling and lack of development of coping skills increases the difficulty of establishing healthy relationships as an adult. It may not be until they seek help as disturbed adults that they are made cognizant of the root of their emotional problems.

## Can we treat child maltreatment when alcohol or other drugs are a problem?

Research has shown that when families exhibit both of these behaviors, the problems must be treated simultaneously in order to insure a child's safety. Although ending the drug dependency does not automatically end child maltreatment, very little can be done to improve parenting skills until this step is taken. It should be noted that the withdrawal experienced by parents who cease using alcohol or other drugs presents specific risks. The effects of withdrawal often cause a parent to experience intense emotions, which may increase the likelihood of child maltreatment.[18] During this time, lasting as long as two years, it is especially important that resources be available to the family.

### *How can we prevent these problems?*

Aside from promoting awareness of the link between parental alcohol or other drug problem and child maltreatment and cross-training professionals in the recognition and treatment of both problems, prevention services need to be available for all. Among the preventive efforts Prevent Child Abuse America believes to be most effective are:

- prevention education for all children, adolescents, and young adults.

- direct access to supportive services for all children of parents with alcohol or other drug problems before child maltreatment occurs, with an emphasis on validation of feelings, supporting self-esteem, and intensive parenting and prevention education and support for all new parents.

- access to self-help groups and other supportive services for all parents under stress and all victims and survivors of abuse.

- education of all who work with children and families, including teachers, service providers, obstetricians, pediatricians, and emergency room personnel, regarding the interplay between a parent's alcohol or other drug problems and child maltreatment.

### *Notes*

1.  National Institute of Alcohol Abuse and Alcoholism. 1994. *Alcohol Health & Research World* 18 (3): 243.

2.  Substance Abuse and Mental Health Services Administration, U.S. Department of Health and Human Services. 1995. *National Household Survey on Drug Abuse: Population Estimates 1994*. Research Triangle Park, NC: Research Triangle Institute.

3.  Russell, M., C. Henderson, and S. B. Blume. 1984. *Children of Alcoholics: A Review of the Literature*. New York: Children of Alcoholics Foundation, Inc.

4.  Lung, C. T., and D. Daro. 1996. *Current Trends in Child Abuse Reporting and Fatalities: The Results of the 1995 Annual Fifty State Survey*. Chicago, IL: Prevent Child Abuse America.

5.  Children of Alcoholics Foundation, Inc. 1996. *Collaboration, Coordination and Cooperation: Helping Children Affected by Parental Addiction and Family Violence*. New York: Children of Alcoholics Foundation.

6. Bijur, P. E., M. Kurzon, M. D. Overpeck, and P. C. Scheidt. 1992. "Parental Alcohol Use, Problem Drinking and Child Injuries." *Journal of the American Medical Association* 23: 3166–171.

7. West, M., and R. Prinz. 1987. "Parental Alcoholism and Childhood Psychopathology." *Psychological Bulletin* 102(2): 204–18.

8. Behling, D. W. 1979. "Alcohol Abuse as Encountered in 51 Instances of Reported Child Abuse." *Clinical Pediatrics* 18(2): 87–91.

9. Children of Alcoholics Foundation, Inc. 1992. *Help for Inner-City Children of Addicted Parents*. New York: Children of Alcoholics Foundation, Inc.

10. National Institute of Alcohol Abuse and Alcoholism. 1993. *Eighth Special Report to U.S. Congress on Alcohol and Health*. (March): 221.

11. SAMHSA, Center for Substance Abuse Prevention. 1993. "Toward Preventing Perinatal Abuse of Alcohol, Tobacco and Other Drugs." *USDHHS Technical Report*, No. 9, p. 1.

12. Children of Alcoholics Foundation, Inc. 1990. *Children of Alcoholics in the Medical System: Hidden Problems, Hidden Costs*. New York: Children of Alcoholics Foundation, Inc.

13. Russell, M., C. Henderson, and S. Blume. 1985. *Children of Alcoholics: A Review of the Literature*. New York: Children of Alcoholics Foundation, Inc.

14. Werner, E. E. 1986. "Resilient Offspring of Alcoholics: A Longitudinal Study from Birth to Age 18." *Journal of Studies on Alcohol* 47(1): 34–40.

15. Briere, J. 1996. "A Self-Trauma Model for Treating Adult Survivors of Severe Child Abuse." In *The APSAC Handbook on Child Maltreatment* (pp. 140–57) edited by J. Briere, L. Berliner, J. A. Bulkley, C. Jenny, and T. Reid. Newbury Park, CA: Sage.

16. Kelley, S. J. 1996. *Do Substance Abusing Mothers Experience Increased Parenting Stress?* Paper presented at the International Congress of the International Society on the Prevention of Child Abuse and Neglect. Dublin, Ireland.

17.  Ziegler, E., and J. Kaufman. 1987. "Do Abused Children Become Abusive Parents?" *American Journal of Orthopsychiatry* 57(20): 187–92.

18.  Zuskin, R., and D. DePanfilis. 1987. "Working with CPS Families with Alcohol or Other Drug (AOD) Problems." *The APSAC Advisor* 8(1): 7–11.

## Section 15.5

# *Talking to Young Children about Domestic Violence: When a Parent Goes to Jail*

Burt, Tracy. "Talking to Young Children about Domestic Violence: When a Parent Goes to Jail," April 1999. This article originally appeared in the Santa Clara County Domestic Violence Council Children's Committee Newsletter and on the Support Network for Battered Women's website, www.snbw.org. Reprinted with permission.

*Tracy Burt, Ed. M., Children's Program Coordinator,*
*Support Network for Battered Women*

Children's developmental capacities influence how they create meaning about the world around them. Recent research has shown that most all children who live in homes with domestic violence are aware of the violence, even when their parents believe they are not. Rather than avoiding a dialogue with children about domestic violence, we can choose to bridge them to appropriate understanding of difficult events in their lives. We owe it to them to give them honest answers that respect their developmental capacities.

In general children will usually ask for what they need to know. When answering questions about the criminal consequences of domestic violence, young children will benefit from the following guidelines:

• Connect the batterer's absence to children's concrete experiences and framework of understanding. For example, "Jail is like a time-out for adults." Children younger than four will be unable to think abstractly and thus need such concrete references.

- Differentiate consequences for adults from consequences for children. "When adults make big (or serious) mistakes, they have to be in jail. Children are still learning and have more chances."

- Tell them that when one person hurts other people, they have to be separated in order to keep people safe. Everyone, child and adult, has the right to a safe body.

- Keep it simple. Use short sentences and avoid elaborating. Try to answer only the question asked. Wait for the child to ask you for more information.

- If appropriate and depending on your comfort level with the truthfulness of this statement, tell them that jail is supposed to be a place where adults can learn how to stop hurting other people. If the domestic violence situation has been particularly lethal, and future contact with the batterer will be avoided at all costs, also tell the child that the batterer has hurt his or her partner so much that he will not be allowed to see her again.

When we answer children's difficult questions honestly and appropriately we respect their right to know the truth and we also validate their reality. Without this validation they will integrate trauma into their worldview in potentially detrimental ways. However, merely talking honestly to children about domestic violence is not enough. Most children and families will benefit from family therapy, group counseling and/or individual counseling. It is vital to refer children and parents to resources that will support them in their healing process and prevent the recurring cycle of violence in the future.

Chapter 16

# Repressed Memory Controversy

## Chapter Contents

# Section 16.1

# *The Repressed Memory Controversy*

Barnett, Ola W., Cindy L. Miller-Perin, and Robin D. Perrin. *Family Violence Across the Lifespan: An Introduction,* pp. 97–98, copyright © 1997 by Sage Publications, Inc. Reprinted by permission of Sage Publications, Inc.

**1989** The California Court of Appeal extended the statute of limitations under the doctrine of "delayed discovery," allowing individuals claiming a history of CSA [child sexual abuse] during childhood to sue their parents. Individuals must be able to demonstrate that memories of the event were repressed (by providing certification by a licensed mental health professional).

**1990** Nineteen-year-old Holly Ramona accused her father, Gary Ramona, of repeatedly raping her between the ages of 5 and 8. Holly's memories of the abuse surfaced while she was a college student receiving therapy for depression and bulimia. Over the course of several months of therapy, Holly experienced flashback memories of her father sexually molesting her. Just before accusing her father, Holly received the hypnotic drug sodium amytal and recounted multiple episodes of abuse by her father. After the allegations surfaced, Gary Ramona lost his $400,000-a-year job, his daughters refused to interact with him, and his wife divorced him.

**1992** The False Memory Syndrome (FMS) Foundation was established to provide information and support to more than 2,300 families. The group contends that there is a "rash" of individuals who have been falsely accused of sexual abuse.

**1994** The Napa Valley Superior Court jury ruled that Holly Ramona's memories were "probably false" and that although her therapists had not implanted the memories, they had negligently reinforced them (Butler, 1994). Gary Ramona was awarded $500,000 of the $8 million he sought in damages.

This chronology of events effectively illustrates some of the dilemmas associated with the repressed memory debate. Are Holly and others like her victims of CSA? Or are the adults being accused the victims of false memories? There is little consensus regarding these questions among legal, medical, and mental health professionals. In one camp, there are experts who believe that repressed memories are quite common and result from either repression of negative feelings associated with the abuse or amnesia associated with dissociative defenses (i.e., multiple personality disorder) of a traumatic event (Briere & Conte, 1993). In the other camp are the critics of repressed memories who claim that such memories may be due to fantasy, illusion, subsequent contextual cues, or the result of implantation by a therapist or other perceived authority figure (Ganaway, 1989; Loftus, 1993).

In support of the argument that repressed memories exist, Herman and Schatzow (1987) found that 64% of female incest survivor patients did not have full recall of their sexual abuse and reported some degree of amnesia. One fourth of these women reported severe memory deficits or complete amnesia for the event. Approximately 75% of the women obtained evidence to corroborate their abuse reports such as confirmation from other family members, discovering that a sibling had also been abused, or a confession by the perpetrator. A more recent study conducted by Briere and Conte (1993) also showed a substantial rate of repressed memories in a clinical sample of sexual abuse victims (59%). Such studies, however, are limited due to the retrospective and self-report nature of the data and the fact that the individuals were in therapy. An additional study, however, followed a community sample of 100 victims of CSA who reported abuse in their childhood and found that 17 years later, 38% did not recall the previously reported incident (Williams, 1992).

Critics of repressed memories, on the other hand, emphasize the limitations of such studies: specifically, the problem that participants in clinical samples are attempting to remember "a memory for forgetting a memory" (Loftus, 1993, p. 522). Other potential sources of repressed memories have been suggested. For example, some claim that popular writings exaggerate sexual abuse as "nearly universal" (Bower, 1993b) and contain unvalidated claims such as "If you are unable to remember any specific instances but still have a feeling that something abusive happened to you, it probably did" (Bass & Davis, 1988, p. 21). Proponents of false memories claim that such statements are dangerous given the malleability of memory. Research has shown that memory is subject to distortion from stress, incentives to keep secrets, and suggestion (Loftus, 1993; Perry, 1992).

Others contend that popular writings encourage emotional confrontations with alleged perpetrators (Loftus, 1993) and in general are written as part of a "sexual abuse industry" to create victims (Travis, 1993). Since 1989, a total of 19 states have passed legislation allowing people to sue for recovery of damages for injury suffered as a result of CSA remembered for the first time during adulthood, and an estimated 300 lawsuits involving formerly repressed memories had been filed as of September 1993 (Bower, 1993a). Some have suggested that the motivation behind these lawsuits is fame and fortune (Davis, 1991; Lachnit, 1991) rather than justice.

The final argument offered by critics of repressed memories is the notion that therapists may "implant" memories through either overt or covert suggestions. Therapists may inadvertently communicate to their clients their own belief that repressed memories are common, and clients might subsequently assume that it is likely to have happened to them (Loftus, 1993). Others have suggested that therapists may overtly implant a memory of CSA by diagnosing abuse after too brief an evaluation, the use of leading questions, or the use of questionable assessment or therapeutic techniques such as hypnosis and sodium amytal (Butler, 1994; Loftus, 1993).

Unfortunately, the debate over whether memories of CSA are repressed or false remains unresolved, and it is unlikely that the question will receive a clear answer in the near future. To date, there is no definitive way of knowing whether a given memory is true or false. Both sides do agree, however, in the importance of improving methods to assess and treat victims of CSA and to continue seeking empirical knowledge to uncover the realities regarding repressed memories. An APA [American Psychological Association] task force was recently appointed to examine what is known about repressed memories and included a panel of both skeptics and believers. A preliminary report from the group indicated that they had reached a consensus regarding the extremes of the debate: "Both ends of the continuum on people's memories of abuse are possible...It is possible that under some cue conditions, early memories may be retrievable. At the other extreme, it is possible under some conditions for memories to be implanted or embedded" (DeAngelis, 1993).

## References

Bass, E., and L. Davis. (1988). *The Courage to Heal*. New York: Harper & Row.

Bower, B. (1993a). "Sudden Recall: Adult Memories of Child Abuse Spark Heated Debate." *Science News* 144: 177–92.

Bower, B. (1993b). "The Survivor Syndrome." *Science News* 144: 202-04.

Briere, J., and J. Conte. (1993). "Self-Reported Amnesia for Abuse in Adults Molested as Children." *Journal of Traumatic Stress* 6: 21–31.

Butler, K. (1994, June). "Clashing Memories, Mixed Messages." *Los Angeles Times Magazine*, p. 12.

Davis, L. (1991). "Murdered Memory." *Health* 5: 79–84.

DeAngelis, T. (1993). "APA Panel is Examining Memories of Child Abuse." *APA Monitor* 24: 44.

Ganaway, G. K. (1989). "Historical Versus Narrative Truth: Clarifying the Role of Exogenous Trauma in the Etiology of MPD and its Variants." *Dissociation* 2: 205–20.

Herman, J. L., and E. Schatzow. (1987). "Recovery and Verification of Memories of Childhood Sexual Trauma." *Psychoanalytic Psychology* 4: 1–14.

Lachnit, C. (1991, April). "'Satan Trial': Jurors Rule for Two Sisters." *Grange County Register* 1: 26.

Loftus, E. F. (1993). "The Reality of Repressed Memories." *American Psychologist* 48: 518–37.

Perry, N. W. (1992). "How Children Remember and Why They Forget." *The APSAC Advisor* 5: 1–2, 13–16.

Travis, C. (1993, January). "Beware the Incest-Survivor Machine." *New York Times*, p.1.

Williams, L. M. (1992). "Adult Memories of Childhood Abuse: Preliminary Findings from a Longitudinal Study." *The APASAC Advisor* 5: 19–21.

## Section 16.2

# Questions and Answers about Memories of Childhood Abuse

"Questions and Answers about Memories of Childhood Abuse," APA Public Communications, American Psychological Association. Copyright © 1995 by the American Psychological Association. Reprinted with permission.

Following are some questions and answers that reflect the best current knowledge about reported memories of childhood abuse. They will help you better understand how repressed, recovered, or suggested memories may occur and what you can do if you or a family member is concerned about a childhood memory.

### Can a memory be forgotten and then remembered? Can a "memory" be suggested and then remembered as true?

These questions lie at the heart of the memory of childhood abuse issue. Experts in the field of memory and trauma can provide some answers, but clearly more study and research are needed. What we do know is that both memory researchers and clinicians who work with trauma victims agree that both phenomena occur. However, experienced clinical psychologists state that the phenomenon of a recovered memory is rare (e.g., one experienced practitioner reported having a recovered memory arise only once in 20 years of practice). Also, although laboratory studies have shown that memory is often inaccurate and can be influenced by outside factors, memory research usually takes place either in a laboratory or some everyday setting. For ethical and humanitarian reasons, memory researchers do not subject people to a traumatic event in order to test their memory of it. Because the issue has not been directly studied, we can not know whether a memory of a traumatic event is encoded and stored differently from a memory of a nontraumatic event.

Some clinicians theorize that children understand and respond to trauma differently from adults. Some furthermore believe that childhood trauma may lead to problems in memory storage and retrieval. These clinicians believe that dissociation is a likely explanation for a memory that was forgotten and later recalled. Dissociation means that a memory is not actually lost, but is for some time unavailable for retrieval. That is, it's in memory storage, but cannot for some period of time actually be recalled. Some clinicians believe that severe forms of child sexual abuse are especially conducive to negative disturbances of memory such as dissociation or delayed memory. Many clinicians who work with trauma victims believe that this dissociation is a person's way of sheltering himself or herself from the pain of the memory. Many researchers argue, however, that there is little or no empirical support for such a theory.

## *What's the bottom line?*

First, it's important to state that there is a consensus among memory researchers and clinicians that most people who were sexually abused as children remember all or part of what happened to them although they may not fully understand or disclose it. Concerning the issue of a recovered versus a pseudomemory, like many questions in science, the final answer is yet to be known. But most leaders in the field agree that although it is a rare occurrence, a memory of early childhood abuse that has been forgotten can be remembered later. However, these leaders also agree that it is possible to construct convincing pseudomemories for events that never occurred.

The mechanism(s) by which both of these phenomena happen are not well understood and, at this point it is impossible, without other corroborative evidence, to distinguish a true memory from a false one.

## *What further research is needed?*

The controversy over the validity of memories of childhood abuse has raised many critical issues for the psychological community. Many questions are at this point unanswered. This controversy has demonstrated that there are areas of research which should be pursued; among them are the following:

- Research to provide a better understanding of the mechanism by which accurate or inaccurate recollections of events may be created;

- Research to ascertain which clinical techniques are most likely to lead to the creation of pseudomemories and which techniques are most effective in creating the conditions under which actual events of childhood abuse can be remembered with accuracy;

- Research to ascertain how trauma and traumatic response impact the memory process;

- Research to ascertain if some people are more susceptible than others to memory suggestion and alteration and if so, why.

Much of this research will profit from collaborative efforts among psychologists who specialize in memory research and those clinicians who specialize in working with trauma and abuse victims.

### If there is so much controversy about childhood memories of abuse, should I still seek help from a mental health provider if I believe I have such a memory?

Yes. The issue of repressed or suggested memories has been overreported and sensationalized by the news media. Media and entertainment portrayals of the memory issue have succeeded in presenting the least likely scenario (that of a total amnesia of a childhood event) as the most likely occurrence. The reality is that most people who are victims of childhood sexual abuse remember all or part of what happened to them. Also true is the fact that thousands of people see a psychologist every day and are helped to deal with such things as issues of personal adjustment, depression, substance abuse and problems in relationships. The issues of childhood abuse or questionable memory retrieval techniques never enter into the equation in the great majority of therapy relationships.

### What should I know about choosing a psychotherapist to help me deal with a childhood memory or any other issue?

The American Psychological Association has released to the public the following advice to consider when seeking psychotherapy services.

First, know that there is no single set of symptoms which automatically indicates that a person was a victim of childhood abuse. There have been media reports of therapists who state that people (particularly women) with a particular set of problems or symptoms must have been victims of childhood sexual abuse. There is no scientific evidence that supports this conclusion.

Second, all questions concerning possible recovered memories of childhood abuse should be considered from an unbiased position. A therapist should not approach recovered memories with the preconceived notion that abuse must have happened or that abuse could not possibly have happened.

Third, when considering current problems, be wary of those therapists who offer an instant childhood abuse explanation, and those who dismiss claims or reports of sexual abuse without any exploration.

Fourth, when seeking psychotherapy, you are advised to see a licensed practitioner with training and experience in the issue for which you seek treatment. Ask the therapist about the kinds of treatment techniques he or she uses and how they could help you.

## How can I expect a competent psychotherapist to react to a recovered memory?

- A competent psychotherapist will attempt to stick to the facts as you report them. He or she will be careful to let the information evolve as your memory does and not to steer you toward a particular conclusion or interpretation.

- A competent psychotherapist is likely to acknowledge that current knowledge does not allow the definite conclusion that a memory is real or false without other corroborating evidence.

## What credentials should I look for when selecting a mental health provider?

You should choose a mental health professional as carefully as you would choose a physical health provider. For example, licensed psychologists have earned an undergraduate degree and have completed 5–7 years of graduate study culminating in a doctoral degree and including a one-year, full-time internship. All psychologists are required to be licensed or certified by the state in which they practice and many states require that they keep their training current by completing continuing education classes every year. Members of the American Psychological Association are also bound by a strict code of ethical standards.

Once the provider's competency has been established, his or her experience dealing with the issues you want help with is important. Also important is your level of comfort with the provider. Psychotherapy is a cooperative effort between therapist and patient, so a high level of personal trust and comfort is necessary. However, you should be concerned if your therapist reports to you that a large number of his or her patients recover memories of childhood abuse while in treatment.

347

There are a number of good ways to get a referral to a mental health professional. Your state psychological association will be able to provide you with referrals to psychologists in your community. Many state associations are located in their state capital. Also, because so many physical ailments have psychological components, most family physicians have a working relationship with a psychologist. Ask your doctor about a referral. Your church or synagogue and school guidance program or university counseling centers also usually maintain lists of providers in the community.

# Chapter 17

# *Prevention and Treatment Strategies*

## *Chapter Contents*

# Section 17.1

# *An Approach to Preventing Child Abuse*

Prevent Child Abuse America (formerly National Committee to Prevent
Child Abuse), *Fact Sheet No. 15*, copyright © December 2000.
Reprinted with permission.

Prevent Child Abuse America is committed to preventing child
abuse before it occurs. Since child maltreatment is a complex problem with a multitude of causes, an approach to prevention must respond to a range of needs. Therefore, Prevent Child Abuse America
has designed a comprehensive strategy comprised of a variety of community-based programs to prevent child abuse. Reflective of the
phases of the family life cycle, this approach provides parents and
children with the education and support necessary for healthy family functioning. Based on what is known or believed to enhance an
individual's ability to function within the family unit, several program
areas contributing to the strategy can be identified. Beginning with
the prenatal period, these programs offer a continuum of educational,
supportive and therapeutic services for parents and children endur-
ing throughout the school years. Although a community may not
choose to offer services in all program areas, as a group they respond
to the needs of all family members.

## *The Prevention Programs*

### *Support programs for new parents*

The purpose of support programs for new parents, such as perinatal support programs, is to prepare individuals for the job of parenting.
Such programs should include supports during both the pre- and postnatal periods to ease the difficulties associated with having a new
infant at home. Prenatal and postnatal medical care is clearly important, particularly since low-birth-weight babies, drug-exposed babies
and babies otherwise sick in infancy are at risk for being abused. Many
prospective parents now participate in prenatal care programs that
go beyond the medical needs of the pregnant mother and the growing fetus to include attention to the demands of parenting. Prenatal

programs can build on existing medical programs and educate about-to-be parents in child development, parent-child relationships, and adult relationships.

Currently, home visitation is the most innovative and holistic prevention program used in approaching the difficulties of educating and supporting the at-risk family, while at the same time making a wide range of community and professional services available to the family. [*See* Section 17.3.] This strategy is a comprehensive program in which services vary widely in both scope and content. An array of services may be offered, including nurse visitation to monitor the health of an infant and mother, in-home parenting education, and the intervention of a social worker for the purpose of preventing the placement of an infant in foster care. Most importantly, home visitation programs strive to create social networks for new parents by connecting them with other center-, community-, and hospital-based prevention programs. This helps break down the social isolation experienced by many new parents, especially those in poverty-stricken communities. Social isolation is a proven risk factor for child abuse.

## *Education for parents*

Since 1989, the family support movement has pointed to an increasing need among all American families for support, advice, and role models. Consequently, many parent education and support programs have encouraged the participation of all families, without regard to specified risk. By targeting all families, rather than low-income or otherwise at-risk groups, parent education and family support programs have achieved the broad-based backing necessary to underwrite statewide programs.

Nationally known programs that target at-risk families such as Parent Effectiveness Training (P.E.T.), the Parent Nurturing Program, and Systematic Training for Effective Parenting (S.T.E.P.) have various approaches toward parenting education and are distinct in their use of such teaching tools as reward and punishment, praise, and specific encouragement. Such parent-focused interventions with well-specified training components aimed at improving child-rearing competence and stress management have been supported by empirical findings as effective measures for reducing risk factors associated with physical child abuse.

Many groups that provide parenting education, such as natural childbirth groups, community-based prevention programs, and mental health services also can provide social support systems for families either at risk for or in treatment for abuse. Mutual support, or self-help groups also provide a network of support to members in adjusting to new roles, problems, or changes in family circumstances. These groups can help members expand their social contacts, improve their feelings of self-esteem, and increase their knowledge of child development.

## Early and regular child and family screening and treatment

Because abusive behavior is often cyclic, many health and developmental problems in early childhood can lead to behavioral, educational, and psycho-emotional problems in later adolescence and adulthood, which could lead to the recurrence of abusive behavior. Also, many abused children at first appear acquiescent, cooperative, shy, affectionate, and "normal," but this apparent serenity may mask multiple psychological problems. For this reason, detecting and treating health and developmental problems early in life is important. Early childhood screening and treatment programs should be seen as a continuation of the preschool screening services, such as those offered by a home visitor. The purpose of such programs should be to detect problems children may be having, including abuse and neglect, and to ensure that these children receive the necessary health, mental health, and other services that will best protect them from becoming abusive parents, while at the same time remaining sensitive to the possibility that a child may be inappropriately labeled, with long-term negative consequences.

## Child care opportunities

The purpose of child care or day care programs is to furnish parents with regular or occasional out-of-home care for their children. While child care is a necessity in households in which all adults are employed, such services also are beneficial for parents who do not work outside the home but who find continuous child care responsibilities very stressful. Child care programs also provide opportunities for children to learn basic social skills. Head Start programs in particular provide a rich mix of child care and child development services.

## Programs for abused children

It has been argued that prevention of abuse is in part tied to providing therapeutic treatment to children or young people who have been abused or neglected. To minimize the long-term effects of abuse, age-appropriate treatment services should be available to all maltreated children.

Treatment programs for abused children include therapeutic day school programs as well as day hospital programs, residential programs, and home and clinic setting treatment. These programs most often concentrate on improving the cognitive and developmental skills of younger children and psychodynamic treatment for children in older age groups.

## Life skills training for children and young adults

The purposes of life skills training are first to equip children, adolescents, and young adults with interpersonal skills and knowledge that are valuable in adulthood, especially in the parenting role; and second, to provide children with skills to help them protect themselves from abuse. Knowledge and skills can be imparted in a variety of ways; irrespective of the specific techniques, educational classes or supports would be provided through the school systems and through adult education centers.

Skill and knowledge building should be stressed in the areas of child development, family and life management, self-development, self-actualization, and methods of seeking help. For adolescents in particular, education in sexuality, pregnancy prevention, and issues related to parenting should be provided.

## Family support services

Lacking a support network in times of crisis puts families at significantly greater risk for abuse or neglect. To provide immediate assistance to parents in times of stress, crisis care programs should be available on a 24-hour basis and should include the following services: telephone hot line, crisis caretakers, crisis baby-sitters, crisis nurseries, and crisis counseling. Through these programs, parents facing immediate problems could receive immediate support to alleviate the stresses of a particular situation. Help should be available over the phone or through in-person counseling.

The program also should offer parents the options of having some-one come into their homes on a temporary basis to assist with child and home care or of taking the child to a crisis nursery. Because crisis care is temporary and short-term, such programs should be equipped to refer parents to long-term services as needed.

## Public information and education

While hospitals, schools, and community agencies have a critical role to play in implementing this child abuse prevention strategy, they cannot fully shoulder the responsibility. Educational campaigns are necessary to make the public aware of the seriousness of the problem and its implications as well how individuals can make a difference. The effectiveness of the preceding prevention strategy will only be realized when there is a fully aware public, committed to preventing child abuse.

Adapted from: Cohn Donnelly, A. (1997). *An Approach to Preventing Child Abuse.* Chicago, IL: Prevent Child Abuse America.

## Section 17.2

# *How to Reduce Abuse and Neglect of Children With Disabilities*

Beach Center on Families and Disability, University of Kansas, Lawrence, copyright © 1998. Used by permission.

Child abuse and neglect has gained increasing public attention. But what hasn't been acknowledged is the disability connection: At least one-quarter of disabilities are caused by abuse and neglect. Does disability cause abuse? Said Jim Garbarino, a noted researcher in the field, "It depends." General principles, general relationships, general causal statements are always conditioned by that particular mix within an individual of a unique constellation of factors, variables, and characteristics." Experts do know abuse and neglect is a serious problem for children with disabilities. According to the National Council on Abuse and Neglect, children with disabilities experience abuse and neglect 1.7 times more frequently than children without disabilities. Other reports state prevalence rates from 3% to 70%. Shedding light on this under-investigated field is crucial and has implications for child abuse and neglect as a whole.

## *What to Look for*

Signs of abuse and neglect related to children with disabilities are similar to abuse of children who are not disabled. Common physical indications include bruises, sexually transmitted diseases, dental injuries, welts, lacerations, and fractures. Behavior signs, such as aggression, withdrawal, eating disorders, avoidance of specific people or places, self-destructive acts, fearfulness, or atypical attachment are tipoffs. The same behaviors can also be characteristic of disabilities making identification of abuse more difficult. Evaluations, therefore, must be done carefully by knowledgeable professionals. These "easy target" children are often isolated, may have poor communication skills, and need a variety of adult care. Behavior problems, excessive caregiving demands, language comprehension problems, difficult developmental stages, and other factors can put children with disabilities into a high-risk category for abuse and neglect. Also, familial

355

alcohol or drug use, isolation, a history of violence, and other psychological environmental stresses have been associated with child abuse and neglect.

## What to Do

**Resource awareness.** Anyone suspecting child abuse should report the abuse and be made aware that there are abuse telephone hotlines. To ward off abuse before it happens, families need to know what support is available. The Individuals With Disabilities Education Act, for example, provides for early intervention for infants and toddlers and special education for school-age children. Supplemental Security Income offers financial help for children with severe disabilities, and states offer money, services, or both, depending on the state. Parents also can talk with a parent in a similar situation who "has been there" and wants to share information in one of the nation's numerous Parent to Parent programs. To increase awareness, agencies can use public service announcements, easily understood materials, local human service agencies for information and referral, and other means to get information out.

**Resource availability.** Services that support families include disability-related training, early intervention, early childhood special education, counseling, respite care, informal supports, child evaluations, case management, and help in securing benefits. Ideally, all involved providers should collaborate and include nonviolent strategies for handling challenging behaviors in every training program. The justly praised home-visiting programs can significantly reduce maltreatment, especially if started at birth to help ensure parent-child attachment and newborn-care techniques. Service providers need to treat families with the greatest possible respect and emphasize family strength because often families labeled at risk have negative feelings about involvement with a prevention program.

**Inclusion.** More vulnerable to outside and internal pressures, isolated families experience abuse and neglect far more than others. Correspondingly, if maltreatment happens, fewer potential observers can report it. Unfortunately, people with disabilities are often discouraged from fully participating in schools and social gatherings, and, so then are their families. Support of inclusion and integration of the child and family in the community is one more prevention against abuse and neglect.

**When a child is out of the home setting.** Safeguards and protections should be built into organizational design, policies, recruitment, in-service training, counseling, and supervising. Staff should be taught to practice positive behavior management techniques, including specialized training in nonviolent self-defense strategies. Punitive or aversive behavioral techniques (sensory deprivations, restraint, electric shock, etc.) should not be allowed. To support staff workers, administrators should have screening procedures for job applicants, peer consultation, initial and ongoing training, effective staff/student/ client ratios, and clear, consistent policies and procedures. An open environment that welcomes families has proven to be very effective in reducing abuse and neglect.

**Legal issues.** To further improve investigation and possible prosecution, agency recordkeeping must be upgraded. Too often, professionals do not file reports because of uncertainty, fear, vague reporting statutes, and other reasons. Prosecutors and child protection service personnel must be informed and vigorously pursue prosecution of these cases. All involved personnel need training in disability concerns, especially in communicating with children who are nonverbal or have communication difficulties.

Information for this fact sheet was derived from the National Symposium on Abuse and Neglect of Children With Disabilities co-sponsored by The Beach Center on Families and Disability and The Erikson Institute. If you are interested in more information concerning families who have children with disabilities, please contact the Beach Center on Families and Disability at 3111 Haworth, University of Kansas, Lawrence, KS 66045, 785-864-7600, Beach@dole. lsi.ukans.edu. See other fact sheets, research briefs, and publications at our Internet site:
http://www.lsi.ukans.edu/beach/beachhp.htm.

# Section 17.3

# Prenatal and Early Childhood Nurse Home Visitation

U.S. Department of Justice, Office of Justice Programs. Publication No. NCJ 172875, November 1998.

*David Olds, Ph.D., Peggy Hill, and Elissa Rumsey*

To prevent youth crime and delinquency, it is important to understand how antisocial behavior develops and design programs to interrupt that developmental pathway. The most serious and chronic offenders often show signs of antisocial behavior as early as the preschool years (American Psychiatric Association, 1994). Three important risk factors associated with early development of antisocial behavior can be modified: adverse maternal health-related behaviors during pregnancy associated with children's neuropsychological deficits, child abuse and neglect, and troubled maternal life course.

The Prenatal and Early Childhood Nurse Home Visitation Program, developed by David Olds and his colleagues (Olds, Kitzman et al., 1997; Olds, 1988; Olds and Korfmacher, 1997), is designed to help low-income, first-time parents start their lives with their children on a sound course and prevent the health and parenting problems that can contribute to the early development of antisocial behavior. Several rigorous studies indicate that the nurse home visitation program reduces the risks for early antisocial behavior and prevents problems associated with youth crime and delinquency such as child abuse, maternal substance abuse, and maternal criminal involvement.

Recent evidence shows that nurse home visitation even reduces juvenile offending (Olds, Henderson et al., 1998). Beginning in the mid-1970s, a series of randomized clinical trials was designed to develop and test the program model (Olds, Kitzman et al., 1997; Olds, 1988; Olds and Korfmacher, 1997). In each of these studies conducted in Elmira, N.Y., and later in Memphis, Tenn., women were randomly assigned to either home visitation by nurses during pregnancy and the first 2 years of their children's lives or comparison services such as free transportation for prenatal care and developmental screening and referral for their infants. Results from the Elmira and Memphis studies indicate that this program of nurse home visitation can promote healthy maternal and child functioning early in life (Olds, Henderson, Tatelbaum et al., 1986, 1988; Olds, Henderson, Chamberlin et al., 1986) and reduce the likelihood that children eventually will develop serious antisocial behavior (Olds, Eckenrode et al., 1997; Olds, Pettitt et al., 1998) including criminal offending (Olds, Henderson et al., 1998). A third trial conducted in Denver, Colo., which is nearing completion, compares the results achieved when employing trained paraprofessionals instead of nurses when following the same program model.

This section describes the model nurse home visitation program and explains how it successfully reduces the risks for early development of antisocial behavior and maternal and juvenile offending. Evidence is also presented detailing the program's effectiveness in reducing those risks. Most striking, this section shows how a program of prenatal and early childhood nurse home visitation has reduced both maternal and juvenile offending.

## *Program Overview*

Nurses begin visiting low-income, first-time mothers during pregnancy and continue visits until a child is 2 years old. These visits help pregnant women improve their health, which makes it more likely that their children will be born free of neurological problems. Parents receiving home visits also learn to care for their children and to provide a positive home environment. This means making sure children are nurtured, live in a safe environment within and around the home, are disciplined safely and consistently, and receive proper health care. Nurses also teach young parents to keep their lives on track by practicing birth control and planning future pregnancies, reaching their educational goals, and finding adequate employment.

## *Key Program Components*

The elements of the nurse home visitation program have been refined over the past 20 years, with visit-by-visit written protocols to guide nurse home visitors. Research and experience indicate that the following elements of the program are fundamental to its effectiveness:

- The program focuses on low-income, first-time mothers.

- Trained, experienced, mature nurses with strong interpersonal skills make home visits.

- Home visits begin during pregnancy and continue for 2 years after a child is born.

- Home visitors see families at home every 1 to 2 weeks.

- Home visitors focus simultaneously on the mother's personal health and development, environmental health, and quality of caregiving for the infant or toddler.

- Home visitors involve family members and friends in the program and help families use other community health and human services when needed.

- A full-time nurse home visitor carries a maximum caseload of 25 families.

- A nursing supervisor provides supportive guidance and oversees program implementation.

- Detailed records are kept on families and their needs, services provided, family progress, and outcomes.

## *Reducing Risks for the Development of Antisocial Behavior in Childhood*

How does the nurse home visitation program reduce risks for antisocial behavior that begins in childhood? This section summarizes how the program reduces three major risk factors: adverse maternal health-related behaviors during pregnancy that are associated with neuropsychological impairment in children, child abuse and neglect, and a troubled maternal life course.

### *Neuropsychological Impairment*

Children who exhibit antisocial behavior very early in life are more likely than other children to have impaired neurological functioning. Signs of neurological impairment include poor motor functioning, attention deficits, hyperactivity, impulsivity, and impaired language and cognitive functioning (Moffitt et al., 1996). In many cases, these problems can be traced to poor prenatal health conditions that interfere with the development of the fetal nervous system (Olds, 1997; Wakschlag et al., 1997; Fergusson, Horwood, and Lynskey, 1993; Milberger et al., 1996; Weitzman, Gortmaker, and Sobol, 1992).

The nurse home visitation program helps pregnant women improve their diet and cut down on cigarette smoking or the use of alcohol or illegal drugs that can hurt the developing fetus (Olds, Henderson, Tatelbaum et al., 1986). Cigarette smoking during pregnancy is especially dangerous because it is related to intellectual impairment in young children. In the Elmira trial, which served primarily Caucasian families, the 3- and 4-year-old children of women who did not receive a nurse home visitor and who smoked 10 or more cigarettes per day during pregnancy had impaired intellectual functioning compared with children of women who did not smoke (Olds, Henderson, and Tatelbaum, 1994a). Children of mothers who smoked 10 or more cigarettes when they signed up for the program and then received a nurse home visitor during pregnancy were not intellectually impaired. Data indicate that these women improved their diets and reduced their smoking by approximately three cigarettes a day (Olds, Henderson, and Tatelbaum, 1994b).

Cigarette smoking by a mother during pregnancy also has been linked to an infant's compromised neurological functioning. Compromised neurological functioning makes it harder for infants to signal their needs and regulate their emotions and behavior (Olds, Pettitt et al., 1998). When asked to evaluate how fussy and irritable their children were at 6 months of age, mothers who did not receive nurse home visitors and who smoked 10 or more cigarettes per day during pregnancy reported more fussiness and irritability in their children than did nonsmoking mothers without a nurse home visitor. In contrast, mothers who smoked 10 or more cigarettes per day when they started the program and who received home visits by a nurse during pregnancy reported far less irritability and fussiness in their children than did their counterparts in the control group (Olds, Pettitt et al., 1998). These findings suggest that the guidance mothers received from their nurse home visitors not only helped them cut down or stop smoking, it also improved their infants' soothability, which made infant care much easier.

### Child Abuse and Neglect

Abused and neglected children are at higher risk for developmental pathways marked by persistent behavior problems and academic failure, followed by chronic delinquency, adult criminal behavior, antisocial personality disorder, and violent crime (Widom, 1989; Maxfield and Widom, 1996; Kelley, Loeber et al., 1997; Kelley, Thornberry, and Smith,

1997). The program studied in the Elmira clinical trial has reduced the rates of child abuse and neglect and less serious forms of caregiving problems by helping young parents deal with depression, anger, impulsiveness, and substance abuse problems. It also helped them reflect on how they were parented themselves; learn about normal child development; and develop the skills needed to "read" their baby's signals, anticipate their baby's needs, and parent effectively (Olds, Henderson, Chamberlin et al., 1986; Olds, Eckenrode et al., 1997).

For children from birth through age 15, the Elmira program reduced state-verified cases of child abuse and neglect by 79 percent among mothers who were poor and unmarried (Olds, Eckenrode et al., 1997). In the second year of life (age 13 to 24 months), nurse-visited children had 56 percent fewer visits to an emergency room for injuries and ingestions than children not receiving home visits by nurses (Olds, Henderson, Chamberlin et al., 1986). During the 2-year period after the program ended (from the second through the fourth year of life), children from nurse-visited families were 40 percent less likely to be seen in a physician's office for injuries, ingestions, or social problems, and they had 35 percent fewer visits to the emergency room.

In the Memphis test of the program, which served African-American families, corresponding positive effects on parental caregiving and reductions in childhood injuries were seen during the first 2 years of the children's lives. Because Memphis has a very low rate (approximately 3 percent) of officially verified cases of child abuse and neglect, it was not possible to make valid and reliable comparisons between program participants and control group families. The data obtained from the nurse-visited families, however, strongly suggest a reduction in poor caregiving practices or behavior, including a reduction in child abuse and neglect (Kitzman et al., 1997).

## Troubled Maternal Life Course

A mother's personal development and lifestyle choices influence whether her child will develop antisocial behavior. Young women who become parents as adolescents and have recent welfare experience are more likely to have children who engage in a variety of antisocial and delinquent behaviors and who are expelled from school than are their low-income, nonwelfare, adolescent-mother counterparts (Furstenberg, Brooks-Gunn, and Morgan, 1987). Mothers who are unmarried, do not graduate from high school, and have three or more children are more likely to have children who exhibit behavioral problems.

The nurse home visitation program reduces these risk factors by helping young parents develop the confidence and skills necessary to set and achieve goals such as completing their education, finding work, and avoiding unplanned subsequent pregnancies (Olds, Eckenrode et al., 1997). The nurses help young parents consider multiple options, make good choices about the environment in which they will raise their children, and take steps to create the kind of lives they want for themselves and their children.

During the first 15 years after delivery of their first child, low-income, unmarried women in the Elmira trial who received nurse home visits had fewer subsequent children (1.1 versus 1.6), longer intervals between the births of the first and second children (65 versus 37 months), 30 fewer months on welfare (60 versus 90 months), 44 percent fewer behavioral problems because of their use of drugs and alcohol, 82 percent fewer arrests, and 81 percent fewer convictions than those in the control group, as shown by state records. Results of the first phase of the ongoing Memphis replication study indicate that the program's effects on maternal life course (especially reductions in the rates of subsequent pregnancies and births) are being reproduced (Kitzman et al., 1997).

## Cumulative Risk

The kinds of problems described above often combine to increase the total risk for the development of antisocial behavior in childhood. The figure on the next page presents an overview of the factors that can increase risk early in a child's life and shows how a program of home visitation by nurses may prevent such a negative developmental process from unfolding.

For example, subtle damage to the developing fetal nervous system can interfere with children's capacity to respond effectively to their parents' efforts to care for them. This establishes patterns of frustration and anger that interfere with the development of secure attachment (Rodning, Beckwith, and Howard, 1989; Sanson et al., 1993; Moffitt, 1993a, 1993b). To compound the problem, the parents of children with neuropsychological impairment are more likely to provide inconsistent discipline and may themselves be impatient and irritable. There are many possible causes for such dysfunctional caregiving, including genetic links, overwhelming stress, or substance abuse (Moffitt, 1993b). Poor parenting practices can lead to vicious cycles of interaction in which the child's problems with emotional and behavioral regulation contribute to parental child abuse

363

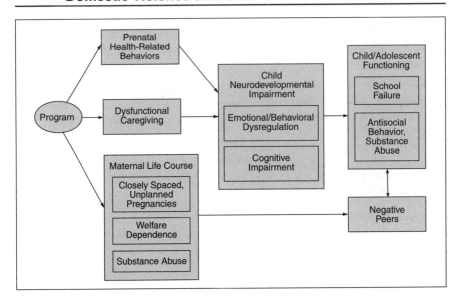

or neglect that further intensifies the child's emotional and behavioral imbalances.

Poor caregiving occurs more frequently when parents experience financial difficulties (Conger et al., 1993) and have larger families (Hirschi, 1994). In such cases, children's risks for antisocial behavior are further increased by their exposure to environments that are often associated with poverty and that may surround them with criminal influences (Felner et al., 1995; Hirschi, 1994; Moffitt, 1993a, 1993b).

Children from low-income households that are characterized by aggression and include family members with a history of school failure are more likely to be placed in low-level reading groups. This placement tends to worsen their aggressive behavior and academic problems, because these groups are likely to be made up of other children with similar problems and include classroom disruptions that interfere with education (Eder, 1983). Vulnerable children then become even more susceptible to rejection by prosocial peers and to negative peer influences (Dishion et al., 1995; Coie et al., 1995). When parents with limited social skills are confronted by school officials about their children's disruptive school behavior, they are more likely to harshly reject their children, which pushes the children further toward delinquency and crime (Coie, 1996).

Preventing the accumulation of risk factors from such a wide variety of sources is possible through comprehensive programs like the model of nurse home visitation described in this section. By attending to health, social, and environmental issues all at once, nurse visitors can help families get off to a strong start that enables their children to develop and mature into healthy, productive individuals. In some cases, the positive skills families develop seem to neutralize the negative influence of other risk factors that are harder to reduce or eliminate.

Moreover, for the first time there exists solid, scientifically validated evidence that prenatal and early childhood nurse home visitation services prevent crime and delinquency (Olds, Henderson et al., 1998). As described in a 15-year followup of the Elmira nurse home visitation program, the long-term effects of the program on children's criminal and antisocial behavior are substantial and have groundbreaking implications for juvenile justice and delinquency prevention. Adolescents whose mothers received nurse home visitation services over a decade earlier were 60 percent less likely than adolescents whose mothers had not received a nurse home visitor to have run away, 55 percent less likely to have been arrested, and 80 percent less likely to have been convicted of a crime, including a violation of probation (Olds, Henderson et al., 1998). They also had smoked fewer cigarettes per day, had consumed less alcohol in the past 6 months, and had exhibited fewer behavioral problems related to alcohol and drug use.

## *Program Costs and Cost Savings*

The nurse home visitation program costs an estimated $3,200 per family per year during the startup phase (first 3 years) and $2,800 per family per year once nurses are completely trained and working at full capacity. Costs vary from site to site, depending primarily on nursing salaries in the community where the program is run. When the program focuses on low-income women, the government's costs to fund the program are recovered by the time the first child reaches age 4, primarily because of the reduced number of subsequent pregnancies and related reductions in use of government welfare programs (Olds et al., 1993). A report from The RAND Corporation estimates that by the time children from high-risk families reach age 15 the cost savings are four times the original investment because of reductions in crime, welfare expenditures, and health care costs and as a result of taxes paid by working parents (Karoly et al., 1998).

## Growing National Interest

Many states and cities have expressed an interest in adopting the nurse home visitation program because it has proven so successful in preventing crime and violence and other serious health and social problems. Three components of the U.S. Department of Justice's Office of Justice Programs—the Office of Juvenile Justice and Delinquency Prevention (OJJDP), the Bureau of Justice Assistance, and the Executive Office for Weed and Seed—are supporting implementation of the program in six high-crime, urban areas as part of its national Weed and Seed and Safe Futures initiatives. By summer 1998, agencies serving low-income neighborhoods in Fresno, Los Angeles, and Oakland, Calif.; Clearwater, Fla.; St. Louis, Mo.; and Oklahoma City, Okla., were implementing the nurse home visitation program.

OJJDP also funds an initiative at the Center for the Study and Prevention of Violence at the University of Colorado, which recently named the nurse home visitation program 1 of 10 "blueprint" programs after a rigorous evaluation demonstrated its effectiveness in preventing violence and success in replication across sites. The center is developing instructions to help communities plan and implement blueprint programs. OJJDP will provide the center with approximately $5 million over 3 years to assist selected communities in implementing blueprint programs.

## Summary

This cost-effective program of home visitation by nurses, tested over the past 20 years, has the proven ability to reduce the development of antisocial behavior in childhood and later crime and delinquency. It has been effective in reducing three major categories of risk related to antisocial behavior: adverse maternal prenatal health-related behaviors; child abuse and neglect; and troubled maternal life course (unintended successive pregancies, reduced work-force participation, welfare dependence, substance abuse, and criminal behavior).

## For Further Information

For further information about the nurse home visitation program and the research demonstrating its effectiveness, contact:

Peggy Hill, Associate Director
Kempe Prevention Research Center for Family and Child Health
1825 Marion Street
Denver, CO 80218
303-864-5207
E-Mail: Hill.Peggy@tchden.org

For further information about OJJDP's Blueprints Violence Prevention Project publications or training and technical assistance program, contact:

Center for the Study and Prevention of Violence
Institute of Behavioral Science
University of Colorado at Boulder
Campus Box 442
Boulder, CO 80309-0442
303-492-8465
303-443-3297 (Fax)
Web site: www.Colorado.EDU/cspv/blueprints/
E-Mail: cspv@colorado.edu

## Acknowledgments

David Olds, Ph.D., is Professor of Pediatrics, Psychiatry, and Preventive Medicince at the University of Colorado Health Sciences Center and Director of the Kempe Prevention Research Center for Family and Child Health. He has devoted his career to investigating methods of preventing health problems in low-income families and developmental problems in children.

Peggy Hill, M.S., is the Associate Director of the Kempe Prevention Research Center for Family and Child Health. She has experience in community organization and in-home visitation program design, management, evaluation, and training. Ms. Hill assists in translating research into practice and supporting national dissemination of the nurse home visitation program.

Elissa Rumsey, M.S., is a program manager in the Research and Program Development Division at OJJDP. Ms. Rumsey manages a demonstration and evaluation of the prenatal and early childhood visitation model at five Weed and Seed sites and one Safe Futures site.

The authors wish to thank Charles Henderson, Jr., John Eckenrode, Pamela Morris, and Jane Powers, Cornell University; Robert Cole, Harriet Kitzman, and Kim Sidora, University of Rochester; Lisa Pettitt, University of Denver; and Dennis Luckey, University of Colorado Health Sciences Center, for their contributions to this research on prenatal and early childhood nurse home visitation.

## *References*

American Psychiatric Association. 1994. *Diagnostic and Statistical Manual of Mental Disorders,* 4th ed. Washington, DC: American Psychiatric Association.

Coie, J. 1996. "Prevention of Violence and Antisocial Behavior." In *Prevention of Psychological Disorders,* edited by R. Peters and R. J. McMahon. London: Sage Publications, pp. 1–18.

Coie, J., R. Terry, K. Lenox, J. Lochman, and C. Hyman. 1995. "Childhood Peer Rejection and Aggression as Predictors of Stable Patterns of Adolescent Disorder." *Development and Psychopathology* 7(4): 697–713.

Conger, R. D., K. J. Conger, G. H. Elder, Jr., F. O. Lorenz, R. L. Simons, and L. B. Whitbeck. 1993. "Family Economic Stress and Adjustment of Early Adolescent Girls." *Developmental Psychology* 29(2): 206–19.

Dishion, T. J., D. Capaldi, K. M. Spracklen, and F. Li. 1995. "Peer Ecology Of Male Adolescent Drug Use." *Development and Psychopathology* 7(4): 803–24.

Eder, D. 1983. "Organizational Constraints and Individual Mobility: Ability Group Formation and Maintenance." *Sociological Quarterly* 24(3): 405–20.

Felner, R. D., S. Brand, D. L. DuBois, A. M. Adan, P. F. Mulhall, and E. G. Evans 1995. "Socioeconomic Disadvantage, Proximal Environmental Experiences, and Socioemotional and Academic Adjustment in Early Adolescence: Investigation of a Mediated Effects Model." *Child Development* 66(3): 774–92.

Fergusson, D. M., L. J. Horwood, and M. T. Lynskey. 1993. "Maternal Smoking Before and After Pregnancy: Effects on Behavioral Outcomes in Middle Childhood." *Pediatrics* 92(6): 815–22.

Furstenberg, F. F., J. Brooks-Gunn, and S. P. Morgan. 1987. *Adolescent Mothers and Their Children in Later Life.* Cambridge, MA: Cambridge University Press.

Hirschi, T. 1994. "Family." In *The Generality of Deviance,* edited by T. Hirschi and M. R. Gottfredson. New Brunswick, NJ: Transaction Publishers, pp. 47–69.

Karoly, L. A., S. S. Everingham, J. Hoube, R. Kilburn, C. P. Rydell, M. Sanders and P. W. Greenwood. 1998. *Investing in Our Children: What We Know and Don't Know about the Costs and Benefits of Early Childhood Interventions.* MR-898. Santa Monica, CA: The RAND Corporation.

Kelley, B. T., R. Loeber, K. Keenan, and M. DeLamatre. 1997 (December). *Developmental Pathways in Boys' Disruptive and Delinquent Behavior.* Bulletin. Washington, DC: U.S. Department of Justice, Office of Justice Programs, Office of Juvenile Justice and Delinquency Prevention.

Kelley, B. T, T. P. Thornberry, and C. A. Smith. 1997 (August). *In the Wake of Childhood Maltreatment.* Bulletin. Washington, DC: U.S. Department of Justice, Office of Justice Programs, Office of Juvenile Justice and Delinquency Prevention.

Kitzman, H., D. L. Olds, C. R. Jr. Henderson, C. Hanks, R. Cole, R. Tatelbaum, K. M. McConnochie, K. Sidora, D. W. Luckey, D. Shaver, K. Engelhardt, D. James, and K. Barnard. 1997. "Effect of Prenatal and Infancy Home Visitation by Nurses on Pregnancy Outcomes, Childhood Injuries, and Repeated Childbearing: A Randomized Controlled Trial." *Journal of the American Medical Association* 278(8): 644–52.

Maxfield, M. G., and C. S. Widom. 1996 (April). "The Cycle of Violence: Revisited 6 Years Later." *Archives of Pediatric and Adolescent Medicine* 150(4): 390–95.

Milberger, S., J. Biederman, S. Faraone, L. Chen, and J. Jones. 1996. "Is Maternal Smoking during Pregnancy a Risk Factor for Attention Deficit Hyperactivity Disorder in Children?" *American Journal of Psychiatry* 153(9): 1138–42.

Moffitt, T. E. 1993a. "Adolescence-Limited and Life-Course-Persistent Antisocial Behavior: A Developmental Taxonomy." *Psychological Review* 100(4): 674–701.

369

Moffitt, T. E. 1993b. "The Neuropsychology of Conduct Disorder." *Development and Psychopathology* 5(1-2): 135–51.

Moffitt, T. E., A. Caspi, N. Dickson, P. Silva, and W. Stanton. 1996. "Childhood-Onset Versus Adolescent-Onset Antisocial Conduct Problems in Males: Natural History from Ages 3 to 18 Years." *Development and Psychopathology* 8(2): 399–424.

Olds, D. 1988. "The Prenatal/Early Infancy Project." In *Fourteen Ounces of Prevention: A Casebook for Practitioners,* edited by R. Price, E. Cowen, R. Lorion, and J. Ramos-McKay. Washington, DC: American Psychological Association.

Olds, D. 1997. "Tobacco Exposure and Impaired Development: A Review of the Evidence." *Mental Retardation and Developmental Disabilities Research Review* 3(3): 257–69.

Olds, D., J. Eckenrode, C. R., Jr., Henderson, H. Kitzman, J. Powers, R. Cole, K. Sidora, P. Morris, L. Pettitt, and D. Luckey. 1997. "Long-Term Effects of Home Visitation on Maternal Life Course and Child Abuse and Neglect: 15-year Follow-up of a Randomized Trial." *Journal of the American Medical Association* 278(8): 637–43.

Olds, D., C. Henderson, R. Chamberlin, and R. Tatelbaum. 1986. "Preventing Child Abuse and Neglect: A Randomized Trial of Nurse Home Visitation." *Pediatrics* 78(1): 65–78.

Olds, D., C. R. Henderson, R. Cole, J. Eckenrode, H. Kitzman, D. Luckey, L. Pettitt, K. Sidora, P. Morris, and J. Powers. 1998. "Long-Term Effects of Nurse Home Visitation on Children's Criminal and Antisocial Behavior: 15-year Follow-up of a Randomized Trial." *Journal of the American Medical Association* 280(14): 1238–44.

Olds, D., C. Henderson, C. Phelps, H. Kitzman, and C. Hanks. 1993. "Effect of Prenatal and Infancy Nurse Home Visitation on Government Spending." *Medical Care* 31(2): 155–174.

Olds, D. L., C. R. Henderson, and R. Tatelbaum. 1994a. "Intellectual Impairment in Children of Women Who Smoke Cigarettes during Pregnancy." *Pediatrics* 93(2): 221–27.

Olds, D. L., C. R. Henderson, and R. Tatelbaum. 1994b. "Prevention of Intellectual Impairment in Children of Women Who Smoke Cigarettes during Pregnancy." *Pediatrics* 93(2): 228–33.

Olds, D., C. R. Henderson, R. Tatelbaum, and R. Chamberlin. 1986. "Improving the Delivery of Prenatal Care and Outcomes of Pregnancy: A Randomized Trial of Nurse Home Visitation." *Pediatrics* 77 (1): 16–28.

Olds, D., C. Henderson, R. Tatelbaum, and R. Chamberlin. 1988. "Improving the Life-Course Development of Socially Disadvantaged Mothers: A Randomized Trial of Nurse Home Visitation." *American Journal of Public Health* 78(11): 1436–45.

Olds, D., H. Kitzman, R. Cole, and J. Robinson. 1997. "Theoretical Foundations of a Program of Home Visitation for Pregnant Women and Parents of Young Children." *Journal of Community Psychology* 25(1): 9–25.

Olds, D., and J. Korfmacher. 1997. "The Evolution of a Program of Research on Prenatal and Early Childhood Home Visitation: Special Issue Introduction." *Journal of Community Psychology* 25(1): 1–7.

Olds, D., L. M. Pettitt, J. Robinson, J. Eckenrode, H. Kitzman, R. Cole, and J. Powers. 1998. "Reducing the Risks for Antisocial Behavior with a Program of Prenatal and Early Childhood Home Visitation." *Journal of Community Psychology* 26(1): 65–83.

Rodning, C., L. Beckwith, and J. Howard. 1989. "Characteristics of Attachment Organization and Play Organization in Prenatally Drug-exposed Toddlers." *Development and Psychopathology* 1(4): 277–89.

Sanson, A., D. Smart, M. Prior, and K. Oberklaid. 1993. "Precursors of Hyperactivity and Aggression." *Journal of the American Academy of Child and Adolescent Psychiatry* 32(6): 1207–16.

Tygart, C. E. 1991. "Juvenile Delinquency and Number of Children in a Family: Some Empirical and Theoretical Updates." *Youth & Society* 22: 525–36.

Wakschlag, L. S., B. B. Lahey, R. Loeber, S. M. Green, R. A. Gordon, and B. L. Leventhal. 1997. "Maternal Smoking during Pregnancy and the Risk of Conduct Disorder in Boys." *Archives of General Psychiatry* 54(7): 670–76.

Weitzman, M., S. Gortmaker, and A. Sobol. 1992. "Maternal Smoking and Behavior Problems of Children." *Pediatrics* 90(3): 342–49.

Widom, C. S. 1989. "The Cycle of Violence." *Science* 244: 160–66.

## Section 17.4

# *Parents Anonymous<sup>SM</sup>: Strengthening Families*

U.S. Department of Justice, Office of Justice Programs.
Publication No. NCJ 171120, April 1999.

*Teresa Rafael, M.S.W., and Lisa Pion-Berlin, Ph.D.*

*The Office of Juvenile Justice and Delinquency Prevention (OJJDP) is dedicated to preventing and reversing trends of increased delinquency and violence among adolescents. These trends have alarmed the public during the past decade and challenged the juvenile justice system. It is widely accepted that increases in delinquency and violence over the past decade are rooted in a number of interrelated social problems—child abuse and neglect, alcohol and drug abuse, youth conflict and aggression, and early sexual involvement—that may originate within the family structure. The focus of OJJDP's Family Strengthening Series is to provide assistance to ongoing efforts across the country to strengthen the family unit by discussing the effectiveness of family intervention programs and providing resources to families and communities.*

Parents Anonymous, Inc., the oldest national child abuse prevention organization, is dedicated to strengthening families through innovative strategies that promote mutual support and parent leadership. Founded in 1970 through the joint efforts of a courageous parent who sought help in providing a safe and caring home for her children and a social worker who believed that parents are their own best agents of change, Parents Anonymous, Inc., currently leads a dynamic national network of affiliated community-based groups with weekly meetings for parents and children. Each year, approximately 100,000[1] parents and their children come together in Parents Anonymous<sup>SM</sup> groups to learn new skills, transform their attitudes and behaviors, and create long-term positive changes in their lives. These weekly groups are led by parents and professionally trained facilitators and are free of charge to participants. While the parents are meeting, their children are usually engaged in specialized programs to promote healthy growth and development, and free childcare is provided in sites in which these programs are unavailable. Many state and local Parents Anonymous$^{SM}$ programs operate 24-hour telephone helplines to provide an immediate response to parents seeking help. Parents Anonymous$^{SM}$ also raises awareness and educates the public on critical issues and community solutions and joins with community, state, and federal policymakers to promote effective services for families across America.

Parents or adults in parenting roles (e.g., grandparents, aunts, uncles, foster parents, stepparents, or older siblings) who are concerned about their parenting abilities and seeking support, information, and training are welcome at Parents Anonymous$^{SM}$ groups, whatever the age of their children or their current circumstances. Groups are ongoing and open ended; parents can join at any time and participate as long as they wish. Group participation is not restricted by age, educational level, income, problems experienced by the parents or children, or any other specific criteria. Because the groups are community based, participants mirror the ethnic, geographical, and cultural nature of their neighborhoods.

Parents Anonymous$^{SM}$ responds to the diverse needs of families (married or single parents, stepparents, teenage parents, and divorced parents) by providing group meetings in neighborhood family centers, churches, clinics, schools, housing projects, prisons, homeless shelters, and Head Start centers. In addition, group members discuss parenting concerns in English, Spanish, French, and several Southeast-Asian and American Indian languages. A Parents Anonymous $^{SM}$ group can become a valuable resource for any parent, regardless of culture or language, who is having difficulty providing a safe and caring home.

## Organizational Structure

### The National Network

Parents Anonymous, Inc., the national organization, is a private, nonprofit agency located in Claremont, Calif. Through a variety of strategies and mechanisms, the organization provides training, technical assistance, materials, national media exposure, advocacy, national networking opportunities, and coordination of Parents Anonymous$^{SM}$ programs at state and regional levels. Through local, city, county, and state partnerships, Parents Anonymous, Inc., selects, monitors, and assists a dynamic national network of organizations that share responsibility for promoting, maintaining, developing, and expanding programs in local areas.

These organizations provide volunteer management (including recruitment, screening, training, recognition, and evaluation), promote parent leadership, develop community-based groups, provide outreach to parents, and form close links with other resources and organizations in their communities. With regard to shared leadership, parents work with professionals in planning, implementing, and evaluating program services through prescriptive leadership roles. In addition, Parents Anonymous, Inc., is integrally involved in major national system reform initiatives addressing the need for change in the child protective services system and in other child welfare arenas. Through consultation, training, and technical assistance to local communities and public child welfare systems, Parents Anonymous, Inc., helps others understand and incorporate sound principles into their work with families and children to ensure responsive service planning, implementation, oversight, and evaluation.

### *National Parent Leadership Activities*

In 1995, Parents Anonymous, Inc., developed the diverse National Parent Leadership Team, consisting of parents who demonstrated leadership in their local groups and organizations and who expressed an interest in expanding their leadership role. The leadership team provides training for professionals and other parents; participates in public education, outreach, and advocacy activities; and serves as the editorial board for *The Parent Networker* newsletter. The team advises Parents Anonymous, Inc., regarding program and organization issues that affect families and works with local, state, and national media to ensure that the voices of parents are heard on issues that are related to families and children. Based on the success of the national team, several state or local Parents Anonymous[SM] organizations have developed parent leadership teams to accomplish similar goals locally.

## Program Components

### *The Parent Group Leader*

Based on the principle of shared leadership, each group must have a parent leader who, in addition to being a group member, also serves as a cofacilitator of the group and promotes leadership among all group members. Other parent leadership activities may be shared so that multiple parents have the opportunity to practice and strengthen their leadership skills, which allows parents to give back to others and increase their self-esteem.

## *One Mother's Search Leads to Help for Hundreds of Thousands of Parents*

The story of Jolly K., the founding parent of Parents Anonymous [SM], is one that has provided hope and inspiration to thousands of parents throughout the country. In 1970, Jolly was searching for help in providing a safe and caring home for her two daughters and was particularly worried about her behavior toward her 6-year-old daughter. After many fruitless attempts to locate help in changing her behavior, Jolly was finally assigned to the caseload of Leonard Lieber, a clinical social worker at a California state mental health clinic. Jolly and Leonard met in traditional therapy sessions for several months. When Jolly expressed frustration about her lack of progress, Leonard encouraged Jolly to suggest alternative solutions. Jolly realized that if she could meet with other parents with similar problems, they could explore solutions together.

She and Leonard met with other mothers with whom he was working and who were also seeking to improve their parenting abilities—Jolly led the discussion and Leonard served as a resource and facilitator. At the end of 2 hours, the parents attending this first meeting felt encouraged and hopeful and decided to continue meeting under the following guidelines:

- They would make a commitment to stop behaviors they deemed unacceptable or abusive.

- They would exchange telephone numbers and be available to each other day or night, especially in times of crisis.

- They would meet in donated space and would welcome, free of charge, any other parents who wanted to attend.

In Redondo Beach, Calif., they placed the first advertisement in a local newspaper, "For Moms Who Lose Their Cool With Their Kids, Call..." This gave birth to a national movement that has helped millions of parents and children all across America. Through their courage and tenacity, the parents in the first Parents Anonymous [SM] group demonstrated that, by helping each other, they could find the strength to become the parents they wanted to be. Jolly and Leonard began to speak to community groups and the media. They and others told the story of the significant positive changes that were taking place in families when parents participated in Parents Anonymous [SM] groups.

## The Professionally Trained Facilitator

Each Parents Anonymous<sup>SM</sup> group has a professionally trained facilitator who meets with the group each week and is available to the parent leader and other group members between meetings. The facilitator commits to working with the group for a minimum of 1 year and may be a volunteer given release time by his or her employer or paid a stipend. Facilitators bring a variety of skills and talents to their work with Parents Anonymous<sup>SM</sup>. They are primarily practicing professionals with expertise in social work, counseling, healthcare, mental health, teaching, or related fields. They possess personal characteristics that embody the principles of Parents Anonymous<sup>SM</sup>. They are knowledgeable about child abuse, juvenile delinquency, group dynamics, family systems, child development, and local community resources. Above all, they must be capable of working with parents in the unique Parents Anonymous<sup>SM</sup> model of shared leadership and be flexible and accepting.

In addition, the facilitators are mandated to report child abuse and must be comfortable doing so to protect the safety of children in a way that continues to promote the strength of parents. When it is necessary to report child abuse, it is important for facilitators to focus on the parent's role in protecting his or her child, encourage the parent to self-report, and involve the parent with child protective services

## The Parents Anonymous<sup>SM</sup> Principles

Parents Anonymous<sup>SM</sup> programs are based on the following four guiding principles:

- **Parent Leadership.** Parents recognize and take responsibility for their problems, develop their own solutions, and serve as role models for other parents.

- **Mutual Support.** Help is reciprocal, in that parents give and receive support from each other, creating a strong sense of community.

- **Shared Leadership.** Parents and professionals build successful partnerships to share responsibility, expertise, and leadership roles.

- **Personal Growth.** Parents make significant long-term positive change through identifying their options, exploring their feelings, and acting on their decisions in an atmosphere of belonging, trust, and acceptance in which healthy interactions are modeled.

in any other way possible. This helps ensure that the parent continues to be responsible for the child's safety and well-being, even if it is necessary for the parent to ask for help from child protective services in fulfilling that role.

The facilitator is an integral part of the group. He or she serves as a role model, provides links to other community resources, and helps create a sense of safety and positive growth in the group. The nature of the facilitator's role differs significantly from the traditional role of human service professionals, in that it is based on a true partnership with parents and is designed to promote individual parent leadership and strengthen the functioning of the group.

## Community-Based Volunteer Support

Volunteers make up the core support for programs by facilitating groups, operating children's programs, providing childcare, and answering telephone response lines. Moreover, volunteers provide their skill and expertise on boards of directors, fund-raising committees, and public relations campaigns. Their valuable assistance contributes to the cost effectiveness of the program and a high level of community ownership, supports local replication of the model, and ensures that parents and their children have access to Parents Anonymous[SM] programs. Through volunteering, community members are given a vehicle with which to respond to the needs of their neighbors and to invest in strengthening families and children. Approximately 30,000 volunteers across the country donate an estimated $10 million worth of services annually.

## Specialized Children's Programs

According to an annual database survey given to all Parents Anonymous[SM] affiliates, specialized Parents Anonymous[SM] children's programs help approximately 22,000 children and youth gain problem-solving skills, increase their positive social interaction skills, and learn to better understand and manage their emotions. These activities lead to greater self-esteem and more positive interactions with others. Some programs also emphasize building other skills. In Oregon, for example, the programs teach drug and alcohol refusal skills to youth to prepare them to resist peer pressure. Because the children's programs are held in conjunction with the parent groups, the need for childcare is not a

377

barrier to parental attendance. As noted before, sites without specialized programs offer free childcare.

### Public Awareness and Outreach

Parents Anonymous, Inc., and its national network conduct public awareness activities and reach out to potential parent participants through news and feature coverage in local and national media; distribution of brochures, pamphlets, newsletters, and fliers; production and distribution of informational videos; and training programs for professionals in healthcare, social services, education, and other disciplines to encourage their referrals of parents. Parents reach out to other parents through public speaking, newspaper articles, and media interviews; share their successes; and encourage others to join or support Parents Anonymous^SM programs across the country.

### Parents Anonymous^SM Helplines

Parents Anonymous, Inc., and its national network provide telephone helplines for parents seeking information and referral to local groups. These toll-free telephone services provide a necessary lifeline for parents seeking help. Annually, Parents Anonymous^SM provides immediate support and referrals to approximately 90,000 parents through Parents Anonymous^SM helplines.

### Participant Profile

Parents Anonymous^SM is a viable resource for thousands of mothers and fathers—33 percent of the program participants are male, and 67 percent are female (see figure). Parents Anonymous^SM reaches out to families of color in local communities, including those on reservations, with an almost even split between Caucasian parents (51 percent) and all other groups combined (49 percent). The percentage of people of color in Parents Anonymous^SM groups far exceeds the racial/ethnic breakdown of the general U.S. population. Twenty-one percent of the participants are African-American, 22 percent are Hispanic, 5 percent are American Indian, and 1 percent are Asian/Pacific Islander. Parents Anonymous^SM programs integrate the values, languages, and strengths of local communities with a strong commitment to providing culturally responsive services that meet the diverse needs of the nation's families. This commitment is demonstrated by the wide range of populations served and locations of groups. Twenty-six percent of all Parents Anonymous[SM] groups serve specialized populations of parents, while 74 percent reach out to all parents in their target community.

Parents join Parents Anonymous[SM] groups for multiple reasons:

- They are seeking help because they want to change their behavior toward their children. This can range from parents who are feeling too much stress to parents who have harmed their children or fear they might harm them.

- A family member, friend, social worker, teacher, healthcare provider, daycare worker, religious leader, or other individual encouraged them to attend.

- They want help, information, and support in managing specific behavioral, health, or other issues facing their family.

- They are mandated by a court order or child protective services agreement to attend.

## Breakdown of Participants

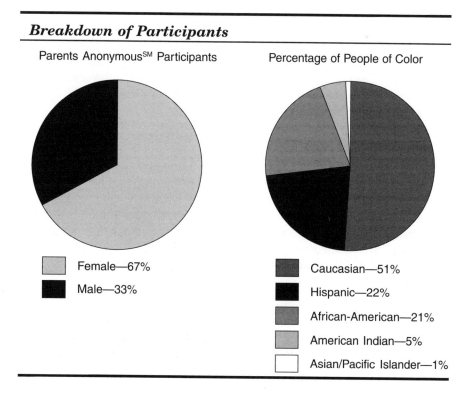

Parents Anonymous[SM] Participants

- Female—67%
- Male—33%

Percentage of People of Color

- Caucasian—51%
- Hispanic—22%
- African-American—21%
- American Indian—5%
- Asian/Pacific Islander—1%

## A Typical Parents Anonymous^SM Meeting

*It is sometimes easiest to understand a program when given an example to review. Below is an example of what a newcomer may experience when attending his or her first Parents Anonymous^SM group meeting.*

When Karen starts to feel overwhelmed with her role as a parent, she knows that she needs help. A trusted friend tells her about Parents Anonymous^SM programs and Karen decides to attend a meeting. She leaves her two children in the care of a well-trained children's program worker and, after getting them settled, joins seven other parents and a facilitator to begin the 2-hour group meeting. No forms are handed out, no one insists that personal information be provided, and no fee is required to participate. The group meeting begins when one parent, the parent group leader, reads from an opening statement: "This Parents Anonymous^SM group is part of a national network of parents who support and encourage positive change and growth in family relationships. Any concerns will be discussed in a caring and supportive manner. Confidentiality and anonymity are to be respected, except when the health or safety of a family member is at risk."

Group members indicate the amount of time they need to discuss the issues they want to cover during the next 2 hours. All newcomers are invited to participate but also are assured that they may just listen. As parents talk about their individual situations, Karen gains an understanding of who they are, what brought them to Parents Anonymous^SM, and what goals they hope to achieve. For example:

- Susan is a 19-year-old single mom with a 10-month-old baby. The baby's father is no longer involved in her life, and Susan is learning how to provide a safe and caring home for herself and her new baby. She has no immediate family members in the area and has little support or relief from the constant stress she feels. With the information and support she gains from the group, Susan feels more confident and has an extended network of other parents she can call during the week if she is unsure of herself or feels at the end of her rope. She has even enrolled in a nearby nursing school to pursue her dream of working in the medical field.

- Alishia and Robert, the only couple in the group, have three children; the oldest one, a 15-year-old, seems to have become a different person. Her normally sunny disposition and helpful nature have disappeared, and she is often surly, insolent, and angry. Susan has helped them understand the emotional changes teens experience, as she is only a few years away from being that same age. Alishia and Robert are learning to set limits while remaining empathetic with their daughter. Life at home has become much better for the entire family.

- Manuel is the father of two children, ages 6 and 10. He and his wife recently divorced, and Manuel realized he had a habit of leaving the job of parenting to his wife. Now that the children are with him on weekends, he must create a new relationship with them and help them deal with the pain and grief of the divorce. He wants to become a strong and competent parent even though he has limited time with his children. He knows they are angry and confused, and he also realizes how much he loves them and how important they are to him.

- Barbara is an outpatient in a drug-abuse treatment program. She participated in a Parents Anonymous<sup>SM</sup> group during the 4-week, inpatient portion of the treatment program and joined this community group when she returned to her own neighborhood. As she gained a new awareness of her life beyond her use of drugs, she realized that her addiction had seriously impaired her ability to be a safe and caring parent to her children. She is determined to learn all she can in order to be the best parent she can be.

- Samantha is in the group because she lost control one day and struck her 11-year-old son, leaving a mark on his arm. His school counselor contacted child protective services (CPS), and when the CPS worker visited the home to assess the situation, she realized that this parent could benefit from the program and asked the judge to mandate that Samantha attend. Each week, for 3 months, Samantha asked the facilitator to sign an attendance form, which she gave to her social worker to demonstrate her compliance with the court order. After the mandated period was completed, she continued to attend and recently celebrated her second anniversary as a member.

- Randy attends because his oldest son was convicted of a misdemeanor. His son's probation worker stressed the importance of strong, positive parenting skills in helping the youth avoid future problems and recommended the program. Randy attends the group, and although his wife works evenings and is unable to participate, she supports Randy's involvement and learns from him. Thus far, their son has improved in his schoolwork and made new friends who are a more positive influence on him. Best of all, he is now a healthy role model for his two younger brothers. Randy has attended the group for a year and is the parent group leader.

- Maria is the group facilitator. She is a social worker, and her agency provides release time for her to meet with the group each week. Maria became a facilitator 2 years ago and finds it the most rewarding professional role she has ever held. She works closely with the parent group leader and encourages leadership among all the parents in the group. She serves as a resource to the parents during group meetings, and helps build links with other community services.

After listening to the discussion for an hour or so, Karen decides to share her concerns and finds that the group is supportive and has valuable information to share—some from their own experience and some learned in other settings. Several parents recommend resources they have found to be useful, and the facilitator encourages her to talk further with the parents who seem to be the most helpful to her.

At the end of the meeting, a list is passed around with names and telephone numbers on it, although providing this information is not mandatory. Susan tells Karen she'll call her to find out more about a suggestion Karen made—a method that helped her children get to sleep when they were the age of Susan's child.

As Karen leaves, she recognizes that her sense of helplessness has been replaced with hope, and fear with pride of accomplishment.

---

## *The Parents Anonymous*<sup>SM</sup> *Group Model*

To reduce the blame and shame parents sometimes experience, Parents Anonymous<sup>SM</sup> offers help through support systems with other parents. Parents Anonymous<sup>SM</sup> group members determine the content of each meeting, usually through formal agenda building at the beginning of each session, although multiple strategies may be employed. Thus, the topics discussed on any given day relate specifically to the needs and interests of the group members present. This allows for valuable discussion because members often can share their own expertise in particular areas with other members seeking assistance. The group model capitalizes on the learning style of adults—adults learn best when they perceive they need to know about a topic—and adult learning is reinforced when a new skill can be practiced immediately and ongoing support and feedback are available to promote long-term change.

At Parents Anonymous[SM] meetings, parents discuss communication, discipline, child development, parental roles, effective strategies for helping children achieve independence and self-control, methods for successfully dealing with the everyday stresses of parenting, and any other issues that affect their parenting behavior. Parents Anonymous[SM] is equally as appropriate for parents who are under stress and need information and support as for parents who have experienced difficulties requiring professional intervention from child protective services or courts. Because all aspects of parents' lives may affect their relationship with their children, all relevant topics are open for discussion. To reinforce and solidify their new skills, parents practice new behaviors at home and discuss the results at the meeting each week. Attitudes dramatically change and form the basis for integrating new knowledge and skills, helping parents to successfully foster the healthy growth and development of their children.

Parents are given an opportunity to experience the safety and caring of the group, to be trusted and to know others who are trustworthy, and to take charge of their lives and their families while knowing that the group members will be available to help them as needed. Parents find an environment where they can talk about their serious concerns and specific events and behaviors that may be problematic. In this setting, new behaviors are learned and incorporated into daily life. Through the mutual support of the group, parents grow stronger by developing new self-images that are positive, capable, and responsible.

Through interactions with their peers, parents identify their options, examine their attitudes toward childrearing, and learn positive ways of relating to their children. Group members and the facilitator also exchange telephone numbers; this offers 24-hour support to parents when they experience a crisis or stress. The strong peer connections parents build within the group often are reinforced through telephone calls and other personal contacts outside the group. The foundation of the group is reciprocity—in addition to receiving help from the group, every parent has the opportunity to offer help to other group members and become a leader. Parents who reach out and provide help thus benefit as much as or more than the parents who receive their assistance.

When necessary, courts mandate parents to attend parenting classes; Parents Anonymous[SM] is one resource. The mutual support environment of a Parents Anonymous[SM] group has been proven effective in reducing resistance and breaking through denial of the need for personal change.

Becoming a parent is a major developmental transition for anyone. In an ideal world, all young people would grow up in nurturing, supportive homes with positive role models who would fully prepare them to be loving and responsible parents to their own children. Unfortunately, reality for many is very different. Many parents are still struggling to reconcile issues related to their own development and may be so overwhelmed with their own needs and fears that they are unable to focus as much as necessary on meeting their children's needs. If a parent's self-image is still that of a child who needs approval, support, and acceptance, it is unlikely that information about positive parenting techniques will elicit significant change. If anything, parents may feel rage, grief, and loss about their childhoods as they learn more about what is necessary for the well-being of children. Parents with many unmet needs may not be motivated to attend a parenting class. They may need to understand the benefits to their own lives in order to participate.

Parents Anonymous<sup>SM</sup> addresses these issues by providing a safe and supportive place in which parents can unload excess emotional baggage from their life experiences so that they can focus on their role as parents and the joys and responsibilities inherent in that role. Once that transition takes place, parents are often ready and eager for help and support as they work to become more effective caregivers. Furthermore, many parents find Parents Anonymous<sup>SM</sup> a valuable resource following participation in structured, time-limited parent education classes.

### *Barriers to Change*

Much is known about risk factors facing parents and children and about ways to develop the protective factors that can overcome the impact of risk factors. However, risk factors often present a barrier to obtaining support and taking advantage of educational opportunities. For example, the following challenges—often faced by families involved in public child welfare systems and the courts—also can be barriers to seeking and using the help that is available:

- Social and emotional isolation.
- Lack of assurance about what is "normal," perhaps leading to harsh self-judgment, self-protectiveness, or fear of speaking out.

- Family rules about keeping secrets and lack of trust in others.
- Lack of resources.
- High stress and frequent crisis situations.
- Lack of awareness of options for change, and lack of hope in the possibility of change.
- Exposure to people who inappropriately use power and control, which leads to a sense of helplessness and lack of trust in authority figures.
- Unmet needs from one's own childhood.

All Parents Anonymous^SM programs are confidential unless the health or safety of a child is at risk. Based on state law, Parents Anonymous^SM facilitators are required to report suspected child abuse and neglect. It is the policy of Parents Anonymous^SM that parents are always made aware of the reporting requirements when they attend their first Parents Anonymous^SM group. In those situations serious enough to warrant a report, concerns are initially discussed with the parent involved, who is encouraged and supported in making a self-report. If he or she is unwilling or unable to do so, the facilitator will make the report and will continue to provide support to the parent. Suspected situations of child abuse and neglect may be identified when:

- A parent discloses a particular concern about his or her behavior.
- An emerging pattern of behavior leads to concern about a parent's ability to cope in a healthy way with the stresses of parenthood.
- A child in childcare exhibits signs of or verbally reports abuse or neglect.

The need to make a report provides an opportunity to promote the parent's role, responsibilities, and power in managing his or her interaction with the child by keeping the parent involved in the process as much as possible. The child's safety is always the primary concern, but parents are encouraged to participate in the report, including making a self-report when appropriate.

## Positive Outcomes for Families

One goal of Parents Anonymous^SM is to prevent or end juvenile delinquency and child abuse problems in families. To reach this goal, parents learn that it is a sign of strength to ask for help. They learn to use appropriate community resources and to build supportive, positive peer relationships for themselves and their children. They learn to establish reciprocal relationships, which helps them maintain positive peer associations and avoid overburdening the friends and family members who make up their personal support system. Parents gain a sense of their own power and use it to improve their ability to care for their children, avoid violent reactions to their children, protect them from violence inflicted by other adults, and use parenting practices that promote healthy outcomes for their children.

### *Demonstrated Effectiveness of Parents Anonymous[SM]*

Research suggests that Parents Anonymous[SM] is a promising approach to strengthening families and preventing child abuse and neglect, although only a small number of studies have been conducted. Behavior Associates (1976) administered a one-time survey to 613 program participants and asked them a range of questions about their self-esteem, feelings about parenthood and children, satisfaction derived from parenthood, knowledge of child development, social contacts and use of community resources, frequency and severity of abuse, perceived benefits of membership in the program, and background characteristics.

Participants reported improved parenting behavior, an immediate reduction in physical abuse, a positive change in physical and verbal interactions with their children, improved self-esteem, increased social contacts, more help-seeking behavior, and greater use of community facilities for childcare. Also, it was found that participants' expectations of children's behavior became more developmentally appropriate. The findings suggest that these positive results are more pronounced as time spent in the program increases.

A second study found that Parents Anonymous[SM] is a key element in service delivery plans for parents (Cohn, 1979). This study used data collected from case managers who were asked a variety of questions about their clients when they began and terminated services. Case managers were asked to rate their clients on a variety of parental attitudes, situations, and behaviors thought to be causally related to child abuse and neglect (e.g., parental stress, having a sense of the child as a person, appropriate behavior toward the child, and knowledge of child development). At service termination, case manager reports indicated that parents who participated in Parents Anonymous[SM] were more likely to improve on these measures than those who did not participate. The researchers did caution that parents may self-select into this self-help service (the study was not able to study the effects of motivation), but also suggest that the nature of the service helps parents resolve important problems.

OJJDP and Parents Anonymous, Inc., have recognized the need to conduct an updated, rigorous evaluation of the program. In 1999, OJJDP will sponsor a national evaluation of Parents Anonymous[SM] and build on the findings of past research.* Important advances in evaluating Parents Anonymous[SM] will include collecting information from multiple sources, conducting post-program followups on participants, and using a comparison group.

## *Benefits of Having a Parents Anonymous[SM] Group in Your Community*

- Families will have free, immediate access to ongoing, long-term support and education based on their own identified need for help.

- Parents will learn new communication skills, discipline techniques, and effective parenting strategies.

- Parents, as their own agents of change, will develop a personal support system through a network of parents who assist each other with everyday needs.

- Parents will be in charge of their own growth and development and can participate for as long as they find it useful.

- Parents will have an opportunity to develop their leadership abilities and become stronger leaders in their homes and in the community.

- Children will have access to a program that is structured to develop self-esteem, teach cooperative play, and build confidence.

---

* Ed. note: As of May 2000, efforts are underway to organize this evaluation, which will be a three-year effort. Initial results should be available sometime in the summer of 2001. Findings from the complete project may be expected sometime in 2003. (Editor's communication with Dean Hoffman, Program Manager, Research and Program Development Division, Office of Juvenile Justice and Delinquency Prevention, U.S. Department of Justice.)

- Professionals in the fields of juvenile justice, health, education, and social service will gain an excellent, cost-effective ongoing resource for families with whom they work.

- Professionals who facilitate groups will gain training and experience in working in true partnership with families through the Parents Anonymous℠ model of shared leadership.

- Communities will create effective programs for families in need, and volunteers will benefit from the opportunity to support and strengthen families through their efforts.

- Program participants, volunteers, and staff will have the opportunity to join with thousands of their peers across the country by participating in the national network and benefiting from training, materials, consultation, and numerous other activities designed to strengthen their community programs.

## Two Examples of Parents Anonymous℠ Programs

Juanita Chávez, M.S.W, A.C.S.W

### Parents Anonymous℠ Serving Hispanic Families in East Los Angeles

The majority of people who live in East Los Angeles are Mexican, and theirs is one of the oldest Mexican communities in the United States. Residents include recent immigrants (documented and undocumented) and members of families who have been in this country for two, three, four, or more generations. Many families settled in this area long ago and remained here, often with several generations living in the same community. In addition to the Mexican and Salvadoran residents residing in the immediate area, Salvadoran residents from downtown Los Angeles also use the culturally relevant services in East Los Angeles.

Some immigrant parents do not understand the laws regarding child protection and may become involved with child welfare agencies or law enforcement officials regarding their treatment of their children, particularly around the use of disciplinary practices. This creates resentment and a sense that their role as parents is being undermined by outside influences. Because some immigrants are undocumented, there is the additional fear that the Immigration and Naturalization Service (INS) will deport them if they become involved with public social service agencies or law enforcement.

Poverty is another issue facing many families in East Los Angeles. Parents who are undocumented immigrants often must work in jobs that pay less than the minimum wage. In many families, including those of immigrants and long-term residents, both parents are wage earners, but the family income remains at or below the poverty level. It is not unusual for older children to have jobs to help support their families. To stretch their resources, several generations often live together in one house.

Parents Anonymous, Inc., has joined with a social service agency located in East Los Angeles to provide a Parents Anonymous[SM] program there. Most of the agency's employees are bilingual and bicultural, and many are intimately familiar with the community.

The agency initially provided parent education classes, and staff members observed that some parents attended several sequential series of classes. After talking with them, the staff realized that these parents were using the classes to meet their long-term needs for support and continued growth as they made critical changes in their lives. Parents reported they preferred not to repeat parent education classes, because of the structure and fixed curriculum, but it was their only option for involvement with others.

In response to the needs of families in the community, a Spanish-speaking Parents Anonymous[SM] group was developed and based at the affiliated social service agency, which is located near public transportation and has ample room for both the parent group and the children's program. The children's program is provided by agency staff. Parents Anonymous, Inc., provides training, program materials, outreach and referral, and ongoing support for the program.

Other agency staff refer parents they work with to the Parents Anonymous[SM] program. In addition, the agency uses culturally appropriate outreach and recruitment materials and distributes them in schools and the community. All materials clearly state that the Parents Anonymous[SM] program is conducted in Spanish.

## Parents Anonymous[SM] Serving American Indian Families in Montana

Montana has seven reservations that are home to several different Indian tribes. Unemployment on these reservations is as high as 89 percent, with the result that most families live below the poverty level. To pursue greater job opportunities, parents often have to leave the reservation and their extended family, so the cost of remaining close to family members can be very high. Inadequate housing is another major issue facing many families. Sometimes, several generations of one family live in a small house that may not have indoor plumbing, electricity, or other conveniences that are common outside the reservation. Given the high level of stress, it is not unusual for families to move from house to house because of intrafamilial conflicts. In addition, as in the general population, issues regarding substance abuse cause stress in the American Indian community.

This Parents Anonymous^SM program began when a social worker, acting as a community organizer, identified key leaders in the community and invited them to a 2-day conference to develop responses to the needs of families on Montana reservations. She worked closely with tribal chiefs and elders and used her own familial contacts and those of her colleagues to build stronger connections between attendees. Because of her age and life experience, the community organizer is a respected elder, and this increases her credibility. Thus, development of the Parents Anonymous^SM program gained significant benefit from the support of elders, chiefs, and tribal councils. More than 250 participants attended the conference and agreed to work together to create additional programs to help strengthen families.

Tribal councils are significantly involved in the development of local Parents Anonymous^SM groups in Montana. For example, they help identify locations that will be most inviting for parents. By their involvement, they sanction Parents Anonymous^SM groups in their communities. Other (mostly government) agencies that are working with American Indian families are excellent referral sources. Parents Anonymous^SM also helps families use other services. Because of these close relationships, staff cooperate with each other and with families to help coordinate available services and to ensure that Parents Anonymous^SM continues to be recognized as a vital community resource.

On one reservation, a healthcare clinic sponsors the Parents Anonymous^SM group through the Bureau of Indian Affairs. The group meets in a local Catholic church, but the facilitators are employees of the clinic. The program also provides meals for both parents and children. This use of the traditional "breaking of the bread" is an excellent strategy to recruit and retain families.

For American Indian families in Montana, cultural norms regarding elders as leaders sometimes create discomfort regarding formal identification of parent group members as parent leaders. Therefore, the Parents Anonymous[SM] model is implemented with a change in title for the parent group leader; while maintaining a high commitment to the principle of parent leadership, parent leaders may use the title "parent helper" instead.

The high level of poverty makes it hard to recruit volunteers for the program. Many members of the community are so focused on meeting their basic needs that they have little time or energy to commit to volunteer work. Mostly, agency staff and tribal council staff facilitate each group. Moreover, paid staff provide childcare and limited transportation to group meetings and to other family-oriented cultural events on the reservations.

Among the American Indian families living on reservations in Montana, cultural norms dictate a reluctance to seem too intrusive to another person by maintaining direct eye contact. To encourage parents to attend, and to lessen the need for constant eye contact, American Indian groups in Montana incorporate many creative activities into their meetings. For example, a group on the Blackfoot Reservation quilts and sews together while they discuss their children and families. This activity gives parents something to look at, lessens eye contact, and thereby avoids feelings of intrusiveness.

Also, as many people know each other so well, they are often already aware of the primary issues each family is facing and may know each other's family members. For example, a parent may make a brief statement, sometimes using only the first name of a child, "Georgie." Another parent may acknowledge they understand what the first parent is thinking and support them by saying, "Ah, that Georgie." Still another parent might join in the conversation and say, "My Michael is doing the same thing." Each member of the group may be fully aware of the concerns felt by the other parents. Then, a fourth parent might say, "When my child had this problem, this is what I did…" Because the group meets in a very small community where people know a lot about each other's lives, they do not need to say much to each other to share their feelings and information.

## Additional Relevant Research

Research on mutual assistance-shared leadership groups such as Parents Anonymous[SM] has revealed that such groups are a more effective intervention strategy than pure self-help or traditional therapy. For example, Yoak and Chesler (1985) found that mutual assistance groups with shared leadership enjoyed greater longevity than groups led by a single individual, either a professional or a parent member. Borkman (1990), one of the major theorists and researchers in the area of mutual assistance groups, stated that increased access to and availability of self-help groups are important to promote for the public, especially for ethnic/racial minority groups and the economically disadvantaged.

## Parents Anonymous[SM] and OJJDP: A Vital Partnership

Parents Anonymous, Inc., and the Office of Juvenile Justice and Delinquency Prevention (OJJDP) began working together in 1994 to advance the Parents Anonymous[SM] model of shared leadership and mutual support in ethnically and culturally diverse settings throughout the country because strengthening families is the first principle of OJJDP's *Comprehensive Strategy for Serious, Violent, and Chronic Juvenile Offenders* (Wilson and Howell, 1993). Parents Anonymous[SM] has become a valuable partner in working toward that goal. The OJJDP publication *Family Life, Delinquency, and Crime: A Policymaker's Guide* (Wright and Wright, 1995) focuses on the following points:

- Positive parenting practices appear to act as buffers by preventing delinquent behavior and assisting adolescents involved in such behavior to avoid continued delinquency.

- Children raised in supportive, affectionate, and accepting homes are less likely to become deviant.

- Children who are rejected by their parents, grow up in homes with considerable conflict, are abused, or are inadequately supervised are at greatest risk of becoming delinquents.

- Children's behavior has a role in this dynamic, in that children who are troublesome are more likely to be rejected by parents, creating an escalating cycle that may lead to delinquency.

- The presence of a capable mother who is self-confident and affectionate and who has leadership skills provides a buffer against delinquency.

Research demonstrates that strengthening families is an essential component in the effort to prevent juvenile delinquency. By supporting the expansion of Parents Anonymous^SM, OJJDP has helped ensure that many more families have access to this promising program. Through its partnership with OJJDP, Parents Anonymous^SM has made important progress toward reducing the risk of juvenile delinquency by:

- Developing new groups that focus on serving families of color, and developing more than 40 new programs in the Parents Anonymous^SM national network in such diverse settings as Head Start centers and prisons that focus on strengthening families and children.

- Providing intensive public awareness and outreach to thousands of parents, professionals, and volunteers through national and local print and electronic media.

- Conducting site visits, focus groups, written surveys, and intensive telephone interviews with successful programs serving families of color to identify the best practices for developing groups in diverse settings and publishing and disseminating a new manual, *Strategies for Best Practice,* that incorporates those findings.

- Increasing the ethnic and cultural diversity of the National Parent Leadership Team membership to ensure a stronger voice for parents who represent a wide variety of backgrounds and experiences.

- Creating a families-of-color task force consisting of parent and professional representatives from the national network who meet regularly to assist with planning, implementing, and evaluating programs and materials for families of color.

- Producing and distributing new publications such as a media bulletin and a program bulletin and publishing relevant articles in *Innovations* and *The Parent Networker,* newsletters distributed to thousands of parents, professionals, policymakers, and advocates throughout the country.

- Convening two Parents Anonymous^SM national leadership conferences, an executive directors' meeting, and two regional conferences (in Georgia and Arizona)—all offering an intensive focus on promoting, maintaining, developing, and expanding Parents Anonymous^SM programs.

- Developing closer working relationships with Court Appointed Special Advocate (CASA) programs and with local courts working with children and families.

In 1996, the University of Utah selected Parents Anonymous^SM as a model family-strengthening program to prevent juvenile delinquency. The program was highlighted through workshops and a plenary presentation at two national Strengthening America's Families conferences at which community representatives were encouraged to develop new local programs. In addition, Parents Anonymous^SM is a member of OJJDP's National Training and Technical Assistance Center and a resource for sites participating in OJJDP initiatives.

## *Conclusion*

Parents Anonymous, Inc., was created to provide training, technical assistance, and consultation to states, communities, agencies, and individuals with an interest in replicating the Parents Anonymous^SM model in their local communities. Professionals who seek effective models for strengthening families and who believe in the power of parents to be their own agents for change have become involved in local programs. Thousands of these professionals have gained significant benefit from their work with parents, transforming their beliefs, perspectives, and direct practice methods of strengthening families by being more responsive and supportive to parents. These professionals regard their involvement in Parents Anonymous^SM as one of their most challenging and rewarding experiences. Today, Parents Anonymous, Inc., continues to lead a dynamic national network of programs that was built on one mother's legacy and that reaches out to parents across America.

## *For Further Information*

For further information, contact:

Parents Anonymous, Inc.,
675 West Foothill Boulevard, Suite 220,
Claremont, CA 91711,
909-621-6184,
909-625-6304 (fax),
Parentsanon@MSN.com (e-mail),
www.parentsanonymous-natl.org.

The following publications and resources are available for free (individual copies):

- *Innovations.* The Parents Anonymous<sup>SM</sup> organizational newsletter distributed throughout the national network and to other professionals, organizations, policymakers, and parents.
- *The Parent Networker.* A newsletter published twice each year by and for parents that is distributed to all parents participating in Parents Anonymous<sup>SM</sup> groups.
- *Strengthening Families in Partnership With Communities.* A general information brochure that provides an overview of Parents Anonymous<sup>SM</sup> principles and the program model (1997).

The following publications are available for $15 each:

- *Parent Leadership: A Voice for Change.* A media bulletin designed for parents, professionals, and community volunteers who want to use the media and public speaking opportunities as a means to reach out to other parents, educate the community, and help shape policies affecting families and children (1997).
- *Parents Anonymous: The Model for Effective Parent Education.* A program bulletin to help professionals, volunteers, and parents use the program in the best way possible (1997).

The following publications are provided only to recognized Parents Anonymous<sup>SM</sup> programs:

- *I Am a Parents Anonymous<sup>SM</sup> Parent.* A handbook given to all parents who attend Parents Anonymous<sup>SM</sup> groups (1998).

- *Manual for Group Facilitators.* A manual used in training group facilitators that provides an in-depth discussion of the program model, the roles of the facilitator and parent group leader, issues of group development, and clinical issues that may arise in a group (1993).

- *The Parent Group Leader.* A brief introduction to the role of the parent group leader (1993).

- *Strategies for Best Practice.* A useful manual for developing Parents Anonymous^SM groups; it highlights strategies that respond to the unique strengths and needs of individual communities (1997).

- *Strengthening America's Families.* A video that captures the success stories of several Parents Anonymous^SM families who have demonstrated enormous courage and tenacity to change their lives (1996).

## References

Behavior Associates. 1976. *Parents Anonymous Self-Help for Child Abusing Parents Project: Evaluation Report for Period May 1, 1974–April 30, 1976.* Tucson, AZ: Behavior Associates.

Borkman, T. 1990. "Self-Help Groups at the Turning Point: Emerging Egalitarian Alliances with the Formal Health Care System." *American Journal of Community Psychology* 18(2): 321–82.

Cohn, A. H. 1979. "Essential Elements of Successful Child Abuse and Neglect Treatment." In *Child Abuse and Neglect,* vol. 3. Oxford, England: Pergamon Press, Ltd., pp. 491–96.

Wilson, J. J., and J. C. Howell. 1993. *Comprehensive Strategy for Serious, Violent, and Chronic Juvenile Offenders.* Summary. Washington, DC: U.S. Department of Justice, Office of Justice Programs, Office of Juvenile Justice and Delinquency Prevention.

Wright, K. N., and K. E. Wright. 1995 (August). *Family Life, Delinquency, and Crime. A Policymakers Guide.* Research Summary. Washington, DC: U.S. Department of Justice, Office of Justice Programs, Office of Juvenile Justice and Delinquency Prevention.

Yoak, M., and M. Chester. 1985. "Alternative Professional Roles in Health Care Delivery: Leadership Patterns in Self-Help Groups." *Journal of Applied Behavioral Science* 21(4): 427–44.

*Teresa Rafael, M.S.W., is Vice President of Programs and Lisa Pion-Berlin, Ph.D., is President and Chief Executive Officer of Parents Anonymous, Inc., Claremont, Calif. Juanita Chávez, M.S.W., A.C.S.W., author of the sidebar on sample Parents Anonymous<sup>SM</sup> programs, was, until her death in March 1998, a valued Senior Program Associate at Parents Anonymous, Inc. In her memory, Parents Anonymous, Inc. has established the Juanita Chávez Award to recognize staff members or volunteers from Parents Anonymous<sup>SM</sup> community-based organizations who demonstrate exemplary dedication and commitment to promoting parent leadership.*

# Section 17.5

# *Responding to a Disclosure of Child Abuse*

Reprinted with permission from the National Network for Child Care—NNCC. Reilly, J. & Martin, S. (1995). Responding to a disclosure of child abuse. Fact sheet 95-12. Reno, Nevada: University of Nevada Cooperative Extension.

*Jackie Reilly, M.S.*
*Youth Development Specialist*
*University of Nevada Cooperative Extension*

*Sally S. Martin, Ph.D.*
*State Extension Specialist*
*Human Development and Family Studies*
*University of Nevada Cooperative Extension*

"My uncle burned me with his cigarette."

What do you say, what should you do...when children tell you they have been abused?

## *When a child discloses*

Hearing a disclosure—a child telling you that someone has abused or hurt him—can be scary. How you respond can be critical. A lot of thoughts may run through your mind.

- You may be worried about the child and yourself.

- You may be unsure of how to respond or what to say.
- You may be unsure of the child's comments and information.
- You may not be sure if the child has been abused.
- You may be angry with the parent or alleged abuser.
- You may even want to take the child home with you.

How you respond is very important. Responding to a disclosure of abuse or neglect is a big responsibility. This fact sheet has suggestions about how to respond in ways that help the child, her parents, and yourself.

### *Children often are reluctant to tell about abuse*

In over 80% of the cases of physical abuse, emotional abuse or neglect, the birth parents are the abusers. The majority of perpetrators in sexual abuse cases are non-related caregivers, that is, baby-sitters, stepparents, boyfriends, girlfriends or adoptive parents.

Children often love the person who is abusing them and simply want the abusive behavior to stop. Because they love and care about the person, they may be reluctant to get the person in trouble. Many perpetrators tell children to keep the abuse a secret and frighten them with unpleasant consequences.

Children may start to tell someone about the abuse. If the person reacts with disgust or doesn't believe them, they will stop disclosing the events. Then they may not tell anyone about it until they feel brave enough or have established a sense of trust with someone. This may delay them from seeking help. If a child begins to tell you about possible abuse, please listen carefully.

### *He or She?*

We give equal time and space to both sexes! That's why we take turns referring to children as "he" or "she. " So keep in mind that even if we say "he" or "she" we are talking about all children.

### Ideas that can help

- Find a place to talk where there are no physical barriers between you and the child.

- Be on the same eye level as the child.

- Don't interrogate or interview the child.

- Be tactful. Choose your words carefully, don't be judgmental about the child or the alleged abuser. Listen to the child. Do not project or assume anything. Let the child tell her own story.

- Find out what the child wants from you. A child may ask you to promise not to tell anyone. Be honest about what you are able to do for the child.

- Be calm; reactions of disgust, fear, anger, etc., may confuse or scare a child.

- Assess the urgency of the situation. Is the child in immediate danger? Safety needs may make a difference in your response.

- Confirm the child's feelings. Let him know that it is okay to be scared, confused, sad, or however he is feeling.

- Believe the child and be supportive.

- Assure the child that you care. Some children will think you may not like them anymore if they tell you what happened. Let her know that you are still her friend and that she is not to blame.

- Tell the child it is not his fault. Many children will think that the abuse happened because of something they did or did not do. Don't over dramatize.

- Tell the child you are glad he told you.

- Tell the child you will try to get her some help.

- Let the child know what you will do. This will help build a sense of trust, and he will not be surprised when he finds out that you told someone.

- Tell the child you need to tell someone whose job it is to help with these kinds of problems.

- Report your suspicions to the appropriate agency.

## Section 17.6

# What Should I Know about Reporting Child Abuse and Neglect?

American Humane Association *Fact Sheet,* November 1997.
Reprinted with permission.

### Taking the First Step

Deciding whether or not to report suspected child abuse can be a difficult and confusing process, yet it is the important first step toward protecting a child who might be in danger. Professionals who work with children are required by law to report suspected neglect or abuse. About 20 states require that every citizen who suspects a child is being abused or neglected must report. However, regardless of whether or not you are among those who are mandated to report, accurate reporting of the suspected maltreatment of any child is a moral obligation. "Reasonable suspicion" based on objective evidence is all that is needed to report. That evidence might be your firsthand observation or statements made by a parent or a child.

Unfamiliarity with state reporting laws and ignorance of the dynamics of abuse and neglect are two of the most frequent reasons given for nonreporting. Frustration with lack of response by child welfare professionals to a complaint, and an unwillingness to "get involved" are other reasons given for failure to report. Others include not wanting to "make things worse for the child," an unwillingness to provide the time-consuming court testimony that might be necessary, or a reluctance to risk angering the family. All of these reasons are understandable yet any one of them could lead to the death of a child that might otherwise have been prevented if the person with the information had only reported it.

### What Happens After I Make the Decision to Report Suspected Child Abuse and/or Neglect?

Several events might take place before and after the initial complaint is filed. First of all, depending on where you live, you might report suspected abuse and/or neglect to your local child protective agency. These agencies are sometimes called Social Services, Human

Rehabilitative Services, Human Welfare, or Children and Family Services. If you feel that a child is in an emergency situation, you should call your local law enforcement immediately.

The person responding to your call may ask you several questions about what you are reporting. This is done to ensure that enough information is available for the investigative team to be able to make decisions concerning whether or not abuse and/or neglect has occurred. You might be asked to give names of the family and child; your reasons for suspecting abuse; the names, addresses, and telephone numbers of other witnesses; your relationship to the alleged victim; any other previous suspicious injury to the child; or your name, address, and phone number. Anonymous reports can be made in every state, however, child welfare agencies generally try to discourage anonymity for many reasons. Not knowing the identity of the reporter denies the child welfare worker the opportunity to get more information during the investigative process or to call the reporter as a crucial evidentiary witness if the case goes to trial.

Unfortunately, over the last several years many child welfare agencies have been severely underfunded and understaffed. Sometimes the investigation of abuse and neglect complaints will be prioritized according to the immediate risk to the child. Be patient. You may have to call more than once.

## Who Investigates Complaints of Child Abuse and Neglect?

The state or county agency that provides child protective services has the legal authority granted it by law or charter which gives them an obligation to provide services when needed and which grants them the right "to explore, study and evaluate" the facts. Child welfare workers base their decision on whether or not to remove a child from the family on two issues:

1. What is the immediate danger or risk to child?

2. What is the motivation, capacity, and intent of the alleged perpetrator?

During the investigative process, the child welfare worker may call on a variety of supportive assistance from individuals and organizations in the community. It then becomes the responsibility of the child welfare worker to organize or provide any needed services for the child and the family.

## What Happens to the Child and Family?

With the enactment of Public Law 96-272, it is legally mandated that child welfare workers make all "reasonable efforts" to reunite the family whenever possible. If, after a thorough investigation, it is determined that the child is in need of substitute care, then the child is placed in temporary foster care or in another safe placement alternative until the immediate danger has passed and services can be provided for the child and family. Sometimes criminal child abuse charges have to be filed depending on the nature and the severity of the abuse/neglect. There is a range of legal penalties for child maltreatment that varies from ordering the perpetrator into therapy to incarceration.

## Will I Be Able to Find Out What Happens to the Child?

Persons who have reported suspected child maltreatment should be allowed to know whether or not their suspicions were founded and what steps the investigation agency took to protect the child. However, there is a great deal of confusion over whether or not information from child welfare cases should be shared. Legally, there is no impediment to providing general feedback to the child abuse/neglect reporter. Some states have even gone so far as to implement laws that require the child welfare agencies to report back to the reporters. Many times, child welfare agencies, overburdened with high caseloads and too many time demands, will not report back the results of their investigations. Other agencies will wrongly say that they cannot release the results of their investigations because the information is confidential. If the agency does not voluntarily provide such information to you, then you will have to request it. Mandated reporters of child abuse, because they have an ongoing legal obligation to report, need to know the circumstances of an investigation so that they can keep track of any conditions that might further endanger the child.

Professionals who work with child victims may have to know information in order to treat the victims in their care. The most difficult confidentiality issue to resolve concerns the reporting individual's need to know vs. the family's right to privacy. So, the distinction is usually made to provide less specific information to individuals outside the child welfare professional community. This means that if the reporter is a family friend, neighbor, or relative, then the information won't be provided in detail. The child welfare agency may give feedback that indicates that the reporter was right in making a referral and that the agency will be working with the family.

## *What Happens If I Report and the Case Is Unsubstantiated?*

All states have laws that protect the reporter of suspected abuse or neglect from legal liability as long as the report was made "in good faith" and not maliciously. Only a small percentage of reports are deliberately false. Another percentage of cases may be classified as "unsubstantiated." This means that there might not have been sufficient information regarding the allegation or the identity of the family, or that the state law contained narrow criteria for substantiating a case. In addition, a case may not be substantiated because services were provided to the child but no court action was taken, or because there was a lack of resources to assist the child or family. Criteria for substantiation varies from state to state because there is no uniform national system for case reporting.

If you are unsure of what the legal and societal definitions of abuse/ neglect are in your community, contact your local child welfare agency for information. In addition, the American Humane Association can offer you more information on what you can do, and what we are doing to assure that children's interests and well-being are fully, effectively, and humanely guaranteed. **Knowing how, when, and what to report about child abuse and neglect may make a life or death difference for a child.**

## Section 17.7

# *Just In Case....Parental Guidelines In Case Your Child Might Someday Be the Victim of Sexual Abuse or Exploitation*

The instructions in this section provide information for the family and the school about what to do if a child indicates that he or she has been the victim of sexual abuse or exploitation. They are calm, straightforward instructions that will not alarm or frighten your child. **We want families and children to be careful...we do not want them to be afraid.**

There is always a chance that a child may disclose past acts of exploitation or general feelings of fear. If this happens, we want you to be prepared to help the child. How you react to a child's disclosure of sexual exploitation or fear is a very important part of child protection. Follow the guidelines below if a child indicates that he or she may have been the victim of sexual abuse or exploitation.

### Don't

- panic or overreact to the information disclosed by the child. With your help and support, you will both make it through these difficult times.

- criticize the child. The worst thing you can do is to express anger at the child having violated previous instructions. Outbursts such as "I told you not to go into anyone's home!" will only hurt your ability to help.

### Do

- **Respect the child's privacy.** Accompany the child to a private place where he or she can relate the story. Be careful not to discuss the incidents in front of people who do not need to know what happened.

- **Support the child and the decision to tell the story.** It is normal for children to fear telling others—especially parents. Make it clear that telling you what happened was the right thing to do and that you will protect the child from future harm. Remember, often a child molester or exploiter will tell the child that bad things will happen if the child ever tells anyone what has happened. The child is especially fearful of punishment, panic, or the loss of the parents' love.

- **Show physical affection, and express your love and confidence with words and gestures. Avoid** challenges starting with why, such as "Why didn't you tell me this before?" or "Why did you let it happen?" **Give positive messages**, such as "I'm proud of you for telling me this," "I'm glad it wasn't worse," or "I know you couldn't help it."

- **Explain to the child that he or she has done no wrong.** The child may well have feelings of guilt and responsibility and assume that he or she is to blame for what happened. Most children are enticed or tricked into acts of exploitation, and they think they should have been smarter or stronger.

- **Remember that children seldom lie about acts of sexual exploitation.** It is important that the child feel that you believe what he or she has told you.

- **Keep open the lines of communication with the child.** In the future, it will be vitally important that the child believe that you are sympathetic, understanding, supportive, and optimistic so that he or she will be comfortable in making additional disclosures and in discussing feelings.

## Steps to Take

- If you think the child has been physically injured, seek out appropriate medical attention. Remember, often we do not realize that a child who has been sexually exploited is also physically injured. Do not guess. Let the professionals make an independent judgment about treatment.

- You must alert the child protection, youth services, child abuse, or other appropriate social services organizations. The police, sheriff's office, or other law-enforcement agency must **also** be notified.

- Consider the need for counseling or therapy for the child. To ignore the incident, to "sweep it under the rug," to act as if it did not happen is not going to help the child deal with the exploitation. In deciding what counselors to use, look for someone who is experienced in cases of sexual victimization. Ask about the number of children they have counseled.

# Part Four

# Sibling and Parent Abuse

# Chapter 18

# *Sibling Abuse*

*Vernon R. Wiehe*

*My memories of growing up at home focus a lot on the way my brother who was 3 years older than me treated me. He would hit, punch, and slap me continually. If I complained to my parents about it they would say things like "You must have done something to deserve it" and "Fight your own battles and don't get us involved." After a while I started to fight back but he was so much bigger and stronger than me. I couldn't hold my own against him. Besides, then my parents had reason to excuse his actions because they saw me hitting him. This behavior continued until my brother joined the army immediately after graduation from high school. Later, I left for college and married. I have nothing to do with my brother now. I don't care if I ever see him again. He made my childhood miserable. Also, I have never forgiven my parents for allowing this to happen, but we just don't talk about it now.*

*When I was in grade school, I was somewhat overweight. My older sister, who was not heavy, started to tease me about my weight. She called me "Lardo." After a while my younger brother picked up on the name and began calling me this name. My weight was a frequent topic of discussion in our family. My parents would say things like "You have such a pretty face, if only you got rid of that extra weight" and "No one is going to date you when you get into high school unless you start losing weight." My parents even expected me not to have dessert when everyone in the family would eat a piece of cake my mother baked for dinner.*

*One time my older sister called me "Lardo" at school in front of some of my friends. Everyone laughed. I wanted to cry, but I knew I couldn't because it would only make matters worse. That evening I told my mother what had happened and her response was that I deserved it if I didn't lose weight. She told me that others also would call me that if I gained any more weight. I was very hurt by what she said. She doesn't know it, but I even thought of committing suicide.*

*I am now 23 years old, single, and working as a secretary in a large office. The emotional abuse I experienced from my siblings, which my mother would not stop, has made me a "loner." I go to my job, go home, and stay in my apartment. I'm thinking of joining a group for overweight people as a way to deal with my low self-esteem.*

*      *      *

*When I was about 7 years old, my brother told me he wanted to teach me something. He would baby-sit me in the evening while my mother worked a second job from which she didn't get home until after midnight. My parents were divorced, and since my Dad never paid child support my mother had to work two jobs. My brother, who was about 14 at the time, took his pants down and showed me his erect penis. He proceeded to tell me what adults do when they have sex and touched my vaginal area. Although he acted like he was doing me a big favor, he also warned me that if I ever told our mother about this he would kill me.*

*My sexual abuse by my brother continued until I started to menstruate. He never would penetrate me but he often would come into my bedroom when I had just gone to bed, lay on top of me, and rub back and forth simulating intercourse. Then he would masturbate or sometimes make me do it. I was too scared to tell my mother because my brother was a bully and I didn't know what he might do to me.*

These are accounts of adults who as children were victims of a type of family violence that has largely gone undetected—the physical, emotional, and sexual abuse of one sibling by another.

This chapter discusses this type of family violence in terms of the various forms of sibling abuse, parental reactions to the problem, understanding sibling abuse, the victim's response to the abuse, its effect on the victims, the treatment of survivors, distinguishing sibling abuse from normal sibling rivalry, and ways this problem can be prevented.

There is very little research on the subject of sibling abuse, even though this type of abuse occurs more frequently than child and domestic abuse (Straus et al., 1980). Research on sexual abuse in the form of incest studies has been done; however, many of these studies do not differentiate among the family members who were the perpetrator (parent, stepparent, cousin, sibling). Hence, the information presented here is based on my research involving 150 adult survivors of sibling abuse. These survivors responded to questionnaires sent to counseling and mental health centers throughout the United States at which they were seeking help for problems resulting from their physical, emotional, or sexual abuse by a sibling.

The data from these questionnaires were analyzed using qualitative rather than quantitative data analysis. The goal of qualitative analysis is to understand the research topic from the perspective of the participants involved—their thoughts, emotions, and firsthand experiences. Qualitative data analysis is descriptive in nature with minimal use of statistics, a characteristic of quantitative analysis (Royse, 1995). Anecdotal accounts from the survivors portray their emotions, enable learning about the problem of sibling abuse from their perspective, and impart the impact of the abuse on their lives. Thus, comments from survivors of sibling abuse who participated in the research illustrate the various themes in this chapter.

## The Research Participants

Who were the people seeking help from counseling and mental health centers for the effects of sibling abuse on their lives and who agreed to respond to the research questionnaire? Obviously, this was not a random sample but one biased in the direction of individuals

411

who recognized that what they experienced from a sibling was abuse and who were experiencing problems in living resulting from their sibling's behavior toward them.

Of the 150 respondents, 89% (134) were female, average age was 37, and 85% (127) were Caucasian, 13% (20) African American, and 2% (3) other racial or ethnic backgrounds. Over one quarter (27%, or 41) were single, 47% (73) identified themselves as married, and 3% (4) indicated they were cohabiting with someone; 21% (31) were divorced. Only 1 person was widowed.

The respondents represented a well-educated group of persons: Only 16% (24) had a high school education or less, whereas 50% (75) had attended college or had completed an undergraduate degree; an additional 34% (51) held graduate degrees.

It was not possible to control for the socioeconomic status of the respondents' parents because many had no knowledge of their parents' income given the different times when the respondents were children. The educational level achieved by the parents, however, gives some indication of their social status: 57% (85) of their mothers had a high school education or less, and 43% (65) had attended college, completed college, or held graduate degree; the fathers' educational level was nearly identical, with only one more father having attended or completed college.

Although the questionnaire indicated that people could respond anonymously, 71% (107) provided their names, addresses, and phone numbers, indicating their willingness to be contacted for a possible follow-up letter or phone call.

## Incidence of Abuse

How frequently does physical abuse by a sibling occur? National statistics based on reported cases do not exist because generally cases of physical or emotional sibling abuse do not come to the attention of the authorities. Rather, abusive behavior between siblings is excused as sibling rivalry, and mandatory reporting of these incidents is not required. Intrafamilial sexual abuse statistics, which would include sibling sexual abuse, generally do not distinguish among the various family members who were the perpetrators.

Several studies in the family violence literature, however, give some indication of the extent to which sibling abuse occurs. In a survey of 57 randomly selected families, a high level of physical violence between siblings was found, as reported in families' comments and in diaries they kept for a week (Steinmetz, 1977).

Similarly, in a nationwide study of violence in 2,143 American families, the researchers found that violent acts between siblings occurred more frequently than either parent-child (child abuse) or husband-wife (partner abuse) violence in that 53 of every 100 children per year physically attack a brother or sister (Straus et al., 1980).

Likewise, a study reported by *U.S. News & World Report* found that 138,000 children, ages 3–17, used a weapon on a sibling over a 1-year period. If such attacks had occurred outside the family, they would have been considered assaults; however, because they occurred between children within a family they were basically ignored ("Battered Families," 1979).

## Physical Abuse

Forms of sibling physical abuse discussed using survivors' comments are labeled most common, unusual, and injurious or life threatening.

### Most Common Forms

The most common forms of physical abuse reported by adult sibling abuse survivors consisted of hitting, slapping, shoving, punching, biting, hair pulling, scratching, and pinching. Survivors also reported having been hit with objects such as broom handles, rubber hoses, coat hangers, hairbrushes, belts, and sticks and being threatened and stabbed with broken glass, knives, razor blades, and scissors.

A 40-year-old woman described her memories of physical abuse by her brother:

> When I was three or four, my brother pushed me down some stone steps. I had approximately 30 stitches in my knee. As I grew older, my brothers typically would slug me in the arm. I was not to cry or everyone went to their rooms. My older brother would usually hit me in the stomach, push me down on the floor and hold me down while he continued to hit me in the stomach and on the arms.

A female survivor from New Mexico described the abuse she experienced from an older brother:

413

*He would engage me in wrestling matches daily, typically punching me in the stomach until I could not breathe, torturing my joints—wrists, knees—spitting on me, putting his knees on my arms and pinning me down and beating on my chest with his knuckles.*

A male respondent described the physical abuse he received from an older brother and identified the source from which the brother learned this behavior:

*Usually the abuse would consist of getting beat up by my brother with his fists or being slapped around with the inside of his hands, a practice he learned from our parents, along with being kicked in the rear.*

### Unusual Form

An unusual form of sibling abuse that survivors reported was tickling. Tickling generally is not regarded as a form of abuse, but it can in fact become physically abusive under certain conditions. Tickling can be pleasant, even erotic, or it can be painful. The unpleasantness often associated with tickling is due to the fact that the nerve fibers that respond to tickling are the same ones that respond to pain (Farrell, 1985). Tickling can be pleasant when it occurs in a context of trust and mutual respect. In such a context, the victim trusts that the perpetrator will stop the behavior at the victim's request.

But tickling becomes painful and abusive if the victim has no control over the situation. When the victim requests that the tickling cease but the perpetrator continues to engage in the behavior, it is abusive. As reported by survivors in this research, some perpetrators even restrained their victims, such as pinning them to the floor. Often, there was little the victims could do because of their smaller size or weaker strength in relation to their perpetrators.

Several survivors described having serious reactions to the tickling they experienced from a sibling. An adult woman reported that a sister, 3 years older, would physically abuse her as a child by punching, slapping, and pinning her down on the floor. Most disturbing, however, was the fact that the sister would tickle her to the point that she would vomit.

Another survivor reported that

*I was unmercifully tickled by my brother who held down every limb and body part that wiggled and covered my mouth when I*

414

*cried and yelled for help. He pulled my hair after I pulled his,*
*thinking that would hurt him and he would stop.*

This survivor said that her mother ignored what her brother did, calling it playing, even though she tried to convince her mother that it was not playful activity. The survivor reported that this abuse affects her even now as an adult. She does not like to be touched by other people, especially when they hug her or hold her in any way reminiscent of being restrained.

### Injurious or Life-Threatening Forms

Some physical abuse between siblings had an injurious or life-threatening aspect to it. Play among siblings sometimes escalates into aggressive behavior and can result in injury. All children probably at some time or another are injured while playing, even accidentally by a sibling. Survivors described incidents where siblings shot them with BB guns, attempted to drown them, smothered them under pillows until they nearly suffocated (in one instance needing mouth-to-mouth resuscitation), and repeatedly hit them in the stomach until they lost their breath.

These incidents, however, must be distinguished from what often happens when children play and someone becomes injured. First, the experiences occurred frequently and were typical of the interactions between the siblings. Although children may at some time suffer some type of physical injury in childhood while playing with a sibling, it is generally an isolated or single incident. For the sibling abuse victims, the abuse was typical of the behavior they experienced from a sibling.

Second, the perpetrator's reaction to the injury the victim suffered must be considered. In most abusive instances, the perpetrator laughed at the victim. This reaction further "injured" the victim by giving the message that the behavior had an intentional element to it.

Finally, the experience must be understood in the context of the parents' reaction. When children are injured by a sibling when playing, parents comfort them, take care of their injuries, and punish the sibling who perpetrated the injury. At the very least, parents make an attempt to determine what happened. But when parents react to an injurious or life-threatening incident with nonchalance, denial of the suffering the victim experienced, or even blame the victim for what happened, the incident becomes abusive.

A 55-year-old woman described a physically abusive incident in childhood from a sister that resulted in injury. The scars from this injury remain today as a reminder to her of the physical abuse she experienced from this sister as a child:

*I climbed on the chicken coop and a nail penetrated my foot. It went all the way through my foot. I was literally nailed to the coop. My older sister saw me and laughed and told me that's what I deserved. She left and wouldn't help me down. After a long time my older brother came by, helped me get down and took me to the hospital for help and a tetanus shot. I was so afraid I would get lockjaw. I still have the scar on my foot.*

*Once my sister was ironing. She was a teenager. I was between four and five. I was curious as to what she was doing. I put my hands flat up on the ironing board and she immediately put the hot iron down on my hand. She laughed and told me to get lost. I still have the burn scar on my left hand.*

A woman in her late 40s described the injurious abuse she suffered from an older brother as a child and her parents' response to it:

*When I was two or three, my mother went to visit my father who was in the Army and my brother and I were left in the care of my grandparents. My brother was helping my grandfather paint a fence and he painted me from head to toe with dark brown paint. I remember the paint was in my hair, face, clothing, etc. and I had to be scrubbed down with turpentine and repeated baths. Some of my hair had to be cut to get the paint out. My brother laughed and teased me about all of this. Later, during another incident my brother wrote his name on my bare back with his woodburning kit. He seemed to treat me as an object rather than as a person with any feelings. My abuse continued through high school. My brother would twist my arms or pin me down and bend my arms or legs to get me to do things he wanted me to do, such as his chores or to cover for him by lying to my parents. These incidents usually happened when my parents weren't home. When I reported them to my parents, he would say I was making it up to get him in trouble. Then we would both be punished. I knew my parents didn't know how to handle the problem, so I quit reporting to my parents. I would just arrange to go to a friend's house or have a friend over when my parents were going to be out.*

Another survivor reported, "I have photographs of my brother pushing me down and trying to 'playfully' strangle me when I was an infant." This same woman remembers that as a child of 4 to 6 years old, her brother would restrain her and in a threatening but supposedly playful manner put his hands around her neck, as if to choke her to death. She indicated that as an adult she remains very frightened of men and has a phobia about anyone touching her neck. She also stated, based on her experience with her sibling, that she is not willing to have more than one child.

Respondents told of siblings smothering them with a pillow, another form of life-threatening physical abuse. This particular behavior seems to have occurred when siblings were playing together on a couch or bed. The frightening response of the victim to what initially might be described as playful activity became a clue for some perpetrators of the power and control they could exert over their sibling.

> *I remember my brother putting a pillow over my head. He would hold it and laugh while I struggled to get out from under him and the pillow. I remember being terrified. I honestly thought he would smother me to death. This occurred frequently.*

### Victims' Responses to Their Physical Abuse

How did the victims who experienced physical abuse from a sibling respond to it? Several responses will be identified.

#### Protecting Themselves

As one would expect, the most typical response was that the victims would attempt in whatever ways possible to protect themselves from the physical assaults. A young woman from New York described how she tried to protect herself from a sister who was a year older: "My sister would beat me up, and I would sit on my bed with my knees up guarding myself until she stopped."

#### Screaming and Crying

Another typical, natural reaction was that the victim screamed or cried out for help. Unfortunately, this reaction often provoked the perpetrator to intensify the physically abusive behavior. Following is a typical scenario: An older brother is beating on a younger sibling. If the younger sibling cries or screams for help, the beating intensifies under the warning, "Take it like you should!" or "If you cry, I'll give you more." Some children may learn or model this behavior from their parents and the way in which they have been punished by them. A parent punishes a child by spanking. After the child is spanked, the parent warns the child not to cry: "If you don't stop crying, I'll really give you something to cry about."

### Separating Themselves from the Perpetrator

The position of powerlessness in which sibling abuse victims often found themselves with older and stronger siblings prompted many of them to respond in the only way they could, by separating themselves from the perpetrator and at times literally hiding in order to avoid being abused. The victims would lock themselves in their bedroom, if they were fortunate enough to have their own room, or they would spend as much time as possible away from home with friends.

Victims appeared to live in constant fear of further abuse. Attempts to scream or cry out for help often only resulted in further abuse. The only way some of the victims could cope with the abuse was always to distance themselves from the sibling. As children, life involved sensing the mood of an abusive sibling and staying as far away from the sibling as possible as a means of self-protection.

A survivor described her efforts at self-protection from an older abusive brother:

> I became a very withdrawn child. I would retreat to my room and read. If my brother was involved in a game, I wouldn't play. If he was in a particular room, I would go to a different one.

An adult woman described the abuse she experienced as a child on a daily basis from an only sibling, a brother 4 years older:

> My brother would hit me, bite me, wrestle me, etc., anytime my parents were out of sight. The times which were most frightening for me were after school or the period between the time we arrived home from school and my parents came home from work, about two to three hours. I would run to my room and lock the door or go to a friend's house so he wouldn't terrorize me.

### Abusing a Younger Sibling in Turn

The response of some victims to their abuse by a sibling was to inflict the same abuse on another sibling. This behavior can be understood in two ways. One, the victim used the older sibling's behavior as a model and in turn became a perpetrator. Social learning theory states that violence or abuse is often a learned behavior. The behavior may be learned from parents—if they are abusive to each other— from an older sibling who may be abusive, from peers, or from television, movies, and videos (Huston et al., 1992; Irwin & Gross, 1995; Paik & Comstock, 1994). A continuing pattern is established, and unless the parents intervene, abuse can potentially become a normal way for older siblings to interact with younger siblings. Second, the behavior may be understood as a psychological defense. The victim assumes the characteristics of the aggressor by shifting from a passive victim role to an active aggressive role by inflicting the same behavior on another victim. The end result is that the siblings are in a constant state of conflict. A young adult woman described the process with her sibling in this way:

> *The worst fights started around the time I was in third grade. I got a lot of abuse from my older brother. Then I would turn around and abuse my sister. I would get her twice as hard as what I received. As we got older, it got worse. I would have knives pulled on me. Then I would turn around and pull a gun on one of the others. I would take my anger out on my sister or younger brother. I became very violent especially toward my sister.*

### Telling Their Parents

Many of the victims of sibling physical abuse told their parents about the abuse, but the parents refused to help the victim. Indeed, reporting the physical abuse often resulted in the victim being further victimized. A typical parental response was to blame the victim for it. "You must have done something to deserve it," a parent would respond. Obviously, such a response provided the victim no protection from future physical assaults and discouraged the child from ever again telling the parents about the abuse.

Another common parental response was to become very angry and discipline both the perpetrator and the victim with corporal punishment. In some instances, the perpetrator would be so severely corporally punished (whipped, beaten with a belt) by a parent that the victim felt badly for having reported the abuse to the parent. These parental responses also led the victim to conclude that it did not pay to report physical abuse.

419

Undoubtedly, many children who are physically abused by a sibling do report the behavior to their parents, and the parents effectively intervene. The parents' intervention may involve examining the situation with the sibling, determining what provoked the abuse, perhaps identifying the contribution of each sibling to the incident that escalated to abusive behavior, and helping the siblings consider ways the altercation could have been avoided. This "problem-solving approach," discussed later, is an effective way for parents to intervene in sibling-abusive situations.

## Emotional Abuse

A frequently heard jingle states, "Sticks and stones may break my bones, but words will never hurt me." Although physical abuse may leave bruises and other evidence, there are no outwardly visible marks from emotional abuse. However, the jingle is very incorrect when it states that words, the basic component of emotional abuse, do not hurt.

### Definition

The term emotional abuse or psychological maltreatment is often labeled *teasing* when it occurs among siblings (or peers). Individuals who identified themselves as victims of emotional abuse by a sibling frequently reported that they were "teased" by the sibling. The term now denotes not only a behavior that often occurs among children but is a catch-all word to denote a number of behaviors. Current synonyms for the verb *to tease* indicate the specific types of actions that constitute this behavior: *to belittle, intimidate, annoy, scorn, provoke.*

Researchers in the field of child abuse have identified emotional abuse as more prevalent and potentially even more destructive than other forms of child abuse and as often underlying physical and sexual abuse (Claussen & Crittenden, 1991; Garbarino & Vondra, 1987; Hart & Brassard, 1987). This is equally true in sibling relationships. Generally, emotional abuse among siblings includes the following behaviors: name-calling, ridicule, degradation, exacerbating a fear, the destruction of personal possessions, and the torture or destruction of a pet.

Emotional abuse is difficult to identify. Accepted legal standards are not available either for proving that emotional or behavioral problems resulted from emotional abuse or for determining the seriousness of emotional abuse (Corson & Davidson, 1987; Navarre, 1987). Also, because emotional abuse leaves no physical evidence, to an outside observer a family may appear to be operating well psychosocially, but within the family one sibling may be emotionally abusing another.

Detecting emotional abuse by a sibling is complicated by the fact that professionals and parents have tended to accept emotionally abusive behavior as a phenomenon that occurs in all children's interactions with their siblings and their peers. The teasing and verbal put-downs in which siblings engage with each other and with children in general, although disliked by parents, is often accepted as normal behavior. Between siblings this behavior is simply excused as sibling rivalry.

When parents excuse or overlook emotional abuse that occurs between siblings, the victims are given the message that this behavior is really not abusive. Different child-rearing practices and cultural values may reinforce denial that certain behaviors or styles of communication between siblings are emotionally abusive. Even victims of emotional abuse sometimes deny this form of abuse.

A similar phenomenon happened historically with the physical abuse of children by adults. This form of abuse was overlooked because children were viewed as the property of their parents and what occurred behind the closed doors of the family residence was considered the family's private business. Children who experienced severe beatings by their parents and other forms of physical assault were forced to conclude that they deserved this behavior or that these were proper forms of discipline, despite the physical and emotional suffering the victims endured. Within the past several decades, as society began recognizing adult-child physical abuse as a social problem, victims have been able to seek help for the effects of physical abuse on their lives, and society has taken steps to prevent such abuse. As long as sibling emotional abuse (as well as all forms of sibling abuse) is not recognized for what it is, victims are forced to conclude that this is normal behavior or that they deserve such treatment from their siblings.

## *Interaction of Emotional, Physical, and Sexual Abuse*

Eleven people, or 7% of the 150-person sample, indicated that they had only been emotionally abused. Although the three forms of sibling abuse—physical, emotional, and sexual—were treated separately in the research questionnaire, the respondents indicated that one form of sibling abuse rarely occurred in isolation. (The only exception was that some survivors did not report being sexually abused by a sibling.) Generally, several forms of abuse occurred in interaction with the others. Thus, 71% (107) indicated that they had been emotionally, physi-

421

cally, and sexually abused. Combined with the 11 persons who indicated that they had been only emotionally abused, this means that 78% (118) of the sample had been emotionally abused.

The interaction of emotional and physical abuse is demonstrated by the following comments of a survivor of abuse from a brother 3 years older:

> *I can't remember a time when my brother didn't taunt me, usually trying to get me to respond so he would be justified in hitting me. Usually he would be saying I was a crybaby or a sissy or stupid or ugly and that no one would like me, want to be around me, or whatever. Sometimes he would accuse me of doing something and if I denied it, then he would call me a liar. I usually felt overwhelmingly helpless because nothing I said or did would stop him. If no one else was around, he would start beating on me after which he would stop and go away. I felt helpless to stop any of it.*

Another survivor described how her brother, 9 years older, used emotional abuse in connection with sexual abuse:

> *The emotional abuse stemmed directly from the sexual abuse. The earliest memory was when I was about five years old. It is difficult for me to be specific about a single event since it is hard for me to remember many instances. I've blocked a lot out of my mind. But I always remember being afraid of being rejected by my parents. My brother was the oldest and he made me believe that my parents would always believe him over me since I was only five and he thirteen. So, you see, he always had some sort of power over me emotionally and physically. As a child and adolescent I was introverted and never really shared my inner feelings with anyone. I felt like dirt and that my needs, concerns, and opinions never mattered, only those of other people. I was always in fear of both forms of abuse (emotional and sexual). I learned to prepare myself for both. I'm so resentful that I had to do this to survive mentally in my home. My brother would always present himself in these situations as being perfect—mature, responsible, brave—a model brother. Then, I'd feel like an immature, non-credible child. He's saying things like how my parents thought he was so special, being the oldest. And, that if I told on him, I would destroy the entire family; my parents would divorce; I would be sent to a foster home. He had such emotional*

*control over me in that sense that I "obeyed" him and never told. He had control over my self-image and my body.*

### Extent of the Problem

The research questionnaire asked respondents to identify how frequently emotional abuse occurred in their family while they were growing up. Their responses revealed that emotional abuse in the form of name-calling, ridicule, and degradation was a common pattern in the relationship between siblings and in some instances between the parents and the siblings. Respondents repeatedly used words like *constant* and *always* when describing the emotional abuse they experienced from a sibling. Many of the respondents spent their childhood years in a climate of name-calling, ridicule, and mockery:

*I was constantly being told I was no good, a pig, whore, slut—all sexually oriented negatives. I was constantly emotionally being degraded.*

*       *       *

*I can't remember a time when I was growing up when my brother didn't taunt me.*

*       *       *

*From my earliest memories, age five or so, my siblings called me names and said degrading things to me.*

### Forms of Emotional Abuse

Name-calling, ridicule, degradation, exacerbating a fear, destroying personal possessions, and torturing or destroying a pet are forms of emotional abuse discussed and illustrated with survivors' experiences of these forms of abuse.

#### Name-Calling

Nearly every individual in the sample who was emotionally abused by a sibling made reference to being called names. The perpetrator appeared to use name-calling as a way to belittle or degrade the victim. (Degradation, discussed later, also occurred without name-calling.) The name-calling generally focused on some attribute of the victims, such as their height, weight, physical characteristics, intelligence, or inability to perform a skill. The second case example that opened this chapter reflects emotional abuse focusing on a sibling's weight problem. Survivors recounted experiences with name-calling:

*When I was six, my mother realized I needed glasses. For the next several years my brothers told me I was ugly and taunted me with a lot of names referring to being unattractive.*

*   *   *

*I was heavy as a young child, about seven or eight years old. My brother called me "Cow." He was asked to mark all the children's socks with our names so for mine he drew the face of a cow. He called me a Spanish word which I understood meant "whore."*

*   *   *

*My sister would verbally harass me—you're ugly, stupid, fat, etc. If I did accomplish something, she would turn things around and prove that I had failed or been a fool.*

### Ridicule

Ridicule appeared to be a sport to some siblings and a form of emotional abuse that survivors recalled with painful emotions. Ridicule is defined here as words or actions used by the perpetrator to express contempt, often along with laughter directed against the victim. Several survivors recalled being ridiculed by siblings:

*My sister would get her friends to sing songs about how ugly I was.*

*   *   *

*Life as a child consisted of constant taunts and ridicule on issues such as things I said, clothes I wore, my friends, etc.*

*   *   *

*I was ridiculed by my older brothers and sisters for just being. Ridicule and put-downs were "normal" for our family.*

### Degradation

This form of emotional abuse deprives individuals of their sense of dignity and worth. Many survivors reported that their siblings told them that they were "worthless" and "no good." Degradation was emotionally devastating to the victims both at the time the abuse was occurring and even years later as adults. The survivors' comments indicate that the degrading messages they received as children from a sibling continued to haunt them into their adult years. It was as if the message from their abusive sibling became a self-fulfilling prophecy. This was especially true for those survivors whose parents did not intervene in the abusive behavior but ignored it, accepted it as normal behavior, or worst of all participated in it.

Children who degrade their siblings do not seem to realize how this behavior affects the victims. Those abused in this way may react by appearing as if the degrading comments have no effect. This stoical reaction perhaps is at the root of the jingle, "Sticks and stones may break my bones but words will never hurt me." By taking a defensive stance, the victim denies the emotional pain caused by the verbal assault. Unfortunately, however, this reaction often only reinforces or encourages the perpetrator to continue the emotionally abusive behavior.

Children are especially vulnerable to degrading remarks because it is during their childhood years that they are developing a positive sense of self-worth and self-esteem. Unfortunately, interactions with peers in play and at school often do not facilitate this development. Verbal put-downs between siblings (and peers) often occur so frequently that parents and others in authority tend to accept them as normal. A parent's failure to stop such behavior gives a message to the perpetrator that this is acceptable behavior. The behavior can therefore be expected to continue unless some action is taken to discontinue it.

Many sibling abuse survivors reported that their emotional abuse as a child continued into their adulthood. "Labeling theory" explains that one child in a family may be labeled the scapegoat or as outside the family circle. The nicknames they were given by their siblings as children often remained with them as adults. Similarly, the labels that children acquired that focused on a specific personality trait or physical characteristic that distinguished them from their peers continued to haunt them into adulthood:

> *I was being constantly told how ugly, dumb, unwanted I was. Already about two years of age, I was told, "No one wants you around. I [my sister] wish you were dead. You aren't my real sister, your parents didn't want you, either, so they dumped you with us." I grew up feeling, if my own family doesn't like me, who will? I believed everything my sister ever told me—that I was ugly, dumb, homely, stupid, fat—even though I always was average in weight. I felt no one would ever love me. When you're little, you believe everything you're told. It can last a lifetime.*

\*            \*            \*

*I was told that I was no good, that no one loved me, that I was adopted (which was not true), that my parents did not really want me. My parents were always gone and emotionally unavailable, partially due to alcohol abuse, so that I was often left in the care of my two older brothers.*

\*            \*            \*

*My brothers loved to tease me to tears. They were ruthless in their teasing and did not let up. They teased me for being ugly. They teased me for being sloppy. They teased me for just being. This was the worst.*

A young adult male who identified himself as being gay experienced degrading comments from a brother when he was growing up:

*My brother would tell me what a sissy or faggot I was; that I wasn't a man, and then would laugh. He would tell others to taunt me, to bait me. He would bring me to tears.*

Survivors who experienced emotional abuse in the form of degradation reported having a pervasive feeling during childhood that they should not exist, like the survivor quoted earlier whose older brothers teased her "for just being." The transactional analysis (TA) school of psychology refers to this as "Don't Be," a "game" some parents even engage in with a child (Berne, 1967). A subtle message is given to a child in a variety of ways that life would be much better if the child were not around. The parents would have fewer financial expenses or there would be less tension in the home. This destructive and emotionally damaging "game" is also played by siblings against one another. When this "game" is analyzed from a reality perspective, its extreme psychological destructiveness can be understood. Although a child is not responsible for his or her existence, the "game" carries an underlying wish for the child's destruction.

Another form of degradation that occurred, especially by older siblings toward younger siblings and especially brothers toward their sisters, was to "use" the sibling. Sisters described their brothers as "lording it over" them. A brother would command his sister to do things on his behalf, such as household chores that he was expected to do. The failure of the victim to comply with the perpetrator's demands at times resulted in physical abuse. In essence, a brother would be exerting power and control over his sister. A survivor who was raised on a farm in the Midwest in a very religious family of eight children provides an example of this. She reported that she had to wait on her older brothers in the house, even if she had been working all day in the fields. Her parents instructed her to obey her older brothers in their absence. "It was as if my brothers could do no wrong." The older brothers took advantage of her, not only by demanding that she do tasks for them but by tricking her out of her allowance and eventually sexually abusing her.

*Exacerbating a Fear*

Older siblings would often exacerbate a fear that a younger sibling had, such as a fear of being lost, fear of the dark, or fear of strangers. Sibling perpetrators would use fear as a means of having power and control over the victim, thereby getting the sibling to do what they wanted. Perhaps the perpetrators were modeling this behavior after their parents because some parents coerce their children to comply with their wishes by manipulating the child through fear. The following comments by survivors illustrate the power of siblings' use of fear:

*My older siblings would take my sister and me out into the field to pick berries. When we would hear dogs barking, they would tell us they were wild dogs and then they'd run away and make us find our own way home. We were only five or six, and we didn't know our way home.*

\*           \*           \*

*I remember very clearly that my older sister, who was seven years older, would go to the telephone and pretend to call a man she called "Mr. Krantz." He ran an institution, she said, for "bad children" and my sister said she was going to send me there, banishing me from the family. I was terrified.*

One research respondent wrote that an older sister played upon her fear of the dark to force her to do the older sister's household tasks and in general to control her. The victim was afraid of the dark, but her older sister would allow her to sleep with her as long as she did everything her older sister demanded. The victim was caught in a bind. The parents were not aware of this arrangement, but she knew that if she told her parents about it, her sister would not allow her to sleep with her and she would be alone with her fear of the dark. The survivor indicated that she acquiesced to her sister's control and repeatedly became the victim of her emotional abuse.

### *Destroying Personal Possessions*

A child's possessions, such as a bicycle, toys, or clothing, are valued and have special meaning for the child. Everyone remembers a favorite toy, book, or blanket from their childhood. Some adults may still have these objects. These objects were often used by sibling perpetrators as a means of emotional abuse.

Yet even though the perpetrator destroys a sibling's prized object, the actual target of the abuse is the sibling. In Freudian terms, the object becomes "cathected," or invested with the emotions and feelings of the owner. Thus, harming the object is actually harming the individual who treasures the object.

One adult male participating in the research related how as a small child he experienced this form of emotional abuse from an older brother. His older brother took a pair of Mickey Mouse ears he treasured, deliberately broke them, and then laughed about it. Initially, this seems humorous. Why should an adult continue to hold on to the fact that his older brother destroyed his Mickey Mouse ears when they were children many years ago?

The destruction of the toy per se is not the point. To understand what the victim is saying and to empathize with what he is expressing in his statement, several factors must be considered. First, the destructive behavior was only one in a series of continual abusive incidents directed at the victim; this was not a one-time event. (A single abusive incident, however, may be harmful, such as sexual molestation by a sibling.)

Second, the destruction of the Mickey Mouse ears must be viewed in the context of the deliberateness of the perpetrator's action. Respondents to the research repeatedly wrote of the delight that perpetrators took in destroying something that was meaningful to them. The incident was not an accident; the deliberateness with which it occurred made it abusive.

Finally, the incident must be considered in light of its impact on the victim. The victim was deeply hurt by his brother's behavior. Again, the destruction of the Mickey Mouse ears per se was not the point, but its impact on the victim, who was the real target of the abusive behavior, is important. The statement often made when something like this happens indicates how people experience its impact: "How could someone do this to *me*!"

Survivors gave other examples of a sibling being emotionally abusive through the destruction of personal possessions:

*My sister would take my things and wreck them, cut my clothes up to fit her and blackmail me to do her housework.*

*         *         *

*My brother would cut off the eyes, ears, mouth and fingers of my dolls and hand them to me.*

### Torturing or Destroying a Pet

Although the torture or destruction of a pet may resemble the destruction of prized possessions, it involves the abuse of life, an animal's life. This implies an even greater degree of cruelty toward the object, although the emotional pain the sibling experienced may be the same.

Survivors reported the torture and destruction of their pets by a sibling as examples of emotional abuse:

*My second-oldest brother shot my little dog that I loved dearly. It loved me, only me. I cried by its grave for several days. Twenty years passed before I could care for another dog.*

*         *         *

*My older brother would come to my room and tear up my toys. He would beat my dog after tying his legs together and wrapping a cloth around its mouth to tie it shut. My brother would tell me I was stupid and say, "Why me, why me? Why did I get a sister so stupid and dumb?" My brother also would tell me he hated me and wished I were dead.*

*         *         *

*My brother took my pet frog and stabbed it to death in front of me while I begged him not to. Then he just laughed!*

## Victims' Responses

Earlier, victims of physical abuse indicated that they responded to their siblings' abuse by protecting themselves, screaming and crying, separating themselves from the perpetrator, abusing a younger sibling, and telling their parents. Victims of emotional abuse responded to their abuse in these ways and also by fighting back and internalizing the abusive message.

### Fighting Back

Unlike survivors of physical abuse, sibling survivors of emotional abuse reported that they fought back and in turn emotionally abused the perpetrator by name-calling, ridicule, and degrading comments. Victims of physical abuse did not respond this way because generally they were younger than their abusers and did not have the strength to effectively fight back.

A survivor wrote that an older sister would "yell swear words and names" at her as one aspect of her verbal abuse. At the age of 8 or 9, she was shocked by her sister's language but she soon "gave as good as I got, swear-word-wise." Another respondent reported, "I retaliated with equally mean words."

An adult woman wrote about how she handled her sister's emotionally abusive comments:

*I would turn the emotional abuse around on my sister. I would make her cry and go into hysterics. She would just go crazy. The more I got from my older brother, the more and more I would give my sister.*

This survivor's comment may explain why some parents view emotional abuse among their children as "normal sibling rivalry." Parents conclude that since all the siblings are engaging in emotionally abusive behavior it must be normal. Survivors reported that in some instances their parents even joined in by calling them names or making fun of them as their siblings were doing. Emotional abuse in these families became a normal way of interacting—normal, yet pathological in its destructiveness to the individuals involved.

### Internalizing the Abusive Message

A response unique to victims of emotional abuse was to accept and internalize the abusive messages they were receiving. The victims accepted the name-calling, ridicule, and especially the degrading comments as if what was being said were true. The perpetrator's abuse became a self-fulfilling prophecy for the victim. Accepting the message as reality confirmed the victims in their role as victims into which the perpetrators had initially put them.

One survivor reported that "I believed *everything* my sister ever told me. I was dumb, homely, stupid, fat. No one would ever love me." This survivor stated that now at age 41, as a reasonably bright adult woman, she still believes most of her abusive sister's comments, that she is no good, dumb, and ugly. She still feels that her worth as a person is only as good as what she does. As she describes it, in her adult life she is constantly trying to prove with her actions that she is worth something.

## Sexual Abuse

Sibling sexual abuse was defined in this research as inappropriate sexual contact, such as touching, fondling, indecent exposure, attempted penetration, intercourse, rape, or sodomy, between siblings.

### Research on Sibling Incest

The term incest is generally thought of as referring to sexual relations between fathers and daughters. Most of the literature on incest focuses on the parent-child relationship, even though researchers feel that sibling incest is more common (Finkelhor, 1979; Justice & Justice, 1979; Meiselman, 1978). The lack of attention to this type of sexual abuse may be due to the reluctance of families to report to authorities the occurrence of sibling incest, minimization of the problem by parents, the threat under which victims are placed when it occurs, and the perception that sexual contact between siblings is within the normal range of acceptable sexual play or exploration between siblings (Adler & Schutz, 1995; Doyle, 1996).

Studies on sibling incest have been hampered by (a) their small sample size, which makes it difficult to generalize the data from the sample to the general population and (b) the absence of comparison groups. For example, Adler and Schutz (1995) studied 12 males who were sibling incest offenders referred for evaluation and treatment to a hospital-based outpatient clinic. The sample came from middle- to upper-middle-class, suburban, primarily Caucasian families where the majority had parents married to each other and living in the home. The offenders had no previous records with juvenile justice authorities. Other studies on sibling incest, however, report previous offender contact with the juvenile system, the physical absence of a parent and low socioeconomic status (Becker, Kaplan, Cunningham-Rathner, & Kavoussi, 1986; Finkelhor, 1979; O'Brien, 1991). Although no one in

Adler and Schutz's (1995) sample reported having been sexually abused, a history of intrafamilial physical abuse by one or both parents was present. Other studies of sibling sexual abuse, however, report that rates of prior sexual victimization on the part of the perpetrators ranged from approximately 25% to 50% of the sample (Becker et al., 1986; Smith & Israel, 1987; O'Brien, 1991). Although the perpetrators denied using verbal threats to intimidate their victims, 75% of the victims reported that they had been verbally threatened to maintain silence about the sexual abuse.

O'Brien (1991) studied the characteristics of 170 adolescent male sexual offenders who had been referred for evaluation and/or treatment to an outpatient mental health clinic. The offenders were subdivided into three groups: sibling sexual abusers, child molesters, and nonchild offenders. Compared with the child molesters and nonchild offenders, the sibling sexual abusers admitted committing more sexual crimes, had longer offending careers, and generally engaged in more intrusive sexual behavior, such as vaginal penetration. O'Brien concluded that this was because the sibling victim is easily available to the perpetrator and the context of secrecy in which the sexual abuse occurs in the family prevents early disclosure.

Cole (1990) studied a volunteer sample of 122 adult women from 28 states who had been sexually abused by a brother and 148 women sexually abused by their father. The mean age of the onset of the sexual abuse for the brother-sister survivors was 8.2 years compared to 5.2 years for the father-daughter survivors. Approximately one third of both groups experienced the sexual abuse for 4 to 10 years and did not disclose the abuse for 20 years or more. The sibling sexual abuse survivors reported feeling more responsible for their abuse as compared to their father-daughter survivor counterparts.

Finally, Doyle (1996) studied 12 women who during individual or group therapy revealed sexual abuse by a brother. Although sibling sexual abuse is generally thought to be perpetrated by an older brother, Doyle found that 4 of the 12 perpetrators were younger brothers abusing older sisters.

## Incidence of Abuse

Adults are generally assumed to be the perpetrators of child sexual abuse and most likely are closely known by the victim. However, an early study on incest reported that brother-sister sexual relationships may be five times more common than father-daughter incest (Gebhard, Gagnon, Pomeroy, & Christenson, 1965).

Several studies on the extent of sexual abuse in general give some indication of the extent to which sibling sexual abuse occurs. Finkelhor (1984a) reported that the incidence of sexual abuse in general is basically unknown. Estimates are that 35% of all girls by the time they reach adulthood have been sexually abused. This includes incidents where the perpetrators are siblings. A survey of 796 undergraduates attending six New England colleges found that 15% of the females and 10% of the males reported some type of sexual experience involving a sibling (Finkelhor, 1980). Fondling and touching the genitals were the most common activities in all age categories. Twenty-five percent of the incidents could be regarded as exploitive because force was used and because of the large age disparity between the individuals involved. Forty percent of the students reported that they had been less than 8 years old at the time of the sexual experience. However, 73% of the experiences occurred when at least one partner was older than 8, and 35% occurred when one partner was more than 12 years of age.

These studies probably grossly underestimate the extent of sibling sexual abuse because feelings of embarrassment and shame connected with the event prevent both perpetrators and victims from talking about it. Many adults also may no longer remember childhood sexual incidents with a sibling. The information on sibling sexual abuse frequently comes from reports filed in court against a perpetrator. However, these cases barely represent the extent to which this problem occurs because most incidents of sexual abuse by siblings go not only unreported but undetected by parents.

Studies on the incidence of child sexual abuse by adults indicate that most incidents are never disclosed. The cases that come to the attention of the courts, mental health clinics, and support groups for sexual abuse survivors appear to be the exception rather than the norm. As the comments by respondents in the present research reveal, the same is true for victims of sexual abuse by a sibling.

Of the 150 respondents in this research, 67% (100) indicated that they had been sexually abused by a sibling while growing up, compared with 33% (50) who had been physically and/or emotionally abused.

Why were so many more of the respondents survivors of sexual abuse as compared to survivors of physical and emotional abuse? One reason may be that many of the individuals participating in the research were already in treatment for their abuse at counseling centers or were affiliated with support groups for people who experienced abuse. Survivors of sexual abuse may seek treatment for their abuse more readily than survivors of physical or emotional abuse. Even between siblings, sexual abuse is recognized by society as *abuse*, unlike physical and emotional abuse, which are often ignored and overlooked. For example, the meaning of the term *incest* is commonly understood to mean illicit sexual activity between family members, including that between brothers and sisters. But the meaning of the terms *emotional abuse* and *physical abuse* between siblings is not commonly understood. Thus, it may be easier for persons who have been sexually abused to acknowledge their victimization than it is for those who have been physically and emotionally abused. Also, the trauma from sexual abuse may be more severe than that from physical or emotional abuse and thus may cause victims to more readily seek treatment for its impact on their lives.

Sexual abuse did not occur in isolation for those survivors responding to this research. Three percent (5) indicated that they had been both physically and sexually abused, 11% (16) had been both emotionally and sexually abused, and 37% (55) had been physically, emotionally, and sexually abused. Other research has found similar results in that victims were not only sexually abused but also physically and emotionally abused (Brassard & Galardo, 1987; Claussen & Crittenden, 1991). Goodwin (1982) found that in 50% of incest cases reported to a protective service agency there was also evidence of physical abuse or neglect.

The interaction of sexual and physical abuse can be seen in the survivors' comments. Some were threatened with physical harm and even death by their sibling perpetrator if they reported the sexual abuse to their parents. The interaction of sexual and emotional abuse is exemplified by the comment of one respondent whose sexual molestation by a brother 10 years older, including forceful vaginal penetration, began when she was 3 or 4 years old: "Later, when I was about seven or eight years old, he would tease me by asking me if I was a virgin and laughing when I said no. It was humiliating."

Although far more females than males reported having experienced sexual abuse from a sibling, males also are sexually abused (Rosencrans, 1997). In their review of eight random-sample community surveys that had interviewed both men and women regarding sexual abuse during childhood, Finkelhor and Baron (1986) found a much higher percentage of males who had been sexually abused than the present study found. Approximately 2.5 women were sexually abused for every man. Among all victims of sexual abuse, 71% were females and 29% were males. A study of boys and girls who were sexually abused revealed that, although the majority of all victims were sexually abused within the family, boys were more likely than girls to be victimized by someone outside the home (36.7% vs. 10.9%) (Faller, 1989). Researchers found in a sample of 375 individuals who had been physically or sexually abused before age 18 that females were almost 3 times more likely than males to experience any type of abuse and over 11 times more likely than males to report sexual abuse (Silverman, Reinherz, & Giaconia, 1996). Clinicians generally agree that the sexual abuse of boys is underreported due to stereotypical expectations regarding masculinity and the fear that disclosure on the part of the victims may give them the appearance of being homosexual.

### Earliest Memories

Survivors reported that, as best as they can remember, the earliest incident of sexual abuse by a sibling occurred when they were 5 to 7 years old. This may be merely the earliest incident that survivors could recall; their sexual abuse may actually have begun at a much earlier age. Some survivors reported being aware that they were sexually abused as infants, but they did not indicate how they became aware of this. For example, one survivor recalled, "Sexual abuse was a part of my life from the time I was an infant. The age of three months is the earliest memory I have."

Parents often think of children as beginning to engage in sexual activity when they reach adolescence or become sexually mature—not at age 4 or 5. Parents may rationalize that their children are not interested in or knowledgeable about sex at such an early age. Even though a child is not yet sexually mature and does not exhibit any interest in sex, the child still can become a victim of sexual abuse.

In most incidents of sibling sexual abuse reported in this research, the perpetrator was an older brother or sister, generally 3 to 10 years older than the victim. The sexual abuse of the younger sibling may have been prevented if the victim's parents had provided the child information about preventing sexual abuse, such as forcefully to say no and to report the incident immediately to them.

The following comments describe survivors' earliest memories of their abuse:

*I was four years old and my older brother told me that he wanted to show me something that Mom and Dad did. I refused. Then he offered to pay me a quarter and said that I would like*

435

*it. If I turned him down, it was clear that he would hurt me. So I gave in and he made me perform oral sex with him.*

\*　　　　　\*　　　　　\*

*My brother threatened to kill me if I told our parents about him molesting me. I was three or four years of age at the time; he was about eighteen. He showed me the butcher block we kept in the cellar with the ax and blood. He said he'd kill me there if I told.*

\*　　　　　\*　　　　　\*

*My earliest memory is of my brother sneaking into my bed while we were on vacation and were sharing one bedroom. This happened while my parents were still out on the town. I pretended I was asleep, and it was very difficult to determine what to do about it because of the physical pleasure but inappropriate and selfish behavior on his part.*

### Typical Experiences

Only a few survivors participating in this research reported that their sexual abuse by a sibling was a one-time event. In most instances, the abuse continued and proceeded to other and different kinds of sexual abuse, often accompanied by physical and emotional abuse. The repetitious nature of the sexual abuse for siblings resembles that of children who are victims of sexual assault by an adult male, such as their father or another family member. The sexual assault is generally repeated and continues until the child is old enough forcibly to prohibit the behavior or until the sexually abusive behavior is discovered and appropriate interventions occur.

The sexual abuse that siblings experienced generally was accompanied by physical threats of harm or even death voiced by the perpetrator if they told their parents. This is a significant way in which sibling sexual abuse differs from adult-child sexual abuse. Adult sexual abuse of children generally occurs in the context of the perpetrator telling the victim that he or she is special and that the sexual activity will be a secret they alone share. Threats of harm may occur; however, through enticement, the child victim becomes entrapped in the perpetrator's web of abuse (Gonzalez et al., 1993; Petronio et al., 1996; Summit, 1983).

Several respondents described how their sexual abuse by an older sibling progressed during their childhood:

*I can't remember exactly how the sexual abuse started but when I was smaller there was a lot of experimenting. He would do things to me like putting his finger in my vagina. Then, as I got older, he would perform oral sex on me.*

\*     \*     \*

*Initially I was forced to masturbate him one night, but from then on it moved quickly to oral sex on him and eventually rape.*

Clarification should be made about the use of the term *rape*. In most states, rape is legally defined as the penetration of the penis into the vagina under force or the threat of force. Based on a growing understanding of sexual abuse and its effect on victims, rape is now being defined more broadly, consistent with feminist thought (Russell, 1986). Thus, rape may refer to any sexual activity between a perpetrator and a victim in which force, the threat of force, or threats in general are used. (An example of a threat in general is the perpetrator warning the victim not to tell anyone about their sexual activity because he might be sent to jail.)

The more inclusive meaning of the term has important implications for both the prosecution of perpetrators and the treatment of the victims. In terms of prosecuting the perpetrator, his use of aggression, force, or threats brings his behavior into the realm of rape, regardless of the nature of the activity. For example, fondling a victim's genitals can no longer be labeled less harmful than sexual intercourse because the consequences are the same: The victim's right to privacy has been abused by means of an aggressive act. In other words, the victim has been raped. Likewise, the implication for the treatment of the victim is that regardless of the nature of the activity a victim of sexual abuse is a victim of an aggressive act. The respondent quoted earlier used the word rape in the legal sense: sexual intercourse under the threat of force. Actually, she had already been a victim of rape when she was forced to engage in masturbation and oral sex against her wishes.

The following survivors' comments describe their typical experiences of sexual abuse by a sibling.

*It began as games and grew to "look and feel." As I became older, he played with my breasts and then fondled my genitals, always wanting but never achieving intercourse. He showed me with his fingers how it would feel.*

\*     \*     \*

*I would try to put off going to bed. I would try to cover up tight with my blankets. My brother would come into my room and touch me all over. I would pretend that I was asleep. After he left, I would cry and cry.*

Sibling sexual abuse is a phenomenon that can occur in families regardless of their socioeconomic status. The following comment is by a survivor whose mother had completed several years of college and whose father held a graduate degree from a university:

*It became much more frequent as he got older. It mostly happened when I was in sixth to ninth grade, ages eleven to fifteen. I knew he would try, so I would lock myself in my room. He would pick the lock and force me to the ground or bed. I can remember yelling at him, or crying, or begging, or throwing myself down and saying, "Go ahead," which he did, or saying I would tell. His response was, "Well, if you're going to tell, I might as well go ahead." I tried everything I could think of, for example, appealing to his morals as a brother. One time I remember holding a knife to myself. He got it away, always laughing. He'd force off my clothes, rub and suck my breasts, put his penis between them, and rub. He would perform oral sex on me often. I remember sucking his penis once. He did not come in my mouth. He would rub his penis all over my vulva and press against my vagina. He never inserted it, just pressed against it. I kept a calendar during his senior year of high school. I had made it a "countdown" of when he'd move out upon graduation with the numbers going down.*

A common tactic of perpetrators was to isolate the victim in order for the sexual abuse to occur. One respondent described how her older brother would know when to attack her:

*He would always seem to know when I was alone and when no one could hear. I would always know when he entered a room when it would happen. He would make me terrified. I would think, "Oh, no, not again!" He'd try to compliment me in a sexual way. Complimenting a 4- to 6-year-old on her "great breasts" was not what I'd call a turn-on. He'd either undress me or make me undress myself. He would undress and make me touch his erection. I hated that because he'd force me to do it and would hold my hand against it to almost masturbate him. He never orgasmed, though. He'd touch me, almost like he was examining me. A few times he had oral sex on me. He attempted intercourse*

438

*but that was difficult. He'd force my legs apart. I was always so scared because my muscles were so tight and my opening was so small. He never really could enter without severe pain. I would say he was hurting me, which he was, and I'd cry in hopes he'd stop. Sometimes he did. Other times he would force himself inside of me so that I would hurt for days.*

Although most of the survivors were females, the following comment is from an adult male survivor:

*My brother caught me masturbating once. That's when the sexual abuse began. At night he would have me fondle him, masturbate him and fellate him, depending on what he wanted. He threatened to tell Mom about catching me masturbating if I didn't go along. The abuse went on about a year or two. It was always at night. He would lay on his back. A streetlight would shine across his body through the curtains, and he would call me to come "do" him. I felt like I was on stage with the streetlight and trapped in a bad part. I hated him immensely. Finally, after a year or so I told him he could tell whomever he wanted but I wouldn't do it anymore. The abuse stopped, but the damage was done. My feelings would haunt me into high school, college, and my marriage.*

## Survivors' Responses to Their Sexual Abuse

Survivors' responses to sexual abuse by a sibling differed from their responses to emotional and physical abuse. In cases of emotional abuse, for example, a typical response was to fight back verbally and in turn to ridicule and call the perpetrator names. Generally, this was not effective and only served to further victimize the victim because the perpetrator intensified the abuse or shifted to other tactics. Victims of sibling physical abuse were often unable to fight back due to limitations in size and strength compared to their perpetrators. Thus, they resorted to hiding or withdrawing into themselves to get away from the perpetrator and the physical abuse.

In cases of sexual abuse, none of the survivors reported that they fought back. Undoubtedly, some siblings do fight back against sexual abuse by another sibling. Those who do are demonstrating their empowerment by their ability to say no, which may distinguish them from the sexual abuse survivors who comprised the sample discussed here.

439

An assertive verbal response can be an effective way for a child to prevent sexual abuse.

A common response of female victims of sibling sexual assault was to feign sleep. This response was also frequently reported by child victims of sexual assault by adult males within their household. These children often "play possum" as a way of coping with the assault, lacking the ability to use force to ward off their assailant (Summit, 1983). This behavior may also be a psychological defense against the emotional pain and suffering the victim experiences. It was as if she were saying, "If I am asleep, I won't be aware of what is happening. It won't hurt me as much." This response, however, often works against the victim later if she attempts to prosecute the perpetrator. Unfortunately, children are frequently attacked by attorneys and discredited by juries in the prosecution of sexual abuse cases because they made no protest or outcry. Such accusations only add to their guilt and self-blame. Thus, the entire sexual assault, the traumatic incident as well as the investigation that follows it, can be psychologically devastating for a child victim.

A more frequent response was to acquiesce or to submit to the sexual abuse. This response must be seen within the context of the abuse. First, the victims, especially young siblings, often were not aware of what they were doing when an older sibling engaged them in sexual play. Only after the event, sometimes many years later, when they began to experience shame and guilt for their involvement in the behavior did they begin to feel like a victim. They frequently coped with their feelings of shame and guilt by blaming themselves for participating in the behavior, but in reality they may have had no other option, considering their lack of information about or empowerment over sexual assault.

Second, as stated earlier, sibling sexual abuse often occurred within the context of threats. An older sibling would threaten a younger sibling that if the parents were told the victim would be harmed or both would be punished. The latter tactic left the victim feeling partly responsible for the sexual activity. Thus, the victim was frequently set up to pretend as if nothing had happened lest the victim experience retaliation from the perpetrator and from their parents for reporting the incident. One survivor wrote,

> *Once my mother was suspicious [about my being sexually abused by my brothers]. She confronted my brothers and they denied it. She told them she would ask me. Then she waited several*

*days. During that time they told me I'd better not tell her or they'd get me into trouble.*

Although the victim is pressured into remaining silent, this does not alleviate the emotional trauma associated with the sexual abuse. Rather, it forces the victim silently to bear the anxiety, shame, guilt, and other emotions. The only visible sign of this situation on the part of the victim may be a tendency to withdraw, to want to be alone. Thus, withdrawn behavior is an important clue for parents, teachers, and other adults who are in contact with children that something is bothering the child about which he or she is not able to or dare not talk. The withdrawn behavior may indicate that the child is attempting to repress the emotions surrounding a painful experience.

One survivor described how she handled her victimization from a brother for many years:

*I had no recollection of the sexual abuse from my brother until I was pregnant with my daughter. I then started having very graphic nightmares about my brother raping me. I was about three or four years old in the dreams. He was on top of me, holding me down and forcing himself into me. I was crying and screaming at him to stop. He would say, "You know you like it." I thought I was a pervert to have those dreams, so I didn't tell anyone about them until when my daughter was about a year old. I was physically abusing her, and I went to Parents Anonymous for help. The sponsor asked me if I had been sexually abused. I said I hadn't, but I told her about the nightmares. She said she thought it had really happened. With her support and encouragement, I asked my sisters first. They said he had abused them, but there was no penetration. Then I confronted him. I told him just exactly what was in the dreams, down to the last detail. There was a silence; then he said, "You are right. I did that."*

## Sexual Curiosity

Is any contact of a sexual nature between siblings sexual abuse? Some contacts may be described as sexual curiosity. All children explore their bodies and to some extent and at some time may engage in visual or even manual exploration of a sibling's body. This is one way that children discover sexual differences or verify what they have been told by their parents about the differences between boys and

441

girls. Two small children exploring each other's bodies does not pre-destine them to a life of emotional chaos and suffering. For example, 4-year-old Tim was observed by a nursery school attendant showing his penis to Sue, who was the same age. When the children became aware that the attendant had seen their behavior, Tim's reaction was to blame Sue, saying she had asked him to do this. Sue denied it. The nursery school attendant reported the activity to the teacher who took the children aside and talked with them about their sexuality at a level that they could understand and reviewed with them an earlier discussion in which all the children had participated on the subject of good touches and secret touches.

Sexual activity may be viewed relative to the age and psychoso-cial developmental level of a child. Among preschool-age children (ages 0–5), patterns of activity include intense curiosity, seen in taking ad-vantage of opportunities to explore their universe. This may be ex-pressed in the sexual behaviors of masturbation and looking at others' bodies. Among primary-school-age children (ages 6–10), activities in-clude game playing with peers and continuing to seize opportunities to explore their universe. Sexual behaviors for this age group may include masturbation, looking at others' bodies, sexual exposure of themselves to others, and even sexual fondling of peers or younger children in a play or gamelike atmosphere. Among preadolescent chil-dren (ages 10–12) and adolescents (ages 13–18), behaviors focus on individuation including separation from parents and family and de-veloping relationships with peers. Among adolescents, this includes practicing intimacy with peers of the same or opposite sex. Sexual behaviors for these developmental stages include masturbation, an intense interest in voyeuristic activities involving viewing others' bodies through pictures, films, or videos (some of which may be por-nographic), or attempts at "peeking" in opposite-sex locker/dressing rooms. Open-mouth kissing, sexual fondling, simulated intercourse, and intercourse involving penetration are sexual activities engaged in at these developmental stages (Sgroi, Bunk, & Wabrek, 1988).

Sexual activity among consenting participants probably presents the least risk of unfavorable consequences. But often young children appear to consent but actually do not because they cannot anticipate unfavorable consequences from their behavior. In many instances, what appears to be consent may actually be only passive consent, or the inability to make a rational decision because of limited cognitive skills and life experiences.

One factor affecting children's psychosexual development is societal attitudes toward sexuality demonstrated by parents. Some adults are very uncomfortable with sexual issues and thus attempt to handle them with their children by pretending this area of life does not exist. At the other end of the continuum, some advocate open sexual activity in the presence of children and even encourage children to engage in sexual activity. But neither approach guarantees healthy psychosexual development.

Because of the impact of sexual abuse by an adult, a peer, or sibling on a child's later adult psychosocial functioning, it is important for parents to take a proactive approach to sexuality with their children by providing them information about sex that is appropriate to their age and psychosocial development, empowering them with the knowledge and ability to discriminate between good touches and secret touches, and providing an atmosphere at home where their sexual concerns and problems can be discussed.

## Parental Awareness of Sibling Abuse

Prior to discussing parental reactions to sibling abuse, the question should be asked if the parents were even aware that abuse was occurring between or among the siblings in their family. Among the 150 participants in the study discussed here, 71% (70) of those surviving sibling physical abuse and 69% (81) of those surviving sibling emotional abuse felt their parents were aware of what was happening, which is understandable because it is difficult to hide these types of abuse. However, regarding sexual abuse, only 18% (18) of the survivors felt their parents were aware of this behavior, which finding is also understandable because the sexual abuse occurred only when the parents were away from home or during the night when parents were asleep.

The parents' lack of awareness of siblings' sexual abuse was also often due to the inability of the victims to inform their parents about what was happening. One would think that children could surely tell their parents, but the data indicate the contrary. Many victims could not tell their parents for several reasons, one of which is that at the time the sexual abuse was occurring the victim often did not perceive it as abuse. The victim was not cognitively or emotionally mature enough to understand that it was indeed abuse. This was especially true of young children. However, the way the survivors in this research perceive the sexual activity now as adults, looking back on their childhood, is very different from the way they perceived it when they were children. For example, this is true of a survivor who was 7 years old during her first sexual incident with her older brother. He took her into the woods while their mother was working and he "played dirty" with her by touching her on her breasts and genitals and making her do likewise to him, Afterward, he threatened to kill her if she told anyone. The survivor, now as an adult, recalled her reaction to the sexual abuse at the time: "I didn't even realize what he was doing. To me it was like brushing my hair." As an adult, however, this survivor's reaction to the abuse is very different. She is aware that this was an abusive incident, the first of many. Looking back on these experiences, she is very angry that as a small child she was used by her brother. As a result, she experiences feelings of low self-esteem.

A second reason why children frequently did not tell their parents about sibling sexual abuse is that the abuse often occurred in the context of abuse of authority. Some of the perpetrators, older brothers of the victims, were acting as baby-sitters for their younger sisters when they abused them sexually. The younger sibling had been instructed by the parents to obey the older brother. Siblings wrote,

> *I remember a vague feeling that my brother was more important than me and I should keep quiet and do what he wanted.*

> \*            \*            \*

> *I was taught to do as people told me.*

A third reason why children did not tell their parents was that the perpetrator threatened the victim with retaliation if he or she told, like the survivor who recounted being abused in the woods by her brother. In the context of a physical threat, the victim was fearful that if the abuse were reported to the parents, the sibling perpetrator might act on the threat. Moreover, if the abuse occurred while the perpetrator was baby-sitting the victim, the victim feared that if left in the care of the perpetrator at a later time the perpetrator would punish the victim for reporting the abuse (Gonzalez et al., 1993; Petronio et al., 1996).

Note the comments of survivors of sibling sexual abuse that occurred in the context of a threat, such as this male survivor who recalled how his older brother threatened him:

> *He would lay me down, put his big fist by my face and he would say, "if you scream, this is what you'll get." Then he would masturbate me.*

And from this female survivor:

*I would be in my bed asleep. He would jump in the bed with me. I would try and push him out. I was just not strong enough and he would always keep a baseball bat or knife with him.*

A fourth reason why victims did not tell their parents about the abuse is that they blamed themselves for what happened. Some survivors in this research spoke of experiencing pleasurable physical feelings during the sexual encounters with a sibling. Because they derived sexual pleasure from the experience, often of an autonomic nature, the survivors blamed themselves for contributing to the abuse. They were afraid to report the activity to their parents lest their abusive sibling in self-defense would tell their parents of this participation. Moreover, to keep the victim from telling the parents, the perpetrator often blamed the victim for not resisting the sexual advances. "You could have stopped it [sexual abuse], if you had wanted," perpetrators defensively would say as they attempted to shift the blame for the abuse from themselves to the victim. Generally, the survivors participating in this research had not been empowered by their parents by being informed about good touches and secret touches so as to resist sexual advances effectively.

A final reason why the victims did not tell their parents is that the climate in the home made it impossible for them to report it. One survivor did the best she could to communicate with her parents about the sexual abuse:

*I remember every time my parents went out, I'd sit in my parents' room while they got ready and I'd ask them, "Do you really have to go out tonight? Can't you stay home?" That's as close as I could get to telling them or asking for their protection.*

Another victim felt the climate in the home was such that she could not tell her parents what was happening:

*Somehow they should have provided a family atmosphere in which their children—me at this point—could have approached them with the situation without being fearful of getting into trouble.*

445

## Parental Reactions to Sibling Abuse

How did the parents who were aware of the abuse occurring in their homes between the siblings respond? Six different parental responses are identified and discussed.

### *Ignoring or Minimizing the Abuse*

A typical parental response to sibling physical and emotional abuse was to ignore or minimize it. Parents often excused the behavior on the basis that it was merely sibling rivalry. "Boys will be boys; children will be children," victims were told by their parents. While it is true that certain behaviors are accepted as appropriate for children because of their level of maturity, the abuse of one sibling by another should not be. Nothing excuses or justifies the abuse of one person by another.

Several survivors provided comments regarding this parental response:

> *They ignored or minimized the abuse. They told me, "Boys were boys and needed to clear their system."*

*       *       *

> *I told them once and they didn't believe me and they would leave me alone with him again. Then I really suffered for telling on him. I soon learned not to tell.*

*       *       *

> *My parents saw my brother's physical abuse of me as normal sibling rivalry and did not correct any of what he did. If they were around when it was occurring, they would just say we had to learn to get along better.*

### *Blaming the Victim*

Other parents responded to the abuse that was occurring by acknowledging it when it was reported to them but then blaming the victim for its occurrence. This parental response was reported frequently by sibling abuse survivors in this research and by survivors in other studies of sibling abuse (Laviola, 1992; Loredo, 1982). When parents blamed the victim, the victim became a victim a second time; this is known as "revictimization." The unfortunate outcome of this parental response is that perpetrators are absolved of responsibility for their actions and are given the implicit message that the behavior was appropriate or that the victim deserved what the perpetrator did. The perpetrator in essence is given license to continue the behavior. Survivors wrote,

*My parents would usually break it up when my brother was abusing me but with me being the oldest, I'd always get accused of causing the problem and be told that I should set a better example and I wouldn't get hurt.*

*　　　　　*　　　　　*

*I was hurt by the abuse I received from a younger sister, but my sister was not blamed or it was turned around that I had done something to cause it. She was never wrong.*

*　　　　　*　　　　　*

*My parents didn't know [often about the abuse] but they would have blamed me or at least made excuses for my brother. My mother would say, "Men are hunters, don't trust any, not even your own brother." But she meant it in general, not for her son, the "King."*

## Inappropriately Responding to the Behavior

The manner in which some parents responded to the abusive behavior occurring between or among siblings was ineffective and in some instances exacerbated the abuse. For example, survivors reported that their parents used severe corporal punishment on the perpetrator in an attempt to stop the physically or emotionally abusive behavior against a sibling. One survivor reported that when she told her parents about the physical abuse she was receiving from her older brother, her father beat the brother so badly that she resolved never to tell her father again. A two-stage process of self-blame resulted from her father's action. First, the victim blamed herself for her brother's severe beating because she had reported his behavior to her father. Second, she blamed herself for the abuse, feeling that perhaps she may in some way have caused him to treat her this way.

Another survivor described a similar situation:

*My older brothers received a severe beating when I told my parents how they were abusing me. The severity of the beating, how-*

447

*ever, discouraged me from ever reporting again what happened because I wanted to avoid a more violent outcome.*

Yet another inappropriate response to sibling abuse was for the parents to abuse the perpetrator. For example, if the perpetrator was hitting or calling the victim names, the parents would do the same to the perpetrator. This approach appears to be based on the myth that giving perpetrators a dose of their own medicine will teach them to stop the behavior. Some parents use this form of behavioral control with small children. They may bite a child who has bitten them or encourage a child who has been slapped to slap back. Unfortunately, this form of discipline establishes no new behavioral patterns for the child. Rather, mimicking the perpetrator's aversive or abusive behavior reinforces this behavior in the child. Just as violence sometimes begets more violence, the violence in this form of punishment encourages continued violence. The perpetrator may become angrier as a result of this form of discipline and likely ventilate this anger once again on the victim or on someone else, as occurred for this survivor:

*My parents would yell at her and pinch and bite her to "teach" her how it felt so she'd stop doing it. It only made it worse for me though. They'd clean my wounds and tell me a story to tell my teacher to explain my bandages and markings.*

Some survivors reported that when they told their parents about the abuse they experienced from a sibling, all the children were indiscriminately punished, which only further victimized the victim and did not protect the victim from additional abuse.

*Dad would yell at us and threaten us with a belt if we didn't shut up. Anger was not directed at my brother who abused me but at all the kids. I learned to cry silently because of my Dad. The belt was worse than my brother's abuse.*

Research on the effects of parental punishment of sibling aggression or fighting indicates that parents are more likely to punish the older sibling rather than the younger (Felson & Russo, 1988). This tendency to punish the older or more powerful sibling, the researchers found, generally results in more frequent aggression because the younger siblings do not hesitate to be verbally or physically aggressive, knowing the parents will identify with them and punish the older sibling. A more effective approach, the researchers found, is for parents to intervene in the fighting but not to engage in punishment.

## *Joining in the Abuse*

Perhaps the saddest parental response, especially to emotional abuse such as name-calling and ridicule, was to join the perpetrator in abusing the victim. The effect on the victims was devastating, for they were further victimized by the very parents from whom they sought protection. Victims could turn for protection to no one else. The crying and the sadness these victims felt is understandable:

*My mother would pick up on it [the abuse] and also make fun of me.*

\*　　　　　　\*　　　　　　\*

*When I was six and started school, the girls took me into the bathroom and put me in the toilet to wash me. Then they called me "Stink-weed." I was crushed. When I got home, I talked about it. Even my whole family laughed at me and called me that daily. It still hurts. It's something I'll never forget. They still remind me of it.*

## *Disbelieving the Abuse Was Occurring*

When some victims of sibling abuse, especially sexual abuse, reported the abuse to their parents, the parental response was disbelief. Again, the effect of this response was further victimization. Not only were they victims of their parents' disbelief and failure to protect them, but they were victims of the perpetrator's continuing behavior. Two survivors recalled the effect of being disbelieved by their parents:

*When I tried to tell my father about it, he called my mother and brother into the room, told them my accusations, and asked my brother if it was true. Naturally, he said I was lying, and my mother stood there supporting him. Nothing happened, except that I got beaten later by my mother for daring to say anything and for "lying." My brother knew that from then on there was nothing he couldn't do to me. He was immune from punishment. Never again did I say a word since to do so would only have meant more abuse from them both. I concluded it was better to keep my mouth shut.*

\*　　　　　　\*　　　　　　\*

*When I tried to tell them about the beatings I was taking, they didn't believe me and they would leave me alone with him again.*

449

*So when it came to the sexual abuse, I didn't think they would believe me.*

### Indifference

Another parental response to sibling abuse in the family was indifference. Some parents may simply not have known what to do; others' indifference may have stemmed from their own overwhelming problems or from being under so much stress that they did not have the energy to look beyond their own problems. One survivor commented on this parental response:

*I told my mother about my older brother molesting me about two years after it happened and she asked me what I expected her to do about it. I never bothered to tell her about other things that happened because obviously she didn't care.*

## Understanding Sibling Abuse

How can we understand why one sibling would physically, emotionally, or sexually abuse another? Following are reasons drawn from the survivors' accounts of their abuse that help us to understand why sibling abuse occurs.

### The Abuse of Power and Control Over Others

A commonality in all forms of sibling abuse, whether it be physical, emotional, or sexual, as well as of all types of family violence—child, partner, and elder abuse—is the abuse of power and the pathological need of the perpetrator to control another person. The abuse of power focuses on a more powerful individual abusing a less powerful one. In sibling abuse, as the comments of respondents indicated, this often was an older sibling abusing a younger sibling. In most instances, power was related to the gender of the perpetrator, with a male sibling abusing his sister.

Female survivors of sibling abuse reported what appeared to be an underlying assumption of their brothers; namely, that the latter had a right to assert their will over their sisters. Physical force and verbal abuse were seen as appropriate ways to achieve this goal. In instances of sexual abuse, brothers tended to view their sisters as sexual objects rather than as individuals.

## Inappropriate Expectations

The most frequently cited reason for sibling abuse, generally of a younger sibling by an older sibling, was that the older sibling was in charge of the younger at the time the abuse was occurring. The older sibling was baby-sitting the younger when the parents were away from home at night or immediately after school before the parents returned home from work. The parents had inappropriate expectations of the older sibling in that this child was not capable of handling the responsibility of caring for a younger sibling. Several survivors described what happened to them when an older sibling baby-sat them:

> *When my parents went out dancing or to my aunt's home on a Saturday night, my two older brothers baby-sat us six children. Not long after they left, my brothers would tell us to go to bed. It was too early, so we didn't want to go to bed. When we resisted, we were hit. I was punched and slapped by my oldest brother. If I defended myself by hitting back, my oldest brother would grab my wrists in the air as he screamed at me that he would hit me more. He would be telling me what to do and to go to bed. I would be crying hard even more and would go to bed.*

*             *             *

> *My mother would go to bingo leaving my sister (three years older) in charge with specific chores to be done. She would make us do the work. If it didn't get done when she said, she would hit us with a belt. Leaving her in charge gave her every right to do whatever she wanted.*

## Modeling Parental Behavior

Respondents reported that the physically and emotionally abusive behavior they experienced from their sibling was no different from the way their parents treated each other. One survivor wrote,

> *How could I expect my brother to treat me differently other than being physically and emotionally abusive when this is the kind of behavior we as kids saw our parents continually engage in toward each other?*

A review of research on parents who are abusive toward each other reveals a high likelihood that the parents also will abuse their children (O'Keefe, 1995; Ross, 1996; Saunders, 1994). In domestic violence studies, about 50% of the men who batter their partners are also reported to abuse their children. Slightly more than a third of the battered women, on average, reported having abused their children. To these findings, based on the current research, should be added the fact that in families where there is spousal and child abuse it is highly likely that sibling abuse also is occurring. This can be explained in two ways. First, the children may be modeling their behavior toward each other after their parents' behavior. Second, research shows that children who witness parental violence tend to have more behavioral problems than children not exposed to parental violence (Hughes et al., 1989; Jouriles, Barling, & O'Leary, 1987; O'Keefe, 1995; Suh & Abel, 1990). Sibling abuse may be one manifestation of such behavioral problems.

### Parents Overwhelmed by Their Own Problems

Another reason for sibling abuse is that parents are often so overwhelmed by their own problems that they are unaware of what is happening between or among siblings. The parents may not have the energy or the ability to handle the situation. Some of the parents of survivors in the research were coping with alcohol problems, mental illness, financial difficulties, and marital problems, as these comments indicate:

*My family was very chaotic. My father was an alcoholic. My mother died when I was eleven years old. My father had many lovers and was gone a lot of the time.*

*      *      *

*I don't think my mother knew how badly I was being hurt by an older sister and I was afraid to tell her for fear of retaliation. She was busy trying to survive on practically nothing and deal with her own emotional problems, and probably she had systemic lupus then, even though it wasn't diagnosed for another fifteen years or so. But I think she didn't want to know how bad things were because she was powerless to change her circumstances.*

Research suggests that adolescent sibling sexual abuse perpetrators often come from discordant families. Worling (1995) compared 32 adolescent male sex offenders who assaulted younger siblings with 28 males who offended against nonsibling children. Adolescent sibling-incest offenders reported significantly more marital discord, parental rejection, use of physical punishment, a more negative and argumentative family atmosphere, and general dissatisfaction with family relationships than did their nonsibling sexual offender counterparts. The researcher suggests several possible explanations for the relationship between discordant families and sibling-incest perpetrators. First, children who live with abusive and rejecting parents may turn to each other for comfort, nurturance, and support. As these children enter adolescence, a risk of sexualizing these relationships may occur. Second, intrafamilial offenders may be seeking some form of retribution within their families for the abuse and rejection they have suffered. Third, the adolescents may be modeling their aggressive behavior toward their siblings after what they observe in their parents' relationship to each other as well as to their children. Fourth, although the research data did not suggest this, the sibling-incest offenders may be exposed to more sexualized behaviors in the home, such as family nudity, pornography, or witnessing parental sexual acts.

Although parents' inability to intervene effectively in sibling abuse may be a reflection of their psychological problems, the problem is better viewed from a broader perspective, such as from an ecological or social-situational perspective (Garbarino, 1977; Parke & Collmer, 1975; Wiehe, 1989) that views the family as a system within the larger social system of which it is a part. A mutual dependence exists between a family and its social environment, and interdependent interactions occur between the two systems. The psychosocial development of individual family members, as well as that of the family as a whole, occurs in the context of the physical, social, political, and economic characteristics of society. Thus, parenting cannot be viewed only from the perspective of psychological functioning. Rather, external social forces impacting on each parent also must be considered. For example, inadequate opportunities for vocational training may require parents to work two or more unskilled jobs. Inadequate housing may prevent siblings of age and gender differences from having adequate privacy. Psychiatric hospitalization, outpatient mental health treatment, or substance abuse treatment programs may not be available or a person may be unable to pay for such treatment. Latchkey programs for children who return home from school before their parents return home from work may not be available, thus forcing an older sibling to care for younger siblings. Under these difficult social circumstances, problems arise that can affect the children in terms of their relationships with their parents and toward each other as siblings.

## Contribution of the Victim

Another causal factor associated with sibling abuse is the victim's own contribution to the abuse, particularly to physical and emotional abuse. This causal factor is known in the literature on child abuse as the interactional theory (Parke & Collmer, 1975).

When an adult abuses a child, the adult does not necessarily abuse all the children in a family. Frequently, the abuse is selective and directed at one specific child. Certain physical characteristics may make a child more prone to abuse. Some children also may exhibit behaviors that make them targets for abuse. In these cases, abuse often becomes cyclical and escalates. This in turn reinforces the child's behavior, which may prompt more emotional and physical abuse of that child. Research supports the hypothesis that some behavioral patterns of abused children tend to invite further abuse (Bakan, 1971; Patterson, 1982).

It is important to note that the interactional theory of child abuse *does not blame the child for the abuse.* Blaming the child implies that in some way the child deserves what occurred, but no one deserves to be abused. Rather, the interactional theory identifies and analyzes factors contributing to the abuse for the purpose of helping prevent and treat the abuse.

The interactional theory, generally applied to the abuse of children by adults, also applies to sibling abuse. Some siblings may be more prone to abuse by another sibling because of physical characteristics. In name-calling and ridicule, as noted in survivors' comments, physical characteristics such as height or weight frequently become the targets of a sibling's emotional abuse. Likewise, the behavior of some siblings may set up situations in which abuse is more likely to occur. For example, when a younger sibling makes excessive demands on an older sibling for attention or repeatedly uses another sibling's possessions without permission, incidents of abuse may occur. Again, this is not to blame the younger sibling for the abuse; rather, it is to place responsibility on the parents to be aware of such interactions and to effectively intervene. Using the problem-solving approach, discussed later, may help determine ways the siblings are expected to relate to each other.

## Ineffective Interventions

As has been previously mentioned, the inability of parents to intervene and effectively stop sibling abuse because they do not know how is a factor relating to sibling abuse. This does not mean the parents in the research sample were not interested in or concerned about the abuse; rather, the way they tried to stop it was ineffective. Consequently, the abuse continued and in some instances escalated out of control. Behaviors such as verbal put-downs, name-calling, hitting, and slapping occur to some extent between siblings in all families. This is not abnormal, and effective parental intervention generally stops the behavior. Parents may take the problem-solving approach with their children, which conveys the message that the behavior should be avoided and will not be tolerated in the family. The parents' intervention also prevents the behavior from escalating into a pattern of abuse.

Ineffective interventions by contrast do not give this message. The children are not instructed on how to avoid the abusive behavior. When severe corporal punishment is used, such as giving the perpetrator a beating, the abuse may even escalate. The perpetrator becomes angry at the victim for reporting what happened and in retaliation escalates the abuse. The victim may be forced to not report abuse in the future for fear of retaliation. Survivors wrote,

*My older brothers received a severe beating when I told my parents how they were abusing me. The severity of the beating, however, discouraged me from ever reporting again what happened because I wanted to avoid a more violent outcome.*

   \*     \*     \*

*My parents were so busy abusing themselves and each other and us that it was only natural that as siblings we would abuse each other.*

Some respondents described the atmosphere in their home as a "battleground." A culture of violence developed for all family members living in this atmosphere. Verbal and physical assaults become a typical pattern of interaction—between husband and wife and between parents and children. Researchers are becoming aware that often more than one type of violence occurs in a family, such as spousal abuse and child abuse (Sutphen, Wiehe, & Leukefeld, 1996; Wiehe, 1997a). In families where both of these types of violence are occurring, drug and alcohol abuse generally are prominent. These families have been identified as "multiple abuse families." Based on survivors' comments, sibling abuse also is prevalent in these families.

### *Sibling Abuse Viewed as Normal*

Some parents accepted physical abuse between siblings as normal because they felt that the sibling perpetrator was "going through a phase." They excused the behavior as appropriate for males, or they accepted the behavior as "normal sibling rivalry":

*The abuse was considered normal behavior by my parents, who had no idea what normal might be. I might add that the physical abuse by my siblings was much less than the emotional and sexual abuse by them.*

Sibling rivalry has been around for as long as there have been brothers and sisters. Literature is filled with examples of siblings attacking one another. The biblical story of Cain and Abel is just one example. The fact that sibling rivalry is so universal suggests to some parents that sibling abuse is normal. Sibling rivalry is normal; sibling abuse is not.

Why does rivalry between siblings occur? According to Adele Faber and Elaine Mazlish (1988) in *Siblings Without Rivalry: How to Help Your Children Live Together So You Can Live Too,* the presence of another sibling in the home casts a shadow upon the life and well-being of the firstborn. A sibling implies there will be *less*—less attention from the parents, less time with the parents, less energy for meeting the firstborn's needs. The first child may even think that the parents love the second child more. Thus, the new sibling implies a threat. Psychologist Alfred Adler referred to the birth of a second child as a "dethroning" of the firstborn.

## Effects of Abuse on the Survivor

How does sibling abuse in childhood affect the survivors as adults? "Time heals all wounds" runs an old adage; however, the number of individuals seeking help from mental health professionals and joining support groups for the abused disproves this statement. Physical, emotional, or sexual abuse by a sibling can have devastating effects on survivors, whether the perpetrator of the abuse was an adult or a sibling, as research documents (Bagley & Ramsay, 1986; Beitchman et al., 1992; Briere & Runtz, 1990; Meuenzenmaier, Meyer, Struening, & Ferber, 1993; Moeller et al., 1993; Mullen, Martin, Anderson, Romans, & Herbison, 1996). The emotional pain the abuse causes never seems to go completely away, even when the survivor seeks psychotherapy. Survivors simply learn to cope with the pain, but the memory of the abuse does not disappear: "I get so angry just thinking about how humiliating, degrading this was. And my brother has been dead for twenty years."

Prior to discussing the effects that being physically, emotionally, or sexually abused by a sibling as a child had on the survivors as adults, some comments should be made about the effects of the abuse on the victims at the time the abuse was occurring or shortly thereafter. Several studies provide a description of the immediate effects of abuse by an adult on a child victim that may also be applicable to victims of sibling abuse. The behavior of 93 prepubertal children evaluated for sexual abuse and 80 non-abused children was examined using the Child Behavior Checklist approximately 4 months after the sexually abused children had been clinically seen for their abuse (Dubowitz et al., 1993). The sexually abused children had significantly more behavior problems than their nonabused counterparts, including depression, aggression, sleep and somatic complaints, hyperactivity, and sexual problems.

Similarly, in a study of school-age children who had been physically abused as compared to a nonabused sample, the abused children displayed pervasive and severe academic and social/emotional problems (Kurtz et al., 1993). They performed poorly on standardized tests of language and math skills, received low performance assessments by teachers, and were more likely than their nonabused counterparts to have repeated one or more grades. A number of the children who were age 14 and up already had dropped out of school. The research concluded that, because physically abused children are often angry, distractible, anxious, and lack self-control, it is extremely difficult for these children to learn.

The abuse can affect victims in the years immediately following the abuse rather than waiting until adulthood, as the survivors in the present research reported. For example, in a 17-year longitudinal study of 375 people who had been physically and sexually abused before age 18 by a family member (mother, father, sibling, stepparent, uncle, cousin), those who were abused, as compared to their nonabused counterparts, demonstrated significant impairments in functioning at both ages 15 and 21, including depression, anxiety, psychiatric disorders, emotional-behavioral problems, suicidal ideation, and suicide attempts (Silverman et al., 1996).

## *Poor Self-Esteem*

Nearly every respondent to the research, whether a victim of physical, emotional, or sexual abuse from a sibling, referred to poor self-esteem. From their responses, it would appear that low self-esteem is a universal effect of sibling abuse.

Low self-esteem appears to be an effect of all types of abuse whether by an adult or a sibling. Research on the effects of parents' psychological maltreatment of their children found that the children tended to feel unwanted, inferior, unloved, and inadequate—symptoms that can affect a person's psychological development (Garbarino, Guttman, & Seeley, 1986). Similarly, survivors reported that the abuse they experienced as children from a sibling left them feeling they were in some way inferior, inadequate, and worthless:

*I lack self-esteem and self-confidence. I cling to my husband and am afraid of a lot of things.*

\*　　　　　　\*　　　　　　\*

*The abuse contributed to my low self-esteem and self-confidence. I still have difficulty accepting credit for successes. I have a continuing sense of being worthless and unlovable, despite evidence to the contrary.*

\*　　　　　　\*　　　　　　\*

*I feel unwanted, unloved. I feel like no one could love me. I feel no one needs or wants me. I feel like no one cares!*

## *Problems in Relationships With the Opposite Sex*

Women who were physically, emotionally, or sexually abused by a brother reported that the abuse affected their attitude toward males. The survivors' attitudes may be described as distrustful, suspicious, fearful, and even hateful. The emotions the women experienced stemming from their abuse by a brother are in turn transferred to all men. This disgust and distrust of men has significantly affected their ability to relate to and especially to form intimate relationships with them. The abuse that some respondents experienced from a brother while growing up even influenced their decision not to marry.

An underlying fear and suspicion of men pervades the female survivors. Their fear of entrapment by men, which the survivors reported, may stem from the restraints their brothers placed on them while physically abusing them, such as pinning them to the floor. It may also stem from the entrapment they felt in their family when they pleaded in vain for protection from the abuse. As has been seen, when victims reported their sexual abuse by a brother to their parents, they often were not provided protection but were blamed for what happened, which may have heightened their feeling of entrapment.

Several survivors described how their childhood abuse has affected their relationships with the opposite sex:

*I am uncertain of men's real intentions. I see them as a source of pain.*

        *               \**               \**

*I have a lot of fear of men and tend to use my mind and intellect to push men away and intimidate them the same way I was intimidated. I have a lot of difficulties in my relationships with men. I tend to disagree a lot and to be very afraid and contemptuous of a man's need for me.*

## Difficulty With Interpersonal Relationships

Some survivors have difficulty relating not only to members of the opposite sex but to anyone, regardless of gender. Difficulties in interpersonal relationships impair these survivors' ability, say, to hold a job. Others reported compensating for their poor feelings of self-worth by trying too hard to please others.

The survivors commented about their inability to handle anger appropriately in interpersonal relationships. They frequently used the words *rage* and *anger* when describing their reactions to their childhood abuse by a sibling. Some survivors spoke of this anger being with them constantly and having a need to suppress these feelings. Other research shows that one outcome frequently experienced by incest survivors is the suppression of anger, which creates more symptoms for them as compared to survivors who appropriately express their angry feelings (Scott & Day, 1996). Survivors mentioned their fear of (a) expressing any anger, (b) others' anger, and (c) what they described as their own uncontrollable outbursts of anger. The victims related their present anger to that felt in three phases of their life: the anger they felt as a child but were not able to express because of their parents' inappropriate response to their abuse by a sibling; a continual festering of this anger throughout their adult years, the source of which they often did not know until they sought professional help; and the anger toward their sibling that they still experience today for the abuse they suffered. Although many of the survivors have sought professional help, their anger is still a factor with which they must continually cope:

*I'm afraid that everyone is going to abuse me in some way. I don't trust anyone. I feel in everything people say or do that they want to hurt me. I always want to take the blame for any mistake made, or I feel that everyone is blaming me.*

\*        \*        \*

*It has made me very cynical and untrusting of those who attempt to get close quickly. I grew up feeling if your own family doesn't like or want you, who will?*

### Repeating the Victim Role in Other Relationships

A significant effect of sibling abuse is that the survivors as adults enter into relationships in which they are revictimized. Many survivors choose friends and mates that place them in situations where they again become victims of abuse. This phenomenon relates to the survivors' feelings of low self-esteem and worthlessness. Their behavior gives the message to others that they are worthless and deserve to be used and abused.

Research on adult-child sexual abuse indicates that the victims are likely to continue being abused as adults (Faller, 1989; Herman & Hirschman, 1977; McGuire & Wagner, 1978; Summit & Kryso, 1978). Child sexual abuse survivors may internalize their victimization to the extent that they regard the abuse as something they deserved. Thus, they unconsciously choose mates who continue to abuse them. A similar phenomenon occurs among women who have been battered by their husbands. They frequently leave one abusive relationship and enter into another, thereby continuing their role of victim (Walker, 1994). The following comments confirm this behavior:

*I now know that my brother hurt me because he needed something desperately from me that he felt he didn't have himself. He felt weaker than me. I tend to pick men now who are weaker than me and need a lot. Then I push them away. I also pick men who have a covert sadistic streak.*

\*        \*        \*

*It took me into my thirties before I began to see a pattern from
the abuse I experienced from an older sister. I chose a first husband who abused me. Also, I tend to constantly be doing too
much as if to make me feel better.*

## Continued Self-Blame

Survivors who blame themselves for the sexual abuse often continue this pattern into adulthood. Intellectually, they know that such
thinking is absurd, but emotionally they cannot accept the fact they
did not stop the sexual abuse (Agosta & Loring, 1988). Survivors find
themselves repeatedly thinking that they allowed themselves to be
sexually abused, even though in reality there probably was little at
the time that they could have done to prevent it. One survivor wrote
about her self-blame for the sexual abuse she experienced from an
older brother:

*I was told by several women and especially by my older sister
that it was my fault because of the way I dressed and carried
myself. I am very self-conscious now as an adult of how I dress. I
do not like or wear short skirts. I prefer turtleneck sweaters and
high-necked blouses. I do not accept compliments very well from
men, other than my husband.*

One respondent at the age of 4 was paid a quarter by her older
brother to perform oral sex. She complied largely out of fear that if
she didn't he would hurt her. She commented, "I have punished myself for 22 years for taking that quarter from him. I don't like myself."

### Sexual Dysfunction

Survivors of sexual abuse by a sibling in particular noted that the
abuse has affected their sexual functioning. Two extreme reactions
were reported: One was avoidance of all sexual contact, and the other
was sexual compulsivity. Some female survivors reported that because
of their sexual abuse by an older brother they have an aversion to sex,
sometimes even in marriage:

*I have been deeply affected by the sexual abuse from my brother.
Even after years of therapy, it's hard for me to be truly open
sexually with a man. I often experience shame and disgust
around sex and tend to focus on the man's experience and plea-*

461

*sure rather than on my own. I have a hard time initiating sex. I often experience myself as a sexual object to be used and contemptuously discarded by men.*

Others use sex as a weapon:

*I became very sexually active after leaving home at age 20. I did not want to have meaningful or strong relationships with anyone but to have sex with many men and never see them again, so that they might have a feeling of being used and hurt.*

The findings of several studies on adults who were sexually abused as children support the comments of survivors of sibling sexual abuse in this research about sexual problems (Bagley & Ramsay, 1986; Briere & Runtz, 1988; Kinzl et al., 1995). Briere (1984) and Meiselman (1978), using samples of adults who had been sexually abused as children and control groups of persons who had not been sexually abused, found that the sexual abuse survivors had a higher percentage of sexual problems than the control group. Sarwer and Durlak (1996) investigated 359 married adult women who sought sex therapy with their partners. A high percentage of these women had experienced sexual abuse as a child. The study also found that childhood sexual abuse involving physical force and penetration were predictive of an increased likelihood of sexual dysfunction. Studies also indicate that an unusually high percentage of both male and female prostitutes report being sexually abused as children (Blume, 1986; Janus, 1984; Silbert & Pines, 1983).

## Eating Disorders, Alcoholism, and Drug Abuse

Survivors reported that sibling abuse has affected their adult lives in the form of eating disorders:

*I have an eating disorder in the form of bulimia and am at times anorexic. These problems have to do with the denial of needs and the shame and hate I have regarding taking things into my body.*

Research shows a relationship between sexual abuse as a child and bulimia nervosa in adult women. For example, 38 women who were receiving treatment for incest abuse were compared with a control group of 27 women also in treatment but denied having been sexually abused. The incest victims were significantly more likely to binge, vomit, experience a loss of control over their eating habits, and report dissatisfaction with their bodies as compared to those in the control group. The incest victims also more frequently engaged in other maladaptive behaviors such as the abuse of alcohol, suicidal gestures, self-mutilation and smoking (Wonderlich et al., 1996). Similarly, 72 women suffering from bulimia nervosa were compared with a matched control group of 72 women not displaying bulimic symptoms (Miller, McCluskey-Fawcett, & Irving, 1993). Rates of self-reported sexual abuse were significantly greater in the women diagnosed as bulimic. The researchers suggested that the eating disorder may have developed in an attempt to cope with sexual victimization.

Other survivors reported problems with alcohol and drugs. One wrote, "I still tend to blunt my feelings or drown them in booze. I am in Alcoholics Anonymous."

Numerous studies show a relationship between being sexually abused as a child and later drug abuse (Boyd et al., 1993; Boyd et al., 1994; Covington & Kohen, 1984; Harrison et al., 1997; Widom et al., 1995). For example, in a sample of recovering chemically dependent women, researchers found that 68% of the 60 respondents had been recipients of unwanted sexual contacts from family and nonfamily members (Teets, 1995).

## Depression

Survivors repeatedly referred to experiencing depression as adults that they directly associate with their childhood abuse from a sibling. Researchers have found a similar relationship between childhood sexual abuse and adult depression in adult survivors of childhood sexual abuse by adults known to the victim. In a nonclinical sample of 278 university women, 15% had sexual contacts with a significantly older person before the age of 15. Those who had a sexual abuse history showed greater depressive symptomatology than those who had not experienced sexual abuse. Their depression appeared to relate to a sense of powerlessness they felt at the time of the abuse and that they continued to experience in adulthood (Briere & Runtz, 1988).

When the 150 participants in the research discussed here were asked if they had ever been hospitalized for depression, 26% (39) responded affirmatively. Because so large a proportion had been hospitalized for depression, it may be assumed that even more had sought help for depression on an outpatient basis.

Some survivors' depression was so severe that it led to suicide attempts. Over 33% of the sexual abuse survivors reported having attempted suicide. Research reports even higher suicide-attempt rates for victims of sexual abuse by adults (Briere, Evans, Runtz, & Wall, 1988; DeYoung, 1982). When asked how her sexual abuse by a sibling affects her as an adult, a 42-year-old woman responded, "Terribly! I have seriously considered suicide. I experience severe depression requiring medication."

### Posttraumatic Stress Disorder

Survivors reported that they experience anxiety attacks and flashbacks of their abuse by a sibling, which are symptoms of postraumatic stress disorder (PTSD), a psychosocial dysfunctioning experienced by individuals who have been traumatized. Anxiety attacks were reported by survivors when they were in situations with someone wanting to be intimate with them or in more general interpersonal relationships with peers and bosses. The anxiety seemed to be reminiscent of encounters the survivors had with their sibling perpetrator where they felt they could not escape from the physical or sexual abuse that was about to occur. Survivors described flashbacks of their sexual abuse by a brother occurring especially when they were engaged in sexual activity:

*Until recently sexual intercourse was not very enjoyable. Well, I would enjoy it but could never achieve an orgasm. Sometimes sex would become so emotionally upsetting that in the middle of it I would remember the past and the moment would be destroyed and I'd usually cry.*

$$* \qquad\qquad * \qquad\qquad *$$

*Sometimes I will be thinking about what my brother did to me and when my husband approaches me for sex, I will push him away. I find myself daydreaming about the whole nightmare of my sexual abuse. It's like it's still happening and never going to stop.*

Other research shows that a high number of individuals who experienced child sexual abuse also show the symptomatology of PTSD. In one study that assessed 117 help-seeking adult survivors of childhood sexual abuse to determine the relationship between their sexual abuse and PTSD, 72% met full *DSM-III* criteria for current and 85% for lifetime posttraumatic stress disorder, based on PTSD intensity scores (Rodriguez et al., 1996). Other studies have reported a similar relationship between child sexual abuse and posttraumatic stress disorder with in some instances even higher rates (Beitchman, et al., 1992; O'Neill & Gupta, 1991; Saunders, 1991).

## Distinguishing Abusive Behavior from Normal Behavior

This chapter has focused on the abusive behavior of one sibling toward another, including behaviors that involved physical, emotional, and sexual abuse. The question may appropriately be asked whether these behaviors were really abuse or normal sibling interactions or even, in the case of sexual abuse, are some of the actions merely sexual curiosity between siblings?

Some siblings hit, slap, and punch each other. Siblings at times may call each other names. The critical question then is how can one distinguish between normal sibling interactions and sibling abusive behaviors? Four criteria will be presented to answer this question.

A word of caution is in order regarding these criteria. The criteria should not be applied in an "either/or" or absolute manner. Human behavior is very complex and does not lend itself to easy scrutiny. Many shades of gray can be found in sibling interactions, and questions as to whether a specific behavior is abusive will remain. Based on the physical pain and emotional suffering survivors of sibling abuse experienced, it would be wise to err in the direction of protecting the victim in cases of uncertainty.

Before trying to distinguish between normal and abusive behavior, the specific behavior must be identified. The specific behavior may be identified by isolating what is occurring from the emotions surrounding the behavior, such as anger, hurt, or shame. The following are three examples of sibling interactions, each of which illustrates a specific behavior.

**Example 1:** Two siblings, 2 and 4 years old, are constantly fighting over toys. When the 4-year-old chooses a toy with which to play, the 2-year-old wants the same toy. A struggle ensues and one of them, generally the 2-year-old, ends up crying.

**Example 2:** Sue is 14 years old. She is very angry at her parents about the limits they have set on her dating. Her parents require that she do no individual dating but go out with boys only in mixed groups. Also, they have established a weekend evening curfew of 10 p.m. But Mitzi, Sue's 17-year-old sister, is allowed to go on dates alone with a boy to a movie or a school activity. Her weekend curfew is 11 p.m. Sue is very jealous of Mitzi's privileges, and every weekend she reminds her parents about how unfairly they are treating her. Furthermore, the two girls wage a constant battle over this issue. Recently, the parents overheard Sue calling Mitzi "an ugly bitch" after a heated discussion of their different dating privileges,

**Example 3:** A mother notices that her 4-year-old son is fascinated by his new baby sister when her diaper is being changed. He seems very curious about the baby's genital area and is always present when diapers are changed.

What specific behavior is occurring in each of the above examples? In the first example, the behavior is *fighting*, in the second, *name-calling*, and, in the third, *observation*, and although the example does not state this, the 4-year-old boy probably also is *questioning* the mother about the differences in genitalia that he is observing.

### Criterion 1: Is the Behavior Age-Appropriate?

The first criterion for distinguishing abusive behavior from non-abusive behavior is the behavior's age-appropriateness. Consider the first example: Is it appropriate for a 2-year-old and a 4-year-old to be struggling over toys? Yes, it is. The 2-year-old is probably simply mimicking his older sibling in play. With whatever toy his older sibling plays, he too wants to play. It is easier to do what "big brother" is doing, and it is probably more fun, even though "big brother" doesn't feel this way.

Consider the second example. Jealousy and fighting over differences in privileges are quite age-appropriate between adolescents. They are both struggling with their own identities and attempting to try their wings outside the safe nest of their home. Sue, at age 14, does not view herself as less mature than Mitzi and sees no reason why she shouldn't have the same privileges. But name-calling is hardly an appropriate way for Sue to handle her anger, although it is not uncommon.

A word of caution at this point: Even though fighting and jealousy between siblings can be expected to occur, they should not be ignored. Nonabusive behavior can escalate into abusive behavior if effective parental intervention does not occur. Ignoring the behavior will not make it go away. Moreover, constant fighting between siblings is unpleasant not only for those involved but for those around the behavior.

The critical question is how to intervene. For parents who are having difficulty handling dysfunctional sibling interactions, various avenues of assistance are available. Parent education courses are available through community mental health agencies, churches, and other educational resources. Books that focus on sibling relationships are available at bookstores or public libraries, Examples of such books are *Siblings Without Rivalry* (Faber & Mazlish, 1988), *How to Talk So Kids Will Listen & Listen So Kids Will Talk* (Faber & Mazlish, 1982), and *Help! The Kids Are at It Again: Using Kids' Quarrels to Teach People Skills* (Crary, 1997).

Consider the third example: Observation and questioning on the part of a 4-year-old are normal, as is sexual curiosity. The child who has never seen a clitoris may be expected to ask why his sister is different. If the 4-year-old child wants to touch his baby sister's clitoris, an effective parental response may be to differentiate for the child appropriate and inappropriate touches. This example highlights the importance of children having sexual information regarding appropriate and inappropriate touching relevant to their psychosocial development.

Age-appropriate behavior can be determined by professionals with a knowledge of child development and by books on child development (Vander Zanden, 1993; Zastrow & Kirst-Ashman, 1997). Determining what is age-appropriate behavior can also occur through parents talking to other parents and sharing information on their children's behavior. The parents of a mentally retarded child, for example, told their friends that their 4-year-old would sometimes crawl on the floor and bark like a dog or meow like a cat. The parents saw this as an example of his retardation. The friends, however, pointed out that their 4-year-old child, who was not mentally retarded, frequently did the same thing. As a matter of fact, they said he had once asked if he could try eating out of a bowl on the floor like the family pets. Thus, the first set of parents learned that this was age-appropriate behavior for their 4-year-old.

However, some behavioral interactions between siblings are not age-appropriate and should be considered abusive. Consider the following examples. A 10-year-old brother destroys his 3-year-old sister's dolls by pulling out their hair, tearing off a leg or arm, or stabbing them with a knife. An 8-year-old sister composes a song about her younger brother who is overweight. The words make fun of him and call him "tubby." She sings it whenever she is around him and in front of his friends. A 14-year-old boy fondles the genitals of his 3-year-old sister behind a shed in the backyard.

These examples portray three behaviors: the destruction of toys, ridicule through name-calling, and sexual fondling. In light of the age of the participants, especially the perpetrators, these are not age-appropriate behaviors. A 10-year-old boy should have learned to respect the toys of other children and not destroy them. Likewise, an 8-year-old girl may delight in some teasing, but in this instance the teasing is vicious in nature as it is done before her brother's peers. And a boy fondling the genitals of his younger sister is not appropriate behavior at any age. By the age of 14, a boy should be aware of sexual differences between boys and girls and between good touches and secret touches. Moreover, the fact that the behavior is occurring in a clandestine setting implies that the perpetrator has some awareness that the behavior is inappropriate. Also, the younger child is not mature enough to decide whether she wishes to participate.

### Criterion 2: How Often and How Long Has the Behavior Been Occurring?

Fighting, name-calling, teasing, and even some sexual exploration occur between siblings at some time or another and may be considered normal sibling rivalry or simple sexual curiosity. But frequency and duration of the behavior may turn a nonabusive behavior into an abusive one. When fighting, name-calling, teasing, and sexual exploration occur frequently over a long period of time, the behavior becomes abusive, especially if the perpetrator is admonished to stop but doesn't.

This does not mean that a single occurrence of a potentially abusive behavior between siblings, such as sexual activity, should be minimized. In some instances, sexual abuse by a sibling is only a single occurrence, but its effects on the survivor are serious and can affect the individual into adulthood. Recall the survivor who at the age of four was paid a quarter by her older brother for performing oral sex and who complied largely out of fear of retaliation: "I have punished myself for 22 years for taking that quarter from him. I don't like myself." Thus, frequency and duration should not be used as the *only* criteria in determining whether a behavior is abusive.

How long is too long, and how frequently is too frequently? A definite period of time or number of occurrences would be helpful, but such a pat answer is not available. When a child complains on more than one occasion about the behavior of a sibling, the parents should explore the complaint. Likewise, when parents begin to feel uncomfortable about a behavior in which a child is engaging toward a sibling, the time has come to intervene. A critical element in both of these situations is the observation of a *pattern* of behavior that is occurring over a period of time. Ignoring dysfunctional sibling behaviors will not necessarily make them disappear.

## Criterion 3: Is There an Aspect of Victimization in the Behavior?

A *victim* is someone who is an unwilling, nonconsenting object of abusive behavior and is hurt or injured by the action or actions of another. The research respondents who were abused by a sibling think of themselves as *victims* of their sibling's actions. They vividly recalled what they had experienced many years before. They were the targets of their sibling's physical assaults, the butt of their ridicule, or the object of their sexual abuse.

An individual in the victim role may be a dupe or may have been placed in a gullible position by the other person. Many of the respondents, especially those sexually abused by a sibling, had been placed in the victim role because of their powerlessness. They were duped or enticed to participate in sexual activity, were threatened, or were taken advantage of because of their age. These victims often had little choice but to acquiesce to their sibling's sexual demands because they felt there was nothing else they could do or were not mature enough to realize what was happening.

A victim, an unwilling participant, may not even be able to give or withhold consent. The fact that a victim participates in an activity does not mean that the participation was voluntary. A child may be unable to consent verbally to an older sibling's sexual advances because he or she is simply too young. For example, a 2-year-old child is not able to protest her older brother's sexual explorations. Likewise, a mentally retarded or emotionally disturbed adolescent who is the continual object of jokes and ridicule by a sibling may not be able to fend off these verbal assaults.

The question of whether an individual is being victimized can often be determined by assessing how the perpetrator gained access to the individual. If access was gained through game playing, trickery, deceit, bribery, or force, the person who is the object of the behavior is a victim. For example, a 4-year-old girl is bribed with candy to go to a tree house that her brother and his friends have built in the backyard; when she gets there, she is asked to remove her panties and expose herself. An older brother constantly acquires money from a younger sibling on the pretense that the coin size determines its value. In both instances, the sibling is a victim and the behavior is abusive.

Another indication of victimization is the emotions surrounding a behavior that the sibling feels. A sibling called a name by another sibling may experience embarrassment or hurt, yet others who are the targets of name-calling may not be offended by the terms used. A husband and wife, for example, may call each other names that out of context would be offensive but in context are terms of endearment. The emotional reaction of the person who is being called the name may be an important clue as to whether he or she is being put into a victim role.

Individuals who have been targets of abusive behavior may not realize their victimization until long after the act. A prepubertal young girl who is sexually abused by an older sibling may not realize the consequences of the activity in which she is involved. She may become aware of her victimization only after she experiences sexual dysfunctioning in her relationships with the opposite sex or in other problems in living.

Victims commonly blame themselves for their victimization. Many of the respondents to the research not only blamed themselves for what happened but were blamed by the perpetrator or their parents. A parallel may be drawn to wives abused by their husbands. A wife may excuse and thereby tolerate her husband's abusive behavior by telling herself that she deserved his anger because she did not have dinner ready on time or was insensitive to his wishes. That she is a victim may not become clear to her until later when she joins a group for abused women and realizes that she cannot always please her husband, that his expectations are unrealistic, and that his actions are abusive. Sibling abuse victims, too, may have difficulty realizing their victimization if their parents blame them and do not protect them.

### Criterion 4: What Is the Purpose of the Behavior?

The motivation of one sibling to engage in a behavior with another sibling is tied to the purpose the behavior serves.

In most instances of emotional abuse by a sibling, the purpose is to belittle the victim with name-calling or ridicule. This is destructive behavior and therefore abusive. If the victim provoked the perpetrator, both individuals are engaging in abusive behavior and are placing themselves in their roles of victim and perpetrator. Obviously, there are more appropriate ways for siblings to settle differences between themselves. For example, taking a problem-solving approach is an effective way to break abusive behavior between siblings.

When an older sibling, generally a male, sexually abuses a sibling for the purpose of achieving sexual gratification, the purpose of the behavior is not observation but sexual pleasure. Survivors of childhood sexual abuse by a sibling reported that the perpetrator received sexual satisfaction, such as through masturbation, by viewing or touching a younger sibling's genitals. In most instances of sexual abuse reported by these research respondents, the individual who was the target of the behavior was victimized and the behavior was age-inappropriate. Such behavior must be regarded as abuse.

Sexual exploration with the intent of sadism or suffering is also abusive behavior. An older sibling may insert objects into the anus or vagina of a younger sibling with the intention of seeing the sibling suffer. The perpetrator may or may not masturbate. Again, the activity sets one sibling up as a victim.

In some incidents of sexual abuse, an additional person besides the sibling perpetrator may be involved. Children may be requested or forced to engage in sexual activity because it gives a third party sexual gratification. An older sibling, for example, may encourage two younger siblings to engage in sexual play while the older sibling watches. Or one sibling may encourage another to abuse a third sibling physically or emotionally. In these instances, the behavior is abusive because of the purpose the behavior served for the dual perpetrators.

A word of caution on the purpose the behavior serves for the perpetrator: Children are frequently not able to conceptualize the purpose of behaviors in which they engage. When parents ask a young child who has done something with serious consequences "Why did you do that?" the child often responds, "I don't know." Although partially defensive, the response may also indicate that cognitive limitations prevent the child from identifying why he or she did something. Children may not yet perceive cause and effect; rather, they engage in behavior at an impulsive level with little thought for the consequences. Nor have children had the range of experiences that enable them to anticipate consequences, especially undesirable ones. In other words, they lack the maturity to look beyond their own behavior to the consequences.

*Supplementary Questions*

The following questions may also help in distinguishing abusive behavior from normal behavior:

- In what context did the behavior occur?
- What preceded the behavior?
- What was the victim's contribution to what occurred?
- Was the perpetrator imitating something he or she had seen?
- Was the behavior planned or spontaneous?
- Has the behavior ever occurred before?
- How did the victim feel about what occurred?
- What was the perpetrator's reaction to what occurred?
- Has the perpetrator been confronted in the past about this behavior?

## Problem Solving as an Intervention in Sibling Abuse

The acronym SAFE provides a guide for parents to intervene effectively in sibling interactions that have the potential of becoming abusive. Each letter represents a step in the problem-solving process.

"S" stands for *s*top the action and set a climate for problem solving. When two siblings are engaged in hitting, slapping, pushing, name-calling, and other potentially abusive behaviors, it may be necessary for a parent to stop the behavior. Separating the children by having them go to their own rooms or engage in activities by themselves for a period of time may prevent the behavior from escalating into abuse. A climate for problem solving can be set by assuring the siblings that, based on the frequency with which this behavior has occurred, there is a need to discuss their actions toward one another. After dinner or before the family begins to watch TV in the evening may be an appropriate time to sit down together to talk about the behavior and to consider alternatives to resolving the problems that occur between or among the siblings.

"A" stands for *a*ssess what is happening. An assessment should occur in the family meeting of the facts and feelings regarding what happens prior to the siblings becoming embroiled in a conflict and engaging in aversive verbal or physical behavior. All siblings involved in the conflict should talk about what happens as well as how they were feeling at the time and after the conflict.

"F" represents *f*ind out what will work. This is the core of the problem-solving process. The central question is "What can you do to avoid the negative physical and verbal interactions that occur?" Although parents may be tempted to present simple solutions to the problem, they should skillfully involve the children in analyzing the conflicts and what they can do to avoid them. A recent conflict can serve as the basis for this discussion.

In this aspect of the problem-solving process, the family may wish to determine some basic rules that all must follow. For example, no one borrows toys, clothing, or other possessions from another sibling without expressed permission from that person. When the door to a bedroom or bathroom is closed, no one enters without permission from the person in the room. Frequently, conflicts develop around the completion of household chores assigned to siblings such as taking out the trash, setting the table, and washing the dishes. Mounting a chart on the refrigerator clearly identifying who is responsible for what task on what day and establishing consequences for not fulfilling responsibilities often help reduce these conflicts.

"E" stands for *e*valuating a few days or a week later whether or not what was determined in the family problem-solving conference is being implemented. Evaluation is important and may provide clues as to how to fine-tune the outcomes determined in the problem-solving process so as to make them a viable means of preventing sibling rivalry from becoming sibling abuse.

The problem-solving process is not a one-time event for a family; it may need to be used frequently as siblings and parents confront problems in living together. The participation of all family members in the process makes all responsible for their behavior and assists them to function as a family unit with minimal conflict.

## Treating Survivors

Although the treatment of survivors of sibling physical, emotional, and sexual abuse in essence does not differ from the treatment of survivors of adult-child physical, emotional, and sexual abuse, several factors are relevant for mental health professionals working with sibling abuse survivors.

## *Uncovering Sibling Abuse*

Numerous sibling abuse survivors who read my first book on the subject (Wiehe, 1997b) have written expressing appreciation that my research has brought the problem of sibling abuse out into the open. Two words that many survivors used when expressing their appreciation for the research on sibling abuse were that the research *validated* or *affirmed* for them that what they experienced from a sibling as they were growing up was not sibling rivalry but sibling abuse. A survivor from Montana wrote,

> *I am a sibling abuse survivor and can now say that after having found your book in the library and having read it. I have looked for years in the literature for something written about the way my older brother treated me and even today as an adult continues to do so. Even a therapist I went to for a short period of time denied what I experienced was really abuse but "just a bad case of sibling rivalry." Your book affirms for me that I am an abuse survivor and I am now in meaningful therapy with a group of other survivors.*

I include these comments so that mental health professionals can become aware of the confusion that exists over the differences between sibling rivalry and sibling abuse, and even worse, the denial that sibling abuse does occur. This sense of confusion and denial is found not only among parents of victims but even among mental health professionals to whom some survivors turn for treatment for the effects of their abuse by a sibling.

Perhaps what these comments most importantly demonstrate is the need for mental health professionals to be aware that sibling abuse does exist. Evidence of sibling abuse may occur, for example, in family therapy sessions where a therapist, focusing on problems affecting the family as a whole, may overlook and fail to explore the aversive behaviors that are occurring between the siblings. Also, in cases of spousal and child abuse, based on the theory that violence is a learned behavior, exploration of the relationship of the siblings toward each other should occur because the children may be modeling in their relationship to their siblings the behavior that the parents are engaging in with each other and with the children.

Therapists should keep in mind when assessing clients' problems that sibling abuse can be an etiologic factor affecting the problems in living some adults may be experiencing and for which help is being sought. How should an assessment to determine if sibling abuse occurred in childhood be done? A therapist might be tempted to directly ask "Were you ever physically, emotionally, or sexually abused by a sibling?" Experience shows, however, that such a direct question in many instances provokes a defensive denial. Individuals are reluctant to state they are victims of abuse unless the abuse has been very blatant. Also, as the comments of survivors indicate, survivors often do not identify the aversive treatment they experienced from a sibling as abuse, and some survivors blame themselves for the abuse they experienced, thus making them reluctant to say that they were victimized by a sibling.

A more indirect but effective way to assess whether or not sibling abuse occurred is for a therapist to ask a client first to describe pleasant memories they have of their childhood associations with their siblings. Following a discussion of these memories, the therapist should ask the client to describe unpleasant memories of childhood associations with their siblings. The unpleasant memories provide the therapist the opportunity to explore selected memories in depth and to assess whether or not these memories are indicative of abuse. The latter assessment can be made using the criteria previously discussed for distinguishing sibling rivalry from sibling abuse: Were the behaviors age-appropriate? How long and how often did the behavior occur? Was the client a victim of the sibling engaging in the behavior? What purpose did the behavior serve? Such an assessment allows the therapist to determine if physical, emotional, or sexual sibling abuse occurred and if there may be an association between these abusive behaviors experienced by the client and the problems in living that the client is currently experiencing. The identification of effects of sibling abuse discussed earlier may also assist the therapist in the latter task.

## A Differential Effect of Sibling Abuse

Numerous effects of sibling sexual abuse reported by survivors have been identified earlier. However, a significant difference in the context in which sibling sexual abuse occurs as compared to adult-child sexual abuse may create a differential effect in adult survivors. The context in which sibling sexual abuse occurs is usually that of a threat. Recall the comments of survivors in earlier sections of this chapter who reported that their older brothers threatened to harm them in various ways or to make their sexual victimization look as if it were their fault if the victimization became known to the parents. Yet, because most perpetrators of adult-child sexual abuse, whether intra- or extrafamilial, are known to the victim, the context in which the sexual abuse occurs usually involves the victim implicitly trusting the perpetrator because of the loving relationship between the two persons, such as a grandfather and his granddaughter, or because of the authority role of the perpetrator, such as the scout leader and a scout. The loving relationship context may be reinforced by the perpetrator giving the victim gifts, such as candy, special favors, or privileges. This violation of trust that occurs in adult-child sexual abuse significantly affects the survivor's ability to trust others (Agosta & Loring, 1988).

Because sibling sexual abuse generally occurs in the context of a threat, the victim becomes entrapped in the desire to please the perpetrator or feels that she must comply for the sake of her own safety (Summit, 1983). The outcome of this scenario for adult survivors of sibling sexual abuse frequently is self-blame for allowing oneself to become entrapped. There initially may be denial that sexual abuse occurred or a reluctance to discuss the victimization because the survivor is embarrassed that she allowed the abuse to occur. (Thus, the manner in which sibling abuse is assessed, as discussed earlier, is important to the information the therapist can gather.) Regarding the survivor's self-blame for the sexual abuse, in reality she may have had no choice but to comply because, developmentally speaking, she cognitively did not understand what was happening, was operating under a threat, or had not been empowered by her parents to prevent sexual victimization.

One effect of this context of fear in which sibling sexual abuse occurs is that the adult survivor expresses a fear of others, especially individuals who represent power or authority, such as teachers and employment supervisors. One adult survivor of sexual abuse reported that she changed jobs, and in some instances even cities where she lived, over six times in the space of a few years. Her fear of authority and her need to please her superiors at work were so intense that she misinterpreted any criticism as failure and reacted with fear, with the result that she would defensively take flight and seek other employment and even residency. She reported that until she sought therapy for the effects of the abuse, she was not aware of the intense fear that she was living under that pervaded many of her adult interpersonal relationships.

476

## Substance Abuse

Numerous survivors of sibling abuse reported that they were experiencing problems with drugs and alcohol as an effect of their abuse. Although the participants in this research were adults (average age 37), the problem of substance abuse may have started much earlier in life, considering the participants experienced their abuse as young children. Other research also reports a significant relationship between adolescent chemical dependency and a history of abuse. For example, a review of 250 cases at a rural midwestern chemical dependency treatment center revealed that 70% of the patients had some history of abuse, with 27% having experienced child/adolescent physical abuse and 9% sexual abuse (Potter-Efron & Potter-Efron, 1985). Other studies have likewise found high rates of abuse in chemically dependent adolescents (e.g., Cavaiola & Schiff, 1989).

Therapists treating chemically dependent adolescents may wish to pay close attention in their assessment to the possibility of abuse perpetrated by a parent, another adult, or even a sibling. Cavaiola and Schiff (1989), based on their study of chemically dependent adolescents who were abused, provide insight for mental health professionals treating such clients:

> *While alcohol and drugs may play a self-enhancing role in chemical dependence, it appears that for the abused chemically dependent adolescent, the self-enhancement or self-medicating role of these chemicals is short-lived. In these adolescents the chemical dependence is the first layer of defense; it must be removed before an attempt can be made to work through the repetitive trauma of abuse. This work is similar to working with a burn victim or multiple surgical case because of difficult scarring and adhesions. The therapeutic work is long-term and enduring in nature. (p. 333)*

Cavaiola and Schiff also caution that chemically dependent adolescents do not readily reveal having been abused. The researchers report that, on average, the abused adolescents did not disclose the specifics of their abuse trauma until approximately the fourth week of residential chemical dependence treatment. The abuse and chemical dependency wreaked havoc on the adolescents' self-esteem. The struggle for appropriate self-esteem, sobriety, and recovery from victimization can be a lifelong process for these adolescents (Cavaiola & Schiff, 1989).

### Stages of Therapy

The stages that survivors go through in therapy for the sexual abuse they experienced from an adult as a child (Sgroi, 1989c) are very similar to those for sibling abuse survivors, with slight modifications due to the context in which the abuse occurs, as discussed earlier. These stages are acknowledging the reality of the abuse, overcoming secondary responses to the abuse, forgiving oneself (ending self-blame and punishment), adopting positive coping behaviors, and relinquishing survivor identity. They do not necessarily occur in an orderly fashion with one following the other but may occur in a cyclical manner with repetitions or with survivors reworking aspects of an earlier stage later in therapy.

#### Acknowledging the Reality of the Abuse

As discussed earlier, this is perhaps the most critical aspect of sibling abuse because of the denial from significant other persons in the survivor's life that the aversive behaviors experienced from a sibling as a child was really abuse. Following exploration of these behaviors, the therapist's validation or affirmation of them by labeling them abusive can free up the survivor's emotional energy to begin coping with the effects of the abuse.

Various protective coping mechanisms are used by survivors in order to deny the reality of the abuse they experienced (Sgroi & Bunk, 1988). These mechanisms consume enormous amounts of emotional energy. Protective coping mechanisms include distancing oneself from emotions associated with the abuse, such as fear, shame, or anger; continually giving to and caring for others but not allowing oneself to accept nurturance, as often seen in a constant activity or "busyness" in life; denying the seriousness of the abuse experienced or even denying that the events occurred; and self-blame for what happened.

#### Overcoming Secondary Responses to the Abuse

In this stage of recovery, denial of abuse at the time of the event is distinguished from *contemporary denial* occurring in therapy. In contemporary denial, the survivor continues to deny or excuse what happened as abuse. Support for this denial may come from family members when told the survivor is seeking therapy for childhood abuse, or it comes from the perpetrator when asked to apologize and assume responsibility for his or her behavior. Group therapy is helpful to survivors in this recovery stage, for they can confront each other about the defensive mechanisms they are engaging in based on their own personal experiences in going through this therapeutic stage (Sgroi, 1989c).

## Forgiving Oneself

In this stage of the therapeutic process, if survivors are able to forgive themselves for the abuse that occurred and relinquish self-blame, a freeing-up process occurs. Sgroi (1989c) identifies specifically how this process occurs in the context of group therapy:

- The survivor receives acceptance of the validity of one's childhood victimization and current responses to it.

- Caring from others is also received, coupled with a message that the survivor is viewed by other members of the group as good and not blameworthy or deserving of punishment for the abuse experienced.

- The survivor receives feedback from group members regarding their self-blaming and self-punishing behaviors.

- Concrete suggestions for substituting self-blaming behaviors with self-affirming behaviors are also received by the survivor in the context of the group members' wishes that the survivor will choose to stop practicing self-punishment.

- Group members extend forgiveness to the survivor for the childhood sexual victimization and current secondary responses to it. This stage in the therapeutic process represents a recognition that the survivor has become a self-abuser and now is ready to move away from that emotional state.

## Adopting Positive Coping Behaviors

Exploration focuses on alternative ways to handle the effects of the abuse. This may include acknowledging the futility of getting family members and especially the perpetrator to recognize that what the survivor experienced was abuse. Those who participated in the research reported here experienced frustration in trying to get their perpetrator to acknowledge responsibility for his or her sexual abuse of them and finally concluding that distancing themselves from the perpetrator and even other family members who were supportive of the perpetrator's denial was a more effective way of coping with the abuse.

479

*Relinquishing Survivor Identity*

Sgroi (1989c) states this stage can be summarized in the following comment a survivor may make who has successfully completed the therapeutic process:

> I am a human being, a person with strengths and weaknesses, good qualities and faults; a person who makes mistakes but also has useful and positive accomplishments. I was sexually abused when I was a child and that is an important part of my history. But that was then; this is now, and I no longer need to identify myself as a survivor. Instead it is more accurate for me simply to identify myself as a person and a self—no more and no less." (p. 128)

## Preventing Sibling Abuse

How can sibling abuse be prevented? Survivors suggested several ways in which this can occur.

### *Building Awareness of the Problem*

Nearly every survivor commented that people must be made aware that sibling abuse does occur and that all interactions between or among siblings do not fall under the category of normal sibling rivalry. Respondents also emphasized that sibling abuse can occur in any family regardless of socioeconomic status, race, or religion. Sibling abuse is more likely to occur in multiproblem or dysfunctional families; however, no family with more than one child is entirely exempt from the problem. Although it was not possible to determine the socioeconomic background of the survivors participating in this research at the time they were abused by a sibling, the respondents appeared to have come from middle-income families because their parents were quite well educated, with 43% having attended college or graduate school. The survivors also rated their families as moderately religious, as evident in this comment: "My problem and others is that we come from religious, 'looking good' families on the outside but where there was a lot of pain and dysfunctioning on the inside."

## *Listening to Children and Believing Them*

The sibling abuse survivors participating in the research frequently lamented their parents' reaction to the abuse, as the following comments reflect:

*If only my parents had listened to me. If only they had believed me when I told them what was happening.*

*          *          *

*I would tell my mother about the way my brothers were treating me, but she always brushed it off. I really don't think she cared what they did. At least that's the message I got from her. It didn't pay for me to tell her my troubles.*

Research on reports of children being sexually abused by adults has found that an overwhelming majority of the reports are true. Actually, very few reports that children make about being sexually abused by an adult are false. For example, when the cases of 287 children who alleged they had been sexually abused were reviewed, only 28 (less than 9%) could not be substantiated (Cantrell, 1981). Children may report their sexual abuse rather tentatively and over a period of time, but parents should not regard that the report is not true (Gonzalez et al., 1993).

## *Providing Good Supervision to Children in the Absence of Parents*

Sibling abuse occurred most frequently when an older sibling was baby-sitting a younger sibling after school before the parents arrived home from work or in the evening when the parents went away. One survivor stated,

*Parents should wake up and realize that just because a child is the oldest doesn't mean they can take care of the younger children. My folks would always leave us with my older sister. This is when I and my other brothers and sisters suffered. My sister felt she could do anything she wanted to us. She did.*

It may be appropriate for an older brother or sister to act as a baby-sitter when the parents go away for an evening, but the parents must provide an environment in which this sibling can appropriately and effectively act as a substitute parent. Optimally, parents should discuss with the sibling in charge as well as with other siblings the rights and responsibilities of each—for example, the appliances they may use, their bedtime, and whether or not friends are allowed to visit. Equally important, parents should evaluate how effectively the older sibling handled his or her responsibilities while they were gone. This evaluation should not occur in the presence of all the siblings because sibling sexual abuse often occurs in the context of a threat. A younger sibling, when asked by her parents how an older sibling functioned as a baby-sitter, may not be able to reveal what happened for fear of retaliation from the older sibling.

Communities can provide parents who must work latchkey programs after school, thereby avoiding placing siblings in charge of each other. These programs are often government subsidized or operated by parent organizations and may be located in a school or a neighborhood church. Latchkey programs provide children a snack after school, supervised recreation, and assistance with homework. Often, these programs are free to low-income parents or have a sliding-scale fee to make them affordable. Parents can find out about them from their local child care resource and referral agency. Some communities have established telephone support services for children who are home alone after school. Staffed by volunteers, the services can handle a wide range of children's problems, including those with siblings.

### Giving Children Appropriate Sex Instruction

Information about sexuality appropriate to a child's age and developmental stage is important in preventing sibling abuse. Providing information about sexuality is not a one-time event but must be imparted at different times in a child's life, appropriate to the age of the child and the age of the siblings with whom the child interacts. Such instruction empowers children to be in control of their sexuality and decreases the chance for sexual victimization.

A positive attitude about sex also implies that individuals have a right to privacy or times and places where they can be alone. Parents, for example, must set rules or expectations about privacy in the use of a bathroom, a setting for sexual abuse mentioned by several research respondents.

A healthy attitude about sex also implies that parents respond appropriately when sexuality is debased in films, videos, and TV programs, in sexually slanted innuendoes that one sibling may make toward another, and in sexually oriented jokes. The survivors of sexual abuse indicated that their parents' failure to confront these factors, especially the sexual innuendoes of a sibling, established a climate in the family in which sexual abuse would be tolerated. The survivors appeared to be saying that because their parents allowed these unhealthy aspects of sexuality to exist in the family, the perpetrator perceived that the sexual abuse of another sibling might also be tolerated.

## Giving Children Permission to Own Their Own Bodies

Children have a right to own their own bodies. They have the right to be hugged, kissed, and touched in appropriate places on their bodies in an appropriate manner by appropriate people. The converse is equally true. Children have the right *not* to be hugged, kissed, or touched in inappropriate places on their bodies in an inappropriate manner by inappropriate people. Thus, children must be given permission to say no to inappropriate and especially secret touches. Programs with these goals in mind are being effectively conducted in many schools throughout the country.

## Violence-Proofing the Home

Society is very violent, as seen daily on television, movies, and videos and in newspapers and magazines. Just as a room can be made soundproof or a building waterproof, so can parents strive to violence-proof the home. Obviously, a family cannot keep out every mention of violence; however, parents can develop a sensitivity to the violence that enters the home, such as through television or videos. Violence begets violence, and a constant exposure to violence not only desensitizes children to violence but may even act as a stimulus to engage in violent (abusive) behavior toward siblings.

Another important way that parents can help reduce violence is to be sensitive to how siblings treat each other. Verbal put-downs of one sibling by another (emotional abuse) are often a prelude to physical abuse. Put-downs that are gender associated can be a prelude to sexual abuse in which a brother inappropriately assumes the right and power to dominate and abuse a sister.

Nor should pushing, shoving, hitting, or other acts of violence go unnoticed or tolerated. Children can be given the message, in a nurturing context, that physical abuse is an unacceptable form of behavior and that when differences occur, problem solving is the appropriate way to handle disagreements.

## Summary

Research has shown that violence between siblings occurs more frequently than that between spouses and between parents and children. Yet this type of violence, termed sibling abuse, has largely gone unnoticed. Adult survivors of childhood abuse by a sibling report that the abuse adversely affected their lives, for they often experience low self-esteem, depression, problems with drugs and alcohol, and problems in interpersonal relationships. Parents can effectively intervene in sibling abuse by first being aware that not all interactions are simply attributable to sibling rivalry. A problem-solving approach can help siblings resolve differences that normally occur in any family, thus reducing the chances of normal sibling rivalry escalating into sibling abuse.

## References

Adler, N., and J. Schutz. "Sibling Incest Offenders." *Child Abuse & Neglect* 19 (1995): 811–19.

Agosta, C., and M. Loring. "Understanding and Treating the Adult Retrospective Victim of Child Abuse," 115–35. In S. Sgroi, ed. *Vulnerable Populations*. Volume 1. Lexington, Mass.: Lexington Books, 1988.

Bagley, C., and R. Ramsay. "Sexual Abuse in Childhood: Psychosocial Outcomes and Implications for Social Work Practice." *Journal of Social Work and Human Sexuality* 4 (1986): 33–47.

Bakan, D. *Slaughter of the Innocents*. San Francisco: Jossey-Bass, 1971.

"Battered Families: A Growing Nightmare." *U.S. News & World Report* (January 1979): 60, 61.

Becker, J., M. Kaplan, B. Cunningham-Rathner, and R. Kavoussi. "Characteristics of Adolescent Incest Sexual Perpetrators." *Journal of Family Violence* 1 (1986): 85–97.

Beitchman, J., K. Zucker, J. Hood, G. DaCosta, D. Akman, and E. Cassavia. "A Review of the Long-Term Effects of Child Sexual Abuse." *Child Abuse & Neglect* 16 (1992): 101–18.

Berne, E. *Games People Play*. New York: Grove, 1967.

Blume, E. "The Walking Wounded: Post-Incest Syndrome." *SIECUS Report XV* 1 (September 1986): 5–7.

Boyd, C., F. Blow, and L. Orgain. "Gender Differences among African-American Women Substance Abusers." *Journal of Psychoactive Drugs* 25 (1993): 301–05.

Boyd, C., B. Guthrie, J. Pohl, J. Whitmarsh, and D. Henderson. "African-American Women Who Smoke Crack Cocaine: Sexual Trauma and the Mother-Daughter Relationship." *Journal of Psychoactive Drugs* 26 (1994): 243–47.

Brassard, M., and M. Galardo. "Psychological Maltreatment: The Unifying Construct in Child Abuse and Neglect." *School Psychology Review* 16 (1987): 127–36.

Briere, J. *The Effects of Childhood Sexual Abuse on Later Psychological Functioning: Defining a Post-Sexual Abuse Syndrome*. Paper presented at the National Conference on Sexual Victimization of Children, Washington, D.C., May 1984.

Briere, J., D. Evans, M. Runtz, and T. Wall. "Symptomatology in Men Who Were Molested as Children: A Comparison Study." *American Journal of Orthopsychiatry* 58 (1988): 457–61.

Briere, J., and M. Runtz. "Symptomatology Associated with Prior Sexual Abuse in a Nonclinical Sample." *Child Abuse & Neglect* 12 (1988): 51–59.

Briere, J., and M. Runtz. "Differential Adult Symptomatologies Associated with Three Types of Child Abuse Histories." *Child Abuse & Neglect* 14 (1990): 357–64.

Cantrell, H. "Sexual Abuse of Children in Denver, 1979: Reviewed with Implications for Pediatric Intervention and Possible Prevention." *Child Abuse & Neglect* 5 (1981): 75–85.

Cavaiola, A., and M. Schiff. "Self-Esteem in Abused Chemically Dependent Adolescents." *Child Abuse & Neglect* 13 (1989): 327–34.

Claussen, A., and P. Crittenden. "Physical and Psychological Maltreatment: Relations among Types of Maltreatment." *Child Abuse & Neglect* 15 (1991): 5–18.

Cole, A. *Brother-Sister Sexual Abuse: Experiences, Feeling Reactions, and a Comparison to Father-Daughter Sexual Abuse*. Unpublished doctoral dissertation, Union Institute, Cincinnati, Ohio, 1990.

Corson, J., and H. Davidson. "Emotional Abuse and the Law," 185–202. In M. Brassard, R. Germain, and S. Hart, eds. *The Psychological Maltreatment of Children and Youth*. Elmsford, N.Y.: Pergamon, 1987.

Covington, S., and J. Kohen. "Women, Alcohol, and Sexuality." *Advances in Alcohol and Substance Abuse* 4 (1984): 41–56.

Crary, E. *Help! The Kids Are at It Again: Using Kids' Quarrels to Teach People Skills*. Seattle, Wash.: Parenting Press, 1997.

De Young, M. *The Sexual Victimization of Children*. Jefferson, N.C.: McFarland, 1982.

Doyle, C. "Sexual Abuse by Siblings: The Victims' Perspectives." *Journal of Sexual Aggression* 2 (1996): 17–32.

Dubowitz, H., M. Black, D. Harrington, and A. Verschoore. "A Follow-Up Study of Behavior Problems Associated with Child Sexual Abuse." *Child Abuse & Neglect* 17 (1993): 743–54.

Faber, A., and E. Mazlish. *How To Talk So Kids Will Listen & Listen So Kids Will Talk*. New York: Avon, 1982.

Faber, A., and E. Mazlish. *Siblings Without Rivalry: How to Help Your Children Live Together So You Can Live Too*. New York: Avon, 1988.

Faller, K. "Characteristics of a Clinical Sample of Sexually Abused Children: How Boy and Girl Victims Differ." *Child Abuse & Neglect* 13 (1989): 281–91.

Farrell, L. "The Touching Truth about Tickling." *Mademoiselle* (April 1985): 54, 56.

Felson, R., and N. Russo. "Parental Punishment and Sibling Aggression." *Social Psychology Quarterly* 51 (1988): 11–18.

Finkelhor, D. *Child Sexual Abuse: New Theory and Research*. New York: Free Press, 1984.

Finkelhor, D. *Sexually Victimized Children*. New York: Free Press, 1979.

Finkelhor, D. "Sex among Siblings: A Study of Prevalence, Variety, and Effects." *Archives of Sexual Behavior* 9 (1980): 171–93.

Finkelhor, D., and L. Baron. "Risk Factors for Child Sexual Abuse." *Journal of Interpersonal Violence* 1 (1986): 43–71.

Garbarino, J. "The Human Ecology of Child Maltreatment: A Conceptual Model for Research." *Journal of Marriage and the Family* 39 (1977): 721–35.

Garbarino, J., E. Guttman, and J. Seeley. *The Psychologically Battered Child*. San Francisco: Jossey-Bass, 1986.

Garbarino, J., and J. Vondra. "Psychological Maltreatment: Issues and Perspectives," 25-44. In M. Brassard, R. Germain, and S. Hart, eds. *The Psychological Maltreatment of Children and Youth*. Elmsford, N.Y.: Pergamon, 1987.

Gebhard, P., J. Gagnon, W. Pomeroy, and C. Christianson. *Sex Offenders: An Analysis of Types*. New York: Harper & Row, 1965.

Gonzalez, L., J. Waterman, R. Kelly, J. McCord, and M. Oliveri. "Children's Patterns of Disclosures and Recantations of Sexual and Ritualistic Abuse Allegations in Psychotherapy." *Child Abuse & Neglect* 17 (1993): 281–89.

Goodwin, J. *Sexual Abuse: Incest Victims and Their Families*. Boston: John W. Wright, 1982.

Harrison, P., J. Fulkerson, and T. Beebe. "Multiple Substance Abuse among Adolescent Physical and Sexual Abuse Victims." *Child Abuse & Neglect* 21 (1997): 529–39.

Hart, S., and M. Brassard. "A Major Threat to Children's Mental Health—Psychological Maltreatment." *American Psychologist* 42 (1987): 160–65.

Herman, J., and L. Hirschman. "Father-Daughter Incest." *Signs: Journal of Women in Culture and Society* 4 (1977): 735–56.

Hughes, H., D. Parkinson, and M. Vargo. "Witnessing Spouse Abuse and Experiencing Physical Abuse: A 'Double Whammy'?" *Journal of Family Violence* 4 (1989): 197–209.

Huston, A., E. Donnerstein, H. Fairchild, N. Feshbach, P. Katz, J. Murray, E. Rubenstein, B. Wilcox, and D. Zuckerman. *Big World, Small Screen: The Role of Television in American Society*. Lincoln, Neb.: University of Nebraska Press, 1992.

Irwin, A., and A. Gross. "Cognitive Tempo, Violent Video Games, and Aggressive Behavior in Young Boys." *Journal of Family Violence* 10 (1995): 337–50.

Janus, M. "On Early Victimization and Adolescent Male Prostitution." *SIECUS Report XII* 1 (September 1984): 8–9.

Jouriles, E., J. Barling, and K. O'Leary. "Predicting Child Behavior Problems in Maritally Violent Families." *Journal of Abnormal Child Psychology* 15 (1987): 165–73.

Justice, B., and R. Justice. *The Broken Taboo: Sex in the Family*. New York: Human Sciences Press, 1979.

Kinzl, J., C. Traweger, and W. Biebl. "Sexual Dysfunctions: Relationship to Childhood Sexual Abuse and Early Family Experiences in a Nonclinical Sample." *Child Abuse & Neglect* 19 (1995): 785–92.

Kurtz, P., J. Gaudin, J. Wodarski, and P. Howing. "Maltreatment and the School-Aged Child: School Performance Consequences." *Child Abuse & Neglect* 17 (1993): 581–89.

Laviola, M. "Effects of Older Brother-Younger Sister Incest: A Study of the Dynamics of 17 Cases." *Child Abuse & Neglect* 16 (1992): 409–21.

Loredo, C. "Sibling Incest," 177-88. In S. Sgroi, ed. *Handbook of Clinical Intervention in Child Sexual Abuse*. Lexington, Mass.: D. C. Heath, 1982.

McGuire, L., and N. Wagner. "Sexual Dysfunction in Women Who Were Molested as Children: One Response Pattern and Suggestions for Treatment." *Journal of Sex & Marital Therapy* 1 (1978): 11–15.

Meiselman, L. *Incest: A Psychological Study of Causes and Effects with Treatment Recommendations*. San Francisco: Jossey-Bass, 1978.

Meuenzenmaier, K., I. Meyer, E. Struening, and J. Ferber. "Childhood Abuse and Neglect among Women Outpatients with Chronic Mental Illness." *Hospital and Community Psychiatry* 44 (1993): 666–70.

Miller, D., K. McCluskey-Fawcett, and L. Irving. "The Relationship between Childhood Sexual Abuse and Subsequent Onset of Bulimia Nervosa." *Child Abuse & Neglect* 17 (1993): 305–14.

Moeller, T., G. Bachmann, and J. Moeller. "The Combined Effects of Physical, Sexual, and Emotional Abuse During Childhood: Long-Term Health Consequences for Women." *Child Abuse & Neglect* 17 (1993): 623–40.

Mullen, P., J. Martin, J. Anderson, S. Romans, and G. Herbison. "The Long-Term Impact of the Physical, Emotional, and Sexual Abuse of Children: A Community Study." *Child Abuse & Neglect* 20 (1996): 7–21.

Navarre, E. "Psychological Maltreatment: The Core Component of Child Abuse," 45-56. In M. Brassard, R. Germain, and S. Hart, eds. *The Psychological Maltreatment of Children and Youth.* Elmsford, N.Y.: Pergamon, 1987.

O'Brien, M. "Taking Sibling Incest Seriously," 75-92. In M. Patton, ed. *Family Sexual Abuse: Frontline Research and Evaluation.* Newbury Park, Calif.: Sage, 1991.

O'Keefe, M. "Predictors of Child Abuse in Maritally Violent Families." *Journal of Interpersonal Violence* 10 (1995): 3–25.

O'Neill, K., and K. Gupta. "Posttraumatic Stress Disorder in Women Who Were Victims of Childhood Sexual Abuse." *Irish Journal of Psychological Medicine* 8 (1991): 124–27.

Paik, H., and G. Comstock. "The Effects of Television Violence on Antisocial Behavior: A Meta-Analysis." *Communication Research* 21 (1994): 516–46.

Parke, R., and C. Collmer. "Child Abuse: An Interdisciplinary Analysis," 509-90. In E. Hetherington, ed. *Child Development Research.* Chicago: University of Chicago Press, 1975.

Patterson, G. *Coercive Family Process.* Eugene, Ore.: Castalia, 1982.

Petronio, S., H. Reeder, M. Hecht, and T. Ros-Mendoza. "Disclosure of Sexual Abuse by Children and Adolescents." *Journal of Applied Communication Research* 24 (1996): 181–99.

Potter-Efron, R., and P. Potter-Efron. "Family Violence as a Treatment Issue with Chemically Dependent Adolescents." *Alcoholism Treatment Quarterly* 2 (1985): 1–5.

Rodriguez, N., S. Ryan, A. Rowan, and D. Foy. "Posttraumatic Stress Disorder in a Clinical Sample of Adult Survivors of Childhood Sexual Abuse." *Child Abuse & Neglect* 20 (1996): 943–52.

Rosencrans, B. *The Last Secret: Daughters Sexually Abused by Mothers.* Brandon, Vt.: Safer Society Press, 1997.

Ross, S. "Risk of Physical Abuse to Children of Spouse-Abusing Parents." *Child Abuse & Neglect* 20 (1996): 589–98.

Royse, D. *Research Methods in Social Work.* Chicago: Nelson-Hall, 1995.

Russell, D. *The Secret Trauma.* New York: Basic Books, 1986.

Sarwer, D., and J. Durlak. "Childhood Sexual Abuse as a Predictor of Adult Female Sexual Dysfunction: A Study of Couples Seeking Sex Therapy." *Child Abuse & Neglect* 20 (1996): 963–72.

Saunders, E. "Rorschach Indicators of Chronic Childhood Sexual Abuse in Female Borderline Patients." *Bulletin of the Menninger Clinic* 55 (1991): 48–71.

Scott, R., and H. Day. "Association of Abuse-Related Symptoms and Style of Anger Expression for Female Survivors of Childhood Incest." *Journal of Interpersonal Violence* 11 (1996): 208–20.

Sgroi, S. "Stages of Recovery for Adult Survivors of Child Sexual Abuse," 111-30. In S. Sgroi, ed. *Vulnerable Populations*. Volume 2. Lexington, Mass: Lexington Books, 1989.

Sgroi, S., and B. Bunk. "A Clinical Approach to Adult Survivors of Child Sexual Abuse," 137-86. In S. Sgroi, ed. *Vulnerable Populations*. Volume 1. Lexington, Mass: Lexington Books, 1988.

Sgroi, S., B. Bunk, and C. Wabrek. "Children's Sexual Behaviors and Their Relationship to Sexual Abuse," 137-86. In S. Sgroi, ed. *Vulnerable Populations*. Volume 1. Lexington, Mass.: Lexington Books, 1988.

Silbert, M., and A. Pines. "Early Sexual Exploitation as an Influence in Prostitution." *Social Work* 2 (1983): 285–89.

Silverman, A., H. Reinherz, and R. Giaconia. "The Long-Term Sequelae of Child and Adolescent Abuse: A Longitudinal Community Study." *Child Abuse & Neglect* 20 (1996): 709–23.

Smith, H., and E. Israel. "Sibling Incest: A Study of the Dynamics of 25 Cases." *Child Abuse & Neglect* 11 (1987): 101–08.

Steinmetz, S. *The Cycle of Violence: Assertive, Aggressive, and Abusive Family Interaction*. New York: Praeger, 1977.

Straus, M. A., R. J. Gelles, and S. K. Steinmetz. *Behind Closed Doors: Violence in the American Family*. Garden City, N.Y.: Anchor, 1980.

Suh, E., and E. Abel. "The Impact of Spousal Violence on the Children of the Abused." *Journal of Independent Social Work* 4 (1990): 27–34.

Summit, R. "Child Sexual Abuse Accommodation Syndrome." *Child Abuse & Neglect* 7 (1983): 177–93.

Summit, R., and J. Kryso. "Sexual Abuse of Children: A Clinical Spectrum." *American Journal of Orthopsychiatry* 48 (1978): 237–51.

Sutphen, R., V. Wiehe, and C. Leukefeld. *Dual Violence Families: The Relationship between Spouse Abuse, Child Abuse and Substance Abuse*. Paper presented at the National Conference on Child Abuse and Neglect, Washington, D.C., September 1996.

Teets, J. "Childhood Sexual Trauma of Chemically Dependent Women." *Journal of Psychoactive Drugs* 27 (1995): 231–38.

Vander Zanden, J. *Human Development*. New York: Knopf, 1993.

Walker, L. *Abused Women and Survivor Therapy: A Practical Guide for the Psychotherapist*. Washington, D.C.: American Psychological Association, 1994.

Widom, C., T. Ireland, and P. Glynn. "Alcohol Abuse in Abused and Neglected Children Followed Up: Are They at Increased Risk?" *Journal of Studies on Alcohol* 56 (1995): 207–17.

Wiehe, V. *Multiple-Violence Families*. Paper presented at the Conference on Vulnerable Families, Seattle, Wash., April 1997a.

Wiehe, V. *Sibling Abuse: The Hidden Physical, Emotional, and Sexual Trauma*. Second edition. Thousand Oaks, Calif.: Sage, 1997b.

Wiehe, V. "Child Abuse: An Ecological Perspective," 139–47. In R. Pardeck, ed. *Child Abuse and Neglect: Theory, Research and Practice*. New York: Gordon & Breach, 1989.

Wonderlich, S., M. Donaldson, D. Carson, D. Staton, L. Gertz, L. Leach, and M. Johnson. "Eating Disturbance and Incest." *Journal of Interpersonal Violence* 11 (1996): 195–207.

Worling, J. "Adolescent Sibling-Incest Offenders: Differences in Family and Individual Functioning When Compared to Adolescent Nonsibling Sex Offenders." *Child Abuse & Neglect* 19 (1995): 633–43.

Zastrow, C., and K. Kirst-Ashman. *Understanding Human Behavior and the Social Environment*. Fourth edition. Chicago: Nelson-Hall, 1997.

Chapter 19

# Parent Abuse

*Richard J. Gelles*

## Parent Abuse

The idea of children attacking their parents is so foreign to our conceptions of parent-child relations that it is difficult for most of us to believe that such behavior occurs. Parents are granted the position of authority and power in the family's status hierarchy. Parents command control of the family's resources, such as money, power, status, and violence. According to the sociologist William Goode, violence is a legitimate resource at the disposal of family members, and it will be used whenever other attempts at alleviating a conflict fail. It is logically assumed, however, that the use of violence to resolve conflicts is brought into play by the typically dominant members of the family to ensure submission of those in their care. Goode argues that wives and children could, and sometimes do, use force but it does not occur frequently due to greater normative disapproval of children and wives using force against the father or husband.

> The rebellious child or wife knows the father or husband is stronger, and can call on outsiders who will support that force with more force... The force or threat they command is not only

their own strength but that of the community, which will back up the traditional family patterns. (Goode, 1971, pp. 625–26)

The societal attitudes concerning who uses violence within the family partially explains why this form of violence has been one of the least researched and consequently why, until recently, not very much was known about its extent, patterns, and causes.

Goode's (1971) quote alludes to other social attitudes that hinder recognition of parent abuse as a hidden form of family violence. Not only do children lack control of the family's resources, but they are also thought of as smaller and having less physical strength. This observation alone is enough to make us think that children are not physically capable of injuring their parents. However, what research is available graphically demonstrates that children can and do inflict injury on their parents. For example, one clinical study reports on the case of an 11-year-old boy who became aggressive toward his mother after she spanked him for disobeying orders. He reportedly pushed her down, broke her coccyx, and then proceeded to kick her in the face while she was on the floor (Harbin & Madden, 1979). Carol Warren (1978), in her investigation of 15 battering adolescents between the ages of 12 and 17 who were admitted to a psychiatric hospital, found that what these children lacked in physical strength, they more than made up for with speed and weapons. One 12-year-old "poured gasoline in the bathroom while his mother was in there, threw in a match, and shut the door" (p. 6). These examples demonstrate that physical size and strength are not always the best indicator as to who will be violent in a family.

Goode (1971) also quite accurately states that there is greater normative disapproval of children using violence against a parent than of a parent using violence against their children. The community supports parental rights and obligations while imposing strong sanctions against children who violate traditional family patterns concerning the legitimate use of force. Children abusing their parents is so counter-normative that it is extremely difficult for parents to admit that they are being victimized by one of their children. Unless the children commit lethal acts or acts of extreme violence, it is rare that the behavior of violent children and adolescents comes to the public's attention. Discussion and reporting of such acts is almost a taboo subject because many parents are ashamed of their own victimization. Parents are afraid that others will blame them for their children's violent behavior. Parents of abusive children are believed to suffer from tremendous anxiety, depression, and guilt. Henry Harbin and Dennis Madden (1979) examined 15 families identified as having an adolescent between the ages of 14 and 20 who was assaulting a parent. All these families were trying desperately to maintain an illusion of family harmony. Parents would occasionally admit to being abused by their children immediately following a particularly aggressive episode, but the "veil of denial" would rapidly reappear. Parents would try endlessly to protect their abusive offspring. Harbin and Madden identified four ways in which the veil of denial and protection manifested itself: (a) the families would try to avoid all discussion of the violent episodes, (b) all the family members would attempt to minimize the seriousness of the aggressive behavior, (c) the parents would avoid punishment for the abusive behavior, and (d) the families refused to ask for outside help for either themselves or for their child. The role of denial and the creation of an image of a peaceful and loving family plays an important part in abusive families. This role allows the family to continue functioning even though the family must continually deny the reality of violence (Ferreira, 1963). Admission of violent behavior on the part of the offspring or the parent may introduce the threat of family separation. The denial of reality serves as a defense mechanism to protect the family from outside observers and influence.

## *Extent of Violence Toward Parents*

The investigations of violence toward parents that have been conducted all report the same result: The rate of child-to-parent violence, although less than parent-to-child abuse, is large enough to warrant attention. The U.S. Department of Justice (1980) estimated that of the 1.2 million incidents of violence between relatives, 47,000 involved children's violence against parents. An examination of restraining order defendants in Massachusetts found that almost one-third of all the restraining orders issued between September 1992 and June 1993 were requested by parents against their children (Cochran, Brown, Adams, & Doherty, 1994).

Surveys of adolescents and parents find rates of violence and abuse against parents ranging from 5% to 12%. Mulligan (1977) reports that 12% of the college students she questioned used at least one form of violence against a parent while they lived at home during their senior year of high school. Charles Peek and his colleagues (Peek, Fisher, & Kidwell, 1985) analyzed data collected from more than 1,500 parents of white male high school sophomores, juniors, and seniors as part of the Youth in Transition Survey. They found that between 7% and 11% of the parents reported being hit. Straus et al. (1980) found that 10% of the children 3 to 17 years of age in their sample performed at least one act of violence against a parent during a 1-year period (see Table 1). Our own statistics (Cornell & Gelles, 1982), generated from a nationally representative sample of families who had a teenager living at home between the ages of 10 and 17, agreed with the findings of the other studies—9% of parents reported at least one act of violence. This translates into approximately 2.5 million parents being struck at least once a year. A statistic was also calculated for the more severe forms of violence. Approximately 3% of the adolescents were reported to have kicked, punched, bit, beat up, or used a knife or gun against a parent. Although this percentage appears quite small, when it is projected to the total number of adolescents between ages 10 and 17 living in two-parent households, it means that 900,000 parents are being abused each year. Robert Agnew and Sandra Huguley (1989) analyzed data from the 1972 National Survey of Youth and reported that roughly 5% of the adolescents in the survey hit one of their parents in the previous year.

***Table 1. Incidence of Hidden Forms of Family Violence (in percentages)***

| Violent Acts | Sibling to Sibling | Parent to Adolescent | Adolescent to Parent |
|---|---|---|---|
| Any violence | 82 | 46 | 9 |
| Pushed or shoved | 74 | 25 | 6 |
| Slapped | 48 | 28 | 3 |
| Threw things | 43 | 4 | 4 |
| Kicked, bit, or punched | 42 | 2 | 2 |
| Hit or tried to hit with an object | 40 | 7 | 2 |
| Beat up | 16 | 1.3 | 0.7 |
| Threatened with a knife or gun | 0.8 | 0.2 | 0.3 |
| Used a knife or gun | 0.3 | 0.2 | 0.2 |

**Source:** Based on data from Straus et al. (1980).

Children not only hit and assault their parents, they kill them as well. A National Institute of Justice analysis of murder victims and defendants in the 75 largest urban counties in the United States found that 2% of all family murder victims were parents killed by their children (Dawson & Langan, 1994). For the period 1977 to 1986, approximately 1 of 11 family homicides nationwide were parents killed by their children (Heide, 1989).

Some of the cases of children killing their parents have generated enormous publicity. The most recent case is that of the Menendez brothers in Los Angeles, who were convicted of the shotgun killings of their parents. In this case, as in others, such as Richard and Deborah Jahnke in Wyoming or Cheryl Pierson on Long Island, New York, the children claimed that the killings were the result of years of physical, emotional, or sexual abuse at the hands of their parents.

### *Factors Related to Violence Toward Parents*

Who is violent? Harbin and Madden (1979) found that the majority of children who attack a parent are between the ages of 13 and 24, although they also report on children as young as 10 years old inflicting injury on their parents. Researchers agree that sons are slightly more likely to be violent and abusive than daughters. In Massachusetts, nearly two thirds (64%) of the restraining orders in parent abuse cases were issued for mothers against their sons (Cochran et al., 1994).

Sons' rates of severe violence against a parent appears to increase with age, whereas for daughters the rates of severe violence decline with age. Agnew and Huguley (1989) found that as boys grew older, they were somewhat less likely to hit their mothers and more likely to hit their fathers. This suggests, perhaps, that boys do take advantage of increased size and strength that comes with adolescent growth. A social explanation could be that the boys and girls are adhering to the cultural norms that reward aggressiveness in teenage boys but negatively sanction the use of violence among teenage girls.

Irrespective of who is the victim of a parricide—mother, father, stepfather, or stepmother—sons are overwhelmingly the killers. More than 85% of the offenders in parricide are sons (Heide, 1989, 1995).

Researchers generally found that mothers are more likely to be hit and assaulted than fathers (Cornell & Gelles, 1982; U.S. Department of Justice, 1994a). An examination of police reports of formal complaints about adolescent aggression toward parents found that the modal pattern was male adolescent violence toward mothers (Evans & Warren-Sohlberg, 1988). Finally, a survey of adolescents concludes that mothers are more likely to be victims of their children's violence but that fathers are the more likely victims of older male children (Agnew & Huguley, 1989).

Whereas mothers are more likely to be hit by their children than are fathers, fathers, whether biological or stepfathers, are more likely to be killed by their children who are under the age of 30 than are mothers or stepmothers. If the offender is over 30 years old, the victim is more likely to be the mother or stepmother as opposed to the father or stepfather (Heide, 1989, 1995).

Clinical observations of adolescents who had abused a parent found that most families had some disturbance in the authority structure within the family. Adolescents had been granted too much control. Abused parents seemed to be turning to young or immature children for decision making. This tremendous responsibility on the shoulders of young people seemed to generate extreme frustration. Harbin and Madden (1979) claim that the physical attacks on the parent were often an attempt by the adolescents to either control the family or to punish the parents for placing them in the decision-making role in the first place. Many of the abusive children had very poor self-concepts; whenever they were challenged or made to feel insecure, anxiety was created, often resulting in violent episodes.

In those instances when children, especially adolescent children, kill their parents, the key underlying factor is that the child has been severely abused (Heide, 1995; Mones, 1991). In a smaller number of cases of parricide, the child is severely mentally ill or has an antisocial personality disorder (Heide, 1995).

Although child abuse and spouse abuse have been found to be related to many social, family structural, and situational factors, adolescent violence does not seem to vary in any meaningful way with these same factors. Adolescent violence cannot be explained using the same social factors that explain adult violence. The data do appear to indicate, as noted in the previous paragraph, that the rates of parent abuse are related to the frequency of other forms of family violence in the home. The more violence children experience or witness, the more likely they are to strike out at a parent. These findings are consistent with the theory that families who view violence as a legitimate way to resolve conflict run a greater risk of experiencing all forms of family violence, including parent abuse. Adolescents who have friends who assault parents, who approve of delinquency under certain conditions, who perceive the possibility of being arrested as low, and who are weakly attached to their parents have been found to be the most likely to use violence toward their parents (Agnew & Huguley, 1989).

## References

Agnew, R., and S. Huguley. "Adolescent Violence Towards Parents." *Journal of Marriage and the Family* 51 (1989): 699–711.

Cochran, D., M. E. Brown, S. L. Adams, and D. Doherty. *Young Adolescent Batterers: A Profile of Restraining Order Defendants in Massachusetts*. Boston: Massachusetts Trial Court, Office of the Commissioner of Probation, 1994.

Cornell, C. P., and R. J. Gelles. "Adolescent to Parent Violence." *Urban Social Change Review* 15 (1982): 8–14.

Dawson, J. M., and P. A. Langan. *Murder in Families*. Washington, D.C.: Bureau of Justice Statistics, 1994.

Evans, E. D., and L. A. Warren-Sohlberg. "A Pattern of Adolescent Abusive Behavior Towards Parents." *Journal of Adolescent Research* 3 (1988): 201–16.

Ferreira, A. "Family Myth and Homeostasis." *Archives of General Psychiatry* 9 (1963): 451–63.

Goode, W. "Force and Violence in the Family." *Journal of Marriage and the Family* 33 (1971): 624-36.

Harbin, H., and D. Madden. "Battered Parents: A New Syndrome." *American Journal of Psychiatry* 136 (1979): 1288-91.

Heide, K. M. *Why Kids Kill Parents: Child Abuse and Adolescent Homicide*. Thousand Oaks, Calif.: Sage, 1995.

Heide, K. M. "Parricide: Incidence and Issues." *The Justice Professional* 4 (1989): 19–41.

Mones, P. *When a Child Kills: Abused Children Who Kill Their Parents*. New York: Pocket Books, 1991.

Mulligan, M. *An Investigation of Factors Associated with Violent Modes of Conflict Resolution in the Family*. Unpublished master's thesis, University of Rhode Island, 1977.

Peek, C., J. L. Fisher, and J. S. Kidwell. "Teenage Violence Towards Parents: A Neglected Dimension of Family Violence." *Journal of Marriage and the Family* 47 (1985): 1051–58.

Straus, M. A., R. J. Gelles, and S. K. Steinmetz. *Behind Closed Doors: Violence in the American Family*. Garden City, N.Y.: Anchor, 1980.

U.S. Department of Justice. *Domestic Violence: Violence between Intimates*. Washington, D.C.: U. S. Department of Justice, Bureau of Justice Statistics, 1994.

U.S. Department of Justice. *Intimate Victims: A Study of Violence among Friends and Relatives*. Washington, D.C.: Government Printing Office, 1980.

Warren, C. *Battered Parents: Adolescent Violence and the Family*. Paper presented at the Pacific Sociological Association, Anaheim, Calif., April 1978.

# Part Five

# Elder Abuse

Chapter 20

# Definitions, Incidence, and Prevention

## Chapter Contents

## Section 20.1

# *What Is Elder Abuse?*

National Center on Elder Abuse, 1996. Used by permission.

## *What Are the Major Types of Elder Abuse?*

Federal definitions of elder abuse, neglect, and exploitation appeared for the first time in the 1987 Amendments to the Older Americans Act. These definitions were provided in the law only as guidelines for identifying the problems and not for enforcement purposes. Currently, elder abuse is defined by state laws, and state definitions vary considerably from one jurisdiction to another in terms of what constitutes the abuse, neglect, or exploitation of the elderly. In addition, researchers have used many different definitions to study the problem. Broadly defined, however, there are three basic categories of elder abuse: (1) domestic elder abuse; (2) institutional elder abuse; and (3) self-neglect or self-abuse. In most cases, state statutes addressing elder abuse provide the definitions of these different categories of elder abuse, with varying degrees of specificity.

Domestic elder abuse generally refers to any of several forms of maltreatment of an older person by someone who has a special relationship with the elder (e.g., a spouse, a sibling, a child, a friend, or a caregiver in the older person's own home or in the home of a caregiver.)

Institutional abuse, on the other hand, generally refers to any of the above-mentioned forms of abuse that occur in residential facilities for older persons (e.g., nursing homes, foster homes, group homes, board and care facilities). Perpetrators of institutional abuse usually are persons who have a legal or contractual obligation to provide elder victims with care and protection (e.g., paid caregivers, staff, professionals).

Definitions and legal terminologies vary from state to state in regards to the types of domestic elder abuse that the National Center on Elder Abuse (NCEA) recognizes as well as their signs and symptoms:

## Physical Abuse

Physical abuse is defined as the use of physical force that may result in bodily injury, physical pain, or impairment. Physical abuse may include but is not limited to such acts of violence as striking (with or without an object), hitting, beating, pushing, shoving, shaking, slapping, kicking, pinching, and burning. In addition, the inappropriate use of drugs and physical restraints, force-feeding, and physical punishment of any kind also are examples of physical abuse.

Signs and symptoms of physical abuse include but are not limited to:

- bruises, black eyes, welts, lacerations, and rope marks;
- bone fractures, broken bones, and skull fractures;
- open wounds, cuts, punctures, untreated injuries in various stages of healing;
- sprains, dislocations, and internal injuries/bleeding;
- broken eyeglasses/frames, physical signs of being subjected to punishment, and signs of being restrained;
- laboratory findings of medication overdose or under utilization of prescribed drugs;
- an elder's report of being hit, slapped, kicked, or mistreated;
- an elder's sudden change in behavior; and
- the caregiver's refusal to allow visitors to see an elder alone.

## Sexual Abuse

Sexual abuse is defined as non-consensual sexual contact of any kind with an elderly person. Sexual contact with any person incapable of giving consent is also considered sexual abuse. It includes but is not limited to unwanted touching, all types of sexual assault or battery, such as rape, sodomy, coerced nudity, and sexual explicit photographing.

Signs and symptoms of sexual abuse include but are not limited to:

- bruises around the breasts or genital area;
- unexplained venereal disease or genital infections;
- unexplained vaginal or anal bleeding;
- torn, stained, or bloody underclothing; and
- an elder's report of being sexually assaulted or raped.

505

## Emotional or Psychological Abuse

Emotional or psychological abuse is defined as the infliction of anguish, pain, or distress through verbal or nonverbal acts. Emotional/psychological abuse includes but is not limited to verbal assaults, insults, threats, intimidation, humiliation, and harassment. In addition, treating an older person like an infant; isolating an elderly person from his/her family, friends, or regular activities; giving an older person the "silent treatment"; and enforced social isolation are examples of emotional/psychological abuse.

Signs and symptoms of emotional/psychological abuse include but are not limited to:

- being emotionally upset or agitated;
- being extremely withdrawn and non-communicative or non-responsive;
- unusual behavior usually attributed to dementia (e.g., sucking, biting, rocking); and
- an elder's report of being verbally or emotionally mistreated.

## Neglect

Neglect is defined as the refusal or failure to fulfill any part of a person's obligations or duties to an elder. Neglect may also include failure of a person who has fiduciary responsibilities to provide care for an elder (e.g., pay for necessary home care service) or the failure on the part of an in-home service provider to provide necessary care. Neglect typically means the refusal or failure to provide an elderly person with such life necessities as food, water, clothing, shelter, personal hygiene, medicine, comfort, personal safety, and other essentials included in an implied or agreed-upon responsibility to an elder.

Signs and symptoms of neglect include but are not limited to:

- dehydration, malnutrition, untreated bed sores, and poor personal hygiene;
- unattended or untreated health problems;
- hazardous or unsafe living condition/arrangements (e.g., improper wiring, no heat, or no running water);

- unsanitary and unclean living conditions (e.g. dirt, fleas, lice on person, soiled bedding, fecal/urine smell, inadequate clothing); and

- an elder's report of being mistreated.

## Abandonment

Abandonment is defined as the desertion of an elderly person by an individual who has assumed responsibility for providing care for an elder, or by a person with physical custody of an elder.

Signs and symptoms of abandonment include but are not limited to:

- the desertion of an elder at a hospital, a nursing facility, or other similar institution;

- the desertion of an elder at a shopping center or other public location; and

- an elder's own report of being abandoned.

## Financial or Material Exploitation

Financial or material exploitation is defined as the illegal or improper use of an elder's funds, property, or assets. Examples include but are not limited to cashing an elderly person's checks without authorization/permission; forging an older person's signature; misusing or stealing an older person's money or possessions; coercing or deceiving an older person into signing any document (e.g., contracts or will); and the improper use of conservatorship, guardianship, or power of attorney.

Signs and symptoms of financial or material exploitation include but are not limited to:

- sudden changes in bank account or banking practice, including an unexplained withdrawal of large sums of money by a person accompanying the elder;

- the inclusion of additional names on an elder's bank signature card;

- unauthorized withdrawal of the elder's funds using the elder's ATM card;

- abrupt changes in a will or other financial documents;

507

- unexplained disappearance of funds or valuable possessions;
- substandard care being provided for bills unpaid despite the availability of adequate financial resources;
- discovery of an elder's signature being forged for financial transactions and for the titles of his/her possessions;
- sudden appearance of previously uninvolved relatives claiming their rights to an elder's affairs and possessions;
- unexplained sudden transfer of assets to a family member or someone outside the family;
- the provision of services that are not necessary; and
- an elder's report of financial exploitation.

## Self-neglect

Self-neglect is characterized as the behavior of an elderly person that threatens his/her own health or safety. Self-neglect generally manifests itself in an older person as a refusal or failure to provide himself/herself with adequate food, water, clothing, shelter, personal hygiene, medication (when indicated), and safety precautions. The definition of self-neglect excludes a situation in which a mentally competent older person, who understands the consequences of his/her decisions, makes a conscious and voluntary decision to engage in acts that threaten his/her health or safety as a matter of personal choice.

Signs and symptoms of self-neglect include but are not limited to:

- dehydration, malnutrition, untreated or improperly attended medical conditions, and poor personal hygiene;
- hazardous or unsafe living conditions/arrangements (e.g., improper wiring, no indoor plumbing, no heat, no running water);
- unsanitary or unclean living quarters (e.g., animal/insect infestation, no functioning toilet, fecal/urine smell);
- inappropriate and/or inadequate clothing, lack of the necessary medical aids (e.g., eyeglasses, hearing aids, dentures); and
- grossly inadequate housing or homelessness.

## *Why Does Elder Abuse Occur and Who Are the Perpetrators?*

Elder abuse, like other types of domestic violence, is extremely complex. Generally a combination of psychological, social, and economic factors, along with the mental and physical conditions of the victim and the perpetrator, contribute to the occurrence of elder maltreatment. Although the factors listed below cannot explain all types of elder maltreatment because it is likely that different types (as well as each single incident) involve different casual factors, they are some of the causes researchers say are important.

### *Caregiver Stress*

Caring for frail older people is a very difficult and stress-provoking task. This is particularly true when older people are mentally or physically impaired, when the caregiver is ill-prepared for the task, or when the needed resources are lacking. Under these circumstances, the increased stress and frustration of a caregiver may lead to abuse or willful neglect.

### *Impairment of Dependent Elder*

Some researchers have found that elders in poor health are more likely to be abused than those in good health. They have also found that abuse tends to occur when the stress level of the caregiver is heightened as a result of a worsening of the elder's impairment.

### *Cycle of Violence*

Some families are more prone to violence than others because violence is a learned behavior and is transmitted from one generation to another. In these families, abusive behavior is the normal response to tension or conflict because they have not learned any other ways to respond.

### *Personal Problems of Abusers*

Researchers have found that abusers of the elderly (typically adult children) tend to have more personal problems than do non-abusers.

Adult children who abuse their parents frequently suffer from such problems as mental and emotional disorders, alcoholism, drug addiction, and financial difficulty. Because of these problems, these adult children are often dependent on the elders for their support. Abuse in these cases may be an inappropriate response by the children to the sense of their own inadequacies.

## *Who Are the Abusers?*

More than two-thirds of older abuse perpetrators are family members of the victims, typically serving in a caregiving role.

## *Is Elder Abuse a Crime?*

Depending on the statute of a given state, elder abuse may or may not be a crime. However, most physical, sexual, and financial/material abuses are considered crimes in all states. In addition, depending on the type of the perpetrator's conduct and its consequences for the victims, certain emotional abuse and neglect cases are subject to criminal prosecution. However, self-neglect is not a crime in all jurisdictions, and, in fact, elder abuse laws of some states do not address self-neglect.

## *For Help Regarding Elder Abuse*

When domestic elder abuse occurs, it can be addressed—if it comes to the attention of authorities. Although each state has a different system to address elder abuse, the following are some of the agencies that have been established by federal, state and local governments to help:

### *Which State and Local Agencies are Helping Victims and Their Families Involved in Elder Abuse?*

In most states, the APS (Adult Protective Services) agency, typically located within the human service agency, is the principal public agency responsible for both investigating reported cases of elder abuse and for providing victims and their families with treatment and protective services. In most jurisdictions, the county departments of social services maintain an APS unit that serves the need of local communities.

However, many other public and private agencies and organizations are actively involved in efforts to protect vulnerable older persons from abuse, neglect, and exploitation. Some of these agencies include: the state unit on aging; the law enforcement agency (e.g., the police department, the district attorney's office court system, the sheriff's department); the medical examiner/coroner's office; hospitals and medical clinics; the state long-term care ombudsman's office; the health agency; the area agency on aging; the mental health agency; and the facility licensing/certification agency. Depending on the state law governing elder abuse, the exact roles and functions of these agencies vary widely from one jurisdiction to another. Finally, because funds under the federal elder abuse prevention program are distributed to area agencies on aging (AAAs) in many parts of the country, the extent of these agencies' involvement with elder abuse is likely to increase in the future.

Although most APS agencies also handle adult abuse cases (where clients are between 18 and 59 years of age), nearly 70 percent of their caseloads involve elder abuse. The APS community is relatively small compared with the groups working for other human service programs, but it is composed of a few thousand professionals, nationwide.

### Adult Protective Services

In most jurisdictions, either APS, the Area Agency on Aging, or the county Department of Social Services is designated as the agency to receive and investigate allegations of elder abuse and neglect. If the investigators find abuse or neglect, they make arrangements for services to help protect the victim.

### State Elder Abuse Hotlines

Many states have instituted a 24-hour toll-free number for receiving reports of abuse. Calls are confidential. [*See* Chapter 39, Hotlines and Organizations.]

### Law Enforcement

Local police, sheriff's offices, and prosecuting attorneys may investigate and prosecute abuse, particularly in cases involving sexual abuse or assault. In states whose statutes make elder abuse a crime, there may be a requirement to report suspected abuse to a law enforcement agency.

### *Long-Term Care Ombudsman Program*

Since passage of the 1975 Older Americans Act, every state has had a long-term care ombudsman program to investigate and resolve nursing home complaints. The program has also been working toward extension of services to board and care facilities and, in some areas, to those who receive professional care at home. Check with your State Unit on Aging or Area Agency on Aging to see if the long-term care ombudsman program in your area can help in any given instance. [*See* Chapter 39, Hotlines and Organizations.]

### *Information and Referral*

Every Area Agency on Aging operates an information and referral (I & R) line that can refer people to a wide range of services for people 60 and older. I & R services can be particularly helpful in locating services that can help prevent abuse and neglect.

### *National and State Information*

Often people who want to help older relatives or friends don't live near them. Long-distance caregivers can call a nationwide toll-free Eldercare Locator number (1-800-677-1116) to locate services in the community in which the elder lives. In addition, some states have established a statewide toll-free number to provide centralized aging services information for residents of their states.

### *Medicaid Fraud Control Units (MFCU)*

Every State Attorney General's Office is required by federal law to have a MFCU to investigate and prosecute Medicaid provider fraud and patient abuse or neglect in health care programs which participate in Medicaid, including home health care services.

# Section 20.2

# *The National Elder Abuse Incidence Study*

National Center on Elder Abuse, 1998.

## *Introduction and Background*

America's burgeoning elder population has affected every segment of the social, political, and economic landscape. Public debate of the issues surrounding the special needs of the approximately 44 million persons in this country age 60 years and over has heightened national awareness and concern. As a result, public policies relating to issues such as retirement security, affordable long-term care, and quality of life are changing to meet the unique needs of the aging population. Yet, as the public looks toward improving the lives of the elderly, abuse and neglect of elders living in their own homes have gone largely unidentified and unnoticed. The National Elder Abuse Incidence Study has shed new light on this significant problem with the finding that **approximately 450,000 elderly persons in domestic settings were abused and/or neglected during 1996. When elderly persons who experienced self-neglect are added, the number increases to approximately 551,000 in 1996.** Additionally, through this study we have learned that:

- Female elders are abused at a higher rate than males, after accounting for their larger proportion in the aging population.

- Our oldest elders (80 years and over) are abused and neglected at two to three times their proportion of the elderly population.

- In almost 90 percent of the elder abuse and neglect incidents with a known perpetrator, the perpetrator is a family member, and two-thirds of the perpetrators are adult children or spouses.

- Victims of self-neglect are usually depressed, confused, or extremely frail.

The National Elder Abuse Incidence Study (NEAIS) was conducted by the National Center on Elder Abuse at the American Public Human Services Association (formally known as the American Public Welfare Association) and the Maryland-based social science and survey research firm, Westat. The Administration for Children and Fami-

513

lies (ACF) and the Administration on Aging (AoA) in the U.S. Department of Health and Human Services jointly funded this research. The study asked the fundamental question: What is the incidence of domestic elder abuse and neglect in the United States today? In public health and social research, the term "incidence" means the number of new cases occurring over a specific time period. The NEAIS used a rigorous methodology to collect national incidence data on what has been a largely undocumented phenomenon, and it provides the basis to estimate the incidence of domestic elder abuse and neglect among those aged 60 and above in 1996.

The NEAIS originated in 1992 when Congress, through the Family Violence Prevention and Services Act of 1992 (P.L. 102-295), directed that a study of the national incidence of abuse, neglect, and exploitation of elderly persons be conducted under the auspices of the Administration for Children and Families. ACF consulted with the federal Administration on Aging, resulting in the two agencies combining resources and expertise to support the national study. Because the legislative mandate primarily was concerned with the prevention of violence in domestic settings, the study focused only on the maltreatment of non-institutionalized elderly. Elders living in hospitals, nursing homes, assisted-living facilities, or other institutional or group facilities were not included in the study.

In order to maximize the utility of the research, the study also collected and analyzed data about elder self-neglect in domestic settings, and these findings are reported separately from the findings for abuse and neglect. In the NEAIS, the phrase "elder maltreatment" generally refers to the seven types of abuse and neglect that are measured in the study—physical abuse, sexual abuse, emotional or psychological abuse, financial or material exploitation, abandonment, neglect, and self-neglect. An early task of the NEAIS was to develop standardized definitions for each specific type of abuse and neglect, which are provided later in this article.

Prior attempts to generate national data on domestic elder abuse in the United States relied on state-compiled statistics of suspected abuse, with considerable variations in definitions and comprehensiveness of reporting systems. These earlier studies, frequently designed to estimate the prevalence (i.e., the total number of cases at a designated time period) of elder abuse rather than the incidence (i.e., the new cases occurring over a specific period of time), varied considerably in their research questions, methodology, sources of data, analysis, and findings. Accordingly, comparisons of earlier research with the NEAIS findings should be done cautiously.

The NEAIS gathered data on domestic elder abuse, neglect, and self-neglect through a nationally representative sample of 20 counties in 15 states. For each county sampled, the study collected data from two sources: (1) reports from the local Adult Protective Services (APS) agency responsible for receiving and investigating reports in each county: and (2) reports from "sentinels"—specially trained individuals in a variety of community agencies having frequent contact with the elderly. The NEAIS study design and methods are described more fully later in this article.

The NEAIS research is groundbreaking because it provides, for the first time, national incidence estimates of elder abuse, which can serve as a baseline for future research and service interventions in this critical problem. Its findings confirm some commonly held theories about elder abuse and neglect, notably that officially reported cases of abuse are only the "tip of the iceberg," or a partial measure of a much larger, unidentified problem. The NEAIS final report offers insight into critical questions, including: who are the victims of elder abuse and neglect, and who are the perpetrators? Who are the reporters of abuse and neglect? What are the characteristics of self-neglecting elders? What is the extent of the problem of abuse, neglect, and self-neglect in our communities and what forms do they take?

## National Elder Abuse Incidence Estimates

To arrive at the most accurate estimate of the national incidence of elder abuse and neglect in 1996, researchers added two numbers: (1) reports submitted to APS agencies and substantiated (i.e., determined to have occurred or be occurring) by those agencies, and (2) reports made by sentinels and presumed to be substantiated. Consistent with three national incidence studies on child abuse and neglect, this methodology assumes the sentinel reports represent substantiated reports. Because the incidence estimate is statistically derived from the nationally representative sample, researchers also calculated the standard error to establish the range of the incidence estimate within a 95 percent confidence interval.[1]

---

1. The standard error of the estimates of APS agencies is relatively low because of the large number of actual reports (1,466) by those agencies in the sample, while the standard error for the sentinel data is relatively large because of the smaller number of reports (140) in the study sample. The range of the "true" value, at the 95 percent confidence level, for an estimated number is plus and minus two times the standard error.

Using the identical methodology, researchers also separately calculated the estimated national incidence of elder abuse, neglect, and/or self-neglect in 1996. Both incidence estimates are for unduplicated elderly persons. In other words, individuals are counted only once, even if: (1) they were abused and neglected and/or self-neglecting, (2) more than one report were received about the same incident, or (3) different incidents were reported for the same elderly person during the study period.

## *Estimated Incidence of Elder Abuse and/or Neglect in 1996*

**The best national estimate is that a total of 449,924 elderly persons, aged 60 and over, experienced abuse and/or neglect in domestic settings in 1996.** Of this total, 70,942 (16 percent) were reported to and substantiated by APS agencies, but the remaining 378,982 (84 percent) were not reported to APS. From these figures, one can conclude that over five times as many new incidents of abuse and neglect were unreported than those that were reported to and substantiated by APS agencies in 1996. The standard error suggests that nationwide as many as 688,948 elders or as few as 210,900 elders could have been victims of abuse and/or neglect in domestic settings in 1996.

## *Estimated Incidence of Elder Abuse, Neglect, and/or Self-Neglect in 1996*

**The best national estimate is that a total of 551,011 elderly persons, aged 60 and over, experienced abuse, neglect, and/or self-neglect in domestic settings in 1996.** Of this total, 115,110 (21 percent) were reported to and substantiated by APS agencies, with the remaining 435,901 (79 percent) not being reported to APS agencies. One can conclude from these figures that almost four times as many new incidents of elder abuse, neglect, and/or self-neglect were unreported than those that were reported to and substantiated by APS agencies in 1996. The standard error suggests that nationwide as many as 787,027 elders or as few as 314,995 elders could have been abused, neglected, and/or self-neglecting in domestic settings in 1996.

## Abuse and Neglect Reported by APS Agencies

### Characteristics of Victims of Domestic Elder Abuse

Of 236,479 reports of abuse, neglect, and self-neglect to APS in 1996, 48.7 percent, or 115,110 reports were **substantiated after investigation,** 39.3 percent were unsubstantiated, and 8.2 percent were still under investigation at the end of 1996. The remaining 3.8 percent of reports had other outcomes (e.g., suspected victim died, could not be located, or had moved away).

Of the 115,110 substantiated reports in 1996 for which information was available, 61.6 percent (70,942) were reports of incidents in which elders were maltreated by other people (also called "perpetrators"), while the remaining 38.4 percent (44,168) were incidents of self-neglecting elders. Of the 70,942 unduplicated substantiated reports of elder abuse attributable to perpetrators (which excludes self-neglect), the most common types were: neglect (34,525), emotional/psychological abuse (25,142), financial/material exploitation (21,427), and physical abuse (18,144).

While the substantiation rate for all types of investigations of elder abuse combined was 48.7 percent, the **substantiation rates for different types of maltreatment** varied considerably, as follows: physical abuse—61.9 percent; abandonment—56.0 percent; emotional/psychological abuse—54.1 percent; financial/material abuse—44.5 percent; and neglect—41.0 percent. (The substantiation rate for sexual abuse was not statistically significant.)

A wide variety of **reporters of domestic elder abuse** were found in the 70,942 substantiated reports of abuse and neglect. The most frequent reporters were family members, who were responsible for 20.0 percent of all reports, followed by hospitals (17.3 percent), and police and sheriffs (11.3 percent). In-home service providers, friends/neighbors, and physician/nurses/clinics each reported between 8 and 10 percent of total reports. The remaining reports were made by out-of-home service providers, banks, public health departments, and other reporters.

Hospitals (19.8 percent) and friends/neighbors (19.1 percent) were the most frequent **reporters of substantiated reports of self-neglect** in 1996. Police/sheriff, in-home service providers, and physicians/nurses/clinics each reported 12 percent of total reports. Out-of-home providers, family members, banks, the victims themselves, and other reporters made the remaining reports.

517

The report examines the **age of victims** of different types of abuse reported to APS. The oldest elders (those over 80 years of age), who made up about 19 percent of the U.S. elderly population in 1996, were far more likely to be the victims of all categories of abuse, with the exception of abandonment. They accounted for over half the reports of neglect (51.8 percent), and 48.0 percent of financial/material abuse, 43.7 percent of physical abuse, and 41.3 percent of emotional/psychological abuse. In all types of abuse and neglect, elderly victims in the 60–64 and 65–69 age groups accounted for the smallest percentages.

**Female elders** were more likely to be the victims of all categories of abuse, except for abandonment. While making up about 58 percent of the total national elderly population in 1996, women were the victims in 76.3 percent of emotional/psychological abuse, 71.4 percent of physical abuse, 63.0 percent of financial/material exploitation, and 60.0 percent of neglect, which was the most frequent type of maltreatment. A majority of the victims of abandonment were men (62.2 percent).

In 1996, **white elders** were 84.0 percent of the total elder population, while black elders comprised 8.3 percent, and Hispanic elders were 5.1 percent. While white elders were the victims in eight out of ten reports for most types of maltreatment, black elders were overrepresented in neglect (17.2 percent), financial/material exploitation (15.4 percent), and emotional/psychological abuse (14.1 percent). Hispanic elders and those from other racial/ethnic groups were underrepresented among victims in all types of maltreatment.

The study found that elders who are **unable to care for themselves** were more likely to suffer from abuse. Approximately one-half (47.9 percent) of the substantiated incidents of elder abuse involved elderly persons who were not able to care for themselves, 28.7 percent were somewhat able to do so, and 22.9 percent were able to care for themselves. For the national elderly population as a whole, the federal government estimates that 14 percent have difficulties with one or more activities of daily living.[2] Approximately six out of ten substantiated elder abuse victims experienced some degree of **confusion** (31.6 percent were very confused, or disoriented, and 27.9 percent were sometimes confused). This represents a high degree of potential mental impairment among this group of abused elders, particularly when compared with the estimated 10 percent of the total national elderly population suffering with some form of dementia.

---

[2] Nov. 1997 U.S. Census Bureau report on disability status of persons 65 years and older in 1994–95.

About 44 percent of all substantiated abused elders were gauged to be **depressed** at some level, with about 6 percent of them severely depressed. This compares with the estimated 15 percent of all elders nationally who are depressed at any one time. One-third of substantiated elder abuse victims (35.4 percent) displayed no signs of depression.

## Characteristics of Perpetrators of Domestic Elder Abuse

Overall, men were the perpetrators of abuse and neglect 52.5 percent of the time. Of the substantiated cases of abuse and neglect, **males were the most frequent perpetrators** for abandonment (83.4 percent), physical abuse (62.6 percent), emotional abuse (60.1 percent) and financial/material exploitation (59.0 percent). Only in cases of neglect were women slightly more frequent (52.4 percent) perpetrators than men.

The **age category** with the most perpetrators was the 41 to 59 age group (38.4 percent), followed by those in the 40 years or less group who were perpetrators in more than one quarter of reports (27.4 percent). About one-third of perpetrators (34.3 percent) were elderly persons themselves (60 and over). Perpetrators of financial/material exploitation were particularly younger compared to other types of abuse, with 45.1 percent being 40 or younger and another 39.5 percent being 41–59 years old. Eighty-five percent of the perpetrators of financial/material exploitation were under age 60.

About three-fourths (77.4 percent) of domestic elder abuse perpetrators in 1996 were white, and less than one-fifth (17.9 percent) were black. Other minority groups accounted for only 2 percent of the perpetrators, while the race of 2.7 percent of perpetrators was unknown.

Data show that **family members** were the perpetrators in nine out of ten (89.7 percent) substantiated incidents of domestic elder abuse and neglect. Adult children of elder abuse victims were the most likely perpetrators of substantiated maltreatment (47.3 percent). Spouses represented the second largest group of perpetrators (19.3 percent). In addition, other relatives and grandchildren, at 8.8 percent and 8.6 percent respectively, were the next largest groups of perpetrators. Non-family perpetrators included friends/neighbors (6.2 percent), in-home service providers (2.8 percent), and out-of-home service providers (1.4 percent). The report provides details about the relationship of perpetrators to the victims for the different types of maltreatment.

## *Characteristics of Self-Neglecting Elders*

Self-neglect was included in the NEAIS and a common definition and signs and symptoms were adopted for it, as with all the specific types of abuse and neglect. Self-neglect is characterized as the behaviors of an elderly person that threaten his/her own health or safety. Self-neglect generally manifests itself in an older person's refusal or failure to provide himself or herself with adequate food, water, clothing, shelter, safety, personal hygiene, and medication (when indicated).[3]

Approximately two-thirds (65.3 percent) of substantiated self-neglecting elders were female, compared with women being 58 percent of the overall elderly population. About two-thirds (65.1 percent) of self-neglecting elders were 75 years or older (or almost twice their proportion of the overall elderly). The largest proportion of self-neglecting elders were in the oldest age category of 80 and over (44.7 percent), while the proportion decreased in each declining age group, with only 6.3 percent of self-neglecting elders being in the 60–64 year age group (compared to their being 23 percent of the total elderly population).

Self-neglecting elders were predominately white (77.4 percent), while 20.9 percent were black and 1.7 percent were other or unknown. The black elderly are two-and-a-half times more likely to be self-neglecting than their proportion of the elderly population.

Not surprisingly, most (93.3 percent) self-neglecting elders have difficulty caring for themselves. Of these elders, 34.3 percent are not capable of caring for themselves, while 59.0 percent are somewhat able to care for themselves. Three out of ten self-neglecting elders (29.9 percent) are very confused or disoriented, while 45.4 percent are sometimes confused. Three-quarters (75.3 percent) of substantiated self-neglecting elders suffer from some degree of confusion.

## *Abuse and Neglect Reported by Sentinel Agencies*

The remaining findings from the NEAIS address elder abuse reported by 1,156 sentinel reporters in the 248 sentinel agencies. Since sentinel data are not officially reported to the APS agencies, they are not officially substantiated. Sentinels were, however, carefully trained to screen out incidents that would not be supported. The unduplicated

---

[3] For purposes of this study, the definition of "self-neglect" excludes a situation in which a mentally competent older person (who understands the consequences of her/his decisions) makes a conscious and voluntary decision to engage in acts that threaten her/his health or safety.

sentinel reports were relatively small in number (140) and, therefore, standard errors are relatively high.

## *Characteristics of Elderly Victims of Nonreported Domestic Abuse and Neglect (Sentinel)*

Neglect was highest among those 80 years and over (60.0 percent). Physical, emotional, and financial abuse were found at higher rates among those aged 60 to 70 than among those 80 and older.

As with APS reports, a majority of victims of all types of abuse were women, as reported by sentinels. Although women represented about 58 percent of the total U.S. elderly population in 1996, over 80 percent of the physical abuse recognized by sentinels, over 90 percent of the financial abuse, over 70 percent of the emotional abuse, and over 65 percent of the neglect cases was found among women rather than men. Abandonment was also more frequent for women (65.4 percent), in contrast to substantiated APS reports, which show men were more likely to be abandoned (62.2 percent).

The data do not show that rates of unreported abuse and neglect are higher among minorities than among nonminorities. Rather, minorities, which collectively accounted for 15.5 percent of the total elderly population in 1996, were victims of abuse, as reported by sentinels, between 3.6 and 7.6 percent depending on the type of abuse.

Data from sentinel reports reveal that only one-third (33.8 percent) of the victims were **able to care for themselves,** another one-third (33.1 percent) were somewhat able to care for themselves, and 18.8 percent were not able to care for themselves. (Sentinels were unable to make a determination 14.2 percent of the time.) Individuals experiencing neglect, abandonment, and self-neglect were most often reported by sentinels as not able or only somewhat able to care for themselves. Two-thirds (67.7 percent) of those that were physically abused were thought to have the ability to care for themselves, suggesting that such abuse is not perpetrated on just the most vulnerable individuals.

Sentinels reported, through observation not diagnosis, that over one-third (36.6 percent) of alleged victims were not **confused,** about an equal proportion (37.9 percent) were sometimes confused, and a relatively small percentage (7.5 percent) were very confused or disoriented. Sentinels were unable to make one of these choices 18.0 percent of the time. Confusion was most common among those who experienced neglect, abandonment, and self-neglect.

521

In noting observations of **depression,** sentinels were unable to make a determination for a third of the elders they saw. Sentinel data show that 20.0 percent of the alleged victims were not depressed, 41.4 percent seemed to be moderately depressed, and a relatively small proportion (5.5 percent) appeared severely depressed. Signs and symptoms of moderate or severe depression were relatively high across all forms of abuse and neglect, but did not stand out for any one category when standard errors are taken into account.

### Characteristics of Perpetrators of Nonreported Abuse and Neglect (Sentinel)

As with APS reports, perpetrators reported by sentinels were most frequently **family members** (89.6 percent), including the adult children (30.8 percent), spouses (30.3 percent), and a parent (24.0 percent). Parents are possible abusers of elders because elders were defined as persons aged 60 and over, and some persons in their 60s and 70s had parents in their late 70s and 80s.

Friends, neighbors, and service providers were believed to be responsible for the abuse and neglect 10 percent of the time.

The most common age range for perpetrators was the middle years, ages 36 to 59 (45.5 percent), with 28.6 percent of abuse being committed by people 60 and older, and 15.3 percent by those 35 and younger.

Nearly twice as many men as women were reported as perpetrators of abuse and neglect by sentinels (63.1 percent compared to 35.4 percent).

## Conclusions

The results of the National Elder Abuse Incidence Study (NEAIS) strongly confirm the validity of the "iceberg" theory of elder abuse that has been accepted in the aging research community for 20 years or more. The contribution the NEAIS has made to our understanding of the extent of elder abuse and neglect is graphically depicted by the large new middle area in Figure ES-1 below.

**Figure ES-1. Iceberg theory showing NEAIS identified unreported abuse and neglect, excluding self-neglect**

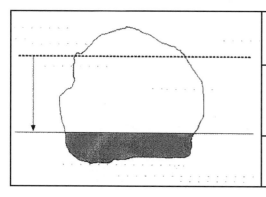

| | |
|---|---|
| | *Reported abuse and neglect:* 70,942 estimated new incidents substantiated by APS |
| | *Unreported abuse and neglect:* 378,982 estimated new incidents reported by sentinels but not reported to APS. |
| | *Unidentified and unreported new incidents.* |

## The NEAIS findings lead to the following conclusions:

Domestic elder abuse and neglect is a significant problem. NEAIS research shows that about 450,000 unduplicated elders experienced abuse and neglect in domestic settings in 1996. More than five times as many of these incidents of abuse and neglect were unreported than were reported to and substantiated by APS agencies.[5]

When elders who experienced only self-neglect are included with those that were abused and neglected, the number increases to 551,000 unduplicated elder persons in 1996. Almost four times as many of these incidents were unreported than were reported to and substantiated by APS agencies.[6]

The NEAIS has measured a large and previously unidentified and unreported portion of elder abuse and neglect, and also has learned much about the characteristics of the victims and perpetrators of abuse and neglect.

At the same time, it was not possible to identify and report on **all** previously hidden domestic elder abuse and neglect. Clearly, the

---

[5] Using precisely developed standard errors, the NEAIS estimates that as many as 688,948 or as few as 210,900 elder persons may have been abused and/or neglected in domestic settings in 1996.

[6] When self-neglecting elders are added, the estimate range is that as many as 787,027 or as few as 314,995 elder persons may have been abused, neglected, and/or self-neglecting in domestic settings in 1996.

NEAIS has not measured abuse, neglect, and self-neglect among those most isolated elders who do not leave their homes or who rarely come in contact with others in the community.

Several of the characteristics of abused and neglected elderly persons are particularly worrisome and challenge us to prevent and intervene in this tragedy:

- Our oldest elders (80 and over) are abused and neglected at two to three times their proportion of the elderly population.

- Female elders are abused at a higher rate than males.

- Almost half of substantiated abused and neglected elderly were not physically able to care for themselves.

- In almost nine out of ten incidents of domestic elder abuse and neglect, the perpetrator is a family member. Adult children are responsible for almost half of elder abuse and neglect.

Elderly self-neglect also is a problem, as evidenced by about 139,000 unduplicated reports (some of the self-neglecting elderly may also be counted as being abused and/or neglected). Most victims of self-neglect are unable to care for themselves and are confused. This is a difficult and troubling problem, which warrants further research and study.

Despite the study's identification of over five times as many unreported incidents of elder abuse and neglect as incidents that were reported to and substantiated by APS agencies, some professionals and researchers in the aging field may have expected this multiplier to be larger than NEAIS found. The NEAIS estimate may be lower than those expectations because:

- Elder abuse and neglect are not as hidden and under-reported to APS agencies as they were at the time of earlier studies. Between 1986 and 1996, for example, official reports of abuse and neglect made to APS agencies throughout the country increased by 150 percent, while the total number of elderly persons aged 60 and over increased by only 10 percent. A much larger proportion of new incidents of domestic elder abuse and neglect was reported to official APS agencies in 1996 than was reported 10 years ago.

- Still more of the unidentified and unreported area of the iceberg remains to be revealed, especially instances of abuse and neglect among seriously isolated elderly persons and those with little contact with community organizations.

## Limitations of NEAIS

The NEAIS study design had some limitations that prevented it from making a definitive estimate of all incidents of elder abuse and neglect, including:

- The sentinel approach tends to cause a certain amount of "undercount" in the detection of domestic elder abuse because there are no community institutions in which most elders regularly assemble and from which sentinels can be chosen and elders observed (unlike schools in child abuse research).

- Sentinels cannot observe and report abuse and neglect of elders who are isolated and/or have no or very limited contact with any community organizations.

- Resource constraints for conducting the NEAIS limited the number of counties and sentinels sampled and the length of the reporting period. Consequently, the relatively small number of sentinel reports resulted in incidence estimates with wide confidence bands. Increasing the sample size and reporting period in future such studies would further improve the precision of incidence estimates through the calculation of narrower confidence bands.

## Implications of Findings and Future Research Questions and Issues

The findings of the NEAIS suggest a number of important issues for policy development, practice, and training in addressing the problems of elder abuse, neglect, and self-neglect. Because states and localities historically have had responsibility for elder abuse reporting, investigation, and services, most of the implications are for state and local governments. These issues are discussed in the full report. Finally, the report raises a number of research questions and issues for researchers and service providers, including suggesting areas for future research of the incidence and nature of elder abuse and neglect.

## Conclusion

The NEAIS has documented the existence of a previously unidentified and unreported stratum of elder abuse and neglect, thus confirming and advancing our understanding of the "iceberg" theory of elder abuse. NEAIS estimates that for every abused and/or neglected elder reported to and substantiated by APS, there are over five abused and/or neglected elders that are not reported. The study also documents similar patterns of underreporting of self-neglecting elders. NEAIS acknowledges that it did not measure all unreported abuse and neglect. Our collective challenge—as policy makers, service providers, advocates, researchers, and our society as a whole—is to utilize this information to better the lives of our elderly citizens.

## Section 20.3

# *Elder Abuse Prevention*

Administration on Aging, U.S. Department of Health and
Human Services, 1998.

## *Service Delivery*

State legislatures in all 50 states have passed some form of legislation (e.g., elder abuse, adult protective services, domestic violence laws, mental health commitment laws) that authorizes the state to protect and provide services to vulnerable, incapacitated, or disabled adults.

In more than three-quarters of the states, the services are provided through the state social service department (adult protective services). In the remaining states, the State Units on Aging have the major responsibility. Agencies receive and screen calls for potential seriousness. Some states operate hotlines 24 hours a day, 7 days a week. [*See* Chapter 39, Hotlines and Organizations.] The agency keeps information received in reports of suspected abuse confidential. If mistreatment is suspected, an investigation is conducted (in cases of an emergency, usually within 24 hours). On the basis of a comprehensive assessment, a care plan is developed which might involve, for example, obtaining a medical assessment of the victim; admitting the victim to the hospital; assisting the victim in obtaining needed food, heat, or medication; arranging for home health care or housekeeping services; calling the police; or referring the case to the prosecuting attorney.

Once the immediate situation has been addressed, the adult protective services agency (APS) continues to monitor the victim's situation and works with other community agencies serving the elderly to provide ongoing case management and service delivery. The older person has the right to refuse services offered by APS, unless he or she has been declared incapacitated by the court and a guardian has been appointed.

## Where to Go for Help

If, as a concerned citizen or a practicing professional serving the elderly, you suspect that abuse has occurred or is occurring to an older person whom you know, report your suspicions to the local APS agency. In most states, certain professionals are mandated to report abuse. If the suspected incident involves an older person living in an institutional setting, call the office of the local long-term care (LTC) ombudsman.

You can find the telephone number for the APS office by calling directory assistance and requesting the number for the department of social services or aging services. To reach a LTC ombudsman, call the Area Agency on Aging (AAA), which is listed in the government section of your telephone directory, usually under "aging" or "elderly services." [*Or see* "Elder Abuse Reporting Numbers" in Chapter 39.]

It is essential to call the office with jurisdiction over the geographical area where the elder lives. If you cannot find the number for either of these offices or you are unsure of the office that has jurisdiction over the geographical area in which the older person lives, you can obtain the correct telephone number by calling the **Eldercare Locator** at **1-800-677-1116**, sponsored by the Administration on Aging (AoA). It is helpful to provide the address and zip code number of the older person's residence.

## AoA's Involvement in Elder Abuse Prevention

The AoA administers the Older Americans Act (OAA). The AoA's key priority areas are building systems of home and community-based long-term care; promoting consumer empowerment and protection;

and serving as a focal point for aging information and education. The OAA supports a nationwide "aging network," consisting of the AoA, including its **Regional Offices**; the 57 **State Units on Aging** (SUAs); 655 AAAs; 221 Tribal Organizations, representing over 300 Tribes; and more than 27,000 community service providers.

The OAA provides formula grant funds to SUAs to support state elder abuse prevention activities, authorized by Title VII, Vulnerable Elder Rights Protection Activities. The OAA also funds discretionary project grants, authorized by the Title IV, Training, Research, and Discretionary Projects and Programs.

## State Elder Abuse Prevention Activities

The State Elder Abuse Prevention Program, created by the 1987 Amendments to the OAA, was consolidated into the new Vulnerable Elder Rights Protection Activities, Title VII, when the OAA last was reauthorized in 1992. Title VII provides the states discretion in setting priories for spending these moneys. For the most part, states have focused their elder abuse prevention activities in four areas:

- **professional training,** e.g., skill-building workshops for adult protective services personnel; workshops designed to introduce specific professional groups, e.g., law enforcement, to aging and elder abuse issues; statewide conferences open to all service providers with an interest in elder abuse; and development of training manuals, videos, and other materials;

- **coordination among state service systems and among service providers**, e.g., creation of elder abuse hotlines for reporting; formation of statewide coalitions and task forces; and creation of local multidisciplinary teams, coalitions, and task forces;

- **technical assistance**, e.g., development of policy manuals and protocols that outline the proper or preferred procedures; and

- **public education**, e.g., development of elder abuse prevention curriculum for elementary and secondary students; and development and delivery of elder abuse prevention public education campaigns, including radio and television public service announcements, posters, flyers, and videos with training materials suitable for use with community groups.

## The Size of the Problem

The National Center on Elder Abuse (NCEA) reports an increase of 150 percent in state-reported elder abuse nationwide over a 10-year period, from 1986 to 1996. However, because abuse and neglect is still largely hidden under the shroud of family and personal secrecy, it is grossly underreported.

To gain a fuller understanding of this national problem, the AoA and the Administration for Children and Families jointly funded NCEA, together with its subcontractor Westat, Inc., to conduct the nation's first elder abuse incidence study.

On October 5, 1998, the Assistant Secretaries for Aging and Children and Families, Jeanette C. Takamura and Olivia Golden, announced release of the **National Elder Abuse Incidence Study** prepared for the Administration on Aging and the Administration for Children and Families. This study, requested by Congress, was conducted by the National Center on Elder Abuse at the American Public Human Services Association (formerly the American Public Welfare Association) in collaboration with Westat, Inc., a Maryland-based social science and survey research firm.

**This study estimates that at least one-half million older persons in domestic settings were abused and/or neglected, or experienced self-neglect during 1996, and that for every reported incident of elder abuse, neglect or self-neglect, approximately five go unreported. The report may be viewed on the internet at: http://www.aoa.gov/abuse/report/** [*See* Section 20.2 for the reports's Executive Summary.]

Copies may be obtained through the **National Aging Information Center** (330 Independence Ave., SW, Washington DC 20201—Tel. 202-619-7501—FAX 202-401-7620—web **http://www.aoa.gov/naic/publist.html**

**E-Mail:** aoainfo@aoa.gov
**Internet Web Site:** http://www.aoa.gov

# Part Six

# Prevention and Treatment Strategies for Individuals, Communities, and Government

# Chapter 21

# *Individual Initiatives*

## *Chapter Contents*

## Section 21.1

# *Partner Violence: What Can You Do?*

*Angela Browne, Ph.D. and Laura S. Brown, Ph.D.*

## *Introduction*

Until the mid-1970s, no one talked much about abuse between adult partners. We were taught to think that criminal violence occurred on the streets or in bars. Home was thought to be a safe place. Now we know that violence in the home is very frequent. More than 4 million American women a year are physically attacked by their male partners; violence can also happen in same sex relationships, and some men are beaten in heterosexual relationships, although what is most common is that women are battered by men. Some of these assaults are severe. From 1990 through 1994 the deaths of nearly 11,000 people age 18 and over resulted from one partner killing another, with women almost twice as likely to be victims of such fatal partner violence as men. Violence between partners happens in all groups in society. No group is immune. If your intimate partner has beaten you, you are not alone.

## *How Do I Know If I'm At Risk?*

Violence in a relationship is never okay and never justified. A "little slap" is violence. So is pushing, shoving, throwing things, threatening violence, or forcing a partner to engage in sexual activities against her or his will. All of these things, along with punching, kicking, biting, choking, burning, and injury with weapons, have happened to victims of partner violence. If violence or a threat of violence of any kind has happened more than once or twice, it is extremely likely to happen again. It may get more frequent or more severe. If this describes you and your relationship, you are at risk.

## Am I Overreacting?

Very often abusers will tell victims that they are overreacting and causing the batterer to become violent. You are not overreacting or causing the violence. It is normal to feel frightened and angry when your spouse or partner is violent with you. Your reactions to earlier abuse are no excuse for someone to be violent toward you.

## Why Don't I Just Leave?

This is a common question that people ask about victims and victims ask of themselves. It is almost always more complicated than just leaving. Sometimes the batterer will not allow you to leave and may threaten to kill you or other family members if you do. These are not always idle threats. Research tells us that women are more likely to be killed by their battering mates at the time these women try to leave. You may still feel love and compassion for the abuser and worry about hurting that person's feelings. You may be afraid to be alone and on your own. You may worry about how to support yourself and your children without the batterer. You may blame yourself, wrongly, for causing the violence and feel ashamed and afraid of exposing yourself. It may be against your religious or other beliefs to end a marriage or committed relationship. It's important for you to get help in learning how to resolve these issues for yourself.

## What Can I Do?

***If you are the victim of violence:***
- Begin to think about how you can plan for your own safety and happiness. Waiting for abusers to change and trying harder to please them will not work.
- Find out what resources are available in your area for victims of partner abuse. At a safe time, when the abuser is not around, call a local battered women's shelter or domestic violence hotline. Tell them what has happened; ask them what your choices are to protect yourself and to end the violence. Think about the answers to your questions and call again if you need to know more.

- If you are considering leaving your abuser, make safety plans before you talk about separation. Discuss the abuser's pattern of violence with someone at a shelter or crisis line and think about what risks there might be if you talk about leaving. Try to keep enough money in a protected place to use when you need it to get to safety. Some victims find it best to go to a shelter where they can be safe before they tell the abuser that they are leaving.

- If you can do this safely, encourage the abuser to go to a group for batterers. There are now many such groups for men who batter their partners. Some large cities also have groups for gay men and lesbians who batter their partners and for people from particular ethnic or religious groups. In such a group, batterers can get help from experts specially trained to treat violent people and may learn to change their beliefs and behaviors. You still may need to live apart from the batterer while that person is in the group. Changing patterns of violence can take a long time. (Call the National Domestic Abuse Hotline for information on groups in your area; see Hotlines and Organizations in Chapter 39).

- If you think you are in immediate danger, you probably are. You are expert at sensing when things are getting really bad. Flee at once to a safe location or call the police if you can. When police arrive, ask what legal protections are available to you, and use whatever you need to be sure you are safe. Don't let the police leave you alone with the abuser once they've arrived. If you are hurt, ask for medical help. Be sure that the doctor or nurse makes a record of your injuries and notes that those injuries were the result of an assault, not falling down stairs or bumping into a door.

### *If you are an abuser:*

- Get help to end your violent behavior. Hurting the people you love will cost you their trust and respect and your own self-respect as well. You may lose your loved ones permanently. No one likes to be violent or to get hurt.

- Realize that you can change. Others have gone through this and found ways to stop their patterns of violence. Their lives and relationships with those they love have gotten better. Call a state or local domestic violence hotline (you don't have to give your name to get information) and ask for referrals to a batterer's group or to expert therapists in your area. Be honest with the people running the group or with an individual therapist about your history of violence. Tell the leader or therapist that your violent behaviors are the ones you want to change. Don't wait until a judge requires you to go to treatment.

### If you are a friend or family member:

- You can do something. Encourage the victim to get to safety and help keep that person safe. Confront the abuser if you can do it safely (you may want to have someone else with you when you do this). Don't accept excuses for violence from people you love.

- Call the National Domestic Abuse Hotline or a local hotline and gather information about local resources and support services. Advise the victim about her options and assistance available to her and her children.

- Call the police if the victim cannot. Sometimes this can help stop or reduce the violence.

### For anyone:

- Become knowledgeable about violence between partners. Support local initiatives to reduce violence and help victims to become safe. A list of books that you might find helpful follows.

## Resources

Browne, A. (1987). *When Battered Women Kill*. New York: Free Press.

Jones, A., and S. Schechter (1992). *When Love Goes Wrong: What to Do When You Can't Do Anything Right*. New York: Harper Collins.

Lobel, K., ed. (1986). *Naming the Violence: Speaking Out about Lesbian Battering*. Seattle, WA: Seal Press.

NiCarthy, G. (1982). *Getting Free: A Handbook for Women in Abusive Relationships*. Seattle, WA: Seal Press.

NiCarthy, G. (1987). *The Ones Who Got Away—Women Who Left Abusive Partners*. Seattle, WA: Seal Press.

Sonkin, D. J., and M. Durphy (1989). *Learning to Live Without Violence: A Handbook for Men*. San Francisco: Volcano Press.

Walker, L. (1979). *The Battered Woman*. New York: Harper & Row.

White, E. C. (1985). *Chain, Chain, Change: For Black Women Dealing with Physical and Emotional Abuse*. Seattle, WA: Seal Press.

## Section 21.2

# *What Can Each of Us Do?*

U.S. Department of Justice, 1996.

## *What Can Each of Us Do?*

• Call the police if you see or hear evidence of domestic violence.

• Speak out publicly against domestic violence.

• Take action personally against domestic violence when a neighbor, a co-worker, a friend, or a family member is involved or being abused.

• Encourage your neighborhood watch or block association to become as concerned with watching out for domestic violence as with burglaries and other crimes.

• Reach out to support someone whom you believe is a victim of domestic violence and/or talk with a person you believe is being abusive.

• Help others become informed by inviting speakers to your church, professional organizations, civic group, or workplace.

• Support domestic violence counseling programs and shelters.

Adapted from: "Preventing Domestic Violence" by Laura Crites in *Prevention Communique*, March 1992, Crime Prevention Division, Department of the Attorney General, Hawaii.

## *What Can You Say to a Victim?*

• I'm afraid for your safety.

• I'm afraid for the safety of your children.

• It will only get worse.

• We're here for you when you are ready or when you are able to leave.

• You deserve better than this.

• Let's figure out a safety plan for you.

Adapted from: Sarah Buel, Esq., in "Courts and Communities: Confronting Violence in the Family," Conference Highlights, National Council of Juvenile and Family Court Judges, 1994.

## Section 21.3

# *What You Can Do*

Family Violence Prevention Fund, undated. Reprinted with permission.

### *What You Can Do: Talking With a Victim*

There are people who are currently suffering from domestic violence in every community in this country, including your own. Whether you know it or not, some of the people in your life may be facing this devastating problem—maybe a friend, a co-worker, or the kid who plays on your block. For many reasons, it is often difficult for a woman to admit she is being abused by someone she lives with. But there are lots of signs you can watch for that might indicate something is wrong—perhaps she frequently has unexplained injuries, or the explanations she offers for them don't quite make sense; perhaps her child is upset a lot and won't say why; perhaps you've noticed that she often cancels plans at the last minute without saying why, or that she seems afraid of making her partner angry.

If your friend, relative or neighbor is being abused by her partner, then she and her children need help—and it is up to all of us to lend a hand. What should you do? There are lots of ways to help her:

- Ask direct questions, gently. Give her ample opportunity to talk. Don't rush into providing solutions.

- Listen—without judging. Abused women often believe their abusers' negative messages. They may feel responsible, ashamed, inadequate, and may be afraid they will be judged.

- Let her know that you support and care about her, that she's not responsible for the violence, that only the abuser can stop the violence—and that there are steps she can take to protect herself and her children.

- Explain that physical violence in a relationship is never acceptable, at any time. There's no excuse for it—not alcohol or drugs, not financial pressures, not depression, not jealousy.

- Make sure she knows that she's not alone—that millions of American women from every ethnic, racial, and socioeconomic group suffer from abuse, and that many women find it difficult to leave.

- Also explain that domestic violence is a crime—as much of a crime as robbery or rape—and that she can seek protection from the justice system.

- If she has children, reinforce her concern for them, letting her know that domestic violence is damaging to children. In fact, you may want to reach out to support her children, and let them know you're there for them, too.

- Let her know that it is likely that, in spite of his promises, the violence will continue and, probably, escalate.

- Emphasize that when she is ready, she can make a choice to leave the relationship, and that help is available.

- Provide her with information about local resources—the phone number of the local domestic violence hotline, support groups, counseling, shelter programs, and legal advocacy services.

- She may need financial assistance, or help finding a place to live, or a place to store her belongings. She may need assistance to escape. Decide if you feel comfortable helping out in these ways. If you don't, you can still advise her to keep some money stored in a secret place so that she has access to it in an emergency—perhaps in a separate bank account (with statements mailed to a P.O. box or a friend's house) or tucked away in the trunk of her car.

- If she is planning to leave, remind her to take important papers with her, such as birth certificates, passports, health insurance documents, etc.

- Contact your local domestic violence program yourself for advice or guidance.

- If she remains in the relationship, continue to be her friend while at the same time firmly communicating to her that she and her children do not deserve to be in this violent situation. Encourage her to ask her doctor to document the abuse in her medical records; if she does decide to leave her abuser, these records will make it easier for her to obtain custody of her children or to press charges if she chooses to do so.

- If you see or hear an assault in progress, call the police.

- If you see an assault on the street, try to draw public attention by honking the horn of your car loudly and repeatedly until a crowd forms, the police arrive or he stops battering her. Because these assaults are often dangerous, assess the situation carefully before deciding to intervene.

## What You Can Do at the Doctor's Office

We all have a role to play in stopping domestic violence. The next time you visit your family doctor or other health care provider, ask what she or he is doing to address domestic violence and encourage them to ask all their patients if there is violence in their lives. Ask him or her to place posters about domestic violence in the waiting room, and materials about what to do if you're a victim of domestic violence in the restrooms so that women can take them anonymously, without feeling ashamed. Get involved. The person who needs help next time may be your own sister, daughter, grandmother or brother. Make sure that your community is prepared to help them and all other victims and survivors.

## What You Can Do at Work

Often, a working woman is a battered woman. Whether you know it or not, some of your co-workers may be facing violence at home. There are things we all can do to help: Create an environment in which she can feel comfortable coming forward for help by putting posters condemning domestic violence in public places, drinking from coffee mugs which sport anti-domestic violence messages, or wearing THERE'S NO EXCUSE FOR DOMESTIC VIOLENCE t-shirts on casual days at work.

You can also investigate whether your company's policies are supportive of battered women—whether, for example, your employee assistance program includes domestic violence services or referrals, or whether security guards at work have been trained to be responsive to the special safety needs of battered women. If not, speak to your human resources director or appropriate manager about the possibility of implementing such policies and safeguards. Lastly, if you suspect a co-worker is either a victim or perpetrator of domestic violence, talk to them and let them know that help is available.

## *What You Can Do to Address the Problem with Men*

For too long, wife beating has been a subject of laughter in locker rooms, at sporting events, and even in board rooms. But that is beginning to change. You can help. If you hear a male friend make a joke about domestic violence, take a stand. Tell him it isn't funny. If you feel too uncomfortable to speak up, body language can communicate disapproval almost as loudly as words. Turn away from the person making the joke, or frown instead of laughing and don't respond. By letting him know that you will not participate in his joke, you are sending the powerful message that domestic violence isn't a laughing matter, and that he should feel ashamed to treat it that way. If enough people send the same message, we can all really begin to change the way domestic violence is thought about and talked about—by both men and women.

Above all, if you know someone who is abusive, make it your responsibility to talk to him about it and tell him that his behavior is offensive to you. Remember that while confronting a man you know abuses his wife is difficult, it's more difficult to be the wife.

## *What You Can Do in Public*

There are lots of ways you can take action against domestic violence publicly. If you have a car, you can put a THERE'S NO EXCUSE FOR DOMESTIC VIOLENCE bumpersticker on it to tell the world domestic violence is not acceptable. You can wear t-shirts that sport the same message to softball games, to jog in, and to keep cool in the summer. Donate food and clothing—especially professional wear—to battered women's shelters to help battered women transition into the workforce; and when you travel, collect the soap and shampoo found at most hotels to donate, as well.

You can also make a personal commitment to talk about domestic violence—whether it is with a friend you suspect is either a victim or perpetrator of abuse, or in your workplace with co-workers who might be convinced to get involved as well. Ask a pastor to make domestic violence the subject of a sermon, civic and women's groups to address the subject, and inquire about programs at local schools. If we all agreed to simply raise the issue more often, we could really begin to create a world in which victims of battering know they are not alone and men who batter know that their behavior is not okay.

## *What You Can Do With the Media*

Lately, many television newscasts, programs and specials have addressed domestic violence, often examining new aspects of the problem, like the impact of domestic violence on the workplace or the responsibility of men to get involved. Such programs go a long way toward raising awareness about the problem, encouraging victims of domestic violence to feel safe enough to come forward for help, and emphasizing that we all have a role to play in stopping domestic violence. Editors and producers are very sensitive to the likes and dislikes of their viewing and listening audiences, so when a thoughtful story appears about domestic violence in your local media, you can really make a difference by writing or calling to let them know how much you liked the program. That kind of feedback makes it much more likely that similar stories will be produced in the future.

You can also call the public service director of your local television and radio stations, and editors or publishers at local newspapers and magazines, to ask them to print public service announcements (PSAs) about domestic violence to raise awareness about the problem and let victims know where they can find help. The Family Violence Prevention Fund has created television, radio and print PSAs which have been sent to the media all over the country. Make sure your local television and radio stations, as well as local newspapers and magazines, are airing and printing them in your community; if not, request that they be ordered through The Advertising Council in New York.

Likewise, monitoring the media for damaging and irresponsible coverage of domestic violence can make a difference, as well. Language is a powerful tool. For years, battered women's advocates have worked to convince journalists not to refer to incidents of abuse as "lovers' quarrels," "domestic discord," "domestic conflict" or other terms that minimize the violence and terror. In large parts, those efforts have made a difference, and the tone and tenor of coverage have improved significantly over the years. Still, such language does continue to appear in news reports across the country. If language demeaning the seriousness of domestic violence appears in your local media, challenge it aggressively each time through letters-to-the-editor and calls to news producers and station managers. Tell them that "domestic discord" doesn't leave women with broken bones and black eyes; violence does.

# Chapter 22

# *A Community Checklist: Important Steps to End Violence Against Women*

On July 13, 1995, the U.S. Department of Justice created the Advisory Council on Violence Against Women to help promote greater awareness of the problem of violence against women and its victims, to help devise solutions to the problem, and to advise the federal government on implementing the 1994 Violence Against Women Act. From police to doctors to clergy, the Advisory Council's 47 members draw on the many different professions that can help fight violence against women and assist victims.

Members of the Advisory Council have created working groups that focus on different segments of the community and what they might do to address the problem of violence against women. At the third meeting of the Advisory Council, held on July 18, 1996, each subgroup created a checklist of important steps communities can take to end violence against women. We are grateful for their input and for the commitment of each member to this issue.

This checklist identifies actions that can be taken by the religious community, colleges and universities, law enforcement, health care professionals, the sports industry, and through the media. We also recognize that there are many other facets of the community that can have a significant effect in this effort. The initial distribution of this booklet took place during October 1996 in recognition of National Domestic Violence Awareness Month.

---

U.S. Department of Justice, Violence Against Women Office, October, 1996.

This is not intended to be an exhaustive list but is meant to offer some straightforward, practical suggestions that we believe can make a difference in communities across the country. By coming together as a community, exchanging ideas, and coordinating efforts, we can begin to end this violence which destroys so many American lives.

—Janet Reno, U.S. Attorney General
and Donna E. Shalala, Secretary
of Health and Human Services

## Religious Community

The religious community provides a safe haven for women and families in need. In addition, it exhorts society to share compassion and comfort with those afflicted by the tragedy of domestic violence. Leaders of the religious community have identified actions to share with the nation to create a unified response to violence against women.

- **Become a Safe Place.** Make your church, temple, mosque or synagogue a safe place where victims of domestic violence can come for help. Display brochures and posters which include the telephone number of the domestic violence and sexual assault programs in your area. Publicize the National Domestic Violence Hotline number, 1-800-799-SAFE (7233) or 1-800-787-3224(TDD).

- **Educate the Congregation.** Provide ways for members of the congregation to learn as much as they can about domestic and sexual violence. Routinely include information in monthly newsletters, on bulletin boards, and in marriage preparation classes. Sponsor educational seminars on violence against women in your congregation.

- **Speak Out.** Speak out about domestic violence and sexual assault from the pulpit. As a faith leader, you can have a powerful impact on people's attitudes and beliefs.

- **Lead by Example.** Volunteer. Volunteer to serve on the board of directors at the local domestic violence/sexual assault program or attend a training to become a crisis volunteer.

- **Offer Space.** Offer meeting space for educational seminars or weekly support groups or serve as a supervised visitation site when parents need to visit safely their children.

- **Partner with Existing Resources.** Include your local domestic violence or sexual assault program in donations and community service projects. Adopt a shelter for which your church, temple, mosque or synagogue provides material support, or provide similar support to families as they rebuild their lives following a shelter stay.

- **Prepare to be a Resource.** Do the theological and scriptural homework necessary to better understand and respond to family violence and receive training from professionals in the fields of sexual and domestic violence.

- **Intervene.** If you suspect violence is occurring in a relationship, speak to each member of the couple separately. Help the victim plan for safety. Let both individuals know of the community resources available to assist them. Do not attempt couples counseling.

- **Support Professional Training.** Encourage and support training and education for clergy and lay leaders, hospital chaplains, and seminary students to increase awareness about sexual and domestic violence.

- **Address Internal Issues.** Encourage continued efforts by religious institutions to address allegations of abuse by religious leaders to insure that religious leaders are a safe resource for victims and their children.

*[Adapted in part from the Nebraska Domestic Violence and Sexual Assault Coalition and the Center for the Prevention of Sexual and Domestic Violence, Seattle, WA. Used with permission]*

## Colleges & Universities

Colleges and universities offer important opportunities to educate young men and women about violence against women. Experiences on campuses will be carried forth to everyday life and will influence future actions. Therefore, every effort to inform students may mean one less victim abused or one less crime committed. Leaders in higher education have identified the following strategies to assist educators across the country in reaching out to students and communities, and to make campuses safe places for women.

- **Make Campus a Safe Place.** Evaluate the safety and security of the campus environment and the quality and availability of resources to insure safety. For example, establish campus escort services through campus security and student government programs.

- **Increase Awareness.** Educate your students, faculty, and staff about the problem of sexual assault and dating violence on college campuses. Provide adequate training on the signs that often accompany abuse, on victims' legal rights and on available resources.

- **Target Special Groups.** Identify target groups (e.g. new students, fraternities and sororities, athletes, etc.) on your campus and develop specialized training and resources for them.

- **Coordinate Resources.** Identify resources addressing violence against women on your campus and bring together local community and university service providers.

- **Encourage Reporting of Violence.** Through orientation and awareness programs on campus, encourage students, faculty and staff to report incidents of violence. Develop effective linkages between campus and community law enforcement personnel.

- **Provide Services to the Campus Community.** Support a coordinated community response to violence against women; ensure that services are comprehensive and appropriate for the entire campus community.

- **Develop an Administration Response to Violence on Campus.** Establish protocols to manage complaints of violence on your campus with care for the victim as the first priority. Your protocol should include a clearly defined process for providing assistance to victims and holding the perpetrators accountable.

- **Review and Revise the Student Code of Conduct and Policies.** Review your campus policies and disciplinary sanctions to assess that violence against women is treated as seriously as other crimes with equally severe punishments.

- **Provide a Voice for Women on Campus.** Provide support for students and faculty to establish victim advocacy groups on campus.

- **Get the Message Out to the Campus Community.** Speak out against domestic violence and sexual assault in your position of leadership on campus. Communicate expectations about appropriate conduct, include them in student policy statements. Post information about available resources in dining halls, health facilities, dormitories, locker rooms, and other places students are likely to see it.

## *Law Enforcement*

Across the country, law enforcement is developing innovative and effective strategies to prevent and prosecute violence against women more effectively. Law enforcement leaders have identified several of these strategies that, if used consistently, may go a long way toward reducing incidents of violence against women.

- **Create a Community Roundtable.** Convene a community roundtable bringing together police, prosecutors, judges, child protection agencies, survivors, religious leaders, health professionals, business leaders, educators, defense attorneys and victim advocate groups, and meet regularly. Create specific plans for needed change, and develop policies among law enforcement, prosecutors, and others that will result in coordinated, consistent responses to domestic violence.

- **Record Domestic Violence.** To help understand and respond to the dimensions of violence against women, develop and require the use of a uniform domestic violence reporting form. It should include an investigative checklist for use in all domestic violence incidents or responses.

- **Continue to Educate.** Create informational brochures on domestic violence and sexual assault, which include safety plans and a list of referral services, for distribution in all court houses, police stations, and prosecutors offices *and* in non-legal settings such as grocery stores, libraries, laundromats, schools, and health centers.

- **Provide Clear Guidance on Responding to Domestic Violence.** Write new or adapt existing protocol policies for police, courts, and prosecutors regarding domestic violence and sexual assault incidents, and train all employees to follow them. Policies should specify that domestic violence and sexual assault cases must be treated with the highest priority, regardless of the severity of the offense charged or injuries inflicted.

- **Ensure Law Enforcement Is Well-Informed.** Designate at least one staff member to serve as your agency's domestic violence and sexual assault contact, with responsibility for keeping current on legal developments, training resources, availability of services and grant funds. Wherever possible, create a unit of employees with special expertise to handle domestic violence and sexual assault cases in prosecutor's offices, police departments, and probation/parole agencies, and ensure that these employees are well trained regarding their responsibilities.

- **Reach Out to Front Lines.** Identify and meet with staff and residents from local battered women's shelters and rape crisis centers to discuss their perceptions of current needs from the law enforcement community. Solicit suggestions for improving the law enforcement response to these crimes.

- **Improve Enforcement by Implementing a Registry of Restraining Orders and a Uniform Order for Protection.** Implement a statewide registry of restraining orders designed to provide accurate, up-to-date, and easily accessible information on current and prior restraining orders for use by law enforcement and judicial personnel. Develop a uniform statewide protection order for more effective and efficient enforcement.

- **Support and Pursue Legislative Initiatives.** Develop and support legislative initiatives to address issues regarding domestic violence and sexual assault including: a) *stalking,* b) *death review teams,* c) *sentencing guidelines,* d) *indefinite restraining orders,* and e) *batterers intervention programs.*

- **Conduct Training.** Conduct on-going multi-disciplinary domestic violence and sexual assault training for police, prosecutors, judges, advocates, defenders, service providers, child protection workers, educators and others. Training should include the victim's perspective and an emphasis on safety planning.

- **Structure Courts to Respond to Domestic Violence/Create Specialized Domestic Violence Courts.** Develop specialized courts that deal exclusively with domestic violence cases in a coordinated, comprehensive manner, where community and court resources can be utilized together to address domestic violence effectively. At a minimum, all court personnel involved with domestic violence cases, including judges prosecutors, public defenders, probation officers, and corrections and parole officers should receive relevant and practical domestic violence training and have an understanding of the dynamics of domestic violence.

## *Health Care Professionals*

Health care professionals are in the critical position of providing services to victims of violence as the first contact point for many of these victims. It is crucial that health care professionals recognize their potential to intervene appropriately. Immediate recognition of the problem and the provision of medical care and referrals to appropriate resources within the community can make all the difference. Leaders in the field have identified the following strategies to make interventions by health care professionals more effective.

- **Incorporate Training into Curricula.** Support the incorporation of domestic violence and sexual assault training in medical, nursing, and allied health care professional education curricula.

- **Make Resources Available to Patients.** Make resource materials available in waiting rooms and restrooms. Include the National Domestic Violence Hotline number 1-800-799-SAFE (7233) or 1-800-787-3224 (TDD).

- **Support Incorporation of Protocols into Accreditation Process.** Support efforts to ensure that domestic violence and sexual assault protocols are addressed through the National Commission for Quality Assurance and the Joint Commission on Accreditation of Hospitals.

- **Encourage Continuing Education on Violence-Against-Women Issues.** Encourage your state licensing boards and various specialty groups to encourage physicians and nurses to allocate Continuing Medical Education (CME) hours to violence-against-women related issues for re-licensure requirements.

- **Involve Medical Organizations and Societies in Increasing Awareness.** Collaborate with health care professional organizations and societies in your area to increase medical school and health care professional involvement in addressing violence against women.

- **Feature Violence Against Women on Meeting Agendas.** Arrange presentations and symposiums on violence against women at various health care specialty annual, regional and local meetings.

- **Highlight Commitment to Violence-Against-Women Issues.** Give awards, citations, and certificates to exceptional organizations and individuals for their continued commitment to addressing violence against women.

- **Develop a Standard Intake Form.** Develop a standardized intake assessment form for health care professionals who interact with victims of domestic or sexual violence. This assessment form would ensure that certain information regarding these incidents is identified and proper resources are utilized.

- **Ensure Employee Assistance Programs Are Responsive to Victims of Domestic Violence.** Determine whether your health care facility's employee assistance program (EAP) includes domestic violence services or referrals. If it does not, speak with your human resources director or the appropriate manager about the possibility of expanding the program to address the needs of employees facing violence in their homes. All EAP personnel should receive domestic violence training and have an understanding of the dynamics of domestic violence.

- **Volunteer.** Provide a health care series on a volunteer basis to community organizations that serve victims of domestic and sexual violence.

## Sports

Today, more than ever, our sports players and organizations have an enormous capacity to influence the minds and behaviors of Americans, both young and old. The reason is simple. For many Americans, professional, college and Olympic athletes are today's heroes. We must utilize this outlet to send a positive message to all Americans about preventing domestic violence and sexual assault. Following are a number of ways communities can work with the local sports industry to help stop the violence.

- **Bring Sports Leagues Together in a Common Cause.** Encourage local sports teams to come together in a joint effort to combat violence against women through joint awareness campaigns and public appearances.

- **Create Strict Disciplinary Policies.** Encourage the creation of disciplinary policies for players on domestic violence and violence against women similar to drug policies. These policies should include stiff sanctions and penalties for committing domestic violence and sexual assault.

- **Push for PSAs During Broadcast of Sporting Events.**
  Write or call sports leagues to support PSAs about violence
  against women during the broadcast of major sporting events,
  including NCAA games.

- **Promote the Distribution of Educational Materials.** Promote
  the distribution of educational materials from local shelters and
  programs to players by offering the materials to the teams.

- **Involve Local Sports Heroes in Community Activities.** Involve local sports heroes in rallies and events which bring attention to the problem of violence against women.

- **Reach Out to Potential Sponsors.** If there are businesses in
  the area that are known for making or selling sporting equipment or clothing, approach them for sponsorship of community
  awareness activities.

## *Media*

The media industry represents much more than television and film
stars. It is the most influential source of information for millions of
Americans. Before we can change people's attitudes about violence
against women and prevent violent behavior, we must not only change
the way violence is portrayed in the media, but also educate members of the media who report on domestic violence and sexual assault
crime. Leaders in the media industry have identified ways in which
communities can work with their local media to encourage responsible reporting of violence against women.

- **Use the Power of Communication.** Contact local television,
  radio, and newspapers urging thoughtful and accurate coverage
  of violence against women, and the provision of educational
  messages about the problem when possible.

- **Urge Action Through the Local Paper.** Through community
  organizations, distribute model op-ed pieces and letters to the
  editor and urge community action for placement of these pieces.

- **Link Media with Experts.** Provide media outlets with a list of
  well-known experts available for interviews, as well as a packet
  of materials with information on a variety of related subject areas, such as local shelters and programs.

- **Organize Public Events.** Plan a public event, such as a community education forum on violence against women, and solicit local media coverage.

- **Encourage Employee Awareness.** Encourage the development of domestic violence awareness programs for employees of media outlets.

- **Build a Bridge Between Media and Law Enforcement.** Urge police chiefs and commissioners to go on the air locally to discuss domestic violence and violence against women.

- **Provide a Forum for Community Leaders.** Encourage community leaders to speak to media about issues of violence against women.

- **Publicize Local Resources During Reporting.** Encourage local media to include the National Domestic Violence Hotline number, 1-800-799-SAFE (7233) or 1-800-787-3224 (TDD), during reporting on incidents of domestic violence.

# Chapter 23

# *Workplace Initiatives*

## *Chapter Contents*

## Section 23.1

# *Domestic Violence in the Workplace*

U.S. Department of Justice, *Violence Against Women Act News*,
June/July 1997.

## *Every Employer's Concern: Domestic Violence in the Workplace*

*Frederica Lehrman\**
*Attorney-at-Law, Shaw,*
*Pittman, Potts & Trowbridge*

Employers who recognize and respond to the needs of employees affected by domestic violence reduce the chance that violence will occur in the workplace, help insure themselves from legal liability, and protect their companies' bottom line by focusing on employees' safety. Acts of domestic violence diminish the injured employee's productivity, attendance, morale, and health. An abused employee and her co-workers are imperiled when the battering partner enters the worksite intent on doing harm. Employers who fail to act to prevent foreseeable violence may be found liable to injured employees and to murdered employees' survivors.

Many employers now have programs that offer assistance to battered employees. The Polaroid Corporation, Marshall's Inc., and Liz Claiborne, Inc. are leaders in the corporate fight against domestic violence. Polaroid retains restraining orders in its own name to keep batterers (even employee batterers) away from the worksite and the injured employee. Marshall's sponsors an annual "Shop 'til it Stops!" day and donates a percentage of the day's sales to stop domestic violence. Liz Claiborne has seminars on domestic violence and helps injured employees find legal assistance.

To protect the safety of battered and other employees, an employer must institute a policy of zero-tolerance for violence that applies to employees and visitors. The employer should require that all threats and acts of violence against employees be reported immediately. Any person who makes a substantial threat, exhibits threatening behavior, or perpetrates a violent act should be removed from the premises. The employer should take action against the perpetrator: criminal prosecution or termination of business relationship or employment are examples of actions that may be appropriate.

All managers and supervisors should be trained to recognize and respond to workplace domestic violence. A manager's failure to implement policies designed to protect workers can lead to legal liability if an employee is injured as a result. (See, e.g., Massic v. Godfather's Pizza, Inc., 844 F.2d 1414 (10th Cir. 1988)).

An informed or perceptive employer can recognize a battered employee even if the employee remains silent about the violence. Clues that an employee is being abused may include repeated bruises or injuries attributed to falling down or being clumsy; inappropriate clothing with long sleeves, sunglasses, or heavy makeup; high rate of absenteeism; lack of concentration; unusual amount of phone calls from a family member and strong reaction to these calls; or a reluctance to participate in informal activities.

When an employer recognizes that an employee is being battered, there are several steps the employer can take. It is essential to create a safe and nonjudgmental environment for the employee to come forward. The employer should ask "How can I help?" Never say, "Why don't you just leave?" Five simple things to say are: "I am afraid for your safety"; "I am afraid for the safety of your children"; "The violence will only get worse"; "I am here for you when you are ready to leave"; "You do not deserve to be abused." The employer should provide information about area resources and make written information available to all employees in such places as restrooms and cafeterias. Employers should make clear that domestic violence is a crime and that employees can get protection from the courts. Safety plans are effective ways to predict and plan responses to violence.

An employer also should be aware of potentially violent employees. In a Minnesota case, a male employee harassed, threatened, and killed a female co-worker. The court found the employee's actions were foreseeable because he had demonstrated a pattern of abusive behavior. The employer was found to be liable to the murdered employee's survivors for failing to protect against a foreseeable threat of violence (Yunker v. Honeywell, 196 N.W.2d 419 (Minn. App. 1993)). Signs that an employee may become violent include exhibiting emotional mood swings and self-destructive behavior; expressing a fear of losing control; harassing others; breaking or smashing objects; and making threats.

If an employee has been threatened and violence is imminent, the employer should call 911 and implement the safety plan. Informing co-workers of the risk will help prepare them to act if the batterer enters the workplace. Photographs of the batterer can be distributed. The threatened employee's phone calls can be screened. If possible, the threatened employee's workstation should be moved away from publicly accessible areas. The employer can provide escorts to and from the parking lot or bus stop.

An employer's quest for workplace safety must include a plan for recognizing and responding to the needs of employees affected by domestic violence. The employer who acts to prevent domestic violence from spilling into the workplace protects the rights and safety of its employees and takes steps to protect itself from the legal liability that may result from violence on the job.

*Ms. Lehrman is an attorney at the law firm of Shaw, Pittman, Potts & Trowbridge in Washington, D.C., and chair of the Domestic Violence Litigation Group of the Association of Trial Lawyers of America.*

## Section 23.2

# *Domestic Abuse: A Workplace Hazard*

U.S. Department of Justice, *Violence Against Women Act News*, June/July 1997.

*Ida L. Castro*
*Director-designate, Women's Bureau*
*U.S. Department of Labor*

Each year nearly 1 million individuals become victims of violent crime while working or on duty. From 1987–92, five percent of the women victimized at work were attacked by a husband, ex-husband, boyfriend, or ex-boyfriend. From 1992–94, seventeen percent of men charged with killing a woman at her job were current or former husbands or boyfriends.

Abusive partners may make it difficult for their victims to work by withholding necessary resources such as money (including the victim's wages) and transportation, leaving bruises in prominent places so a victim is embarrassed to go to work or to an interview, or threatening victims at the workplace. Some victims are also stalked by and receive hostile phone calls or e-mails from current or past abusers at work. Women who are being abused or women who are survivors of abuse may be under severe stress, making it difficult to concentrate at work.

In a study of domestic violence victims, 96 percent of those employed had some type of problem in the workplace as a result of their abuse or abuser. These problems included tardiness (reported by more than 60 percent of respondents), difficulty performing one's job (reported by more than 70 percent of the respondents), being reprimanded for problems associated with the abuse (reported by more than 60 percent), and losing a job (reported by more than 30 percent).

Domestic violence is not only harmful to workers, it is harmful to business. Without effective policies to confront this issue, domestic violence has negative effects on productivity, may increase employer liability for assaults committed at the workplace by abusive partners against their victims or the victims' co-workers, may result in higher health care costs, and may result in high turnover due to employers' termination of employees who are domestic violence victims.

In 1995, the Department of Labor's Women's Bureau developed the *Working Women Count Honor Roll*—a program challenging businesses, nonprofits, unions, and state and local governments to initiate new programs or policies that make real, positive workplace change in the areas women said they needed change the most. More than 1,300 organizations, public and private, large and small, pledged to institute changes affecting more than 2 million workers. Two Honor Roll members, the Commonwealth of Massachusetts and the Services Employee International Union, Local 509, agreed to offer state employees 10 days of paid leave per calendar year to attend necessary legal proceedings or activities when the employee or employee's child is a victim of domestic abuse.

Unions can help domestic violence victims in a variety of ways. They can work with employers to implement screening, counseling, and leave policies, as well as low-cost or free legal assistance; expand benefit programs to include counseling and legal services for union members who are domestic violence victims; sponsor workshops to train employees about domestic violence issues; and widely publicize crisis hotline numbers, outside counseling programs, and women's shelters in the workplace.

The American Federation of State, County, and Municipal Employees (AFSCME), AFL-CIO, DC 37, for example, has been addressing the issue of domestic violence since 1981, when the union established the Municipal Employees Legal Services (MELS) Plan to provide legal aid, child care, and housing to victims of domestic violence. MELS employs social workers to help victims obtain financial help needed to leave an abusive relationship, find housing, and make safety plans. [*See also* Section 23.4]

Private employers, nongovernmental organizations, unions, and government need to recognize and act upon the seriousness of domestic violence and its impact at the workplace. Doing so will save lives, improve workplace morale, increase productivity, and strengthen families.

### *Good Business Sense*

Greg Marshall is a successful businessowner who started his moving and storage company in Austin, Texas, more than 13 years ago. The business expanded and he now has offices in three cities. When one of his employees confided that she was trying to escape an abusive marriage, it made sense to him to help her in any way he could. "It was the right thing to do," says Marshall, "and it made good business sense. She was a good, hard-working and dedicated employee." Marshall extended her paid leave so she could move out of her house and get resettled and offered her the use of his vans and storage facilities—a service he continues to make available to women attempting to leave abusive situations.

## Section 23.3

# *Corporate Sector Responses to Domestic Violence\**

U.S. Department of Justice, *Violence Against Women Act News,*
June/July 1997.

*Nancy E. Issac*
*Research Director*
*Domestic Violence Institute*
*Northeastern University*

*Having moved into an apartment to escape her abusive ex-boy-friend, Jessica knew she had to keep going to work to support herself and her two children. Although he no longer knew where she lived, Jessica's ex-boyfriend knew how to find her at work. He shot and killed her as she was stocking shelves at the local grocery store.*

*Alice felt relatively "safe" working at her office building, where the security staff was careful not to let in any unannounced visitors. Still, her productivity fell as her estranged husband made up to 20 calls a day threatening to kidnap her children from school and burn down her parents' home.*

Domestic abuse follows women to work every day. Yet measuring the dimensions of this problem has proved very difficult: Women often hide or deny their abuse—partly because they fear exposure will negatively impact their employment—and most employers lack knowledge about warning signs of abuse or helpful responses. The results are mutually reinforcing—employers see little need to respond to a problem that appears rarely to occur, and women see little reason to reveal their abuse in an environment that does not communicate awareness and support around this issue.

The goal of the NIJ-funded research discussed here was to examine what role the corporate sector plays in responding to domestic violence ("partner abuse") as an issue affecting the health and safety of employees.

The project researchers used three broad strategies to shed light on this question. First we interviewed approximately 60 corporate professionals to examine the awareness of and attitude toward partner violence and its potential impact on employees' work lives. We then surveyed employee assistance professionals to obtain a broader view of current corporate-sector responses to partner violence. For companies that have one, the employee assistance program (EAP) is the natural locus for response to "troubled" employees. It assists employees with personal problems that are interfering with their ability to function effectively in their jobs.

In the spring of 1995, using the membership list of the Employee Assistance Professional Association, we sent an extensive survey to counselors in internal and external EAPs. We received responses from 307 individuals (an estimated response rate of 53 percent). The EAP sample was 54 percent female, had a mean age of 46.5 (SD=8.4), and came from all regions of the United States. The survey was targeted to the private sector and 91 percent of respondents stated they were from the private sector (for profit, nonprofit, or private-sector labor union).

Finally, we included a case study of Polaroid Corporation, which has been particularly proactive in responding to domestic violence as an issue both for employees and within the community. Provided here are some of the general conclusions of the study, which also offers recommendations for companies interested becoming more responsive.

### Conclusions from the EAP Survey

- A large majority of EAP providers have dealt with specific partner abuse scenarios in the past year, including an employee with a restraining order (83 percent) or an employee being stalked at work by a current or former partner (71 percent).

- While policies or guidelines on "workplace violence" appear to have proliferated, similar documents that specifically address domestic violence and the workplace are rare. While three-quarters of respondents from larger U.S. companies said they had workplace violence policies or guidelines, only 14 percent had policies or guidelines that covered domestic violence. These figures are almost certainly higher than the national prevalence of such policies or guidelines, since they are drawn only from companies that have EAPs and are hence likely to be more responsive to employee problems.

- There is increasing awareness that domestic violence is a problem employees may bring to the EAP. Slightly more than one-quarter (26 percent) of EAPs already have a question about partner abuse on their written intake or history forms. Slightly more than a quarter of respondents reported that their companies' response to partner abuse had changed in the past year, mostly in the direction of increased awareness.

- At larger U.S. firms, significant numbers of EAP staff are already applying a range of policies to accommodate the needs of employees affected by abuse. Two-thirds of internal EAP providers have used leaves of absence or medical leave policies and 41 percent have used short-term disability policies to assist employees affected by abuse.

## *Conclusions Based on Corporate Interviews*

- Although they are aware that domestic violence is a major social problem, most corporate executives and managers in the corporate sector have given little or no thought to its potential impacts on employee health and safety.

Nevertheless, as the findings of the EAP survey demonstrate, there is an important minority of companies that is already taking important steps toward education and awareness.

- In larger companies, awareness of domestic violence appears to be greatest in EAP and security departments. Often individuals in these departments are aware of cases that are unknown to others such as human resources, medical, or legal personnel.

- Little communication about the extent or handling of domestic violence cases appears to occur across company departments. This is true not only for specific incidents (where confidentiality may limit such communications) but with general discussion of the problem and how the company is encountering it.

- Potential barriers to increased corporate response include a lack of awareness, denial, embarrassment, privacy and confidentiality concerns, victim blaming, an expectation that abused women will identify themselves to the company, fear of advocating for a "marginalized" issue, and concern that responding may alienate male employees, negatively impact the company image, or cost too much (especially to external EAP providers).

- EAP staff are motivated to learn more about partner abuse. Although most EAP survey respondents felt their preparation was already good (52 percent) or excellent (21 percent), large majorities were interested in learning more about a wide range of partner abuse issues.

- Interaction with the criminal justice sector in relation to domestic violence is limited. Very few firms have received training from police or other criminal justice professionals, although those who have consider such training helpful. Three-quarters of EAP providers viewed inadequate follow through by the criminal justice system as a moderate or major barrier to dealing with domestic violence cases.

Perhaps the most valuable lesson taught by firms actively responding to domestic violence is that the corporate sector can play a positive and helpful role. By forming alliances with respondents in other sectors and by providing visible responses within their own corporate communities, businesses can increase understanding of the problem, knowledge of resources, and the ability of those affected to seek help.

* This study was supported with grant funding from the National Institute of Justice. Copies of the report are available from the National Criminal Justice Reference Service at 1-800-688-4252; or on-line at www.hsph.harvard.edu/organizations/hcra/hicc.html. (Dr. Issac was with the Harvard Injury Control Center when this study was performed.)

# Section 23.4

# *What Unions Can Do*

American Federation of State, County and Municipal Employees
(AFSCME), December 1996.

## *Labor-Management Efforts*

- Negotiate employer-paid legal assistance for use by abused women.

- If you have an Employee Assistance Program, be sure that it includes services for victims of domestic violence.

- Either independently, or in cooperation with the employer, sponsor workshops about domestic violence. In virtually every community the battered women's shelter will be glad to supply a speaker.

- Work with the personnel or human resources department to ensure that procedures are in place to prevent a victim's telephone number and address being given out to an estranged partner. For example, an employee should be able to request that personnel not give out this information without specific authorization. That notation should be made to all appropriate files and lists so as to minimize inadvertent violations.

- If you work in a profession which directly deals with the problem and you see ways that the services you provide could be more effective, strategize with the union about how to get your ideas implemented.

## *Public Awareness Campaign*

- Make abuse an issue. Invite speakers, show films, and have lunch hour workshops or seminars at a general meeting. Create an environment in your local in which honest, open discussion about abuse is possible.

- Run articles in union newsletters on the issue of abuse, including information on help for batterers and the work of community-based organizations.

- Post the phone number of the shelter or hotline on employee bulletin boards and distribute literature to the members.

### *Work With Shelters*

- Establish links with local shelters, hotlines, and other community sources.

- Introduce materials into the workplace from the local hotlines and shelters—some women may need this information.

- Begin actively supporting your local women's shelters. If there is not one, use union organizational skills to get one started.

- Lobby federal, state and local governments for increased funding for shelters.

- Call your local shelter and ask how the union can help. Money is always scarce, so individual or union donations will be appreciated. Non-monetary contributions such as clothes or toiletries may also be needed.

- Most communities have a hotline. The union might provide volunteers to answer the hotline a few hours per month.

### *Union Training*

- Be sure all members have information about where to refer members for help.

- Help women become more confident by running assertiveness-training workshops.

- Include information about domestic violence as part of your steward training.

## What You Can Do to Support a Co-Worker Who Is Being Abused

Some AFSCME members may be approached by a friend or co-worker who is a victim of domestic violence and wants someone to talk to. The following list of "do's" and "don'ts" may be helpful.

- Believe her.

- Encourage, but don't pressure her to talk about the abuse.

- Respect her need for confidentiality.

- Listen to her. Support her feelings without judging her.

- Let her know that she is not alone. Domestic assault happens to many women.

- Reassure her that the abuse is not her fault. She is not to blame.

- Give her clear messages that she can't change her partner's behavior; apologies and promises will not end the violence; violence is never justifiable.

- Her physical safety is the first priority. Discuss her options and help her make plans for her and her children's safety.

- Give her the time she needs to make her own decisions.

- If she is not ready to make major changes in her life, do not take away your support.

- Give her a list of key community resources that support and work with assaulted women.

- Battered women need our support and encouragement. Some forms of advice can be harmful or dangerous.

- Don't tell her what to do, when to leave, or not to leave.

- Don't tell her to go back and try a little harder.

- Don't rescue her by trying to make her decisions for her.

- Don't offer to try to talk to her partner to straighten things out.

- Don't tell her she should stay because of the children.

## For Stewards

While the signs below could be explained by something other than domestic violence, possible signs that a co-worker is being battered include:

- Bruises she may try to explain as being caused by an accident.

- Frequent or unexplained absences or lateness.

- Frequent personal phone calls that leave her upset.

- A decline in job performance—difficulty concentrating or working effectively.

- Withdrawal from co-workers.

Remember that despite severe on-the-job problems, the co-worker may be reluctant to talk about the abuse because she feels embarrassed or fearful. You might open the discussion by assuring her that the union is there to help and you understand that it is not always possible to separate one's personal life from one's working life. If she does want to confide in you, the previous section on "What You Can Do to Support a Co-Worker Who Is Being Abused" may offer some helpful suggestions. Also offer to be her advocate to get the employer to make some accommodations to help her through the crisis. For example, she may need some time off or may need a temporary change in shift or work location.

If she is reluctant to confide in you, assure her you will still represent her. Encourage her to get help through the Employee Assistance Plan if you have one, or offer to help her tap into available community resources. Discourage any workplace gossip about her situation. Leave the door open to her if she wants to talk in the future.

# Chapter 24

# *Legal Initiatives*

## *Chapter Contents*

# Section 24.1

# *Domestic Violence and the Law*

National Center for Victims of Crime (formerly National Victim Center),
*INFOLINK*, No. 61, copyright © 1997. Reprinted with permission.

## *Overview*

Domestic violence has traditionally been defined as violence in the home, or between family members. As society's definition of family has changed, so has the law's definition of family violence. While some states cling to the traditional view of domestic violence as between spouses or former spouses, increasingly legislatures are expanding the scope of the law to include children, relatives, unmarried persons living together, persons with a child in common, and even those in an "intimate relationship." *(All statutes discussed in this summary are current through 1995 unless otherwise indicated. Source: National Victim Center, Legislative Database.)*

In general, state domestic violence laws prohibit physical abuse and threatened or attempted physical abuse. Many domestic violence laws also bar sexual assault or abuse, emotional or psychological abuse, or even financial exploitation.

Police have been given a more specific role in combating domestic violence in recent years. Frequently, police are required to arrest offenders if they have strong reason to believe that there has been physical abuse. In some states, if police fail to arrest an offender, they are required to file a written report stating their reasons for declining to arrest. Police are typically required to inform victims of their legal rights, to enforce protective orders, and to use all means to prevent abuse. They may also be required to transport the victim to a medical facility or shelter. Police are often required to explain the procedures for obtaining a protective order to the victim, which may include giving the victim a written pamphlet outlining the procedures.

## *Protective Orders*

The standard method of redress for domestic violence victims is obtaining a protective order. These may be short-term, emergency protective orders, or longer term orders issued after a hearing. An emergency protective order in most cases is only issued where the applicant can show that there is a danger of immediate harm unless an order is issued. Such an order ordinarily is valid for only a few days, until a contested hearing can be held. After a hearing, the court may issue a longer term protective order.

A protective order may provide such relief as:

- Prohibiting further abuse;
- Prohibiting contact with the victim;
- Excluding the offender from the victim's home and/or place of work or school;
- Payment by the offender of spousal support, child support, monetary compensation, or payment for alternative housing for the victim; and/or
- Various other forms of relief.

Offenders may be required to participate in counseling, either as part of a protective order or as part of a pretrial diversion program. Successful completion of the counseling program in many states results in the charges against the offender being dropped.

Protective orders in some states are valid only for three months, although the court may be permitted to extend the order if the circumstances warrant. In other states, an order is valid for up to three years.

States enforce their protective orders in a variety of ways, whether by treating a violation of an order as civil or criminal contempt of court, or as a separate felony or misdemeanor. In some states, police are required to arrest an offender if they have reason to believe a protective order has been violated. The law often provides a means for police to verify whether a protective order is in effect. In a number of states, the victim is given a certified copy of the protective order, and another copy of the order is sent to law enforcement. [For additional and more up-to-date information on protective orders, see Section 24.2]

## Protection from Intimidation

State legislatures are becoming increasingly aware of the great potential for victim intimidation posed in cases of domestic violence, and are passing laws to deal with this intimidation. In Rhode Island, a judge is required to make clear to the victim and defendant that prosecution of the domestic violence action is determined by the prosecutor, not the victim. In Texas, a prosecutor's decision whether to file an application for a protective order must be made without considering whether a criminal complaint has been filed by the applicant. Also, in many states, the location of domestic violence shelters is confidential and need not be disclosed, even in court. Arizona imposes a civil penalty of up to $1,000 for the disclosure of information which could identify the location of a shelter. Similarly, the address of the victim is confidential in many states.

As of 1993, all states and the District of Columbia had passed "stalking" laws in an attempt to protect victims, usually women, who are followed, harassed, and threatened over a period of time—often by ex-husbands and ex-boyfriends. In an attempt to assist victims from being stalked by protecting their anonymity, some states, like Pennsylvania, are giving individuals who have been the victims of domestic violence and stalking behavior the option of blocking their phone numbers from being revealed through the popular "caller identification" services. [For more information on stalking laws, see Section 25.5] Other states are limiting the release of information from voter registration and department of motor vehicles records. (This trend in tightening disclosure policies concerning these records follows the passage of the *Driver Protection Act, as incorporated in the Violent Crime Control and Law Enforcement Act of 1994.*)

Many states also consider the communications between a victim and a domestic abuse counselor privileged. There may be exceptions where the counselor learns that a child is being abused, or where the court orders disclosure in a particular case.

## Recent Trends

The law in the area of domestic violence has been expanding in recent years. In a growing number of states, courts must consider any past history of domestic violence in a family when making custody and visitation determinations. More and more often, domestic violence offenders are being prohibited by statute from owning or possessing firearms.

Training for law enforcement, prosecutors, and judges in issues of special concern to domestic violence victims is becoming more prevalent, while medical and mental health professionals are being taught to detect signs of abuse and make appropriate referrals.

Some jurisdictions are using technology to assist domestic violence victims, including providing victims with cell phones to call 911 or other alarm systems to summon help. Many courts are also ordering electronic monitoring of batterers while on bail release or post-conviction release.

Funding for services and counseling for domestic violence victims is another area which has been receiving attention. In California, offenders can be ordered to contribute up to $1,000 to a battered women's shelter. A number of states routinely require the payment of restitution by the offender to cover the cost of mental health counseling incurred by a victim of domestic abuse. Some states even assess an additional marriage license fee which is designated to fund domestic violence programs.

For information on the domestic violence laws in your area, contact your local prosecutor's office, your state Attorney General's office, or your local law library.

## Bibliography

American Medical Association. (1991). "Domestic Violence: No Longer a Family Secret." *Five Issues in American Health*. Chicago, IL: American Medical Association.

American Medical Association, Council on Ethical and Judicial Affairs. (1992). "Physicians and Domestic Violence: Ethical Considerations." *Journal of the American Medical Association* 267(23): 3190–3193.

Attorney General's Family Violence Task Force, Pennsylvania. (1989*). Domestic Violence: A Model Protocol for Police Response*. Harrisburg, PA.

Berry, Dawn B. (1995). *The Domestic Violence Sourcebook*. Los Angeles: Lowell House.

National Victim Center. (1995). "Domestic Violence." *INFOLINK*, No. 14. Arlington, VA: National Victim Center.

National Victim Center and Crime Victims Research and Treatment Center. (1992). *Rape in America: A Report to the Nation*. Arlington, VA: National Victim Center and Crime Victims Research and Treatment Center

Novello, Antonia C. (1992). "A Medical Response to Domestic Violence." *Journal of the American Medical Association* 267(23): 3132.

Stark, James, and Howard Goldstein. (198S). *The Rights of Crime Victims*. New York: Bantam Books.

## Section 24.2

# *Full Faith and Credit for Orders of Protection: Assisting Victims of Domestic Violence*

Full Faith and Credit Project of the Pennsylvania Coalition Against Domestic Violence and the Department of Justice, August 1999.

### *What Is Full Faith and Credit?*

Simply stated, full faith and credit means that:

*A valid order of protection is enforceable where it is issued and in all other **jurisdictions**. This includes all 50 states, Indian tribal lands, the District of Columbia, the U.S. Virgin Islands, Puerto Rico, American Samoa, the Northern Mariana Islands and Guam.*

Under the federal Violence Against Women Act (VAWA), jurisdictions must give full faith and credit to valid orders of protection issued by other jurisdictions. Full faith and credit is a legal term that means jurisdictions must honor and enforce orders issued by courts in other jurisdictions.

*"Any protection order issued that is consistent with subsection (b) of this section by the court of one State or Indian tribe (the issuing State or Indian tribe) shall be accorded full faith and credit by the court of another State or Indian tribe (the enforcing State or Indian tribe) and enforced as if it were the order of the enforcing State or tribe." 18 U.S.C. §2265.*

For the order of protection to be valid, it must meet the following conditions:

- The court that issued the order must have had **personal jurisdiction** over the parties and **subject matter jurisdiction** over the case
- The respondent must have had **notice** and an opportunity to be heard.* **18 U.S.C. §2265(b).**

---

*If the order is **ex parte**, notice and opportunity to be heard must be provided within a reasonable period of time.

"Opportunity to be heard" does not require that the respondent actually appear at a hearing; rather, it requires only that he/she be given an opportunity to appear.

Full faith and credit helps to protect freedom of movement by requiring the justice system to enforce orders of protection throughout the country. If an abuser travels across state or tribal lines and violates a protection order, the abuser can be punished under the laws of the jurisdiction where the violation occurred and also may be charged with federal crimes.

### *What does this mean for survivors of abuse?*

The full faith and credit provision of VAWA can enable survivors of abuse to call on law enforcement officers and the courts to enforce their orders of protection across state or tribal lines. When survivors cross jurisdictional lines to work, travel, or relocate, they often find themselves in on-going danger, since frequently they are pursued or stalked by their abusers. For this reason, VAWA establishes nation-wide enforcement of orders of protection.

### *What does this mean for abusers?*

The full faith and credit provision of VAWA requires police and courts in the enforcing jurisdiction to treat the order as if it were issued in their own state or tribe. This means that if the abuser violates the order, he/she can be arrested and prosecuted if the laws of the enforcing jurisdiction allow this type of enforcement for violations of protection orders.

Tribes do not have criminal jurisdiction over non-Indians. Tribal police do have authority to stop, detain and transport non-Indian offenders to state or federal authorities who have criminal jurisdiction over non-Indian crimes. In addition, some tribes use their civil laws to impose civil fines or orders of exclusion to escort non-Indian abusers off tribal lands.

### *What does this mean for advocates?*

Full faith and credit may be a passport to safety for many survivors of domestic violence so advocates need to be familiar with the federal law and understand how it is being implemented in states and tribes throughout the country. Advocates need to share this information with all survivors. Advocates also need to advise survivors of the dangers they may face when traveling and assist them with appropriate safety planning. Abusers who are determined and willing to cross state or tribal lines in pursuit of their victims may be among the most dangerous. With information about full faith and credit, survivors can make more informed decisions about safety.

### *Advocate Tips*

- Assess the need for enforcement of orders of protection in other jurisdictions including travel for purposes of work, shopping, vacation, and relocation
- Be familiar with the sources of technical assistance on full faith and credit (many are listed in the last page of this document)
- Assist survivors in obtaining clear, enforceable orders from the courts in your jurisdiction
- Know the laws and policies (e.g. registration and filing procedures) for enforcing foreign protection orders in your jurisdiction
- Know how to got this same information about other jurisdictions

---

An important role of the advocate is to help the abused person assess the dangerousness of the situation and develop a safety plan. Most survivors will travel across jurisdictions, so full faith and credit issues need to be addressed in all safety plans.

### Assessing Danger
Factors to consider in determining serious danger/lethality:

- Separation of the parties
- Threats of homicide/suicide
- Possession or access to weapons
- Stalking
- Obsessive or desperate attachment to victim

- Destruction of victim's property
- History of domestic violence and violent criminal conduct
- Drug or alcohol involvement
- Depression or other mental illness
- Abuse of animals

### Safety Planning
Advocates should assist survivors in developing a safety plan. Safety plans should be detailed, specific, and practical. Issues to address include:

- Custody and visitation and legal assistance in these matters
- Plans to leave the jurisdiction
- Travel safety

- Getting a protection order that will be enforceable across jurisdictions
- Phone numbers for domestic violence programs, law enforcement, court clerks, and technical assistance

# Which Orders of Protection Are Enforceable?

Under VAWA, a protection order is defined as: *"any injunction or other order issued for the purpose of preventing violent or threatening acts or harassment against, or contact or communication with, or physical proximity to, another person, including temporary and final orders issued by civil and criminal courts (other than support or child custody orders)..."* 18 U.S.C. §2266.

The full faith and credit provision applies to both civil and criminal orders of protection, whether issued ex parte, after a hearing, or by agreement. Orders may differ from jurisdiction to jurisdiction in form, content, length, layout, or name (e.g., protection from abuse order, no contact order, stay away order, harassment order, restraining order, permanent order, conditions of release order).

## Civil Orders of Protection

**Consent Orders.** If a valid order of protection is issued on behalf of only one party, the federal law does NOT require that the order include a specific finding of abuse to be enforceable across jurisdictional lines. This means that if the victim files a petition for an order of protection and the abuser consents or agrees to the entry of the order, even without admitting to the abuse, the order will still be entitled to full faith and credit.

**Mutual Orders.** Sometimes an order of protection will contain a mutual "no contact" provision or it will direct both parties not to abuse each other. The full faith and credit section of VAWA requires special safeguards for enforcement of this type of order across jurisdictional lines. It states that an order should be enforced against the **respondent** and not the **petitioner**, unless the respondent cross filed a written pleading for an order of protection and the issuing court made a specific finding that each party had abused the other. If such findings were made, the order may be enforced against both parties. 18 U.S.C. §2265(c).

### Advocate Tip

- If you are working with a victim whose abuser filed a petition first, assist the victim, if appropriate, in filing a **cross petition** so the court can make a finding that the victim is entitled to relief and issue an order that can be enforced across jurisdictional lines

• Another option would be to file a separate petition so the victim can get a separate order that would be eligible for full faith and credit

**Custody Provisions.** Orders of protection often include terms that award custody of the minor children to the victim. However, the definition of "protection order" in §2266 of VAWA contains language that specifically excludes custody and support orders from court orders that are entitled to interstate enforcement under full faith and credit. It is unclear whether Congress intended to exclude the custody provisions in orders of protection or only custody orders that are part of separate divorce or custody decrees. Until this issue is clarified, advocates should look to other state, tribal, and federal laws that govern custody and visitation orders to try to determine if a custody order can be enforced in other jurisdictions. Some of the federal laws to check include the **Uniform Child Custody Jurisdiction Act** (UCCJA), the **Uniform Child Custody Jurisdiction and Enforcement Act** (UCCJEA), the **Parental Kidnapping Prevention Act** (PKPA), and the **Indian Child Welfare Act** (ICWA). If a custody provision in an order of protection meets the jurisdictional requirements of either the UCCJA or UCCJEA of the issuing jurisdiction and the PKPA, it is entitled to interstate enforcement. These laws can be quite complex, so advocates should encourage survivors to seek legal assistance.

*For more information concerning custody provisions in orders of protection, contact the Family Violence Department of the National Council of Juvenile and Family Court Judges at (800) 527-3223 or the Commission on Domestic Violence of the American Bar Association at (202) 662-1737.*

### Advocate Tips

You can assist abused persons in their efforts to protect their children in the following ways:

• Assist the survivor in getting legal representation

*Many legal services programs provide direct representation and legal assistance. The Battered Women's Justice Project (Civil) at (800) 903-0111 ext. 2 offers information on how to obtain legal representation.*

- If the order meets the requirements of the UCCJEA or UCCJA and PKPA, request that the court include a statement to that effect in the order of protection

- Assist the survivor in getting a trusted friend, battered women's program representative, or attorney to accept service if the abuser makes an effort to change the order of protection or seeks a separate custody order after the survivor leaves the jurisdiction

- Remind judges and policy makers of the importance of protecting the children of abused persons and the fact that abusers often use children to control their partners

**Criminal Orders of Protection.** The full faith and credit provision of VAWA applies to valid criminal orders of protection. These orders may be part of pre-trial release orders, conditional release orders or probation orders. They also may be separate, independent orders.

Enforcement across state or tribal lines may be problematic, because the way to enforce such orders usually requires a hearing before the court that issued the order. Jurisdictions vary in the type of authority given to police officers to make arrests without a warrant for violations of criminal orders. Few states and tribes have separate provisions in their criminal laws for violation of such orders. If a criminal order is violated across state or tribal lines, the enforcing jurisdiction can probably only hold the perpetrator for extradition, which is a formal legal process to send the offender back to the home (issuing) jurisdiction. Extradition is unlikely to occur when the underlying charge is a misdemeanor crime. Jurisdictions also vary considerably in providing notice to the victim about the existence of criminal orders of protection. Additionally, many criminal orders of protection are not entered into the jurisdiction's protective order registry, so police officers may not be able to obtain confirmation of the order.

*For more information concerning enforcement of criminal orders of protection, contact the Battered Women's Justice Project (Criminal) at (800) 903-0111 ext. 1.*

**Military Orders of Protection.** The federal law does not explicitly cover orders of protection issued on military bases or installations. In fact, most military orders will not meet the requirements for validity under VAWA since they are usually issued by a commanding officer without providing the respondent with an opportunity to be heard. This means that military orders of protection are generally not entitled to full faith and credit. The question that remains is whether military bases are required to enforce orders of protection issued by state or tribal courts. Commanding officers on some bases are directing military police (MPs) to enforce civilian (state or tribal) orders of protection issued against service members. Such enforcement usually consists of informing the local civilian courts or law enforcement agency of the violation and assisting the civilian authorities in investigating and prosecuting the violation in civilian court.

*For more information on policies and enforcement of orders of protection on military bases, contact the Battered Women's Justice Project (Criminal) at (800) 903-0111 ext. 1.*

## Which Laws Apply?

### The jurisdiction that *issues* the order determines:

- Who is protected
- The terms and conditions of the order
- How long the order is in effect

*Examples:*

A survivor obtains an order of protection against her same-sex abuser in State A. She then flees to State B, where same-sex partners are not eligible for orders of protection.

**Q:** Is her order entitled to full faith and credit in State B?

**A:** Yes. Since State A (the issuing jurisdiction) determined she was eligible for an order, State B (the enforcing jurisdiction) must enforce the out-of-state order.

A survivor of domestic violence is granted a lifetime order of protection by an Indian tribe. Four years later, she relocates to a state where the maximum duration of an order is three years.

**Q:** Is her order of protection enforceable in the state?

**A:** Yes. Since the Indian tribe (issuing jurisdiction) determined she was entitled to a lifetime order, the state (enforcing jurisdiction) must enforce the order for the lifetime of the victim.

### The jurisdiction that *enforces* the order determines:

- How the order is enforced
- The arrest authority of responding law enforcement
- Detention and notification procedures
- Penalties or sanctions for violations of the order

*Example:*

A survivor of abuse obtains an order of protection in State A where a violation of an order is a misdemeanor crime. After obtaining the order, the survivor visits a family member in State B, where violation of an order is prosecuted as criminal contempt.

**Q:** If the order of protection is violated in State B, will the abuser be charged with a misdemeanor crime or with criminal contempt?

**A:** Since State B (the enforcing jurisdiction) determines the sanctions for violations of the order, the abuser will be charged with criminal contempt.

## How Is the Federal Law Being Implemented?

At present, there is considerable variation among jurisdictions regarding implementation procedures. Some have enacted full faith and credit laws to implement VAWA while others have developed enforcement protocols. Advocates need to be familiar with full faith and credit legislation and procedures in their own jurisdictions as well as those of neighboring jurisdictions so they can provide accurate information to survivors.

### Registration/Filing

The federal law does NOT require registration or filing of orders of protection, however, a handful of jurisdictions require registration for purposes of enforcement.

**Benefits.** Registration/filing may be necessary to ensure full faith and credit if it is required by state or tribal law. Registration may also help to facilitate proper enforcement by courts and law enforcement agencies. These procedures, however, are relatively new in many jurisdictions so clerks of court and law enforcement personnel may be unfamiliar with how to register or file an order. Advocates should be prepared to assist survivors, if appropriate, in complying with registration or filing procedures.

**Risks.** Registration is not without risks. Filing can be dangerous in certain situations, especially if the abused person is registering the order in a jurisdiction where notice is sent to the abuser or where an order of protection is deemed a public record. It would be time-consuming and difficult, but a diligent abuser could locate the victim by searching court records throughout the jurisdiction. Advocates need to advise survivors who want to keep their whereabouts confidential that registration may be risky.

Registration/filing may not always be practical or even possible. In an emergency, there may not be an opportunity to register or file the order before seeking enforcement.

### Recognition

The federal law does not require **recognition** of orders of protection, however, a number of Indian tribes *recognize* orders from other jurisdictions under the legal principle of **comity**.

*For more information concerning Indian tribes, contact Sacred Circle at (877) 733-7623 or the American Indian Law Center at (505) 277-5462.*

### Certification

A certified copy of an order of protection generally contains a stamp, seal, or signature of the issuing judge or clerk of court and a notation that the copy is an authentic duplicate of the original order of the court. VAWA does not mandate that an order of protection be **"certified"** to be entitled to enforcement across state, territorial, or tribal lines. Nonetheless, many jurisdictions require that a copy of a foreign order be certified for purposes of registration or filing. Therefore, advocates may want to suggest that survivors get certified copies of their orders of protection to ensure proper enforcement.

*For more information related to state and tribal full faith and credit enabling laws or other enforcement procedures, contact the Full Faith and Credit Project at (800) 256-5883.*

## *Advocate Tips*

- Help the survivor to find out whether there are any registration requirements in the jurisdictions where enforcement will be needed

- Get several certified copies of the order of protection, as some jurisdictions may require a certified copy for purposes of filing or registration

- If the survivor does not have a certified copy of the order of protection but wants to register the order in the enforcing jurisdiction, assist in getting a certified copy of the order from the issuing jurisdiction

- If law enforcement cannot arrest for violations of an order before it has been registered or filed in the enforcing jurisdiction, encourage them to arrest for other state or tribal crimes that may have been committed (e.g. trespass, burglary, stalking)

- Keep court officials and local law enforcement informed about the potential risks of registration so that they are encouraged to enforce orders when survivors choose not to register their orders in jurisdictions where registration is optional

- If the laws of a state or tribe require registration or filing for purposes of enforcement, encourage lawmakers to amend their statutes because of safety concerns

## *How Are Orders Enforced?*

### *Law Enforcement*

Law enforcement officers are required to enforce orders of protection from other jurisdictions in the same manner they enforce orders issued within their own jurisdictions.

Before arresting for violation of an order of protection issued in another jurisdiction, officers should verify that a valid order exists (see below), determine whether the order was violated, and enforce the terms of the order pursuant to the laws of the enforcing jurisdiction (e.g. arrest if probable cause exists and if the alleged violation is an arrestable offense).

*For more information concerning law enforcement responsibilities, refer to the International Association of Chiefs of Police (IACP)/De-*

*partment of Justice (DOJ) publication entitled* **A Law Enforcement Officer's Guide to Enforcing Orders of Protection Nationwide.** *Copies of the IACP/DOJ booklet can be obtained by contacting (800) THE-IACP.*

Tribal police (unless they have been cross-deputized or cross-commissioned) do not have authority to arrest non-Indians. Many tribes call in the city, county, or state law enforcement officers to make those types of arrests.

As federal officers, Bureau of Indian Affairs (BIA) officers DO have criminal jurisdiction over non-Indians who commit offenses against Indians, and they exercise that jurisdiction in coordination with the FBI and U.S. Attorneys' offices. The BIA sometimes deputizes qualified tribal police officers who assist in exercising this jurisdiction.

**State, Tribal and Local Electronic Protection Order Registries.** Many states, tribes, and localities have developed computerized databases that contain records of valid orders of protection issued or registered within the jurisdiction. Some jurisdictions also keep records of expired orders. If a state or tribal registry is **accurate** and **up-to-date,** it can be accessed to verify the existence of a protection order in cases where the victim cannot produce a paper copy or where the paper copy does not appear to be valid. It should be noted that not all states and tribes have centralized databases of protection orders so officers should be prepared to take other steps to check the validity of an order.

**The NCIC Protection Order File.** In 1997, the FBI established the National Crime Information Center's (NCIC) Protection Order File. Because state and tribal participation is voluntary and NCIC requires certain data elements to list an order, the national registry does not contain orders from all jurisdictions. As such, the NCIC Protection Order File is an imperfect verification tool. Law enforcement officers who access the national registry to confirm the status of an order need to be aware of its limitations. In particular, advocates should remind officers that:

- Many states and tribes are not yet participating in the FBI registry

- Even if a state or tribe enters orders into the NCIC system, checking the NCIC file or verifying with the state registry may not result in a positive verification for reasons including the following:

  - the data fields in some state or tribal registries may be incomplete or incompatible with the NCIC file

– registries may not always capture 100% of enforceable orders

– there may be a time delay between the issuance of the order and entry into the state or tribal registry or the NCIC file

*For more information concerning the NCIC Protection Order File or state and tribal registries, contact the Full Faith and Credit Project at (800) 256-5883.*

## Verification of an Order by a Law Enforcement Officer

**If the survivor has a paper copy of the order, the officer should enforce the order if it:**

• Contains the names of both parties

• Includes the date it was issued

• Appears to be in effect (i.e., has not expired)

• Specifies terms and conditions with which the abuser must comply

• Contains the name of the issuing court

• Includes a signature of or on behalf of a judicial officer

**If the survivor does *not* have a paper copy of the order, the officer can:**

• Check to see whether the order has been entered into the issuing or enforcing jurisdiction's protection order registry or the NCIC Protection Order File

• Contact the issuing court for verification of the order's validity

• Arrest for all violations of the order and any other crimes that may have been committed

• Alert the prosecutor's office of all crimes committed under the enforcing jurisdiction's criminal code and potential federal domestic violence crimes

• Enforce the protection order based on a good faith belief that the order is valid

**Verifying the terms and conditions of an order of protection**

Although verification is not required under the federal law, it may be required by the enforcing jurisdiction under certain circumstances (e.g., the victim does not have a copy of the order).

## Courts

Courts are required to give full faith and credit to orders of protection from other jurisdictions. This means that the order must be enforced as issued, but that the court should apply the laws of the enforcing jurisdiction if the order is violated. To facilitate implementation of full faith and credit:

- Clerks of court should be familiar with the mandates of the federal law and be prepared to file or register an order upon presentation by a survivor
- Judges should
  - be familiar with full faith and credit when issuing and enforcing orders of protection
  - issue orders that are explicit, clear, comprehensive, and legible
  - include language in orders confirming that the requirements for "validity" under VAWA have been met
  - include notations in orders that the custody provisions meet the requirements of the UCCJA or UCCJEA and PKPA
  - inform both parties orally and in writing that the order is enforceable in all jurisdictions, violations of the order may result in state, tribal, or federal sanctions wherever the violations occur, and enforcement procedures may vary significantly from jurisdiction to jurisdiction
  - inform the protected party that laws and procedures vary among the tribes and encourage the protected party to seek further assistance and information on enforcement procedures if he/she plans to travel across tribal lines
- The relief granted by the issuing jurisdiction must be enforced even if such relief is unavailable under the laws of the enforcing jurisdiction
- The laws and penalties of the enforcing jurisdiction must be followed when imposing sanctions for violations of orders
- If there is a challenge to "validity" (e.g., respondent denies receiving notice), the enforcing court should contact the issuing jurisdiction to verify information
- The issuing jurisdiction should be notified of outcomes of any enforcement proceedings in the enforcing jurisdiction

## Local/State/Tribal/Federal Prosecutors

In most instances, local, state and tribal prosecutors will handle violations of orders of protection that occur across jurisdictional lines. Prosecutors should:

- Obtain information from the victim, local law enforcement, and the issuing jurisdiction
- Obtain information about all pending and past convictions
- Prosecute alleged violations in accordance with the procedures and laws of the enforcing jurisdiction
- Work to ensure victim safety

Some violations also may qualify for federal prosecution, since VAWA created a number of federal domestic violence crimes (see pages 589–91). To determine when a case should be referred to the U.S. Attorney's office, local, state, and tribal prosecutors should contact their federal counterparts and establish working relationships. Decisions about whether to try the case in state, tribal, or federal court will depend on a variety of factors, including differences in sentencing options, witness protection, adequacy of local, state, or tribal remedies, and available victim and investigative resources.

### Advocate Tips

#### Issuing Jurisdiction

- Assist the abused person in getting proof of service
- Work with the court and the survivor to ensure that the terms of the order are clear and specific
- Make sure that the abused person has several certified copies of the order (the court should not charge for these copies)
- Work with the court and the survivor to ensure that the following language is included in the order:

  1. Order is enforceable outside the jurisdiction

  2. Crossing jurisdictional lines to violate the order may be a federal crime under VAWA

  3. Custody provisions are made in compliance with the UCCJA or UCCJEA and PKPA

4. The court had jurisdiction to issue the order

5. The respondent had notice and an opportunity to be heard

- Work with the court and the survivor to ensure that the order includes a prohibition against firearm possession, if applicable under the laws of the issuing jurisdiction
- Work with the court and the survivor to ensure that the order includes required data elements for entry into the NCIC Protection Order File
- Provide copies of §§2265; and 2266 of VAWA for the abused person to carry along with the order
- Encourage survivors to notify enforcing courts of any changes in the terms of their order
- Find out about the laws and procedures of the jurisdiction(s), including any tribal lands where the abused person will need enforcement of the order (this information is available from the state domestic violence coalition, local battered women's programs, and the organizations listed on pages 596–97)
- Inform the survivor about comity and assist in checking on enforcement procedures of tribal jurisdictions to which the survivor may be traveling
- Provide names, addresses, and phone numbers of court clerks, local and federal prosecutors, law enforcement, state coalitions, and local battered women's programs in the jurisdictions where, the abused person may be traveling. *See the list of technical assistance providers on pages 596–97.*

### *Enforcing Jurisdiction*

- Know the laws and procedures of the jurisdiction
- Work with judges, court clerks, prosecutors, and law enforcement to develop a coordinated response for enforcement of orders issued in other jurisdictions
- Check to make sure that the abused person has certified copies of the order and proof of service, or assist in obtaining them
- Inform the abused person of the laws and procedures of the jurisdiction and provide the information needed for the person to decide whether to register the order

- Remind officers that, in most jurisdictions, the protection order can be enforced on its face regardless of whether it is registered/filed in the jurisdiction or listed in a state protection order database or the NCIC Protection Order File (consult the laws and procedures of your jurisdiction)

- Inform the survivor that she/he may need to take the protection order to the tribal court to be recognized, even if she/he has a protection order issued by another tribe

- Inform the survivor that, if appropriate, she/he should take the tribal protection order to the county, state, or other local jurisdiction for registration

- Encourage state, tribal, and federal prosecutors to work together to ensure the most successful prosecution of interjurisdictional cases

- Develop relationships with federal victim/witness coordinators in order to work together to provide victim safety

## Summary of Federal Crimes of Domestic Violence

Advocates need to be familiar with the new federal criminal laws that pertain to domestic violence in order to inform victims of options related to federal criminal prosecution. The contact for assessment of potential federal crimes is the U.S. Attorney's office in your district.

For the following federal crimes, the law defines State to include: a state of the United States, the District of Columbia, a commonwealth, territory, or possession of the United States.

### Interstate Travel to Commit Domestic Violence-18 U.S.C. §2261

*It is a Federal crime for a person to travel interstate, or leave or enter Indian country with the intent to injure, harass or intimidate an intimate partner when in the course of or as a result of the travel the abuser commits a violent crime that causes bodily injury. The abuser must intend to commit the domestic violence at the time of travel. The definition of partner is broad and basically includes a person with whom the abuser has cohabited in an intimate relationship (including a current or former spouse) or a person who has a child in common with the abuser.*

*It is also a Federal crime to cause an intimate partner to cross state lines, or leave or enter Indian country by force, coercion, duress, or fraud if the abuser intentionally inflicts bodily injury on the partner during or as a result of the conduct.*

### Interstate Stalking-18 U.S.C. §2261A

*It is a Federal crime to cross a state line with the intent to injure or harass any person if, during the course of or as a result of the travel, the defendant places the person or a member of the person's immediate family in reasonable fear of death or serious bodily injury. It also is a federal crime to stalk another individual within the special maritime or territorial jurisdiction of the United States (which includes federal reservations).The definition of immediate family is broad and includes a spouse, parent, child, sibling and all other household members who are related to the primary victim by blood or marriage.*

### Interstate Violation of an Order of Protection-18 U.S.C. §2262

*This law basically prohibits interstate travel or leaving or entering Indian country with intent to violate a valid protection order that prohibits credible threats of violence, repeated harassment, or bodily injury. The abuser must intend to violate the order at the time of travel and a violation of the order must occur.*

*It is also a federal crime to cause an intimate partner to cross state lines, or to leave or enter Indian country by force, coercion, duress or fraud, if during or as a result of the conduct, the abuser intentionally inflicts bodily injury on the victim in violation of a valid protection order.*

## *Firearms*

Federal law prohibits an abuser subject to a *qualifying order of protection* from possessing firearms and ammunition. 18 U.S.C. §922(g)(8). Abusers are not banned from possessing guns and ammunition permanently, only for the time that the order of protection is in existence. Additionally, there are "official use" exemptions, which allow law enforcement and military personnel who are subject to an order of protection to possess their service weapon while on duty.

18 U.S.C. §922(g)(9) prohibits gun or ammunition possession by anyone who has been convicted of a *qualifying misdemeanor* crime of domestic violence. The law applies to both federal and state misdemeanors that meet certain conditions. The gun ban is permanent, which means that if a person has been convicted of a qualifying misdemeanor, he/she can never legally possess a gun again unless the conviction has been expunged or set aside or the person has been pardoned or has had his/her civil rights restored. There is no "official use" exemption, so law enforcement officers and members of the military are subject to this law, even while on duty. The federal statute is also retroactive, so it applies to convictions that occurred before the law went into effect.

### *Advocate Tips*

- Advocates should work to have standardized protection order forms adopted which include a warning to the defendant that possession of a firearm or ammunition while subject to a protection order may be a violation of federal law (inclusion of the firearm prohibition in the protection order may facilitate federal prosecution)
- When appropriate, advocates should encourage victims to tell the court that the defendant is in possession of firearms

## Advocate's Guide Glossary of Terms

**Certified**—a stamp, seal, or signature of the issuing judge or clerk of court noting that the copy is an authentic duplicate of the original order of the court.

**Comity**—a legal principle where a sovereign nation decides voluntarily to recognize another jurisdiction's court order.

**Consent Order**—an order of protection which is issued, usually without a finding (legal conclusion) of abuse, but after the respondent consents or agrees to the entry of the order.

**Ex parte Order**—an emergency or temporary order issued at the request of the petitioner without first providing notice or a hearing to the respondent.

**Indian Child Welfare Act (ICWA)**—a law that applies to custody proceedings in state courts involving foster care placement, termination of parental rights, preadoptive placement, and adoptive placement of Indian children. The ICWA may apply to divorces or custody proceedings where custody of the child(ren) is given to a third party. This law is significant because abusers often threaten to use the ICWA against battered women even though the ICWA does not apply to custody proceedings between the parents of the child(ren).

**Jurisdiction (location)**—in this guide, jurisdiction is used most commonly as a general name for the geographic areas impacted by the federal law. This includes all 50 states, Indian tribal lands, the District of Columbia, the U.S. Virgin Islands, Puerto Rico, American Samoa, the Northern Mariana Islands, and Guam.

> **Issuing Jurisdiction**—jurisdiction that grants the order of protection.

> **Enforcing Jurisdiction**—jurisdiction that enforces an order of protection issued by another jurisdiction.

**Jurisdiction**—can also be used as a legal term to refer to the types of authority that a court may exercise.

> **Subject Matter Jurisdiction**—refers to the authority of a court to hear and determine a particular type of case.

> **Personal Jurisdiction**—refers to the power the court may (or may not) have over the parties involved in a particular case.

**Mutual Order**—a single order of protection that includes prohibitions against both the petitioner and respondent.

**Parental Kidnapping Prevention Act (PKPA)**—federal legislation enacted to ensure that jurisdictions honor and enforce custody orders entered by the courts of other jurisdictions so long as both parties received prior notice and were given a chance to be heard. The PKPA prioritizes home state jurisdiction so other jurisdictions have to defer to orders entered by the jurisdiction where the child lived for the six-month period prior to the filing of the action.

**Petitioner**—the person who presents a petition to the court requesting an order of protection.

**Qualifying Misdemeanor**—state or federal misdemeanor crime that has as an element the use or attempted use of physical force or the threatened use of a deadly weapon. 18 U.S.C. §922(g)(9).

**Qualifying Protection Order**—protection order that meets the following conditions: (i) the protected party must be a spouse, former spouse, present or former cohabitant with the respondent, parent of common child, or a child of the respondent; (ii) the order must have been entered after a hearing of which the respondent had notice and an opportunity to appear; (iii) the order must include a finding that the respondent represents a credible threat to the protected party or must include an express prohibition against harassment, stalking, or the use of force that would reasonably be expected to cause injury. 18 U.S.C. §922(g)(8).

**Recognition**—the status granted a court order from another jurisdiction after a tribe determines it is enforceable. The tribe then issues its own order granting recognition.

**Registration/Filing**—refers to a procedure where an order of protection from one jurisdiction is registered or filed with a clerk of court or law enforcement agency in another jurisdiction. In some jurisdictions, the order may be entered into a local or statewide protective order computer registry. Registration usually creates a public record of the order of protection in the enforcing jurisdiction.

**Respondent**—the person against whom an order of protection is filed or issued.

**Tribe**—an Indian nation, Indian tribe, or native sovereign nation.

**Uniform Child Custody Jurisdiction Act (UCCJA)**—a uniform law, enacted with few variations by all of the states, which establishes jurisdiction to render custody orders that are enforceable across jurisdictional boundaries. The UCCJA sets forth four possible bases of jurisdiction without giving priority to any one over the others. Because of this, it is still possible for more than one state at a time to establish jurisdiction over the same parties and facts and for courts to render conflicting orders in the same case. The Act is more than 30 years old and is inconsistent with some provisions of subsequently enacted federal law.

**Uniform Child Custody Jurisdiction and Enforcement Act (UCCJEA)**—a replacement for the UCCJA currently being considered by the states and already enacted by a few. This Act establishes one jurisdictional base as having priority over the others—the state where the child has lived for the six months prior to the filing of the custody case—and builds in a number of protections for victims of domestic violence not available in the UCCJA. For example, the UCCJEA creates a structure of cooperation among the courts of the competing states so that the victim does not have to return physically to the home state in order to litigate in its courts; more comprehensive emergency jurisdiction in the refuge state; and a greater likelihood that the home state will voluntarily relinquish jurisdiction if it would be unsafe for the victim to litigate there.

## Helpful Interventions/Effective Advocacy

### Advocate Checklist

#### Issuing Jurisdiction

- If appropriate, assist the survivor in filing a cross petition if the abuser files for an order first
- Work with the court and the survivor to ensure that the following language is included in the order:

  1. Order is enforceable outside the jurisdiction

  2. Crossing jurisdictional lines to violate the order may be a federal crime under VAWA

  3. Custody provisions are made in compliance with the UCCJA or UCCJEA and PKPA

  4. The court had jurisdiction to issue the order

  5. The respondent had notice and an opportunity to be heard

- Work with the court and the survivor to ensure that the order includes a prohibition against firearm possession, if applicable under the laws of the issuing jurisdiction
- Work with the court and the survivor to ensure that the order includes required data elements for entry into the NCIC Protection Order File

- Work with the judge to ensure that the terms of the order are clear and specific
- Assist the abused person in getting proof of service
- Make sure that the survivor has several certified copies of the order and carries one at all times
- Inform the survivor about recognition/comity and assist in checking on procedures of the particular tribal jurisdiction
- Provide copies of §§2265 and 2266 of VAWA for the survivor to carry along with the order
- Get information about the laws and procedures of the enforcing jurisdiction(s)
- Provide names, addresses, and phone numbers of court clerks, local and federal prosecutors, law enforcement, the state coalition, and local battered women's programs in the jurisdiction(s) the abused person may be traveling
- If the victim has left the issuing jurisdiction, help the victim find someone who will accept service for any future attempts to change the order
- Help the survivor develop a detailed safety plan

### *Enforcing Jurisdiction*

- Know the laws and procedures of the jurisdiction
- Work with judges, court clerks, prosecutors and law enforcement to develop a coordinated response to orders issued in other jurisdictions
- Make sure that the survivor has certified copies of the order and proof of service, or assist in obtaining them
- Inform the abused person of the laws and procedures of the jurisdiction
- If registration is optional or mandatory, provide the information needed for the person to decide whether to register the order
- Remind officers that, in most jurisdictions, the protection order can be enforced on its face regardless of whether it is registered/filed in the jurisdiction or listed in a state protection order database or the NCIC Protection Order File (consult the laws and procedures of your jurisdiction)

- For custody issues, assist the abused person in getting legal representation
- Inform survivor that she/he may need to take the protection order to the tribal court to be recognized, even if she/he has a state protection order or a protection order from another tribe
- Inform survivor that, if appropriate, she/he should take a tribal protection order to the county, state, or other local jurisdiction for registration
- Develop relationships with federal victim/witness coordinators in order to work together to provide victim safety

## Technical Assistance on Full Faith and Credit Implementation

### Assistance to Victims of Domestic Violence

National Domestic Violence Hotline
(800) 799-SAFE
TTY (800) 787-3224
(24 hours/day, for referral to state and local programs)

### Technical Assistance on Full Faith and Credit

Full Faith and Credit Project
(800) 256-5883

International Association of Chiefs of Police
(800) The-IACP

Battered Women's Justice Project (Civil)
(800) 903-0111 ext 2

Battered Women's Justice Project (Criminal)
(800) 903-0111 ext. 1

### Expertise on Tribal Issues

Sacred Circle
(877) 733-7623

Mending the Sacred Hoop
(888) 305-1650

Northern Plains Tribal Judicial Institute
(701) 777-6176

American Indian Law Center
(505) 277-5462

### Expertise on Custody Issues

Family Violence Department of the National Council of Juvenile
and Family Court Judges
(800) 527-3223

Domestic Violence Commission of the American Bar Association
(202) 662-1737

### Expertise on Immigration Issues

National Immigration Project of the National Lawyers Guild
(617) 227-9727

Family Violence Prevention Fund
(415) 252-8900

## Special Issues

### Advocating for Immigrant Survivors of Domestic Violence

When an immigrant survivor tries to obtain or enforce a protection order, she may face difficult issues related to the risk of deportation of her non-citizen abuser and potentially of herself or other household members. Police and courts deal with immigrant victims in very different ways depending on the jurisdiction. Assessing risks and options with immigrant victims is a complicated task.

Survivors of domestic violence who have questions on immigration law should be referred to an attorney who has expertise in immigration and domestic violence issues. Any of the offices of the National Network on Behalf of Battered Immigrant Women (two are listed below) may also be contacted for a phone consultation.

*For technical assistance or more information, call the National Immigration Project of the National Lawyers Guild at (617) 227-9727 or the Family Violence Prevention Fund at (415) 252-8900. Website for the National Network on Behalf of Battered Imigrant Women: http://www.fvpf.org/immigration/national_network.html*

# Section 24.3

# *Teen Dating Violence and the Law*

Excerpted from *National Handbook on Teen Violence and the Law.* Copyright © 1996 National Center on Women and Family Law and NOW Legal Defense and Education Fund. Reprinted with permission.

Some people do not believe that teenagers and college students can get involved in dangerous dating situations from which they cannot remove themselves. Unfortunately, this can and does happen without any advance warning signs to alert the victim and his or her loved ones, as in the case of Jenny.

Jenny was 14 when she fell in love with Mark, a high school senior, and he was her first real boyfriend. They dated and were close for about six months before Jenny first tried to end their relationship, but Mark would not accept no for an answer. The harder Jenny tried to end any contact with Mark, the harder he tried to be around her and to see her.

It got so Mark would show up at the mall whenever Jenny went there with her friends and she would find out he had scared away possible new boyfriends by telling them she was still his. Later Mark began entering Jenny's home when no one was there and going into her bedroom where he would move her things around and leave notes so she would know he had been there. Jenny did not want to worry her parents so she didn't tell them how bad things were getting and how scared she was. Finally Mark left a note one day saying she would not live until Homecoming that year. Again Jenny did not tell her parents. Jenny's father found her viciously stabbed to death on Homecoming evening when he came home from work. Mark was convicted of her murder.[1]

This article was written to help teenagers, college students, their parents, and friends learn about an individual's rights in dating situations or relationships that start to feel uncomfortable or that actually become frightening because a boyfriend or girlfriend threatens, hits, follows or hurts the other person in the relationship. We hope to help you learn legal ways to protect yourself and to help prevent injury or even the death of yourself, a loved one, or a friend.

---

[1] For more about this case, please see *Dating Violence: Young Women in Danger,* "A Parent's Story," pages 21–27, Barrie Levy, ed. (The Seal Press, 1990).

# Can I Get an Order of Protection?

## *Your Relationship with the Abuser*

Unfortunately, not every state will let you get an order of protection against someone you are dating. In many states you need to be married, related to, living with, or have a child in common with that person in order to get an order of protection against him or her. In some states, the person you are living with must be of the opposite sex. There are also states which allow you to get an order of protection against another household member, while other states require that the person be someone you are living with as if married.

In some states, it is enough if you are dating the abuser on a regular basis. In many states that protect people who are dating or living together, you are protected even if you are no longer dating, while in other states you must be dating or living together when the abuse happens.

Finally, a small number of states allow you to get an order of protection against someone with whom you have no relationship if that person is harassing you, or stalking you, or if they have committed a crime against you more than once.

## *What About Gay Relationships?*

If the law in your state allows a person to get an order of protection against someone with whom that person *has resided in the same dwelling*, then it would not matter if you have a gay or straight relationship, or no intimate relationship at all. If your state specifies that you can get an order of protection against someone you are living with who is of the opposite sex, then it clearly would not cover gay relationships.

Still other states have provisions that are unclear. Can two people who are gay be "living together as spouses" or "living together as if married," or "cohabiting"? The answer is not obvious and may differ from state to state. [*See also* Section 12.13.]

## *What about Relatives?*

In many states you can get protection from a relative by blood or marriage, who abuses you, but not in all states. Some states limit the protection to current or former spouses, or parents and children, including stepparent, stepchildren, foster parents and foster children.

There are some states that will protect you against relatives, but only if the relative has resided with you in the same household.

### *People with Disabilities*

Some states have special provisions for those with disabilities. For instance, in Illinois, you can get an order of protection if you are disabled and your personal assistant abuses you. Abuse, in that case, includes denial of medical care or assistance.

### *Your Age and the Abuser's Age*

Most states do not require that you or the abuser be over 18 to get an order of protection, but some states do. In many states, if you are a minor, an adult may be able to file the petition requesting the order for you.

There are some states, however, which do not specify whether minors are permitted to obtain an order of protection, either on their own or by having an adult file the petition for them. You can certainly try to file for an order of protection in those states, although it is not completely certain that you will succeed.

If you need specific answers to any of the issues raised in this section, please contact your local hotline, a local domestic abuse organization, the clerk of the court, or an attorney in your area. [*See* Chapter 39, Hotlines and Organizations.]

## Section 24.4

# *What You Can Do If You Are a Victim of Crime*

U.S. Department of Justice, Office for Victims of Crime,
*OVC Fact Sheet,* May 1999.

*I don't believe half of the American population or even a small portion knows what can happen to you when you are a victim of a crime going through the criminal justice process.*

—A crime victim quoted in *New Directions from the Field: Victims' Rights and Services for the 21ˢᵗ Century,* 1998.

Crime victimization is a frightening and unsettling experience for the millions of Americans whose lives it touches each year. As recently as 1972, there were almost no services available to help crime victims or their survivors repair the damage done to their lives and property, or contend with the traumatic and frustrating ordeal of prosecution of the offender. Today, however, due largely to the dedicated efforts of advocates, lawmakers, and individual victims of crime, there is a tremendous range of services and resources designed to help victims obtain justice and healing. The Office for Victims of Crime (OVC), the U.S. Department of Justice agency that advocates for the fair treatment of crime victims, wants you to know that if you or someone you love is a victim of crime you have rights, you can get help, and you can work for positive change.

## *You Have Rights*

A majority of states have amended their constitutions to guarantee certain rights for crime victims. Typically, these include the following fundamental rights:

- The right to notification of all court proceedings related to the offense.
- The right to be reasonably protected from the accused offender.
- The right to have input at sentencing (in the form of a victim impact statement).

- The right to information about the conviction, sentencing, imprisonment, and release of the offender.
- The right to an order of restitution from the convicted offender.
- The right to notice of these rights.
- The right to standing to enforce these rights.

If you are a victim of or witness to a crime, these rights apply to you. Information about these rights may be obtained through your local victim/witness assistance program (usually located in the prosecutor's office), your State Attorney General's office, or U.S. Attorneys' offices.

## You Can Get Help

Literally thousands of programs now exist in the United States that provide services and sanctuary to crime victims. These programs are located within both state government agencies and private nonprofit or charitable organizations. Services provided through these programs are of two general types—*compensation and assistance.* Crime victim *compensation* programs reimburse victims of crime occurring within the state (including victims of federal crimes) for crime-related expenses. Crimes include violent crimes such as homicide, rape, drunk driving, domestic violence, and child sexual abuse and neglect. Expenses covered are medical costs, mental health counseling, funeral and burial costs, and lost wages or loss of support. Crime victim *assistance* programs provide services including crisis intervention, counseling, emergency shelter, criminal justice advocacy, and emergency transportation. Although compensation and assistance are usually provided to individuals, in certain instances entire communities may be eligible to receive assistance when a multiple victimization occurs. Information about compensation and assistance can usually be obtained through your local prosecutor's office or may be provided to you by your local law enforcement agency when you report an offense. [For contact information, see Chapter 39—Hotlines and Organizations.]

Financial support for many of these crime victims programs is provided through the Crime Victims Fund administered by OVC. The Fund is supported, not by tax dollars, but by fines, penalty assessments, and bond forfeitures collected from convicted federal offenders and is distributed among the states and territories annually.

## You Can Work for Positive Change

The progress that has been achieved to improve the treatment of crime victims is due largely to the efforts of untold thousands of individuals who have turned their victimization into a force for positive change. Victims and survivors of victims of homicide, rape, child abuse, domestic violence, and other serious offenses have transformed their experience into a vehicle for ensuring that victims of similar types of crime are afforded true justice, meaningful assistance, and compassionate treatment before the law. Many of these victims and survivors have volunteered their own time and resources toward such worthwhile activities as creating and staffing programs, conducting legislative advocacy, working in shelters, answering crisis hotlines, and speaking on victim impact panels. Similar opportunities exist in virtually every community. Working for positive change will help ensure that this progress is not lost and that new ground can be broken as greater justice and healing is gained for all victims of crime.

# Section 24.5

# *Compensation for Crime Victims*

U.S. Department of Justice, Office for Victims of Crime, April 1998.

Every state in the country operates a program to help pay for some of the expenses resulting from crimes involving violence or abuse. Victims of assault, rape, domestic violence, child abuse, drunk driving, and other crimes involving personal injury may qualify for this assistance. Families of murder victims also may be eligible for financial help. These programs are called crime victim compensation programs. While each state's program is slightly different, this section will provide some general information about all of the programs. *It's important to check with the program in the state where the crime occurred to determine exactly what the eligibility requirements are and what benefits are available.*

Victims of crime under state, federal, military, and tribal jurisdiction are eligible to apply for compensation. A conviction of the offender is not required. The programs will pay for certain expenses not covered by insurance or another public benefit program. *With very limited exceptions in a few states, crimes solely involving theft or damage to property are not covered.*

## Who May Get Financial Help?

Those eligible for crime victim compensation include:

- A crime victim who has been physically injured.
- In a number of states, a victim who suffers emotional injury as a result of violence or threats, even though no physical injury resulted.
- Family members of a deceased victim and, in some states, any individual who pays for expenses resulting from a victim's injury or death.

## What Are the Eligibility Requirements?

While each state's eligibility requirements vary slightly, victims are generally required to:

- Report the crime promptly to law enforcement. (Most states have a 72-hour reporting requirement.)
- Cooperate in the investigation and prosecution of the crime.
- Be innocent of any criminal activity or misconduct leading to the victim's injures or death.
- File a timely application with the compensation program in the state where the crime occurred, and provide any information requested. *Most states require that the application be filed within 1 year from the date of the crime, but a few states have shorter or longer periods.*

## What Costs May Be Paid?

The following expenses may be covered if they are *not* paid for by insurance or by another public benefit program, and if they result directly from the crime:

- Medical and hospital care, and dental work to repair injury to teeth.
- Mental health counseling.

- Lost earnings due to the crime-related injuries.
- Loss of support for dependents or a deceased victim.
- Funeral and burial expenses.

*Check with the specific state where the crime occurred to determine exactly what costs are covered by the program.*

## What Costs Are Not Covered?

- *Property loss, theft and damage are usually not covered* (unless damage is to eyeglasses, hearing aids, or other medically necessary devices). However, a few states may pay limited amounts for the loss of essential personal property during a violent crime, or for cleaning up the crime scene.
- Expenses paid for by other sources, such as any type of public or private health insurance, automobile insurance, disability insurance, or workers compensation are not covered.
- Except in a very few states, award for pain and suffering are not available.

## Are There Limits on the Assistance Available?

Costs related directly to the crime can be reimbursed up to a maximum level in each state. These maximums typically range from $10,000 to $25,000, though a few states have higher or lower maximums. In addition, there may be limits on some types of benefits, such as mental health counseling or funeral costs.

## How Can a Victim Apply?

Applications can be obtained from the compensation program or from police, prosecutors, or victim services agencies. Many states also have brochures describing their programs. Victims can seek help from victim service programs in completing the application. The application should be submitted to the compensation program as soon as possible. The compensation program will review the application to determine eligibility and to decide what costs can be paid, and will notify the applicant of the program's decision.

For a listing of state victim assistance and compensation programs, see Chapter 39—Hotlines and Organizations.

# Chapter 25

# Legislative and Other Government Initiatives

## Chapter Contents

## Section 25.1

# *Preventing Violence Against Women*

U.S. Department of Health and Human Services *HHS Fact Sheet,*
February 1999.

## *Overview*

Violence against women is an urgent criminal and public health problem with devastating consequences for women, children, and families. To help break the cycle of violence, the Clinton Administration has made stopping domestic violence and violence against women top priorities.

Since taking office, the Administration has worked to eliminate domestic violence from our communities by working to create a system that not only prevents domestic violence but which also ensures that every woman suffering from domestic violence has access to information and emergency assistance, wherever and whenever she needs it.

The cornerstone of this effort is the Violence Against Women Act, included at the President's urging in the Violent Crime Control and Law Enforcement Act of 1994. Under the law, the federal government for the first time adopted a comprehensive approach to fighting domestic violence and violence against women, combining tough new penalties with programs to prosecute offenders and assist women victims of violence.

Initiatives at the Department of Health and Human Services [HHS] are an important part of the Administration's comprehensive strategy. HHS has launched a national toll-free domestic violence hotline, more than tripled resources for battered women's shelters, and worked to raise awareness of domestic violence in the workplace and among health care providers, among others.

The fiscal year (FY) 1999 budget includes $156 million for HHS programs to prevent violence against women, including $1.2 million for the National Domestic Violence Hotline. For HHS programs under the Violence Against Women Act, the Department will receive $88.8 million for grants to states for battered women's shelters, $15 million for programs to reduce sexual abuse among runaway, homeless and street youth, $45 million for grants to states for rape prevention and education programs, and $6 million for coordinated community responses. In addition, $7 million from the Preventive Health and Health Services Block Grant is earmarked for rape prevention programs. The President's FY 2000 budget includes an additional $27.9 million to fund a Department-wide initiative to prevent violence against women from occurring and to provide services to its victims. In total, the Department is requesting $218.2 million for programs to prevent violence against women.

## The Violence Against Women Act

The landmark Violence Against Women Act (VAWA), administered by HHS and the Department of Justice (DOJ), has provided funding to hire more prosecutors and improve domestic violence training among prosecutors, police officers, and health and social services professionals. It has also provided for more shelters, counseling services, and research into causes and effective community campaigns to reduce violence against women.

In addition, VAWA set new federal penalties for those who cross state lines to continue abuse of a spouse or partner, making interstate domestic abuse and harassment a federal offense. VAWA also made it unlawful for any person who is subject to a restraining order to possess ammunition or a firearm, requires states to honor protective orders issued in other states, and has given victims the right to mandatory restitution and the right to address the court at the time of sentencing.

The Department of Health and Human Services and the Justice Department are leading the following initiatives under the Violence Against Women Act:

## Health and Human Services Programs under VAWA

- **Grants for Battered Women's Shelters.** Since 1993, the Clinton Administration has more than quadrupled funding for battered women's shelters, from $20 million in FY 1993 to $88.8 million in FY 1999. These resources will also support related services, such as community outreach and prevention, children's counseling, and linkage to child protection services. The Crime Act provided new resources to extend these services under the existing Family Violence Prevention and Services Act. Overall, the Clinton Administration has granted states, territories, and Native American tribes over $400 million to support the system of 1,400 emergency shelters, safe homes, and related services nationwide.

- **The National Domestic Violence Hotline.** In February 1996, President Clinton launched the National Domestic Violence Hotline, a 24-hour, toll-free service which provides crisis assistance and local shelter referrals for callers across the country. The hotline has received more than 292,000 calls since it was launched, and the majority of these calls are from individuals who have never before reached out for assistance. To support the response to this service, the hotline received $1.2 million in funding for FY 1999. The hotline is operated by the Texas Council on Family Violence, through an HHS grant. The voice number is 1-800-799-SAFE, and the TDD number for the hearing impaired is 1-800-787-3224.

- **Education and Prevention to Reduce Sexual Abuse Among Runaway, Homeless and Street Youth.** This program provides street-based outreach and education, including treatment, counseling and provision of information and referrals to runaways, homeless, and street youth who have been subjected to or are at risk of sexual abuse. The program was appropriated $15 million for FY 1999.

- **Education and Prevention Grants to Reduce Sexual Assaults Against Women.** Under this program, HHS provides grants to states for rape prevention and education programs conducted by rape crisis centers or similar nongovernmental, entities [for a list of these entities, see the Department of Health and Human Services Gateway page at: http://www.hhs.gov.gateway.html]. The funds will support educational seminars, the operation of hotlines, training programs, preparation of informational materials, and other activities to increase awareness of and to help prevent sexual assault. States receiving grants must devote at least 25 percent of their funds to education programs targeted to middle school, junior high school, or high school students. HHS funding for the program in FY 1999 is $45 million. In addition, $7 million from the Preventive Health and Health Services Block Grant is earmarked for rape prevention programs.

- **Coordinated Community Responses to Prevent Intimate Partner Violence.** This program, administered by CDC [Centers for Disease Control and Prevention], will help build new community programs aimed at preventing intimate partner violence, as well as strengthen and better coordinate existing community intervention and prevention programs. The program will also evaluate the impact of comprehensive community programs on preventing intimate partner violence. This program was appropriated $6 million for FY 1999. Under the program, HHS awarded 10 grants in FY 1997 for primary prevention activities in communities.

## Justice Department Programs under VAWA and Related Efforts

- The Justice Department's STOP (Services, Training, Officers, Prosecutors) Violence Against Women grant program assists law enforcement officers and prosecutors in developing better strategies to combat violence against women. The Justice Department [DOJ] has provided $412 million to states and territories to support coordinated approaches to combating domestic violence and sexual assault. In FY 1998, DOJ awarded 56 grants totaling $135 million in formula grants and DOJ awarded 57 grants to tribal governments totaling $4.9 million.

- In FY 1998, DOJ awarded 57 Civil Legal Assistance Grants totaling $11.5 million—one grant to every state, the District of Columbia, American Samoa, Puerto Rico, and the Virgin Islands.

- DOJ awarded states $53.8 million in FY 1998 to encourage policies of arrest of domestic violence offenders at the local level. Justice also provided $19.4 million to fund rural domestic violence programs in FY 1998, up $5.2 million in FY 1997.

- The Clinton Administration has designed a new $46 million Community Policing to Combat Domestic Violence Program. The Justice Department's COPS office is providing funds to over 300 jurisdictions around the country under this initiative to run innovative community policing programs focused on domestic violence.

- DOJ has adopted an implementation strategy involving federal leadership through outreach, research and the provision of training, technical assistance and opportunities for collaboration at the national, state and district levels. The Department's Office of Justice Programs awarded funding for a cooperative agreement with the Battered Women's Justice Project to support the development of a resource clearinghouse and implementation tools. The Department has also funded a regional pilot project in Kentucky to test interstate and intrastate verification systems for facilitating the street level enforcement of protection orders. In addition, the Department has awarded funding for a joint task force of the Conference of Chief Justices and the Conference of State Court Administrators that will focus on full faith and credit. [*See* Section 24.2.]

• In August, 1996, at the direction of the President, the Attorney General developed and presented a plan for a national registry to track sex offenders, including rapists and child molesters. The FBI is currently implementing that plan. [*See* Section 25.4.]

• The Jacob Wetterling Crimes Against Children and Sexually Violent Offender Registration Act, enacted as part of the Crime Act, was amended by the federal Megan's Law, signed by the President on May 17, 1996, and by the Pam Lychner Act, enacted October 1996. Under these statutes, sex offenders and child molesters must register information about their whereabouts with appropriate state law enforcement agencies for ten years after release from prison and state prison officials must notify local law enforcement when they are released or move. States must notify the public about the release of registered sex offenders when necessary for public safety. [*See* Section 25.4.]

• *Violence Against Women Act News* is a monthly publication of the Violence Against Women Office that provides victims' groups, public agencies, and individuals with current information about legislation, programs, and policies concerning domestic violence and sexual assault. First distributed in July 1996, the newsletter is disseminated through a growing list of subscribers and includes examples from the field of how state and local groups are working against violence.

## The Advisory Council on Violence Against Women

The Advisory Council on Violence Against Women was created on July 13, 1995. Co-chaired by Attorney General Janet Reno and Secretary of Health and Human Services Donna Shalala, the Council consists of 47 experts—representatives from law enforcement, media, business, sports, health and social services, and victim advocacy—working together to prevent violence against women.

- **A Checklist for Communities**—On October 1, 1996, the Attorney General and Secretary Shalala announced the creation of a "Community Checklist," to help ensure that every community in the country has resources in place for domestic violence prevention and intervention. [*See* Chapter 22.]

- **Workplace Awareness**—The Workplace Resource Center is organized by the Family Violence Prevention Fund and supported by many corporations, state and local governments, labor unions, and the Advisory Council. The Center provides help and education to employees in the private and public sectors concerning domestic violence—through newsletters, information fairs, and workplace assistance.

The federal government, under the President's direction, has also implemented an Employee Awareness Campaign on Violence Against Women. In October 1997, the Vice President announced new guidelines, created at the President's direction to help federal departments and agencies create a safer work environment. These new guidelines explain how to develop programs to respond to violence against federal employees, including domestic violence as well as threatening, harassing, and intimidating behavior.

To address domestic violence concerns among its own employees, an HHS human resources task force compiled an action guide entitled, "Understanding and Responding to Domestic Violence in the Workplace." The guide assists HHS employees in understanding the nature of the problem, finding help for domestic violence problems, and developing safety plans. It also addresses concerns of co-workers and supervisors.

### *Executive Action on Domestic Violence*

On October 3, 1996, President Clinton urged all states to implement the Family Violence provisions included in the welfare bill he signed on August 22, 1996. To help welfare recipients who are victims of domestic violence move successfully into work, the provisions give states the option to screen welfare recipients for domestic abuse; refer them to counseling and supportive services; and temporarily waive any program requirements that would prevent recipients from escaping violence or would unfairly penalize them. The President also directed the Department of Health and Human Services and the Justice Department to assist states in implementing the provisions. [*See also* Section 7.3.]

## *Federal Anti-Stalking Law and Domestic Violence Gun Law*

On September 23, 1996, President Clinton signed into law the Interstate Stalking Punishment and Prevention Act of 1996, which dramatically toughens the law against stalkers. For the first time, this law makes it a federal crime for any stalker to cross state lines to pursue a victim, regardless of whether there is a protection order in effect, they have committed an actual act of violence, or they are a spouse or intimate of the victim. In addition, on September 30, 1996, the President signed legislation to keep guns away from people convicted of misdemeanor crimes of domestic violence. [*See also* Section 25.5.]

## *Immigration Bill Provision for Domestic Violence Victims*

At the Administration's urging, Congress included a provision in the immigration bill that the President signed on September 30, 1996, to ensure that immigrant women and children who are victims of domestic violence are eligible for vital public health services and are not denied services due to changes in deeming rules. The Administration also succeeded in removing provisions from the bill that would subject battered immigrants to deportation for receiving these vital services. In addition, the immigration bill now makes battered immigrants eligible for cash assistance and Medicaid if the states exercise their option under the welfare law to make legal immigrants eligible for such programs. [*See also* Section 5.2.]

## *Other Efforts at the Department of Health and Human Services*

- HHS is working to increase the ability of battered women, including those on welfare, to obtain and retain employment and access child support, through technical assistance to state welfare and child support administrators and through grant programs. As part of this effort, HHS is working to increase collaboration between domestic violence and welfare agencies.

- HHS is encouraging greater linkages and collaboration between the child welfare, family and intimate violence, and criminal justice fields to protect better both children and parents in homes where violence occurs. As part of this effort, HHS has funded 26 grants over three years to local programs to stimulate collaboration between child welfare agencies and domestic violence providers. These projects primarily train child welfare staff to identify and respond appropriately to instances of domestic violence in their caseloads. In addition, HHS has awarded five child welfare training grants to schools of social work to develop curricula and train social workers in family violence.

- In FY 1997, HHS established a National Technical Assistance Center on Welfare Reform and Disability. One focus of this center is to increase our understanding about linkages between welfare, disability, and domestic violence.

- HHS is working to strengthen the health care system's ability to screen, treat, and prevent family and intimate violence by evaluating and helping to improve training of health professionals. The Agency for Health Care Policy and Research (AHCPR) is supporting research on the effectiveness of team training to help primary care providers identify and manage domestic violence. In another AHCPR study, researchers are examining the relationship between exposure to domestic violence, health status, and use of health care services in Kaiser Permanente's northwest region. As part of this effort, HHS is supporting a National Nursing Violence Against Women Strategy Initiative with participants from national nursing organizations to begin collaborations and develop a national nursing strategy. The first National Nursing Summit on Violence Against Women was held on October 27, 1997.

- HHS is working with the Department of Justice, state and local agencies, and private organizations to increase the knowledge base about family and intimate violence, through data collection and research.

- The Substance Abuse and Mental Health Services Administration (SAMHSA) administers several programs that both research and work to address substance abuse and mental health issues among victims of domestic violence. SAMHSA has developed a comprehensive domestic violence curriculum for training substance abuse, mental health and other health and human service professionals on how to address violence against women. A component of the program is the Violence Data Exchange Team (VDET), which has trained teams in 28 cities to gather, interpret, and report information about local substance abuse-related violence for use in policy making and program planning.

- Since 1993, HHS' Administration for Children and Families (ACF) has funded a network of four domestic violence resource centers. In 1998, ACF expanded their resource centers to include Sacred Circle, the National Resource Center to End Violence Against Native Women. These centers provide information, technical assistance, and research funding on domestic violence.

- **The Violence Against Women Prevention Research Center** will conduct research, provide researchers and practitioners with training in this field, and disseminate information about effective prevention strategies.

- **Coordinated Community Response Projects** in 6 communities were funded by CDC for three years starting in Fiscal Year 1996. Three of these projects were designed for rural and Native American communities to develop and evaluate a coordinated community response. The remaining three were intended for larger communities with existing coordinated responses.

- Community-based Primary Prevention Projects are designed to develop, implement, and evaluate programs that prevent family and intimate violence. Some of these projects will focus on intimate partner violence among ethnic and racial minority populations.

- The National Institute of Mental Health (NIMH) has funded a number of research studies focusing on factors that directly influence the initiation and escalation of physically aggressive behavior in intimate relationships. A number of these projects are investigating complex individual and interpersonal mediational processes in physically abusive intimate partner relationships.

These studies have significant implications for interventions to prevent the occurrence and to ameliorate the mental health consequences of domestic violence by identifying potent targets for intervention; research on helping interventions for victims of violence against women continue to be a research priority to help reduce the extent and consequences of violence against women.

In addition to programs focusing specifically on violence against women, the HHS has a number of related programs, including:

- The Administration on Aging (AoA) has funded the creation and operation of the National Center on Elder Abuse, which focuses on training, technical assistance, research, and information dissemination related to elder abuse, neglect, and exploitation. A previously funded AoA grantee, the Wisconsin Coalition Against Domestic Violence, has integrated its AoA demonstration program serving older women into its permanent ongoing program and provides technical assistance and resources to others who are starting similar programs.

- HHS also funds several programs that aim to strengthen families, prevent the abuse of women and children, and help families provide a healthy and safe environment for children. These programs include the Family Preservation and Support program; Community Schools; and Child Abuse Prevention and Treatment Act grants. AoA funds state elder abuse prevention programs in all 50 states that focus on the prevention of elder abuse, neglect and exploitation, which significantly impact older women. A recent released study funded by AoA and ACF found that—after accounting for their larger proportion in the aging population—older women are abused at a higher rate than males, and are often abused by a family member.

- The Substance Abuse and Mental Health Services Administration (SAMHSA) has published and distributed a best practices guide to help drug addiction counselors recognize when clients are victims or perpetrators of domestic violence, and to help counselors of abused women in need of protection to recognize drug and alcohol addiction.

- AoA also operated the National ElderCare Locator, a national toll-free information and assistance service to assist family members and others to learn about and access services for their loved ones. Included among the information available through the ElderCare Locator is information about programs to identify and prevent elder abuse. The ElderCare locator number is 1-800-667-1116. It operates from Monday through Friday, 9 a.m. to 8 p.m. E.S.T.

## Section 25.2

# *Initiatives to Combat Violence Against Women*

U.S. Department of Justice, Office of Justice Programs, Office for
Victims of Crime, August, 1998.

### *Background*

The Office for Victims of Crime (OVC), in collaboration with other
Office of Justice Programs (OJP) bureaus, and public and private interest groups and agencies, administers funding to programs that
develop strategies, discuss issues, and make recommendations to prevent and combat victimization of women. For the purpose of this fact
sheet, violence against women includes sexual assault, campus crime,
stalking, and domestic violence.

In forming partnerships with other government agencies and organizations, OVC pools resources and support in order to develop new
alternatives and directions for resolving violence against women. For
example, OVC has joined together with the Bureau of Indian Affairs
(BIA) to target family violence in Indian Country. OVC also has formed
a partnership with the Violence Against Women Grants Office
(VAWGO) within the Office of Justice Programs to work on many
projects. One such collaboration funded the Battered Women's Justice Project which conducts training and technical assistance to develop effective law enforcement, prosecution, court, and advocacy
practices on behalf of battered women. OVC grants finance efforts by
communities to create and adopt locally responsive approaches that
encourage collaboration among all sectors. Such sectors include victim service providers, victims' advocates, law enforcement authorities,
health care providers, and community organizations representing
educators, businesses, members of the clergy, and others involved in
the fight to end violence against women.

### *Funding*

OVC's funding is based on the Crime Victims Fund, which is derived, not from tax dollars, but from fines and penalties paid by federal criminal offenders. Nearly 90 percent of the money collected each

year, $363 million in 1997, is distributed as formula grant programs to states to assist in funding their victim assistance and compensation programs. The other portion is placed in a discretionary fund that assists federal crime victims and supports training and technical assistance programs or demonstration projects that can be used as models of "promising practice." Since 1988, OVC has distributed over $2 billion to the states to support victim services and compensation.

## VOCA Victim Assistance Program

*(Formula Grant Programs to the States)*

Through the Victims of Crime Act, OVC funds the VOCA Victim Assistance Program which provides nearly 3,000 local victim services and programs nationwide.These programs offer victims a wide range of services, including crisis counseling, criminal justice advocacy, and shelter. To date, using FY 97 funds, states have funded 1,881 domestic violence programs, 1,484 adult sexual assault programs, 332 rape crisis programs in hospitals, and 675 domestic violence shelter programs for a total of $222,278,099. For information about federal funding available in your state, please contact the agency designated by the Governor to administer the VOCA Victim Assistance Program. In many cases, the same agency has been designated to administer VAWA funding. [For information on contacting state offices, see Chapter 39—Hotlines and Organizations.]

## Discretionary Fund Initiatives

The following list of initiatives shows the collaborative commitment from OVC, OJP offices and agencies, as well as other federal agencies and organizations by devoting resources and attention to building and strengthening the response of communities nationwide to ending violence against women. In addition to sharing information about existing programs, OVC invites those people who touch the lives of crime victims to propose plans that establish practices and provide materials that can be readily used by communities to assist in curbing violence against women. Many of the products produced from these and other OVC grants can be obtained through the OVC Resource Center.

## *Sexual Assault Programs*

### *Sexual Assault Nurse Examiners (SANE) Development and Operation Guide*

#### Minneapolis Research Foundation, Sexual Assault Resource Service

OVC awarded funds to the Sexual Assault Resource Service (SARS) of the Minneapolis Research Foundation to develop a SANE guidebook. The Sexual Assault Nurse Examiners program is an innovative treatment model for sexual assault victims and was developed by SARS in the 1970s. Requests from communities across the nation for information and guidance to develop this program in their own community has prompted the need for this guidebook. The SANE guidebook, available in 1998, leads interested individuals through the process of establishing and operating a SANE program and comprehensively addressing clinical, legal, and operational issues. The second phase of the project will provide technical assistance through a series of 12 to 15 regional training workshops; develop a SANE Web site for dissemination of information and technical assistance; and evaluate program efficacy through statistical tracking of new and existing programs, focusing on outcomes that measure the impact of SANE services on sexual assault victims and their communities.

### *Building Skills for Sexual Assault Responders*

#### Minneapolis Research Foundation, Sexual Assault Resource Service

OVC awarded a training and technical assistance grant to the Sexual Assault Resource Service of the Minneapolis Research Foundation to address the need to improve the quality and continuity of services to victims of sexual assault. The grantee is currently developing a comprehensive training and technical assistance package for crisis response, advocacy, and mental health services that can promote personal recovery and healing. The grantee pilot-tested the training in Colorado in April 1998 and in Minnesota in May 1998. During the second phase of the project, the grantee will modify the curriculum based on results of the pilot-testing and conduct a series of regional training workshops for direct service providers.

*Justice for Deaf Victims of Domestic Violence and Sexual Assault*

## Abused Deaf Women's Advocacy Services

OVC awarded a grant to the Abused Deaf Women's Advocacy Services in Seattle, Washington, to develop a training and technical assistance package for five cities across the country. This project originally started in Seattle providing services and support for deaf victims of domestic violence and sexual assault. Now, the project will work with the deaf communities in Boston, Austin, Minneapolis, Rochester (NY), and San Francisco to replicate the program.

## *Domestic Violence Programs*

*Educating to End Domestic Violence*

## American Bar Association

The American Bar Association (ABA) Commission on Domestic Violence developed a report detailing various innovative programs law schools have implemented to teach about domestic violence and assist victims of domestic violence. The program staff also developed a series of recommendations for replicating these types of initiatives in other schools. This publication, *When Will They Ever Learn? Educating to End Domestic Violence*, was funded by OVC to encourage and assist law schools to establish, develop, and expand curricula in the classroom and clinical programs that both teach students about domestic violence and assist victims.

*Training Lawyers to Respond to Domestic Violence and Elder Abuse*

## American Bar Association

This project involves two divisions of the ABA—the Commission on Domestic Violence and the Commission on the Legal Problems of the Elderly. Both Commissions have joined together to develop a model national training curriculum to improve the responses of general practice and family lawyers to victims of elder abuse and domestic violence. The Commissions will develop, pilot test, revise, produce, and disseminate a model curriculum that can be replicated or adapted by bar associations and other organizations interested in providing this training.

*Battered Immigrant Women Program*

## American Bar Association

The ABA Commission on Domestic Violence, in cooperation with AYUDA (AHELP@), a grassroots agency for Latina victims of domestic violence, are finalizing a curriculum for victim advocates and attorneys on the Battered Immigrant Women Provisions of the Violence Against Women Act (VAWA). The Commission conducted three trainings in 1998 and four trainings in 1999. This curriculum includes information about VAWA's recently issued regulations, immigration law, cultural issues, and ways to assist victims who want to petition for residency. For more information about upcoming training programs, contact the ABA Commission on Domestic Violence at 202-662-1737.

*Domestic Violence: A Training for Dental Professionals*

## University of Minnesota

The School of Dentistry and the Program Against Sexual Violence at the University of Minnesota received grant funding to produce and pilot test a training videotape and curriculum for dentists and ancillary staff on how to effectively intervene with victims of domestic violence.

A comprehensive training packet that will enable dental teams to easily apply the intervention model to their own office setting will accompany the video.

*AMWA Online Health Care Provider Educational Project on Domestic Violence*

## American Medical Women's Association (AMWA)

This program will develop an interactive online physician and health professional education program on domestic violence on the AMWA Web Site. In doing so, AMWA will utilize a curriculum developed by the Family Violence Prevention Fund. For further information contact their web site at http://www.amwa.doc.org/edproj.html.

*Promising Strategies and Practices to Enhance Workplace Response to Victims of Domestic Violence*

## The Family Violence Prevention Fund (FVPF)

Domestic violence hampers a victim's ability to perform in the workplace. This project has created a blueprint to transform workplaces into a supportive environment for victims of domestic violence. In doing so, the FVPF conducted a "victim needs assessment." The project will create materials outlining model policies and programs that can be jointly adopted by employers and labor unions. Finally, the project will work with trade and labor organizations and others to build a network for distributing the model policies and practices. These networking and collaborative activities will serve to increase public awareness of domestic violence as a workplace issue.

*Full Faith and Credit Provision, Violence Against Women Act*

The following three initiatives are organized under the Violence Against Women Act's (VAWA) Full Faith and Credit provision. VAWA provides Full Faith and Credit for all state and tribal protection orders under 18 USC Section 2265. OVC has been working closely with the Violence Against Women Grants Office (VAWGO) to develop programs to assist in the implementation of this provision.

*Full Faith and Credit Training and Technical Assistance Project*

## Pennsylvania Coalition Against Domestic Violence, Inc.

The goal of this project is to develop effective law enforcement, prosecution, court, and advocacy practices to promote accessible, consistent enforcement of civil and criminal protection orders in appropriate state and tribal courts throughout the country. [For more information, see Section 24.2.]

*National Conference, Across State Lines: Collaborating to Keep Women Safe*

In 1997, OVC provided partial funding for a national conference, "Across State Lines: Collaborating to Keep Women Safe." This conference brought together teams of law enforcement and court professionals from over 40 states and territories to begin planning for the implementation of the Full Faith and Credit Provisions of the Violence Against Women Act. The conference also provided needed training and technical assistance to these state teams on the latest issues involving Full Faith and Credit.

*Domestic Violence in Kentucky: Model Law Enforcement Response*

OVC has worked closely with the Community Oriented Policing Services and VAWGO to establish a demonstration program in Kentucky to implement the Full Faith and Credit provisions of the Violence Against Women Act. The program is both an intra-state and inter-state enforcement effort. Kentucky has focused its implementation efforts on the development of model forms, enhancement of its central database of protection orders, training and technical assistance for law enforcement and court personnel, and outreach and education efforts for victims of domestic violence.

*Victim Advocates in a Specialized Domestic Violence Court*

**Criminal Court of New York City**

OVC is working with VAWGO to establish a domestic violence court within the Criminal Court of New York City. The domestic violence court, which will handle misdemeanor offenses and pre-indictment felony contempt cases based on violations of criminal court orders of protection, will be staffed by a dedicated judge who will use the authority of the Court to coordinate and monitor the responses of all of the criminal justice and social service agencies charged with addressing domestic violence. The project will fund victim advocates to work closely with victims and the judge.

*Domestic Violence Fatality Reviews: A National Summit*

## National Council of Juvenile and Family Court Judges

Communities nationwide are requiring a uniform method of investigating and assessing the efficacy of services provided to victims of domestic violence. In response to this need, the State Justice Institute and OVC joined to fund the Family Violence Project of the National Council of Juvenile and Family Court Judges to convene a group of national experts on the issue of domestic violence fatality reviews. This group will compile procedures, protocols, and models resulting from a national forum and use that information to develop an educational training module and informational materials on promising practices for fatality review teams. The finished products will be disseminated nationwide for use by new and ongoing fatality review teams seeking to establish or improve procedures and programs.

*Effective Intervention in Domestic Violence and Child Abuse Cases:*
*Guidelines for Policy and Practice*

## National Council of Juvenile and Family Court Judges

With the support of OVC and the National Center on Child Abuse and Neglect of the Department of Health and Human Services, the Family Violence Project of the National Council of Juvenile and Family Court Judges will develop a set of recommended guidelines on intervening in domestic violence and child abuse cases. The grantee will compile materials from promising programs and provide that information to a multidisciplinary committee of national experts on the subject, which will meet several times to develop the guidelines. Guidelines will be used by child protective services staff, law enforcement, attorneys, courts, family preservation agencies, and battered women's programs.

*National Teleconference on Domestic Violence*

In May 1996, OVC worked closely with the South Carolina United States Attorney's Office to cosponsor a National Teleconference, *"When the Cry Comes..."* to train law enforcement officials and victim advocates on best practices when handling a case of domestic violence. This teleconference aired at 165 locations, in 45 states, across the country, viewed by nearly 4,000 criminal justice professionals and victim advocates. In June 1997, OVC again joined the South Carolina United States Attorney's Office to cosponsor and provide funding for a follow-up teleconference, *"When the Cry Comes...from the Children."* This teleconference provided training to law enforcement officials and victim advocates on handling domestic violence cases when children are involved.

### *Violence Against Women Act Specialist*

OVC funded a Violence Against Women Act specialist position to assist EOUSA in providing training and technical assistance to all presently employed and new Assistant U.S. Attorneys, Federal Victim-Witness Coordinators, Advocates, and Specialists from U.S. Attorneys' Offices nationwide concerning the effective and efficient implementation of relevant provisions of the Violence Against Women Act.

### *Victim Information and Notification Everyday (VINE™) System Support*

OVC is working with the Bureau of Justice Assistance and VINE™ to extend notification services to victims of crime. The VINE™ system is automated to link police, prosecutors, and corrections officials to victims. VINE™ provides confidential notice of inmate status changes, such as release and relocation, which allows victims to take necessary measures of precaution to protect themselves from further harm. This project is intended to improve compliance with victim notification laws and enhances the criminal justice system's response to victims.

## Section 25.3

# *Justice System Initiatives for Child Abuse Cases*

Excerpted from *Breaking the Cycle of Violence: Recommendations to Improve the Criminal Justice Response to Child Victims and Witnesses.* U.S. Department of Justice, Office of Justice Programs, Office for Victims of Crime, June 1999.

## *Multidisciplinary Initiatives*

Cases involving child victims tend to involve multiple agencies and professionals from various disciplines. In such cases, both the professionals and the child victims benefit from effective communication and collaboration. Experience indicates that coordinated responses to child victim cases can:

- Reduce the number of interviews a child undergoes.
- Minimize the number of people involved in a case.
- Enhance the quality of evidence discovered for criminal prosecution or civil litigation.
- Provide information essential to family and child protection service agencies.
- Minimize the likelihood of conflicts among agencies with different philosophies and mandates.[1]

Cases involving child witnesses also involve complex medical issues and family relationships. These cases often involve a number of people and systems, including family members, police, clergy, hospital staff, prosecutors, guardians *ad litem*, civil attorneys, criminal defense attorneys, child protection agencies, family courts, and therapeutic clinicians. Prosecutors and victim advocates have to be particularly diligent in managing the case to monitor and provide for the well-being of the child witness.

---

[1] *Joint Investigations of Child Abuse: Report of a Symposium*, National Institute of Justice, U.S. Department of Justice (p. 3), July 1993.

Many communities have some form of multidisciplinary team (MDT) to effectively manage child abuse cases that involve several agencies. The purpose of multidisciplinary child abuse teams is to reduce duplication of agency procedures and the number of child interviews and to coordinate intervention and services. Apparent inconsistencies in young victims' statements are often caused by the phrasing of questions and differences in the way individuals interpret answers. Jointly conducted or monitored interviews can reduce inconsistencies and improve the quality of information.

Sharing information, expertise, and experiences with other professionals can improve the quality and outcome of child victim cases. Law enforcement officers and prosecutors with limited knowledge of child development stages should consult social workers and therapists who have studied and are experienced with troubled children. They should also meet with pediatricians and medical examiners. Social workers and medical providers may consult with police officers who can provide guidance on investigation and evidentiary issues.

Many states have laws requiring joint investigations and cooperation between law enforcement and child protection agencies in child abuse cases. Other states have laws authorizing creation of multidisciplinary and multiagency child protection teams. Many more states have informal information-sharing arrangements. A formal MDT is not necessary for effective collaboration and information sharing, but the interagency relationships do need to be developed and institutionalized through written policies or memoranda of understanding.

## Children's Advocacy Centers

One of the best examples of a team approach to handling child victim cases is children's advocacy centers. More than 350 communities have established or are in the process of developing children's advocacy center programs. These centers allow law enforcement officers, child protection workers, prosecutors, victim advocates, medical professionals, and therapists to coordinate the investigation, prosecution, and treatment of the child victim. A single or limited number of investigatory interviews are conducted in "child friendly" settings rather than multiple interviews in intimidating environments. The children's advocacy center approach makes it easier for a team of professionals with varied expertise to work together to ensure that maltreatment of children is responded to in the most appropriate way with the least amount of additional trauma to child victims during the various stages of criminal justice intervention. Some centers are affiliated with medical centers and/or have facilities for medical examinations. Many are equipped with one-way mirrors and have videotaping capacity. All children's advocacy centers are furnished with young children in mind. The coordinated approach and team decision-making processes also improve the quality of information and increase the number of successful prosecutions. The Office of Juvenile Justice and Delinquency Prevention (OJJDP) in the U.S. Department of Justice provides funds to communities seeking to establish or strengthen children's advocacy centers. The funds are administered by the National Children's Alliance, which maintains a directory of existing centers. [*See* Chapter 39—Hotlines and Organizations.]

## Child Death Review Teams

Homicide is the leading cause of nonillness death of children under age five. More than half of these child victims are under age two. A significant number of these deaths are initially misidentified as SIDS (Sudden Infant Death Syndrome) or accidental deaths. Until recently, the death of a child as a result of chronic child abuse or severe neglect was not recognized under most state laws as an intentional homicide, nor prosecuted as first-degree murder. Today, more than 23 states and the District of Columbia have adopted "homicide by abuse" laws that do not require proof of specific intent to kill when a child's death results from abuse, thus allowing stiffer sentences, sanctions, and penalties. Child death review teams, first initiated in Los Angeles County in 1978, now exist in all 50 states and the District of Columbia and are charged with examining the circumstances surrounding certain child deaths known or suspected to be preventable or the result of child abuse or neglect. Child death review teams try to correctly determine when children have died from abuse or neglect, identifying risk factors and systemic problems in hopes of preventing future deaths. Most teams consist of representatives from law enforcement, the prosecutor, child protective services, the medical examiner or coroner's office, public health agencies, and emergency medical personnel and pediatricians.

## *Legal Representation for Child Victims*

For children who are the subject of protection proceedings in juvenile or family court, the Child Abuse Prevention and Treatment Act requires states to provide child victims with independent representation. In some communities, children are represented in such cases by an attorney appointed to act as guardian *ad litem*. Courts in hundreds of communities are also using volunteer court-appointed special advocates who perform independent assessments of the children's circumstances and file their own reports with the court. The National Court-Appointed Special Advocate Association is funded by OJJDP to help courts establish a volunteer program and to standardize training for volunteer advocates. The American Bar Association has developed standards and practices for lawyers representing children in abuse and neglect cases. While most of these programs are available only in family or juvenile courts, there has been an increase in the use of independent legal advocacy for child victims in criminal court proceedings.

## *Reform of Juvenile/Family Court Handling of Child Abuse and Neglect Cases*

In recent years, several important developments are helping improve the ability of juvenile and family courts to work with greater effectiveness and speed in cases involving maltreated children. State court systems in 48 states received funding from the Children's Bureau at the U.S. Department of Health and Human Services to evaluate and improve operations in child abuse and neglect-related proceedings. Based upon administrative reforms undertaken by the Hamilton County, Ohio, Juvenile and Family Court, the National Council of Juvenile and Family Court Judges in 1995 developed and published a document entitled "Resource Guidelines: Improving Court Practice in Child Abuse and Neglect Cases." This publication sets forth the essential elements of properly conducted court hearings and describes how courts can more efficiently manage their work to ensure each child receives a fair, thorough, and speedy court process.

Using the "Resource Guidelines" as a blueprint, the Child Victims Model Courts Project of the National Council of Juvenile and Family Court Judges and the OJJPD focus on improving how courts handle child abuse and neglect cases. Since 1995, eighteen courts have adopted the model court practices developed in Hamilton County, Ohio. The model courts practices are characterized by the use of alternative dispute resolution; community-based services; multidisciplinary, court-led meetings and training; court calendar improvements; assignment of a single magistrate for the life of the case; more substantive preliminary hearings; and increased representation for families and children.

Criminal courts can learn from the example of the juvenile and family court innovations to improve system responses to children. Children who are crime victims or witnesses may be involved in both juvenile and criminal courts and benefit from close coordination between the two systems.

## *Model Children's Court, El Paso, Texas*

The Honorable Patricia Macias, Lead Judge for the El Paso Children's Court, guides that community's effort to improve the court's response to abused and neglected children. In all cases requiring foster care placement for abused or neglected children, the Court involves local networks of professionals to provide "front-loaded" services to increase the likelihood of safe permanent homes. A new assessment foster home project has been established to provide a nurturing home environment where the child's special needs can be immediately identified. To ensure that the child's support system is fully involved in the proceedings, the Court provides simultaneous language interpretation for all non-English-speaking court participants, and foster parents testify at each hearing and participate in permanency transition teams. Through such innovations, the court has streamlined court procedures and reduced the length of time children spend in foster care.

## *Use of Victim Assistance Professionals*

Numerous victim assistance programs provide special support services for child victims who are involved in criminal justice system cases. Research indicates that participation of a victim-witness advocate appears to increase guilty verdicts in sexual abuse cases, suggesting that better prepared and more relaxed child victims and child witnesses are more credible at trial[2]. Advocates working with child

---

[2] Dible, D., and R. H. C. Teske, Jr. "An Analysis of the Prosecutory Effects of a Child Sexual Abuse Victim-Witness Program." *Journal of Criminal Justice* 21 (1993): 79–85.

victims and child witnesses should have specialized training and experience with abused and traumatized children. A child advocate or a child interview specialist may provide a great deal of assistance, including the following: interview or help interview child victims or child witnesses; assess safety issues; assess the mental condition and developmental level of the child; as necessary, refer the child for more in-depth psychological assessment; participate in support groups or individual counseling; explain the legal process to the child and the non-offending caretaker; make crisis intervention and social services referrals; conduct court preparation; provide logistical support for the child victim and family, including transportation and assistance with medical and therapy appointments; and support the victim during trial, including accompanying the child to court when he or she testifies. Advocates can also help the victim and/or caretaker complete victim impact statements for sentencing, if desired. Victim advocates can help monitor the child's situation and alert prosecutors when the child is not supported, when stay-away orders are violated, or when the child is threatened or coerced into recanting. Many police departments and prosecutors' offices have their own victim assistance units and advocates who work closely with officers and prosecutors.

## Preparing Children for Court: Court School Programs

Every witness needs some preparation prior to testifying. To bring a child into the complex and often stressful process of testifying in court without careful preparation is unthinkable. A child who knows what to expect and is prepared for his or her role will provide more credible testimony. Child victims and witnesses require extra time and special effort to prepare for court. There are two primary methods of preparing a child—individual preparation by the prosecuting attorney or through a group process that focuses on general orientation programs, such as court school. Individual preparation is best handled by the case prosecutor and a victim advocate. It should be tailored to the specific age and needs of the child. Specific case issues are covered in this type of preparation. Many prosecutors will take the child witness to an empty courtroom to familiarize the child with the setting.

Court school programs are designed to orient the child victim and child witness to the court process and to the role of the witness. These programs are usually facilitated by victim advocates and prosecutors and include a group of children scheduled to testify in the near future. Most programs include role-playing, a courtroom tour, and opportunities to practice answering questions in the courtroom. Individual cases are never discussed, and the program is designed to avoid jeopardizing the child's testimony in any way. Court school programs may use props, such as puppets, child-sized judges robes, coloring/activity books about court, and a wooden model of a courtroom with moveable figures. Court school programs help reduce anxiety in children and normalize what may have been a strange and frightening process. Many programs include a concurrent session for non-offending parents and caretakers to provide information about the court process and how they can support their children.

---

## *Kids' Court, King County, Seattle, Washington*

In King County, Washington, Kids' Court and Teen Court empower child crime victims and their parents through education about the legal process. In the five-hour Saturday court school, children meet with a judge and prosecutor and participate in activities that help them understand the roles of court personnel, discuss their concerns about testifying in court, and feel comfortable in the courtroom. Judges and prosecutors lead discussions about the importance of telling the truth and answer children's questions about the upcoming trial. Children and their parents learn stress reduction techniques to help them through the trial. Kids' Court has developed a comprehensive curriculum and has served over 1,200 children in the last 9 years. It is being replicated in several cities throughout the United States and abroad.

---

## *Special Courtroom Accommodations*

Judges should make efforts to ensure that the trial process and courtroom atmosphere help the child witnesses provide true and accurate information without unnecessary revictimization. Judges need to know and understand the special developmental needs of children. Judges can do many things to prevent trauma to children in court, such as making sure all objections are argued outside the hearing or presence of the child, requiring that all attorneys use developmentally appropriate language when questioning child witnesses, and arranging the courtroom to be less intimidating for the child witness. A simple example of how to arrange the courtroom to avoid intimidating the child witness would be to allow the child to sit in a child-sized chair or to allow the child to sit next to a support person.

Continuances should be limited unless it is in the best interest of the particular child or in the cause of justice. Speedy resolution of child victim cases should be encouraged. In federal cases, when a child will be called to give testimony, judges can designate the case as being of special public importance which gives the case precedence over all others on the judge's calendar (18 U.S.C. §3509(j)). Safe and separate waiting areas should be available to prevent the child from encountering the defendant and the defendant's family. If a separate waiting area is impossible, a victim-witness advocate should remain with the child and caretaker to monitor the situation. Children should be allowed to have a support person in court with them. Judges should take care to ensure that the defense attorney does not unnecessarily subpoena support persons.

Courts should consider alternatives to live testimony. If the child would be too traumatized by seeing the defendant in the courtroom, prosecutors should consider making a motion for him or her to testify via closed circuit television. The use of closed circuit television has advantages and disadvantages. It may help reduce trauma and enable the child to testify more effectively, but it may be less compelling than a child's live presence in the courtroom. Prosecuting attorneys should weigh the advantages and disadvantages of testimony via closed circuit television on a case-by-case basis, always keeping in mind the level of trauma to the child. The federal courts and many states allow videotaped testimony of children under special circumstances; some states include tapes of original forensic interviews with children. These videotapes may be particularly useful when child victims recant their testimony.

### Los Angeles County Children's Court, Los Angeles, California

Children's Court in Los Angeles County, California, was built with the 550 children who come to court each day in mind. Courtrooms have child-size proportions, a lower judge's bench, no jury box, and limited seating. Children who await hearings are protected from contact with offenders through private waiting rooms and seating areas that carry the Disney Channel and other children's programming. During the inevitable delays, an arts program and play rooms safely occupy the children. On site, immediate services and personnel, including school system personnel, mental health providers, and victim advocates are available for planning and consultation with children and families. Dependency Court administrators insist that more important than the new child-friendly facility is the court's philosophy that supports children's involvement in a secure court environment in all court proceedings affecting them.

## Victim Impact Statements: In a Child's Words

A victim impact statement (VIS) from a child can be a powerful evidentiary tool, bringing the full impact of the crime home to the judge or jury in a potent way. Clearly, child victims should not be forced to make a VIS nor be made uncomfortable or fearful while making one. The process of making the VIS actually becomes an important step in the healing process for many children.

In most states and the District of Columbia, children have the right to present a VIS at the time of sentencing or to have an adult present a statement on their behalf. Since most children need help preparing a VIS, a victim advocate can work with the child to develop one that is accurate and age-appropriate. Knowledgeable professionals should assess the substantial body of research documenting the initial and long-term psychological effects of abuse on children and be sure to present this evidence as part of the VIS.

In most cases, the primary impact of abuse is psychological, not financial. However, the treatment of medical and psychological damage resulting from the abuse will often have a significant financial impact on the victim and the victim's family. Therefore, the financial impact portion of the victim impact statement should cover expenditures for medical treatment and psychological counseling expenditures. A restitution order should be requested for these expenditures, with contingencies for possible future medical and psychological expenses related to the crime.

While most VIS are technical documents unlikely to be reviewed directly by children, many children understand and like the idea of writing a letter to the judge describing what happened and how they were affected. Very young children can be encouraged to draw pictures of how they feel about the crime, themselves, or the defendant. Victim-witness advocates may wish to ask the child questions and transcribe the answers. Some courts allow audiotapes or videotapes of children making statements during an interview. Oral statements by the child at sentencing can be effective in helping judges understand the crime's impact. If a severely traumatized or injured child cannot provide a statement or drawing, the caretaker, physician, or therapist should prepare the primary statement and present it as part of an information package. Copies of research articles that document the short- and long-term impact of victimization on children can be attached. Non-offending parents are usually good sources of information on how the abuse affected the child, the siblings, and the entire family. Siblings are often forgotten secondary victims and should be allowed to participate in the process or make their own VIS. Older children should be encouraged to write a letter to the judge expressing their feelings about the crime and the defendant. Some adolescent victims express their feelings and thoughts related to their abusive experience by keeping journals, writing poetry, or creating artwork. Copies of these can be presented as part of their VIS.

## Section 25.4

# *Sex Offender Registration and Notification Laws*

Excerpted from *Violence Against Women Act News*. U.S. Department of Justice, February/March 1998.

*Dena Sacco, Office of Policy Development, USDOJ*

Over the past few years, federal and state governments have made tremendous efforts to develop strong, effective systems to track the whereabouts of convicted rapists and child molesters. Reports indicate that every state now has a sex offender registration system, and a majority of states have established systems for notifying communities about sex offenders. In addition, at the direction of the President, the FBI has established an interim national sex offender registry to enable law enforcement to access information from participating state registries. Although it has been in existence for less than a year, the national registry has over 36,000 records on sex offenders from 24 states, with new states joining the system each month.

There are now four federal laws that set out requirements for state sex offender registration and notification programs. The Jacob Wetterling Crimes Against Children and Sexually Violent Offender

Registration Act (Wetterling Act), which is part of the 1994 Crime Act, provides a financial incentive for states to establish registration systems for convicted child molesters and other sexually violent offenders. Megan's Law, which the President signed on May 17, 1996, requires states to release relevant information that is necessary to protect the public concerning registered sex offenders. Before the enactment of Megan's Law, the Wetterling Act permitted, but did not require, such disclosure. The Pam Lychner Act, which strengthens the Wetterling Act's requirements in many respects and mandates the national sex offender registry, was enacted in October 1996. Finally, provisions of the Commerce-Justice-State Appropriations bill, enacted in November 1997, amended the Wetterling and Lychner Acts to afford states greater flexibility in establishing effective registration systems. It also contains provisions requiring registration for offenders convicted in federal and military tribunals, as well as offenders who live in one state but work or go to school in another.[1]

Each of these laws contains important elements of a comprehensive registration and notification system. To assist the states in interpreting and implementing them, the Department of Justice is working hard to publish guidelines[2] on the laws. Because states that fail to meet the requirements of each law by certain deadlines risk forfeiting 10 percent of their Byrne formula grant funds, the forthcoming guidelines will clarify by what date each specific requirement must be met.

Sex offender registration and notification systems are important law enforcement and public safety tools. By informing local authorities of the identities and whereabouts of convicted sex offenders, registration systems aid in the investigation of sex crimes. Likewise, community notification programs enable communities and parents to take common sense measures to protect themselves and their children.

At the same time, it is important to recognize that other tools also may be effective in conjunction with registration and notification systems. Thus, the department has taken steps to promote the development of comprehensive programs for sex offender management, with the goal of reducing recidivism rates and increasing community safety. In 1996, the Department of Justice, through the Office of Justice Programs, created

---

1. The Wetterling Act, Megan's Law, and the Lychner Act are codified at 42 U.S.C. Sections 14071 and 14072. The Commerce-Justice-State Appropriations Act amendments are in Section 115 of P.L. 105–119.

2. These guidelines effectively will replace those published to implement the Wetterling Act and Megan's Law on July 21, 1997 (62 Fed. Reg. 39009).

the Center for Sex Offender Management. The Center is a national project that supports local jurisdictions in the effective management of sex offenders. It works with jurisdictions around the country that have developed innovative team approaches to sex offender management, with the idea that bringing together law enforcement, treatment providers, courts, and others to manage sex offenders is the most effective way to reduce recidivism and increase community safety. The Center also provides intensive training opportunities and technical assistance for local jurisdictions and produces publications addressing critical topics in the area of sex offender management.

## Section 25.5

# *Federal and State Antistalking Legislation*

Excerpted from *Stalking and Domestic Violence: The Third Annual Report to Congress under the Violence Against Women Act.* U.S. Department of Justice, Office of Justice Programs, July 1998.

In 1990, California became the first state to pass antistalking legislation. Since then all states and the District of Columbia have enacted laws making stalking a crime. In 1996, a federal law was enacted to prohibit stalkers from traveling across a state line in pursuit of their victims.[1] This legislation enabled federal prosecution in instances where the interstate feature of a stalking case created additional challenges to effective state investigation and prosecution of such crimes.

As mentioned previously, state antistalking statutes vary widely. For instance, at least four states and one Territory—Alaska, Michigan, Oklahoma, Wyoming, and Guam—specifically prohibit stalking through electronic means, such as e-mail. Nine states—Alaska, Connecticut, Florida, Iowa, Louisiana, Michigan, Minnesota, New Mexico, and Vermont—permit enhanced penalties in stalking cases involving victims who are minors. As of March 1998, legislation to enact new laws and strengthen existing ones addressing stalking of children is pending in 12 states.[2]

This section summarizes the cases prosecuted under the new federal antistalking statute, offers a comprehensive analysis of state antistalking laws, and concludes with a brief analysis of the challenges mounted against some of these state statutes.[3]

## Federal Antistalking Legislation

The Interstate Stalking Punishment and Prevention Act of 1996 prohibits individuals from traveling across a state line with the intent to injure or harass another person or placing such person in reasonable fear of death or bodily injury as a result of, or in the course of, such travel. Under this law, the Department of Justice has brought charges against nine stalkers as of April 1998. In all of these cases, the stalker was a male. In eight of these cases, the victim was a female. Six of the nine cases involved intimates, former intimates or dating partners, and two cases were related to the workplace.

As of the end of April, four defendants had been sentenced under the federal antistalking statute and defendants in two other federal antistalking cases were waiting to be sentenced. In one of the four cases in which sentences have been imposed, the defendant entered a guilty plea. He was sentenced to six months in a community-based facility and a 3-year term of supervised release. In the second case, the stalker was convicted and received a sentence of 20 years. In the third case, the stalker was convicted on three counts—interstate violation of a protection order, the interstate stalking statute, and the interstate domestic violence provision of the Violence Against Women Act (VAWA). He received a sentence of 87 months. In the fourth case, the defendant was found guilty on six counts, including violation of the interstate stalking law. He was sentenced to 120 months on the stalking charge and 60 months for the remaining five charges. In at least two of the cases, the stalking occurred in a domestic violence context.

The Department of Justice is committed to prosecuting cases involving interstate stalking and plans to pursue these cases vigorously. The federal law fills an important gap in the legal system's ability to respond effectively to stalking crimes.

## State-by-State Analysis of Antistalking Statutes[4]

The federal law notwithstanding, stalking crimes are largely the responsibility of state and local jurisdictions. In the past decade, states have responded to this crime with a myriad of statutory sanctions. The following state-by-state analysis describes the extent to which stalking and related laws have been enacted by the legislatures of the 50 states, the District of Columbia, Puerto Rico, and the Virgin Islands. When appropriate, the analysis contrasts the enactment of stalking statutes with that of laws aimed at domestic violence, a common correlate of stalking behavior.

## Legal Context

Before the enactment of stalking laws, police officers and prosecutors dealt with stalking behavior using a variety of criminal law provisions. These included harassment, (terroristic) threats, criminal trespass, and specialized laws addressing telephone or letter harassment or threats. In a few states, civil law injunctions could also be used to keep stalkers at bay; and the criminal contempt powers of the court were used to enforce these injunctions.

In many jurisdictions, however, these laws failed to adequately address stalking behavior. Civil injunctions were too difficult to obtain. Criminal law penalties were often relatively light, while more serious criminal laws required a high burden of proof as to intent. Most important, stalking behavior was not a high priority with police officers and prosecutors, who often lumped stalking together with similarly unenforced laws against domestic violence.[5]

Stalking laws changed this environment in two important ways. First, the enactment of such laws provided symbolic reinforcement of the seriousness with which legislators considered stalking, effectively increasing its enforcement priority. Second, these laws changed the elements of crime that needed to be proven, adding in a reasonableness test in many states that can be used to prove intent.

Stalking laws do not necessarily replace the earlier harassment, terroristic threats, and similar laws, however. These older statutes still play an important role in enforcement of the laws against stalking behavior. Thus, a full understanding of stalking laws in the 50 states requires inclusion of both stalking and these related statutes. Stalking laws are often supplemented by other laws that provide penalties for stalking-like behavior that lacks some element of stalking. This includes both harassing and threatening behavior.

## Criminal Law Provisions for Stalking

Exhibit 1 lists the types of laws found in each state by penalty and severity level. In 32 states, Guam, and the Virgin Islands, a first conviction for stalking can be a felony. However, in 16 of these states, felony penalties for stalking are restricted (denoted as [R] in exhibit 1) to specific types of stalking, such as where there is bodily injury, weapon use/carrying, or where the stalking constitutes a violation of a protective order. In 22 of these 32 states (including the 16 states with restricted felony penalties), stalking may also be a misdemeanor, depending on the specific behavior involved. In the remaining 18 states that provide only misdemeanor penalties for a first-offense stalking conviction, repeat stalking is a felony in all but 2. In the District of Columbia, a third stalking conviction calls for a maximum 3-year prison sentence.

### *Exhibit 1: State Stalking Laws by Crime Level Seriousness*

| State | Stalking Crime Level |
|---|---|
| Alabama | B or C felony |
| Alaska | C felony (R) or A misdemeanor |
| Arizona | Felony 4 or 5 |
| Arkansas | B or C felony |
| California | Felony or misdemeanor; 2nd has 4 year maximum |
| Colorado | Felony 6; 2nd is Class 5 felony |
| Connecticut | D felony (R) or misdemeanor |
| Delaware | C or D felony (R) or F felony |
| District of Columbia | Misdemeanor; 3 years for 3rd offense |
| Florida | Felony 3 or misdemeanor 1 |
| Georgia | Felony (R) or misdemeanor |
| Hawaii | Misdemeanor; 2nd is C felony |
| Idaho | Misdemeanor; 2nd is felony |
| Illinois | Class 3 (R) or 4 felony |
| Indiana | D felony (R) or A misdemeanor |
| Iowa | D felony (R) or aggravated misdemeanor |
| Kansas | Class 9 (R) or 10 felony |
| Kentucky | D felony (R) or A misdemeanor |
| Louisiana | Felony (R) or misdemeanor |
| Maine | Class D crime; 3rd is class C crime (5-year maximum) |
| Maryland | Misdemeanor (5-year maximum) |

| | |
|---|---|
| Massachusetts | Felony |
| Michigan | Felony or misdemeanor |
| Minnesota | Felony or gross misdemeanor |
| Mississippi | Misdemeanor |
| Missouri | D felony or A misdemeanor |
| Montana | Misdemeanor; 2nd is felony |
| Nebraska | Class 1 misdemeanor; 2nd is Class 4 felony |
| Nevada | B felony or misdemeanor |
| New Hampshire | A misdemeanor; 2nd is B felony |
| New Jersey | 3rd (R) or 4th degree crime |
| New Mexico | Felony (R) or misdemeanor |
| New York | B misdemeanor |
| North Carolina | Misdemeanor A1 or 2; 2nd is felony |
| North Dakota | C felony (R) or misdemeanor |
| Ohio | Misdemeanor 1; 2nd is felony 5 |
| Oklahoma | Felony (R) or misdemeanor |
| Oregon | A misdemeanor; 2nd is C felony |
| Pennsylvania | Misdemeanor; 2nd is felony |
| Rhode Island | Misdemeanor; 2nd is felony |
| South Carolina | Felony (R) or misdemeanor |
| South Dakota | Misdemeanor; 2nd is felony 5 |
| Tennessee | A misdemeanor; 2nd is C felony (if same victim) or E felony |
| Texas | A misdemeanor; 2nd is felony 3 |
| Utah | Felony (R) or misdemeanor |
| Vermont | Felony |
| Virginia | Class 1 or 2 misdemeanor; 3rd is felony 6 |
| Washington | C felony (R) or gross misdemeanor |
| West Virginia | Misdemeanor; 3rd in 5 years is felony |
| Wisconsin | Felony (R) or A misdemeanor |
| Wyoming | Felony (R) or misdemeanor |
| Guam | Felony 2 (R) or 3 |
| Virgin Islands | Felony |

Source: Institute for Law and Justice, Alexandria, VA, March 1998.

### Stalking of Minors

Ten states mention stalking or harassing of a minor in their antistalking statutes; however, only 9 of them provide for enhanced penalties against persons who stalk or harass minors. In five of these states, minors under the age of 16 are covered by the law, while in three other states, coverage is extended to minors under the age of 18. In the ninth state, only minors under the age of 12 are covered by a law providing enhanced felony punishment for stalking. In California, harassing a minor because of the child's parents' employment is a misdemeanor. In Missouri, a special protection order for children is available that includes protection from stalking by a present or former household member; violation of the order is a Class A misdemeanor.

### Related Criminal Laws

Other criminal laws closely related to stalking include those that cover harassment and intimidation.[6] This review indicates the following:

- Harassment laws have been adopted in 25 states and the territory of Guam. In three of these states, harassment may be a felony. In 3 other states, a second harassment offense may also be a felony. In the remainder of the states, harassment is either a misdemeanor or a summary offense (one state).

- Threatening or intimidating behavior is a statutory crime in 35 states, the District of Columbia, Guam, and Puerto Rico. In 17 of these states and Guam, threatening or intimidation may be a felony offense. Two states call for enhanced penalties for repeat offenses.

- Laws specifically directed at telephone threats or harassment have been adopted in 43 states, Guam, and the Virgin Islands. Of these jurisdictions, only two states' laws provide felony sentences. An additional six states make a repeat telephone threat or harassment offense a felony crime.

- Letter threats are the subject of 21 states' and the Virgin Islands' criminal laws. Five of these states make letter threats a felony offense. One state provides misdemeanor penalties for "written" forms of harassment.

- With respect to other stalking-related crimes, one state criminalized threats by facsimile. Three other states have made stalking by e-mail or fax elements of their definition of a stalking crime. The territory of Guam forbids harassment by fax.

## Comparison of State Stalking Statutes to the NIJ Model Antistalking Law

In 1993, the National Institute of Justice (NIJ) sponsored a study conducted by the National Criminal Justice Association to develop a *Model Antistalking Code* to assist States in developing felony-level antistalking laws.[7] The key crime elements of the NIJ-sponsored *Model Code* included:

- A course of conduct involving repeated physical proximity (following) or threatening behavior or both;
- The occurrence of incidents at least twice;
- Threatening behavior, including both explicit and implicit threats; and
- Conduct occurring against an individual or family members of the individual.

The criminal intent to commit stalking is measured by the *Model Code* by examining:

- Intent to engage in a course of conduct involving repeated following or threatening an individual;
- Knowledge that this behavior reasonably causes fear of bodily injury or death;
- Knowledge (or expectation) that the specific victim would have a reasonable fear of bodily injury or death;
- Actual fear of death or bodily injury experienced by a victim; and
- Fear of death or bodily injury felt by members of the victim's immediate family.

The *Model Code* recommends that punishment for stalking crimes be set at the felony level. Other recommendations include:

- Expansion of the fear element to include fear of sexual assault; and
- Enactment of harassment/misdemeanor stalking or intimidation laws to deal with annoying behavior, including aggravated

harassment for persistent behavior that does not rise to felony-level fear.

A comparison of all state stalking laws to the *Model Antistalking Code* provisions requires some translation to match the *Code's* specific use of language to the statutory language used in many states' codes. The major differences between this review and a more formulaic review that allows for no deviation from the *Code's* language involve four points of departure:

1. Many states distinguish between stalking and aggravated stalking; the latter involves especially dangerous behavior, such as weapon possession or physical injury. Many states that make this distinction limit felony penalties to aggravated stalking. This review identifies states that provide felony penalties for stalking *per se* and those that reserve it for aggravated stalking.

2. The *Model Code* uses the phrase "purposefully engages in a course of conduct" to denote an intent to cause fear. Many state laws, however, distinguish between the purposive act that constitutes stalking and the intent to instill fear itself. This review separates these two concepts.

3. The *Model Code* includes "maintaining visual or physical proximity" as a critical element of stalking. Many states, however, use the simpler term "following." Because so few states use the *Model Code's* broader language, the review does not distinguish between the two linguistic terms.

4. The *Model Code* language defining "course of conduct" was viewed as simply a guide because it, too, is rarely explicitly followed. Instead, the review looks for substantial compliance with this language's intent (e.g., use of the phrase "pattern of behavior").

With these changes, a review of state statutory agreement with the *Model Code's* criminal law provisions shows that:

- Only 16 states, Guam, and the Virgin Islands make stalking a felony offense as recommended by the *Model Code*; an additional 16 states make only the most serious stalking incidents a felony.

- Forty-four states, the District of Columbia, Guam, and the Virgin Islands match the *Code's* use and definition of "course of conduct" involving physical proximity.

- Twenty-five states use the *Code's* definition of two or more incidents to specify how many incidents are required to demonstrate repeated behavior as part of a course of conduct; 24 states, the District of Columbia, and the Virgin Islands do not use this definition, although several of these states use the undefined term "repeated" in their laws. One state defines repeated behavior as at least three acts.

- Only 12 states and the Virgin Islands explicitly define "threat" to include implied threats.

- Thirty-two states, the District of Columbia, Guam, and the Virgin Islands make intent to instill fear an element of the crime of stalking. Of those that do not, 14 states adopted the *Code's* requirement that the acts constituting stalking be done purposefully. Only four states do not require some proof of intentional behavior as part of their stalking laws.

- Six states require using a "reasonable person" test to determine the reasonableness of any victim's fear resulting from the stalking behavior.

- Twenty-six states, the District of Columbia, Guam, and the Virgin Islands require fear of death or bodily injury, as recommended by the *Model Code;* five states use similar language to define fear, such as fear for one's physical safety; five other states add fear of sexual assault or battery, as recommended in the commentary to *the Model Code;* nine states protect against emotional distress and related responses, including feelings of annoyance or being threatened. Only six states' statutes do not require that the stalking result in victim fear or some lesser response to the stalking.

- Twenty-six states and Guam extend the scope of fear to include the victim's family, as recommended by the *Model Code.*

Exhibit 2 provides a state-by-state analysis of each of the key *Model Anti-Stalking Code* provisions. An "x" in the statutory provision column indicates that the state's statute generally meets the *Model Code's* recommended language. The absence of an "x" signifies that either the statute makes no reference to the *Model Code* provision in question or the language used is substantially different.

*Exhibit 2. State Stalking Laws' Agreement with Model Stalking Act*

| State | Stalking is Felony Crime | Stalking Has Special Felony Penalty | Stalking is Misdemeanor | Course Conduct/ Pattern Included | Two Events Are Required | Includes "Follow" Acts | Both Actual and Implied Threat | Purposeful Action e.g. to follow) | Indended or Knew of Victim Fear | Reasonable Victim Fear | Actual Fear of Death or Injury | Family of Victim Covered |
|---|---|---|---|---|---|---|---|---|---|---|---|---|
| AL | x | x |   |   |   | x | x | x | x | x | x | x |
| AK | x | x | x | x |   | x |   | x | x[1] |   | x | x |
| AZ | x |   |   | x | x | x | x | x |   | x | x | x |
| AR | x | x |   | x | x | x |   | x |   |   | x | x |
| CA |   | x | x | x |   | x | x | x | x | x | x[2] | x |
| CO | x |   |   | x | x | x |   |   | x | x | x[3] | x |
| CT |   | x | x | x |   | x |   | x | x | x | x[2] |   |
| DE | x | x |   | x | [4] | x | x |   |   | x | x[2] | x |
| DC |   |   | x | x |   | x |   |   | x | x | x |   |
| FL | x | x | x | x |   | x |   |   | x | x | x |   |
| GA |   | x | x | x |   | x | x | x |   | x | x | x |
| GU | x | x |   | x |   | x |   |   | x | x | x | x |
| HI |   | x | x |   | x | x |   |   |   | x | [5] |   |
| ID |   | x | x | x |   | x |   | x |   | x | 5 | x |
| IL | x | x |   |   | x | x |   | x |   | x | x[6] |   |

[1] Reckless language
[2] Safety fear
[3] Fear of physical action threat
[4] Three events required
[5] Stalking victim is annoyed, alarmed, or harassed
[6] Sexual assault fear added

## Exhibit 2. State Stalking Laws' Agreement with Model Stalking Act (continued)

| State | Stalking is Felony Crime | Stalking Has Special Felony Penalty | Stalking is Misdemeanor | Course Conduct/ Pattern Included | Two Events Are Required | Includes "Follow" Acts | Both Actual and Implied Threat | Purposeful Action e.g. to follow) | Indended or Knew of Victim Fear | Reasonable Victim Fear | Actual Fear of Death or Injury | Family of Victim Covered |
|---|---|---|---|---|---|---|---|---|---|---|---|---|
| IN |  | X | X | X |  |  | X |  |  | X | $X^6$ |  |
| IA |  | X | X | X | X | X | X | X | X | X | X | X |
| KS | X | X |  | X |  | X |  | X |  | X | 5 |  |
| KY |  | X | X | X | X |  | X | X | X | $X^5$ |  |  |
| LA |  | X | X | X |  | X | X | X | X | X |  |  |
| ME |  |  | X | X | X | X | X | X | X | X | X | X |
| MD | X |  |  | X |  | X |  |  | X | X | X | X |
| MA | X | X |  | X |  |  |  | X | X | X | X |  |
| MI | X | X | X | X | X | X |  |  |  | X | X | X |
| MN | X |  | X | X | X | X |  |  | X |  | X | X |
| MS |  |  | X | X |  | X |  | X | X | X | $X^2$ |  |
| MO | X |  | X | X |  | X |  |  | X | X | X |  |
| MT |  |  | X | X |  | X |  |  | X | X | X |  |
| NE |  |  | X | X |  | X |  | X | X | X | 7 |  |
| NV | X |  | X | X |  |  |  | X | X | X | X |  |

2 Safety fear

5 Stalking victim is annoyed, alarmed, or harassed

6 Sexual assault fear added

7 Terrified, threatened, or intimidated

## Exhibit 2. State Stalking Laws' Agreement with Model Stalking Act (continued)

| State | Stalking is Felony Crime | Stalking Has Special Felony Penalty | Stalking is Misdemeanor | Course Conduct/ Pattern Included | Two Events Are Required | Includes "Follow" Acts | Both Actual and Implied Threat | Purposeful Action e.g. to follow | Indended or Knew of Victim Fear | Reasonable Victim Fear | Actual Fear of Death or Injury | Family of Victim Covered |
|---|---|---|---|---|---|---|---|---|---|---|---|---|
| NH |  |  | X | X | X | X | X | X | X | X | X |  |
| NJ |  | X | X | X | X | X |  | X | X | X | X | X |
| NM |  | X | X | X | X | X |  | X | X | X | X | X |
| NV |  |  | X | X |  | X |  |  | X | X | X |  |
| NC |  |  | X |  | X | X |  |  | X | X | X |  |
| ND |  |  | X | X | X |  |  | X |  | X | $8$ | X |
| OH |  |  | X | X | X |  |  |  | X |  | $7$ |  |
| OK |  | X | X | X | X | X |  | X |  | X |  | X |
| OR |  |  | X |  |  | X |  |  |  | X | $X^2$ | X |
| PA |  |  | X | X | X | X |  |  | X | X | X | X |
| RI |  |  | X | X |  | X |  | X |  | X | $5$ |  |
| SC |  | X | X | X | X | X |  |  | X | X | $X^6$ | X |
| SD |  | X | X | X |  | X | X |  | X | X | $5$ |  |
| TN |  |  | X | X | X | X |  | X |  | X |  |  |
| TX |  |  | X | X | X |  |  |  | X | X | X | X |

[2] Safety fear
[5] Stalking victim is annoyed, alarmed, or harassed
[6] Sexual assault fear added
[7] Terrified, theatened, or intimidated
[8] Physical harm, fear, or mental distress

## Exhibit 2. State Stalking Laws' Agreement with Model Stalking Act (continued)

| State | Stalking is Felony Crime | Stalking Has Special Felony Penalty | Stalking is Misdemeanor | Course Conduct/Pattern Included | Two Events Are Required | Includes "Follow" Acts | Both Actual and Implied Threat | Purposeful Action e.g. to follow) | Intended or Knew of Victim Fear | Reasonable Victim Fear | Actual Fear of Death or Injury | Family of Victim Covered |
|---|---|---|---|---|---|---|---|---|---|---|---|---|
| UT | | x | x | x | x | x | | x | | x | x | x |
| VT | x | x | | x | x | x | x | x | | x | x[6] | |
| VA | | | x | x | x | | | x | x | x | x[6] | x |
| WA | | x | x | x | | x | | x | x | x | x | |
| WV | | | x | | | x | | x | x | x | | x |
| WI | | x | x | x | x | x | | x | x | x | x | x |
| WY | | x | x | x | | x | | | x | x | [7] | |
| VI | x | x | | x | | x | | | x | x | | |

2 Safety fear
6 Sexual assault fear added
7 Terrified, threatened, or intimidated

### Criminal Procedure Laws

Criminal procedure laws regulate enforcement of criminal laws. They range from specifying how arrests are made to trial procedures to sentencing by the court. Often changes in criminal law require parallel changes in criminal procedure for the legislative intent to be fully realized. Stalking criminal law enactments are no exception.

#### Arrest without Warrant

Under common law, arrest without a warrant occurs in two situations. First, officers may arrest without a warrant, if they see a person committing a crime. Second, police officers may have probable cause to arrest if they believe that an individual committed a crime, but they did not actually see the crime committed by the individual. Different rules apply to warrantless arrest authority where the latter authority is relied upon, depending on the nature of the offense.

#### States with Felony Stalking Laws

Police can arrest without a warrant any person who they have probable cause to believe committed a felony. In 24 states, stalking may be a felony offense. In 11 of these states, stalking of any sort is a felony, and police may arrest a stalker based on probable cause. In the other 13 states, stalking may be either a felony or a misdemeanor, depending on a variety of factors such as use of a weapon, injury, or prior convictions. In these states, police may have to first ascertain the seriousness of the stalking charge before they can arrest based on probable cause.

#### Special Misdemeanor Arrest Authority

Police may arrest without a warrant a stalker charged with a misdemeanor offense on one of two legal bases. First, in 49 states, police may arrest without a warrant a person who they have probable cause to believe committed *misdemeanor domestic violence*, including stalking. Second, in 10 states where stalking may be a misdemeanor offense, police may arrest without a warrant for misdemeanor stalking *per se*, that is, without any domestic violence involvement.[8]

## *Other Criminal Procedure Provisions*

Other criminal procedure provisions include those relating to pretrial release of persons charged with stalking offenses, state registry of stalking protective orders, and training of police in investigating stalking complaints.

### *Pretrial Release*

In 14 states, special pretrial release provisions are set for persons charged with stalking. These include nine states (Alaska, Arkansas, Georgia, Iowa, Maryland, Ohio, Texas, Washington, and West Virginia) that authorize or require issuance of an antistalking protection order as part of any pretrial release order following arrest for stalking. In Illinois, bail may be denied if the stalker is found to be a serious threat to the safety of another person. Bail may also be denied in Georgia on the basis of prior violation of a pretrial release order or of parole/probation conditions. In two states (Montana and Oklahoma), police are not authorized to issue citations or bail release before judicial arraignment. Three states (California, Ohio, and Vermont) require courts to treat stalking as a serious crime in setting a bail level. In other states, the court's authority to issue a no-contact order is inherent in its discretionary authority to impose release conditions.

North Carolina has a unique provision aimed at protecting minors. There, state law provides for issuance of a no-stalking order as part of pretrial release for any person charged with a violent offense against a minor.

### *State Registries of Orders*

In six states, a special registry for stalking orders is established by statute to facilitate police confirmation of the validity of any stalking order.[9] In addition to the stalking order registries, legislation in 33 states (including 5 of the 6 with stalking registries) requires the establishment of a special registry for domestic violence protection orders; these orders may, of course, include antistalking provisions.

### *Training*

Police training about stalking is required in Minnesota. In 30 states, the District of Columbia, and the Virgin Islands, police training on domestic violence is required; this training is often administratively required to include stalking in the context of domestic violence.[10]

## Civil Law Injunctions and Penalties

In many states, criminal law penalties for stalking are complemented by civil law remedies for victims of stalking. Thus, injunctions against stalking behavior are available in 23 states. In the other 27 states, the District of Columbia, Puerto Rico, and the Virgin Islands, stalking may be enjoined as an element of a protection order issued against domestic violence or abuse (see exhibit 3).

In the 23 states with stalking injunction laws, criminal penalties are provided for violating the court order in all but 2 of these states. In the two states without specific criminal penalties for violating an antistalking court order, violations of the order may be punished under the criminal contempt authority of the court to punish violations of any court order (see exhibit 3).

In the remaining state, stalking violations of the court order are punished under the courts' general powers of criminal contempt (see appendix B). One unique provision is found in North Dakota, where State law requires that the stalking law provisions be attached to all domestic violence protection orders.

## Tort Damages

At least four states now specifically provide for a tort action based on stalking behavior. These states are California, Oregon, Texas, and Wyoming.[11] In the remaining states, such actions might be brought either as civil actions for assault or under the courts' inherent power to provide tort remedies for commission of a crime.[12] The key element of a civil assault action is being unreasonably placed in fear of injury.

Among the 27 states with no separate stalking protection order provisions, 3 states specifically provide criminal penalties for stalking violations of a domestic violence protection order. In 23 of the remaining 24 states with only domestic violence orders available, criminal penalties for violating a domestic violence protection order are applicable to stalking violations. In the remaining state, stalking violations of the court order are punished under the courts' general powers of criminal contempt (see appendix B).

## *Exhibit 3: Stalking Protection Orders*

| State | Civil Injunction Available/Penalty |
| --- | --- |
| Arizona | Criminal contempt |
| California | 4-year maximum |
| Colorado | Class 6 felony |
| Florida | Misdemeanor |
| Idaho | Misdemeanor; 2nd is felony |
| Maine | Class D crime |
| Michigan | No penalty |
| Minnesota | Misdemeanor |
| Missouri | Misdemeanor; 2nd in 5 years is Class D felony |
| Montana | Misdemeanor |
| Nebraska | Misdemeanor |
| Nevada | Class C felony |
| New Hampshire | Misdemeanor; 2nd is felony |
| North Dakota | Felony |
| Oklahoma | Misdemeanor |
| Oregon | Class C felony or Class A misdemeanor |
| Rhode Island | Felony |
| South Carolina | Misdemeanor |
| South Dakota | Felony 6 or misdemeanor |
| Virginia | Misdemeanor 1 |
| Washington | Class C felony |
| Wisconsin | Misdemeanor |
| Wyoming | Misdemeanor |

## New Challenges to State Antistalking Laws[13]

All the state antistalking laws withstood legal challenges this past year.[14] In April 1998, the U.S. Supreme Court denied petitions to hear challenges to antistalking laws in the District of Columbia and Virginia. The Court declined to review the two challenges to the state antistalking laws. The challenges were made on the grounds that these laws were constitutionally vague and overbroad.

In the District of Columbia case, Roy L. Jett was convicted of stalking for sending sexually explicit, threatening letters to a woman with whom he had previously been acquainted and also for sending threatening letters to the woman's mother. Jett appealed his conviction of stalking, challenging the statute on a constitutional basis. The D.C. Court of Appeals decided that Jett's rights were not violated because his letters were part of a course of conduct constituting the criminal offense of stalking (See *Roy L. Jett v. United States,* No. 95-CF-1529 [D.C. April 15, 1997]).

In the Virginia case, Michael Parker, who was serving a prison sentence for stalking his former intimate, was convicted of first-offense stalking for repeatedly telephoning her while he was incarcerated. Parker rarely chose to speak during these calls, although he did tell the victim that he "would be out" of jail and that she should "not be afraid." Parker challenged the constitutionality of Virginia's stalking statute on the grounds of vagueness and overbreadth. The court decided that these calls were multiple instances of conduct directed at the victim; they caused a reasonable fear of death, criminal sexual assault, or bodily injury; and Parker intended to cause fear or knew that fear would result from his conduct. The Virginia court dismissed Parker's vagueness challenge to the definition of the reasonable fear statutory element on the grounds that the reasonable fear standard was objective and limited in scope. The Virginia court found no merit in Parker's overbreadth challenge, stating that the purpose of the statute is clear, and the statute is tailored so that it does not substantially infringe upon speech protected by the First Amendment. (See *Parker v. Commonwealth,* 485 S.E.2d 150 [Va. Ct. App. 1997]).

## Conclusion

Every state and the federal government now have enacted laws prohibiting stalking. While all state antistalking laws withstood legal challenges this past year, these laws remain incomplete. In several states, defects in the language of the stalking laws leave them vulnerable to constitutional challenge where courts are unable to provide ameliorating interpretations such as imputing the need for intent or *mens rea* where none exists in the statute. *The Model Antistalking Code* has not been widely followed. It is unclear how these defects are handled in practice by recourse to alternative criminal law approaches such as use of harassment or threatening behavior laws. NIJ is sponsoring ongoing research to help answer this question. Results of this research will be included in future reports.

Other problems include the unavailability of stalking protection orders in most states except in the context of domestic violence. Of course, the courts may have issued such injunctions without explicit statutory authority, combining the court's common law ability to fashion remedies and the criminal law stalking provisions; there is no information currently available on this point. Nor do we know much about the significance of the absence of explicit authority to arrest without a warrant in states where stalking is a misdemeanor offense. Again, ongoing research may provide answers to both these questions.

## References

1. This law was intended to fill a gap in the federal law, which covered interstate domestic violence (18 U.S.C. 2261) but did not extend to essentially similar conduct where the victim either had not had an intimate relationship with the offender or had not obtained a protection order.

2. These states are Arizona, California, Iowa, Kentucky, Massachusetts, Michigan, Minnesota, Missouri, Nebraska, New Jersey, and Oklahoma. This information was compiled by the Violence Against Women office.

3. A complete list of state stalking code citations and constitutional challenges to the statutes as of March 1998 can be found in appendix A of this document.

4. This state-by-state analysis was prepared in March 1998 by Weal Miller of the Institute of Law and Justice, Alexandria, VA.

5. It was not until the 1980s that domestic violence became widely recognized as the serious crime that it is. And it was

not until 1994 that the federal government enacted comprehensive legislation to combat domestic violence.

6.  A review of these laws for all 50 states is summarized in appendix C of *Stalking and Domestic Violence: The Third Annual Report to Congress under the Violence Against Women Act.*

7.  National Criminal Justice Association, *Project to Develop a Model Anti-Stalking Code for States* (Washington, D.C.: U.S. Department of Justice, National Institute of Justice, October 1993.)

8.  Arrest without a warrant for misdemeanor stalking is authorized in Florida, Idaho, Indiana, Maine, Maryland, Missouri, Montana, Nevada, New Hampshire, and Oregon. In South Carolina and Wyoming, police may arrest without a warrant based on probable cause that a stalking order violation has occured.

9.  These include Arizona (local registry for harassment order), Michigan, Ohio (local registry), Oregon, and Washington (antiharassment orders).

10. A survey by the Institute for Law and Justice, under an NIJ grant, found that 20 state agencies setting standards for training local police require specific training in handling stalking cases; another 24 agencies may include training as part of their domestic violence curriculum. In the past 2 years, local agencies have also developed or offered special training on stalking with funds provided under VAWA.

11. In 1993, only Oregon had a tort damage action available for stalking victims, according to the *Model Anti-Stalking Code for States* report.

12. See, for instance, South Carolina Code Annotated § 16-3-1830.

13. The section on challenges to state stalking statutes was prepared by the Office of Policy Development, U.S. Department of Justice.

14. For more information, see Appendix A of *Stalking and Domestic Violence: The Third Annual Report to Congress under the Violence Against Women Act.*

Chapter 26

# *A Guide to Court Watching in Domestic Violence and Sexual Assault Cases*

## *Introduction to Court Watching*

Concerned about the way in which courts are enforcing local laws and handling cases, citizens groups across the country have organized court watching programs. Unlike individuals who go to court as witnesses, victims, defendants or jurors, court watchers do not have a personal stake in the outcome of a case; instead, they go to court to observe proceedings and to assess whether courts are serving their communities fairly. Existing court watching programs monitor anything from audibility of proceedings to the behavior of court personnel to gender bias in the courts. The premise of most community programs is that while judges, jurors, and court personnel want to do the right thing, having residents and citizens evaluating court proceedings encourages fairness for parties involved in court cases and makes courts accountable to the communities they serve.

The specific focus of this chapter is to provide information about developing a court watching program for domestic violence and/or rape and sexual assault cases in your community. The information contained in this manual, however, can help individuals interested in establishing a court watching program for any issue.

## The Importance of Court Watching in Domestic Violence and Sexual Assault Cases

Violence against women is epidemic: two to four million women in the United States are beaten annually, and 13% of adult American women have been victims of forcible rape. The FBI, the Department of Justice, and the American Medical Association report that the numbers of rapes, sexual assaults and incidents of battering are increasing. So, too, is the physical, economic, and psychological cost of this plague. Battering is the single greatest cause of injury for women, and 22% to 35% of women who go to emergency rooms with medical complaints have symptoms which stem from domestic violence. Violence ranks as the number one hurdle facing many women in the job market: 50% of victims lose their jobs or are forced to quit in the aftermath of rape, and 50% of battered women missed work because of the abuse. Violence often deprives women of the joys of exercise, recreation, and friendship that men take for granted. And in the end, violence confines millions of women to lives of fear and insecurity, whether or not they are directly the victims of battering or assault.

Fortunately, states in the last two decades have seen significant reforms in domestic violence and rape laws. Today, laws in all fifty states and the District of Columbia permit battered women to obtain civil protection orders, and most states have changed their rape laws to focus on the behavior of the offender rather than the response of the victim. Legislative reforms notwithstanding, research reveals that in some locations only minor improvements in rates of arrest, prosecution and conviction have followed. Prevailing myths and stereotypes about domestic violence and rape continue to operate in the courtroom and undermine justice for victims. These myths include:

- battered women provoke their partner's violence
- rapists are knife-wielding, sex-starved, mentally deranged strangers
- a battered woman is someone who is beaten up constantly and has serious injuries to show for it
- a real rape victim offers the utmost in physical resistance, suffers savage physical injuries and immediately reports the rape to the police
- it is easy for a battered woman to leave her abuser

- domestic violence committed by women against men is equivalent to the domestic violence men commit against women

- domestic violence against mothers does not affect children

- acquaintance rape is just "bad sex" or "regretted sex," and is not as traumatic as stranger rape

The pervasiveness of violence against women and the failure of the judicial system to respond may leave victims believing that the legal system does not want to and cannot protect them adequately. Court watching is a clear demonstration to law enforcement and the judiciary that the community is concerned about these crimes and committed to addressing them seriously. Court watching is a positive way for concerned groups and individuals to address problems of bias within the system by documenting when these myths and stereotypes are carried into the courtroom and how they undermine justice for victims. Finally, court watching is important because it works. To date, several programs have succeeded in having courts adopt their recommendations and in improving judicial intervention for victims of domestic violence and sexual assault. A listing of relevant court watching programs is included in the back of this chapter.

## *Starting a Court Watching Program*

The following is an outline of action steps necessary to start a court watching program. As a general principle, it is best to try to work within the guidelines of your court system as much as possible.

**Set realistic goals.** Goal setting is one of the first and most important steps in developing a successful court watching program. Whether your mission is to identify why courts allow violent sexual offenders to slip through the system or to make courts respond effectively to domestic violence cases, you will need to develop a set of specific and attainable goals. Some existing programs monitor enforcement of new state domestic violence laws; others monitor how courts treat orders of protection. You may have to observe the courts beforehand or conduct interviews with individuals working with the court system to help you define any gaps or problems in your local courts. Because the stated goals will serve to both direct the work of volunteers and educate the courts and community about the project, it is important to think through your goals carefully. To assist your goal-setting efforts, examples of general and specific goals of existing court watching projects are listed below:

- to compile data on how domestic violence cases and sexual assault cases are handled in a given courtroom, including how the court issues orders of protection and enforces new stalking or domestic violence statutes;

- to make those involved in the judicial process (judges, jurors and other court personnel) aware of the public's interest in how courts handle domestic violence and sexual assault cases;

- to investigate cases which appear to have unusual or problematic outcomes; keep files on repeat offenders and contact judges (and other responsible parties) when public safety may be compromised;[1]

- to educate legislators, advocates, and the general public about court watching conclusions;

- to educate citizen volunteers about the justice system; and

- to create a more informed and involved public.

**Ride a wave of community energy.** Demonstrate a need for a court watching program by spotlighting cases in which there has been inconsistent judicial enforcement of recent changes to domestic violence or rape laws. Alternatively, highlight a specific case or series of domestic violence/sexual assault cases that are troubling to the community or indicative of problems within the system. For example, the Bergen County Commission on Women in New Jersey established the Community Court Watch Project, in part, after a Family Division judge denied a protection order to a battered woman; a few weeks later, the woman's husband beat her to death with a baseball bat.[2]

**Collaborate with groups within the community.** Cooperation among groups is essential for a successful court watching program. In fact, coalitions of groups spearhead most existing court watching projects. The Cook County Court Watch Program in Illinois, one of the most well-established court watching programs in the country, suggests establishing a formal Steering Committee or Board of Directors comprising representatives from a variety of groups with diverse skills (i.e., fundraising, public relations, and legal professionals).

When designing your project, you may want to partner with county commissions on women, bar associations, domestic violence and sexual assault groups, churches and other community organizations.

**Communicate with the courts.** Court watching programs cooperate with and seek input from victim advocates and prosecutors at the District Attorney's office, educators, court administrators and judges. The Board of Directors may want to convene a formal meeting with court administrators to explain the goals of the project and what will be done with the results. You will also want to seek the cooperation of court personnel regarding how to obtain up-to-date court calendars and notify judges whose courtrooms you will observe.

During your meetings and in subsequent correspondence, emphasize to administrators that the program is not out to get a specific judge or clerk. Instead, the focus will be on improving the courts' response to domestic violence and sexual assault cases as a whole.[3]

**Develop a court watching plan of action.** Determine a time frame for court watching, such as three months or a year. An on-going court watching program is ideal; any time less than three months may yield few results. Determine which courts will be monitored. Keep in mind that at the outset of the project, it may be too difficult to observe more than one or two courtrooms. Additionally, it is better to pick courtrooms with a lot of activity, such as misdemeanor courts or courts that hear numerous domestic violence cases. The proceedings in felony or jury courts may be too complicated to begin court watching there.[4] Contact the clerk of the courts to find out which courtrooms have the cases you want to hear and the schedule (days and times) for these cases. Be present and observe a case along its entire course. Be aware that often a case is not completed at one hearing.

**Recruit volunteers.** Go to law schools, universities, and colleges. Solicit the help of social-service organizations and domestic violence and sexual assault centers. Put ads asking for volunteers in the paper and send announcements to local TV and radio stations to make the public aware of the program and to recruit additional volunteers. Work with volunteer agencies in the community.

Many programs begin with ten to twenty volunteers and expand as they become more established. For example, after operating for twenty years, the Fund for Modern Courts—a group of court watching programs in New York State—has expanded its volunteer staff to over 600.

You will need to develop a process to screen volunteers. Most court watching programs recommend that volunteers who observe court proceedings should not have recently been, or currently be, a defendant or complainant in a local court case.

**Raise funds.** Because most court watching staff will be volunteers, you can operate a short-term court watching program with limited funds. However, you will want to have money for supplies and will need to prepare a budget. Seek donations from members of the Steering Committee or Board, bar associations, businesses, corporations, foundations, lawyers, and community organizations. Have members of the Board solicit funds from their contacts and affiliates. The Cook County Court Watching program recommends contacting potential donors by letter and enclosing a copy of the budget. Although you may not receive all the money you ask for, you may have better luck with corporations and foundations if you state a specific dollar amount when soliciting donations.[5] Furthermore, although some organizations and individuals may not be able to provide you with funds, they can donate valuable resources, such as the use of office equipment or other supplies.

If you are interested in extending the duration of your project, consider researching corporations, businesses and foundations in your community to find out which groups or charities they fund. You may want to obtain a not-for-profit, tax exempt status so that all contributions to your project will be tax-deductible.[6] To do this, you will need to incorporate in your state and then apply to the Internal Revenue Service for a "501(c)(3)" status. This process can be complicated, and you may want to consult an accountant or attorney. Your local library may also have resources on how to start a not-for-profit.

**Work with the media.** Send press releases to newspapers and radio stations about the details and goals of the project. Designate and train a contact person who will respond to media inquiries.

**Develop a resource manual for volunteers.** The manual should cover:

- the specific goals of your court watching program;
- a glossary with any legal language and terminology used in the courtroom;
- basic legal concepts, including how the county court system operates and the procedures in the types of proceedings volunteers will monitor (e.g., arraignments, pre-trials, probation hearings, sentencings);

- information on domestic violence and sexual assault, including prevailing myths and stereotypes that affect courtroom proceedings, sample domestic violence complaints, sample orders of protection, and local or state statutes that pertain to domestic violence and sexual assault;

- a confidentiality agreement;

- a map of the court building; and

- a list of judges, indicating whether they preside over district or county court cases.

**Train volunteers.** Court proceedings move quickly, and to someone unfamiliar with terminology and procedures, the process will seem enigmatic. A team comprising legal advocates from domestic violence and sexual assault centers and other legal or court personnel should offer a half-day or full-day formal training for volunteers. Training should cover project design and goals, local laws, judicial disposition, and how to listen and record data objectively. You may have to provide training to monitors on an array of court proceedings, including arraignments, pre-trials, trials, sentencings and probation hearings. A few trips to court with a legal advocate or a fully-trained court watcher are essential to a successful training.

*Tips for Court Watchers:* As a court watcher, your job will be to document what happens in each case on the survey form. You may want to record behavior such as timeliness, ability to be heard, attentiveness to the victim and inappropriate comments or jokes. You will also want to note how much of the proceeding takes place in the judges chambers, the amount of bail set, and any departures from the sentencing guidelines.[7]

Dignified conduct and dress are important. Avoid gesturing, loud comments, unpleasant facial expressions, angry words, emotional confrontations, or any other disruptive behavior.[8] If the outcome of a case is particularly troubling, contact the project coordinator or designated domestic violence representative. In time, you will begin to pick up on the attitude of a court toward domestic violence and/or sexual assault cases. However, the value of your observations is based partly on your being neutral and unbiased, so do not come to a conclusion without looking at as many facts as you can.[9] The detailed information collected from questionnaires of many court monitors will allow your program to analyze data and to identify patterns and long-term trends within the court system.

*Tips for Supervisors:* You are in charge of scheduling court watchers and informing them of the schedule regularly. When scheduling, it is important to ensure that the selected courts are monitored as many days as possible and by many volunteers. In this way, you can obtain a variety of viewpoints and have a complete picture of the courts as they operate day-to-day.[10] You will also be in charge of responding to any cases of particular concern. For example, the Executive Director of WATCH, a court watching program in Minnesota, contacts a judge or a prosecutor to discuss any case with unusual or troubling outcomes.

Schedule volunteers to observe in pairs so that one observer can listen and the other can write. Encourage volunteers to introduce themselves to the judges and their bailiffs as court watchers. Volunteers should identify themselves to the court by wearing nametags.

You will also be in charge of collecting and reading surveys. Volunteers will need to complete a survey for every proceeding they observe and should return surveys soon after the date of observation. In this way, you can follow up with volunteers on any responses while the information is still fresh in their minds.

**Design a survey for court observation.** Because the surveys will determine what data are collected on court proceedings, a good survey instrument is critical to the success of the project. Designing one should not be taken lightly. Visit and observe several court proceedings before trying to draft the survey instrument. The visits will give you a better idea of what data to collect and the pace of the court proceedings. The survey should include both objective and subjective questions and should cover:

- demographic information for the defendant and the complaining witness;
- the relationship of the parties and whether they share children;
- detailed case information, including the type of proceeding (arraignment, hearing or trial), the nature of the alleged abuse, and the case disposition (i.e. restraint against defendant, type of relief granted to the victim);
- judicial and court personnel conduct; and
- court watchers' comments and assessments.

Volunteers should visit the courts to test the survey and make any necessary changes to the questions before officially beginning the program. Because courts are busy and fast-paced, design survey questions so that the observer can record information quickly and accurately.

When writing the survey, keep in mind that you will need to analyze the data gathered from the surveys. You may want to work with a college or a group with statistical expertise to ensure that the survey instrument will allow you to gather the information you desire.

**Hold regular volunteer meetings.** Because volunteers usually will work only in pairs, they will seldom have an opportunity to exchange information, report on difficulties, and gather ideas from other volunteers. In the past, court watching programs have held debriefing meetings regularly, such as once a month, to give volunteers the chance to meet collectively and to ensure consistency and validity of recorded data.

## What to Do with Court Watching Conclusions

**Develop a report analyzing the survey data and make recommendations.** Many court watching programs tabulate the data themselves. Others enlist the help of colleges or computer consultants. Either way, once the data is compiled, convene focus groups comprising court watching monitors, domestic violence experts, attorneys, advocates and others to discuss the significance of the data and to draft recommendations. Compile results in a final report for distribution.

The following are examples of general and specific recommendations from various court watching programs monitoring domestic violence and sexual assault cases:

- reform aspects of state domestic violence laws;[11]
- grant more types of stay-away relief (such as orders of protection), including from work, school and other places;[12]
- include child support, risk assessment, counseling and treatment services as a mandatory component of judicial disposition;[13]
- ensure that the Administrative Office of the Courts requires judges to attend one or more courses on domestic violence;[14]
- establish a drop-in child care center at the courts;[15]
- make information on local domestic violence laws available to victims in a written format, such as a booklet; [16]

- establish a coordinating committee to improve interaction and information sharing among all systems involved in domestic violence intervention;[17]

- educate sheriff's deputies assigned to court security on the special security problems posed by domestic violence cases;[18]

- call on political leaders to seek out female and minority candidates for judgeships, so that the bench reflects the diversity of the community it serves;[19]

- for the safety of victims, witnesses, and the public, ensure that defendants convicted of or pleading to cases that carry a presumptive prison sentence should not be released pending sentencing;[20]

- change the Rules of Criminal Procedure so that when the victim's current address has no relevance to the case, he or she should not be required to provide it;[21] and

- change the rules governing judicial behavior so that judges may be subject to public scrutiny when their actions are in violation of the rules.[22]

**Go to the courts.** Inform judges, administrative offices of the courts, public defenders, district attorneys, judicial educators, etc., about your report. Schedule a meeting with court administrators to discuss the report and how to release the information to the public. In order to maintain your credibility, welcome and influence in the courts, the Cook County Court Watching Program recommends that you reach an agreement with court administrators on whether names of court officials will be kept confidential. You may also want to ask court administrators for a written response to your recommendations, which you can then include in your report to the public.[23]

Make sure judges and other court personnel understand your recommendations and collaborate with community groups to pressure courts to adopt them. Regularly meet with individual court administrators or others involved in the judicial process who can follow up on your recommendations.

Be aware that judges are held to high standards of ethics, both on and off the bench. In the event that a judge's conduct is improper or biased, you can use your data to file a complaint with the Commission on Judicial Conduct, which has the power to discipline judges. Contact your local bar association for details on how to bring complaints against judges.

**Distribute reports to the public.** Send copies of the report with an official statement to libraries, shelters, social service organizations, churches, schools, bar associations, government commissions, and other interested parties. Several court watching programs communicate regularly with the public via newsletters or reports. For example, the Cook County Court Watching Project reports annually to the public in a publication entitled "Citizens Look at Their Courts." Although names of court officials are not included in this report, court watchers' comments are included to highlight pervasive problems and support any recommendations.

**Go to the media.** By informing the media, you will focus public attention on domestic violence and rape, creating additional pressure on the courts to change. Be prepared to receive questions and responses from the media about your report. Designate spokespeople to field both media and public inquiries and train them to do this. Media visibility and public awareness will help you secure volunteers and increase funding.

## Creating Change through Court Watching

As many established court watching programs have found, it does not take an army of volunteers to make a difference—court watching programs have accomplished many of their goals with only a handful of observers. Initiating change and establishing credibility with court personnel takes time and persistence, and success may come slowly. Furthermore, "success" need not be determined exclusively by whether your efforts reformed the court system. In other words, training and educating the community; gathering valuable statistical data on courtroom proceedings; and the response from the media, court personnel, and the community are also part of the "success" of a program.

However, you should be encouraged by the fact that court watching projects have made significant changes within the court system. Some of these accomplishments are listed below:

- As of March 1, 1995, over 100 WATCH volunteers in Minneapolis had monitored more than 3,000 appearances on cases related to domestic abuse, sexual assault and criminal conduct. Judges have repeatedly said that everyone does a better job when WATCH is in the courtroom.

- Church Women United of Rochester, NY, succeeded in having the Family Court opened to their presence. A judge who had opposed the move twenty years earlier recently told them that they would never know how much good opening the Family Court had done for the court system.

- Monitors with the Bergen County program felt that judges were more knowledgeable about domestic violence cases and made a greater effort to protect the victim as a result of court watching. Judges referred, recommended and ordered people to more support services after the first set of court watching recommendations were distributed. Prior to these recommendations, certain agencies were hardly mentioned by the courts.

- As a result of Cook County Court Watch program recommendations, proper procedures were followed when appointing the Public Defender to ensure that the needs of the poor were met.

- Partly as a result of publicity surrounding the recommendations of a monitoring program in New York, construction on a desperately needed new Family Court courthouse was started.[24]

Although you may not achieve results like these overnight, the improvements in the court system today, from mandatory training for court personnel, to reforms in domestic violence dispositions, are in part a result of the persistent efforts of court monitors. Existing court watching programs agree that even if you do not "reform the courts," your presence there will go a long way toward improving public trust and faith in the court system. And in the end, your presence will mean a better, fairer day in court for victims of domestic violence and sexual assault.

## Endnotes

1. WATCH. *Hennepin County Criminal Courts: A View from the Outside*, Minneapolis, MN: April, 1994.

2. Cook County Court Watchers, Inc. *How to Start a Court Watching Project*, (1984).

3. WATCH, *supra* n.1.

4. Cook County Court Watchers, *supra* n.2, at II-2 (1984).

5. *Id.* at I-7.

6. *Id.* at I-9.

7. WATCH, *supra* n.1, at 2.

8. Kentucky Domestic Violence Association, et al. *Model Domestic Violence Court Watch Program,* at 4.

9. Church Women United. *Task Force on Courts,* Rochester, NY: Nov. 1996.

10. Cook County Court Watchers, Inc. *supra* n.2, at III-1.

11. For example, the Public Justice Center Domestic Violence Task Force recommended that a section be added to the relieve available under the Maryland Domestic Violence Act that permitted a judge to hold a protection order hearing when parties seeking an ex parte order are both present.

12. Public Justice Center. *Court Watch: A Report on Civil Protection Orders in Maryland Domestic Violence Cases,* at 2 (Sept. 1995).

13. Bergen County Commission on the Status of Women. *Court Watch II: A Study of the Bergen County Family Court System and the Enforcement of the State of New Jersey Prevention of Domestic Violence Act,* at 34 (Jan. 1995).

14. *Id.* at 35.

15. *Id.* at 34.

16. *Id.* at 35.

17. *Id.* at 36.

18. Cook Count Court Watchers, Inc. *Citizens Look at Their Courts,* at 7 (1994).

19. A Fund for Modern Courts. *Annual Report,* at 8 (1995).

20. WATCH, *supra* n.l, at 3.

21. *Id.* at 5.

22. *Id.* at 12.

23. *Id.* at IV-2.

24. A Fund for Modern Courts, *supra* n.19, at 9.

## *Selected Court Watching Programs*

The following is a partial listing of court watching programs. The list consists of programs that work on an array of issues, not limited to sexual assault and domestic violence. If you would like to add your court watching program to this list or know of a court watching program that should be included, please contact NOW LDEF's Intake Department at (212) 925-6635.

**Bergen County Commission on the Status of Women**
Department of Human Services
21 Main Street, Room 115W
Hackensack, NJ 07601
(201) 646-3700
Monitors domestic violence cases in civil courts. Authored two reports on community court watching.

**Church Women United**
644 Titus Avenue
Rochester, NY 14617
(716) 342-2790

*Works for general court reform and publishes a guidebook on court watching.*

**Cook County Court Watchers, Inc.**
332 South Michigan, Ste. 1140
Chicago, IL 60604
(312) 939-5550

*A twenty-four-year-old multi-issue court watching program. Monitors some domestic violence cases. Distributes manual entitled "How to Start a Court Watching Project" (1984).*

**Council for Court Excellence**
1800 M Street, Ste. 750 South
Washington, DC 20036
(202) 785-5917

*Occasional court watching programs on an array of issues.*

### A Fund for Modern Courts
19 West 44th Street, Ste. 1200
New York, NY 10036
(212) 575-1577

*Since 1975, an umbrella group for numerous court watching programs in New York. Monitors an array of issues and produces an annual report.*

### Kentucky Domestic Violence Association
PO Box 356
Frankfort, KY 40602
(502) 581-7273

*Monitors courts that issue domestic violence orders; publishes manual entitled "Model Domestic Violence Court Watch Program."*

### Maryland Public Justice Center
Domestic Violence Task Force
330 N. Charles St., Ste 500
Baltimore, MD 21201
(410) 625-9409

*Released a report on civil protection orders in Maryland domestic violence cases.*

### Rape and Abuse Crisis Center
715 11th Street, Ste. 306
Moorhead, MN 56560
(218) 299-7224

*Monitors rape and sexual assault cases and publishes information on courtwatching these cases.*

### WATCH
Suite 1001 Northstar East
608 Second Avenue South
Minneapolis, MN 55402
(612) 341-2747

*A Hennepin County program that monitors rape, sexual assault, domestic violence and child abuse cases in criminal court. Distributes reports and newsletters.*

# Part Seven

# Research

# Chapter 27

# *Facing Up to Family Violence*

*Rosemary Chalk and Patricia A. King*

For an alarming number of Americans, the family is a source of fear and physical violence. The 1996 National Incidence Study of Child Abuse and Neglect found 2.8 million reported cases of child maltreatment, a rate of 41.9 per 1,000 children. The rate of domestic violence, according to the most recent National Crime Victims Survey, was 9.3 cases per 1,000 adults. These cases involve both physical and psychological injuries that can extend long beyond the violent events themselves; family violence also contributes to the development of other social problems such as alcoholism, drug abuse, delinquency, crime, teenage pregnancy, and homelessness.

Society's traditional unwillingness to intervene in family matters has given way in the past few decades to a host of efforts to support and protect victims and to deter and rehabilitate offenders. We have witnessed the birth of shelters for battered women, special police units focused on domestic violence, victim advocates in the court system, guidelines for health care providers who see evidence of family violence, and a wide range of other services.

Many of these programs deal with the acute injuries and crisis nature of family violence, when the victim's needs are clearly visible. More recently, however, service providers and policymakers have been

Reprinted with permission from *Issues in Science and Technology*, Chalk et al., "Facing Up to Family Violence" Winter 1998–99, pp. 39–46. Copyright © 1999 by the University of Texas at Dallas, Richardson, TX.

exploring how to develop prevention programs or treatment approaches that can address the long-term consequences of family violence. This shift from acute response to problem prevention and treatment is difficult, especially because the state of research knowledge about family violence and the effectiveness of interventions is not well developed, and service providers seek to balance multiple goals in meeting the needs of children and adults.

As society comes to understand the complex nature of family violence, it is becoming increasingly clear that simply identifying problems and responding to crises will not solve the problem. Many aspects of family violence need more attention. Parenting practices have proven to be highly resistant to change. When alerted to reports of child abuse or neglect, for example, social service and law enforcement agencies must struggle with how to respond to the safety and developmental needs of the child, maintain and support families challenged by instability and stress, and keep their services efficient and inexpensive. In addressing domestic violence, law enforcement agencies and others are looking closely at the comparative benefits of treatment and deterrence, and are often uncertain about how to balance victim safety, fairness for the accused, and community support. Elder abuse has also raised difficult questions about the benefits of separating family members when abuse or neglect has been reported, especially when the abused person is dependent on the relationship for important benefits.

But although serious gaps in our understanding of the origins and causes of family violence still exist, opportunities now exist to improve the nature and effectiveness of interventions in health care, social service, and law enforcement settings. As program sponsors, policy officials, and service providers move forward in building victim support and offender deterrence efforts, a series of challenges needs to be overcome to create an effective service delivery system and an adequate knowledge base that can guide policy and practice.

## Problem Discovery and Crisis Response

The origin of many of the current shortcomings in research can be traced to the way in which the problems of child maltreatment, domestic violence, and elder abuse emerged as a source of social concern. Traditionally defined as a social and legal problem, the issue of child abuse emerged as a topic of major medical concern in the early 1960s, when health professionals became aware that they could detect signs of chronic and traumatic abuse in young children in the form of healed injuries that were no longer visible. With this knowledge, physicians and other child advocates encouraged the federal government to develop a national child abuse reporting system so that health care workers, teachers, and others would be required to report suspected cases of child maltreatment to local social service agencies. Mandatory reporting became the first component of child protection policy.

Defenders of battered women brought the needs and concerns of their clients to the attention of legal officials throughout the states in a different way during the past few decades. Recognizing that violence among intimates was often trivialized or treated as a civil disorder rather than a criminal action, police officials, prosecutors, and judges were urged to reform their response efforts to offer more forceful protection to victims involved in domestic violence cases. With federal resources, victim advocates were supported within law enforcement systems to counsel victims, predominantly women, who often were not aware of their options in bringing charges against a batterer or protecting themselves and their children from assaults and unwanted intrusions. Protective interventions thus became a distinctive component of law enforcement interventions for domestic violence.

Elder abuse, which has never received the level of national attention given to child maltreatment and domestic violence, has nonetheless been a topic of recurring concern among social service and health care agencies. Local agencies responsible for services for the aging have long been troubled by the cases of elder neglect that come to their attention. Service providers consistently search for solutions that can meet the needs of the vulnerable adult, preserve the older person's autonomy and decision-making authority, and retain family support systems where appropriate.

The caseloads associated with these early response efforts quickly became overwhelming. Child protective service and other social workers were assigned dozens of reports of families in trouble. Courts became backlogged as they tried to sort out the intricacies of evidence and the appropriateness of sanctions. Intimate partners or abused elders would cry for help from police one day, only to drop charges the next. Families reported for abuse would be monitored for months without incident, then they would move or disappear within the community, only to surface again as new allegations emerged. Law enforcement officials and social service personnel became frustrated and disillusioned by the lack of success of their efforts as they witnessed patterns of abuse and violence that were seemingly resistant to social controls and counseling.

Although inadequate, these initial interventions into family violence are tremendously important. They represent the first stage of a long-term effort to address an important social problem. They have revealed the scope and multiple dimensions of family violence. They have suggested that numerous pathways lead to violence within the home and that violence that occurs in childhood and among adults may have important linkages. They have indicated that relationships among family members and contextual factors are often important forces in triggering as well as preventing child maltreatment, domestic violence, and elder abuse. And they have demonstrated that the recurrent nature of family violence makes it a problem that will not be "cured" with a single dose of services.

## Understanding the Problem

Before moving on to develop new approaches and improved practices, it is important to take stock of what we have learned from the experience with family violence interventions. But taking stock is not easy. Research in this field involves several disciplines and is fragmented by competing theories that have not yet explained the pathways to family violence in a way that could serve as a basis for effective interventions. Understanding the challenges to research on family violence interventions is an important step in developing a strategic plan that can help build the next wave of interventions in this field.

First, family violence has traditionally been defined as a problem of pathological or criminal behavior rather than one that involves a variety of contributing causes and several stages of disorders. For many years, researchers focused on individual risk factors such as psychological deficits or environmental causes, but they were unable to isolate a single trait or risk factor that characterized a batterer or offending parent. This lack of success suggests that more complex and interactive forces are at work that stimulate, sustain, or moderate violent behavior. But observing family or adult interactions or relationships that emerge over time involves more intensive, and more intrusive, measures and methods that require significant resources and effort.

Second, the absence of large-scale studies describing the distribution and patterns of violence in everyday relationships challenges the development of appropriate measures and methods in the field. Most of the cases that have formed the basis of scientific studies of family violence involve actions that have been reported to the courts, social service agencies, or health professionals. These cases often involve the most serious, and possibly most resistant, forms of violent or abusive behavior. Scientists in this field have generally not had access to large general population samples and appropriate comparison groups that could provide insight into the antecedents of violence in the home.

Third, the tendency to deal with family violence cases as separate incidents rather than as symptoms of a broader social pattern of disorder and dysfunctional behavior has also contributed to the difficulty of developing a research base to identify the origins of family violence. Research remains highly idiosyncratic, often focusing on clinical populations or retrospective memories rather than large research samples with control populations and direct observation.

Fourth, researchers who study family violence are hindered not only by a lack of resources but also by concerns about safety, privacy, ethics, and law. The stigma and bias associated with family violence also raise important concerns in developing large-scale population-based studies in this field. Research on the efficacy of treatment programs in addressing domestic violence, for example, can be problematic when offenders are randomly assigned to jail time, community service, or treatment. Questions about fairness and victim safety, in particular, complicate efforts to duplicate the clinical trial model in judicial settings. The involvement of vulnerable parties in service network and research studies requires consistent vigilance to ensure that appropriate protections exist to keep them from further harm.

Although a few well-defined and rigorous studies aimed at understanding the causes of family violence and evaluating the effectiveness of interventions have emerged, a large research literature consistent with high standards does not yet exist. The absence of this literature complicates the study of interventions, because it is difficult to identify for whom a particular approach might work, under what conditions, and for how long.

## Learning from What We Know

Studies of the effectiveness of family violence interventions commonly focus on the relative effects of individual programs rather than incorporating an appreciation of the complex, systemic, and pervasive nature of this problem within the lives of those affected by it. Although some victims experience acute trauma and other clinical symptoms, for many others the impact of victimization is diffuse and global, compromising their ability to react to stress or other situations that require self-control and the management of anger, fear, or uncertainty. This knowledge suggests that service interventions will need to address family violence as an integral part of the lives of the victims and offenders rather than an isolated component of their behavior or experience.

As they acquire greater awareness of the relationships between different types of abuse (for example, the connection between witnessing domestic violence in the home and using violence as part of adult relationships later in life), researchers and practitioners are hopeful that new opportunities will emerge to apply preventive interventions for children and adolescents who have been exposed to violence before it can become part of their own parenting or intimate behaviors.

In other areas, stronger theories about the causes of family violence can help specify how the targets, scope, and timing of interventions should be designed. For example, improving the quality of or access to parenting education will not help prevent child maltreatment if a large number of offending parents abuse their children as a result of adult depression, anxiety, and social isolation or if parents lack social support in using nonviolent ways to discipline their children. Similarly, a husband who abuses his wife only when he is drunk may require a different type of service response than one who is habitually aggressive to friends and family alike. The latter case may be a strong candidate for law enforcement interventions designed to isolate and punish the offender, whereas the former might be more appropriate for a program that combines elements of marital counseling, anger management, and substance abuse treatment. If different types of offenders are placed in a treatment program that works effectively for only one segment of the total population, the results of the evaluation study will be marginal or mixed, even though the program may be highly effective for a small portion of the total study sample. And if the client base for the program is too small or the follow-up times are too short to demonstrate the scale of the effects that a specific intervention can achieve, promising approaches may be too hastily dismissed when the research evidence is simply insufficient to warrant their continuation.

Definitional and classification issues also reveal areas where research can help inform practice. At present, family violence is often grouped into separate categories that capture isolated and fragmentary parts of the experience of victims and offenders. The broad diversity of these categories makes it difficult to organize existing interventions within frameworks that could strengthen interactions among different service settings. Treatment, prevention, and deterrence interventions use different focal points (the victim, the offender, the family, or the community), different units of measuring behavioral or social change, and different outcomes in assessing whether a selected program is achieving its intended effect.

And there are subcategories within categories. Child maltreatment, for example, covers a broad array of offenses: physical child abuse, sexual child abuse, child neglect, and emotional maltreatment. Treatment or prevention interventions for each of these areas often emerge within frameworks that are differentiated by the types of abuse that are reported. Child sexual abuse cases, for example, are more commonly referred to the police or courts for action, whereas physical abuse and neglect cases generally become the responsibility of social service agencies.

These categories and subcategories reflect the details of a case when it is first recognized or reported, reflecting the emphasis of current interventions on problem identification and acute response. The categories are of little use in understanding the underlying causes or forces at work within the family. Although these arbitrary divisions may be appropriate for legal and social service interventions, they present major challenges to researchers who are more concerned with issues such as the frequency of events, levels of intensity, variety of triggers, nature of relationships, and patterns of response. As researchers move away from case records to population-based studies to determine how hidden dynamics influence the continuum of violence, new categories may emerge that could more appropriately guide service interventions in allocating resources, fostering service interactions, and applying appropriate responses to individuals and families.

Building partnerships between research and practice in the field of family violence requires opportunities for sustained collaboration that can allow scientists and service providers to understand more about the multidimensional nature and sequence of patterns of victimization, trauma, and violence. Service providers point to the absence of coordination and comprehensive approaches within their communities as an obstacle to gaining perspective on the multiple dimensions of family violence. Researchers have consistently expressed concern about the lack of resources invested in work necessary to build longitudinal studies. Although many health, law enforcement, and social service agencies support programs and research in family violence, these efforts are scattered across several sectors and lack sufficient strength to define program priorities, promising directions, and research needs. In the meantime, caseworkers, health care providers, law enforcement officials, and the general public must struggle with what to do when confronted with cases of family violence in their communities.

In the midst of this confusion and uncertainty, however, one fact looms above the others. We are entering a new stage in building the scientific knowledge base necessary to understanding and treating the problem of family violence. Although this research is not yet strong enough to provide clear guidance to those who must make policy or programmatic decisions about specific treatment and prevention interventions, a large set of descriptive and empirical studies has emerged that provides an important foundation for future scholarship and programmatic efforts. Like many of the family violence interventions themselves, scientific research in this field is still young and immature, consisting largely of studies that rely on reports of what was done in the intervention rather than probing more carefully into the outcomes that the treatment or prevention effort sought to achieve, the characteristics of the client base, the pathways by which clients were assigned to the program, and the implementation process of the program itself. Critical tools that provide the foundation of solid evaluation studies in other fields—strong theory, large longitudinal and follow-up studies, reliable measures, and consistent definitions and diagnostic criteria—are only beginning to develop in the field of family violence studies.

## Collaboration and Comprehensive Services

If family violence were an infectious disease, an intensive research effort would gradually become an integral part of the design of treatment and prevention interventions, involving large-scale clinical trials designed to test the strength, efficiency, and effects of various interventions. Problems associated with theory, measurement, sample size, and comparison groups would gradually be resolved as researchers and practitioners acquired greater familiarity with the nature of the phenomenon under study and learned from the experience of selected groups. As the knowledge base expanded, service providers and researchers would find ways to communicate their findings and experiences with each other and discover ways to improve on the first generation of interventions to build stronger, durable, and more effective services. This type of infrastructure development and the integration of knowledge and practice have not occurred in family violence for the reasons discussed above. But we now have the opportunity to build such collaborative efforts, which can incorporate findings from existing research.

Assessing the effectiveness of treatment, prevention, and deterrence interventions for family violence, especially in open-service systems that have little control over which types of clients are assigned to experimental interventions or to standard service practices, requires creative strategies and close collaboration among researchers and practitioners. Yet caseworkers, who often have little opportunity to participate in the design of the evaluation studies of their services, can be understandably resentful of scientific evaluations that require randomized controls or experimental designs that require them to place vulnerable children, adults, or families in service settings that they "know" are not ideal. Likewise, they may be unwilling to collaborate with researchers if they believe that negative study results will undermine the funding base of their program in the future. Similarly, court officials who are concerned with the impact of sanctions and deterrent measures on future violent behavior may be reluctant to use scientific methods to compare the relative effectiveness of treatment and stiffer sanctions if concerns about fairness are not resolved.

An increasing emphasis on the need for integration of health care, social service, and law enforcement interventions in the area of family violence has now fostered an even more daunting task: how to measure the impact and cost-effectiveness of comprehensive community interventions that are designed for specific geographic regions and are affected by multiple service systems within their local settings. Yet despite the obstacles associated with their design and implementation, comprehensive interventions are revealing key opportunities where service providers concerned with family violence can interact more effectively with their counterparts in other service settings. For example, although studies have found a strong link between substance abuse and domestic violence, substance abuse treatment programs rarely address the problems of domestic violence, and batterers' treatment programs often lack the capacity to address the addictive behaviors of their clients. Comprehensive intervention seems to be a promising approach, but research to verify its effectiveness and identify the best mix of components will be difficult.

## Preliminary Lessons

Despite these challenges, research studies are beginning to take a closer and more critical look at the knowledge base associated with family violence interventions. This research base, which includes more than 100 studies conducted over the past two decades that meet minimal standards of scientific rigor, is highlighting specific areas where evaluation studies have provided firm evidence of positive or negative effects of family violence interventions.

Although it is premature to offer policy recommendations for most family violence interventions in the absence of a more rigorous research base, a few lessons can be drawn from current studies:

- Mandatory reporting laws for domestic violence should not be enacted until such systems have been tested and evaluated by research. In spite of extensive experience with mandatory reporting, no reliable evaluation of its effectiveness has been completed. Because a report of violence can sometimes diminish protections or precipitate more violence, particularly when there is no intervention, it is wiser to preserve the discretion of health professionals and other service providers in determining when to report troubled families. Such discretion is particularly important under circumstances where the provision of care is disrupted by the process of notification.

- Early warning systems are needed in judicial settings to detect failure to comply with or complete treatment and to identify signs of new abuse or retaliation against victims. Research has indicated that reports of violent behavior often diminish while a batterer is in treatment, and victims are often more inclined to return to a relationship with a batterer if they know that he is enrolled in a program designed to curb violence in intimate relationships. But if the batterer drops out of the program or fails to enroll after court referral, the victim may be at great risk. Early warning systems would require court oversight to ensure offender compliance with the requirements of treatment referrals and should also address unintended or inadvertent results that may arise from the referral to or experience with treatment. For example, some treatment programs may simply involve marital counseling without ever addressing the violence that occurred in the relationships. Others may lack appropriate supervision within a group treatment program. As a result, a batterer may feel justified in using violence since others report that they act in a similar fashion with their partners. The absence of certification for treatment programs allows the use of practices that lack appropriate research support. Courts need to be vigilant to ensure that offenders are referred only to treatment programs that are known to be adequate.

- Abuse and histories of family violence need to be documented in individual and group health care and social service records, but such documentation requires safeguards. If research continues to suggest that family violence is a significant contributor to health outcomes and family caregiving practices, the need to know about early and chronic histories of family violence will become stronger. This need will have to be balanced against individual privacy and confidentiality concerns. Health professionals are often reluctant to record incidents of violence, viewing such events as legal rather than medical matters. But patterns of violent injury should not be allowed to go unnoticed in medical histories, since they can provide important clues to future health disorders, especially in areas that involve chronic fear, stress, anxiety, trauma, or anger.

- Collaborative strategies among caseworkers, lawmakers, prosecutors, and judges have the potential to improve a batterer's compliance with treatment as well as to make sanctions more effective. Studies of police arrest practices, for example, have indicated that arrest has a greater deterrent effect on future violence than simple counseling or arbitration. Arrests without prosecution, however, can send messages to individuals and communities that family violence is not to be taken seriously. Although challenged by evidentiary standards and victim reluctance to press charges, courts need to find collaborative ways to improve the penalties for family violence and to ensure that adequate treatment programs exist for those who are motivated to change their practices.

- Home visitation programs should be particularly encouraged as part of a comprehensive prevention strategy for child maltreatment, especially for first-time parents living in social settings with high rates of child maltreatment. An array of research studies has been conducted on home visitation services that offer promising findings, but they suggest that the greatest benefits of these services occur only with young, single, and poor mothers. But this group includes many who are highly mobile or reluctant to trust others offering them advice and guidance. We need to learn more about how to engage high-risk parents in prevention services designed to improve their child care-giving skills and also to improve the general quality of their own personal health care, education, and job training, which may require them to spend more time out of the home. [*See* Section 17.3.]

- Although intensive family preservation services are an important part of the continuum of family support services, they should not be required in every situation in which a child is recommended for out-of-home placement. Community agencies need to be able to act quickly and decisively when children are endangered or neglected. The costs of delay can be enormous in short- and long-term consequences. Although some families can recover from difficulties if they are provided with appropriate services and guidance, many others are overwhelmed by their problems and simply cannot care for their children. When faced with recurring patterns of child abandonment and abuse, social service and law enforcement agencies should look for appropriate ways to provide reasonable care for vulnerable family members rather than working solely to preserve the family.

Does this analysis imply that the existing array of treatment and prevention interventions for family violence is misguided and a poor use of public funds? Not at all. It does suggest, however, that greater efforts need to be made to build an evaluation and research capacity that can help inform, question, and guide the development of service interventions. Improved evaluation studies can lead to better and more efficient service interventions that reflect an empirical and comprehensive understanding of the problem of family violence rather than a set of beliefs and anecdotes that lead to single-minded approaches and often result in inconsistent and piecemeal efforts to address the needs of victims and offenders. The development of family violence interventions needs to be seen as an iterative process in which services are initially put into place to respond to immediate needs but are refined and improved over time as a knowledge base emerges through collaboration between the service provider and research communities.

Building the next generation of evaluation studies and service interventions for family violence will require leadership and coordinated strategies within the policy, program, and research communities that cut across traditional disciplines and service settings. Efforts have already begun to integrate the network of health, social service, and law enforcement interventions at the local, state, and national policy levels, but many efforts remain disconnected. The Departments of Justice and of Health and Human Services are now collaborating in funding small-scale studies and the development of improved research measures and training programs, but new initiatives are rare because of the lack of new funds and the absence of innovative strategies that could strengthen interdisciplinary approaches to complex social policy concerns. It is far easier for Congress to appropriate funds for hundreds of community-based programs than to craft a bold research strategy that would integrate biological, psychological, social, behavioral, medical, and criminal justice research focused on family violence. But it must take the more difficult path. In the absence of new research-practice partnerships and an infrastructure capable of supporting long-term studies, we will continue to be faced in the next decade with a profusion of interventions and a limited capacity to examine their effects.

## About the Authors

Rosemary Chalk was study director of the National Research Council Committee on the Assessment of Family Violence Interventions. Patricia A. King, the Carmack Waterhouse Professor of Law, Medicine, Ethics, and Public Policy at the Georgetown University Law Center, was chair of the Committee.

## Recommended Reading

Chalk, R. and P. A. King, eds. *Violence in Families: Assessing Prevention and Treatment Programs.* National Research Council and the Institute of Medicine. Washington, D.C.: National Academy Press, 1998.

Connell, J. P., A. C. Kubisch, L. B. Schorr, and C. H. Weiss, eds. *New Approaches to Evaluating Community Initiatives.* New York: The Aspen Institute, 1995.

Crowell, N. and A. Burgess, eds. *Understanding Violence against Women.* National Research Council. Washington, D.C.: National Academy Press, 1996.

Melton, G. and F. Barry, eds. *Protecting Children from Abuse and Neglect.* New York: Guilford, 1994.

National Research Council. *Understanding Child Abuse and Neglect.* Washington, D.C.: National Academy Press, 1993.

Schuerman, J. R., T. L. Rzepnicki, and J. H. Littell (1994). *Putting Families First.* New York: Aldine de Gruyter, 1994.

Chapter 28

# Findings about Partner Violence from the Dunedin Multidisciplinary Health and Development Study

*Terrie E. Moffitt and Avshalom Caspi*

The 1992-96 National Crime Victimization Survey (NCVS) indicates that in 1996 victimization by intimates—spouses, ex-spouses, boyfriends, girlfriends, and former boyfriends and girlfriends—accounts for about 21 percent of the violent crime experienced by women and about 2 percent of the violence experienced by men. Rates of nonlethal violence are highest among women ages 16–24 and women in low-income households.[1] These statistics highlight the importance of studying partner violence among young adults, both married and unmarried, who represent all socioeconomic backgrounds.

The Dunedin Multidisciplinary Health and Development Study is a 21-year investigation of a representative birth cohort of infants born between April 1, 1972, and March 31, 1973, in Dunedin, a city of approximately 120,000 people on New Zealand's South Island.[2] Perinatal data for 1,139 births were obtained at delivery. When these children were traced at age 3, 91 percent, or 1,037, were assessed, forming the base sample for the longitudinal study. The base sample was composed of 535 (52 percent) males and 502 (48 percent) females. Fewer than 7 percent of the study members identified themselves as nonwhite (Maori or Polynesian). The social class and ethnicity of their families matched those of the South Island's general population.

U.S. Department of Justice. National Institute of Justice publication No. NCJ 170018, July 1999.

The Dunedin cohort was reassessed at ages 5, 7, 9, 11, 13, 15, 18, and 21, with 992 (97 percent) of the 1,020 living members of the age 3 base sample (51 percent male) participating in the last assessment at age 21 in 1993–94. This history of reassessment at regular intervals is especially important for the research on partner violence. Since their childhood, study members have revealed problem behaviors; their confidentiality has never been violated, and they have learned to expect no intervention from the researchers (unless imminent serious danger was posed to themselves or others). As a result, by the time they were 21 years old, they were comfortable giving frank responses to questions about partner violence. This circumstance offers a special advantage over studies involving self-reports from perpetrators held in correctional institutions or remanded for treatment.

This chapter summarizes the findings about partner violence from the Dunedin study. Among the results are that partner violence is strongly linked to cohabitation at a young age; a variety of mental illnesses; a background of family adversity, dropping out of school, and juvenile aggression; conviction for other types of crime, especially violent crime; drug abuse; long-term unemployment; and parenthood at a young age.

## Why Study Partner Violence?

The Dunedin study began to examine partner violence because partner violence research is a natural extension of the study's earlier research on childhood behavior problems and teen delinquency. Although official crime statistics from police and courts suggest that offending declines rapidly during young adulthood, Dunedin researchers suspected that some delinquents' antisocial activities were continuing, but in a form not easily detected by official crime statistics; for example, as abuse of family members or intimates in the home. To test this possibility, a decision was made to examine partner violence among study members as they made the transition to young adulthood, became involved in serious relationships, and began to form new families. Given the unique features of this longitudinal study, it became important to apply the study's resources to understanding the origins of partner violence.

The Dunedin cohort, it is important to note, is a *birth* cohort, not a community sample. Followup was conducted with all individuals in the cohort; for example, those who had and had not used battered women's shelters and those who had and had not been convicted of battery.

When the study members turned 21 years old (phase 21 of the Dunedin study), questions about partner violence were embedded in a 50-minute standardized interview about intimate relationships. Information was gathered on both positive and negative conflict-negotiation behaviors occurring during the past 12 months. Included in the interview were the items of the Conflict Tactics Scales (CTS)[3] and other items from published domestic violence interviews. Although the CTS is controversial,[4] it has been used in numerous clinical studies as well as in U.S. national surveys on the prevalence of domestic violence. The CTS was included because it allowed comparison of the Dunedin findings with research on partner violence in the United States and elsewhere.

## How Trustworthy Are the Data? Do Partners' Reports about Abuse in Their Relationship Agree?[5]

The scientific study of partner abuse is controversial in part because there are concerns about the accuracy of data. Abuse data are usually collected by asking respondents to "self-report" their experiences. The majority of studies usually interview only one member of each couple. Can these self-reports of abuse be trusted? To answer this question, the extent to which partners' responses were in agreement was analyzed.

Prior to phase 21, 474 study members indicated they were involved with a partner they had been dating for at least 6 months, were married to, or were living with. Of these, 360 (76 percent) brought their partners along to participate in phase 21. Study members and their partners were interviewed separately (simultaneously) with identical questions by different interviewers who did not know the responses provided by the other member of the couple—and their confidentiality was guaranteed. Couples did not know before they arrived that they would be asked about partner abuse, eliminating any opportunity to coordinate their responses prior to the interview. Before interviewers turned to the topic of partner abuse, each participant was given the opportunity to decline discussion of that topic, but none of the participants refused. The full set of questions measured both physical and psychological abuse (see exhibit 1).

## Exhibit 1. Item content of physical and psychological partner abuse scales

### Physical Abuse Scale

Participants were asked if they had in the past year:

Physically twisted your partner's arm[a]

Pushed, grabbed, or shoved your partner[a,b]

Slapped your partner[a,b]

Physically forced your partner to have sex[a]

Shaken your partner[a]

Thrown or tried to throw your partner[a]

Thrown an object at your partner[a, b]

Choked or strangled your partner[a,b]

Kicked, bit, or hit your partner with a fist[a,b]

Hit or tried to hit your partner with something[a,b]

Beaten up your partner[a, b]

Threatened your partner with a knife or gun[a, b]

Used a knife or gun on your partner[a, b]

[a] From Margolin's "Domestic Conflict Scale" or "Conflict Inventory" (Margolin, G., B. Burman, R.S. John, and M. O'Brien, *The Domestic Conflict Instrument,* Los Angeles: University of Southern California, 1990).

[b] From Straus's "Conflict Tactics Scales" (Straus, M.A., "Measuring Intrafamily Conflict and Violence: The Conflict Tactics Scales," *Journal of Marriage and the Family* 41(1979): 75–88).

### Psychological Abuse Scale

Participants were asked if they had in the past year:

Damaged a household item or some part of the home out of anger[a]

Deliberately disposed of or hidden an important item of your partner's[a]

Become very upset if dinner/housework/home repair work was not done[a]

Purposely damaged or destroyed your partner's clothes/car/other[a]

Insulted or shamed your partner in front of others[a]

Locked your partner out of the house[a]

Told your partner that he/she could not work or study[a]

Tried to stop your partner from seeing/talking to family or friends[a]

Restricted your partner's use of the car or telephone[a]

Made threats to leave[a]

Tried to turn family, friends, or children against your partner[a]

Ordered your partner around[a]

Frightened your partner[a]

Treated your partner like he/she was stupid[a]

Given in to your partner but planned revenge[a]

Ridiculed your partner[a]

Threatened to hit or throw something at your partner in anger[b]

Told your partner he/she was ugly or unattractive[a]

Become abusive after using drugs or alcohol[a]

Thrown, smashed, hit, or kicked something during a disagreement[b]

Perpetrators' reports of their own abuse behaviors were compared with their partners' reports of victimization to determine if couple members concurred about the perpetrator's behaviors. Couples' responses to the interview showed that agreement about whether specific abusive behaviors had happened was poor, as has been suggested by previous research. Study members and their partners did not agree about whether, for example, one of them had tried to strangle the other. However, agreement improved dramatically when the individual items were summed into scales that counted the variety of different abuse behaviors performed in the past year. Although members of a couple may not recall exactly the same acts, they can agree on whether or not abuse took place and on the extent of the abuse. Agreement was even stronger when random measurement errors were removed statistically.[6] This agreement reveals that disagreement between partners is due to random forgetfulness; neither partner was deliberately misrepresenting the facts in an attempt to mislead the interviewer. The statistical correlations indicate that about 70–80 percent of one partner's report agreed with the other partner's report. Contrary to expectations, agreement between partners did not vary with the perpetrator's gender or with the type of abusive behavior.

These findings suggest that the data gathered may confidently be used for research on the correlates and consequences of partner abuse. The resulting high level of confidence in the data can be attributed to the fact that interviews were conducted in a setting in which participants knew there was no risk of prosecution or requirement to participate in a treatment program if they revealed abuse.

## How Prevalent Is Partner Violence in the Dunedin Sample?[7]

Between one-fifth and one-third of all Dunedin study members reported they had experienced one or more of the behaviors on the CTS physical abuse scale in the past year. Exhibit 2 shows the prevalence rates of physical partner violence by and against men and women. Data from the Dunedin study were compared with data from respondents under age 25 in the 1985 National Family Violence Survey (NFVS; n=397)[8] and respondents under age 24 in the 1983 National Youth Survey (NYS; n=477).[9]

Rates from all three surveys were calculated using the same CTS interview questions, which measured physical violence in the past year. The Dunedin phase 21 rates are shown first for cohabiting and married study members only (n=250) to provide direct comparison

**Exhibit 2. Rates of physical partner violence in three studies**

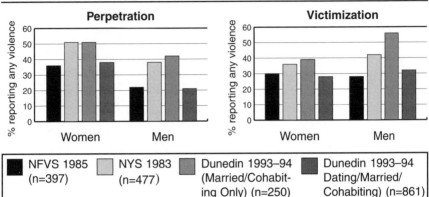

The three studies are the National Family Violence Survey (NFVS), the National Youth Survey (NYS), and the Dunedin Multidisciplinary Health Development Study.

with NFVS and NYS, which included cohabiting and married couples only. Shown fourth are Dunedin rates for married, cohabiting, and dating individuals combined (n=861, excluding 80 study members who had not gone out with anyone in the past year). Exhibit 2 shows that Dunedin prevalence rates are similar to the other two national samples.

When the Dunedin study members were followed up at age 21, they were found to be involved in several types of relationships. Some study members were married, but more were cohabiting without marriage, which has become a common practice for young adults in the 1990s. This offered an opportunity to report the first partner violence data for a representative sample of contemporary unmarried couples who were living together. Most study members were "going out" with someone: Some were in an exclusive relationship; others were "playing the field." About 8 percent had not gone out with anyone in the past 12 months and thus had no opportunity to become involved in partner violence. Exhibit 3 shows the rates of violence for those who were involved in relationships. Given that 48 percent of cohabitating partners and 21 percent of those who were dating experienced partner violence, the colloquial expression "The marriage license is a hitting license" appears to be outdated; the Dunedin study shows that violence cuts across all types of relationships.

**Exhibit 3. Rates of involvement in physical partner violence by relationship type (Dunedin males and females)**

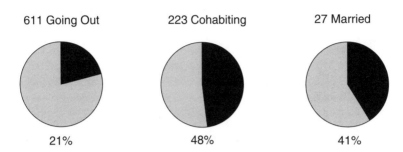

The blackened areas indicate the percentage who have perpetrated any physical violence against a partner during the past year.

Note: Eighty are not shown because they had not dated and had no opportunity for partner violence. Although 992 sample members participated in phase 21, 51 are not represented here because they either were interviewed in the field where the Conflict Tactics Scales could not be given or they refused the interview about partners.

## Is Physical Abuse Strongly Linked with Mental Disorders?[10]

In 1994, the American Psychiatric Association first recognized "physical abuse of an adult" as a "focus of clinical attention." An analysis was conducted to determine whether physical abuse was often "comorbid" with mental disorders among Dunedin study members. (Comorbidity means that a patient suffers from two or more disorders or problematic conditions at once.) Comorbidity between abuse and mental disorders was examined because studies of comorbidity among mental disorders have shown that coexistence of multiple psychiatric problems predicts more severe life impairment, longer duration of the problems, and poorer response to treatment.[11]

Sixty-five percent of Dunedin women who were victims of *severe* physical abuse[12] met criteria for one or more disorders listed in the *Diagnostic and Statistical Manual of the American Psychiatric Association ("DSM–III-R").* Eighty-eight percent of Dunedin men who were perpetrators of severe physical abuse met *DSM-III-R* criteria (see exhibit 4). Abused Dunedin women were three times more likely to suffer a mental illness than nonabused women. The male perpetrators were 13 times more likely to be mentally ill than nonperpetrators.

*Exhibit 4. Rates of mental illness among Dunedin perpetrators and victims of severe physical abuse*

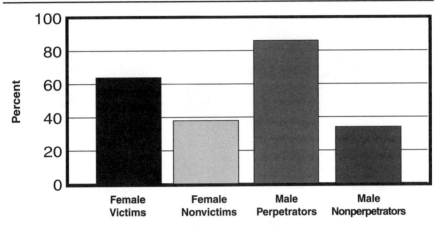

Rates of mental illness among female victims of severe physical abuse, female nonvictims, male perpetrators of severe physical abuse, and male nonperpetrators. The rate for female perpetrators was virtually identical to the rate for female victims, and the rate for male victims was nearly identical to the rate for male perpetrators.

The types of mental illnesses among perpetrators varied; they included anxiety disorders, depression, alcohol and drug dependence, antisocial personality disorder, and schizophrenia.

Research shows that emergency room and general practice medical professionals need to be alert to partner violence. In addition, the Dunedin study findings reveal that more than one-third of candidates for treatment from mental health professionals are involved in domestic violence. Whereas emergency room and general practice physicians usually encounter victims, and only after an injury, mental health practitioners have the opportunity to identify and help victims before they are injured if questions about domestic violence are made a routine part of intake assessment. Moreover, mental health practitioners encounter not only women victims but large numbers of men who are at risk of being perpetrators. If practitioners were trained to screen for partner violence risk, the mental health system might offer prevention as an alternative to prosecution.

## Risk Predictors from the Dunedin Study

When the study members were age 21, the Dunedin researchers examined 24 individual and family characteristics they had previously measured during the study members' childhood and hypothesized these characteristics would predict partner abuse. Early childhood characteristics were measured at study members' birth and at ages 3 and 5. Middle childhood characteristics were measured when study members were ages 7 and 9. Adolescent characteristics were measured when study members were age 15. In addition, study members' mothers answered questions about their own mental health when the members were ages 7, 9, and 15. All of the measures were highly reliable. (Previous reports about research on each risk factor in the Dunedin study have been published and may be obtained from the researchers—see "Full Reports from the Dunedin Multidisciplinary Health and Development Study.")

There were six measures of **family socioeconomic resources.** *Social class* (the socioeconomic status of the parents' occupation on a six-point scale designed for New Zealand) was measured at sample members' birth and when they were ages 7/9* and 15. *Family structure* measured at ages 9 and 15 represents whether or not the sample member lived with both biological parents. *Family structure* measured at birth (taken from hospital records) indicates whether or not the child was born to a married mother.

There were seven measures of **family relations.** *Negative mother-child interaction* was assessed when the sample members were age 3. An observer assessed eight aspects of parenting; for example, if the mother's expression was consistently harsh, if her evaluation of the child was constantly critical or derogatory, or if she was rough or inconsiderate when handling the child. *Family conflict* was measured at ages 7/9 and 15 with the conflict subscale of the Moos Family Relations Index, completed by mothers of the sample members. The conflict subscale contains items such as: "In our family, we believe you don't ever get anywhere by raising your voice," and "Family members sometimes hit each other." A measure of *harsh discipline* at ages 7/9 was constructed from a checklist of disciplinary behaviors. Parents were asked to indicate if they engaged in 10 behaviors, e.g., "smack your child or hit him/her with something," "try to frighten your child with someone like his/her father or a policeman," and "threaten to smack or to deprive your child of something." *Parent-child attachment* was measured when the sample members were age 15 with a 12-item self-report measure from the Inventory of Parent Attachment.

The items measure the adolescents' trust, communication, and alienation in their relationships with their parents. *Mother's mental health problems* were measured with a 24-item questionnaire that sampled a variety of common symptoms of emotional disturbances that was completed by sample members' mothers when the sample members were ages 7/9 and 15.

There were five measures of **educational achievements.** At age 5, *intelligence quotient* (IQ) was assessed with the Stanford-Binet Intelligence Scale. IQ was measured again when the sample members were ages 7/9 with the Wechsler Intelligence Scale for Children-Revised. *Reading achievement* was measured when the sample members were ages 7/9 and 15 by the Burt Word Reading Test, normed for New Zealand children. *Age at leaving secondary school* was the age at which the study member left high school. (Education was compulsory until age 15 in New Zealand.)

There were six measures of **problem behaviors.** *Difficult temperament* was assessed when the sample members were ages 3/5 by psychological examiners who observed each child in a testing session involving cognitive and motor tasks. Following the testing session, examiners rated each child's behaviors. Based on the ratings, the researchers identified a dimension that reflected individual differences in reactions to stress and challenge, impulse control, and the ability to persist in problem solving. Children who scored high on this factor were emotionally unstable, irritable, negative, rough, inattentive, and had difficulty concentrating. The measure of *conduct problems* at ages 7/9 was based on combined parent and teacher ratings of items from the "antisocial" and "hyperactivity" subscales of the Rutter Child Scales. When sample members were age 15, conduct problems were measured with the Conduct Disorder subscale of the Quay and Peterson Revised Behavior Problem Checklist, which was completed by their parents. The items in this subscale reflect aggressive and interpersonally alienated behaviors such as bullying, quarreling, disobeying, and teasing others. *Aggressive delinquency* was measured when the sample members were age 15 with study members' self-reports of aggressive behavior that were obtained in private, individual, structured interviews developed for use in New Zealand. Items for the scale of aggressive behaviors inquired whether the subject ever had set fire to a building, hit a parent, fought in the street or other public place, struggled to escape from a policeman, used force or threats to extort money, or used a weapon in a fight. *Juvenile police contact* from when sample members were between ages 10 and 17 was based on records of police contacts that were obtained from police departments throughout New Zealand. The number of police contacts in this sample ranged from zero to 18. *Substance abuse* was measured when the sample members were age 15 with a "variety" score based on self-reports of buying alcohol while underage, being drunk in a public place, smoking marijuana, sniffing glue, and using other drugs.

\* When the same measurement instrument was used repeatedly at adjacent assessment ages, the researchers were able to combine the two scores to produce a more reliable and accurate composite measure. In this sidebar, the use of such composite measures is denoted by a "/" (e.g., 7/9 indicates that two equivalent measures of study members or their families from assessment ages 7 and 9 were combined).

## Correlations of physical abuse with selected childhood and adolescent characteristics (at age 21)

| | Male Perpetrator | Male Victim | Female Perpetrator | Female Victim |
|---|---|---|---|---|
| **Family Socioeconomic Resources** | | | | |
| Social class at birth | Y | Y | N | N |
| Social class at ages 7/9 | Y | Y | N | N |
| Social class at age 15 | Y | N | N | N |
| Born to unmarried mother | N | N | N | N |
| One parent absent at age 9 | Y | YY | N | N |
| One parent absent at age 15 | Y | Y | Y | Y |
| Composite, with other risk factors controlled | N | N | N | N |
| | | | | |
| **Family Relations** | | | | |
| Negative mother-child interaction at age 3 | N | N | N | Y |
| Family conflict at ages 7/9 | N | Y | Y | Y |
| Family conflict at age 15 | N | N | Y | Y |
| Harsh discipline at ages 7/9 | N | N | Y | Y |
| Parent-child attachment at age 15 | Y | Y | YY | Y |
| Mother's mental health problems at ages 7/9 | N | Y | N | N |
| Mother's mental health problems at age 15 | N | Y | N | N |
| Composite, with other risk factors controlled | N | N | Y | N |

| | Male Perpetrator | Male Victim | Female Perpetrator | Female Victim |
|---|---|---|---|---|
| **Educational Achievements** | | | | |
| Stanford-Binet IQ at age 5 | N | N | N | Y |
| WISC-R IQ at ages 7/9 | Y | Y | N | N |
| Reading achievement at ages 7/9 | Y | Y | N | N |
| Reading achievement at age 15 | Y | Y | N | N |
| Age at leaving secondary school | YY | YY | Y | Y |
| Composite, with other risk | | | | |
|    factors controlled | Y | N | N | N |
| | | | | |
| **Problem Behaviors** | | | | |
| Difficult temperament at ages 3/5 | N | N | N | Y |
| Conduct problems at ages | | | | |
|    7/9 (teacher-parent) | Y | N | N | N |
| Conduct problems at age 15 (parent) | Y | Y | Y | Y |
| Aggressive delinquency at | | | | |
|    age 15 (self) | YY | YY | YY | YY |
| Juvenile police contact | Y | N | Y | YY |
| Substance abuse at age 15 (self) | YY | YY | YY | YY |
| Composite, with other risk | | | | |
|    factors controlled | Y | YY | YY | YY |

Y = yes, a significant risk factor
YY = significant and strong risk factor
N = no risk

## What Are the Risk Factors in Childhood and Adolescence for Partner Abuse?[13]

The unique prospective longitudinal database resources of the Dunedin study provided the necessary means to conduct one of the few prospective studies of risk factors for partner abuse. Risk factors were tested to determine whether they were present before Dunedin participants' abusive behavior began. Previous research on risk factors suffered from two flaws. First, childhood factors have been measured primarily by perpetrators' recall of past family life, which has proved faulty. Adults involved in violence often "remember" their childhoods in ways that provide self-justification for their current behavior. Second, many previous studies have focused on only one risk factor—childhood exposure to parents' violence—while neglecting other important influences on youngsters' development, such as poverty or schooling.

In the early years of the Dunedin study, risk factors were measured long before either the study families or the researchers knew that partner violence would be examined, thereby avoiding any potential bias. The risk measures were grouped into four broad domains: family socioeconomic resources, family relations, educational achievement, and problem behaviors. (See "Risk Predictors from the Dunedin Study.")

Measures were used that had been taken during three developmental periods: early childhood (ages 3–5), middle childhood (ages 7–9), and adolescence (age 15).[14] The pattern of results shows that male perpetrators' backgrounds include primarily poverty and poor school achievement. In contrast, female perpetrators' backgrounds include primarily disturbed family relationships, especially weak attachment, harsh discipline, and conflict between parents. Poverty and school failure were less important. Perpetrators of both sexes have a long history of aggressive behavior problems. For male and female perpetrators, the strongest risk factor is a record of physically aggressive delinquent offending before age 15. However, physically aggressive delinquent offending before age 15 is also the most significant risk factor for victims.

In terms of prevention policy, the finding that partner abuse in adulthood is predictable from certain characteristics during—and even before—adolescence suggests that primary prevention of partner violence should begin as early as youngsters develop an interest in the opposite sex. One clear implication is that children in secondary school (ages 12 to 17) are not too young to learn healthier ways to handle conflicts with partners. Violence education may become as important as sex education for developing healthy relationships. In addition, experiences in different settings (e.g, at home and at school) and in different behavioral domains (e.g., academic achievement and behavior problems) were found to pose risks for partner abuse. This underscores the importance of prevention programs that involve *both* parents and schools.

## Is Partner Violence Closely Linked with Other Kinds of Violence?[15]

Interestingly, each of the risk factors found for partner violence also posed a risk for other kinds of criminal offending by Dunedin study members such as drug, property, and theft offenses and violence against nonpartners. In fact, some researchers and law enforcement personnel question whether there are any risk factors specific to partner violence, as opposed to criminal offending in general. This issue should be resolved before it becomes clear whether a unique theory for partner violence and specialized interventions for its perpetrators are needed.

In the absence of a knowledge base, popular opinion holds that batterers pose less danger to the general public than other violent offenders because their violence stays within the family.[16] As such, law enforcement resource allocation and judicial decisionmaking reflect competition between ensuring the public's safety from street criminals and ensuring the private safety of battered wives. By studying associations between partner violence and violence against other victims who are not intimate partners, the researchers hope to inform policymakers about whether they should think of most partner violence as a special problem arising from the intimate relationship between two adults *or* as part of a pattern of repeated aggression toward others by the perpetrator. If the latter is true, targeting batterers for priority intervention could improve both spouse safety and public safety at once.

The Dunedin study research points to strong links between violence against a partner and a history of violence against other victims. As noted earlier in "What Are the Risk Factors in Childhood and Adolescence for Partner Abuse?" the strongest predictor of partner violence among the many risk factors in childhood and adolescence in the Dunedin study database is a history of aggressive delinquency before

---

***Exhibit 5. Rates of partner violence perpetrated by Dunedin males convicted of any crime***

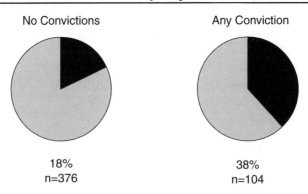

| No Convictions | Any Conviction |
|:---:|:---:|
| 18% | 38% |
| n=376 | n=104 |

Blackened areas show those who perpetrated physical violence against a partner.

---

## Exhibit 6. Rates of partner violence perpetrated by Dunedin males convicted of a violent crime

No Violent Convictions                    Convicted of Violent Offense

20%                                       51%
n=442                                     n=38

Blackened areas show those who perpetrated physical violence against a partner.

age 15. (Aggressive delinquency was measured by the study members' self-reports of assaults at age 15, their parents' reports of their aggressive behavior problems at age 15, and the presence of "333" incident forms—containing charges of assaults by the study member—in the Youth Aid offices of the New Zealand Police).

Researchers checked whether Dunedin study members who were already known to the courts by age 21 were also likely to be perpetrators of partner violence. A search of the New Zealand Police computer files (with each study member's written permission) revealed that by age 21, 141 study members (14 percent) had been convicted of one or more criminal offenses. Among those convicted, 60 percent were repeat offenders. Although most of the convictions were for property crimes, 38 men and 8 women had 113 violence convictions for inciting violence, manual assault, assault with a deadly weapon, rape, robbery, homicide, and threatening with an offensive weapon. Partner violence scores of convicted male study members were compared with those of male study members who were not known to the courts. Exhibits 5 and 6 show that the police and courts already know many of the perpetrators of partner violence because they have been successfully prosecuted for other crimes.

## Gender and Partner Violence: Do Men and Women Hit for the Same Reasons?[17]

As shown in exhibit 2, women report perpetrating partner violence more frequently than men. This was true in the Dunedin study and in both the National Family Violence and National Youth surveys. Exhibit 2 also shows that male victims' reports corroborate this finding.

Such findings about gender similarities in partner abuse have been contested. However, one of the first lessons learned in the Dunedin study is that there are no tidy and distinct groups of victims or perpetrators. Interviewers first asked study members, "Have you done any of these things to your partner?" Next they asked, "Has your partner done any of them to you?" When the data were analyzed, victimized women were 10 times more likely to be perpetrators than other women and male perpetrators also were 19 times more likely to be victims than other men. The data do not include who started each incident or if some of the acts were in self-defense, but it is clear that in most cases of partner violence in this age group, the parties are involved in mutual violence.

Other studies have shown that although partner violence behaviors are similar across genders, consequences differ. Women are much more likely to be physically injured by men than men are to be physically harmed by women.[18] The Dunedin study findings show that although women report perpetrating physical violence, the personal characteristics of male perpetrators are much more deviant. Dunedin study male perpetrators of severe physical violence had extreme levels of polydrug abuse, antisocial personality disorder, dropping out of school, chronic unemployment, poor social support, and violence against victims outside the family. Among men who severely assaulted their partners, 72 percent had used two or more illicit drugs, 56 percent had left secondary school early without any formal certificates or qualifications, 51 percent had assaulted someone else in addition to their partner in the past year, and on average they had been unemployed for 20 months since leaving school. These extreme social and personal problems were not found for Dunedin study female perpetrators.

The Dunedin study findings suggest that although women do report assaulting their partners, women's behavior is generally not accompanied by multiple problems in other areas. The researchers speculate that knowledge about the consequences of partner violence might explain this difference. Most men know that if they hit their partner, she is likely to be injured, the police may be called, and the police are now likely to act swiftly against male perpetrators. As a result, young men whose self-control is compromised by enormous social stress, mental illness, or intoxication will be most likely to risk the consequences of hitting their partner. However, women know that they are unlikely to injure their partner, he is unlikely to call for help, and the police are unlikely to intervene. Thus, there is little to deter an angry young woman from hitting her partner. As such, women of all sorts may be apt to hit their partners, not just women whose judgment is clouded by stress, mental illness, or intoxication. Further research should be conducted to confirm this possible explanation.

## Are Young Parents More Likely to Be Involved in a Violent Relationship than Young Adults Who Have Not Had Children?[19]

One of the most worrisome findings from the Dunedin study is that young adults most likely to be involved in partner violence are also most likely to be parents. Ten percent, or 52, of the study women had a baby by age 21. Five percent, or 25, of the study men were fathers. Of those who were parents, 13 percent, or 6, of the women and 7 percent, or 2, of the men were married, although not necessarily to the person who was the mother or father of their child(ren). Exhibit 7 shows that young mothers were twice as likely as other young women to be physically abused by their male partners. Exhibit 8 indicates that

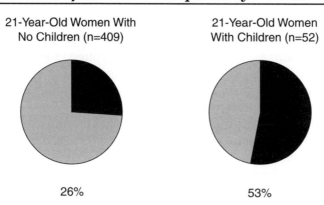

**Exhibit 7. Rates of victimization reported by Dunedin women**

| 21-Year-Old Women With No Children (n=409) | 21-Year-Old Women With Children (n=52) |
| :---: | :---: |
| 26% | 53% |

Blackened areas represent women experiencing physical abuse by their partners.

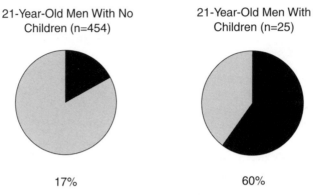

*Exhibit 8. Rates of perpetration reported by Dunedin men*

21-Year-Old Men With No
Children (n=454)

21-Year-Old Men With
Children (n=25)

17%                                   60%

Blackened areas show those men who reported being perpetrators.

those who were fathers were more than three times as likely as those who were not fathers to report being perpetrators of abuse. All of the study women were rearing their children. A few of the men were rearing their children, and other abusive study men were living with a new partner and her children. Presumably some of those children have been exposed to violence between their parent and partner. This finding underscores the importance of services for high-risk adolescents that integrate issues of family planning, parenting, and partner violence to break the cycle of violence transmission to the next generation.

## Conclusion

The Dunedin study findings to date have demonstrated three aspects of violence between partners. First, young people who become involved in a violent relationship tend to come from backgrounds that include family adversity, dropping out of school, and violent juvenile crime. Second, the most violent relationships are found among young parents of small children, especially parents who are unmarried. Third, partner violence is complicated by other problem behaviors, especially long-term unemployment, mental illness, drug abuse, and violence against nonfamily victims.

These findings demonstrate a need for three intervention approaches. First, early interventions with teenagers are needed to teach them not to use violence against partners. Second, interventions with young parents are needed to reduce their stress and protect their small children from exposure to violence at home. Third, perpetrators of partner violence tend to be mentally ill and commit other violent crimes as well, suggesting a need for coordination among police, judicial, and psychiatric interventions.

These research findings have the potential to inform the work of policymakers and practitioners. Policymaking that deters batterers through arrest, prosecution, or therapy requires sound knowledge about how and why individuals become perpetrators and victims. In the Dunedin research, the goal was to improve prediction, understanding, and treatment of partner violence by continuing to study the developmental experiences, personal characteristics, and situational circumstances that lead individuals into partner violence.

## Notes

1.  Greenfeld, L. A., M. R. Rand, D. Craven, P. A. Klaus, C. A. Perkins, C. Ringel, G. Warchol, C. Maston, and J. A. Fox, *Violence by Intimates: Analysis of Data on Crimes by Current or Former Spouses, Boyfriends, and Girlfriends,* Bureau of Justice Statistics Factbook, Washington, DC: U.S. Department of Justice, Bureau of Justice Statistics, March 1998, NCJ 167237.

2.  The study's history is detailed in Silva, P. A., and W. R. Stanton, eds., *From Child to Adult: The Dunedin Multidisciplinary Health and Development Study,* Auckland, New Zealand: Oxford University Press, 1996.

3.  Straus, M. A., "Measuring Intrafamily Conflict and Violence: The Conflict Tactics Scales," *Journal of Marriage and the Family* 41 (1979): 75–88.

4.  See Straus, M. A., and R. J. Gelles, *Physical Violence in American Families,* chap. 4, London, England: Transaction Publishers, 1992, for a discussion of the methodological issues that were initially raised by the Conflict Tactics Scales.

5.  For the full report, see Moffitt, T. E., A. Caspi, R. Krueger, L. Magdol, G. Margolin, P. A. Silva, and R. Sydney, "Do Partners Agree About Abuse in Their Relationship? A Psychometric Evaluation of Interpartner Agreement," *Psychological Assessment* 9 (1997): 47–56.

6. For everything that is measured, there is some slippage between the score the measurement instrument records and the true score. If there were a perfect measurement instrument, all flawed instruments could be tossed out. But there is no perfect instrument, so the best strategy is to use several different measures of the same data and then triangulate among all their results to try to find the true score. Statistical theory assumes that although every measure is flawed, they are each flawed in a different, random way. One score will be too high, another will be too low, and the line score will lie somewhere in the middle.

The Dunedin study used a statistical procedure called "confirmatory factor analysis" to find the true score for perpetrators' self-reports of their own partner violence. Thirteen questions about partner violence were asked, e.g., "Have you hit your partner?" and "Have you used a knife or gun on your partner?" Each question in the interview was assumed to have "random flaws" because the respondent's attention might wander, they might mis-hear the interviewer, misunderstand a word, forget something, circle true when they meant to circle false, etc. These random flaws, however, are distinct from deliberate bias—which is not random—such as lying to conceal the violence or exaggerating violence to get attention.

The confirmatory factor analysis program essentially triangulates among the different answers to the 13 questions to come up with a best estimate of the perpetrator's "true score." The same program was then run on the victim's reports about the perpetrator's behavior to get a "true score" for the perpetrator's abuse from the victim's perspective. Finally, the correlation between the two resulting "true scores" was calculated. Before a confirmatory factor analysis was used to remove random measurement efforts from the perpetrators' and victims' scores, they were correlated at 0.59. After the scores that had been cleaned of random errors were used, they were correlated at 0.83. This difference shows that much of the "disagreement" between partners that researchers worried about is understandable random error. It does not indicate that partners are deliberately trying to misrepresent their violence to researchers. They actually agree very well, if reasonable human error is allowed for. This and the way the program works are explained in detail in Moffitt, T. E., A.

Caspi, R. Krueger, L. Magdol, G. Margolin, P. A. Silva, and R. Sydney, "Do Partners Agree About Abuse in Their Relationship?"

7. For the full report, see Magdol, L., T. E. Moffitt, A. Caspi, D. Newman, J. Fagan, and P. A. Silva, "Gender Differences in Partner Violence in a Birth Cohort of 21-Year-Olds: Bridging the Gap Between Clinical and Epidemiological Approaches," *Journal of Clinical & Consulting Psychology* 65 (1997): 68–78.

8. Fagan, J., and A. Browne, "Violence Between Spouses and Intimates," in *Understanding and Preventing Violence,* vol. 3, ed. A. J. Reiss and J. A. Roth, Washington, DC: National Academy Press, 1994, 115–292.

9. Elliott, D. S., D. Huizinga, and B. J. Morse, *The Dynamics of Delinquent Behavior: A National Survey Progress Report,* Boulder, CO: Institute of Behavioral Sciences, University of Colorado, 1985.

10. For the full report, see Danielson, K. K., T. E. Moffitt, A. Caspi, and P. A. Silva. "Comorbidity Between Abuse of an Adult and DSM-III-R Mental Disorders: Evidence From an Epidemiological Study," *American Journal of Psychiatry* 155 (1998): 131–33.

11. Newman, D., Moffitt, T. E., A. Caspi, and P. A. Silva, "Comorbid Mental Disorders: Implications for Clinical Treatment and Sample Selection," *Journal of Abnormal Psychology* 107 (1998): 305–11.

12. Severe physical abuse was defined as the CTS items likely to cause injury: kicking, biting, hitting with a fist, hitting with an object, beating up, choking, strangling, threatening with a knife or gun, or using a knife or gun.

13. For the full report, see Magdol, L., T. E. Moffitt, A. Caspi, and P. A. Silva, "Developmental Antecedents of Partner Violence: A Prospective Longitudinal Study," *Journal of Abnormal Psychology* 107 (1998): 375–89.

14. Bivariate and multivariate regression were used to test which risk factors predicted self-reports of partner abuse, and for study members whose partner participated, the test was replicated by predicting the partner's reports of abuse.

15. For the full report, see Moffitt, T. E., A. Caspi, and P. A. Silva, in preparation.

16. Fagan, J., and A. Browne, "Violence Between Spouses and Intimates."

17. For the full report, see Magdol, L., T. E. Moffitt, A. Caspi, D., Newman, J. Fagan, and P. A. Silva, "Gender Differences in Partner Violence in a Birth Cohort of 21-Year-Olds."

18. Fagan, J., and A. Browne. "Violence Between Spouses and Intimates."

19. For the full report, see Bardone, A., T. E. Moffitt, A. Caspi, N. Dickson, and P. A. Silva, "Adult Mental Health and Social Outcomes of Adolescent Girls With Depression and Conduct Disorder," *Development & Psychopathology* 8 (1996): 811–19.

## *Full Reports from the Dunedin Multidisciplinary Health and Development Study*

Detailed reports may be obtained from the authors at the following address: Professor Terrie E. Moffitt, Institute of Psychiatry, Social, Genetic and Developmental Psychiatry Research Centre, 111 Denmark Hill, London SE5 8AF England. Please cite the order letters/numbers in bold below.

Bardone, A., T. E. Moffitt, A. Caspi, N. Dickson, and P. A. Silva, "Adult Mental Health and Social Outcomes of Adolescent Girls With Depression and Conduct Disorder," *Development & Psychopathology* 8 (1996): 811–19. **(J81)**

Danielson, K. K., T. E. Moffitt, A. Caspi, and P. A. Silva, "Comorbidity Between Abuse of an Adult and DSM-III-R Mental Disorders: Evidence From an Epidemiological Study," *American Journal of Psychiatry* 155 (1998): 131–33. **(J94)**

Krueger, R. F., T. E. Moffitt, A. Caspi, and A. Bleske, "Assortative Mating for Antisocial Behavior: Developmental and Methodological Implications," *Behavior Genetics* (1998): 173–86. **(J99)**

Magdol, L., T. E. Moffitt, A. Caspi, D. Newman, J. Fagan, and P. A. Silva, "Gender Differences in Partner Violence in a Birth Cohort of 21-Year-Olds: Bridging the Gap Between Clinical and Epidemiological Approaches, " *Journal of Clinical & Consulting Psychology* 65 (1997): 68–78. **(J83)**

Magdol, L., T. E. Moffitt, A. Caspi, and P. A. Silva, "Developmental Antecedents of Partner Violence: A Prospective Longitudinal Study," *Journal of Abnormal Psychology* 107 (1998): 375–89. **(J105)**

Magdol, L., T. E. Moffitt, A. Caspi, and P. A. Silva, "Hitting Without a License: Testing Explanations for Differences in Partner Abuse Between Young Adult Daters and Cohabitors," *Journal of Marriage and the Family* 60 (1998): 41–55. **(J96)**

Moffitt, T. E., and A. Caspi, "Annotation: Implications of Violence Between Intimate Partners for Child Psychologists and Psychiatrists," *Journal of Child Psychology and Psychiatry* 39 (1998): 137–44. **(J93)**

Moffitt, T. E., A. Caspi, R. Krueger, L. Magdol, G. Margolin, P. A. Silva, and R. Sydney, "Do Partners Agree About Abuse in Their Relationship? A Psychometric Evaluation of Interpartner Agreement," *Psychological Assessment* 9 (1997): 47–56. **(J86)**

## *About the Authors*

Terrie E. Moffitt, Ph.D., is a professor in the department of psychology at the University of Wisconsin-Madison and in the Social, Genetic and Developmental Psychiatry Research Centre, Institute of Psychiatry, at the University of London; Avshalom Caspi, Ph.D., is a professor in the department of psychology at the University of Wisconsin-Madison and in the Social, Genetic and Developmental Psychiatry Research Centre, Institute of Psychiatry, at the University of London.

The Dunedin Multidisciplinary Health and Developmental Research Unit is supported by the New Zealand Health Research Council. This research was supported by grant number 94–IJ–CX–0041 from the National Institute of Justice. Additional support was provided by U.S. Public Health Service (USPHS) grant MH–45070 to Terrie E. Moffitt from the Violence and Traumatic Stress Research Branch of the National Intitute of Mental Health, by USPHS grant MH–49414 to Avshalom Caspi from the Personality and Social Processes Branch of the National Institute of Mental Health, by the William T. Grant Foundation, and by the William Freeman Vilas Trust at the University of Wisconsin.

713

Full Reports cited in the Notes in this Research in Brief may be obtained from the authors. See "Full Reports from the Dunedin Multidisciplinary Health and Development Study" for more information.

*Authors' acknowledgments: The authors are grateful to Dunedin Unit investigators and staff and to the study members and their partners. They are also grateful for the assistance of the Dunedin Police over the years and for the help and guidance provided by Police Officer Paul Stevenson, retired.*

*Many individuals helped with this research: Jim Amell, Anna Bardone, Kirstie Danielson, Nigel Dickson, Waleska Echevarria-Troche, Jeff Fagan, Janet Gafford, HonaLee Harrington, Bob Krueger, Lynn Magdol, Gayla Margolin, Marguerite McClelland, Denise Newman, Jay Rodger, Phil Silva, and Ros Sydney.*

# Chapter 29

# *Research on Batterers*

## *Descriptions of Batterers*

One subject that has prompted diverse solutions is how best to investigate batterers. Should information be derived from victims, perpetrators, or other informants? Allied with this question is whether batterers should be characterized as a unique group of men whose violence targets family members only or whether batterers are simply run-of-the-mill, violent criminals.

### *Battered Women's Descriptions of Batterers*

The first attempts by psychologists to examine wife abuse generally consisted of descriptions provided by battered women in counseling. Premised on her discussions with battered women, Elbow (1977), for example, attempted to group maritally violent men into four categories: *controller, defender, approval seeker,* and *incorporator*. Briefly summed up, the controller envisions his wife as an object of control, and she symbolizes the parent who controlled him. The defender, on the other hand, thinks of his mate as both a seductress and hostile other. The value of the approval-seeker's mate is her ability

Excerpted from Barnett, Ola W., Cindy L. Miller-Perrin, and Robin D. Perrin. *Family Violence Across the Lifespan: An Introduction.* pp. 237–38, 238–45, 246–49, copyright © 1997 by Sage Publications, Inc. Reprinted by permission of Sage Publications, Inc.

to reinforce his self-image. She represents the conditional love of the parent. For the incorporator, the mate signifies parental love, and doing without her as a complete loss of the self.

Lenore Walker's (1979) research with battered women enabled her to delineate a sequence of male spouses' battering that she termed the "cycle of violence." The cycle of violence describes interpersonal aggression that intensifies in degree and frequency over time and holds the people involved in an established pattern of behavior. The cycle of violence consists of three phases:

1.  *Tension building.* In this phase, minor incidents of violence may occur along with a buildup of anger. This phase may include verbal put-downs, jealousy, threats, and breaking things and can eventually escalate to the second phase.

2.  *Acute or battering.* In this phase, the major violent outburst occurs. This violence can be seen as the major earthquake. Following the second phase, the couple sometimes enters Phase 3.

3.  *The honeymoon or loving respite.* In this phase, the batterer is remorseful and afraid of losing his partner. He may promise anything, beg forgiveness, buy gifts, and basically be "the man she fell in love with."

### *Batterers' Descriptions of Themselves*

When researchers or practitioners ask men accused of wife beating about their own behavior, the responses provided reveal batterers' tendencies to blame others for their assaults, most especially their female partners, and to downplay the significance and seriousness of their violence.

**The "Blame Game."** The role of blame in a battering relationship is a critical issue because men who blame their female partners are likely to be even more violent than those who do not (Byrne, Arias, & Lyons, 1993). Dutton (1986b) coded wife assaulters' free-form accounts of the causes of their battering and isolated three general classifications: (a) victim provocation, (b) self-blame with denial and minimization of its effects, and (c) self-blame with attributions to some aspect of themselves such as a drinking problem.

Probably the most common explanation given by batterers runs something like this: "I told her not to do it [e.g., staying late after work, mouthing off]. She knew what would happen. She did it anyway. She got what she asked for" (see Barrera, Palmer, Brown, & Kalaher, 1994). This scenario illustrates batterers' propensities to formulate and externalize blame (Sapiente, 1988) and to justify their violence by pronouncing that it is warranted, given the situation (Ptacek, 1988).

**Denial and Minimization.** Batterers also deny the abusive nature of their behavior (Edleson & Brygger, 1986; Wetzel & Ross, 1983). Sonkin, Martin, and Walker's (1985) interpretation of this proclivity is that batterers minimize and deny their assaultive behavior because they themselves disapprove of it. Other research indicates that batterers may be unaware of the true reasons for their abusive behaviors (Barnett, Lee, & Thelen, 1995).

## Similarities and Differences Between Maritally Only Violent and Generally Violent (Panviolent) Men

Another avenue of approach in understanding wife assault has been to contrast batterers' behavior (maritally only violent) with that of violent criminals (generally violent or panviolent men, violent inside and outside the family). Perhaps the tendency to view wife assault as a private matter has obscured the true continuities between maritally only violent and generally violent men.

**Proportion of Family-Only Crime.** Several studies have explored the question of whether spouse abusers are also violent with nonfamily members. In an early inquiry based on interviews with 270 domestic violence victims, Fagen, Stewart, and Hansen (1983) showed that almost half of all spouse abusers had been arrested previously for other violence and that violence in the home was positively correlated with violence toward strangers (also see Shields, McCall, & Hanneke, 1988). Another survey presented consistent data by showing that husbands of women living in shelters tended to have criminal records (Dunford, Huizinga, & Elliott, 1990).

Using a larger sample of 2,291 males from the 1985 National Family Violence Survey data of 6,002 households (Straus & Gelles, 1990), Kandel-Englander (1992) identified 311 men (15%) who had been violent during the previous 12-month period. From the violent group, 208 (67%) had been violent only toward a wife (family), 71 (23%) had been violent only toward a nonfamily member, and 32 (10%) had been violent toward both a wife and a nonfamily individual (panviolent). Thus, the selection of the target (assaulted person) most clearly differentiated the groups.

**Social and Behavioral Differences.** Other surveys have sought to unravel social and behavioral dissimilarities between subsamples of violent men. One study found that men charged with domestic homicide experienced more behavioral problems in childhood (e.g., truancy) than men charged with nondomestic homicide. Both groups were more likely than nonviolent men to have disturbed childhoods, such as a missing parent (Anasseril & Holcomb, 1985). Another account of 85 violent men indicated that generally violent men (panviolent—both wives and nonfamily individuals) and men violent only toward nonfamily individuals were comparable in terms of background characteristics but very dissimilar in terms of other attributes, such as socioeconomic status, drug use, and prior conviction rates (Shields et al., 1988).

## *Becoming and Remaining a Batterer*

The next section of this chapter summarizes some of the socialization practices that contribute to battering and some of the biological forces that generally support male aggression. Socialization forces are paramount in discussing battering behavior because violence may be a learned behavior. Biological support for male aggression, a frequently overlooked topic, needs further elucidation to help provide a more complete understanding of male violence. Research on dyadic or interpersonal relationship variables has generated a relatively large amount of data on topics such as marital dissatisfaction, communication styles, stress, and control issues.

### *Socialization*

A number of researchers have carefully thought about socialization variables that might promote spouse abuse by males. There may be generalized modeling that conveys approval of violence and specific modeling that teaches that certain behaviors are acceptable and certain people are the proper targets (e.g., Kalmuss, 1984).

**Childhood Socialization.** The finding that exposure to violence during childhood is associated with later male-to-female violence is almost universal (e.g., Howell & Pugliesi, 1988; Roberts, 1987; Rouse, 1984; cf. Bennett, Tolman, Rogalski, & Srinivasaraghavan, 1994). In a sample of college students, Briere (1987) was able to link male students' childhood abuse experiences with their likelihood of battering a spouse. Observations of abuse, according to Hotaling and Sugarman (1986), may be a more powerful indicator of future marital violence than experiencing abuse directly, and paternal violence may be a better predictor than maternal violence (see also Barnett, Fagan, & Booker, 1991; Caesar & Hamberger, 1989; Choice, Lamke, & Pittman, 1995; Seltzer & Kalmuss, 1988; Widom, 1989).

Researchers are now beginning to examine other variables related to intergenerational abuse. Harsh treatment as a child, for example, may lead to the development of an antisocial orientation, which, in turn, is associated with chronic (repeated) spousal aggression (Simons, Wu, & Conger, 1995). Most recently, researchers have suggested that anxious attachment during childhood is related to shame in adult batterers (Wallace & Nosko, 1993). In one study, level of male-to-female marital violence was strongly associated with two childhood factors that would be expected to interfere with attachment: (a) the number of separation and loss events experienced, and (b) the presence of paternal substance abuse (i.e., possible erratic caregiving; Corvo, 1992).

Furthermore, a new study has linked parent-to-child shaming and guilt inducement during childhood with chronic adult anger, trauma symptoms, male-to-female marital abusiveness, and borderline personality disorder in adult perpetrators of physical abuse (Dutton, Van Ginkel, & Starzomski, 1995). Although replication studies are needed, these findings provide an important account of the relationship between variability in childhood experiences of abuse and adult individual differences in battering (Dutton et al., 1995).

**Male Socialization and Cultural Factors.** Men can also be socialized to expect their wives to treat them with deference. Male entitlement to power and the use of dominance in marital conflicts to control female partners hinge on sex-role socialization (Birns, Cascardi, & Meyer, 1994).

Influences such as television, movies, magazines, dating partners, and peer groups promote aggression (Kruttschnitt, Heath, & Ward, 1986; Seltzer & Kalmuss, 1988). Men receive a number of messages that encourage them to be tough, aggressive, competitive, and emotionally distant (Scher, 1980; Watts & Courtois, 1981). Some information teaches them to confuse violence with sexuality (Stevens & Gebhart, 1985) and to tune out feelings (except anger; Heppner & Gonzales, 1987). As Breines and Gordon (1983) maintain, however, cultural antecedents should not be accepted as the sole explanation for wife abuse. Not all men who have been socialized to be dominant beat their wives. Indeed, wife beating is not universal in our society. It is used only by some men in some relationships (Maertz, 1990).

Because patriarchal beliefs presumably contribute to spouse abuse, researchers have questioned whether batterers hold more sexist views toward women than nonbatterers. Results seem to depend, however, on the type of scale used. In a controlled study of male spouse abusers, sex-role scores were inconsistent and primarily depended on the test instruments selected (Barnett & Ryska, 1986). Tests assessing masculinity and femininity as separate personality dimensions yielded significant differences between maritally violent and nonviolent men (Rosenbaum, 1986). In contrast, questionnaires combining masculinity and femininity into a single score (e.g., low scores representing masculinity and high scores representing femininity) failed to discriminate between groups (e.g., Caesar, 1988). In this case, a meta-analysis revealed that batterers scored significantly lower on both masculinity and femininity (Sugarman & Frankel, 1993).

Sommer (1990) compared batterers and nonbatterers on four sex-role attitude inventories. An analysis of all the scales combined and individually indicated that the groups varied significantly. She found that batterers do have misogynist attitudes and are more tolerant of interpersonal violence than are nonbatterers.

### Violence, Biology, and Genetics

One question that is receiving increasing research scrutiny is whether the male violence observed in spouse abuse might have some biological basis, rather than being simply a consequence of socialization. Recent discoveries on the relationships between biology and violence raise the age-old "nature-nurture" controversy. Evidence suggests that biological determinants, such as hormones, may influence male violence. Furthermore, there may be a gene-crime relationship and a birth trauma-crime relationship.

**Biological Sex Differences.** It is not surprising that a meta-analysis determined that men are generally more aggressive than women (Eagly & Steffen, 1986). With continued scientific advances, researchers have reported that the major male hormone testosterone forms part of a configuration of components contributing to a general latent predisposition toward aggression but that social factors moderate its influence. Although hormonal distinctiveness might, in part, explain why men are more violent than women, hormone levels do not explain individual variations among men (Booth & Osgood, 1993).

One way to appraise biological contrasts is with genetic studies. In a controversial approach, several investigators have attempted to identify a gene-crime association. Some criminologists, for example, have posited that social factors alone, like poverty, cannot account for certain types of observed differences in rates of crime and have pointed to genetics as a possible explanation (e.g., Wilson & Herrnstein, 1985).

One of the most accurate ways to isolate genetic from environmental contributions to criminality is with adoption studies (Walters, 1992). Children share 50% of their genetic inheritance with each biological parent and none with genetically unrelated persons, such as adoptive parents. Comparing children's behavior with both their biological fathers and their adoptive fathers constitutes an excellent test of the gene-crime relationship. The question is whether the behavior of the adopted boys corresponds more to that of the biological parents or to the adoptive parents.

In a series of analyses conducted in Denmark, Mednick and his colleagues (Mednick, Gabrielli, & Hutchings, 1987) reported that boys whose biological parent had a criminal record were more likely to have been convicted of a crime than were boys whose adoptive parent had been convicted. In other words, the biological parents' genetic contribution had a greater effect on behavior than did the adoptive parents' rearing. In a meta-analysis, Walters (1992) concluded that despite methodological problems with many of the studies, a low-moderate, but significant, association exists between heredity variables and indexes of crime. Based on the analysis of 13 adoption studies, Walters suggests that the individual genetic inheritance of criminal behavior is 11% to 17%.

**Birth Complications and Head Injuries.** There is also evidence that birth complications and head injuries contribute to crime ("Biology and Family," 1996). In a Danish investigation, Kandel and Mednick (1991) examined longitudinal data from a birth cohort study. Adult data included records of violent crimes and property crimes. Background information included factors like the mental health classification of the parents (e.g., character disorder) and pregnancy and birth complications of the individuals. The three comparison groups consisted of 15 violent criminals, 24 property criminals, and 177 nonoffenders. Birth complications did predict adult violent offending but not property crimes, especially in high-risk individuals and repeat violent offenders. Thus, the results suggest a link between birth complications and adult violence. In an analysis of trauma effects in adult males, Rosenbaum and Hoge (1989) uncovered a history of head injury in 61% of the abusers in their sample (see also Warnken, Rosenbaum, Fletcher, Hoge, & Adelman, 1994). Future research might attempt to link physical abuse of males during childhood with the head injuries noted in wife abusers.

## Relationship Factors and Problems in Living

Some of the most striking problems batterers exhibit are those occurring in their personal relationships: hostility, jealousy, insecurity, and emotional dependence. Some batterers experience intemperate levels of stress as a result of events like the wife's "poor" housekeeping. They frequently misperceive such behaviors as a sign of the wife's disregard. In some cases, batterers seem unable to make their needs known verbally, and they may resort to violence as a means of control. These kinds of marital interactions are so intolerable that they precipitate the dissolution of the marriage, the very relationship that the man is fighting to keep.

*Case History: Kim and Kevin—"She Didn't Clean the Lint Trap"*

Kevin was a handsome, 32-year-old cameraman for a local television station. He frequently was called out of town to cover a story and even went overseas occasionally. His beautiful wife, Kim, who earned money modeling, went with him if she wasn't working. They had no children.

On the job, Kevin felt fearful from time to time when he had to shoot at a location in a ghetto neighborhood. He was afraid that local hoods would try to beat him up, and he wouldn't be able to defend himself because he was so *small*. He was anxious about Kim's behavior as well. Other guys were always flirting with her, and she saw nothing wrong with "just being friends" with them. Kevin saw a lot wrong with it, and he warned her to watch her step. Kim also was very sloppy around the house. No matter what he said, she was always forgetting to empty the lint trap on the clothes dryer. It was clear to him that Kim didn't care how he felt, and he felt desperate about doing something to make her "treat him better."

The night Kevin got arrested for beating Kim up (for the first time, we were told) he had come home around 6:30 after several weeks in Australia. He had caught an early flight back to surprise Kim with an expensive pearl ring and some champagne that he bought on the way home from the airport. He really loved her, and he was looking forward to a romantic reunion.

The first thing that went wrong was that Kim was not home. He was both disappointed and suspicious. Perhaps she wasn't at work but was out having a drink with some guy who had picked her up at a bar. He had never actually caught her doing this, but he thought she probably did it a lot when he was out of town. The second thing that happened was that there were some dirty dishes on the counter near the sink, and when he decided to do his laundry, the lint trap had not been emptied again!

At 7:30, he saw Kim coming out of the neighbor's house. He grabbed a shotgun, and ran up and down the side yard, shooting into the air over the neighbor's house. He took a sharp tool out of the garage and sliced his neighbor's tires. By the time the police arrived, Kim was on the living room floor with a broken nose and two broken ribs. Our *5-foot-5-inch* batterer was sitting on the couch, sobbing. Kim was threatening to leave him. He hadn't meant to hurt her, but what other options did he have? (Author's case history)

Kevin's behavior represents a number of problems that many batterers have. He seems to be extremely insecure and jealous. He probably misperceives Kim's behavior as being flirtatious and insensitive to his needs. He also is very stressed and does not seem to know how to handle his feelings. His reaction is to strike out impulsively and violently and then to regret his actions.

**Marital Dissatisfaction.** One of the most common assumptions people make is that happily married men would not hit their wives. Such a belief is intrinsically appealing, of course, but as the case of Kim and Kevin illustrates, it is not always true. On the whole, research on marital satisfaction does show that many maritally violent men score below published normative data on marital satisfaction levels and below that of comparison groups of nonviolent men (e.g., Rosenbaum & O'Leary, 1981b).

Only a handful of experts, however, attribute battering to marital dissatisfaction (see Barnett & Hamberger, 1992; Rosenbaum & O'Leary, 1981b). First, about half of the men who assault their wives highly value their relationships and score above the median on marital satisfaction tests (Locke & Wallace, 1957; Spanier, 1976). Second, men who score very low on marital satisfaction do not necessarily batter their wives. Last, longitudinal data from early marriages reveal that relationship discord is not an antecedent of marital abuse. Repeated abuse, however, may result in relationship dissatisfaction (Riggs & O'Leary, 1989).

**Lack of Verbal Skills and Poor Communication.** Inept communication appears to be another typical problem for some maritally violent men. Many batterers suffer from assertion deficits (e.g., inadequacy in stating one's views forcefully or in making requests appropriately; Dutton & Strachan, 1987; Maiuro, Cahn, & Vitaliano, 1986; Rosenbaum & O'Leary, 1981b), and these deficits are associated with greater verbal hostility (Maiuro, Cahn, & Vitaliano, 1988). Assertion deficits, however, may be more representative of marital dissatisfaction levels than of marital assault levels (O'Leary & Curley, 1986). Across studies, most research indicates that lack of assertiveness is a risk marker for wife assault (Hotaling & Sugarman, 1986).

Misperception of communication is yet another difficulty experienced by violent men (Margolin, John, & Gleberman, 1988). In one study, batterers underestimated the quality and number of caring gestures received from their wives. They saw themselves as "doing more and getting less" in the relationship (Langhinrichsen-Rohling, Smutzler, & Vivian, 1994). Holtzworth-Munroe and Hutchinson (1993) found analogous outcomes in responses of batterers to vignettes of problematic marital situations. Violent husbands attributed more negative intentions to their wives than did husbands in comparison groups. Similarly, when Neidig, Friedman, and Collins (1986) asked the question, "In your day-to-day dealings with other people, what percent of the time do you expect others might try to take advantage of you?" they found that batterers reported higher percentages than comparisons.

Margolin et al. (1988), using Conflict Tactics Scales (CTS; Straus, 1979) subscale scores, classified four groups of men as physically violent, verbally violent, withdrawing, or nonabusive and nondistressed.

In a series of 10-minute, videotaped problem-solving discussions, physically violent men expressed more negative affect (offensive behaviors and harsh voice tones) than did nonviolent men (also see Smith & O'Leary, 1987; Vivian & O'Leary, 1987).

In a related study, Jacobson and Gottman (1993) unexpectedly discovered that during extremely belligerent verbal behaviors, such as yelling, threatening, and demeaning their female partners, batterers were *less* physiologically aroused than comparison groups of nonbattering male partners. This evaluation suggested that verbally combative behaviors may actually be calming, rather than upsetting, to maritally abusive men (see Jacobson et al., 1994).

**Stress and Poor Problem-Solving Skills.** Finn (1985) determined that the relationship between stressors and family violence involves elements such as financial problems, unemployment of males, alcohol problems, pregnancy problems, problems with children, and status inequality. On one measure of stressful events, the Impact of Event Scale (IOE; Horowitz, Wilxer, & Alverez, 1979), batterers had experienced a somewhat larger number of emotionally traumatic events than nonbatterers and had rated their responses to these events as more intense (Kishur, 1989).

Others have suggested that the stress of the relationship itself might trigger some spousal abuse (Rosenbaum & O'Leary, 1981a). Consistent with this supposition, one team of investigators demonstrated that 11 of 14 stress items (e.g., job trouble, small income) significantly differentiated the violent from the nonviolent groups. The primary stressor reported by the maritally violent men was the female partner (Barnett et al., 1991).

Several researchers have posited a relationship between victimization in childhood and subsequent stress vulnerability (Kishur, 1989; van der Kolk, 1988). MacEwan and Barling (1988) proposed that abuse during childhood predisposes individuals to react to stressors with violence (also see Katz & Gottman, 1995). Although the association between childhood abuse, adult stress, and marital violence seems valid, work by Seltzer and Kalmuss (1988) showed that even without exposure to childhood abuse, stress can trigger marital violence.

Results from several sources have shown that when compared to nonbatterers, batterers are poor problem solvers (e.g., Allen, Calsyn, Fehrenbach, & Benton, 1989; Hastings & Hamberger, 1988). In fact, ineffective conflict resolution strategies and high marital distress may serve as mediating factors between observing interparental violence and wife battering (Choice et al., 1995). In one study that subjected men to a variety of problematic marital vignettes, Holtzworth-Munroe and Anglin (1991) found that maritally violent men described less competent responses to a conflict than nonviolent men (cf. Morrison, Van Hasselt, & Bellack, 1987). In particular, maritally violent men exhibited the most difficulty generating adequate responses to situations involving rejection by the wife, challenges from the wife, and jealousy.

    **Power and Control.** Issues of partner control seem to characterize most battering relationships (Tinsley, Critelli, & Ee, 1992). Explanations for the relationship between power and control and battering depend in part on one's theoretical perspective. Feminists contend that men use violence as a means of exerting power and control over their wives (Pence & Paymar, 1986). Learning theorists further point out that when aggression is instrumental in obtaining one's goal, it is reinforcing and therefore likely to increase (Felson, 1992). Others conjecture that feeling powerless in the relationship may serve as a precursor to violence for some men (e.g., Finkelhor, 1983) or that some people have a greater need for power than others (Dutton & Strachan, 1987).

    Research on need for power, based on a modified Thematic Apperception Test and other scales, revealed that wife-assaultive men generate higher need-for-power themes than nonassaultive men (Dutton & Strachan, 1987). In another evaluation, batterers reported feeling powerless and had a very low tolerance for being controlled contrasted with normative data (Petrik, Petrik, & Subotnik, 1994; cf. Allen et al., 1989). In a third inquiry, male batterers' assessment of their female partners' ability to reward them (a measure of interpersonal control) was positively correlated with the severity of male-to-female violence as assessed by the CTS (Claes & Rosenthal, 1990). In their review of published research, Hotaling and Sugarman (1986) found need for power and dominance to be an inconsistent risk marker.

### Individual Differences in Personality and Psychopathology

    Because not all men batter, it is essential to look for individual differences in personality or other variables (O'Leary, 1993). Some have speculated, for example, that battering is a matter of terror about dyadic intimacy (Dutton, 1994). Others maintain that battering is an issue of control (Gondolf & Russell, 1986). Identifying specific problem areas, such as intimacy or control issues, plays an important function in equipping practitioners with a basis for treatment. Some personality traits assessed by researchers are anger and hostility, low self-esteem, jealousy, emotional dependency, and depression. In addition, researchers have used more general personality inventories to assess a broader range of both normal and abnormal traits.

**Anger and Hostility.** Research on anger has been somewhat mixed. Two investigations using the Novaco Anger Scale (Novaco, 1975) did not find significantly higher scores for batterers compared with nonbatterers (Hastings & Hamberger, 1988; Offutt, 1988). In the Hastings and Hamberger (1988) study, male nonalcoholic batterers scored significantly lower than nonabusive males, and in the Offutt (1988) investigation, batterers' scores were higher but not significantly higher. Offutt did find, however, that anger is significantly correlated with CTS scores. The problem with these studies is that batterers may deny or minimize aggression when it is overtly assessed on an anger scale (see Hoshmond, 1987).

Barnett et al. (1991) investigated differences between groups of men who varied in terms of being violent toward female cohabitants, nonfamily members, or no one, and in terms of marital satisfaction level. On the Buss-Durkee Hostility-Guilt Inventory (Buss & Durkee, 1957), maritally violent men differed from maritally nonviolent men on five of the eight dimensions included in the scale: assault, indirect hostility, irritability, resentment, and verbal hostility. The maritally violent men were more hostile overall than any of the other groups (see also Maiuro et al., 1988).

In an analysis using videotaped arguments between a man and a woman, wife assaulters reported more anger evoked in response to the scenario than comparison men, especially in scenes in which the female had verbal power and appeared to be abandoning the male (Dutton & Strachan, 1987).

**Low Self-Esteem.** One suggestion has been that batterers beat women because they are displeased with themselves. Two controlled studies using different instruments produced evidence of lower self-esteem in maritally violent men compared with nonmaritally violent men (Goldstein & Rosenbaum, 1985; Neidig et al., 1986).

**Jealousy and Emotional Dependence.** Many clinicians, researchers, and shelter workers have observed that male spouse abusers suffer from extreme jealousy (Pagelow, 1981a; Wasileski, Callaghan-Chaffee, &

Chaffee, 1982). Some women have reported such extreme levels that their jealous husbands did not allow them to leave their homes (Avni, 1991; Hilberman & Munson, 1978). In an inquiry of lesbian battering, Renzetti (1992) identified a significant relationship between level of jealousy and degree of psychological abuse of a partner.

A recent account by Barnett, Martinez, and Bleustein (1995), however, challenges the role of jealousy in spouse abuse. These investigators found that batterers were not significantly more jealous than a group of unhappily married men who did not beat their wives (see also Murphy, Meyer, & O'Leary, 1994). Instead, jealousy correlated highly with marital dissatisfaction. Maritally violent men in this study, however, did have stronger reasons (e.g., emotional dependence) for staying in their relationships. These findings are congruent with previous research showing that batterers have profound dependency needs (Dutton & Painter, 1993; Margolin et al., 1988) and are more sensitive to themes of abandonment (Holtzworth-Munroe & Hutchinson, 1993).

**Deviations in "Normal" Personality Traits.** Some investigators have tested batterers on personality inventories that assess "normal" personality traits and compared their scores with the test's published norms (e.g., Bersani, Chen, Pendleton, & Denton, 1992). These tests have indicated, for example, that batterers possess interaction styles that are primarily negative. Batterers are significantly less stable emotionally and less socially conforming (Barnett, Wood, Belmont, & Shimogori, 1982). They also are more withdrawn, compulsive, insensitive, and experience many negative emotions such as fear, anxiety, and anger (Schuerger & Reigle, 1988).

It is important to note, however, that research based on normative data (i.e., standardized test scores), rather than on data from comparison groups from the same population, is unreliable. Illustrative of this problem is the finding that when respondents in the comparison group (e.g., nonbattering men from a sample of men undergoing counseling) complete the same questionnaires as individuals in the target group (e.g., batterers undergoing counseling), for instance, the scores of the comparison individuals may not correspond to normative data either. Collectively, the populations sampled may vary from the normative sample in important ways (see Barnett & Hamberger, 1992; Rosenbaum, 1988).

In a study comparing batterers with two nonmaritally violent comparison groups, Barnett and Hamberger (1992) analyzed responses to the California Psychological Inventory (CPI; Gough, 1975). In this survey, batterers clearly displayed different personality traits than nonbatterers in three general areas: intimacy, impulsivity, and problem-solving skills. The implications of this study were that batterers are less well adjusted than nonviolent men. They seem to be rigid, stereotyped, and unresourceful in problem solving-techniques and seem to exhibit difficulty with developing close, intimate relationships anchored on mutuality. They are also likely to be moody, impulsive, self-centered, demanding, and aloof.

**Depression.** Two investigations using comparison groups to assess batterers' moods demonstrated that domestically violent men are substantially more depressed than nondomestically violent men (Hastings & Hamberger, 1988; Maiuro et al., 1988). The level of depression experienced by maritally violent men sometimes extends to suicidal feelings. In one inquiry, men who had killed a family member more frequently tried to kill themselves than men who had killed a non-family member (Anasseril & Holcomb, 1985). Similarly, a Kentucky account of homicide-suicide clusters disclosed that 85% involved family members, with the most likely perpetrator being the current male partner ("Homicides Followed by Suicide," 1991).

**"Abnormal" Personality Traits.** As early as 1974, Faulk demonstrated that homicidal batterers were frequently mentally disturbed (see also Vaselle-Augenstein & Ehrlich, 1992). In one noteworthy investigation, Flournoy and Wilson (1991) analyzed data from various scales on the Minnesota Multiphasic Personality Inventory (MMPI; Hathaway & McKinley, 1940). Their results determined that 44% of the sample of 56 batterers participating in a counseling program obtained scores indicating some deviation from normal, and 56% of the batterers clustered in the normal range (also see Caesar, 1988; Coates, Leong, & Lindsay, 1987).

Using a different assessment of psychopathology, the Millon Clinical Multiaxial Inventory (MCMI; Millon, 1983), Hamberger and Hastings (1986b) contrasted 43 nonviolent community volunteers with 78 alcoholic batterers and 47 nonalcoholic batterers. They were able to classify 88% of their batterer populations as suffering from some level of psychopathology, and they identified several types of personality disorders: passive dependent/compulsive, narcissistic/antisocial, and schizoidal/borderline (also see Offutt, 1988). The term *borderline* implies that there is no dominant pattern of deviance, but there are problems with impulsivity, instability of moods, and so forth. Antisocial disorder is characterized by long-standing problems, such as a disregard for the rights of others, irresponsibility, and resisting authority.

Studies of assaultive males have revealed that about 80% to 90% display diagnosable psychopathology, whereas estimates of psychopathology in the general population range from 15% to 20%. The greater the severity and chronicity of the violence, the greater the likelihood of psychopathology (see Dutton, 1994, for a review).

**Antisocial Personality Disorder.** A synthesis of the findings points to antisocial personality as one of the most typical personality dimensions typifying male batterers (Dutton & Starzomski, 1993; Hamberger & Hastings, 1986). Research on the intergenerational transfer of abuse, assessment of biological traits, personality tests, and measures of psychopathology all implicate antisocial personality orientation/disorder.

According to the Simons et al. (1995) analysis of 451 two-parent families, for example, harsh punishment during childhood is linked with the development of an antisocial personality orientation. Antisocial personality orientation may be the key characteristic that is transmitted across generations and, in turn, results in the well-established link between childhood abuse and adult male battering (Dutton et al., 1995; Simons et al., 1995).

A different line of evidence arising from genetic investigations of criminals also reveals a strong genetic component of antisocial personality disorder underlying criminal behavior (Mednick et al., 1987). Because of the overlap between family and nonfamily violence (general violence), the results of genetic studies on antisocial personality disorder may, by logical extension, apply to maritally assaultive men (Dunford et al., 1990; Fagan et al., 1983; Shields et al., 1988).

Personality tests, of course, evaluate criminals as possessing antisocial tendencies (Megargee, 1966). On the CPI, batterers exhibited a number of characteristics related to antisocial personality disorder, such as inadequate impulse control and self-centeredness (Barnett & Hamberger, 1992). Last, inquiries using psychopathological measures have found evidence for diagnosable antisocial personality disorder in spouse abusers (Hamberger & Hastings, 1986b).

## *Treatment*

For an abuser to make any real changes in his behavior, he must receive appropriate counseling (Dutton, 1986a). Men who batter often find it difficult to recognize verbal and psychological abuse as abuse, and they find it most difficult to change these kinds of behaviors. Much of the work that must be done in effective batterers' programs revolves around recognition of these forms of intimidation and halting nonphysical as well as physical abuse in the relationship.

Because practitioners charged with treating batterers initially had to "jump in feet first," they mainly applied familiar treatments like individual or group counseling. In the late 1970s and early 1980s, treatment programs were developing so rapidly that by the mid-1980s, over 200 such programs existed in the United States alone (Stordeur & Stille, 1989). Out of this fragmented beginning grew the need for program evaluation, and from these assessments came rudimentary principles of treatment.

Behind every batterer is a battered woman who may be in danger. The batterer's participation in counseling in no way guarantees safety for the battered woman with whom he lives. A compelling aspect of batterer treatment programs, therefore, includes consideration of the battered woman's safety (Hamberger & Barnett, 1995). Practitioners have the ethical and legal "duty to warn" and protect potential victims (*Tarasoff v. the Regents of the University of California*, 1976) while maintaining a therapist's primary obligation to protect the client's privacy (see Sonkin, 1989). In an effort to ensure accountability to the victim, some programs have initiated a period of victim safety planning (Hamberger & Hastings, 1990). Victim safety planning includes assisting the battered female partner in thinking through various options that facilitate escape, such as having money hidden somewhere, having a bag packed, and locating a safe home where she and her children may reside temporarily (see Dutton-Douglas, 1991).

## Approaches to Counseling

Practitioners' conceptualizations about the causes of battering (i.e., sociopolitical, interpersonal, and intrapersonal) influence their treatment mode. The goals of programs ordinarily include planning for the victim's safety; empowering men to live emotionally aware, violence-free lives; and preventing intergenerational transmission of violence (Carden, 1994). Caesar and Hamberger (1989) divided therapeutic models into four main categories: feminist, cognitive-behavioral, family, and integrated.

**Feminist Approaches.** Feminist theory views battering as an extreme action falling on a continuum of behaviors intended to allow men to control and oppress women. Followers want to resocialize men to abandon power and control tactics as well as sexist attitudes toward women. Batterers must learn to stop "choosing" violence (e.g., EMERGE, 1980). As an illustration, a man who beats his wife because dinner is late must first learn that he has no right to order his wife to make dinner or to make it on time (Pence & Paymar, 1986). This approach also capitalizes on criminal justice sanctions as an integral part of a successful program (e.g., Schechter, 1982). Critics question its empirical foundation and consider it more of a political statement than a psychological treatment (Dutton, 1994).

In parallel fashion, feminist scholars have criticized psychological explanations on grounds that they serve as excuses for battering (e.g., the "abuse excuse"). They are outspoken in their belief that battering should not be viewed as just an individual problem but also as a social and political problem. Furthermore, they label some psychological treatments, such as training to overcome "skill deficits," as misguided because, in reality, battering stems from the patriarchal system (e.g., Adams, 1988; Goldner, Penn, Sheinberg, & Walker, 1990).

**Cognitive-Behavioral Approaches.** Therapists using a cognitive-behavioral approach apply learning principles to help clients modify behavior identified as problematic by empirically based trait assessments. Simply put, a therapist might be called on to help a client "restructure" his thinking as in the following three-stage example: Initially, a batterer encounters external stimuli such as a wife's failure to have dinner ready on time. He will then internally mediate (interpret) the event (e.g., in terms of past learning, current stress, or drunkenness) as "not caring about how he feels" and decide that he must respond to "force her to treat him better." In the final stage, his external response is to "throw the food in her face."

A cognitive-behavioral approach focuses on restructuring the batterer's thinking so that he will interpret his wife's late dinner differently (e.g., she was ill) and discover other behavioral options (e.g., take the family out to a fast-food restaurant). Other therapeutic techniques involve helping batterers accomplish goals such as managing adverse arousal and learning appropriate assertion and problem-solving skills (Hamberger & Lohr, 1989; Saunders, 1989). Although evaluative research is clouded by high drop-out rates, studies have reported some success in treating batterers with this approach (e.g., Dutton, 1986a; Faulkner, Stoltenberg, Cogen, Nolder, & Shooter, 1992).

**Couples and Systems Approaches.** The least popular approach, systems theory, expands treatment to include marital dynamics and the whole family system as a context for marital violence. Underlying the systems approach is the value placed on preserving the family. From this stance, a batterer's violence is not isolated and ascribed to him alone but somehow is attributable to the "relationship." Two assets of couples therapy are improving communication and allowing male and female therapists to model nonviolent behavior (Geffner & Rosenbaum, 1990).

Adams (1988) criticizes this approach because viewing abuse as an interactional problem of the couple runs the risk of reinforcing a batterer's belief that violence is not really his problem (Willbach, 1989). Critics further point to the dearth of scientific studies documenting effectiveness of these programs and voice concern that violence and safety issues may lose priority (e.g., Edleson & Tolman, 1992). Others suggest that the process can be highly dangerous if it compels battered women to continue interaction with an abusive, controlling, and dangerous partner (Davis, 1984; Dutton-Douglas, 1991; Hansen, Harway, & Cervantes, 1991).

**Treatment for Alcohol Abuse and Criminal Behavior.** At the very least, counselors should make a preliminary assessment of such things as patterns of alcohol use and social and legal problems and make appropriate plans for treatment (Hamberger & Barnett, 1995). Therapists should assess the crime histories of wife assaulters by using a problem identification approach (Quinsey, Maguire, & Upfold, 1987). They should ask questions about arrest records, level of violence, and the selection of targets of violence.

Research consistently shows that spouse abusers have a number of alcohol-related problems (Gelles, 1993). Both genetic (e.g., Bower, 1994) and learning components play a role in alcohol misuse (Vaillant & Milofsky, 1982). Because drunkenness can precipitate battering and be used as an excuse, practitioners must address alcohol treatment. One myth that Zubretsky and Digirolamo (1994) have tried to debunk, however, is that treatment of alcohol or substance abuse problems alone will concomitantly eliminate problems with domestic violence. A batterer trying to stop drinking, in fact, may be more abusive because of the new, added stress of attempting sobriety (see also A.

Davidson, 1994). On the other hand, a treatment consisting of both behavioral marital therapy and treatment for alcoholism for alcoholic husbands and their wives has shown some promise in decreasing violence in men, especially in those who stopped drinking (O'Farrell & Murphy, 1995). These findings are just one more indication of the complexity of the alcohol-violence connection.

## Counseling Outcomes for Group Treatments

A number of domestic violence experts are skeptical about the quality and permanence of behavioral changes made by abusers as a consequence of counseling (e.g., Gondolf, 1988; Gondolf & Russell, 1986; Hart, 1988). Illustrative of just one problem is the tendency for batterers to enroll in a counseling program as a ploy to pressure the female partner into a reconciliation, only to drop the program as soon as the partner has returned (Bowker, 1983; Fagan, 1989). Although most counseling outcome studies use quasi-experimental designs (Carden, 1994), methodology has continually improved over the past decade (Edleson & Tolman, 1992). When discussing batterer treatment outcomes, the traditional catch-22 question, "Are you still beating your wife?" takes on new meaning.

**Recidivism Outcome Studies.** One of the first quasi-experimental studies to tackle this problem originated in Canada. Donald Dutton (1986a) compared postconviction rates over a 3-year period of 50 men who completed a 16-week court-mandated treatment program with those of a comparable group that did not receive treatment. Treated men had a 4% (police reports) or 16% (victim report) recidivism rate compared with nontreated assaulters, who had a 40% rate. In addition, CTS scores completed by both members of the couple demonstrated a significant drop in severe violence from 10.6 times per year before the treatment to 1.7 times per year following the treatment. Generalizability was limited by nonrandom selection of participants, by customary problems inherent in self-report data, and by uncontrollable variation in police decisions to rearrest. Overall, however, Dutton's work represented a striking improvement over anecdotal reports.

In one analysis of reports of female partners over a 2½-year posttreatment period, success rates for ending physical aggression were fairly high (Edleson & Grusznski, 1988). In another survey comparing 120 court-referred abusers with a group of 101 non-referred abusers, court-referred abusers who attended 75% or more of the counseling sessions reduced recidivism (Chen, Bersani, Myers, & Denton, 1990). In a third investigation, 28% of 88 men who had completed a 12-session treatment program engaged in further acts of violence over a follow-up period of 1 year (Hamberger & Hastings, 1990).

**Other Posttreatment Counseling Changes.** Batterers may not only decrease their violence but also make other favorable posttreatment changes. In a 1-year follow-up study, Hamberger and Hastings (1989) reported a dramatic reduction in depressive symptoms following 12 cognitive-behavioral treatment sessions. A no-treatment comparison group, had it been available, would have clarified the findings further. Batterers, however, did not uniformly abandon psychologically abusive behaviors, nor did their scores on tests of pathology change (see also Sommer, 1990).

**The Drop-Out Problem.** The high rate of dropout in batterer programs is rather standard and undermines generalizability of results (e.g., Schuerger & Reigle, 1988). Illustrative of this problem are the results of a study by Gondolf and Foster (1991). They tracked the records of 200 inquiries into batterer programs. From inquiry to first intake session, the attrition rate was 73%. From inquiry to counseling attendance, attrition was 86%, and from inquiry to completion of 12 sessions, 93%. Altogether, only 1% completed the contracted 8-month treatment program.

One investigation following a 16-week spouse abuse abatement program compared violence-free completers with violence-repeating completers (Hamberger & Hastings, 1990). Violence-free completers had fewer alcohol and substance abuse problems during both pre- and posttreatment, and following treatment, they had lower scores for narcissism (self-centered and demanding). On the other hand, variation in outcomes generated by referral (self or mandated) and record of criminal activity failed to discriminate the two groups.

**Court-Mandated Counseling.** It is becoming evident that batterers who are court involved and ordered to treatment differ significantly on a number of dimensions from men who are not court involved and who voluntarily seek treatment. In one survey, for example, non-court-involved men had higher levels of education, employment, and income than court-involved men (e.g., mandated to counseling). Non-court-involved men also had higher levels of outside social support, for example, friends (Barrera et al., 1994). One researcher believes that there is no scientific evidence substantiating the effectiveness of any type of rehabilitative effort with offenders mandated to treatment (Berk, 1993).

Given what is currently known, it is probable that the court must remain involved in any mandated counseling orders. Criminal justice experts advise that diversion into a counseling program and out of the system should not occur before a plea is entered. As long as the abuser is under the control of the court, he can be sentenced without resetting the trial. According to the 1990 Family Violence Project (cited in Pagelow, 1992), without this leverage, a recalcitrant participant may be able to leave treatment with no record at all. Others are recommending longer jail time given that treatment is not uniformly effective (Shepard, 1992).

**Effectiveness of Counseling Programs.** The effectiveness of abuser counseling with or without mandatory arrest remains debatable (Gondolf & Russell, 1986; Neidig et al., 1986; Pirog-Good & Stets, 1986). Nonetheless, court-mandated treatment of wife assault is essential to the criminal justice system's objective of reducing recidivism (Dutton, 1988). If nothing else, arrest challenges a batterer's beliefs that his arrest and conviction were unjust and that his use of violence was justified (Ganley, 1981). It also places the responsibility for change on the batterer, a stance that is compatible with deterrence themes in the criminal justice system (Fagan, 1988). Court-ordered treatment is congruent with social-control models.

Syers and Edleson (1992) pinpointed two crucial variables affecting recidivism: number of previous arrests and duration of court-ordered counseling. Men arrested the first time the police visited the residence, and those mandated into counseling programs for a longer period of time, were significantly less likely to assault their female partners than men not arrested the first time or mandated into shorter counseling programs (see also Steinman, 1991).

The drop-out problem is an especially serious complication. As expected, recidivism is higher for dropouts than completers (e.g., Grusznski & Carrillo, 1988). Completers also diverge from noncompleters in other ways. One investigation found that dropouts were younger, had lower employment levels, and had higher pretreatment levels of police interaction for nonviolent offenses (Hamberger & Hastings, 1989). Pirog-Good and Stets (1986) noted that procedures like allowing clients not to pay for counseling and making use of criminal justice referrals led to higher retention levels than did alternative methods. Given the noticeable variety of outcomes across studies, Hilton (1994) believes that the next step should be to match arrest and treatment decisions to "type" of assaulter.

## References

Adams, D. C. "Treatment Models of Men Who Batter: A Profeminist Analysis," 176–99. In K. Yllö & M. Bograd, eds. *Feminist Perspectives on Wife Abuse.* Newbury Park, Calif.: Sage, 1988.

Allen, K., D. A. Calsyn, P. A. Fehrenbach, & G. Benton. "A Study of Interpersonal Behaviors of Male Batterers." *Journal of Interpersonal Violence* 4 (1989): 79–89.

Anasseril, D., & W. Holcomb. "A Comparison Between Men Charged with Domestic and Nondomestic Homicide." *Bulletin of the American Academy of Psychiatry and Law* 13 (1985): 233–41.

Avni, N. "Battered Wives: The Home as a Total Institution." *Violence and Victims* 6 (1991): 137–49.

Barnett, O. W., R. W. Fagen, & J. M. Booker. "Hostility and Stress as Mediators of Aggression in Violent Men." *Journal of Family Violence* 6 (1991): 219–41.

Barnett, O. W., & L. K. Hamberger. "The Assessment of Maritally Violent Men on the California Psychological Inventory." *Violence and Victims* 7 (1992): 15–28.

Barnett, O. W., C. Y. Lee, & R. E. Thelen. *Gender Differences in Forms, Outcomes and Attributions for Interpartner Aggression.* Paper presented at the 4th International Family Violence Research Conference, Durham, N.H., July 1995.

Barnett, O. W., T. E. Martinez, & B. W. Bleustein. "Jealousy and Anxious Romantic Attachment in Maritally Violent and Nonviolent Males." *Journal of Interpersonal Violence* 10 (1995): 473–86.

Barnett, O. W., & T. A. Ryska. *Masculinity and Femininity in Male Spouse Abusers.* Symposium presented at the annual meeting of the American Society of Criminology, Atlanta, Ga., November 1986.

Barnett, O. W., C. Wood, J. Belmont, & Y. Shimogori. *Characteristics of Spouse Abusers.* Paper presented at the annual meeting of the American Society of Criminology, Toronto, Ontario, Canada, November 1982.

Barrera, M., S. Palmer, R. Brown, & S. Kalaher. "Characteristics of Court-Involved Men and Non-Court-Involved Men Who Abuse Their Wives." *Journal of Family Violence* 9 (1994): 333–45.

Bennett, L. W., R. M. Tolman, C. J. Rogalski, & J. Srinivasaraghavan. "Domestic Abuse by Male Alcohol and Drug Addicts." *Violence and Victims* 9 (1994): 359–68.

Berk, R. A. "What the Scientific Evidence Shows: On Average, We Can Do No Better than Arrest," 323–36. In R. J. Gelles & D. R. Loseke, eds. *Current Controversies on Family Violence.* Newbury Park, Calif.: Sage, 1993.

Bersani, C. A., H. T. Chen, B. F. Pendleton, & R. Denton. "Personality Traits of Convicted Male Batterers." *Journal of Family Violence* 7 (1992): 123–34.

"Biology and Family, Partners in Crime." *Science News* 150, 1 (July, 6, 1996): 11.

Birns, B., M. Cascardi, & S. Meyer. "Sex-Role Socialization: Developmental Influences on Wife Abuse." *American Journal of Orthopsychiatry* 64 (1994): 50–59.

Booth, A. B., & D. W. Osgood. "The Influence of Testosterone on Deviance in Adulthood: Assessing and Explaining the Relationship." *Criminology* 31 (1993): 93–117.

Bower, B. "Alcohol Exposes Its 'Insensitive' Side." *Science News* 145 (1994): 118.

Bowker, L. H. *Beating Wife Beating.* Lexington, Mass.: Lexington Books, 1983.

Breines, G., & L. Gordon. "The New Scholarship on Family Violence." *Signs: Journal of Women in Culture and Society* 8 (1983): 490–531.

Briere, J. "Predicting Self-Reported Likelihood of Battering: Attitudes and Childhood Experiences." *Research in Personality* 21 (1987): 61–69.

Buss, A., & A. Durkee. "An Inventory for Assessing Different Kinds of Hostility." *Journal of Consulting Psychology* 2 (1957): 343–49.

Byrne, C. A., I. Arias, & C. M. Lyons. *Attributions for Partner Behavior in Violent and Nonviolent Couples.* Paper presented at the annual meeting of the Southeastern Psychological Association, Atlanta, Ga., March 1993.

Caesar, P. L. "Exposure to Violence in the Families-of-Origin among Wife Abusers and Maritally Nonviolent Men." *Violence and Victims* 3 (1988): 49–63.

Caesar, P. L., & L.K. Hamberger, eds. *Treating Men Who Batter*. New York: Springer, 1989.

Carden, A. D. "Wife Abuse and the Wife Abuser: Review and Recommendations." *Counseling Psychologist* 22 (1994): 539–82.

Chen, H.,C. Bersani, S. C. Myers, & R. Denton. "Evaluating the Effectiveness of a Court Sponsored Abuser Treatment Program." *Journal of Family Violence* 4 (1990): 309–22.

Choice, P., L. K. Lamke, & J. F. Pittman. "Conflict Resolution Strategies and Marital Distress as Mediating Factors in the Link Between Witnessing Interparental Violence and Wife Battering." *Violence and Victims* 10 (1995): 107–19.

Claes, J. A., & D. M. Rosenthal. "Men Who Batter Women: A Study in Power." *Journal of Family Violence* 5 (1990): 215–24.

Coates, C. J., D. J. Leong, & M. Lindsay. *Personality Differences among Batterers Voluntarily Seeking Treatment and Those Ordered to Treatment by the Court*. Paper presented at the Third National Family Violence Research Conference, Durham, N.H., July 1987.

Corvo, K.N. "Attachment and Violence in the Families-of-Origin of Domestically Violent Men." *Dissertation Abstracts International* 54 (1992): 1950A. (UMI No. 9322595)

Davidson, A. "Alcohol, Drugs, and Family Violence." *Violence Update* 4, 5 (1994): 5–6.

Davis, L. V. "Beliefs of Service Providers about Abused Women and Abusing Men." *Social Work* (May-June 1984): 243–50.

Dunford, F. W., D. Huizinga, & D. S. Elliott. "The Role of Arrest in Domestic Assault: The Omaha Police Experiment." *Criminology* 28 (1990): 183–206.

Dutton, D. G. *The Domestic Assault of Women*. Boston: Allyn & Bacon, 1988.

Dutton, D. G. "The Outcome of Court-Mandated Treatment for Wife Assault: A Quasi-Experimental Evaluation." *Violence and Victims* 1 (1986a): 163–75.

Dutton, D. G. "Wife Assaulters' Explanations for Assault: The Neutralization of Self-Punishment." *Canadian Journal of Behavioral Sciences* 18 (1986b): 381–90.

Dutton, D. G. "Patriarchy and Wife Assault: An Ecological Fallacy." *Violence and Victims* 9 (1994): 167–82.

Dutton, D. G., & S. L. Painter. "Emotional Attachments in Abusive Relationships: A Test of Traumatic Bonding Theory." *Violence and Victims* 8 (1993): 105–20.

Dutton, D. G., & A. J. Starzomski. "Borderline Personality in Perpetrators of Psychological and Physical Abuse." *Violence and Victims* 8 (1993): 327–37.

Dutton, D. G., & C. E. Strachen. "Motivational Needs for Power and Spouse-Specific Assertiveness in Assaultive and Nonassaultive Men." *Violence and Victims* 2 (1987): 145–56.

Dutton, D. G., C. Van Ginkel, & A. Starzomski. "The Role of Shame and Guilt in the Intergenerational Transmission of Abusiveness." *Violence and Victims* 10 (1995): 121–31.

Dutton-Douglas, M. A. "Counseling and Shelter Services for Battered Women," 113–30. In M. Steinman, ed. *Woman Battering: Policy Responses*. Cincinnati, Ohio: Anderson, 1991.

Eagly, A. H., & V. J. Steffen. "Gender and Aggressive Behavior: A Meta-Analytic Review of the Social Psychological Literature." *Psychological Bulletin* 100 (1986): 309–30.

Edleson, J. L., & M. P. Brygger. "Gender Differences in Reporting of Battering Incidents." *Family Relations* 35 (1986): 377–82.

Edleson, J. L., & R. J. Grusznski. "Treating Men Who Batter: Four Years of Outcome Data from the Domestic Abuse Project." *Journal of Social Science Research* 12 (1988): 3–22.

Edleson, J. L., & R. M. Tolman. *Intervention for Men Who Batter*. Newbury Park, Calif.: Sage, 1992.

Elbow, M. "Theoretical Considerations of Violent Marriages." *Social Casework* 58 (1977): 515–26.

EMERGE. *Do You Feel Like Beating Up on Somebody?* Boston: EMERGE, 1980.

Fagen, J. A. "Contributions of Family Violence Research to Criminal Justice Policy on Wife Assault: Paradigms of Science and Social Control." *Violence and Victims* 3 (1988): 159–86.

Fagen, J. A. "Cessation of Family Violence: Deterrence and Dissuasion," 377–425. In L. Ohlin & M. Tonry, eds. *Family Violence*. Chicago: University of Chicago Press, 1989.

Fagen, J. A., D. Stewart, & K. Hansen. "Violent Men or Violent Husbands? Background Factors and Situational Correlates," 49–69. In D. Finkelhor, R. J. Gelles, G. T. Hotaling, & M. A. Straus, eds. *The Dark Side of Families: Current Family Violence Research*. Beverly Hills, Calif.: Sage, 1983.

Faulk, M. "Men Who Assault Their Wives." *Medicine, Science, and the Law* 14 (1974): 180–83.

Faulkner, K., C. D. Stoltenberg, R. Cogen, M. Nolder, & E. Shooter. "Cognitive-Behavioral Group Treatment for Male Spouse Abusers." *Journal of Family Violence* 7 (1992): 37–55.

Felson, R. B. " 'Kick 'Em When They're Down': Explanation of the Relationship Between Stress and Interpersonal Aggression and Violence." *Sociological Quarterly* 33 (1992): 1–16.

Finkelhor, D. "Common Features of Family Abuse," 17–30. In D. Finkelhor, R. J. Gelles, G. T. Hotaling, & M. A. Straus, eds. *The Dark Side of Families: Current Family Violence Research*. Beverly Hills, Calif.: Sage, 1983.

Finn, J. "The Stresses and Coping Behavior of Battered Women." *Social Casework: The Journal of Contemporary Social Work* 66 (1985): 341–49.

Ganley, A. L. *Court Mandated Counseling for Men Who Batter: A Three-Day Workshop for Mental Health Professionals* [Participants' manual]. Washington, D.C.: Center for Women's Policy Studies, 1981.

Geffner, R., & A. Rosenbaum. "Characteristics and Treatment of Batterers." *Behavioral Sciences and the Law* 8 (1990): 131–40.

Gelles, R. J. "Alcohol and Other Drugs Are Associated with Violence—They Are Not Its Cause," 182–96. In R. J. Gelles & D. R. Loseke, eds. *Current Controversies on Family Violence*. Newbury Park, Calif.: Sage, 1993.

Goldner, V., P. Penn, M. Sheinberg, & G. Walker. "Love and Violence: Gender Paradoxes in Volatile Attachments." *Family Process* 29 (1990): 343–64.

Goldstein, D., & A. Rosenbaum. "An Evaluation of Self-Esteem of Maritally Violent Men." *Family Relations* 34 (1985): 425–28.

Gondolf, E. W. "The Effect of Batterer Counseling on Shelter Outcome." *Journal of Interpersonal Violence* 3 (1988): 275–89.

Gondolf, E. W., & R. A. Foster. "Pre-Program Attrition in Batterer Programs." *Journal of Family Violence* 6 (1991): 337–49.

Gondolf, E. W., & D. Russell. "The Case against Anger Control Treatment for Batterers." *Response* 9, 3 (1986): 2–5.

Gough, H. G. *Manual for the California Psychological Inventory*. Palo Alto, Calif.: Consulting Psychologists Press, 1975.

Grusznski, R. J., & T. P. Carrillo. "Who Completes Batterer Treatment Programs? An Empirical Question." *Journal of Family Violence* 3 (1988): 141–50.

Hamberger, L. K., & O. W. Barnett. "Assessment and Treatment of Men Who Batter," volume 14: 31–54. In L. VandeCreek, S. Knapp, & T. L. Jackson, eds. *Innovations in Clinical Practice: A Source Book*. Sarasota, Fla.: Professional Resource Press, 1995.

Hamberger, L. K., & J. E. Hastings. "Personality Correlates of Men Who Abuse Their Partners: A Cross-Validation Study." *Journal of Family Violence* 1 (1986): 323–41.

Hamberger, L. K., & J. E. Hastings. "Counseling Male Spouse Abusers: Characteristics of Treatment Completers and Dropouts." *Violence and Victims* 4 (1989): 275–86.

Hamberger, L. K., & J. E. Hastings. "Recidivism Following Spouse Abuse Abatement Counseling: Treatment Implications." *Violence and Victims* 5 (1990): 157–70.

Hamberger, L. K., & J. M. Lohr. "Proximal Causes of Spouse Abuse: A Theoretical Analysis for Cognitive-Behavioral Interventions," 53–76. In P. L. Caesar & L. K. Hamberger, eds. *Treating Men Who Batter: Theory, Practice, and Programs*. New York: Springer, 1989.

Hansen, M., M. Harway, & N. Cervantes. "Therapists' Perceptions of Severity in Cases of Family Violence." *Violence and Victims* 6 (1991): 225–35.

Hart, B. J. *Safety for Women: Monitoring Batterers' Programs*. Harrisburg, Pa.: Pennsylvania Coalition Against Domestic Violence, 1988.

Hastings, J. E., & L. K. Hamberger. "Personality Characteristics of Spouse Abusers: A Controlled Comparison." *Violence and Victims* 3 (1988): 31–48.

Hathaway, S. R., & J. C. McKinley. "A Multiphasic Personality Schedule (Minnesota) I: Construction of the Schedule." *Journal of Psychology* 10 (1940): 249–54.

Heppner, P. P., & D. S. Gonzales. "Men Counseling Men," 30–38. In M. Scher, G. Stevens, G. Good, & G. A. Eichenfield, eds. *Handbook of Counseling and Psychotherapy*. Newbury Park, Calif.: Sage, 1987.

Hilberman, E., & K. Munson. "Sixty Battered Women." *Victimology: An International Journal* 2 (1978): 460–70.

Hilton, Z. N. "The Failure of Arrest to Deter Wife Assault: What Now?" *Violence Update* 4, 5 (1994): 1–2, 4, 10.

Holtzworth-Munroe, A., & K. Anglin. "The Competency of Responses Given by Maritally Violent Versus Nonviolent Men to Problematic Marital Situations." *Violence and Victims* 6 (1991): 257–69.

Holtzworth-Munroe, A., & G. Hutchinson. "Attributing Negative Intent to Wife Behavior: The Attributions of Maritally Violent Versus Nonviolent Men." *Journal of Abnormal Psychology* 102 (1993): 206–11.

"Homicides Followed by Suicide—Kentucky, 1985–1990." *Morbidity and Mortality Weekly Report* 40 (September 27, 1991): 652–53, 659.

Horowitz, M., N. Wilzer, & W. Alverez. "Impact of Event Scale: A Measure of Subjective Stress." *Psychosomatic Medicine* 41 (1979): 3.

Hoshmond, L. S. T. "Judgment of Anger Problems by Clients and Therapists." *Journal of Interpersonal Violence* 2 (1987): 251–63.

Hotaling, G. T., & D. B. Sugarman. "An Analysis of Risk Markers in Husband to Wife Violence: The Current State of Knowledge." *Violence and Victims* 1 (1986): 101–24.

Howell, M. J., & K. L. Pugliesi. "Husbands Who Harm: Predicting Spousal Violence by Men." *Journal of Family Violence* 3 (1988): 15–27.

Jacobson, N. S., & J. M. Gottman. *New Picture of Violent Couples Emerges from UW Study*. Paper presented at the annual meeting of the American Psychological Association, Toronto, Ontario, Canada, August 1993.

Jacobson, N. S., J. M. Gottman, J. Waltz, R. Rushe, J. C. Babcock, & A. Holtzworth-Munroe. "Affect, Verbal Content and Psychophysiology in the Arguments of Couples with a Violent Husband." *Journal of Consulting and Clinical Psychology* 62 (1994): 982–88.

Kalmuss, D. S. "The Intergenerational Transmission of Marital Aggression." *Journal of Marriage and the Family* 46 (1984): 11–19.

Kandel, E., & S. A. Mednick. "Perinatal Complications Predict Violent Offending." *Criminology* 29 (1991): 519–29.

Kandel-Englander, E. "Wife Battering and Violence Outside the Family." *Journal of Interpersonal Violence* 7 (1992): 462–70.

Katz, L. F., & J. M. Gottman. "Vagal Tone Protects Children from Marital Conflict." *Development and Psychopathology* 7 (1995): 83–92.

Kishur, G. R. "The Male Batterer: A Multidimensional Exploration of Conjugal Violence." *Dissertation Abstracts International* 49 (1989): 2409A. (UMI No. 8814496)

Kruttschnitt, C., L. Heath, & D. A. Ward. "Family Violence, Television Viewing Habit, and Other Adolescent Experiences Related to Violent Criminal Behavior." *Criminology* 24 (1986): 235–67.

Langhinrichsen-Rohling, J., N. Smutzler, & D. Vivian. "Positivity in Marriage: The Role of Discord and Physical Aggression against Wives." *Journal of Marriage and the Family* 56 (1994): 69–79.

Locke, H. J., & K. M. Wallace. "Short Marital Adjustment and Prediction Tests: Their Reliability and Validity." *Journal of Marriage and Family Living* 21 (1957): 251–55.

MacEwan, K. E., & J. Barling. "Multiple Stressors, Violence in the Family of Origin, and Marital Aggression: A Longitudinal Investigation." *Journal of Family Violence* 3 (1988): 73–87.

Maertz, K. F. "Self-Defeating Beliefs of Battered Women." Doctoral dissertation, University of Alberta, Canada. *Dissertation Abstracts International* 51 (1990): 5580B. (UMI No. 8814496)

Maiuro, R. D., T. S. Cahn, & P. P. Vitaliano. "Assertiveness Deficits and Hostility in Domestically Violent Men." *Violence and Victims* 1 (1986): 279–89.

Maiuro, R. D., T. S. Cahn, & P. P. Vitaliano. "Anger, Hostility, and Depression in Domestically Violent Versus Generally Assaultive Men and Nonviolent Control Subjects." *Journal of Consulting and Clinical Psychology* 56 (1988): 17–23.

Margolin, G., R. S. John, & L. Gleberman. "Affective Responses to Conflictual Discussions in Violent and Nonviolent Couples." *Journal of Consulting and Clinical Psychology* 56 (1988): 24–33.

Mednick, S. A., W. F. Gabrielli, & B. Hutchings. "Genetic Factors in the Etiology of Criminal Behavior," 74–91. In S. A. Mednick, T. E. Moffitt, & S. S. Stack, eds. *The Causes of Crime*. Cambridge, England: Cambridge University Press, 1987.

Megargee, E. I., ed. "Undercontrolled and Overcontrolled Personality Types in Extreme Antisocial Aggression." *Psychological Monographs: General and Applied* 80 (1966). (3, Whole No. 611).

Millon, T. *Millon Clinical Multiaxial Inventory Manual*. Minneapolis, Minn.: Interpretive Scoring Systems, 1983.

Morrison, R. L., V. B. Van Hasselt, & A. S. Bellack. "Assessment of Assertion and Problem-Solving Skills in Wife Abusers and Their Spouses." *Journal of Family Violence* 2 (1987): 227–56.

Murphy, C. M., S. L. Meyer, & K. D. O'Leary. "Dependency Characteristics of Partner Assaultive Men." *Journal of Abnormal Psychology* 103 (1994): 729–35.

Neidig, P., D. Friedman, & B. Collins. "Attitudinal Family Violence Characteristics of Men Who Have Engaged in Spouse Abuse." *Journal of Family Violence* 1 (1986): 223–33.

Novaco, R. *Anger Control: The Development and Evaluation of an Experimental Treatment*. Lexington, Mass.: Lexington Books, 1975.

O'Farrell, T. J., & C. M. Murphy. "Marital Violence Before and After Alcoholism Treatment." *Journal of Consulting and Clinical Psychology* 63 (1995): 256–62.

Offutt, R. A. "Domestic Violence: Psychological Characteristics of Men Who Batter." *Dissertation Abstracts International* 49 (1988): 3452B. (UMI No. 8818887)

O'Leary, K. D. "Through a Psychological Lens: Personality Traits, Personality Disorders, and Levels of Violence," 7–30. In R. J. Gelles & D. R. Loseke, eds. *Current Controversies on Family Violence*. Newbury Park, Calif.: Sage, 1993.

O'Leary, K. D., & A. D. Curley. "Assertion and Family Violence: Correlates of Spouse Abuse." *Journal of Marital and Family Therapy* 12 (1986): 281–89.

Pagelow, M. D. *Woman-Battering: Victims and Their Experiences*. Beverly Hills, Calif.: Sage, 1981.

Pagelow, M. D. "Adult Victims of Domestic Violence." *Journal of Interpersonal Violence* 7 (1992): 87–120.

Pence, E., & M. Paymar. *Power and Control: Tactics of Men Who Batter*. Duluth: Minnesota Program Development, 1986.

Petrik, N. D., R. E. Petrik, & L. S. Subotnik. "Powerlessness and the Need to Control." *Journal of Interpersonal Violence* 9 (1994): 278–85.

Pirog-Good, M. A., & J. Stets. "Programs for Abusers: Who Drops Out and What Can Be Done." *Response* 9, 2 (1986): 17–19.

Ptacek, J. "Why Do Men Batter Their Wives?," 133–57. In K. Yllö & M. Bograd, eds. *Feminist Perspectives on Wife Abuse*. Newbury Park, Calif.: Sage, 1988.

Quinsey, V. L., A. Maguire, & D. Upfold. "The Behavioral Treatment of Rapists and Child Molesters," 363–82. In E. K. Morris & C. J. Braukmann, eds. *Behavioral Approaches to Crime and Delinquency*. New York: Plenum, 1987.

Renzetti, C. M. *Violent Betrayal: Partner Abuse in Lesbian Relationships*. Newbury Park, Calif.: Sage, 1992.

Riggs, D. S., & K. D. O'Leary. "A Theoretical Model of Courtship Aggression," 53–71. In M. A. Pirog-Good & J. E. Stets, eds. *Violence in Dating Relationships: Emerging Social Issues*. New York: Praeger, 1989.

Roberts, A. R. "Psychosocial Characteristics of Batterers: A Study of 234 Men Charged with Domestic Violence Offenses." *Journal of Family Violence* 2 (1987): 81–93.

Rosenbaum, A. "Of Men, Macho, and Marital Violence." *Journal of Family Violence* 1 (1986): 121–29.

Rosenbaum, A. "Methodological Issues in Marital Violence Research." *Journal of Family Violence* 3 (1988): 91–104.

Rosenbaum, A., & S. K. Hoge. "Head Injury and Marital Aggression." *American Journal of Psychiatry* 146 (1989): 1048–51.

Rosenbaum, A., & K. D. O'Leary. "Children: The Unintended Victims of Marital Violence." *American Journal of Orthopsychiatry* 51 (1981a): 692–99.

Rosenbaum, A., & K. D. O'Leary. "Marital Violence: Characteristics of Abusive Couples." *Journal of Consulting and Clinical Psychology* 49 (1981b): 63–76.

Rouse, L. P. "Models, Self-Esteem, and Locus of Control of Factors Contributing to Spouse Abuse." *Victimology: An International Journal* 9 (1984): 130–41.

Sapiente, A. A. "Locus of Control and Causal Attributions of Maritally Violent Men." *Dissertation Abstracts International* 50 (1988): 758B. (UMI No. 8822697)

Saunders, D. G. "Cognitive and Behavioral Interventions with Men Who Batter: Applications and Outcome," 77–100. In P. L. Caesar & L. K. Hamberger, eds. *Treating Men Who Batter: Theory, Practice, and Programs.* New York: Springer, 1989.

Schechter, S. *Women and Male Violence: The Visions and Struggles of the Battered Women's Movement.* Boston: South End, 1982.

Scher, M. "Men and Intimacy." *Counseling and Values* 25 (1980): 62–68.

Schuerger, J. M., & N. Reigle. "Personality and Biographic Data that Characterize Men Who Abuse Their Wives." *Journal of Clinical Psychology* 44 (1988): 75–81.

Seltzer, J. A., & D. S. Kalmuss. "Socialization and Stress Explanations for Spouse Abuse." *Social Forces* 67 (1988): 473–91.

Shepard, M. "Predicting Batterer Recidivism Five Years After Community Intervention." *Journal of Family Violence* 7 (1992): 167–78.

Shields, N. M., G. McCall, & C. R. Hanneke. "Patterns of Family and Nonfamily Violence: Violent Husbands and Violent Men." *Violence and Victims* 3 (1988): 83–97.

Simons, R. L., C. I. Wu, & R. D. Conger. "A Test of Various Perspectives on the Intergenerational Transmission of Domestic Violence." *Criminology* 33 (1995): 141–70.

Smith, D. A., & K. D. O'Leary. *Affective Components of Problem-Solving Communication and Their Relationships with Interspousal Aggression.* Paper presented at the Third National Family Violence Research Conference, Durham, N.H., July 1987.

Sommer, J. A. "Men Who Batter: Attitudes toward Women." *Dissertation Abstracts International* 51 (1990): 5592B. (UMI No. 9107514)

Sonkin, D. J., ed. *Domestic Violence on Trial: Psychological and Legal Dimensions of Family Violence.* New York: Springer, 1989.

Sonkin, D. J., D. Martin, & L. Walker. *The Male Batterer: A Treatment Approach.* New York: Springer, 1985.

Spanier, G. B. "Measuring Dyadic Adjustment: New Scales for Assessing the Quality of Marriage and Similar Dyads." *Journal of Marriage and the Family* 38 (1976): 15–28.

Steinman, M. "The Public Policy Process and Woman Battering: Problems and Potentials," 1–18. In M. Steinman, ed. *Woman Battering: Policy Responses*. Cincinnati, Ohio: Anderson, 1991.

Stevens, M., & R. Gebhart. *Rape Education for Men: Curriculum Guide*. Columbus: Ohio State University Rape Education Prevention Project, 1985.

Stordeur, R. A., & R. Stille. *Ending Men's Violence against Their Partners: One Road to Peace*. Newbury Park, Calif.: Sage, 1989.

Straus, M. A. "Measuring Intrafamily Conflict and Aggression: The Conflict Tactics Scale (CT)." *Journal of Marriage and the Family* 41 (1979): 75–88.

Straus, M. A., & R. J. Gelles. *Physical Violence in American Families*. New Brunswick, N.J.: Transaction Books, 1990.

Sugarman, D. B., & S. L. Frankel. *A Meta-Analytic Study of Wife Assault and Patriarchal Beliefs*. Paper presented at the annual meeting of the American Psychological Association, Toronto, Ontario, Canada, August 1993.

Syers, M., & J. L. Edleson. "The Combined Effects of Coordinated Criminal Justice Intervention in Woman Abuse." *Journal of Interpersonal Violence* 7 (1992): 490–502.

Tarasoff v. the Regents of the University of California, 529 P.2d 553 (Cal. 1974), *vac.*, reheard in bank and *aff'd*, 131 Cal Rptr. 14, 551 P.2d 334 (1976).

Tinsley, C. A., J. W. Critelli, & J. S. Ee. *The Perception of Sexual Aggression: One Act, Two Realities*. Paper presented at the annual meeting of the American Psychological Association, Washington, D.C., August 1992.

Vaillant, G. E., & E. S. Milofsky. "The Etiology of Alcoholism: A Prospective Viewpoint." *American Psychologist* 37 (1982): 494–503.

Van der Kolk, B. A. "Trauma in Men: Effects on Family Life," 170–85. In M. B. Straus, ed. *Abuse and Victimization Across the Life Span*. Baltimore, Md.: Johns Hopkins University Press, 1988.

Vaselle-Augenstein, R., & A. Ehrlich. "Male Batterers: Evidence for Psychopathology," 139–54. In E.C. Viano, ed. *Intimate Violence: Interdisciplinary Perspectives*. Bristol, Pa.: Taylor & Francis, 1992.

Vivian, D., & K. D. O'Leary. *Communication Patterns in Physically Aggressive Engaged Couples*. Paper presented at the Third National Family Violence Research Conference, Durham, N.H., July 1987.

Walker, L. *The Battered Woman*. New York: Harper & Row, 1979.

Wallace, R., & A. Nosko. "Working with Shame in the Group Treatment of Male Batterers." *International Group Psychotherapy* 43 (1993): 45–61.

Walters, G.D. "A Meta-Analysis of the Gene-Crime Relationship." *Criminology* 30 (1992): 595–613.

Warnken, W. J., A. Rosenbaum, K. E. Fletcher, S. K. Hoge, & S. A. Adelman. "Head-Injured Males: A Population at Risk for Relationship Aggression." *Violence and Victims* 9 (1994): 153–66.

Wasileski, M., M. E. Callaghan-Chaffee, & R. B. Chaffee. "Spousal Violence in Military Homes: An Initial Survey." *Military Medicine* 147 (1982): 761–65.

Watts, D. L., & C. A. Courtois. "Trends in the Treatment of Men Who Commit Violence against Women." *Personnel and Guidance Journal* 60 (1981): 245–49.

Wetzel, L., & M. A. Ross. "Psychological and Social Ramifications of Battering: Observations Leading to a Counseling Methodology for Victims of Domestic Violence." *Personnel and Guidance Journal* 61 (1983): 423–28.

Widom, C. S. "Does Violence Beget Violence? A Critical Examination of the Literature." *Psychological Bulletin* 106 (1989): 3–28.

Willbach, D. "Ethics and Family Therapy: The Case Management of Family Violence." *Journal of Marital and Family Therapy* 15 (1989): 43–52.

Wilson, J., & R. Herrnstein. *Crime and Human Nature*. New York: Simon & Schuster, 1985.

Zubretsky, T. M., & K. M. Digirolamo. "Adult Domestic Violence: The Alcohol Connection." *Violence Update* 4, 7 (March 1994): 1–2, 4, 8.

# Chapter 30

# *Batterer Programs*

*Kerry Murphy Healey and Christine Smith*

In the late 1970s, activists working with battered women realized that although they might help individual victims, no real progress could be made in reducing the problem of domestic violence unless steps were taken to reform perpetrators and challenge the cultural and legal supports for battering. Batterer intervention programs were established as a first step in changing offenders' behavior and increasing awareness of the problem. For their part, criminal justice agencies have responded by referring an increasing number of batterers to these programs, through pretrial or diversion programs or as part of sentencing.

Although requiring batterers to participate in programs to deter further violence is fast becoming an integral part of the response to domestic violence in many jurisdictions, judges and probation officers may lack sufficient information about the content and structure of these local programs and their goals and methods. In addition, the complexity of state guidelines and standards for batterer programs and the seriousness of the ongoing threat to battered women when offenders' cases are mishandled suggest the need for criminal justice professionals to be knowledgeable about the types of interventions available.

U.S. Department of Justice, National Institute of Justice document no. NCJ 171683. July 1998.

This report is intended to bridge the information gap and thereby enable criminal justice professionals to make informed choices among programs and communicate more effectively with program providers. Program staff should find the report useful as an explanation of the constraints faced by the criminal justice system, its procedures, and its underlying goals—to protect victims and to deter reoffending. In this way, the information should help staff to better align their program practice with criminal justice expectations.

After exploring the nature and causes of domestic violence, the report describes the batterer interventions currently in operation— the larger, "mainstream" programs as well as innovative interventions being explored—examines the theories on which they are based, reviews the most critical issues being debated, and examines criminal justice practices that can improve batterer intervention. The information was obtained from observation of several batterer intervention programs; interviews with program directors, criminal justice professionals, and academics; and extensive review of documents. (See "Sources of Information for the Study.")

## The Nature and Impact of Domestic Violence

Although the legal definition of battering varies from state to state, many intervention providers explain it as a constellation of physical, sexual, and psychological abuses that may include physical violence, intimidation, threats, emotional abuse, isolation, sexual abuse, manipulation, using the children as pawns, economic coercion, and the assertion of male privilege.[1] Only some of these behaviors—most commonly, physical and sexual assault—are illegal in and of themselves.

The cost of domestic violence to society and to the victims is immense. Battering results in physical and psychological injury and sometimes even death; prenatal injuries; physical and psychological harm to children exposed to violence; increased homelessness among women and children; higher health care costs; and corresponding increases in the demands for social, medical, and criminal justice services. Much of the toll is not calculated because, in the estimate of some researchers, as many as six in seven domestic assaults go unreported.[2]

### Who Batters?

Although similar proportions of men and women admit to engaging in violence against their partner,[3] the majority of batterers *ar-*

*rested* are heterosexual men.[4] Prosecutors and probation officers interviewed estimated that between 5 and 15 percent are women, although many are thought to be "self-defending victims" who have been mistakenly arrested as primary or mutual aggressors.[5] A small percentage of those arrested for battering are gay or lesbian.

Efforts to identify key demographic, psychological, and criminal characteristics of men who batter have led some researchers to propose profiles or "typologies" of these men. These tools could help criminal justice professionals and service providers better predict the level of danger and the potential of batterers for reoffending, as well as match batterers with specialized forms of intervention.

### Who Are the Victims?

The victims of battering are disproportionately women. In a single recent year, almost 1 million women, in contrast to 148,000 men, were victimized by intimates (boyfriend, girlfriend, spouse, or ex-spouse).[6] A similar disproportionality holds for murders attributed to intimates: in three of every four instances, the victim was female.[7]

Race is one of the factors that determine the chances a woman will be the victim of intimate violence. African-American women are more likely than women of other races to be victimized, as are women who live in urban areas.[8] Intimate victimization affects younger women (ages 16–24) most frequently.[9] Moreover, the classlessness of domestic violence is a myth, because victims also tend to be poor, with family incomes under $7,000.[10] It may be, however, that victimization of lower income women is more likely to be reported to the police, since women with higher incomes and more status in the community have the resources to deal with domestic violence privately without involving the criminal justice system.[11]

Domestic violence is also associated with low marriage rates, high unemployment, and social problems,[12] and, according to the intervention providers interviewed for this report, women in cross-cultural relationships may also be at unusually high risk.[13] The last factor may be due to cultural differences in expectations about sex roles and acceptable behavior.

## What Works to Stop Battering?

Although some evaluations of batterer interventions have been conducted, researchers concur that the majority of these studies are, inconclusive because of methodological problems.[14] Among the few considered methodologically sound, the majority have found modest but statistically significant reductions in recidivism among men participating in batterer interventions. Frustration with the lack of empirical evidence favoring one curriculum or length of treatment has led some researchers increasingly to look at batterers as a diverse group for whom specially tailored interventions may be the only effective approach.

At the same time, the question of how to evaluate batterer interventions may need to be reframed to include the broader context of criminal justice support. Even if research identifies the perfect match between interventions and offenders, criminal justice and community support will have a crucial impact on the effort's success. Research by Edward Gondolf, who is evaluating four sites in a study sponsored by the Centers for Disease Control and Prevention, points to the importance of systemwide assessments of batterer intervention.[15] Gondolf is particularly concerned about the often long delay between arrest and enrollment in a program. Systemwide evaluation could answer the question of whether the speed of the criminal justice response and program enrollment is more important than either program content or length.

## The Causes of Domestic Violence

The origins of domestic violence are the subject of intense debate. More than in most other fields, in disciplines and professions dealing with domestic violence the theoretical debate affects practice. Each of the three categories of domestic violence theory locates the causes differently: in society and culture (the feminist or profeminist model), in the family (the family systems or interactional model), or in the individual (the psychotherapeutic or cognitive-behavioral model). In the past two decades, a number of practitioners representing specific, divergent theoretical camps have begun to move toward a more integrated, "multidimensional" model of batterer intervention to better address the complexity of the problem. Very rarely do batterer programs reflect a single theory of domestic violence. Among the programs studied for this report, the majority combine elements of different theoretical models.

When criminal justice professionals work with batterer intervention providers, they will find it useful to understand the primary theory of domestic violence that the particular program espouses. It is also useful to understand the content of the intervention programs, which may draw on two or more theories. The mix of types leads experts to caution criminal justice agencies against uncritically accepting an eclectic curriculum and to aim for a coherent approach.

## Major Theories and Related Interventions

Because the three categories of theories dominating the field offer divergent explanations of the root causes of battering, they produce distinct intervention models with different strategies.

### Feminist Approaches

Batterer intervention programs were started in the 1970s when feminists and others brought public attention to the problem of domestic violence and grassroots services began to be established in response. The feminist perspective has influenced most batterer intervention programs. Central to the perspective is a gender analysis of power,[16] which holds that domestic violence mirrors the patriarchal organization of society. In this view, violence is one means of maintaining male power in the family. Feminist programs, which attempt to raise consciousness about society's sex-role conditioning and how it constrains men's behavior, present a model of egalitarian relationships based on trust instead of fear.

Support for the feminist analysis comes from the observation that most batterers, when "provoked" by someone more powerful than they, are able to control their anger and avoid resorting to violence. Further support comes from research showing that batterers are less secure in their masculinity than nonbatterers and from studies documenting the sense of entitlement batterers feel in controlling their partners' behavior.[17]

Critics claim the feminist perspective overemphasizes sociocultural factors to the exclusion of traits in the individual, such as growing up abused.[18] In their view, feminist theory predicts that *all* men will be abusive. Other criticisms hold that feminist educational interventions are too confrontational and as a result self-defeating because they alienate batterers, increase their hostility, and make them less likely to enter treatment. Another concern, revealed in some evaluations, is that the education central to the feminist program may transmit information but not deter violent behavior.

## The Family Systems Model

This model regards the problem behaviors of individuals as a manifestation of a dysfunctional family, with each family member contributing to the problem. Both partners may contribute to the escalation of conflict, with each striving to dominate the other. In this view, either partner may resort to violence. Intervention involves improving communication and conflict resolution skills, which both partners can develop. It focuses on solving the problem rather than identifying the causes.

Of particular concern to feminist and cognitive-behavioral proponents is the format of couples counseling espoused in the family systems model. They believe it can put the victim at risk if she expresses complaints, prevents a frank exchange between counselor and victim, and is conducive to victim-blaming. For these reasons, couples counseling is expressly prohibited in 20 state standards and guidelines for batterer intervention. (For a summary of what these standards cover, see "State Standards for Service Providers.")

## Psychotherapeutic Approaches

These perspectives, which focus on the individual, hold that personality disorders or early traumatic life experiences predispose some people to violence.[19] Being physically abusive is seen as symptomatic of an underlying emotional problem, which may be traced to parental abuse, rejection, and failure to meet a child's dependence needs.

From this perspective, two forms of batterer intervention—individual and group psychodynamic therapy and cognitive-behavioral group therapy—have evolved. The former involves uncovering the batterer's unconscious problem and resolving it consciously. Although a recent study revealed that the approach retained a higher percentage of men in treatment than did a feminist/cognitive-behavioral intervention,[20] critics fault psychodynamic therapy for not explaining what can be done to stop the behavior, allowing the behavior to continue until the underlying problem is solved,[21] and ignoring the cultural acceptability of male dominance.

The cognitive-behavioral approach focuses on the conscious rather than the unconscious and the present rather than the past to help batterers function better by modifying how they think and behave. The approach is compatible with a criminal justice response, simply addressing the violent acts and attempting to change them, without trying to solve larger issues of social inequality or delve into deep-seated psychological problems. Feminists fault the approach for failing to explain why many batterers are not violent in other relationships.

## Pioneering Programs and Their Models

Many of the larger, more established batterer intervention programs are based on the Duluth Curriculum. Other pioneers in batterer intervention, EMERGE and AMEND, share the Duluth Curriculum's basic structure but depart slightly from Duluth in technique and focus. All three of these long-established batterer interventions include a feminist educational approach and, to varying degrees, incorporate cognitive-behavioral techniques.

No single theoretical intervention model has yet proved more effective than any other in reducing recidivism.[22] For this reason, many program directors and criminal justice professionals stress structure over content. They believe that regardless of a program's philosophy or methods, any responsible intervention can help contain batterers' abuse by closely monitoring behavior. Thus it is important to highlight the common structural elements (procedures) of the programs studied for this report.

### *Program Procedures*

Program procedures used by all mainstream programs consist of intake and assessment, victim contact, orientation, group treatment (discussed in the section on "Program content," below), leaving the program, and completion.

**Intake and assessment.** The batterer's first contact with the program occurs when he arranges for an intake interview. First contact with program staff may occur at the courthouse, following contact with a probation officer. In a number of jurisdictions, however, it is the responsibility of the batterer to initiate program and probation contact. Intake assessment, which may last up to 8 weeks, is designed to convince the client to agree to the terms of the intervention, begin the behavior assessment, and screen for other problems. Ideally, the initial session begins to foster rapport between the clinician and the batterer.

Not all batterers are accepted at intake. The most common reason for denying service is that the batterer is part of a group that another program can serve better. For example, batterers who are found to have other problems (such as substance abuse or mental illness) may be referred elsewhere or to a program that addresses these issues in an integrated format. Another common reason for nonacceptance is unwillingness or inability to pay, although some programs offer assistance to those who cannot afford the intake fee and a sliding scale for payments. Some programs consider batterers inappropriate for treatment if they deny having committed violence. Apart from information gathering and initial instruction in program rules, overcoming denial is the primary task of intake.

**Victim contact.** A number of states require that partners be notified at various points in the intervention, and programs with a strong advocacy policy typically contact the partner every 2 or 3 months. Assessments and monitoring often involve separate interviews with the victim to obtain additional information about the relationship. Contacting the victim when the batterer enters the program ensures that she receives accurate information about program goals and methods, can raise her awareness of her situation, and provides her the opportunity to obtain help with safety planning. As part of the ongoing lethality assessment, the batterer's counselor will inform the victim and the probation officer if further abuse is imminent.

Raising the victim's awareness is a key component of victim contact. Just as important, however, is guarding her against false hope that the program can guarantee her partner will change. This caution needs to be balanced against respect for the victim's right to make her own decision, even if that involves remaining with the batterer.

**Orientation.** The assessment process continues during orientation, the initial phase of group intervention. New clients meet together for one or more sessions during which the reeducation process begins; at the same time, counselors more accurately appraise the extent of the batterer's problem. Orientation also establishes rapport between participants and counselors that can reduce the former's defensiveness. In this phase, program goals and rules for participating in the group are spelled out, and batterers are taught the program's underlying assumptions.

Orientation sessions tend to be more didactic than later sessions, which may take on more of a therapeutic tone. Their lecture format is intended to maintain order and avoid digression, as well as to establish norms for participation that can be carried over to the more informal groups. In the orientation sessions, counselors make clear that active participation is required.

**Leaving the program.** Batterers leave the program either because they complete it successfully or are asked to leave. Programs are cautious about terminating a batterer before completion because of the potential danger early release may pose to the victim. However, there are a number of reasons for termination, among them noncooperation, nonpayment of fees, or revocation of parole or probation. The most common reason for the threat of termination is not attending group sessions regularly. Another is violating crucial program rules (for example, being disruptive or aggressive).

Before resorting to termination, a warning may be issued or the batterer may be required to begin the program again. When clients do not attend sessions, or when clients with substance abuse problems fail to maintain sobriety, the probation officer may be informed.

**Completion.** Some programs have specific exit criteria that must be met before completion, such as requiring that the batterer write a "responsibility letter" acknowledging his behavior and read it to the group. In defining completion, some programs distinguish between mere attendance and the accomplishment of intervention goals. Either way, with court-mandated clients the final report to probation indicates whether the client has worked successfully in the program. Completion rates, however, tend to be low.[23] Some programs offer followup or aftercare for clients who complete the program successfully.

### Program Content

Depending on the type of program, the intervention consists of either a set educational curriculum or less structured discussions centered on relationships, anger management skills, or group psychotherapy. The group therapy modality is the intervention of choice.[24]

Of the three mainstream program models, the Duluth Curriculum uses a classroom format to focus on issues of power and control. Violence is viewed as linked to male power and control, and the development of critical thinking skills is emphasized to help batterers understand and change their behavior. By contrast, the two other mainstream models—EMERGE and AMEND—include more indepth counseling and are longer term. As with the Duluth Curriculum, reeducation and skills building are part of these models, but their founders hold that psychoeducational approaches alone do not address the full problem. Thus, EMERGE and AMEND combine cognitive-behavioral techniques with confrontational group processes that force the batterer to accept responsibility for his behavior.

## *The Duluth Curriculum*

Many batterer intervention programs adhere to, or borrow from, a psychoeducational and skills-building curriculum that is a component of the Duluth model developed in the early 1980s by the Domestic Abuse

---

### *State Standards for Service Providers*

As of 1996, more than half the states and the District of Columbia had adopted standards or guidelines governing programs or individuals providing batterer intervention, and 13 others were developing them.

**What the standards govern.** Most standards are designed to institutionalize the current norms of mainstream batterer interventions. They may specify the agency that certifies programs; prescribe the interval for certification renewal; indicate what the court contact or referral, the length of treatment, the screening criteria, and the fee should be; and stipulate elements of program content, such as the curriculum and structure.

**Accommodating innovation.** Local networks of intervention programs and criminal justice agencies that are developing standards may want to avoid standards that stifle innovation. Not enough is known about the efficacy of current interventions to avoid creating new standards that may not accommodate innovation. Ideally, standards should be crafted to foster innovation while providing safeguards for victims. State and local boards governing batterer intervention providers could provide oversight and evaluation of newly proposed interventions and integrate the findings into their practice models. Better evaluations of existing programs would allow standards to focus on performance-based outcomes.

State standards may be controversial because of concern that they result in a "cookie cutter" approach to intervention (when research points to the need for diverse approaches). On the other hand, some advocates argue that having no standards might be more dangerous than having overly restrictive ones.

Intervention Project of Duluth, Minnesota. The model places battering within a broader context of a range of controlling tactics such as intimidation, coercion, threats, and social isolation[25] and emphasizes the importance of a coordinated community response to the problem.

The preset curriculum is taught in classes that emphasize the development of critical thinking skills around several themes, including nonviolence, respect, support, trust, partnership, and negotiation. Two or three sessions are spent on each theme. For each theme, the first session begins with a video demonstration of the specific controlling behavior being highlighted. Discussion centers on the actions used by the batterer depicted in the demonstration to control his partner. During subsequent sessions devoted to the theme, each group member describes his own use of the controlling behavior. Alternative behaviors are then explored.

## EMERGE

EMERGE, of Cambridge, Massachusetts, begins intervention with an orientation phase consisting of educational and skills-building sessions. Clients who complete this phase and admit to domestic violence graduate to an ongoing group that blends cognitive-behavioral techniques with group therapy centered on accountability. The approach is more flexible and interactive than that of programs based on the Duluth model, which uses a preset curriculum.

The programs begin with a long "check-in" conducted in the group session led by a facilitator. New members introduce themselves, describe the incident that brought them to the program, and admit their violence. They are then asked questions that elicit details about the acts of violence they committed. Short check-ins for regular group members follow, centering on their actions of the previous week. There may then be discussion of incidents disclosed by a group member during check-in.

EMERGE focuses on the broader relationship between the batterer and the victim—not simply the abusive behavior. One technique promoting this approach is to require that a client refer to his partner by her first name rather than by her relationship to him (e.g., "my wife") to avoid perceiving her as an object or possession. Each client develops goals that address his favored control tactics, such as behavior signifying extreme jealousy. In establishing the goals, the partner's concerns are incorporated, and the group helps the client develop ways to address these concerns.

## AMEND

AMEND aims to establish client accountability, increase awareness of the social context of battering, and build new skills. Its group therapists use the Duluth cognitive-behavioral techniques, but whereas the ordinary therapy group might try to support the client and help him express his feelings, AMEND group leaders serve as "moral guides" who take directive, value-laden positions—in particular, a firm stand against violence.

AMEND's long-term approach has four stages. The first two consist of several months of education and confrontation intended to break through the batterer's denial. The third stage follows with several months of advanced group therapy in which the batterer begins to recognize his own rationalizations for his abusive behavior and to admit the truth.

Ongoing contacts with the partner are important, because they may be able to reveal relapses or more subtle forms of abuse. The last phase of recovery for those in the advanced group is the beginning of real change. Because this is a difficult time for the client, the group process takes on a more supportive tone. As the client prepares to end therapy, he is encouraged at this, the third stage, to develop a plan that includes a support network to avoid future violence. The fourth and final stage (an optional stage that few men enter) consists of involvement in community service and political action to stop domestic violence.

## Current Trends and Innovations

Practitioners and academics have long been concerned that "one size fits all" intervention is neither effective nor appropriate for the diverse population of batterers. To accommodate diversity, two categories of program refinements are emerging from practitioners' innovations and cooperative field research: those tailored to specific types of batterers ("batterer typologies"), based on psychological profiles or criminal histories, and those tailored to sociocultural differences such as poverty and ethnicity.

### Batterer typologies

Assuming there can be a consensus on groups of individual attributes (typologies), questions remain about how to treat them and whether programs can be modified to meet the needs of every group. Feminist-based programs view the focus on psychological attributes unfavorably, and researchers do not agree on what a typology of batterers might look like.

Although psychological typologies are interesting from a theoretical standpoint, they do not yet offer much assistance to the criminal justice system because of the in-depth assessment needed to identify characteristics and the lack of typology-based interventions available. No consensus on psychological categories for batterers has emerged from the research community. Criminal justice-based typologies offer a more practical frontline approach.

The criminal justice system routinely categorizes offenders, making decisions about the danger they pose and the appropriateness of interventions. However, systematic assessment tools based on an articulated theory of batterer typology have not been available. Recent research may offer a practical, standardized approach that can aid criminal justice agencies in classifying offenders. Using demographic information, criminal histories, and substance abuse data, this research proposes several classification strategies[26] focused on predicting batterers' retention in treatment and the likelihood they will reoffend with the same or another victim.

Categorizing batterers on these two dimensions (risk of dropout and rearrest), researcher John Goldkamp was able to draw some potentially useful distinctions among offenders. For example, he found that more than one-third of the batterers he studied fell into the lowest dropout risk and lowest same-victim rearrest categories. In other words, they should be good treatment prospects and pose little risk to their battering victims. He also found, however, that some offenders who pose little threat to the victim are not likely to stay in treatment.[27] This type of analysis could be helpful to probation officers, prosecutors, and judges in sentencing and assigning batterers to programs (after which there would be additional intake assessment).

### *Tailoring interventions to cultural differences*

The batterer's socioeconomic status, racial or ethnic identity, country of origin, and sexual orientation can affect his expression of domestic violence and his response to treatment. (For example, although domestic violence may be found in all social milieus, there is evidence it is more prevalent among less affluent families.[28]) For this reason, some interventions adapt to accommodate these factors. All programs may be able to improve program retention and decrease resistance to treatment by adopting culturally sensitive approaches that accommodate race, ethnicity, gender, sexual orientation, and socioeconomic status.

**Culturally competent interventions.** Cultural competence in an organization refers to activities the organization undertakes to prepare itself to work with a culturally diverse client population and program efforts that demonstrate preparedness and willingness to work with this population.[29] Culturally competent interventions are those that draw on the strength of the culture, whether it is spirituality, a value placed on family, or communal social systems. Such interventions also address such problems as substance abuse and gender roles condoning wife abuse.

Batterer interventions need to become culturally competent if they are to retain minority referrals and improve minority participation. They can do so by building on the positive values and strengths of minority cultures and by tapping the solidarity felt by members of the same minority culture that can promote mutual support in the group. In sum, culturally competent interventions can be used to diversify and refine interventions.

**Programs for men of African descent.** Some see racially mixed batterer intervention groups as preferable because they believe battering has nothing to do with socioeconomic or race issues. Others reject these groups as allowing men to use cultural differences to avoid identifying with others in the group, thus escaping responsibility for battering. By contrast, African-American groups can enhance participation by enabling men to focus on what they did instead of on social injustice or racism.

If groups consist exclusively of African-Americans, the members are also able to avoid assuming roles that some whites in the group might ascribe to them. With a culturally focused curriculum, African-Americans are able to construct their own reality rather than accept the constructs and limitations society places on them.

**Issues for recent Asian immigrants.** Because of cultural barriers against speaking openly in a group, specialized groups for Asian batterers, who may be recent immigrants, may include initial individual counseling. One-on-one encounters may help avoid humiliating men whose culture places a high value on peer acceptance. The counselors in the programs visited for this report who work with Asian immigrants agreed that the men could not participate effectively in the standard Duluth-style intervention because many of them are averse to group work and abhor confrontation.

Certain cultural values can militate against treatment. According to counselors interviewed for this study who are themselves Asians, domestic abuse is regarded throughout Southeast Asia as a private matter and as socially acceptable; for this reason, some Asian batterers have great difficulty accepting that these behaviors are illegal in the United States. Notions of gender equality are difficult for both women and men to accept. To deal with these and other Asian cultural characteristics, the Asian counselors interviewed for this report had developed a non-confrontational, Socratic method of counseling batterers that relies heavily on metaphors, parables, and analogies.

**Latinos who speak Spanish.** Efforts to make a batterer intervention curriculum relevant to Spanish-speaking Latinos can flounder on the question of which specific Latino culture should be the focus. Because several cultural groups may share certain characteristics—an identity as immigrants, economic instability, and low literacy in their native language—batterer treatment can encompass all of them. In other cases, it is not feasible to create a group based on shared experiences. For example, it may not always be possible that the group leader be the same nationality as that of the participants. The short supply of culturally compatible facilitators is a serious issue for Latino batterer interventions.

Age is also an issue. Among Latino batterers there is a cultural gap between young and older men. Counselors see the young men as less family oriented, more dependent on male friends who portray positive ties with women as a weakness, and more violent.

Strategies used with Latino groups include discussing the batterer's distortion of the concept of "machismo," challenging ownership of the partner, countering excuses for battering based on cultural practices, and discussing and learning to understand the clients' complex family ties.

### Countering the specialized approach

The trend toward increased specialization in intervention is now being challenged by a model based on "attachment theory." As applied to batterers, the theory holds it is possible to develop positive emotions such as trust, intimacy, and commitment and thus overcome the anger, rooted in a sense of powerlessness or worthlessness, that triggers the offending behavior. The Compassion Workshop, based in Silver Spring, Maryland, which uses the model, employs cognitive restructuring to short-circuit the anger before it develops and replace it with compassion. The inclusion of several types of offenders—male and female heterosexual batterers, gay and lesbian batterers, victims, and child abusers—in the same program is one reason the Compassion Workshop is controversial.

## The Criminal Justice Response

Batterer intervention programs alone cannot be expected to deter domestic violence; strong criminal justice support is also needed. The combined impact of arrest, incarceration, adjudication, and probation supervision may send a stronger message to the batterer about the seriousness of his behavior than what is taught in an intervention program. Intervention programs rely on criminal justice support to add force to their work. That support needs to be coordinated systemwide. Coordination is important because victims can be endangered by any breakdown in communication, failure of training, or lack of followthrough by agency representatives.

### Principal Features of a Coordinated, Systemwide Response

In addition to coordination among agencies, the principal features of a supportive criminal justice system include use of victim advocates throughout the system, designation of special units or individuals, and provision of training. To be effective, the response will extend to all components of the system, from law enforcement through probation officers. (See "Key Components of an Integrated Criminal Justice Response to Battering.")

### Criminal justice issues affecting batterer intervention

A number of systemwide issues have an indirect but serious impact on the efficacy of batterer intervention. The experience of the programs studied for this report suggests that by addressing these issues, the criminal justice system can support intervention. The first issue is the time between sentencing and program enrollment, which even in ideal circumstances averages 6 weeks but may take as long as several months. Whatever the cause, if the criminal justice system tolerates slow compliance and noncompliance, it creates an appearance of unconcern for the crime and may also endanger the victim.

Additional actions can be taken at all points in the criminal justice system:

- Probation officers and program directors contacted for this report indicate that tracking participants can be made more efficient. In many jurisdictions, referral practices that give probationers a wide choice of programs may make it difficult to track enrollment. A better approach might be to allow probation officers to assign batterers to a specific intervention.

- Centralized dockets created to handle domestic violence cases present a number of advantages for service delivery. Prosecutors can save time by not having to travel from court to court; probation units located nearby can receive court referrals quickly; judges can become expert in domestic violence issues; and court-based victim advocates would have access to a facility in or near the court to provide support and services for victims.

- Accurate, complete information about the defendant is key to successful adjudication. If they are to make proper decisions concerning plea bargains, sentencing, bail, and supervision, prosecutors, judges, and probation officers need information about previous arrests, substance abuse history, involvement with child protective services, and experience with batterer intervention.

- Opportunities for coordination by the criminal justice system include integrating batterer intervention with court-ordered substance abuse treatment. For cases in which the batterer has a substance abuse problem, courts can mandate not only treatment but also batterer intervention, with probation officers intensively monitoring compliance with treatment. Additionally, at the court level, judges and probation officers can be alert to the danger posed by domestic violence to children and coordinate with child protective services and programs that specialize in domestically abusive families to ensure that batterers' children are safe.

- Low-risk male heterosexuals may be the category of batterer most amenable to standard intervention, but they are not the only category of batterers. Program options are needed for the full range of batterers. Many program providers and probation officers interviewed for this report voiced concern that only a fraction of convicted batterers ever enter interventions. It would be useful if probation officers could work with local intervention providers, when needed, to develop sentencing options for different categories of batterers that include treatment. As sentencing and program options for a fuller range of batterers are developed, they are optimally followed by assessment tools to assign them to appropriate interventions.

## Key Components of an Integrated Criminal Justice Response to Battering[a]

A coordinated, systemwide response to battering, extending from arrest through probation or parole, can reinforce the message of batterer programs and motivate batterers to comply with treatment. The principal features are as follows:

- **Law enforcement.** Officers can be trained to increase their sensitivity to the needs of victims and thoroughly investigate allegations of violence. They can increase their effectiveness if they enforce bench warrants issued for batterers who have violated the terms of their probation.[b]

- **Pretrial screening.** Offenders can be screened before trial to ensure they are not released on their own recognizance or on bail before arraignment. Pretrial services staff can gather as much background information as possible for the prosecutor and judge.

- **Prosecutors.** Some prosecutors can specialize in domestic violence cases. Domestic violence prosecutors need to receive adequate support from police, probation officers, and victim advocates to follow through on cases. Other steps prosecutors can take include pursuing cases without victim testimony, if necessary; using "vertical prosecution"; keeping files containing such information as previous arrests and convictions; using victim advocates to aid in case preparation; pursuing probation revocation; and requesting offender participation in batterer intervention programs as a condition of probation or other sentence.

- **Victim advocates.** Victim advocates could be made available at all stages of the criminal justice process. Based in the specialized criminal justice units, they would contact the victim as soon as possible, explain the criminal justice system, gather evidence, assist with safety planning, and notify the victim of key events in the case. They could also make their case history records available to prosecutors.

- **Judges.** Judges could be assigned to specialized domestic violence dockets and issue sentences that include jail time, mandatory participation in batterer intervention programs, or other sanctions. Judges could be most effective if they respond forcefully to batterers who do not abide by the terms of their sentences; make referrals to appropriate programs; are familiar with state standards for batterer programs; and keep alert to possible co-occurrence of battering and child abuse. Courts could process domestic violence cases quickly and require prompt enrollment in programs when this is part of the sentence.

- **Probation officers.** If organized in specialized units with reduced caseloads, probation officers could provide intensive probation supervision. To supervise batterers as effectively as possible, probation officers could increase their understanding of domestic violence issues, batterer interventions, and emerging batterer typologies. Thoroughly prepared presentencing reports are a necessity, as is quickly obtaining information about batterers sentenced to probation, monitoring sobriety through urine screens, and developing assessment tools or referral policies to assist in assigning batterers to programs. Probation officers could also take the lead in establishing meetings with batterer intervention service providers.

### Notes

[a]For a more detailed description of an integrated criminal justice response to domestic violence, see Gelb, A., *The Quincy Court Model Domestic Abuse Program Manual,* Swampscott, MA: Production Specialists, n.d.

[b]Because enforcement commonly has little or no direct contact with batterer intervention programs, this report does not include an indepth discussion of the police response to domestic violence.

## *The Key Role of Probation: Supervision*

Probation officers are the most critical link between the criminal justice system and batterer interventions.[30] Assigning them to specialized units dedicated to domestic violence cases can help them do a better job, although many who work in such units still feel their caseloads are too heavy to provide the necessary services and supervision. If caseloads were reduced, officers could work closely with victims, who may have special needs. Probation officers may also have to face the problem of how to intervene with clients who are refused service.

In one program visited for this study, the probation department emphasizes coordination among other criminal justice agencies, batterer intervention programs, substance abuse treatment programs, social services, victim advocates, and the community.[31] Key department policies include preparation of thorough presentencing reports urging judges to impose strict probation conditions, maximum-intensity supervision, and rigorous monitoring of compliance. This program also emphasizes substance abuse as a factor exacerbating recidivism.

### Collaboration among Community Partners

The greatest contribution batterer intervention programs make may not be with individual offenders but with their ability to bring together major actors in the criminal justice and community services sectors to work together to reduce domestic violence. This collaboration can be informal, taking the form of monthly meetings of probation officers, program providers, and victim advocates to discuss issues of mutual concern. Less frequently, such meetings could be held with domestic violence committees in neighboring jurisdictions to exchange information.

Criminal justice agencies can also work with the city- or county-level committees that in a number of communities are charged with coordinating domestic violence policy. Some of these committees make policy; others are a forum for information exchange. In some states, they are empowered by state standards to certify batterer interventions.

At the state level, criminal justice agencies can work with state committees and task forces on domestic violence that address policy issues such as legal reforms. These committees may also be charged with developing drafts of standards for certification of batterer interventions.

## Notes

1. These elements common to abusive behavior are reflected in the definitions of domestic violence developed by two major practitioners. The definition developed by Anne Ganley, one of the first mental health providers to establish a batterer treatment program, is in her "Understanding Domestic Violence," in *Improving the Health Care Response to Domestic Violence: A Resource Manual for Health Care Providers*, produced by the Family Violence Prevention Fund and the Pennsylvania Coalition Against Domestic Violence, n.d. The feminist perspective is summarized in the model pioneered by Ellen Pence of Duluth, Minnesota ("The Power and Control Wheel"). See Pence, E., "Batterers' Programs: Shifting from Community Collusion to Community Con-

frontation," unpublished monograph, Duluth, MN: Domestic Abuse Intervention Project, February 1988.

2.  *Statistics Packet: Third Edition,* Philadelphia: National Clearinghouse for the Defense of Battered Women, February 1994.

3.  Crowell, Nancy, and Ann Burgess, eds., *Understanding Violence Against Women,* Washington, DC: National Academy Press, 1996: 32. In a recent study, Murray A. Straus offers an explanation for the discrepancy between evidence that men and women are approximately equal in their assault rates and evidence that men are more likely to assault than are women. He proposes that the latter evidence comes from studies that measure experiences more likely to result in physical injury, which in turn are more likely to be inflicted by men. Such studies, which Straus calls "crime studies," include the National Crime Victimization Survey and the National Violence Against Women in America study. They also reveal lower overall rates of assault than do the other, "family conflict" studies. See Straus, Murray A., "The Controversy over Domestic Violence by Women: A Methodological, Theoretical, and Sociology of Science Analysis," in *Violence in Intimate Relationships,* ed. X. B. Arriaga and S. Oskamp, Thousand Oaks, CA: Sage Publications, 1999.

4.  Because the majority of interventions discussed here are designed for male batterers, the term "batterer" will be matched with a male pronoun unless female offenders specifically are being discussed.

5.  Goldkamp, J. S., *The Role of Drug and Alcohol Abuse in Domestic Violence and Its Treatment: Dade County's Domestic Violence Court Experiment, Final Report,* Philadelphia: Crime and Justice Research Institute, June 1996; Busey, Tina, "Treatment of Women Defendants," *The Catalyst* (Spring 1993): 3–4; and Busey, Tina, "Women Defendants and Reactive Survival Syndrome," *The Catalyst* (Winter 1993): 6–7.

6.  Greenfeld, Lawrence A., et al., *Violence by Intimates: Analysis of Data on Crimes by Current or Former Spouses, Boyfriends, and Girlfriends,* Bureau of Justice Statistics Factbook, Washington, DC: U.S. Department of Justice, Bureau of Justice Statistics, March 1998: v, NCJ 167237.

7. Ibid.

8. Ibid: 13, 14. Crowell and Burgess (*Understanding Violence Against Women*) also note the higher rates of intimate homicide of African-American women (page 27).

9. Greenfeld, *Violence by Intimates*: 13.

10. Ibid: 14.

11. See Butler, C., "Myths about Woman Abuse," in *For Shelter and Beyond,* 2d ed., Boston: Massachusetts Coalition of Battered Women's Groups, n.d.: 21.

12. Belluck, Pam, "A Woman's Killer Is Likely to Be Her Partner, a New Study in New York Finds," *New, York Times,* March 31, 1997.

13. See Linn, M. W. L., and C. I. Tan, "Holding up More Than Half the Heavens: Domestic Violence in Our Communities, A Call for Justice," in *The State of Asian America: Activism and Resistance in the 1990s,* ed. K. Aguilar-San Juan, Boston: South End Press, n.d.: 321.

14. For a recent analysis of evaluations of batterer treatment programs, see Davis, Robert C., and Bruce G. Taylor, *Does Batterer Treatment Reduce Violence? A Synthesis of the Literature,* unpublished paper, February 24, 1998. (The research was conducted for Victim Services and sponsored by the National Institute of Justice.) There is also a discussion in *Violence in Families: Assessing Prevention and Treatment Programs,* ed. Rosemary Chalk and Patricia A. King, Washington, DC: National Academy Press, 1998: 178–80.

15. Interview with Edward Gondolf, October 22, 1996.

16. Pence, E., and M. Paymar, *Education Groups for Men Who Batter: The Duluth Model,* New York: Springer, 1993.

17. Gondolf, E.W., and J. Hanneken, "The Gender Warrior: Reformed Batterers on Abuse, Treatment, and Change," *Journal of Family Violence* 2(2)(1987): 177–91.

18. Dutton, D., "Patriarchy and Wife Assault: The Ecological Fallacy," *Violence and Victims* 9(2)(1994): 167–82.

19. Russell, M., "Wife Assault Theory, Research, and Treatment: A Literature Review," *Journal of Family Violence* 3(3) (1988): 193–208.

20. Browne, K., D. G. Saunders, and K. M. Staecker, "Process-Psychodynamic Groups for Men Who Batter: Description of a Brief Treatment Model," unpublished manuscript, University of Michigan, January 26, 1996.

21. Dutton, "Patriarchy and Wife Assault"; and Adams, D., "Treatment Models for Men Who Batter: A Profeminist Analysis," in *Feminist Perspectives on Wife Abuse,* ed. K. Yllö and M. Bograd. Newbury Park, CA: Sage Publications, 1988.

22. See Browne, Saunders, and Staecker, "Process-Psychodynamic Groups for Men Who Batter," and Gondolf, E.W., "Multi-Site Evaluation of Batterer Intervention Systems: A Summary of Preliminary Findings," manuscript, Mid-Atlantic Training Institute, October 24, 1996.

23. Eisikovits, Z. C., and J. L. Edelson, "Intervening with Men Who Batter: A Critical Review of the Literature," *Social Service Review* 37(1989): 384–414; and Feazell, C. S., R. S. Mayers, and J. Deschner, "Service for Men Who Batter: Implications for Programs and Policies." *Family Relations* 33(1984): 217–23.

24. Gondolf E.W., *Men Who Batter: An Integrated Approach to Stopping Wife Abuse,* Holmes Beach, FL: Learning Publications, Inc., 1985. The group is the modality of choice because it combats implicit approval of abuse perceived to be held by people outside the group, because successful group members can serve as role models, and because the group functions as a source of support for the offender.

25. Paymar, M., *Violent No More: Helping Men End Domestic Abuse,* Alameda, CA: Hunter House, Inc., 1993; and Pence, E., "Batterers' Programs: Shifting from Community Collusion to Community Confrontation."

26. Goldkamp, *The Role of Drug and Alcohol Abuse.*

27. Ibid.: 202. Gondolf developed a computerized method for scoring risk of dropout and arrest.

28. Straus, M., R. Gelles, and S. Steinmetz, *Behind Closed Doors: Violence in the American Family,* New York: Doubleday, 1980.

29. Williams, O., and L. Becker, "Domestic Partner Abuse Treatment Programs and Cultural Competence: The Results of a National Survey." *Violence and Victims* 9(3) (1994): 287–96.

30. Probation officers are involved in the majority of court-mandated batterer treatment cases, but in many other cases this is not so.

31. Gelb, A., *The Quincy Court Model Domestic Abuse Program Manual,* Swampscott, MA: Production Specialties, n.d.

## *Sources of Information for the Study*

Information was obtained from observations of batterer intervention programs and a number of other sources, including interviews with key program directors and staff and a review of the literature on the topic. All data on program enrollment, completion, and success rates were provided by the staff of the programs discussed in this report. The 13 programs in five states that were selected for this study represent a range of approaches:

- EMERGE, in Quincy, Massachusetts, and AMEND, in Denver, two of the largest and most established programs, are modified continually to keep up with the most recent trends in batterer intervention.

- Domestic Abuse Intervention Services of Des Moines is based on the "Duluth model."

- Family Services of Seattle, also based on the Duluth model, serves low-income clients.

- Harborview Medical Center, in Seattle, is based on a public health model of intervention.

- House of Ruth, in Baltimore, is based on the Duluth model and serves interracial clients.

- The Third Path, in Arapahoe County, Colorado, treats high-risk offenders based on a batterer typology and using psychological approaches.

- The Compassion Workshop, in Silver Spring, Maryland, uses cognitive restructuring techniques to address "attachment abuse."

In addition to these eight, five smaller programs serving specialized populations were studied in Seattle. They are discussed in the section "Current Trends and Innovations."

Other sources of information were as follows:

- Telephone interviews with directors of 22 batterer intervention programs located throughout the country.

- Interviews with more than 60 criminal justice professionals, batterer program directors and service providers, battered women's advocates, and domestic violence policymakers at the sites of the 13 programs.

- Interviews with experts in the field of batterer intervention from institutions of higher education throughout the country.

- Review of the literature and of state and local criminal justice protocols on batterer intervention.

Information was also obtained from observing training programs and from presentations on domestic violence policy for service providers and criminal justice professionals.

## *About the Authors*

*Kerry Murphy Healey, Ph.D., is a consultant with Abt Associates Inc., and Christine Smith is a Senior Analyst with Abt. The study was conducted under NIJ contract OJP–94–C–007. The full report on which this summary was based,* Batterer Intervention: Program Approaches and Criminal Justice Strategies *(Issues and Practices, National Institute of Justice, February 1998, NCJ 168638), is available from the National Criminal Justice Reference Service, 800-851-3420, and can be downloaded from the NIJ Web site at www.ojp.usdoj.gov/nij. The full report contains a chapter on additional sources of information about batterer interventions.*

Chapter 31

# Childhood Victimization: Early Adversity, Later Psychopathology

*Cathy Spatz Widom*

Childhood physical abuse, sexual abuse, and neglect have both immediate and long-term effects. Different types of abuse have a range of consequences for a child's later physical and psychological well-being, cognitive development, and behavior. But there is another side to the issue: Because these crimes often occur against a background of more chronic adversity, in families with multiple problems, it may not be reasonable to assume that before being victimized the child enjoyed "well-being." Parental alcoholism, drug problems, and other inadequate social and family functioning are among the factors affecting the child's response to victimization. Gender differences add to the complexity. Disentangling all these factors is difficult, as researchers have found.

Clearly, more needs to be learned about the long-term consequences of childhood victimization and the processes linking it to outcomes later in life. This article discusses what is known from earlier studies and also presents the findings of more recent research.[1]

## Consequences and What Gives Rise to Them

Child maltreatment has physical, psychological, cognitive, and behavioral consequences. Physical consequences range from minor

U.S. Department of Justice, National Institute of Justice *Journal*, January 2000.

injuries to brain damage and even death. Psychological consequences range from chronic low self-esteem, anxiety, and depression to substance abuse and other self-destructive behavior and suicide attempts. Cognitive effects include attention problems, learning disorders, and poor school performance. Behavioral consequences range from poor peer relations to physical aggression and antisocial behavior to violent behavior. These consequences are influenced by such factors as gender differences and the context in which victimization occurs.

**Gender differences.** Differences between men and women in manifesting the effects of childhood victimization have received only limited attention from scholars. Some researchers, exploring how men and women differ in showing distress, have suggested there is some conformity to traditional notions of male and female behavior.[2] Some have noted that differences between men and women in manifesting the consequences of abuse may parallel gender differences in the way psychopathology is expressed. Thus, aggression (in males) and depression (in females) may express the same underlying distress, perhaps reflecting gender-specific strategies for maintaining self-esteem in the face of perceived rejection.[3]

Differences in the way boys and girls react to abuse have been reported in a few studies. In one, boys were found to have more externalizing and girls to have more internalizing symptoms.[4] An examination of depression and conduct disorders in sexually abused children revealed that girls were more likely than boys to develop depressive disorders and less likely to develop conduct disorders.[5]

**Family and community—the context.** The long-term impact of childhood trauma may depend on the larger—family or community—context.[6] In a study of children kidnapped and held underground, preexisting family pathology was identified as a factor in the victims' long-term adjustment. Four years after the incident, the children from troubled families were more maladjusted than those from healthier families.[7] The findings of other research were not as clear; rather, subsequent maladjustment was linked more to whether victimized children received appropriate play materials and maternal involvement than to whether they were abused.[8] Parental alcoholism is another contextual factor linked to child abuse[9] and to alcoholism later in life in the offspring.[10]

In the same way, practices of the community and the justice and social service systems may have long-term effects. Researchers have called attention to the ways in which children who are members of racial and ethnic minorities encounter discrimination, which diminishes their self-esteem and exacerbates the effects of victimization.[11] Elsewhere, researchers have suggested that victimized children are more likely to develop problem behavior in adolescence partly because of juvenile justice system practices that disproportionately label them as juvenile offenders and adjudicate them as such.[12]

## How the Study Is Being Conducted

The study is based on a "prospective cohort design," so-called because it follows a group of people (a cohort) for an extended period, enabling researchers to examine sequences of development over time. In the case of this study, the design helps sort out the effects of childhood victimization from other, potentially confounding effects traceable to different causes. The subjects were told they were part of a study of the characteristics of people who had grown up in the area in the late 1960s and early 1970s.

The cases of children who were abused and/or neglected were drawn from county juvenile and adult criminal court records in a metropolitan area of the Midwest between 1967 and 1971. The children were young—age 11 or younger—at the time of the incident.

*The comparison group.* To create a control group against which to compare the abused and neglected children, a group of children who had not been reported as victimized but who were similar in other respects to the study subjects were identified. To match children younger than school age at the time of the incident, county birth records were used. To match school-age children, records of more than 100 elementary schools were used.

*Sample size and characteristics.* The original sample consisted of 1,575 people, of whom 908 were study subjects and 667 were controls. Of these, 1,196 were interviewed for the study. Just under half the interviewees were female, about two-thirds were white, and the mean age at the time of the interview was 28.7. There were no differences between the abused/neglected group and the controls in gender, race/ethnicity, or age.

*Some caveats.* Because the study findings were based on court cases, they most likely represent the most extreme incidents of childhood abuse and neglect. What is more, they were processed before enactment of child abuse laws, when many cases went unreported and thus never came to the attention of the authorities. The findings are therefore not generalizable to unreported or unsubstantiated cases of abuse and neglect.

Because cases brought before the courts disproportionately represent people at the lower end of the socioeconomic spectrum, the study's subjects and controls were drawn from that stratum. For this reason, it would be inappropriate to generalize to cases involving people from other socioeconomic strata.

## Studying the Long-Term Effects in Depth

In a systematic study of the long-term consequences of early childhood abuse and neglect, the author is examining the experiences of more than 900 people who were victimized in childhood. Begun in 1986, the study first focused on the extent to which, as the victims grew into adulthood, they became involved in delinquency and crime, including violent crime.[13] The current focus is on how their intellectual, behavioral, social, and psychological development was affected. This second phase began in 1989, more than 20 years after the victimization. (See "How the Study Is Being Conducted.")

### *Figure 1: IQ Scores— Abused/Neglected Group and Control Group*

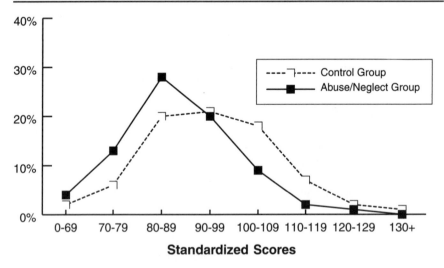

Standardized Scores

Note: Number = 1,185

IQ scores are based on the Quick Test. See Ammons, R.B., and Ammons, C.H., "The Quick Test (QT): Provisional Manual," *Psychological Reports* 11 (1962): 11–162 (monograph supplement 7-VII).

**Intellectual performance.** When tested at about age 29, the study subjects and the comparison group both scored at the lower levels of the IQ scale with the majority in both groups below the standard mean of 100 (see figure 1, page 780). Those who were abused or neglected, however, scored significantly lower than the comparison group, and these lower levels persisted irrespective of age, sex, race, and criminal history.

Overall, both groups averaged 11.5 years of schooling, but the abused and neglected group completed significantly fewer years. Thus, the childhood victims were less likely to have completed high school: Fewer than half, in contrast to two-thirds of the people in the control group.

**Behavioral and social development.** The occupations of both groups ranged from laborer through professional. In the sample overall, the median job level was that of semiskilled worker, with fewer than 7 percent in the two groups holding managerial or professional jobs (see figure 2). The abused and neglected individuals had not done as well as the control group: Significantly more of them held menial and semiskilled jobs. Conversely, a larger proportion of people in the

*Figure 2: Occupational Status—*
*Abused/Neglected Group and Control Group*

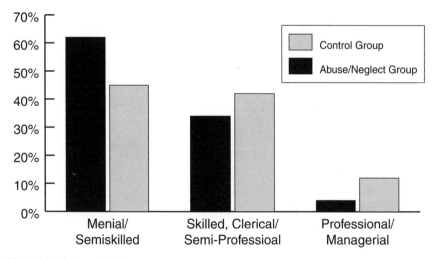

Note: Number = 1,167

Occupational status was coded according to the Hollingshead Occupational Coding Index. See Hollingshead, A.B., "Four Factor Index of Social Class," New Haven, CT: Yale University Working Paper, 1975.

control group held higher level jobs, ranging from skilled worker through professional.

Unemployment and underemployment disproportionately affected the abused and neglected group (see figure 3). In both groups, more than one-fifth had been unemployed in the 5-year period before they were interviewed for the study. Not surprisingly, people in the control group were more likely than the victims to be employed. For underemployment, the story is similar: Significantly more victims of childhood abuse and neglect were underemployed in the 5 years before the interview than were controls.

The quality of interpersonal relations also is affected by childhood victimization, and here again there are no surprises (see figure 4, page 783). Using marital stability as the measure of success, child abuse and neglect victims did not do as well as control group members. Almost 20 percent of the controls reported a stable marriage, compared to only 13 percent of the abuse and neglect group. Frequent divorce and separation were also more common among abused and neglected people.

As reported in previous research, childhood victimization also increases the risk of criminal behavior later in life—as measured by

### Figure 3: Employment History— Abused/Neglected Group and Control Group

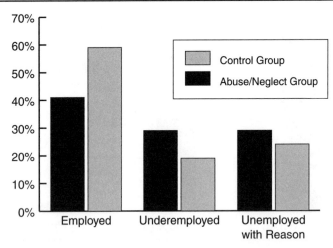

Note: Number = 1,196

Employment history findings are based on a measure used in Robins, L.N., and D.A. Regier, eds., *Psychiatric Disorders in America: The Epidemiological Catchment Area Surveys,* New York: Free Press, 1991: 103.

arrests for delinquency and adult criminality, including violent crime.[14] The current study confirms these findings. The odds of arrest for a juvenile offense were 1.9 times higher among abused and neglected individuals than among controls; for crimes committed as an adult, the odds were 1.6 times higher (see table 1, page 784). Childhood abuse or neglect increases the risk of being arrested for violent crime, whether in the juvenile or adult years, as well as for crime in general. It is perhaps most important to note, however, that a substantial proportion of the abused and neglected children did not become delinquents or criminals.

**Psychological and emotional fallout.** Suicide attempts, diagnosis of antisocial personality disorder, and alcohol abuse and/or dependence were some of the measures of psychopathology. The abused and neglected individuals were significantly more likely than the controls to have attempted suicide and to have met the criteria for antisocial personality disorder (see table 2, page 785), findings irrespective of age, sex, race, and criminal history. High rates of alcohol abuse were found in both groups (more than 50 percent in each), although the abuse/neglect victims were not at greater risk than the controls, a finding that departs from other research but that methodological differences might explain.[15]

*Figure 4: Marital History— Abused/Neglected Group and Control Group*

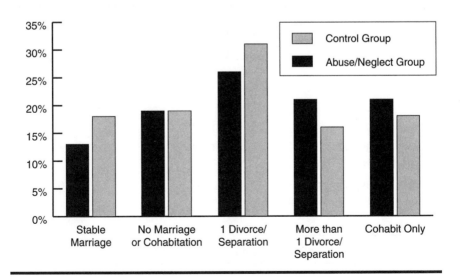

As other research has shown, gender can affect the development of psychopathology in abused and neglected children later in life. The current study revealed some of these gender-based differences. Females abused and neglected in childhood were more likely than controls to attempt suicide, to abuse alcohol or be dependent on it, or to suffer from an antisocial personality disorder. Like females, male victims were found at greater risk than controls of attempting suicide and developing an antisocial personality disorder, but they were not at greater risk of developing alcohol problems (see table 3, page 786).

The findings of males' higher risk for antisocial personality disorder and females' higher risk for alcohol problems parallel previous research revealing conformity to gender roles. However, the finding that females are, like males, at risk for antisocial personality disorder (as well as criminal behavior)[16] may call for reconsidering the assumptions of externalizing and internalizing as the respective pathways of male and female response.

**The context of victimization.** The findings confirmed earlier research identifying context as a factor influencing the long-term outcome for victims. This became evident in analyzing the relationships among childhood victimization, having a parent who had been arrested, and the likelihood of the offspring's developing antisocial personality disorder. The analysis revealed that among people who had a parent with a history of arrest, abuse or neglect in childhood

## *Table 1: Childhood Victimization and Later Criminality*

|  | Abuse/Neglect Group (676) | Control Group (520) |
|---|---|---|
|  | % | % |
| Arrest as juvenile | 31.2*** | 19.0 |
| Arrest as adult | 48.4*** | 36.2 |
| Arrest as juvenile or adult for any crime | 56.5*** | 42.5 |
| Arrest as juvenile or adult for any violent crime | 21.0* | 15.6 |

* p≤ .05 **p≤ .01 *** p≤ .001

Note: Numbers in parentheses are numbers of cases.

did not increase the likelihood of their developing an antisocial personality disorder (see table 4, page 787).

However, where there was no parental criminality, being abused and/or neglected did increase the risk for this disorder. This complicates attempts to understand the consequences of childhood victimization and also suggests multiple factors in the development of antisocial personality disorder.

A different picture and set of relationships were found for alcohol abuse. When parental alcohol/drug abuse, childhood victimization, and subsequent alcohol problems in offspring were analyzed, the parents' substance abuse problem emerged as the critical factor in the development of the same problem in the children, and this held true whether or not the child had been victimized (see table 5, page 787). The study also showed that, as a group, the children who were abused or neglected were no more likely than controls to develop alcohol problems, whether or not the parent had the same problem.

The strong influence of parental characteristics on the offspring, regardless of victimization, warrants more careful consideration, but is consistent with earlier literature on the genetic transmission of alcoholism.

## Multiple Mechanisms

The study generated more—and more systematic—evidence that the consequences of childhood victimization extend well beyond childhood

*Table 2: Childhood Victimization and Later Psychopathology*

| | Abuse/Neglect Group (676) | Control Group (520) |
|---|---|---|
| | % | % |
| Suicide attempt | 18.8*** | 7.7 |
| Antisocial personality disorder | 18.4*** | 11.2 |
| Alcohol abuse/dependence | 54.5*** | 51.0 |

*p≤ .05 **p≤.01 ***p≤ .001

Note: Numbers in parentheses are numbers of cases.

Diagnoses of antisocial personality disorder and alcohol abuse/dependence were determined by using the National Institute of Mental Health DIS-III-R diagnostic interview.

and adolescence, persisting into young adulthood. Such victimization affects many functions later in life, and what was revealed in this study most likely represents only the tip of the iceberg, which further research could bring to light. On the other hand, some expected outcomes (such as increased risk for alcohol problems in abused and neglected children) did not materialize, raising questions for further study.

**Disentangling the pathways.** One of the difficulties in assessing risk of negative consequences is sorting out the children's multiple problems and those of their parents. As previous research has shown, adverse effects interact, so that the combined effects of two types of problems may be greater than their sum.[17] Whether this interaction effect applies to childhood victimization is not known, although it is likely.

This study has not yet tried to distinguish among the many mechanisms by which childhood victimization affects development and psychopathology. When it comes to the influence of contextual factors, children may simply be modeling their parents' behavior. But it also is possible that abuse or neglect may produce immediate effects that then irremediably affect subsequent development, which in turn may affect still later outcomes.

*Table 3: Childhood Victimization and Later Psychopathology, by Gender*

|  | Abuse/Neglect Group | Control Group |
|---|---|---|
|  | % | % |
| Females | (338) | (224) |
| Suicide attempt | 24.3*** | 8.6 |
| Antisocial personality disorder | 9.8* | 4.9 |
| Alcohol abuse/dependence | 43.8** | 32.8 |
| Males | (338) | (276) |
| Suicide attempt | 13.4** | 6.9 |
| Antisocial personality disorder | 27.0** | 16.7 |
| Alcohol abuse/dependence | 64.4 | 67.0 |

*p≤ .05 **p≤ .01 ***p≤ .001

Note: Numbers in parentheses are numbers of cases.

Diagnoses of antisocial personality disorder and alcohol abuse/dependence were determined by using the National Institute of Mental Health DIS-III-R diagnostic interview.

### Table 4: Antisocial Personality Disorder in Offspring— Relation to Parental Criminality

|  | Abuse/Neglect Group | Control Group | Row Significance |
|---|---|---|---|
|  | % | % |  |
| Either parent arrested | 21.9 (365) | 18.8 (170) | n.s. |
| Neither parent arrested | 14.2 (365) | 7.4 (350) | *** |
| Column significance | * | *** |  |

*p≤ .05 **p≤ .01 ***p≤ .001 n.s. = not statistically significant.

Note: Numbers in parentheses are numbers of cases.

Diagnoses of antisocial personality disorder and alcohol abuse/dependence were determined by using the National Institute of Mental Health DIS-III-R diagnostic interview.

### Table 5: Alcohol Abuse/Dependence in Offspring—Relation to Parental alcohol/Drug Problems

|  | Abuse/Neglect Group | Control Group | Row Significance |
|---|---|---|---|
|  | % | % |  |
| Either parent alcohol/ drug problem | 63.2 (389) | 56.6 (196) | n.s. |
| Neither parent alcohol/ drug problem | 42.6 (284) | 47.5 (324) | n.s. |
| Column significance | *** | * |  |

*p≤ .05 **p≤ .01 ***p≤ .001 n.s. = not statistically significant.

Note: Numbers in parentheses are numbers of cases.

Diagnoses of antisocial personality disorder and alcohol abuse/dependence were determined by using the National Institute of Mental Health DIS-III-R diagnostic interview.

is likely that this path leads to abusive behavior in the home, manifested in spouse or child abuse. In other instances there may be a delayed reaction, occurring years later.

Abuse or neglect may encourage certain dysfunctional ways of coping. An example is impulsive behavior that in turn gives rise to deficiencies in problem solving or in school performance, less than adequate functioning on the job, or antisocial personality disorder. Adaptations that might serve well at one stage of development may no longer do so at a later stage, placing the person at risk for further unfavorable situations or subsequent victimization that may trigger psychopathology.

Some early, adverse experiences may be indirect, creating byproducts. They may change the environment or the family situation, which in turn may predispose a person to problem behavior. They also may expose the child to further harmful experiences. In this way, the consequences may be due not so much to the abuse or neglect, but to the chain of events it triggers.

No doubt there are many other mechanisms by which abuse and neglect affect a child. Hopefully, future models that explain long-term consequences will examine some of them, because finding a single mechanism that explains all cases of abuse and neglect is highly unlikely.

## *Notes*

1. This article summarizes the author's "Childhood Victimization: Early Adversity and Subsequent Psychopathology," in *Adversity Stress, and Psychopathology,* ed. B. P. Dohrenwend, New York: Oxford University Press, 1998: 81–95.

2. Downey, G., et al., "Maltreatment and Childhood Depression," in *Handbook of Depression in Children,* ed. W. M. Reynolds and H. F. Johnson, New York: Plenum, 1994: Dohrenwend, B. P., and B. S. Dohrenwend, "Sex Differences in Psychiatric Disorders," *American Journal of Sociology* 81 (1976): 1447–54 Horwitz, A. V., and H. R. White, "Gender Role Orientations and Styles of Pathology Among Adolescents," *Journal of Health and Social Behavior* 28 (1987):158–70: and Widom, C. S., "Sex Roles, Criminality, and Psychopathology," in *Sex Roles and Psychopathology,* ed. C. S. Widom, New York: Plenum, 1984: 87–213.

3. Downey et al., "Maltreatment and Childhood Depression."

4. Friedrich, W. H., A. J. Urquiza, and R. L. Beilke, "Behavior Problems in Sexually Abused Young Children," *Journal of Pediatric Psychology* 11 (1986): 47–57.

5. Livingston, R., "Sexually and Physically Abused Children," *Journal of the American Academy of Child and Adolescent Psychiatry* 26 (1987): 413–15.

6. Briere, J., and M. Runtz, "Symptomatology Associated With Childhood Sexual Victimization in a Nonclinical Adult Sample," *Child Abuse and Neglect* 12 (1988): 51–60; Harris, T., G. W. Brown, and A. Bifulco, "Loss of Parent in Childhood and Adult Psychiatric Disorder: A Tentative Overall Model," *Development and Psychopathology* 2 (1990): 311–28; Terr, L. A., "Chowchilla Revisited: The Effects of Psychiatric Trauma Four Years After a School-Bus Kidnapping," *American Journal of Psychiatry* 140 (1983): 1543–50.

7. Terr, "Chowchilla Revisited."

8. Gibbin, P. T., R. H. Starr, and S. W. Agronow, "Affective Behavior of Abused and Controlled Children: Comparison of Parent-Child Interactions and the Influence of Home Environment Variables," *Journal of Genetic Psychology* 144 (1984): 69–82.

9. Famularo, R., et al., "Alcoholism and Severe Child Maltreatment," *American Journal of Orthopsychiatry* 56 (1986):481–85; Reider, E. E., et al., "Alcohol Involvement and Violence Toward Children Among High-Risk Families," Paper presented at the annual meeting of the American Psychological Association, New Orleans, Louisiana, August 11–15,1989.

10. Goodwin, D. W., et al., "Alcohol Problems in Adoptees Raised Apart from Alcoholic Biological Parents," *Archives of General Psychiatry* 28 (1973): 238–43, Goodwin, D. W., et al., "Alcoholism and Depression in Adopted-Out Daughters of Alcoholics," *Archives of General Psychiatry* 34 (1977): 751–55; Cloninger, C. R., et al., "Psychopathology in Adopted-Out Children of Alcoholics: The Stockholm Adoption Study," in *Recent Developments in Alcoholism,* Vol. 3, M. Galanter, ed., New York: Plenum, 1985.

11. Wyatt, G. E., "Sexual Abuse of Ethnic Minority Children: Identifying Dimensions of Victimization," *Professional Psychology: Research and Practice* 21 (1990): 338–43.

12. Smith, C. P., D. J. Berkman, and W. M. Fraser, *A Preliminary National Assessment of Child Abuse and Neglect and the Juvenile Justice System: The Shadows of Distress,* Washington, D.C.: U.S. Department of Justice: Office of Juvenile Justice and Delinquency Prevention, 1980.

13. Widom, C. S., "The Cycle of Violence," *Science* 244 (1989): 160–66.

14. These findings, based on the study of 1,196 of the original 1,575 subjects (the 908 abuse/neglect victims plus the 667 in the control group), should not be confused with findings from studies published previously (Widom, "Cycle of Violence," and Maxfield, M. G., and C. S. Widom, "The Cycle of Violence: Revisited Six Years Later," *Archives of Pediatrics and Adolescent Medicine* 150 [1996]: 390–95), which report on the entire original sample of 1,575.

15. See Widom, C. S., T. Ireland, and P. J. Glynn, "Alcohol Abuse in Abused and Neglected Children Followed-Up: Are They at Increased Risk?" *Journal of Studies on Alcohol* 56 (1995): 207–17.

16. These findings are not shown here. See Maxfield and Widom, "The Cycle of Violence: Revisited."

17. Rutter, M., "Protective Factors in Children's Response to Stress and Disadvantage," in *Primary Prevention of Psychopathology: Social Competence in Children,* Vol. 3, ed. M. V. Kent and J. E. Rolf, Hanover, NH: New England Press, 1979: 49–74.

## About the Author

Cathy Spatz Widom is a professor of criminal justice and psychology at the State University of New York at Albany. She is widely recognized for her work on the cycle of violence.

The author wishes to thank Patricia J. Glynn and Suzanne Luu for their help in the preparation of this article.

The research described in this article was supported by grants from the U.S. Department of Justice, National Institute of Justice (86-IJ-CX-0033, 89-IJ-CX-0007, and 94-IJ-CX-0031), and the U.S. Department of Health and Human Services, National Institute on Alcohol Abuse and Alcoholism (AA09238) and National Institute of Mental Health (MH49467).

Chapter 32

# Victims of Childhood Sexual Abuse—Later Criminal Consequences

*Cathy Spatz Widom*

## Issues and Findings

Previous research established evidence for a "cycle of violence": people who were abused and neglected in childhood are more likely than those who were not to become involved in criminal behavior, including violent crime, later in life. This chapter examines the criminal consequences in adulthood of a particular type of childhood victimization: sexual abuse. It traces the same individuals studied initially, using official records of arrest and juvenile detention.

## Key Issues

- Whether sexual abuse—more than other forms of childhood victimization—makes people more likely to become involved in delinquent and criminal behavior later in life.

- Whether sexual abuse during childhood makes it more likely that these victims will be charged with a sex crime as an adult.

- Whether there is a pathway from being sexually abused as a child, to running away as a juvenile, to being arrested for prostitution as an adult.

U.S. Department of Justice, Office of Justice Programs, Publication No. NCJ 151525, March 1995. This publication is the second in a series of research briefs on the cycle of violence.

791

- People who were sexually victimized during childhood are at higher risk of arrest for committing crimes as adults, including sex crimes, than are people who did not suffer sexual or physical abuse or neglect during childhood. However, the risk of arrest for childhood sexual abuse victims as adults is no higher than for victims of other types of childhood abuse and neglect.

- The vast majority of childhood sexual abuse victims are not arrested for sex crimes or any other crimes as adults.

- Compared to victims of childhood physical abuse and neglect, victims of childhood sexual abuse are at greater risk of being arrested for one type of sex crime: prostitution.

- For the specific sex crimes of rape and sodomy, victims of physical abuse tended to be at greater risk for committing those crimes than were sexual abuse victims and people who had not been victimized.

- What might seem to be a logical progression from childhood sexual abuse to running away to prostitution was not borne out. The adults arrested for prostitution were not the runaways identified in this study.

### *Target Audience:*

Law enforcement officials, child protection service professionals, researchers, judges, family counselors, and victim service organizations and agencies.

Over the past 25 years, much has been written about the "cycle of violence" or the "intergenerational transmission of violence." These terms refer to the possible negative consequences later in life for children who are sexually or physically abused or neglected. These consequences include an increased potential for violent behavior. In earlier work the researcher examined criminal records on more than 1,500 individuals to determine whether the experience of abuse or neglect during childhood increased the likelihood of arrest as a juvenile or young adult. The research clearly revealed that a childhood history of physical abuse predisposes the survivor to violence in later years, and that victims of neglect are more likely to engage in later violent criminal behavior as well.

Of all types of childhood maltreatment, physical abuse was the most likely to be associated with arrest for a violent crime later in life. The group next most likely to be arrested for a violent offense were those who had experienced neglect in childhood, a finding of particular interest. Though a more "passive" form of maltreatment, neglect has been associated with an array of developmental problems, and the finding extended that array to include greater risk of later criminal violence.[1]

## Focus on Sexual Abuse

This chapter reports the findings from an analysis of a specific type of maltreatment—childhood sexual abuse—and its possible association with criminal behavior later in life.[2] Using the same cases of individuals studied previously, the researcher sought to find out whether those who had been sexually abused were more likely to engage in later delinquent and criminal behavior than those who had experienced the other types of abuse. Is there an "inevitable" or likely progression from being sexually victimized in childhood to being charged with an offense in adulthood, particularly sex offenses.

This examination is part of a two-phase study of the long-term consequences of childhood abuse and neglect. The findings reported here are from the first phase, which used the arrest records of juveniles and adults to measure the criminal consequences of being maltreated. In the second phase, now underway, interviews are being conducted in an attempt to draw a more complete picture of such consequences. The researcher is looking at criminal behavior that may not have been included in official records and at other negative outcomes, including mental health, educational, substance abuse, and other problems. (See Chapter 31.)

## Evidence from Other Studies

The link between childhood sexual abuse and negative consequences for the victims later in life has been examined in clinical reports and research studies in the past two decades. Frequently reported consequences include acting-out behaviors, such as running away, truancy, conduct disorder, delinquency, promiscuity, and inappropriate sexual behavior. Studies of prostitutes have also revealed an association between sexual abuse during childhood and deviant and criminal behavior.

These and other findings have been the basis for theories linking childhood sexual abuse to the development of deviant and criminal behavior later in life. Among researchers as well as clinicians, acceptance of this link is fairly widespread. However, as a review of research into the impact of childhood sexual abuse has indicated, the empirical evidence may not be sufficient to justify this acceptance.[3] And, a recent review of the long-term effects of childhood sexual abuse—which cited sexual disturbance, depression, suicide, revictimization, and postsexual abuse syndrome—noted criminal consequences only in passing.[4]

## The Need for a New Approach

The methods used to conduct these studies make interpretation difficult. For one thing, most used retrospective self-reports of adults who had been sexually abused as children; that is, they relied on the subjects' own recall. Retrospective accounts of sexual abuse may be subject to bias or error. For example, unconscious denial (or repression of traumatic events in childhood) may prevent recollection of severe cases of childhood sexual abuse. It is also possible that people forget or redefine their behaviors in accordance with later life circumstances and their current situation.

Another difficulty with these methods lies with their reliance on correlation. They involve data collection at only one point in time. In examining the relationship between sexual abuse and later delinquent behavior or adult criminality, it is important to ensure the correct temporal sequence of events; that is, to make certain that the incident of childhood sexual abuse clearly preceded (not followed) delinquency. Thus, multiple data collection points are needed. The few studies that do not rely on retrospection have investigated consequences only over relatively short periods of time.

Perhaps the most serious methodological shortcoming is the frequent lack of appropriate control or comparison groups. Childhood sexual abuse often occurs in the context of multiproblem homes, and sexual victimization of children may be only one of these problems. Without control groups, the effects of other family characteristics, such as poverty, unemployment, parental alcoholism or drug problems, or other inadequate social and family functioning, cannot be easily disentangled from the specific effects of sexual abuse.

## The Present Study

The study posed three questions designed to shed light on the possible long-term criminal consequences of childhood sexual abuse:

- **Is there a higher risk of criminal behavior later in life?**
  Compared to early childhood experiences of physical abuse and
  neglect (and also compared to children who did not experience
  maltreatment, at least as documented by official records), does
  sexual abuse in early childhood increase the risk of delinquent
  and criminal behavior?

- **Is there a higher risk of committing sex crimes?** Are childhood sexual abuse victims more likely to commit such crimes as
  prostitution, rape, and sodomy?

- **Is there a link between sexual abuse, running away, and
  prostitution?** Is there a significant and direct relationship between early childhood sexual abuse, being arrested as a runaway as an adolescent, and, in turn, being arrested for
  prostitution as an adult?

## How the Study was Conducted[5]

The study examined the official criminal histories of a large number of people whose sexual victimization during childhood had been
validated. These victims of sexual abuse were compared to cases of
physical abuse and neglect and to a control group of individuals who
were closely matched in age, race, sex, and approximate family socioeconomic status.

### The Groups Selected for Study

The subjects were 908 individuals who had been subjected as children to abuse (physical or sexual) or neglect, and whose cases were
processed through the courts between 1967 and 1971. All were 11
years of age or younger at the time of the incident(s).

The research used a "matched cohorts" design. Such studies involve
selecting groups of subjects who are similar (matched) to each other
but who differ in the characteristic being studied. The "cohort" of children who had been abused or neglected was matched with the control group, which consisted of children who had not been abused or
neglected.

Both groups were followed into adolescence and young adulthood
to determine if they had engaged in delinquent behavior or had committed crimes as adults. At the time they were chosen for the study,
none of them had as yet engaged in delinquent or criminal behavior.

The major aim of this analysis was to determine whether sexual abuse during childhood puts victims at greater risk for criminal behavior later in life than do the other types of maltreatment.

### Sources of Information about Maltreatment

Because it was important to use substantiated cases of physical and sexual abuse and neglect, the study relied on the official records of agencies that handled these cases. Detailed information about the abuse and/or neglect incident and family composition and character-istics of study subjects was obtained from the files of the juvenile court and probation department. The records of the sexual abuse cases were obtained from the juvenile court and from the adult criminal court of a metropolitan area in the Midwest.[6]

Like all sources of information, official records have certain limi-tations. Some incidents are not reported to law enforcement or social service agencies. Moreover, the cases studied were processed before the child abuse reporting laws were passed, when many cases of sexual abuse were not brought to the attention of the authorities. For these reasons, the findings cannot be interpreted as applying to all incidents. It is more likely that they represented only the serious and extreme cases—those brought to the attention of the social service and crimi-nal justice systems.

### Types of Maltreatment

The *sexual abuse* cases represented a variety of charges, from rela-tively nonspecific ones of "assault and battery with intent to gratify sexual desires" to more specific ones of "fondling or touching in an ob-scene manner," sodomy, incest, and the like. The *physical abuse* cases included those involving injuries such as bruises, welts, burns, abra-sions, lacerations, wounds, cuts, bone and skull fractures. The *neglect cases* reflected the judgment of the court that the parents' deficien-cies in child care were beyond those found acceptable by community and professional standards at the time. They represented extreme failure to provide adequate food, clothing, shelter, and medical attention.

### Subgroups Created for the Study

A case was identified as involving sexual abuse if there was evi-dence in the records that the charge had been substantiated. Of these cases, most involved sexual abuse only, but some involved physical abuse and/or neglect in addition. Because exposure to these different types of abuse may have different consequences, distinctions were made. Cases involving only sexual abuse are referenced as *Sexual Abuse Only*. The others are referred to as *Sexual Abuse Plus* (sexual abuse plus physical abuse or neglect). (See Table 1.)

## The Sources of Information for Delinquency and Crime

Finding out whether the subjects had become delinquent and/or committed crime as adults required identifying accurate sources of information about these types of behavior. The researcher decided to use official arrest records as the source, for a number of reasons. They are relatively easy to locate and contain reasonably complete information. The source of information about delinquent juveniles was the files of the juvenile probation department.

## Criminal Consequences

In general, people who experience any type of maltreatment during childhood—whether sexual abuse, physical abuse, or neglect—are more likely than people who were not maltreated to be arrested later in life. This is true for juvenile as well as adult arrests. Twenty-six percent of the people who were abused and/or neglected were later arrested as juveniles, compared with only 16.8 percent of the people who were not. The figures for adults also indicate a greater likelihood of arrest among people who were maltreated during childhood.

### Table 1: Types of Child Victimization Cases

| Type | Number of Cases |
|---|---|
| Physical Abuse and Neglect | 70 |
| Physical Abuse Only | 76 |
| Neglect Only | 609 |
| Sexual Abuse Only | 125 |
| Sexual Abuse Plus (Sexual Abuse with physical abuse and/or neglect) | 28 |
| **Total** | **908** |

For certain specific offenses, the likelihood of arrest is also greater among people who were abused and/or neglected. For example, 14.3 percent of the people who were abused or neglected as children were later charged with property crimes as juveniles, while this was true for only 8.5 percent of the controls. A similar difference in the rate of property crime arrests was found among adults. Childhood abuse and neglect were also associated with later arrest for drug-related offenses. More than 8 percent of the individuals abused or neglected as children were arrested for these offenses as adults, compared to only 5.2 percent of the control group.

### Sexual Abuse

All types of abuse and neglect in childhood put people at greater risk for arrest later in life. But an important finding of this study is that, in cases of sexual abuse, the risk is no greater than for other types of maltreatment. (See Table 2.) In other words, the victims of sexual abuse are no more likely than other victims to become involved with crime.

A breakdown of the types of offenses reveals one exception. People who were victimized during childhood by either physical abuse or

### Table 2: Likelihood of Arrest Depending on Type of Abuse Experienced

| Type of Abuse Subjects | Number of Arrests | Any Juvenile Arrest % | Any Adult Arrest % |
|---|---|---|---|
| All cases of Abuse and Negect | 908 | 26.0*** | 28.6*** |
| Any Sexual Abuse | 153 | 22.2 | 20.3 |
| Any Physical Abuse | 146 | 19.9 | 27.4 |
| Any Neglect | 609 | 28.4 | 30.7 |
| Control Group | 667 | 16.8 | 21.0 |

Note: The asterisks indicate instances in which the differences between all cases of abuse/neglect and the control groups were statistically significant.

***$p<.001$ (The probability is less than 1 in 1,000 that the occurrence could have happened by chance.)

neglect in *addition to* sexual abuse (the Sexual Abuse Plus group) were more likely than those subjected to other types of maltreatment (and also more likely than the controls) to be arrested as runaways during their juvenile years.

## Likelihood of Arrest for Sex Crimes

Could it be that additional breakdowns of types of offenses would reveal greater risk for individuals who were sexually abused in childhood? Previous research indicating that these people are more likely to be arrested for sex crimes suggests this might be the case.

### Sex Crimes in General

Arrest records revealed that, compared to children who had not been victimized, those who had been were more likely to be arrested for sex crimes. Thus, experiencing any type of abuse/neglect in childhood increases the risk for sex crimes. Children who were sexually abused were about as likely as neglect victims to be arrested for any sex crime and less likely than victims of physical abuse. (See Table 3.)

Calculating the *odds* that abused and neglected children will subsequently be arrested for sex crimes as adults confirmed the statistics on likelihood of arrest. For abused and neglected children in general, the odds of being arrested as adults for a sex crime were higher than for nonvictims. Among sexually abused children, the odds were 4.7 times higher. Among physically abused children, the odds of arrest as adults for a sex crime were only a bit less—more than four times higher than for the controls. Neglected children were also at increased risk of subsequent arrest for a sex crime (2.2 times the rate for the controls). (See Table 3.)

### Specific Sex Crimes

The study also looked at various types of sex crimes, and the breakdown revealed more complexity. The differences among the groups in arrest for one particular sex crime, prostitution, were significant. Arrests for this crime were rare, but child sex abuse victims were more likely to be charged with it than were victims of physical abuse and neglect. (See Table 4.) The same is true for the odds. Among children who were sexually abused, the odds are 27.7 times higher than for the control group of being arrested for prostitution as an adult.[7] For rape or sodomy, childhood victims of physical abuse were found to be at higher risk of arrest than either other victims or the controls, and the odds of arrest for these crimes were 7.6 times higher than for the controls.

### From Sexual Abuse to Running Away to Prostitution—Is the Path Inevitable?

It may seem logical to assume that children who are sexually abused follow a direct path from being victimized to becoming a runaway as an adolescent, and then becoming a prostitute as an adult. The findings of the current research support the first part of this relationship; 5.8 percent of abused and neglected children became runaways, compared with only 2.4 percent of the controls.

As noted earlier, the researcher found that sexually abused children were more likely than other victims to be arrested for prostitution as adults, and the odds were higher that a sexually abused child would be charged with prostitution as an adult. But are juvenile run-

### Table 3: Likelihood and Odds of Being Arrested for Any Sex Crime[a]

| Type of Childhood Victimization | Number of Subjects | Likelihood[b] % | Odds[c] |
|---|---|---|---|
| Any Sexual Abuse | 153 | 3.9 | 4.7 |
| Any Physical Abuse | 146 | 6.2 | 4.1 |
| Any Neglect | 609 | 3.6 | 2.2 |
| Control Group | 667 | 1.6 | — |

[a] Sex crimes include prostitution, incest, child molestation, rape, sodomy, assault and battery with intent to gratify, peeping, public indecency, criminal deviant conduct, and contributing to the delinquency of a minor.

[b] $p < 0.2$

[c] The numbers are odds ratios. They depict the odds that a person who has experienced a certain type of childhood abuse of neglect will commit a sex crime. Thus, for example, the odds that a childhood sexual abuse victim will be arrested as an adult for any sex crime is 4.7 times higher than for people in the control group, who experienced no victimization as children. (In calculating these odds, sex, age, and race were taken into account.)

aways subsequently charged with prostitution? The researcher looked at all runaways in the sample studied, both the victimized groups and the control group. When some of these runaways became adults, they were charged with sex crimes. None of the runaways were arrested for prostitution, however.

Thus, the findings do not support the notion of a direct causal link between childhood victimization, becoming a runaway, and in turn being arrested for prostitution. Some adults were found to be arrested for prostitution, but they were not the runaways in this sample.

## Understanding the Aftermath of Childhood Sexual Abuse

All types of childhood abuse and neglect put the victims at higher risk for criminal behavior. However, the particular type of victimization suffered by children who are sexually abused does not set them apart. It does not put them at an even higher risk of arrest, for they are no more likely than children who are physically abused or neglected to be charged with a crime later in life.

The same is true for sex crimes. People victimized by sexual abuse as children are also significantly more likely than nonvictims to be arrested for a sex crime, although no more so than victims of physical abuse and neglect.

*Table 4: Likelihood and Odds of Being Arrested for a Specific Sex Crime*

| Type of Childhood Victimization | Number of Subjects | Prostitution Likelihood[a] % | Odds[b] | Rape or Sodomy Likelihood % | Odds[b] |
|---|---|---|---|---|---|
| Any Sexual Abuse | 153 | 3.3 | 27.7 | 0.7 | c |
| Any Physical Abuse | 146 | 0.7 | c | 2.1 | c |
| Any Neglect | 609 | 1.5 | 10.2 | 1.1 | c |
| Control Group | 667 | 0.1 | — | 0.4 | — |

[a] p<.003

[b] See Note C on table 3.

[c] Not statistically significant. All other findings on odds were significant at the p<.05 level.

This similarity among all three groups of maltreatment victims suggests that for sexual abuse victims, the criminal effect later in life may result not from the specifically sexual nature of the incident but rather from the trauma and stress of these early childhood experiences or society's response to them.

### For Prostitution, the Likelihood is Greater

For prostitution, findings were consistent with those of previous studies: childhood sexual abuse victims run a greater risk than other maltreatment victims of being arrested for prostitution. The percentage of sexual abuse victims arrested for this offense was low, however (3.3 percent).

### From Runaway to Prostitute?

As noted earlier, while the findings support the existence of a link between sexual abuse in childhood and becoming a runaway as a juvenile, they do not support a subsequent link to adult prostitution. That is, being arrested as an adolescent runaway does not predispose people who were sexually abused as children to be arrested for prostitution as adults.

The current research is limited because of its exclusive reliance on official criminal histories. Certainly, such records underestimate the number of runaways, since many of them may be brought to the attention of social service agencies without being arrested. For this reason, other types of data should be examined. However, the fact that none of the runaways identified in this study were arrested for prostitution (while other individuals were) suggests that the connection is at least not as strong as would have been previously thought.

### Other Sex Crimes

Childhood sexual abuse victims were not at greater risk later in life of arrest for rape or sodomy. Rather, the findings reveal an association between these crimes and childhood physical abuse, not sexual abuse. Males who were physically abused in childhood showed a greater tendency than other abused and neglected children and the controls to be arrested for these types of sex crimes. This is consistent with earlier findings regarding the "cycle of violence," which indicated that physical abuse in childhood is associated with the highest rates of arrest for violence later in life.[8] Thus, the violent aspect of rape rather than its sexual component or sexual motivation may explain the association. Indeed, practitioners and clinicians who work with these victims commonly refer to rape as a crime of violence, not simply a sex crime.

## Patterns of Offending

Tentative evidence is offered here to support the notion that when sexual abuse is differentiated by type, the subsequent patterns of juvenile and adult offending are also different. The *Sexual Abuse Plus* group tended to be at greater risk for running away, particularly compared to the other abuse and neglect groups and the controls. Other analysis showed this group more often victimized by family members or relatives in their own homes than the *Sexual Abuse Only* group. If one's home is abusive in multiple ways, it is not surprising that the victims would resort to running away as an escape.

These tentative differences suggest that studies of the long-term consequences of childhood sexual abuse might find it worthwhile to disaggregate sexual abuse experiences into groups consisting exclusively of sexual abuse and groups consisting of sexual abuse in conjunction with other childhood victimization. Future research might examine the question of whether the effect of multiple forms of abuse is additive.

## Criminal Behavior Is Not the Inevitable Outcome

The link between early childhood sexual abuse and later delinquent and adult criminal behavior is not inevitable. Although it is clear that individuals who were sexually abused in childhood are at increased risk of arrest as juveniles and adults, many do not become delinquents or adult criminals. In fact **the majority of the sexually abused children in this study do not have an official criminal history as adults.** Long-term consequences of childhood sexual abuse may be manifest across a number of domains of psychological distress and dysfunction, but not necessarily in criminal behavior. Delinquency and criminality represent only one possible type of outcome of childhood sexual abuse. A number of researchers have described depression, anxiety, self-destructive behavior, and low self-esteem among adults who were sexually abused in childhood. Further research with these samples is underway to document the long-term effects of childhood victimization in a broad array of outcomes. [*See* Chapter 31.]

## *Implications for Policy*

In planning and implementing treatment and prevention programs for children who are sexually abused, practitioners need to keep in mind that these children are in no sense destined for later involvement in criminal behavior. Like other victims of abuse and neglect, the majority will manifest no such negative outcome, at least as evidenced by official records of arrest. However, interventions need to be grounded in the knowledge that childhood victims of sexual abuse, as well as other types of abuse and neglect, are at increased risk for criminal involvement compared to nonvictims.

The need to avoid projecting criminal outcomes for sexually abused children has to be balanced by awareness of the particular risks they face. For example, interventions for sexually abused children should be informed by knowing that the likelihood of becoming a juvenile runaway is not only greater than among nonvictims, but also greater than for other types of childhood maltreatment victims. In developing interventions, it is also important to consider the higher risk for later prostitution that sexual abuse victims face. The health threat posed, not only with respect to the more conventional sexually transmitted diseases, but particularly to HIV infection, makes the need for prevention interventions directed at childhood sexual abuse even more urgent.

*According to this study, child victims arrested as runaways are not arrested for prostitution as adults.*

As the example of prostitution makes clear, outcomes later in life may differ with the type of victimization experienced in childhood. This makes it evident that not all types of childhood maltreatment are alike and makes it incumbent on practitioners to craft responses that meet particular needs. While practitioners need to be aware that sexually abused children are at greater risk of becoming juvenile runaways, they also need to temper that awareness with the knowledge that these runaways are not necessarily "tracked" into prostitution as adults.

Information from the interview phase of the study is likely to bring further nuances to light. If running away does not necessarily lead to prostitution, it may nonetheless place the victim at risk in ways that are not documented in the arrest record.

The interviews may also shed light on intervening factors that mediate between the experience of victimization in childhood and behavioral outcomes in adulthood. Again, prostitution is an example. Since prostitutes have diverse backgrounds, it is unlikely that any single factor (for example, childhood victimization) explains their entrance into this type of life. While early sexual abuse places a child at increased risk, many other factors play a role, and these factors may emerge in the interviews. If such factors are identified, they would necessarily affect the way practitioners intervene for child victims.

## Future Directions

Researchers have recently begun to acknowledge that studies of the impact of childhood abuse (including sexual abuse) find substantially large groups of individuals who appear to have experienced little or no long-term negative consequences. There are a number of possible explanations, among them inadequate measurement techniques on the part of the researchers. It is also possible that some factors or characteristics of the abuse incident (less severity, for example), or some characteristics of the child (having effective coping skills, for example) or the child's environment (having a close relationship with a supportive person, for example) may have served as a buffer from the long-term consequences. Protective factors in the lives of abused and neglected children need to be uncovered.

Future studies need to examine cases in which children appear to have overcome, or been protected from, the negative consequences of their early childhood experiences with abuse. The knowledge from such studies would have important implications for developing prevention and treatment programs for children who experience early childhood victimization. These "protective factors" are being explored as part of the study now being conducted by the present researcher.

## Notes

1. A summary of this research is in Widom, Cathy Spatz, *The Cycle of Violence*, Research in Brief, Washington, D.C.: U.S. Department of Justice, National Institute of Justice, October 1992. The document can be obtained from the National Criminal Justice Reference Service, Box 6000, Rockville, MD 20849-6000; call 800-851-3420 or order through the Internet at lookncjrs@aspensys.com.

2. A fuller presentation is in Widom, C. S., and Ames, M. A., "Criminal Consequences of Childhood Sexual Victimization," *Child Abuse and Neglect* 18 (1994): 303–18.

3. Browne, A., and D. Finkelhor, "Impact of Sexual Abuse: A Review of the Research," *Psychological Bulletin* 99 (1986): 66–77.

4. Beitchman, J. H., et al., "A Review of the Long-Term Effects of Child Sexual Abuse," *Child Abuse and Neglect* 16 (1992): 101–18.

5. A full description of the research design is in Widom, Cathy Spatz, "Child Abuse, Neglect, and Adult Behavior: Research Design and Findings on Criminality, Violence, and Child Abuse," *American Journal of Orthopsychiatry* 59 (1989): 355–67.

6. Of the 153 cases of sexual abuse, 40 were processed in juvenile court and 113 in adult criminal court.

7. In calculating the odds, the researcher controlled for the person's sex, race, and age, as these factors may affect the likelihood of being arrested for a crime.

8. See Widom, *Cycle of Violence*: 3.

*Findings and conclusions of the research reported here are those of the authors and do not necessarily reflect the official position or policies of the U.S. Department of Justice.*

Chapter 33

# Preventing Child Sexual Abuse

## Research Inconclusive about Effectiveness of Child Education Programs

### Introduction

In this report, we describe and synthesize reviews of the research literature on education programs designed to help children avoid becoming victims of sexual abuse. We describe these reviews, report their findings on the effectiveness of education programs in preventing sexual abuse, and report their assessments of the supportability of conclusions drawn from existing research studies.

### Background

The problem of child sexual abuse has received increasing attention in recent years. Deriving accurate estimates of the magnitude of the problem is difficult, however, because research has indicated that abuse tends to be underreported, definitions of what constitutes sexual abuse and the ceiling age used (e.g., whether abuse occurred prior to age 16 or 18) may vary across studies, and there are numerous other methodological difficulties in collecting data on this subject. These caveats provide a context for the abuse figures that follow: The U.S. Department of Health and Human Services reported that about 140,000 new cases of child sexual abuse were reported to and deter-

U.S. General Accounting Office, Publication No. GAO/GGD-96-156, July 1996.

mined to be indicated or substantiated by state child protection agencies in 1994.[1] It has also been reported that between 25 and 35 percent of all sexually abused children are under the age of 7 and that 75 percent of the victims are abused by someone they know.[2]

Since the early 1980s, there has been a tremendous growth in sexual abuse prevention programs targeted at children of preschool and elementary school age. In 1989, 18 states mandated school-based child sexual abuse prevention programs.[3] Surveys of school administrators have found that 48 to 85 percent of school districts offer these programs.[4] The programs, typically delivered in classroom settings, are based on the assumption that children will be able to protect themselves from sexual abuse if they are taught to recognize instances of abuse and are trained in personal safety skills. Programs may also focus on helping children who are victims of past or ongoing sexual abuse, by encouraging them to disclose these incidents to parents or other responsible adults.

The growth in prevention programs has proceeded faster than the evaluation of their effectiveness. Questions exist about whether children learn and retain material taught in the programs, and whether

---

[1] U.S. Department of Health and Human Services, National Center on Child Abuse and Neglect, *Child Maltreatment 1994: Reports from the States to the National Center on Child Abuse and Neglect* (Washington, D.C.: U.S. Government Printing Office, 1996). The figure of 140,000 sexual abuse cases was based on responses from 47 states and the District of Columbia. Connecticut, Maryland, and West Virginia did not provide figures on the number of substantiated or indicated sexual abuse cases. A substantiated or indicated case represents a type of investigation disposition in which sufficient evidence is established under state law to conclude that maltreatment occurred, that the child is at risk of maltreatment, or that there is reason to suspect maltreatment. State agencies differ in how they report incidence data, with some counting each incident of abuse once regardless of the number of children involved, and others counting each child involved separately. Some children may be counted more than once if multiple incidents of abuse are reported during the year.

[2] S. Wurtele, "Sexual Abuse." In *Handbook of Prevention and Treatment with Children and Adolescents: Intervention in the Real World Context,* eds. R.T. Ammerman and M. Hersen (New York: Wiley, 1997).

[3] J. Kohl, "School-based Child Sexual Abuse Prevention Programs," *Journal of Family Violence,* Vol. VIII (1993), pp. 137–50.

[4] Deborah A. Daro, "Prevention of Child Sexual Abuse," *The Future of Children,* Vol. IV, No. 2 (Summer/Fall 1994), pp. 198–223; D. Helge, *Child Sexual Abuse in America—A Call for School and Community Action* (Bellingham, Washington National Rural Development Institute, 1992).

informed children are truly capable of resisting abusive behavior directed at them by older and stronger offenders. Demonstrating empirically that prevention programs work is a difficult and challenging task. Methodological obstacles include selecting the criteria for judging success of the program, ruling out alternative explanations for results obtained by using a comparison group of children who were similar to those exposed to the education program except that they did not receive instruction, and studying children for a long enough period to ensure that the program has lasting effects. There are also ethical obstacles to determining program effectiveness. These include the issue of denying a comparison group of children a potentially beneficial education program. Ethical considerations also arise in trying to measure accurately whether young children can use what they have learned to resist offenders. Some argue that exposing young children to a simulated abusive episode, while potentially a good measure of children's capability to respond to an actual assault, may be unduly traumatic, or may desensitize children to dangerous situations.

## *Results in Brief*

We identified 16 reviews that provided qualitative or quantitative summaries of research on education programs designed to prevent sexual abuse. The reviews discussed the studies in terms of program effectiveness and methodological adequacy.

There was general consensus among the reviews that there was not as yet any direct evidence that these programs were effective in preventing the occurrence of child sexual abuse. The reviews focused on whether children could acquire knowledge about sexual abuse and learn skills that might prove useful in an abusive situation, as well as whether programs prompted victimized children to disclose ongoing or past abuse. There was general consensus that children could learn concepts about abuse, although it was clear that some concepts were more difficult to grasp than others. For example, children had a difficult time grasping the concept that abuse could be perpetrated by a family member. There was less consensus about whether knowledge was retained over the long term, whether children could learn skills for resisting abuse, and whether children would disclose new instances of abuse after participating in the program. Finally, the reviews generally agreed that programs were more effective in teaching concepts to older children, and that concepts and skills could be grasped better when taught with active participation (e.g., modeling or role-playing techniques) than with more passive methods (e.g., films or lectures).

Most reviews reported that methodological limitations in the research precluded conclusions about the effectiveness of education programs in preventing sexual abuse. The problems identified may be grouped into two broad categories: (1) limitations in the outcome measures used, and (2) limitations in the design of studies.

A majority of the research reviews noted that the outcome measures used in evaluation studies were not valid indicators of prevention. These reviews emphasized the need to develop measures that would directly indicate whether sexual abuse was avoided following education programs. The reviews also criticized the reliance on verbal self-report measures because studies have found little correspondence between what children say they will do and their actual behavior. More generally, the reviews noted the lack of standardization of outcome measures in this field, including the tendency of evaluators to develop new and unique outcome measures for each study, and their failure to measure or report information on the statistical properties of the testing instruments (such as test reliability) that would enable other researchers to refine the instruments and replicate earlier results. The reviews pointed to the need for systematic data collection about disclosures of sexual abuse and about potential negative side effects produced by the programs.

All the research reviews identified design weaknesses in the studies. Chief among these was the absence of comparison groups (against which to compare groups exposed to an education program) and, alternatively, the use of comparison groups of children who differed in systematic ways from the children receiving the education program. The latter situation made it difficult to judge whether differences in outcomes were a result of the program or were an effect of selecting only certain kinds of children for the program. Half of the reviews noted that some studies failed to pretest children on measures of knowledge, skills, and anxiety prior to their introduction to the program. This made it difficult to establish a baseline against which to compare changes that occurred as a result of participation in the program. A number of reviews identified inadequate follow-up periods. Only a few studies collected follow-up information on children's knowledge for periods longer than 3 months.

## Scope and Methodology

To examine the effectiveness of education programs to prevent child sexual abuse, we collected, reviewed, and analyzed information from

16 research reviews issued between 1986 and 1996. These reviews were identified through a multistep process that included contacting known experts in the sex offense research field, conducting computerized searches of several online databases, and screening over 100 studies on sexual abuse prevention programs. We sent the list of reviews to two experts, who have done extensive research in the field, to confirm the comprehensiveness of our list of research reviews.[5]

We used a data collection instrument to systematically collect information on the research reviews of education programs. We collected information on program targets, settings and objectives; methods of presentation and characteristics of presenters; outcome measures; methodology issues; follow-up periods; and conclusions reached from these reviews.

We sent a draft of this report to the two experts previously consulted, and one additional expert, to ensure that we had presented the information about the reviews and research articles accurately.[6] Their comments were incorporated where appropriate. We did not send a draft to any other agency or organization because we did not obtain information (other than study citations) from such organizations for use in this study. We did our work between October 1995 and June 1996 in accordance with generally accepted government auditing standards.

## Description of the Research Reviews

The 16 research reviews covered about 135 studies on education programs designed to help children prevent sexual abuse. Of these studies, 65 were cited in two or more reviews, and 34 were cited in five or more reviews. Given the widely varying levels of detail provided in the research reviews, we could not always determine whether reference was being made to an evaluation of an education program or to other types of studies on education programs (e.g., descriptions of programs, or specific materials available for use by schools or parents). We therefore could not precisely determine the total number of studies on education programs covered in these research reviews. We also did not determine how many studies covered in the 16 research

---

[5] Dr. David Finkelhor, Family Research Laboratory, University of New Hampshire, Durham, New Hampshire, and Dr. Sandy K. Wurtele, Department of Psychology, University of Colorado, Colorado Springs, Colorado.

[6] Dr. Jeffrey J. Haugaard, Department of Human Development and Family Studies, Cornell University, Ithaca, New York.

reviews were duplicative in terms of researchers publishing multiple articles based on the same set of data. The earliest study included in a research review was published in 1979; the most recent was published in 1995.

Almost all of the research reviews provided narrative assessors of original research studies, with approximately one-half providing a tabular summary of at least some of the studies covered. Two reviews performed a meta-analysis, a statistical aggregation of the results from multiple studies, to derive an overall quantitative estimate of the effectiveness of education programs.

Most research reviews did not restrict their coverage to a single type of setting (classroom, home, or other community setting), specific target group (children, teachers, or parents), or specific outcome measure (knowledge, skills, or disclosures of abuse). The two reviews that employed meta-analysis focused specifically on knowledge and skills acquired by children. Two other research reviews limited their coverage to published studies.

## Research Reviews Found No Direct Evidence That Education Programs Prevent the Occurrence of Child Sexual Abuse

Fifteen of the 16 research reviews concluded that there was no evidence from the empirical studies they reviewed that demonstrated the effectiveness of education programs in actually preventing the occurrence of child abuse. This did not mean that the programs were ineffective, but rather that none of the studies had been designed so that the link between what was taught in education programs and actual prevention of sexual abuse could be adequately tested. The one review that did not offer a conclusion about prevention was limited in scope in that it only reviewed program effects on knowledge and skills.

Most education programs aim for more short-term objectives than prevention of sexual abuse, and nearly all of the research reviews included some discussion of these short-term objectives. Fourteen of the 16 reviews discussed the goal of teaching children concepts about sexual abuse (defining "appropriate" and "inappropriate" forms of touching, defining what are "private parts," and informing children that abuse could be committed by people known to them). Fifteen of the reviews discussed the goal of teaching children skills for resisting or avoiding abusive situations (saying "no," physical defense, or leaving the scene). Fourteen of the 16 reviews discussed the programs' goal of encouraging children to disclose past or ongoing incidents of abuse to parents or other responsible adults.

Thirteen of the 16 reviews concluded that education programs were generally effective in teaching children new concepts about sexual abuse. Eight of the reviews concluded that these programs were effective in teaching children skills, such as saying no or leaving the scene. Many reviews noted that some concepts were more difficult to learn than others—for example, the concept that abuse could come from someone in the child's family was particularly difficult for children to grasp. Most of the reviews discussed whether knowledge and skills gained in programs were retained by children over the long term. Nine of the reviews concluded that studies showed that knowledge or skills could be retained for periods ranging from 3 months to 1 year. Four other reviews concluded that results for long-term retention were mixed or that the research was inconclusive. Reviewers who concluded that children made knowledge or skills gains after participating in education programs nevertheless cautioned that little was known about whether these gains made children any more capable of resisting actual attempts at sexual abuse. Of the 14 reviews that looked at disclosures, four noted that there was at least tentative support for the conclusion that programs were effective in encouraging children to disclose past or ongoing incidents of sexual abuse. The remainder either offered no conclusions or noted that the findings were inconclusive. Many of the reviews, including those with positive conclusions regarding disclosure, also noted that more systematic research was needed in this area.

Half of the reviews discussed side effects of education programs, both negative and positive. Some critics of education programs have raised concerns that children who participate in these programs may have increased anxiety or fear that abuse might "happen to them," may become oversensitive to appropriate situations involving touch, or may develop negative attitudes towards sexuality. Proponents of education programs have argued that programs may make children feel safer and more able to protect themselves or more willing to discuss sexual abuse concepts with their parents. Five of the eight reviews that discussed side effects concluded that there was little evidence of negative side effects, and three concluded that the research findings on this topic were mixed. Five reviews mentioned possible positive side effects, including increased discussion of child sexual abuse between children and parents.

Most of the reviews included some discussion of the techniques used to present concepts or skills to children. These techniques vary considerably, ranging from classroom lectures; to films, puppet shows, or theatrical performances; to programs that involve more active participation by children, such as role-playing abusive scenarios or rehearsing behaviors that might be used to avoid or resist abuse. Twelve of the 16 reviews concluded that children who participated in programs that used more active techniques (e.g., modeling, role-playing, or behavior rehearsal) made greater knowledge or skill gains than children participating in programs that used more passive techniques (e.g., lectures or films).

A majority of the reviews did not specifically mention, for at least some of the studies they reviewed, the total length of the education program or the total number of sessions involved. Those reviews that discussed program duration and frequency of sessions noted that programs varied considerably, from single sessions lasting less than an hour, to ones presented over several days. Nevertheless, education programs typically are short in duration and limited in intensity. One review noted that a school-based education program is "most likely offered during one session of less than 2 hours duration."[7] None of the reviews had specific conclusions regarding the optimum duration or intensity of programs, although several noted that programs that involved multiple sessions, periodic "booster" sessions to review material covered in earlier sessions, and/or active participation were most likely to have positive results.

All of the reviews discussed programs targeted towards elementary school children, and 15 of 16 reviews discussed programs targeted towards preschool children. Eleven of 16 reviews concluded that education programs were more likely to be effective with older children than with younger ones. Nevertheless, some reviews concluded that preschool-age children could gain knowledge about sexual abuse if they participated in programs that included repetition, active learning techniques, and parent education.

Discussion of programs targeted at adolescents, parents, and teachers and other professionals was much more limited in the research reviews. Only two of the reviews discussed programs targeted towards high school or junior high school students, eight reviews discussed programs that involved some components of parent education, five reviews discussed programs targeted at teachers, and two reviews

---

[7] S. Wurtele, 1997, p. 11.

discussed programs targeted towards school counselors, nurses, or childcare workers in residential institutions. Noting that most education programs were focused on children, and that most were delivered in school settings, several reviews suggested that programs might be more effective if they were linked with comprehensive community efforts to prevent child sexual abuse.

Only two reviews attempted to quantify the overall effectiveness of education programs, and they did so using a statistical aggregation technique called meta-analysis. Each meta-analysis found that participants in both preschool and elementary-school programs made knowledge gains that were either moderately or substantially greater than those of comparison groups.[8] One of the meta-analyses further reported that programs that used more active formats (modeling and role-playing) were more effective than those that used passive formats (lecture, films, and stories).[9]

Most reviewers, even those who were quite positive about the effectiveness of programs in teaching concepts and skills, agreed that more work was needed before firm conclusions could be reached. They cited the methodological limitations of studies as a major obstacle to drawing firm conclusions about program effectiveness.

## Research Reviews Identified Methodological Limitations in Evaluating the Effectiveness of Education Programs

The research reviews found that conclusions about the effectiveness of education programs were impeded by methodological weaknesses in the studies. The problems identified may be grouped into two broad categories: (1) limitations in the outcome measures used and (2) limitations in the design of studies.

### *Limitations in Outcome Measures*

A majority of the research reviews noted that the outcome measures used in evaluation studies were not valid indicators of prevention. These reviews emphasized that most research studies measured whether children learned concepts about sexual abuse and personal safety skills, but that no study had developed reliable and valid mea-

---

[8] J. D. Berrick and R. P. Bard, 1992; T. Heidotting and S. W. Soled, in preparation.

[9] T. Heidotting and S. W. Soled, in preparation.

sures to examine whether education programs resulted in long-term reductions in the incidence of sexual abuse.[10]

The reviews noted other limitations in measures of more proximal outcomes—i.e., gains in knowledge and skills. Five reviews criticized the primary research studies for their overreliance on verbal self-report measures. Such measures are widely used, both to test for gains in knowledge about sexual abuse and to test whether children say they will use the self-protection strategies that they have learned in education programs. But self-reports may be unreliable measures of what children have learned and what they are capable of doing. Some studies have found little correspondence between what children say they will do and their actual behavior. The reviews recommended supplementing verbal self-report measures with behavioral measures that could more reliably indicate how children would behave in actual encounters with an abuser.

Twelve of the reviews discussed studies that had attempted to test children's behavior using "real life simulations." In these, children were lured by potential abductors who were associates of the researcher. Reviewers cautioned that these kinds of measures have several limitations. Since they measure children's responses to strangers, and since research shows that most sexual abuse is perpetrated by persons known to the victim, they may not be valid measures of children's ability to resist most abusers. And there are potential ethical problems. For example, such simulations may unduly frighten chil-

---

[10] A survey conducted by the National Center on Child Abuse Prevention Research asked federally appointed liaisons for child abuse and neglect in each state and the District of Columbia to provide data on the number of children reported for sexual abuse (C. Lung and D. Daro, *Current Trends in Child Abuse Reporting and Fatalities: The Results of the 1995 Annual Fifty State Survey,* National Committee to Prevent Child Abuse, 1996). The results showed that the number reported as sexually abused grew in the 1970s and 1980s, reaching a high point of over 400,000 cases in 1991, and then declined in recent years to around 300,000 cases in 1995. In addition, of all reported cases of abuse and neglect, the proportion involving sexual abuse has dropped from 16 percent in 1986 to 10 percent in 1995. One expert reviewer of our draft report commented that a possible explanation for these declines might be the efficacy of sexual abuse prevention programs. However, there are as yet no research data demonstrating a causal link between outcomes of prevention programs and changes in incidence rates. Without such data, it is difficult to tell whether decreases in the number of reported sexual abuse cases are due to the effectiveness of prevention programs, changes in how data are recorded, changes in the appeal process, changes in definitions of information and referral calls, or other possible explanatory factors.

dren, on the one hand, or may desensitize them to truly dangerous situations, on the other.[11]

One review mentioned a recent set of studies that used a different method for collecting data on children's resistance skills in real-life situations.[12] The investigators conducted a national telephone survey of children ages 10 to 16 in which they queried them about their experiences with sexual abuse and with prevention programs. The survey found that 67 percent of respondents had been exposed to a prevention education program in the course of their schooling. Approximately 40 percent of the children who were exposed to a prevention program reported specific instances where they used the information or skills taught in the programs to protect themselves. Children who reported being victimized were more likely to use self-protection strategies if they had received comprehensive prevention instruction, which included opportunities to practice the skills in class, multiday presentations, and materials to take home to discuss with parents. While the findings are suggestive, the reviewer stated that the study relies on self-report information with no independent confirmation of such reports, and the findings apply only to older children (those aged 10 to 16).

Several reviews pointed to the need for systematic data collection on whether children were more likely to disclose past or ongoing instances of abuse after exposure to an education program. A 1996 review noted that too few researchers provide information about disclosures during or subsequent to education programs, and that

---

[11] Two expert reviewers of our draft report commented that researchers who intend to use behavioral measures face a host of logistical and ethical challenges. For example, they both noted that it is very difficult to devise behavioral measures of resisting abuse and that simulating the perpetration of child sexual abuse for research purposes may be unethical. One of the reviewers also noted that obtaining approval from human subject protection committees and obtaining parental consent to use such behavioral measures may be difficult. Even if parents consent, researchers still have a responsibility to debrief the study participants when the study is concluded. Researchers are reportedly struggling with determining the best ways to debrief children, many of whom may not be able to fully understand the explanation given.

[12] David Finkelhor, Nancy Asdigian, and Jennifer Dziuba-Leatherman, "The Effectiveness of Victimization Prevention Instruction: An Evaluation of Children's Responses to Actual Threats and Assaults," *Child Abuse and Neglect*, Vol. XIX, No. 2 (1995), pp. 141–53; David Finkelhor and Jennifer Dziuba-Leatherman, "Victimization Prevention Programs: A National Survey of Children's Exposure and Reactions," *Child Abuse and Neglect*, Vol. XIX, No. 2 (1995), pp. 129–39.

those who do report disclosures report only the actual number or percentage and fail to provide additional information (e.g., type of abuse, past versus ongoing, consequences of disclosure, disposition of case).[13]

More generally, several reviews noted the lack of standardization of outcome measures in this field. Investigators have tended to develop new and unique outcome measures for each new study, making it difficult to compare findings and make overall generalizations about program effectiveness.[14] This problem has been compounded because many studies have failed to measure or report information on the statistical properties of the testing instruments (for example, test reliability). Such information would enable other researchers to refine the instruments and replicate earlier results.

### *Limitations in Study Design*

All of the research reviews identified design weaknesses in the studies. Over half the reviews noted, for at least some of the studies they reviewed, the absence of comparison groups (against which to compare groups exposed to an education program) or the use of comparison groups of children who differed systematically from children who were exposed to the program. This made it difficult to judge whether differences in outcomes were a result of the program or were an effect of selecting only certain kinds of children for the program. Some more recent reviews noted that absent or inadequate comparison groups was more a problem in earlier studies, and that a number of well-designed studies now existed.

---

[13] S. K. Wurtele, 1997.

[14] Outcomes have been assessed in different ways, depending on the types of program effects the researcher is investigating. Researchers have developed questionnaires to assess changes in *knowledge of sexual abuse concepts,* which may include items covering definitions of sexual abuse descriptions of victims and perpetrators, and other concepts (e.g., "The victim is never at fault."). Measures used to assess *knowledge of prevention skills* may include descriptions of hypothetical encounters with adults, followed by questions about whether these situations are safe or unsafe and what would be an appropriate response on the part of the child. Some researchers have enacted a role-play of an unsafe encounter and required children to say "no," leave the situation, and immediately tell a parent about the incident. Children's scores are based on the degree to which they perform the response correctly. As described above, *actual resistance behavior* has been measured by the use of simulated stranger abductions, where children's responses are observed and coded for correctness.

Eight of the reviews noted that some studies failed to pretest children on measures of knowledge and skills, or on measures of fear and anxiety, before exposing them to the education program. Without a baseline measure, it is difficult to determine whether post-program knowledge, skill, or fear levels changed as a function of program participation.

A number of reviews identified inadequate follow-up periods. They reported that only a few studies collected follow-up information on children's knowledge for periods longer than three months, with the longest follow-up period being 18 months. There was also a large variation in the follow-up period used across studies. Reviews noted that it is important to establish whether programs have lasting effects, as well as to determine what kinds of ongoing education are required to maintain or enhance initial program effects. In addition, some reviews pointed out that follow-up studies need to pay more attention to side effects or unforeseen consequences of participation. Although the reviews that discussed side effects found little evidence of initial negative consequences, many reviews noted that there was as yet little information on the long-term consequences of participation.

## Conclusions

A growing number of studies are being done on the effectiveness of child sexual abuse education programs, many of which were assessed in the research reviews described and synthesized in this report. The most optimistic reviews have concluded that education programs showed some promise for imparting knowledge to children about sexual abuse, as well as teaching them personal safety skills for preventing sexual abuse. However, nearly all these reviews reported that definitive conclusions could not be drawn because no study yet had developed measures of whether these programs were effective in reducing the incidence of child sexual abuse. There was consensus that to demonstrate the effectiveness of sexual abuse education programs more and better research would be required.

## Research Reviews Used in the Synthesis

Berrick, Jill D., and Richard P. Barth. "Child Sexual Abuse Prevention: Research Review and Recommendations." *Social Work Research and Abstracts* Vol. XXVIII, No. 4 (December 1992): 6–15.

Carroll, Leslie A., Raymond G. Miltenberger, and H. Katherine O'Neill. "A Review and Critique of Research Evaluating Child Sexual Abuse Prevention Programs." *Education and Treatment of Children* Vol. XV, No. 4 (November 1992): 335–54.

Conte, Jon R., and Linda A. Fogarty. "Sexual Abuse Prevention Programs for Children." *Education and Urban Society* Vol. XXII, No. 3 (May 1990): 270–84.

Conte, Jon R., Carole Rosen, and Leslee Saperstein. "An Analysis of Programs to Prevent the Sexual Victimization of Children." *Journal of Primary Prevention* Vol. VI, No. 3 (Spring 1986): 141–55.

Daro, Deborah A. "Prevention of Child Sexual Abuse." *The Future of Children,* Vol. IV, No. 2 (Summer/Fall 1994): 198–223.

Finkelhor, David, and Nancy Strapko. "Sexual Abuse Prevention Education: A Review of Evaluation Studies." In *Prevention of Child Maltreatment: Developmental and Ecological Perspectives,* eds. D. J. Willis, E. W. Holden, and M. Rosenberg (New York: John Wiley and Sons, 1992), pp. 150–67.

Heidotting, Terri, and Suzanne W. Soled. "School-based Sexual Abuse and Personal Safety Prevention Programs for Children: A Meta-analysis" (unpublished).

Kolko, David J. "Educational Programs to Promote Awareness and Prevention of Child Sexual Victimization: A Review and Methodological Critique." *Clinical Psychology Review* Vol. VIII (1988): 195–209.

MacMillan, Harriet L., et al. "Primary Prevention of Child Sexual Abuse: A Critical Review. Part II." *Journal of Child Psychology and Psychiatry* Vol. XXXV, No. 5 (1994): 857–76.

O'Donohue, William, James H. Geer, and Ann Elliott. "The Primary Prevention of Child Sexual Abuse." In *The Sexual Abuse of Children. Volume II: Clinical Issues,* eds. William O'Donohue and James H. Geer (Hillsdale, New Jersey: Lawrence Erlbaum Associates, Inc., 1992), pp. 477–517.

Reppucci, N. Dickon, and Jeffrey J. Haugaard. "Prevention of Child Sexual Abuse: Myth or Reality." *American Psychologist* Vol. XLIV, No. 10 (October 1989): 1266–75.

Tharinger, Deborah J., et al. "Prevention of Child Sexual Abuse: An Analysis of Issues, Educational Programs, and Research Findings." *School Psychology Review* Vol. XVII, No. 4 (1988): 614–34.

Tutty, Leslie M. "Are Child Sexual Abuse Prevention Programs Effective? A Review of the Research." *Revue Sexologique* Vol. 1, No. 2 (1993): 93–114.

Wurtele, Sandy K. "Sexual Abuse." In *Handbook of Prevention and Treatment With Children and Adolescents: Intervention in the Real World Context,* eds. R. T. Ammerman and M. Hersen (New York: Wiley, 1997).

Wurtele, Sandy K. "School-based Sexual Abuse Prevention Programs: A Review." *Child Abuse and Neglect* Vol. XI (1987): 483–95.

Wurtele, Sandy K., and Cindy L. Miller-Perrin. *Preventing Child Sexual Abuse: Sharing the Responsibility* (Lincoln, Nebraska: University of Nebraska Press, 1992).

Chapter 34

# Cycle of Sexual Abuse: Research Inconclusive about Whether Child Victims Become Adult Abusers

This report summarizes the results of, and discusses the methodologies used in, the studies that have been done on the cycle of sexual abuse—that is, on the likelihood that individuals who were victims of sexual abuse as children will become sexual abusers of children in adulthood.

This report does not address a follow-on question that was raised concerning ways to prevent sexually abused children from becoming adult sexual offenders against children, because the existence of a cycle of sexual abuse was not established by the research studies we reviewed.

## Background

Sexual abuse can have negative consequences for children during the time of abuse as well as later in life, according to several recent research reviews.[1] Initial effects reportedly have included fear, anxiety, depression, anger, aggression, and sexually inappropriate behavior in at least some portion of the victim population. Long-lasting consequences reportedly have included depression, self-destructive behavior, anxiety, feelings of isolation and stigma, poor self-esteem, difficulty in trusting others, a tendency toward revictimization, substance abuse, and sexual maladjustment.

---

U.S. General Accounting Office, Publication No. GAO/GGD-96-178, September 1996.

In addition, researchers have noted that there is widespread belief that there is a "cycle of sexual abuse," such that sexual victimization as a child may contribute to perpetration of sexual abuse as an adult. Such a pattern is consistent with social learning theories—which posit that children learn those behaviors that are modeled for them—and also with psychodynamic theories which suggest that abusing others may help victimized individuals to overcome childhood trauma. Critics have argued that empirical support for the cycle of sexual abuse is weak, and that parents are unduly frightened into thinking that little can be done to mitigate the long-term effects of sexual abuse. There remain many unanswered questions about the risk posed by early sexual victimization, as well as about the conditions and experiences that might increase this risk (such as number of victimization experiences, age of the victim at the time of the abuse, and whether the abuse was perpetrated by a family member). There are also questions about factors that may prevent victimized children from becoming adult perpetrators (such as support from siblings and parents or positive relationships with other authority figures). Answers to such questions would be useful in developing both prevention strategies and therapeutic interventions.

Studying the relationship between early sexual victimization and later perpetration of sexual abuse is methodologically difficult. If researchers take a retrospective approach, and ask adult sex offenders whether they experienced childhood sexual abuse, there are problems of selecting a representative sample of offenders, finding an appropriate comparison group of adults who have not committed sex offenses but are similar to the study group in other respects, minimizing errors that arise when recalling traumatic events from the distant past, and dealing with the possibility that offenders will purposely overreport childhood abuse to gain sympathy or underreport abuse to avoid imputations of guilt. A prospective approach—selecting a sample of children who have been sexually abused and following them into adulthood to see whether they become sexual abusers—overcomes some of the problems of the retrospective approach, but it is a costly and time-consuming solution. In addition, researchers choosing the prospective approach still face the challenge of disentangling the effects of sexual abuse from the effects of other possible problems and stress-related factors in the backgrounds of these children (e.g., poverty, unemployment, parental alcohol abuse, or other inadequate social and family functioning). This requires the selection of appropriate comparison groups of children who have not been sexually abused and children who have faced other forms of maltreatment, as well as the careful measurement of a variety of other explanatory factors.

## Results in Brief

We identified 25 studies that provided quantitative information relevant to the question of whether persons who were sexually abused as children were at heightened risk of becoming sexual abusers of children in adulthood. Of these studies, 23 were retrospective—that is, they began with a sample of known adult sex offenders of children and sought to determine whether they were sexually abused themselves during childhood. Only two studies were prospective. These began with samples of sexually victimized children and tracked them into adulthood to determine how many became sex offenders.

A number of the retrospective studies found that a substantial percentage of adult sex offenders of children said they had been sexually abused as children. However, a majority of the studies found that most offenders said they had not been sexually abused during childhood. These studies varied in terms of their estimates of the percentages of such offenders who had been abused, from zero to 79 percent, partly because of differences in the types of offenders studied and in how childhood sexual abuse was defined and measured. In general, because they had several methodological shortcomings, these studies offered insufficient evidence that being sexually abused as a child led directly to the victim's becoming an adult sex offender. The two prospective studies employed analytic methods that were better suited to establishing such a link than were the retrospective studies. Respectively, about seven percent and 26 percent of sexually abused children in these studies were found to be sex offenders as adults. However, the various design and measurement problems of the prospective studies precluded the drawing of definitive conclusions from them as well.

Nevertheless, overall, the retrospective studies, prospective studies, and research reviews indicated that the experience of childhood sexual victimization is quite likely neither a necessary nor a sufficient cause of adult sexual offending. The two prospective studies concluded that the majority of victims of sexual abuse during childhood did not become sex offenders as adults. Therefore, childhood sexual victimization would not necessarily lead to adult sexual offending. In addition, the majority of retrospective studies concluded that most adult sex offenders against children did not report that they were sexually victimized as children.

Therefore, childhood sexual victimization would probably not be sufficient to explain adult sexual offending. While some studies indicated that sexual victimization in childhood may increase the risk that victims will become sexual offenders as adults, other studies found that many other conditions and experiences might also be associated with an increased risk. For example, one prospective study we reviewed found that children who were neglected were even more likely than children who were sexually abused to commit sex offenses as adults.

## Scope and Methodology

We collected, reviewed, and analyzed information from available published and unpublished research on the cycle of sexual abuse. Identifying the relevant literature involved a multistep process. Initially, we identified experts in the sex offense research field by contacting the Department of Justice's Office of Juvenile Justice and Delinquency Prevention and Office of Victim Assistance, the National Institute of Mental Health's Violence and Traumatic Stress Branch, the American Psychological Association, and academicians selected because of their expertise in the area. These contacts helped identify experts in the field, who in turn helped identify other experts. We also conducted computerized searches of several on-line databases, including ERIC (the Education Resources Information Center), NCJRS (the National Criminal Justice Reference Service), PsycINFO,[2] Dissertation Abstracts, and the National Clearinghouse on Child Abuse.

We identified 40 articles on the cycle of sexual abuse issued between 1965 and 1996. Four of these reviewed the literature in the area; of these, two were published in 1988, one was published in 1990, and one was published in 1991. Of the remaining articles, 23 presented findings from retrospective research studies, which began with a sample of known adult sex offenders of children and sought to determine (by asking the offenders) whether they were sexually abused during childhood. Another four presented findings from two prospective research studies, which began with samples of sexually victimized children and tracked them into adulthood to determine how many became sex offenders. Of the original 40 articles, we excluded five because they presented findings only, or primarily, on adolescent sex offenders against children, and an additional four because we were unable to obtain them.

For the studies in our review, we recorded the quantitative results, summarized the methodologies used, and summarized the authors' conclusions about the cycle of sexual abuse. Each study was reviewed by two social scientists with specialized doctoral training in evaluation research methodology. Conclusions in this report are based on our assessment of the evidence presented in these studies.

We sent the list of research articles to two experts, both of whom have done extensive research in the field, to confirm the comprehensiveness of our list of articles. In addition, as a final check, we conducted a second search of computerized on-line databases in March 1996 to ensure that no new research articles or reviews had been published since our original search in October 1995.

We sent a draft copy of our report for comment to the two experts previously consulted, as well as to one additional expert, to ensure that we had presented the information about the research studies accurately.[3] Their technical comments were incorporated where appropriate. We did not send a draft to any agency or organization because we did not obtain information from such organizations for use in this study. We did our work between October 1995 and August 1996 in accordance with generally accepted government auditing standards.

## Results Inconclusive about the Relationship Between Childhood Sexual Victimization and Adult Sexual Offending Against Children

There was no consensus among the studies we reviewed that being sexually abused as a child led directly to the victim's becoming an adult sexual abuser of children. However, some studies did conclude that it might increase the risk that victims would commit sexual abuse later. A majority of the retrospective studies noted that most sex offenders had not been sexually abused as children, and the two prospective studies showed that the majority of victims of sexual abuse during childhood did not become sex offenders as adults. The four review articles we obtained, which collectively covered roughly two-thirds of the 25 studies we reviewed, concluded that the evidence from these studies was insufficient to establish that being sexually abused as a child is either a necessary or a sufficient condition for the victim's becoming a sexual abuser as an adult.

## *Retrospective Studies Varied in Groups Studied, Definitions of Sexual Abuse Used, and Results Obtained*

We reviewed 23 retrospective studies.[4] All but one of the retrospective studies focused on adult male sex offenders, and in most studies the offenders sampled were imprisoned or in some type of treatment program. However, these studies varied considerably in the types of child sexual abusers studied, whether control or comparison groups were used, and if so, the types of individuals in these groups.[5]

The retrospective studies also varied considerably in their findings and conclusions. The percent of adult sex offenders against children identified as being sexually abused as children themselves ranged from zero to 79 percent. This variation partially reflects differences across studies in how childhood sexual abuse was defined, as well as other differences in study methodology.[6] This variation may also reflect the differences in the types of child sex offenders studied. For example, both Hanson and Slater (1988) and Garland and Dougher (1988) concluded from their reviews of retrospective studies that offenders who selected male children as victims were more likely to have been sexually abused themselves than were offenders against female children.

A few of the studies found that sex offenders of children were more likely to have been sexually abused as children than were members of control groups composed of noninstitutionalized nonoffenders. However, many studies found that, when compared with other types of sex offenders (e.g., rapists or exhibitionists) and other types of nonsexual offenders (i.e., men incarcerated for nonsexual crimes), adult sex offenders of children were not necessarily more likely to have been sexually abused as children.

According to several researchers, the relationship between childhood sexual victimization and adult perpetration of sexual offenses against children is complex and requires measurement and analysis of a host of factors. For example, it has been postulated that adult sexual offending is not simply a result of the experience of childhood sexual victimization, but also of other factors such as age at onset of the abuse, nature of the abuse, stability of the caregiver, and/or physical abuse.[7] Studies that collect data on such additional factors may add to our understanding of what types of sexual abuse, perpetrated under what conditions against what types of child victims, are associated with what types of adult sexual offending against what types of victims under what types of conditions. However, while such retrospective studies can help explore factors possibly related to adult sexual offending, they cannot establish the importance of these factors in predicting adult sexual offending. The reason for this is discussed in the following section.

### Retrospective Studies Had Several Shortcomings

The retrospective studies we reviewed had several shortcomings that precluded our drawing any firm conclusions about whether there is a cycle of sexual abuse. First, the studies focused on known sex offenders of children (i.e., offenders who have been detected, arrested, or convicted, or who had been referred or had presented themselves for treatment), and these offenders may not be typical or representative of all sex offenders against children. Second, self-reports of childhood sexual abuse obtained from known sex offenders are of questionable validity. Known offenders may be motivated to overreport histories of abuse to gain sympathy or to excuse their own offenses.[8] Third, where comparison or control groups were used, attempts to match group members to sex offenders of children on factors possibly related to being sexually abused or abusive were typically limited; few of the studies attempted to control for such factors statistically.

Finally, one of the major shortcomings of these retrospective studies is that they cannot reveal how likely it is that a person who has been sexually abused as a child will become a sexual abuser in adulthood. For example, even if 100 percent of sexual abusers of children were sexually abused as children, this would not necessarily mean that sexual abuse causes abused children to become abusers themselves. It may be that only a small percentage of sexually abused children become sex offenders against children. Determining how likely victims of childhood sexual abuse are to become adult sex offenders requires that a sample of sexually abused children be followed forward in time, rather than the histories of sex offenders be traced backward.

### Prospective Studies Used Better Methodologies, but Results Were Inconclusive

Our review of the literature identified two research studies (described in four articles) that have used a prospective approach in examining the cycle of sexual abuse. One of these studies is part of a larger study of the cycle of violence.[9]

Widom is the primary researcher in the larger study, which is still ongoing. It involves a cohort of 908 substantiated cases of child abuse (physical and/or sexual) or neglect processed through the courts between 1967 and 1971.[10] These abuse/neglect cases were restricted to children who were 11 years of age or younger at the time of the abuse or neglect incident. They included 153 sexually abused children, 160 physically abused children, and 697 neglected children.[11] This prospective study also includes a control group of 667 individuals who had no record of abuse or neglect and who were either born in the same hospitals or attended the same elementary schools as the abused children. The control and study group members were matched on sex, age, race, and approximate family socioeconomic status.

Local, state, and federal official arrest records containing information recorded up to June 1994 were used to determine how many of the study and control group members were arrested for sex offenses. Table 1 shows results pertaining to sex offenses from the most recent analyses based on this larger study.[12] The study did not distinguish whether the sex offense was perpetrated against a child or an adult.[13]

Compared to the control group, a higher percentage of those who had been sexually abused, physically abused, or neglected as children were arrested as adults for any sex crime, for prostitution, and (among males) for rape or sodomy. To determine how different the study groups were from the control group, Widom statistically controlled for such differences between the groups as age, race, and sex; calculated odds ratios; and performed statistical tests. The results indicated that the differences between the sexually abused group and the control group in the odds of arrest for any sex crime or for rape or sodomy separately were not statistically significant. Sexually abused children were significantly more likely to have been arrested for prostitution, however. Twenty-three to 27 years later, sexually abused children were nearly four times more likely to have been arrested for prostitution. On the other hand, members of the childhood neglect study group were significantly more likely than members of the control group to have been arrested for any sex crime or for prostitution.

Because it could allow researchers to discern the likelihood of victims becoming abusers, the prospective approach is methodologically superior to the retrospective approach. Widom's study, however, has several limitations. First, published work from the study has so far relied solely on official arrest data, which may fail to identify some offenders (those who avoid detection or arrest).[14] Second, the study groups of victimized children were identified by using records of substantiated cases of abuse or neglect that were processed through the state courts. Such cases may represent only the most severe instances of abuse and may not be generalizable to all children who have been abused or neglected.[15] Finally,

## Table 1: Results from the Research of Widom and Colleagues on the Cycle of Sexual Abuse

| Adult arrests | Sexually abused (N = 153) Odds ratio[a] | Pct. | Physically abused (N = 160) Odds ratio[a] | Pct. | Neglected (N = 697) Odds ratio[a] | Pct. | Controls (N = 667) Odds ratio[a] | Pct. |
|---|---|---|---|---|---|---|---|---|
| Any sex crime[b] | 1.4 | 6.5% | 1.4 | 11.0% | 2.1 | 13.1% | NA[d] | 6.0% |
| Prostitution | 3.7* | 3.9% | 0.9 | 1.4% | 5.0* | 3.6% | NA[d] | 0.6% |
| Rape or sodomy[c] | 1.9 | 4.2% | 2.4 | 4.7% | 1.8 | 3.6% | NA[d] | 2.1% |

Note 1: When criminal history checks were conducted in 1994, fewer than 1 percent of the individuals in the sample were under 25 years of age.

Note 2: An asterisk (*) denotes statistical significance.

[a] Odds ratios reflect the differences between groups in the odds or likelihood of becoming a sex offender. For example, an odds ratio of 1.4 indicates that sexually abused children are nearly 1-1/2 times as likely as children in the control group to become adult sex offenders. Odds ratios are based on logistic regression analysis, with all three types of abuse in the equation (comparisons are with controls). These equations also control for age, sex, and race.

[b] Sex crimes include prostitution, incest, child molestation, rape, sodomy, assault and battery with intent to gratify, peeping, public indecency, criminal deviant conduct, and contributing to the delinquency of a minor.

[c] Percentages and odds ratios are for males only.

[d] Not applicable

Source: Data provided by C.S. Widom, 1996.

the number of sexually abused males in the abused/neglected sample was small (a total of 24). Statistical comparisons based on small numbers of cases should be interpreted with caution, since small sample sizes may not yield reliable estimates.

We located one other study that used a prospective design and followed sexually victimized children into early adulthood. This study sampled 147 boys under the age of 14 who were seen in the emergency room of an urban hospital because of sexual abuse between 1971 and 1975.[16] The researchers also collected data on a comparison sample of boys of the same race and roughly the same age who were seen in the same emergency room at roughly the same time for reasons other than sexual abuse. In the period 1992 to 1994, official juvenile and adult arrest records for the entire victim and comparison sample were collected, and the researchers attempted to locate and interview as many of the men as possible.[17] Fifty of the 147 boys in the victim sample, and 56 of the 147 boys in the comparison sample, were interviewed. They were asked to self-report instances of sex-offending, and were also asked a number of other questions about their family of origin, sexual history, history of sexual victimization, psychological functioning, drug and alcohol use, and criminal behavior.[18]

As shown in Table 2, the study found little difference between the victim and comparison samples in the percentages that were arrested for, or that self-reported, sex offenses. According to the researchers, one explanation for this finding is that the victim and comparison

---

### Table 2: Results from the Research of Williams and Colleagues on the Cycle of Sexual Abuse

| Outcome variable | "Official" victim sample (N = 50) | "Official" comparison sample (N = 56) | All sexual abuse victims (both samples) (N = 69) | Nonvictims in comparison sample (N = 33) |
|---|---|---|---|---|
| Arrested for sex offense[a] | 14% | 13% | 16% | 6% |
| Self-reported sex offense[b] | 14 | 14 | 13 | 15 |
| Any sex offense[c] | 26 | 20 | 24 | 18 |

[a] Includes any arrest for a sex offense as a juvenile or as an adult. Sex offenses included rape, involuntary deviate sexual intercourse, sexual assault, indecent assault, indecent exposure, and incest.

[b] Includes all individuals who self-reported having committed a sex offense, whether they were arrested for the offense or not. Study group members were asked to report on any initiation or occurrence of sexual contact with children under the age of 12 and any sexual contact with adolescents or adults when physical force, threats of force, or the coercion of adult or supervisory authority was used to achieve the sexual contact.

[c] Includes all individuals who were arrested for a sex offense and those who were not arrested but who self-reported sex offenses.

Source: L. M. Williams et al., 1995.

samples are not as different as originally intended with respect to their having been victims of child sexual abuse. For instance, in the comparison group, 40 percent of the 56 men interviewed reported that they had themselves been sexually abused. Furthermore, 55 percent of the men in the victim sample did not recall, or at least did not report to interviewers, that they had been sexually abused. When the researchers reanalyzed the data and compared all victims (from both the victim sample and the comparison sample) with the remaining nonvictimized members of the comparison group, they did not find a significant difference between the two groups in the likelihood of becoming a sex offender. These findings must also be interpreted with caution, however, because no-difference findings are sometimes attributable to comparing small samples rather than to a real absence of difference between groups.

The generalizability of these findings may be limited since the sample of sexually abused boys (and the matched comparison group) is neither a random sample nor a sample that is representative of the general population of children at risk of such abuse. Over 80 percent of the boys sampled were African-American, and a disproportionate number of the men who were interviewed were from poor families and had criminal records. About one-third of the interviewed men who were sexually abused as boys, and about one-fifth of all of the men interviewed, were incarcerated at the time of interview.

The Williams et al. study is instructive in that it points to a number of difficulties involved in conducting prospective studies of the relationship between childhood victimization and adult offending. These difficulties include (1) the need to determine whether members of comparison groups were victims of sexual abuse, and (2) the need to employ more than a single outcome measure of offending. Of 15 men who self-reported any sex offense, only five had an arrest record for a sex offense; and of 14 men who had been arrested for a sex offense, only 5 self-reported a sex-offending behavior.

## Conclusions

A number of studies have been done on the cycle of sexual abuse, many of which were reviewed in this report. Most of the studies were retrospective in design; that is, they began with a sample of known sex offenders of children and sought to determine whether they were sexually abused during childhood. The chief limitation of the retrospective studies is that studying a known group of sexual offenders cannot provide any direct information about the extent to which children who are sexually abused become sexual offenders as adults. The two studies we reviewed that were prospective in design attempted to overcome this limitation by identifying samples of sexually victimized children and tracking them into adulthood to determine how many became sex offenders. These studies also had limitations, which made it difficult to reach any definitive conclusions about the cycle of sexual abuse. However, in spite of their limitations, overall, the retrospective studies, prospective studies, and research reviews did indicate that the experience of childhood sexual victimization is quite likely neither a necessary nor a sufficient cause of adult sexual offending. Further research would be necessary to determine what kinds of experiences magnify the likelihood that sexually victimized children will become adult sexual offenders against children and, alternatively, what kinds of experiences help prevent victimized children from becoming adult sexual offenders against children.

## Research Articles Used in This Review

### Research Reviews

Garland, Randall J., and Michael J. Dougher. "The Abused/Abuser Hypothesis of Child Sexual Abuse: A Critical Review of Theory and Research." *Adult Human Sexual Behavior With Children and Adolescents: Biosocial Dimensions,* ed. J. R. Feierman (New York: Aldine de Gruyter, 1988), pp. 488–509.

Hanson, R. Karl. "Characteristics of Sex Offenders Who Were Sexually Abused as Children." *Sex Offenders and Their Victims,* ed. R. Langevin (Oakville, Ontario: Juniper Press, 1991), pp. 77–85.

Hanson, R. Karl, and S. Slater. "Sexual Victimization in the History of Child Sexual Abusers: A Review." *Annals of Sex Research* 1 (1988): 485–99.

Williams, Linda Meyer, and David Finkelhor. "The Characteristics of Incestuous Fathers: A Review of Recent Studies." In *The Handbook of Sexual Assault: Issues, Theories, and Treatment of the Offender,* eds. W. L. Marshall, D. R. Laws, and H. E. Barbaree (New York: Plenum Press, 1990), pp. 231–55.

## Retrospective Approach

Alford, Jane, Mary Grey, and C. James Kasper. "Child Molesters: Areas for Further Research." *Corrective and Social Psychiatry and Journal of Behavior Technology Methods and Therapy* Vol. XXXIV (1988): 1–5.

Baker, D. *Father-Daughter Incest: A Study of the Father.* San Diego: California School of Professional Psychology, 1985. *Dissertation Abstracts International*, 46, 951B.

Ballard, D. T., et al. "A Comparative Profile of the Incest Perpetrator: Background Characteristics, Abuse History, and Use of Social Skills." In *The Incest Perpetrator: A Family Member No One Wants to Treat*, ed. A. L. Horton, et al. (Newbury Park, CA: Sage, 1990), pp. 43–64.

Bard, Leonard A., et al. "A Descriptive Study of Rapists and Child Molesters: Developmental, Clinical, and Criminal Characteristics." *Behavioral Sciences and the Law* Vol. V, No. 2 (1987): 203–20.

Bennett, S. R. *Cognitive Style of Incestuous Fathers.* Lubbock, Texas: Texas Tech University, 1985. *Dissertation Abstracts International*, 47, 778B.

Condy, Sylvia, R., et al. "Parameters of Sexual Contact of Boys With Women." *Archives of Sexual Behavior* Vol. XVI (1987): 379–94.

Dhawan, Sonia, and W. L. Marshall. "Sexual Abuse Histories of Sexual Offenders." *Sexual Abuse: A Journal of Research and Treatment* Vol. VIII, No. 1 (1996): 7–15.

Dutton, D. G., and S. D. Hart. "Evidence for Long-term, Specific Effects of Childhood Abuse and Neglect on Criminal Behavior in Men." *International Journal of Offender Therapy and Comparative Criminology* Vol. XVI, No. 2 (1992): 129–37.

Faller, Kathleen Coulborn. "Why Sexual Abuse? An Exploration of the Intergenerational Hypothesis." *Child Abuse and Neglect* Vol. XIII, No. 4 (1989): 543–48.

Frisbie, Louise V. *Another Look at Sex Offenders in California.* Sacramento: California Department of Mental Hygiene, Mental Health Research Monograph No. 12, 1969.

Gaffney, Gary R., Shelly F. Lurie, and Fred S. Berlin. "Is There Familial Transmission of Pedophilia?" *Journal of Nervous and Mental Diseases* Vol. CLXXII (1984): 546–48.

Gebhard, P. H., et al. *Sex Offenders: An Analysis of Types.* New York: Harper and Row, 1965.

Greenberg, David M., John M. W. Bradford, and Susan Curry. "A Comparison of Sexual Victimization in the Childhoods of Pedophiles and Hebephiles." *Journal of Forensic Sciences* Vol. XXXVIII, No. 2 (March 1993): 432–36.

Groff, M. G., and L. M. Hubble. "A Comparison of Father-Daughter and Stepfather-Stepdaughter Incest." *Criminal Justice and Behavior* Vol. XI (1984): 461–75.

Groth, A. Nicholas. "Sexual Trauma in the Life Histories of Rapists and Child Molesters." *Victimology: An International Journal* Vol. IV, No. 1 (1979): 10–16.

Kirkland, Karen D., and Chris A. Bauer. "MMPI Traits of Incestuous Fathers." *Journal of Clinical Psychology* Vol. XXXVIII, No. 3 (1982): 645–49.

Langevin, R., and R. A. Lang. "Psychological Treatment of Pedophiles." *Behavioral Sciences and the Law* Vol. III, No. 4 (1985): 403–19.

Lee, R. N. "Analysis of the Characteristics of Incestuous Fathers." *Dissertation Abstracts International* Vol. XLIII, No. 2343B (1982). University Microfilms No. DA-8227677.

McCarty, Loretta M. "Mother-Child Incest: Characteristics of the Offender." *Child Welfare* Vol. LXV, No. 5 (September/October 1986): 447–58.

Overholser, James C., and Steven J. Beck. "The Classification of Rapists and Child Molesters." *Journal of Offender Counseling, Services and Rehabilitation* Vol. XIV, No. 2 (1989): 169–79.

Segborn, Theoharis K., Robert A. Prentky, and Richard Boucher. "Childhood Sexual Abuse in the Lives of Sexually Aggressive Offenders." *Journal of the American Academy of Child and Adolescent Psychiatry* Vol. XXVI (1987): 262–67.

Tingle, David, et al. "Childhood and Adolescent Characteristics of Pedophiles and Rapists." *International Journal of Law and Psychiatry* Vol. IX (1986): 103–16.

Williams, Linda Meyer, and David Finkelhor. *The Characteristics of Incestuous Fathers.* Durham, N.H.: University of New Hampshire, 1992.

## Prospective Approach

Widom, Cathy Spatz. "Childhood Sexual Abuse and Its Criminal Consequences." *Society* Vol. XXXIII, No. 4 (May/June 1996): 47–53.

Widom, Cathy Spatz. *Victims of Childhood Sexual Abuse—Later Criminal Consequences: Research in Brief.* Washington, D.C.: U.S. Department of Justice, National Institute of Justice, March 1995.

Widom, Cathy Spatz, and M. Ashley Ames. "Criminal Consequences of Childhood Sexual Victimization." *Child Abuse and Neglect* Vol. XVIII, No. 4 (1994): 303–18.

Williams, Linda Meyer, et al. *Juvenile and Adult Offending Behavior and Other Outcomes in a Cohort of Sexually Abused Boys: 20 Years Later.* Philadelphia, PA: Joseph J. Peters Institute, 1995.

## References

1.  See J. H. Beitchman et al, "A Review of the Long-Term Effects of Child Sexual Abuse," *Child Abuse and Neglect*, Vol. XVI (1992), pp. 101–18; A. Browne and D. Finkelhor, "Impact of Child Sexual Abuse: A Review of the Research," *Psychological Bulletin*, Vol. XCIX, No. 1 (1986), pp. 66–77; and D. Finkelhor, "Early and Long-Term Effects of Child Sexual Abuse: An Update," *Professional Psychology: Research and Practice*, Vol XXI, No. 5 (1990), pp. 325–30.

2.  A database of the American Psychological Association covering the literature in psychology and the behavioral sciences.

3.  The two experts who reviewed the comprehensiveness of our list of articles were Dr. R. Karl Hanson, Senior Research Officer in Corrections Research at the Department of the Solicitor General of Canada, and Dr. Cathy Spatz Widom, Professor of Criminal Justice and Psychology at the State University of New York at Albany. The third expert consulted was Dr. Robert A. Prentky, Director of Clinical and Forensic Services at the Joseph J. Peters Institute in Philadelphia.

4.  R. K. Hanson and S. Slater (1988) and R. K. Hanson (1991) reviewed 14 of the 23 retrospective studies covered in this report, and five others. R. J. Garland and M. J. Dougher (1988) reviewed seven of these 23 studies, and two others. L. M. Will-

iams and D. Finkelhor (1990) reviewed three of these 23 studies, and three others. (See bibliography for full citations.)

5. Some studies looked at child sex offenders defined quite broadly, while others looked at specific types of offenders (e.g., incestuous fathers, homosexual pedophiles, or heterosexual pedophiles). Some studies did not use control or comparison groups. Others compared sex offenders to men incarcerated or in treatment for nonsexual offenses, to men clinically depressed, to college students who dated minimally, or to law enforcement officers, among others. Seven of the 23 studies compared sex offenders to a control group of noninstitutionalized men drawn from the general population.

6. Some studies simply asked study group members whether they had been sexually abused as children, and left it to the individuals themselves to determine what constituted sexual abuse. Other studies asked study group members whether they had been involved sexually as children, or before age 13 or age 16, with a person five or more years older than themselves. Studies involving incest offenders sometimes asked offenders whether they had been involved in incestuous relationships as children. However, these relationships may not have involved older adults or may not have been coercive in nature. Further, sexual abuse victimization experiences were not always limited to acts involving physical contact. For example, in one study, childhood sexual victimization included being solicited by adult males or females through words, gestures, or some other sexual approach.

7. See, for example, R. A. Prentky and R. A Knight, "Age of Onset of Sexual Assault: Criminal and Life History Correlates," in *Sexual Aggression: Issues in Etiology, Assessment, and Treatment*, eds. G. C. N. Hall, R. Hirschman, J. R. Graham, and M. S. Zaragoza (Washington, D. C.: Taylor and Francis, 1993), pp. 43–62; and R. A. Prentky et al., "Developmental Antecedents of Sexual Aggression," *Development and Psychopathology* Vol. I (1989): 153–69.

8. One research study suggested that some sex offenders may claim to have been victims of child sexual abuse when they were not. See: Jan Hindman, "Research Disputes and Assumptions about Child Molesters," *National District Attorney Association Bulletin*, Vol. VII, No. 4 (1988), pp. 1–3. Hindman

studied convicted adult child molesters treated at an Oregon clinic between 1980 and 1988. Offenders were required to write a detailed sexual history, including information on whether they were abused as children. Since 1982, offenders have also been told that they will be subject to polygraph testing, that their written autobiography must conform with the polygraph test, and that they will be sent back to jail if they do not pass the test. A higher percentage of offenders who wrote their sexual histories before the polygraph requirement was instituted in 1982 claimed that they had been sexually victimized as children (67 percent) than of those who were told that their sexual histories would have to conform with the polygraph test (29 percent).

9.  On the cycle of sexual abuse, see C. S. Widom and M. A. Ames, 1994; C. S. Widom, 1995; and C. S. Widom, 1996. On the cycle of violence generally, see M. G. Maxfield and Cathy Spatz Widom, "The Cycle of Violence: Revisited Six Years Later," *Archives of Pediatrics and Adolescent Medicine* (April 1996); Cathy Spatz Widom, *The Cycle of Violence: Research in Brief* (Washington, D.C.: U.S. Department of Justice, National Institute of Justice, October 1992); Cathy Spatz Widom, "Child Abuse, Neglect, and Adult Behavior: Research Design and Findings on Criminality, Violence, and Child Abuse," *American Journal of Orthopsychiatry*, Vol. LIX (1989), pp. 355–367; Cathy Spatz Widom, "The Cycle of Violence," *Science*, Vol. CCXLIV (1989), pp. 160–166; and Cathy Spatz Widom, "Does Violence Beget Violence?: A Critical Examination of the Literature," *Psychological Bulletin*, Vol. CVI (1989), pp. 3–28.

10.  The study has relied on the official records of agencies that handled these cases. Detailed information about the abuse and/or neglect incident and family composition and characteristics was obtained from the files of the juvenile court and probation department, the authority responsible for cases of abused, neglected, or dependent and delinquent children. The records of the sexual abuse cases were obtained from the juvenile court and from the adult criminal court of a metropolitan area in the Midwest. If there was evidence in the records that the charges of sexual abuse had been investigated and found to be true, the case was coded as involving sexual abuse.

11. Some individuals in each of these groups experienced more than one type of maltreatment. Thus, the numbers add up to more than 908 individuals.

12. C. S. Widom, 1996; C. S. Widom, personal communication.

13. To strengthen the study, Widom is extending data collection in a number of ways. Future analyses will include participant self-report data, which will allow corroboration of the results from official arrest data and potentially provide more precise information on the nature of the sex offenses committed (i.e., whether they involve child or minor victims, etc.).

14. We noted in footnote 13 that Widom is undertaking new analyses that will make use of self-report data on commission of sex offenses to supplement official arrest data.

15. Abuse and/or neglect cases that are substantiated at the court level may not be representative of all cases because over half of child maltreatment reports are not substantiated by social services investigators, and the vast majority of cases substantiated by local or county departments of social services never reach the court level. (See J. Leiter, K.A. Myers, and M. Zingraff, "Substantiated and Unsubstantiated Cases of Child Maltreatment: Do Their Consequences Differ?" *Social Work Research*, Vol. XVIII, No. 2 (June 1994), pp. 67–82; and M.T. Zingraff et al., "Child Maltreatment and Youthful Problem Behavior," *Criminology*, Vol. XXXI, No. 2 (May 1993), pp. 173–202.) In addition, Widom states that the cases included in her study were processed before the child abuse reporting laws were passed, and many cases of sexual abuse were not reported. Some researchers have suggested using all substantiated reports of abuse and neglect (not just those that reach the court level), or including unsubstantiated reports, in research on the consequences of abuse and neglect. However, Widom has warned that using unsubstantiated reports might introduce bias because these reports leave open the question of whether abuse or neglect actually occurred and are likely to be biased toward the less serious end of the continuum. (See C.S. Widom, "Sampling Bias and Implications for Child Abuse Research," *American Journal of Orthopsychiatry*, Vol. LVIII (1988), pp. 260–270.) Furthermore, if prospective studies find little support for the cycle of sex abuse among the most severe

cases—those that have been substantiated at the court level—it is not likely that strong support for such a relationship will be found using less severe cases.

16. L. M. Williams et al., 1995.

17. The researchers checked official arrest records from the city's juvenile court, its adult probation department, and the National Criminal Information Center. Sex offenses included rape, involuntary deviate sexual intercourse, sexual assault, indecent assault, indecent exposure, and incest. It appears that arrest records were examined for all members of the victim and comparison sample. However, Williams et al. only present arrest information for sample members who were located and interviewed.

18. In an effort to protect men who did not remember childhood abuse that had occurred or might not want others to know about it, the researchers did not reveal the fact of childhood victimization to men who did not bring it up on their own. Study group members were told that they had been selected for a follow-up study of men who received emergency room services in the hospital in the early 1970s.

# Chapter 35

# *Economic Costs of Abuse*

## *Chapter Contents*

## Section 35.1

# *Measuring the Costs of Domestic Violence Against Women*

Institute for Women's Policy Research, copyright © December 1996.
Reprinted with permission.

Beginning in the late 1960s and early 1970s, the women's movement fought to redefine domestic violence, historically considered a private family problem, as a public issue. The success of this movement in bringing spouse abuse to the attention of the public resulted in the passage of laws such as the Family Violence Prevention and Services Act of 1984 and the Violence Against Women Act of 1994. These laws have assisted victims in making greater claims on services, brought more attention to issues of domestic violence, and led to efforts to collect data on the extent of the domestic violence problem and to estimate its costs.

*Measuring the Costs of Domestic Violence Against Women and the Cost-Effectiveness of Interventions*, based on a collaborative research effort by the Institute for Women's Policy Research (IWPR); Victim Services, Inc.; and the Domestic Violence Training Project, reports on the methods and data available to build an economic model for measuring the direct and indirect societal costs of domestic violence and to assess the cost-effectiveness of interventions. The project focused on the following areas of service use: health care, child welfare, homelessness, criminal justice, and social services (i.e. employment training). Additionally, IWPR reviewed available research concerning costs that are not directly measurable, such as the cost to employers of absenteeism and decreased productivity that result from domestic violence.

### *Prevalence of Domestic Violence*

A variety of national studies attempts to document the prevalence of domestic violence. Although definitions of spouse abuse and domestic violence against women are contested and difficult to measure, research by Stark and Flitcraft and by Stout shows that as much as 20 percent of the adult female population suffers from this abuse, while a survey by the Commonwealth Fund shows that over eight percent of women living with or married to a man reported abuse in the previous year. Between 1992 and 1993, of all acts of violence against women by a lone offender, 29 percent were committed by an intimate (defined as a husband, ex-husband, boyfriend, or ex-boyfriend; See Table 1).

### Defining Domestic Violence

The definition of domestic violence is a crucial element in determining what to include in a measure of the associated costs. Yet no consensus exists as to the actual definition of domestic violence against women. Domestic violence is increasingly defined as a course of coercive conduct existing in any intimate relationship, past or present, that includes not only physical force, but also a pattern of mental abuse and control including intense criticism, "put downs" and verbal harassment, sexual coercion and assaults, isolation due to restraint of normal activities and freedom, and denial of access to resources. Although the joint-study authors would recommend this broad definition in the calculation of direct and indirect costs, the studies reviewed in the report vary in their definitions, with some using a narrow definition and others a broad definition.

### Estimated Costs of Domestic Violence

Straus and Gelles estimated the losses due to domestic violence, including the costs of secondary medical treatment and lost worker productivity, to be between $5 and $10 billion, annually. As part of a study on the cost of crime to victims, Miller, Cohen, and Wiersema estimated the annual losses due to domestic violence to be $67 billion. In this later study, the cost breakdown is presented in three categories—medical, other tangible, and quality of life—and includes only those costs incurred by the victim. All of these efforts to estimate costs are based on the limited data available.

### Direct and Indirect Costs

The economic costs of domestic violence can be split into two types—*direct costs* and *indirect costs*. The economic model developed in the joint study uses Max, Rice, and MacKenzie's definition of direct costs as the value of the goods and services used in treating or preventing domestic violence and indirect costs as the value of goods and services lost because of domestic violence.

## Table 1. Estimates of the General Prevalence of Domestic Violence

**Study:** National Crime Victimization Survey, 1987–1991 (Bachman, 1994)

**Methodology**: Nationally representative survey, interviews

**Unit of Analysis:** 400,000 individual women over the age of 12 years

**Prevalence:** The average annual rate (1987–1991) of violent victimizations per 1,000 women was 5.4 for victimizations by intimates, 1.1 by relatives, and 7.6 by acquaintances. Of all victimization events against women, 28% were committed by intimates, 5% by relatives, and 35% by acquaintances.

**Study:** National Crime Victimization Survey, 1992–1993 (Bachman & Saltzman, 1995)

**Methodology**: Nationally representative survey, interviews—uses new methodology

**Unit of Analysis:** 50,000 households and 100,000 individuals over the age of 12 years

**Prevalence:** The average annual rate (1992–1993) of violent victimizations per 1,000 women was 9.3 for victimizations by intimates, 2.8 by relatives, and 12.9 by acquaintances. Of all victimization events against women, 29% were committed by intimates, 9% by relatives, and 40% by acquaintances.

**Study:** Commonwealth Fund Survey on Women's Health (Commonwealth Fund,1993)

**Methodology**: 1991 nationally representative survey

**Unit of Analysis:** 2,500 women and 1,000 men, ages 18 and older

**Prevalence:** 84 per 1,000 women living with or married to a man reported abuse in the last year (1991).

## Direct Costs

Direct costs can be calculated by multiplying the *prevalence* of domestic violence (the total number of cases in a given time period) by the *cost* of the services used as a result of the violence. This is a useful method for determining the efficacy of intervention strategies because, once a baseline cost is established (much like a baseline mammogram), the analyst can evaluate any change in the cost (either from a decline in prevalence or a decline in costs) from one year to the next after the implementation of the new intervention.

Table 2 includes a variety of numbers that can be substituted for institutional prevalence and the cost of services. These data should be considered only as illustrative of how the cost model might be applied; further review of the validity of these figures and the comparability of these studies' findings must be done before calculating reliable total cost figures.

## Indirect Costs

In determining the indirect economic costs of domestic violence, researchers need to impute two kinds of values: 1) the cost of lost productivity and 2) the cost of mortality. Although much of the data on productivity losses are based on small-scale studies and the overall prevalence of domestic violence among working women is not available, some beginning calculations for these losses due to domestic violence can be made. For instance, the finding that 30 percent of abused working women lose their jobs or that 50 percent of abused working women report being unable to attend school can be coupled with information on women's average earnings by age to yield estimates of productivity losses (see Table 3).

## Indirect Social and Psychological Costs

Analysts argue that the indirect costs of domestic violence to women, to communities, and to society also include losses in the quality of life. These indirect social and psychological costs to women fall into three categories: loss of control over one's environment; alienation from one's self, friends, family, and community; and loss of one's ability to pursue future aspirations. Analysts would also have us consider losses to communities and society, including women's increased dependency, their lack of power, and restraints on their activities. Al-

## Table 2. Direct Costs of Domestic Violence

| Service | Usage | Cost |
|---|---|---|
| HEALTH CARE: Emergency room care | 19% of women with injuries who present themselves at ER are victims of abuse (Stark & Flitcraft, 1991). | A study at Rush Medical Center in Chicago estimated an average charge for medical services to abused women, children, and older people as $1,633 per person per year, excluding psychological or follow-up costs (Meyer, 1992). |
| CHILD WELFARE: Foster care | Of the 256,000 children in foster care (1995 est.), an estimated 50 percent are victims of abuse (Committee on Ways & Means, 1994). | $2.5 billion federal foster care expenditures under Title IV-E in 1993 (Committee on Ways & Means, 1994). |
| HOMELESSNESS: Emergency shelters | 11%–64% of homeless women are victims of abuse (D'Ercole & Struening, 1990). | The Women Against Abuse Center in Philadelphia reported an annual budget of $2.5 million, or $68 per person per day ("Women's Shelters," 1994). |
| HOMELESSNESS: Supported housing (transitional, Section 8, public housing) | 17%–70% of housed mothers are victims of abuse (Bassuk & Rosenberg, 1988). | $6,588 million was allocated for FY1995 in total subsidies for public housing. The monthly appropriation rate per occupied unit is $481 (U.S. HUD, 1995). |
| CRIMINAL JUSTICE SYSTEM: Arrests by police | 5%–16% of domestic violence calls result in arrest in the District of Columbia (Baker, Cahn & Sands, 1989). | The New York City Police Department made 12,724 domestic violence arrests in 1989, at an average cost of $3,241 per arrest (Zorza, 1994). |
| CRIMINAL JUSTICE SYSTEM: Prison and detention costs of batterers | 20,170 male prisoners were incarcerated for harming an intimate in 1991 (U.S. DOJ, 1994). | Average annual operating expenditures per inmate (nationwide) in 1990 were $15,513 (U.S. DOJ, 1992). |
| SOCIAL SERVICES: Job training | 16%–84% of women in training are victims of abuse (Raphael, 1995). | $1,500 per person for JTPA training. |

## Table 3. Examples of Indirect Costs

| Service | Usage | Cost |
|---------|-------|------|
| Job Loss of Victim | 24%–30% of abused working women lose their jobs (Shepard & Pence, 1988; Stanley, 1992). | U.S. Bureau of the Census, 1993a, provides data on women's earning scales, by age. |
| Disruption at Work Place | 75% of victims are harassed at work by their abuser (Friedman & Couper, 1987). | U.S. Bureau of the Census, 1993a, provides data on women's earning scales, by age. |
| Poor Work Habits | 64% of battered women arrived an hour late 5 times per month (Stanley, 1992). | U.S. Bureau of the Census, 1993a, provides data on women's earning scales, by age. |
| Lost Productivity Due to Premature Mortality | 35% of female homicide victims are murdered by an intimate or other relative (Bachman & Saltzman, 1995). | U.S. Bureau of the Census, 1993a, provides data on women's earning scales, by age. |

though quantifying these losses is difficult, it is necessary in order to get a full picture of the costs of domestic violence.

## The Relationship Between Domestic Violence and Welfare and Job Training

For many battered women, welfare is the only alternative income source, and the only immediate way for them to free themselves from financial dependence on their abusers. Given the prominent role of economic independence as a factor in battered women's ability to leave abusive relationships, further research is needed to examine the role of welfare in the well-being of battered women and the training supports needed to help them lead safe, independent lives.

Studies by NOW Legal Defense and Education Fund and by Raphael show that anywhere from 20 to 80 percent of women in welfare-to-work programs around the country were victims of domestic abuse. This has important implications for the effectiveness of training and education programs. Many women, once enrolled in these programs, may be prevented from participating by their partners. Additional support services may be needed at the training site, without which enrollees may not be able to complete training programs within expected time limits.

Federal changes to welfare policy in the Personal Responsibility and Opportunity Reconciliation Act of 1996 allow (but do not require) a state to include "battering and extreme cruelty" among those conditions which exempt recipients from time limits imposed on the receipt of cash assistance. Waivers may be granted in cases where any requirement would make it harder for welfare recipients to escape domestic violence or unfairly penalize past, present, or potential domestic violence victims. The Family Violence Amendment to the welfare bill contains no limitation on how many waivers a state may grant in cases of domestic violence.

## The Need for Further Research

To our knowledge, there are no national studies that determine the direct costs of domestic violence against women; no national studies to determine the extent of the lost production in firms, households, and communities from this source of violence against women; and insufficient data to assess whether services are cost-effective in reducing the prevalence of abuse. The claim that domestic violence against women is a legitimate social problem requiring substantial investment by the public and private sectors needs to be supported by credible information on both the number of individuals affected and the economic cost to victims, institutions, taxpayers, and society. Without such information, policymakers, taxpayers, foundations, private firms, and the medical, criminal justice, and social service establishments will likely be unwilling to allocate increasingly scarce resources to address this problem.

By demonstrating the effect of domestic violence on individuals and society, reliable estimates of the direct and indirect costs of abuse will help to strengthen the argument for intervention by a wide range of social institutions (government, health care, business). Based on its preliminary review of the literature, the joint study suggests that estimates of some of the costs can be made. Estimates of all these costs are worth pursuing as a means of educating funders, policymakers, businesses, and the general public. To make progress in estimating the indirect social costs of domestic violence, research needs to be stimulated more widely in the field.

## References

Bachmann, R. *Violence Against Women: A National Crime Victimization Survey Report*. Washington, D.C.: Bureau of Justice Statistics. NCJ-145235. January 1994.

Bachmann, R., and L. E. Saltzman. *Violence Against Women: Estimates from the Redesigned Survey*. Washington, D.C.: Bureau of Justice Statistics. NCJ-154348. August 1995.

Baker, K., N. Cahn, and S. J. Sands. *Report on District of Columbia Police Response to Domestic Violence*. Joint project of the D.C. Coalition Against Domestic Violence and the Women's Law and Public Policy Fellowship Program at Georgetown University Law Center, funded by the Revson Foundation, 1989.

Bassuk, E., and L. Rosenberg. "Why Does Family Homelessness Occur? A Case-Control Study." *American Journal of Public Health* 78, 7 (1988): 783–87.

Committee on Ways and Means, U.S. House of Representatives. *The Green Book, Overview of Entitlement Programs*. Washington, D.C.: U.S. Government Printing Office, 1994.

The Commonwealth Fund. *The Commonwealth Fund Survey of Women's Health*. New York: The Commonwealth Fund, Commission on Women's Health, July 14, 1993.

D'Ercole, A., and E. Struening. "Victimization among Homeless Women: Implications for Service Delivery." *Journal of Community Psychology* 18, 2 (1990): 141–52.

Friedman, L. N., and S. Couper. *The Cost of Domestic Violence: A Preliminary Investigation of the Financial Cost of Domestic Violence*. New York: Victim Services Agency, 1987.

Max, W., D. Rice, and E. Mackenzie. "The Lifetime Cost of Injury." *Inquiry* 27 (1990): 332–43.

Meyer, H. "The Billion Dollar Epidemic." *American Medical News*. The American Medical Association (January 6, 1992).

Miller, T. R., M. A. Cohen, and B. Wiersema. *Crime in the United States: Victim Costs and Consequences.* Final Report to the National Institute of Justice, May 1995.

NOW Legal Defense and Education Fund. *A Leadership Summit: The Link Between Violence and Poverty in the Lives of Women and Their Children.* April 28, 1995.

Raphael, J. *Domestic Violence: Telling the Untold Welfare-to-Work Story.* Chicago: Taylor Institute, 1995.

Shepard, M., and E. Pence. "The Effect of Battering on the Employment Status of Women." *Affilia* 3, 2 (1988): 55–61.

Stanley, C. *Domestic Violence: An Occupational Impact Study.* Unpublished report prepared for the Domestic Violence Intervention Services, Inc., in Tulsa, Okla.

Stark, E., and A. H. Flitcraft. "Spouse Abuse." In M. Rosenberg and M. A. Fendley, eds. *Violence in America.* New York: Oxford University Press, 1991.

Stout, K. D. "Intimate Femicide: Effect of Legislation and Social Services." *Affilia* 4, 2 (1989): 21–30.

Straus, M. A., and R. J. Gelles. "The Costs of Family Violence." *Public Health Reports* 102, 6 (1987): 638–41.

U.S. Bureau of the Census. "Money Income of Households, Families, and Persons in the United States." *Current Population Reports,* Series P-60. Washington, D.C.: U.S. Government Printing Office, 1993. Average earnings by age for full-time, year-round female workers in 1992: 15–24 years old—$14,698, 25–34 years old—$21,990, 35–44 years old—$24,189, 45–54 years old—$24,531, 55–65 years old—$22,623, 65 and older—$21,548. Average earnings by age for full-time, year-round male workers in 1992: 15–24 years old—$15,769, 25–34 years old—$26,533, 35–44 years old—$34,945, 45–54 years old—$38,219, 55–65 years old—$35,351, 65 and older—$35,256.

U.S. Department of Housing and Urban Development (U.S.HUD). "Comparison of Public Housing Subsidies with Certificate Subsidies." Issue Brief No. 1. Washington, D.C.: Office of Policy Development and Research, U.S. Department of Housing and Urban Development, 1995.

U.S. Department of Justice. *Census of State and Federal Corrections Facilities, 1990.* Washington, D.C.: Bureau of Justice Statistics, 1992. NCJ-137003

U.S. Department of Justice. *Violence between Intimates.* Washington, D.C.: Bureau of Justice Statistics, 1994. NCJ-149529

"Women's Shelters: Demand Up, Donations Down." *Working Woman* (November 1994).

Zorza, J. "Women Battering: High Costs and the State of the Law." *Clearinghouse Review* (1994). Special issue.

## Section 35.2

# *Poverty, Welfare, and Battered Women: What Does the Research Tell Us?*

*Prepared by Eleanor Lyon, Ph.D.*

While domestic violence cuts across social groups defined by race, ethnicity, and economic circumstances, it is clear that the combined experience of poverty and violence raises particularly difficult issues for women. Several studies in the past ten to fifteen years have documented the importance of economic resources for battered women's decision-making. Gondolf's (1988) study of the exit plans of 800 women who had used Texas battered women's shelters, for example, found that access to an independent income, along with child care and transportation were primary considerations; only 16% of the women with their own income planned to return to their batterers. Similarly, shelter programs have reported that a majority of shelter residents use welfare in their efforts to end the violence in their lives (Raphael 1995). Despite these indications, research which explores the connections between domestic violence against impoverished women and their use of welfare is still in its early stages.

What follows is a brief summary of several very recent studies, focusing on the extent and impact of domestic violence among poor women and women on welfare. The overview concludes with implications of this research for the new Temporary Aid to Needy Families (TANF) welfare program. This review is not exhaustive (see Raphael and Tolman 1997, for a more detailed summary), and necessarily does not include research which is currently in process but incomplete. The studies were originally conducted for varying reasons; they use different samples of women, and document violence and its impacts in different ways. All of them show disturbingly high rates of domestic violence in the lives of impoverished women, along with high rates of physical and mental health and other problems. In combination, however, the studies also provide indications of women's astounding resiliency. The picture which emerges at this stage of knowledge is complex: a majority of women on welfare have experienced violence by intimate partners and in childhood, and have been affected in widely different ways and to different degrees. These impacts, in turn, have varying implications for women's use of welfare and need for particular supports or temporary relief from TANF/program requirements.

## How Prevalent Is Domestic Violence Among Poor Women and Women Receiving Welfare?

In nearly all of the studies which have addressed the issue, well over half of the women receiving Aid to Families with Dependent Children (AFDC) reported that they had experienced physical abuse (defined as a continuum from causing fear of being hurt to slapping or hitting through more physically injurious acts) by an intimate male partner at some point during their adult lives; most also reported physical and/or sexual abuse in childhood. When women were asked about more recent violence from their male partners, the rates remained high—from 19.5% to 32%. The specific behaviors counted differ from one study to the next, and measures of recent violence vary, as well. The studies agree, however, that current or recent domestic violence is prevalent among poor women and especially among those receiving AFDC. More specifically:

- *In Harm's Way? Domestic Violence, AFDC Receipt and Welfare Reform in Massachusetts,* a probability sample of 734 women receiving AFDC in 40 of 42 welfare offices in the state, found that 64.9% had experienced physical abuse (using the state's legal definition of "hit, slapped, kicked, thrown, shoved, hurt badly enough to go to a doctor, used weapon in a frightening way, forced sexual activity, or 'made you think you might be hurt'") by an adult male partner during their lives, and 19.5% reported such abuse during the past year (Allard et al. 1997).

- *The Passaic County Study of AFDC Recipients in a Welfare-to-Work Program: A Preliminary Analysis,* a sample of 846 women in an AFDC Job Readiness program in Passaic County, New Jersey, found that 57.3% reported they had experienced physical abuse by an intimate male partner as adults, and 19.7% of those currently in a relationship stated they were being abused physically (just over 65% reported they were currently involved in a relationship with a man). In this study, the term "physical abuse" had been discussed during the program, but was not defined on the survey (Curcio 1997).

- The Worcester Family Research Project, a study of 436 homeless and housed women, of whom 409 received AFDC, found that over 60% of the entire sample reported severe physical violence (slapped at least 6 times, kicked, bit, hit with a fist, hit with an object, beaten up, or more injurious acts) by an intimate male partner in adulthood. Nearly a third (32.4%) reported such violence by their "current or most recent partner" within the past two years (Browne and Bassuk 1997).

- The Effects of Violence on Women's Employment, a random survey of 824 women (one-third currently receiving AFDC, two-thirds not) in one of Chicago's low-income neighborhoods, found that women who were receiving AFDC were more likely than the others to experience domestic violence: 33.8% of the AFDC recipients and 25.5% of the non-recipients had experienced "severe aggression" (kicking, hitting, biting, beating, injuring, raping, and threatening with or using a weapon) by a partner in adulthood. Further, of those currently in a relationship, 19.5% of the recipients and 8.1% of the non-recipients had experienced severe aggression (the same acts, excluding biting and raping) in the last 12 months (Lloyd 1996).

- Other studies of AFDC recipients have reported similar findings (see Raphael and Tolman 1997). For example, 60% of a representative sample of the Washington state caseload reported some type of physical or sexual abuse as adults; 55% stated they had been physically abused by an intimate partner. In 50% of Oregon AFDC cases reviewed because of apparent lack of progress toward work, women reported they had been physically or sexually abused at some point during their lives. Finally, 58% of women who entered a Chicago welfare-to-work program over a one-year period reported current domestic violence (Raphael 1995).

These studies demonstrate that women receiving welfare have experienced high rates of violence of varying kinds by a male partner; the Chicago study found that the rates were higher than those experienced by other low-income women from the same neighborhood. More recent abuse has been measured in multiple ways: most studies have asked about events during the last year, but the Worcester study reported recent violence for the past two years; only the Passaic County study asked about current abuse.

## What Is the Connection Between Welfare and Domestic Violence?

While these studies have documented high rates of domestic violence among welfare recipients, most research has not yet thoroughly investigated the role that welfare plays in the lives of abused women, or the role domestic violence plays in their use of welfare or their ability to sustain employment. Two recent studies have begun to shed more light on these questions.

First, the Worcester study (Saloman et al. 1996) looked at length of stay on welfare, and at the number of episodes of welfare receipt. Over all, less than a third of the women had remained on welfare for a cumulative total of five years or more. However, the study found that women who had experienced physical violence by a partner were more likely to have remained on welfare for a combined total of five years or longer; this relationship was strongest among homeless women. Nearly 82% of the homeless longer-term recipients had experienced domestic violence, compared to just over 56% of those who had received welfare less than five years.

The Worcester study also investigated "cycling" (more than one episode of welfare receipt) among those who had combined totals of two years or more. It found that a lifetime history of violent victimization was a strong determinant of cycling. Women who had experienced physical or sexual abuse in childhood were significantly more likely to "cycle," as were housed women who experienced physical violence by a partner. While it is far from definitive, this last finding could support perceptions that women may use welfare strategically in response to their partner's violence.

The second study started with a sample of 3,147 domestic violence incidents reported to Salt Lake City police. Over three years, between 24% and 27% of the women victims sought AFDC. More to the point, between 38% and 41% of them had their cases opened within a year (before or after) of the reported incident. This proximity suggests a possible connection between domestic violence and welfare receipt for some of these women: they sought AFDC as a way to gain independence following a reported incident, or the independence they found through welfare contributed to a subsequent episode prompted by an abuser's desire to regain control (Brandwein 1997). More research is needed to explore the meaning of these connections.

In short, the data that address the ways that women who turn to welfare include it among their immediate responses to domestic violence are still limited. The available data suggest that most recently battered women receiving welfare have not been long-term recipients, although they are more likely to have multiple episodes of violence.

## What Effects of Domestic Violence Are Found Among Women Receiving Welfare?

Some research has investigated welfare recipients' physical and mental health, aspects of their current and past intimate relationships that could affect their participation in training and employment, and their work experience. Again, the studies have measured and analyzed these characteristics in different ways. Although AFDC recipients who have ever experienced domestic violence have generally higher rates of difficulties than others, the potential implications for TANF waiver or exemption policy are complex.

### *Impacts on Physical Health*

Across studies, many AFDC recipients have reported physical health problems. The Worcester study (Bassuk et al. 1996), for example, found rates of reported asthma, anemia, hypertension, ulcers, and histories of alcohol or drug abuse or dependency at substantially higher rates than among the general population, but comparisons between abused and non-abused women have not been published. Asthma, at over 22%, was the most prevalent health problem. The Massachusetts study (Allard et al. 1997) found that 31.7% of abused women and 21.4% of non-abused women reported a current "physical disability, handicap, or other serious physical, mental, or emotional problem." However, there was no difference between the abused and non-abused groups in having "a condition that makes her unable to work." Finally, the Chicago study (Lloyd 1996) found that 19.8% of the total sample had a "work-limiting disability," compared to 23.9% of those who had experienced severe aggression in the last 12 months.

### *Impacts on Mental Health*

The impact of domestic violence on AFDC recipients' mental health has also been measured in multiple ways. In general, the studies have found higher rates of depression and drug or alcohol abuse among abused women than among those who report no abuse. Current drug and alcohol problems, for example, were reported by 18.7% of the currently abused women compared to 10.1% of the entire sample in the Passaic County study (and about 4% of the entire Worcester sample). That study also found current "severe depression" among 54.1% of those in an abusive relationship, compared to 31.8% of the total sample. Similarly, current depression was reported by 42.3% of the women in the Chicago study who had experienced severe aggression in the past 12 months, compared to 37.3% of those who had ever experienced severe aggression, and 24.8% of the entire sample.

AFDC recipients who have experienced domestic violence are more likely than others to be depressed and show other signs of emotional impact. However, the lower rates for those whose abuse is not current suggest that these effects are not permanent. The Massachusetts study compared women who had been abused within the past 12 months with those whose abuse occurred more than 12 months previously, and found that the second group had significantly higher scores of self esteem and "mastery," and lower levels of symptoms of depression and anxiety than those who were most recently abused (Allard et al. 1997). While these scores still did not reach those of the never abused group, the suggestions of recovery are important, especially since not all of these women had received sustained professional or other support. It is likely that more evidence of recovery would be found after a period longer than 12 months.

## Potential Impact of Relationships on Training or Work

AFDC recipients who are currently being abused report substantially more potential interference with work or training than those who are not. The Passaic County study (Curcio 1997) is clear on this issue: 39.7% of the currently abused women (14.6% of the sample were currently abused) reported that their partner tries to prevent them from obtaining education and training; this was reported by 12.9% of the total sample. About two-thirds of the currently abused women in this study also reported that their partner controls their life. Similarly, the Massachusetts study (Allard et al. 1997) found that 21.7% of the women who had been abused in the past 12 months (19.5% of the total sample) reported having a current or former partner who wouldn't like her going to school or work, compared to 12.9% of those whose abuse occurred more than a year ago, and 1.6% of the women who had never been abused. More dramatically, the Chicago study (Lloyd 1996) found that, among recipients who were currently in a relationship, 8% reported that their partner had prevented them from going to school or work in the past 12 months, 2% said that their partners had harassed them by telephone at work, and the partners of 1.7% had appeared at work to harass them. These women were employed significantly fewer hours than the others.

Not surprisingly, the research also shows that AFDC recipients who have been abused are more likely to have a variety of kinds of conflicts with their current or former partners. The Massachusetts study (Allard et al. 1997) found that over half (52%) of the women who had been abused in the last year had also argued with a man about child support, visitation or custody in the past year, compared to 20% of those who had never been abused. Such arguments are commonly protracted, can include violence or its threat, and play a part in abusers' efforts to control mothers' behavior. However, comparisons between women who had been abused in the past year with those who were abused more than a year prior to the study found that the second group was also significantly less likely to have had such arguments in the past year. This suggests again that the recent abuse is a critical consideration to women's current well-being, as well as an abuse history. The impacts of abuse do diminish with time, and reductions can be seen within 12 months for significant numbers of women. Current studies have not yet indicated what factors are associated with these reductions, however.

## Work Experience and Interest

These studies document high levels of employment interest and experience among AFDC recipients. At least two-thirds of the women report having an employment history—over 88% in the Massachusetts study. In fact, over 70% of the recipients in this study had held full-time jobs, and the women with abuse histories were significantly more likely to have been employed, and employed full-time (73.5% compared to 64.5%), than the women who had never been abused (Allard et al. 1997). Further, 89.4% of the women in this study reported that they would prefer to go to school or work, rather than stay home full-time with children; there was no difference in this respect between women with abuse histories and those who had never been abused. The two groups were also equivalently likely to have had schooling or training for particular work and to be currently enrolled in a program.

The Chicago study (Lloyd 1996) also looked closely at the relationship between employment and abuse in its low-income neighborhood sample. It found no significant difference between women who had experienced physical abuse by a partner (either in the past 12 months or ever in their lives) and those who did not report such abuse in current employment, job status, days absent from work, or number of weeks unemployed in the past year. Notably, in response to an open-ended question, just 20% of the women who had been abused reported that the abuse had negative effects on their education and employment.

However, the women in this study who had experienced abuse were more likely to have ever been unemployed when they wanted to be working, to have lower personal income, and to have received AFDC, food stamps, and Medicaid in the past year. In addition, the women whose partners had threatened them with physical harm or had used a weapon against them were employed in significantly lower status jobs than others; this effect was especially pronounced among women whose partners had used a knife or gun against them.

Notably, Lloyd (1997) also found that some of the women who had experienced abuse increased their labor force participation, while others decreased their employment efforts due to partner interference. Still others did not change. Women make decisions about work involvements based on the combination of options they have available.

In sum, the evidence available to date suggests a complex relationship between domestic violence and employment experience, and there is still more to learn about the role of a woman's race, ethnicity, ability/disability, immigration status, religious affiliation, and age in employment experience. Among AFDC recipients, women who report abuse are at least as likely to have work experience as those who have not, to have received job-related training, and to express a preference for school or work. Among poor women, those who experienced domestic violence had more spells of unemployment, more job turnover, lower personal incomes, and were more likely to receive AFDC and other assistance than others; nonetheless, they had equivalent levels of current employment, absenteeism, and job status.

## Summary Considerations

As these studies document, women who have experienced domestic violence are prominent among AFDC caseloads. Women who have experienced abuse are more likely than others to have a variety of physical and mental health problems, to have ongoing arguments with their partners, to have partners who oppose or interfere with school or employment, and to have more frequent periods of unemployment and welfare receipt; in some cases, the physical, emotional, and employment effects have been prolonged and extreme. However, the studies also provide evidence of many women's remarkable resiliency: over time the physical and emotional effects have declined, and women have continued to seek and achieve employment. The studies also document their active efforts to use available resources, such as police and protective orders, to stop their partners' violence.

Clearly, some women face extreme circumstances and will need special supports and considerations, such as additional advocacy and services, or short or long-term waivers/exceptions from welfare or child support time limits or requirements. The studies just reviewed, while providing a wealth of valuable information, do not say what percentage of ever- or currently-abused women will require special considerations—there is no definitive profile or formula to identify them. However, it is unlikely that they will constitute a majority of women receiving TANF support.

Given the myriad ways women may seek support, it is important to provide women seeking financial assistance with maximum options through flexible policies that can respond on a case-by-case basis. Economic independence and employment are central considerations in women's safety: options should include training and placement which respond to immediate and longer-term needs, as well as safely enforced child support where appropriate. Assisting battered women will require sensitivity to differences in women's strengths and needs,

861

which can be achieved by providing safe and confidential opportunities for communication, and attention to what individual women say they need to achieve both safety and self-sufficiency. To build helpful responses, agencies will also need to recognize that abused women, depending on a complex array of circumstances, will operate according to different time frames. More research will be necessary to identify what will be most helpful policy to assist their route to self-sufficiency. Such research will need to investigate more thoroughly how women's race, ethnicity, age, ability/disability, religious affiliation, and immigration status affect their experiences and decisions. Such research, however, will not replace the importance of listening to and being guided by the women themselves and responding to the differences in their histories and circumstances.

Drawing on the studies outlined in this paper, as well as the research about battered women in general, TANF and Child Support Enforcement agency staff should assume: 1) that not all abused women coming into contact with their offices will have problems that interfere with their ability to take steps toward self-sufficiency; 2) that some formerly abused women will have lingering safety concerns or trauma that will interfere with job training or employment or make paternity establishment or vigorous child support dangerous; 3) that not all women who have left an abusive relationship are now safe (the post-separation period can be very dangerous for many battered women, with significant numbers experiencing ongoing threats and abuse); and 4) that not only women who experience current or past abuse have the kinds of problems reviewed here: these studies show that, while these difficulties are found at higher rates among women who have been abused, they are also found for other impoverished women and women receiving welfare benefits.

States can play a critical role in identifying the prevalence of domestic violence in their caseloads, in tracking and evaluating the granting of waivers or exceptions to TANF and child support enforcement requirements, and in documenting the success and difficulties of battered women in attaining employment. We need to know a great deal more about how waivers, exceptions, or special services will be used by states and how battered women are helped to move to a situation of safety and, ultimately, from welfare to work.

## About the Author

Eleanor Lyon has conducted research and evaluation related to domestic violence, violence against women, and criminal justice and social policy for twenty years. She is a research consultant for several projects for the National Resource Center on Domestic Violence, and is Research Associate at the Village for Families and Children, Inc. in Hartford, CT. She is co-author of *Safety Planning with Battered Women: Complex Lives, Difficult Choices* (1998), from Sage Publications.

**Note:** The views expressed in this paper, as in all papers disseminated through the Welfare and Domestic Violence Technical Assistance Initiative, are solely those of the author. The author expresses appreciation for the contributions of Jill Davies, Anne Menard, Jody Raphael, and Susan Schechter.

## References:

Allard, M. A., R. Albelda, M. E. Colten, and C. Cosenza. 1997. *In Harm's Way? Domestic Violence, AFDC Receipt, and Welfare Reform in Massachusetts*. A report from the University of Massachusetts, Boston (McCormack Institute).

Bassuk, E., L. Weinreb, J. Buckner, A. Browne, A. Saloman, and S. Bassuk. 1996. "The Characteristics and Needs of Sheltered Homeless and Low-Income Housed Mothers." *JAMA* 276: 640–46.

Brandwein, R. 1997. *The Use of Public Welfare by Family Violence Victims: Implications of New Federal Welfare "Reform."* Paper presented at the Fifth International Family Violence Research Conference. Durham, New Hampshire.

Browne, A. 1995. "Reshaping the Rhetoric: The Nexus of Violence, Poverty, and Minority Status in the Lives of Women and Children in the United States." *Georgetown Journal on Fighting Poverty* III (Fall): 17–23.

Browne, A., and S. Bassuk. 1997. "Intimate Violence in the Lives of Homeless and Poor Housed Women: Prevalence and Patterns in an Ethnically Diverse Sample." *American Journal of Orthopsychiatry* 67: 261–78.

Curcio, C. 1997. *The Passaic County Study of AFDC Recipients in a Welfare-to-Work Program.* Passaic County, N.J.: Passaic County Board of Social Services.

Gondolf, E., with E. Fisher. 1988. *Battered Women as Survivors: An Alternative to Treating Learned Helplessness.* Lexington, MA: Lexington.

Lloyd, S. 1996. *The Effects of Violence on Women's Employment.* A report from the Institute for Policy Research, Northwestern University.

Lloyd, S. 1997. "The Effects of Domestic Violence on Women's Employment." *Law & Policy* 19, 2 (April): 139–68.

Pearson, J., and E. A. Griswold. 1997. "Child Support Policies and Domestic Violence." *Public Welfare* (Winter): 26–32.

Raphael, J. 1995. "Domestic Violence and Welfare Receipt: The Unexplored Barrier to Employment." *Georgetown Journal on Fighting Poverty* III: 29–34.

Raphael, J. 1996. "Prisoners of Abuse: Policy Implications of the Relationship between Domestic Violence and Welfare Receipt." *Clearinghouse Review* 30: 186–94.

Raphael, J., and R. Tolman. 1997. *Trapped by Poverty / Trapped by Abuse: New Evidence Documenting the Relationship between Domestic Violence and Welfare.* From the Project for Research on Welfare, Work, and Domestic Violence: A Collaboration between Taylor Institute and the University of Michigan.

Saloman, A., S. Bassuk, and M. Brooks. 1996. "Patterns of Welfare Use among Poor and Homeless Women." *American Journal of Orthopsychiatry* 66: 510–25.

Chapter 36

# Issues and Dilemmas in Family Violence

## Introduction

Psychology provides a unique perspective for understanding and stopping family abuse and violence, and the American Psychological Association (APA) joins a host of other professional groups expressing grave concerns about the magnitude and the effects of family violence. Violence at home is linked to violence in other settings, and for individual victims it is strongly correlated with a number of serious short-term and long-term health and mental health problems.

The knowledge base about violence and the family has expanded rapidly in recent years. Nonetheless, in this area of study and practice, many recurring issues and dilemmas arise that blend concepts not only from research findings, but also from clinical reports, service delivery systems, value orientations, cultural traditions, and human experience. A few of those complicated issues and dilemmas are briefly outlined here. The APA Presidential Task Force on Violence and the Family encourages readers to participate with colleagues from many disciplines in discussion, debate, and study of the problems posed by these issues and dilemmas, and to work thoughtfully toward solutions to the problems. Clearly, the solutions must take into account scientific evidence, clinical experience, genuine concern for human welfare, and substantial wisdom in balancing conflicting interests and viewpoints.

*Issue 1: How can we describe, study, and stop violent be-havior taking place within the family when privacy is one of our most precious rights?*

> *There is inevitable tension between the right of family privacy and the need to expose family violence—to stop its occurrence, to help victims, and to conduct research.*

The sanctity of home and family is something we value. At home we expect warmth, comfort, solace, and protection from harm. Further, we treasure the right to live as we wish without interference from others, but that right can help perpetuate the violence that occurs in some families. The right of privacy, especially when it is buttressed with secrecy and isolation, can prevent professionals and the community at large from learning about the complex dynamics involved in family violence and abuse, and it prevents the victims inside from receiving the assistance that they need. Abuse thrives on closed boundaries and secrecy.

Studies suggest that more violence occurs among low-income families, but it may be that researchers know more about poor families because they are less able to maintain secrecy than those who have more resources. For example, the vice president of an important company may hit a child hard enough to inflict serious injury, but the injury is treated in the office of a family physician and not reported. A mother on welfare or a laborer collecting unemployment, however, may inflict the same injury to a child but would have to take that child to a nearby hospital clinic. One family will be shielded from public view, the other will be counted in the statistics on child abuse.

Balancing the right of privacy with the need for intervention in family violence warrants thoughtful reflection on the part of policymakers and other individuals concerned about abuse. Differences in class, culture, and economic resources should not influence our ability to stop family violence, understand its dynamics, protect its victims, and facilitate healing for all who are affected.

*Issue 2: If violence is learned behavior, who teaches it?*

> *Many people charge that images in the media, ineffective laws, or weak law enforcement is responsible for violence in our soci-*

*ety, but they are unwilling to consider that their own behavior may foster aggression and violence.*

It is important to go beyond blaming others for the proliferation of violence and to examine individual behavior and social norms to better understand how violent behavior is taught and reinforced.

Learning to accept and use violence is a complex process in which each person could be teaching violent responses without realizing it. When parents demean and strike each other or their children, when children are encouraged to be bullies or fight back on the playground, when children have easy access to real or toy guns and other weapons, violence is being taught. When stereotypes and prejudice frame interactions with people who are different from ourselves, the scene is being set for violence. Glorifying war and relishing violence in competitive sports may reinforce violent behavior. Several decades of research has documented that violence in television, film, and other mass media is one way in which the culture teaches violence. When violence and sexual aggression are combined in the media, in popular song, in multimedia computer games, and in the vernacular, the message of violence, including sexual assault, is reinforced. It is often difficult for well-intentioned parents of older children and teenagers to overcome the violent messages that are being taught by their peers and by the larger society.

In recent decades the ways in which men and women interact with each other and live their lives have changed extensively. The women's movement, combined with the reality of more women entering the workforce and becoming financially independent, has caused many women to change their expectations about how much they want to yield to or serve men. While some men have changed their expectations of their partners, others have not. The resulting differences in how couples perceive family roles may cause conflict, and persons who have learned to resolve conflict by physical violence may continue to do so, thus modeling for their children that violent behavior is appropriate when one feels justified that his or her opinion should prevail.

Studies show that more negative than positive behaviors are acted out in dysfunctional families, and in abusive families these negative behaviors occur in clustered patterns, usually expressed by males to females. In homes where there is no violence, people treat each other in a kinder and more pleasant way. In a practical sense, this means that changing the communication patterns in families to convey more positive messages and affirm what each person does right is a step toward violence prevention.

The process by which violence is taught is circular: It begins in the family, expanding through the culture of the larger society in which children grow and mature, and then again is reinforced or discouraged in the family. Our search for ways to stop violence calls for a close look at ourselves and our community and family traditions, as well as institutional practices and public policies that perpetuate violent attitudes, images, and behaviors.

### Issue 3: Is it abusive to spank a child?

*Tension exists between the deeply ingrained value that spanking is appropriate and necessary discipline for a child and the psychological knowledge that, if violence is learned behavior, even spankings can teach children that it is okay to use some kinds of violence, even with people they love.*

According to surveys, the majority of people believe that sometimes a child needs to be disciplined with a spanking. Many who believe in spanking feel that children who are not spanked will not develop the moral values that are appropriate for their culture. They see spanking as a punishment that can stop undesirable behavior, but psychological research shows that behavior is shaped far more effectively by rewarding positive behavior than by punishing negative acts.

While spanking may have the short-term positive effect of stopping undesired behavior, there are risks involved in spanking, because it may have unintended consequences. Although most parents who spank have good intentions, they may actually cause harm by training their children to deal with conflict by using violence. Spanking demonstrates to the child that the person who is supposed to love him or her the most, who has social authority over the child, and who is the most responsible for the child's well-being, also has the right to physically hurt the child. The message is confusing: "If you love someone and need to correct or control them, then in certain situations it is okay to hurt them." In other words, spanking a child increases the likelihood that when the child becomes an adult, he or she may use physical force for control or discipline.

## *Issue 4: Why don't battered women just take their children and leave?*

*Many believe that violent abuse can be stopped by simply leaving the home, but research indicates that leaving does not stop the abuse.*

"Why does she stay?" may be the most frequently asked question about battered women. The underlying assumption in that question is that if the woman leaves, it would somehow stop the man's violence and, conversely, if she stays, she is in some way responsible for what happens to her. There are a variety of reasons why women don't leave their partners—for example, no social supports, nowhere to go, no money, and the psychological effects of battered woman syndrome. Nonetheless, the most important reason that women stay with batterers is that they are terrified to leave—they know that leaving may not stop the violence and may even make it worse.

A large proportion of reported domestic violence happens after the partners are separated. Since threats and violence are control strategies used by the batterer, the woman's leaving may threaten his sense of power and increase his need to control the woman and children. There is evidence, for example, that many stalking crimes involve abusive former spouses, boyfriends, or domestic partners. Child custody and visitation arrangements also may become an ongoing scenario for intimidation, threats, and violent behavior. Threats may be made to hurt the children and other family members. Often the battered woman returns to the batterer out of fear of increased violence and loss of control of the children as well as optimistic submission to his charm and his promises never to hurt her again.

This issue poses dilemmas for personal safety and for public policy, and it requires coordinated responses on the part of individual support systems, social services, mental health services, law enforcement, and the justice system. Otherwise, battered women who leave home will continue to be harmed, and battered women who stay will continue to be harmed!

*Issue 5: When parents separate after an abusive relationship, shouldn't fathers have as much right as mothers to be granted physical custody of and visitation rights with their children?*

*Tensions exist between children's need for contact with their father and their need to be protected from the physical, sexual and psychological abuse that is common in families where there have been other forms of violence such as woman abuse.*

Although most people believe that fathers should have equal access to their children after the termination of a relationship between the parents, the equal-access option is based on the assumption that the fathers will act in their children's best interests. However, that is a naive assumption in situations where family violence has occurred.

Fathers who batter their children's mothers can be expected to use abusive power and control techniques to control the children, too. In many of these families, prior to separation, the men were not actively involved in the raising of their children. To gain control after the marital separation, the fathers fight for the right to be involved. Often children who have been exposed to violence in the family are frightened to confront their father's negative or abusive behavior, and mothers cannot protect them. Sometimes the father tries to alienate the child from the mother by using money and other enticements, negative comments, or restricted access to the telephone during visitation with him. Other times, fathers may threaten or actually kidnap the child to punish the mother for leaving, or to try to force her to return.

Most people, including the battered woman herself, believe that when a woman leaves a violent man, she will remain the primary caretaker of their children. Family courts, however, may not consider the history of woman abuse relevant in awarding custody. Recent studies suggest that an abusive man is more likely than a nonviolent father to seek sole physical custody of his children and may be just as likely (or even more likely) to be awarded custody as the mother. Often fathers win physical custody because men generally have greater financial resources and can continue the court battles with more legal assistance over a longer period of time.

Family courts frequently minimize the harmful impact of children's witnessing violence between their parents and sometimes are reluctant to believe mothers. If the court ignores the history of violence as the context for the mother's behavior in a custody evaluation, she may appear hostile, uncooperative, or mentally unstable. For example, she may refuse to disclose her address, or may resist unsupervised visitation, especially if she thinks her child is in danger. Psychological evaluators who minimize the importance of violence against the mother, or pathologize her responses to it, may accuse her of alienating the children from the father and may recommend giving the father custody in spite of his history of violence.

Some professionals assume that accusations of physical or sexual abuse of children that arise during divorce or custody disputes are likely to be false, but the empirical research to date shows no such increase in false reporting at that time. In many instances, children are frightened about being alone with a father they have seen use violence towards their mother or a father who has abused them. Sometimes children make it clear to the court that they wish to remain with the mother because they are afraid of the father, but their wishes are ignored.

Research indicates that high levels of continued conflict between separated and divorced parents hinders children's normal development. Some practitioners now believe that it may be better for children's development to restrict the father's access to them and avoid continued danger to both mothers and the children.

## *Issue 6: Is it possible to have delayed memories of being sexually abused as a child?*

*Clinical reports suggest that sexual abuse victims may forget the abusive experiences, then remember them later in their lives, but empirical research findings cannot explain this phenomenon by anything we currently know about memory.*

Controversy about adult recollections should not be used to obscure the reality and prevalence of child sexual abuse. Data from a variety of sources provide evidence that as many as 20 percent of American women and 5 to 10 percent of American men experienced some form of sexual abuse as children. Most adults retain conscious memory (whether total, partial, or with fluctuating accessibility) of the abuse, although they may not fully understand it or disclose it. Some sexual abuse victims, however, do appear to have total memory loss for the experience; this phenomenon has been noted even in cases where the abuse was reported to authorities at the time of its occurrence. In either case, delayed recall or delayed disclosure may result.

Some professionals assert that delayed memories of abuse are essentially inaccurate and constitute "false memories." They cite the variable, inaccurate, and reconstructive nature of memory, and they do not believe that memories of trauma are significantly different from memories of nontraumatic events. Some also charge that delayed memories recovered while an adult is in therapy may have been suggested or implanted by the therapist.

Recently the media have widely reported stories of adults who seem to have forgotten incidents of sexual abuse from childhood and then remember the experiences, either spontaneously or in the course of receiving mental health care. Often these stories are reported in such a way that there appears to be a great likelihood that the recollected memories are of events that did not, in fact, happen at all. As a result, many people are confused about whether childhood sexual abuse is common and if it is, about the reasons it may go undetected or unreported until the victim reaches adulthood.

Delayed recall should not automatically be assumed to be a false or implanted memory. On the other hand, the memory should not automatically be interpreted as a literal, historical reality.

Having reviewed the research literature on trauma and on memory, the APA Working Group on the Investigation of Memories of Childhood Abuse issued an Interim Report that reached these conclusions:

- Most people who were sexually abused as children remember all or part of what happened to them.

- However, it is possible for memories of abuse that have been forgotten for a long time to be remembered. The mechanisms by which such delayed recall occurs are not currently well understood.

- It is also possible to construct convincing pseudomemories for events that never occurred. The mechanisms by which these pseudomemories occur are not currently well understood.

- There are gaps in our knowledge about processes that lead to accurate or inaccurate recollection of childhood sexual abuse.

### Issue 7: Are mandatory reporting laws helpful or harmful to families?

*Reporting child abuse cases to child protection authorities often is the only means to initiate interventions. Inadequate follow-up by an overburdened system, however, sometimes intensifies the pain, disruption, and uncertainty in the lives of abused children and their families, and it is destructive to the therapeutic process without contributing help or protection.*

Psychologists who work in schools, clinics, and private offices are required by law to report any suspected incidents of child abuse. However, the difficulties in getting appropriate intervention when such reports are made and the damage to the therapeutic relationship are often discouraging to mental health professionals. Abused children find it difficult to disclose the violence they experience, and when they do find a trusted person to whom they disclose the information, they often feel betrayed when it is reported to the authorities.

Observing the overwhelming burden on the child protection system, service providers sometimes fear that making a report will hinder a child's recovery rather than assist in it. Family members often are separated from each other by the system and may not continue treatment with the reporting professional. Investigations may be conducted poorly by minimally trained caseworkers who have little understanding of family dynamics or their clients' cultural characteristics. Reports indicate that outright bias may affect the handling of poor families, and relatively few child protection agencies can afford to provide sufficient services to re-direct a child's or family's life toward healthy functioning.

Many people who work with abused children are discouraged by the lack of resources for dealing with reports of abuse. The system may protect some of the more seriously physically abused children from being killed, but many children who are removed from their homes experience longstanding disruption and uncertainty, and remain in foster care for years. Rarely do these children receive any psychotherapy or other treatment, and even less frequently do they receive help to reduce the trauma aftereffects such as nightmares, poor concentration in school, cognitive confusion, intrusive memories, and other acute anxiety and depression symptoms associated with abuse. Although treatment plans are usually ordered in juvenile court proceedings, rarely is access to psychotherapy or other treatment readily available to parents, even when they are motivated to seek help.

Many professionals question the merits of mandatory reporting for cases of child abuse; yet they know that if a report is not made, it is unlikely that victims or perpetrators will enter any system of care, protection, and rehabilitation.

### Issue 8: How much do emotions influence what professionals know and do about violence in the family?

*Service providers and researchers who deal with family violence often feel torn as they try to maintain professional attitudes and responses at the same time that they feel outrage, disgust, fear, and sadness because of their constant exposure to personal stories of abuse.*

Family violence elicits very strong feelings. Even professionals trained to respond to trauma sometimes experience vicarious and secondary traumatization from repeated exposure to the effects of family violence through their clients. Dealing with their own intense emotions has not always been recognized as part of therapists' professional experience, and they have been trained to remain "neutral." Consequently, they become uncomfortable and concerned when they have the natural feelings that occur when working with violence victims. In such situations they may "tune out" the effects of violence just as victims do, minimizing the seriousness of the event and signaling the limits of emotional tolerance. But the intense feelings that arise when dealing with violence issues actually provide clues that something is wrong indeed. If professionals have too little emotion and compassion, they are not able to help the victims. If they have too much emotion, they are overwhelmed by the magnitude and intensity of the problems.

### Issue 9: How does society want police to respond to family violence?

*Many who want to help stop violence in homes do not want to involve families in the criminal justice system, but making an arrest is the action that is most likely to get protection and help for victims as well as interventions to control perpetrators' behaviors.*

Expectations about how law enforcement agencies should deal with family violence have changed in recent decades. In the late 1960s and early 1970s, specific programs were implemented that focused on conflict resolution at the scene and follow-up with social service referrals. Useful in some cases, these methods often were not helpful when a woman was being battered by her partner. In the 1980s, following the recommendations of the Attorney General's Task Force on Family Violence, a change of emphasis occurred, switching from mediation to arrest and prosecution of family violence cases. Thus law enforcement officers became the gatekeepers for this new criminalization of family violence, and now most people enter the system when an arrest is made.

Many law enforcement officers responding to a family violence call find it frustrating because even when they make an arrest, the abuse may still continue. But if the officer does not make the arrest, women and children remain unprotected, and few perpetrators have a chance for any kind of intervention or treatment. Although it is possible to obtain a civil restraining order in domestic violence or elder abuse cases, or to obtain juvenile court intervention in child abuse cases, treatment usually cannot be mandated by court order in the same way that it can be ordered as a condition of probation in criminal cases.

Most families only want the violence to stop; they do not want subsequent involvement with a system they perceive as intrusive, unhelpful, and punitive. Yet if arrests are not made and treatment is not ordered, the abuser's behavior has few external controls and is likely to continue.

## Issue 10: Does mandated treatment work?

*Presumably a person must want to change in order to benefit from therapy, but most studies of involuntary, offender-specific treatment programs indicate that many participants do make important changes in their behavior.*

When courts order perpetrators into treatment programs it changes the nature of the usual therapy relationship. Nonetheless, some offenders who go through treatment do stop their violent behavior. Psycho-educational models that are cognitively and behaviorally oriented seem to be most effective in helping many offenders stop their physical violence. Some of these offenders, however, continue their psychological abuse after treatment and do not give up their misuse of power and control in the relationship.

No empirical data exist about stopping coercive and cruel sex in abusive relationships, although clinical experience suggests that unless sexual abuse is specifically dealt with in therapy, changes do not usually occur.

There are many different types of treatment programs, some of which may be useful for one person but not for another, and most communities have difficulty providing appropriate treatment programs for all batterers. Rarely is a proper assessment made of the type of battering in the relationship or of the perpetrator's mental status in order to link that knowledge to a recommendation for the most suitable treatment program available in the community for a specific individual. Studies show that few batterers who are court-ordered to receive treatment ever see a therapist or complete the prescribed treatment program.

### Issue 11: Is abuse an excuse?

*Generally people feel compassion for abuse victims, along with understanding and forgiveness for some of their undesirable behaviors, but often those attitudes conflict with the need to hold people personally accountable for their behavior.*

Are people not taking responsibility for their own behavior and using abuse as an excuse? Some say that society has begun to blame prior abuse for all reprehensible behavior, thus creating a victim-culture which rewards remaining a victim rather than healing and getting on with life. They point to the proliferation of television talk show hosts who interview victims of all kinds of abuse as encouraging the victim-culture attitude, as well as to legal defenses using evidence of child or adult abuse as another example.

People who are abused suffer many consequences, and in some cases those consequences may bring harm to other people. While most abused persons do not become violent, the absence of treatment or other helpful interventions for victims of abuse appears to be related to their later involvement in violence or other destructive behaviors. Treating patterns of violence and victimization can be extremely difficult, requiring multidimensional approaches to change motivation and behavior, and careful, sustained follow-up. A long-term view, then, calls for a commitment to providing ways for victims to resolve the negative feelings and patterns of behavior that often result from a history of abuse. After sufficient and appropriate assistance is provided, victims can be expected to seek help for themselves and to take individual responsibility for their own behavior.

### Issue 12: Should practitioners be concerned about legal risks when they work with family violence?

*It is an important but complicated task to protect competent therapists from frivolous or malicious grievances and lawsuits, and at the same time protect consumers from incompetent or unscrupulous therapists.*

Psychologists can help persons who experience family violence, but the growing number of personal threats, official grievances, ethics complaints, and lawsuits against therapists by clients and/or their families is having a chilling effect on the practice of psychology. Indeed, clinicians increasingly feel they are in jeopardy when they deal with clients who bring up family violence issues.

Working with abuse situations is especially problematic: A therapist is legally mandated to report child abuse, and some jurisdictions require similar reporting of spouse or elder abuse. Sometimes when protective authorities begin to investigate an individual case, however, the therapist faces the risk of angry retaliation from the family. The situation is even more complicated when practitioners work with adults who were abused as children and the controversial area of recovered memories is part of the situation. Consequently, many therapists are practicing "lawsuit therapy," carefully screening their actions and words to minimize the risk of being sued, and potentially compromising the quality of care they offer to their clients. Some other therapists simply refuse to deal with family violence cases, referring such clients to other practitioners.

Mass media reporting and entertainment portrayals of therapy often reflect a "spin" that damages the credibility of psychotherapy. Some of the reporting might lead the public to believe that there is an epidemic of bad therapy instead of an epidemic of child abuse.

Regrettably, there are a small number of practitioners, including some psychologists, who are unethical or whose practices do not meet appropriate standards of care, and some who are untrained or even unscrupulous in handling family violence issues. It is important for the well-being of their clients, as well as for the integrity of our profession, that clients can seek redress for such practitioners' harmful or unethical practices.

In some cases, however, state licensure and grievance procedures are being used to promulgate unfounded charges and deliberate harassment against therapists who work with victims of abuse. This situation, coupled with inadequacies in the processes for investigating and resolving complaints, can inflict damaging expenses and embarrassment even for therapists who ultimately are cleared of all charges.

At least one advocacy group is known to have mounted a campaign to promote lawsuits against psychotherapists by providing instructions and supportive materials for initiating legal action. The same group also has organized a nationwide initiative to introduce model legislation that could jeopardize the practice of psychotherapy, with state legislatures setting standards for practitioners and limiting the types of therapy deemed appropriate for violent families ordered by the court to receive treatment.

Two recent reports by the APA ad hoc Committee on Legal and Ethical Issues in the Treatment of Interpersonal Violence address these matters: *Potential Problems for Psychologists Working With the Area of Interpersonal Violence;* and *Professional, Ethical, and Legal Issues Concerning Interpersonal Violence, Maltreatment, and Related Trauma.*

## APA Presidential Task Force on Violence and the Family

When Ronald E. Fox, PhD, assumed the Presidency of the Association early in 1994, he chose Psychology and Families to be the theme of his presidential year. He appointed a Presidential Task Force on Violence and the Family to make an important contribution to that theme. The Task Force membership included:

Lenore E. Walker, EdD, Chair
Denver, Colorado

J. Renae Norton, PsyD, Vice Chair
Cincinnati, Ohio

Christine A. Courtois, PhD
Washington, DC

Mary Ann Dutton, PhD
Bethesda, Maryland

Ronald E. Fox, PhD
Chapel Hill, North Carolina

Robert A. Geffner, PhD
Tyler, Texas

W. Rodney Hammond, PhD
Atlanta, Georgia

John Chris Hatcher, PhD
San Francisco, California

Janis V. Sanchez, PhD
Norfolk, Virginia

Geraldine Butts Stably, PhD
San Bernardino, California

The Task Force was administered in the APA Public Interest Directorate; Jacquelyn H. Gentry, PhD, was Staff Director.

The Task Force released its final report, *Violence and the Family,* in February 1996. The 156-page publication outlines findings on child abuse, dating violence, partner abuse, and elder abuse. The book is divided into four major subsections— Understanding Family Violence, Victims of Family Violence, Interventions, and Recommendations. The Interventions section covers victims, survivors, and perpetrators; the intersection of family violence, psychology and the law; and promoting violence-free families. The Task Force offers recommendations on public policy and intervention, prevention and public education, clinical services, training, and psychological research.

A single copy of *Violence and the Family* can be obtained from the APA Public Interest Initiatives Office, 750 First Street NE, Washington, DC 20002; phone 202-336-6046. The cost for each additional copy is $5.00.

Chapter 37

# Reducing Violence: A Research Agenda

## Introduction and Overview

Violence in America is a public health problem of the highest magnitude. Today 1 in every 10,000 people will become the victim of homicide, a rate that has doubled since World War II. America's youth are especially vulnerable. Nearly 3 in every 10,000 young males will be murdered. Among minority males between the ages of 16 and 25 who live in impoverished areas of large cities, the rate is more than 10 times higher—one in every 333. These young men are more likely to die by homicide than from any other cause.

Family violence and abuse are among the most prevalent forms of interpersonal violence against women and children. Each year about 4 million women experience a serious assault by an intimate partner, and abuse accounts for about 10% of the injuries to children under age 7 who are treated in emergency rooms.

The annual rate of rape is estimated at 7.1 per 1,000 adult women, and there is cause for alarm regarding increasing reports of violence toward elderly persons cared for at home. Further, pervasive fear has dampened the quality of life as more and more Americans feel that there are no places left which are safe and free from the threat of violence.

Policymakers, health and criminal justice officials, and community leaders want to take action to reduce violence, but their actions need to be based on a better understanding of the causes of violent behavior and how to prevent it. In recent years substantial research efforts have yielded important findings about violence:

- Aggressive, antisocial behavior in early childhood often foretells a life of violence.

- Certain physiological characteristics may predispose a child to be more or less aggressive, but these predispositions are greatly moderated by the environment in which the child grows up.

- Attitudes, beliefs, and values about violence do, as expected, noticeably influence violent behavior.

- Children who grow up in deprived environments, where poverty, frustration, and hopelessness are endemic, are at much greater risk of later involvement in violence than other children.

- Most women, elderly people, and children encounter violence in the home more than in any other location. The perpetrator of that violence is most likely to be another family member.

- Violence begets violence. Children in abusive families, who witness everyday violence in homes and neighborhoods and day by day absorb the media's representations of violence, are at great risk for becoming violent themselves.

- Even as children can be taught to be violent, they can be taught to be nonviolent.

- Children raised without consistent supervision and appropriate discipline are more likely to behave aggressively and to act violently as adults.

These research results, which represent significant advances, have provided the foundation for many existing psychological interventions that attempt to reduce violence. But intervention programs are only as good as the knowledge base on which they are built. That foundation is still missing key blocks of information about what causes violence and how to prevent it.

## The Causes of Violence

Violent behavior can seldom be traced to any one cause. We need to learn more about which factors converge to push individuals toward violence. These factors roughly fall into four groups:

1) *Biobehavioral factors*—the biological influences on the propensity toward aggression and violence;

2) *Socialization factors*—the processes through which children learn patterns of thinking, behaving, and feeling from their early life experiences;

3) *Cognitive factors*—the ideas, beliefs, and patterns of thinking that emerge as a child grows up; and

4) *Situational factors*—the characteristics of the environment, such as stress or violence that stimulate violent behavior.

Each set of factors is not independent. Each influences and is influenced by the others. Dividing the factors into four sets merely provides a convenient way to organize a research agenda for the next decade. Basic research in each of these four areas, coupled with applied research on prevention and treatment methods, can move us a giant step forward towards reducing violence.

## Building the Knowledge Base

### Biobehavioral Factors

Every newborn is unique, an amalgam of physiological characteristics inherited from its parents that have been altered by conditions during gestation and delivery. Neuroanatomy and brain chemistry differ across individuals, and influence emotions, impulsivity, and tendencies toward aggressive behavior. As the child grows and encounters new experiences, these inborn biological and psychological characteristics continue to change. Neuroscientists have learned much about how physiology affects behavior, but have also discovered that experience alters physiology—even the very structure of the brain. Recent advances in the neurosciences have offered tantalizing clues to the reciprocal influences of biological functioning and social environment on child development. How these interactions lead to violent

883

behavior is not understood, but enough has been learned to direct scientists toward productive new lines of inquiry.

Aggressive behavior has been associated with some kinds of brain damage resulting from birth trauma, tumors, or traumatic head injuries. Specific neurophysiological deficits have been linked to violence, such as lesions in the amygdala of the brain. The association between aggression and many of these deficits in neurophysiological functioning is particularly strong in individuals who have repeatedly committed violent crimes. Less extreme aggressive behavior has also been linked to naturally occurring variations in neurophysiological and hormonal functioning. Testosterone, a male hormone, has received particular attention because it seems to be correlated with a tendency to dominate others, although recent evidence suggests that a high testosterone level is as much a consequence of dominance as a cause. Hyperactivity and attention deficits in early childhood are statistical indicators of greater risk for adolescent aggressive behavior. A slow heart rate and low physiological arousability have been linked to adolescent aggression, perhaps because they make children harder to socialize with rewards and punishments. Exciting new research has shown that aggressive young adults are likely to have lower levels of the neurotransmitter serotonin in the brain, although the role of serotonin in childhood aggression has not been sufficiently studied. Substantial research evidence demonstrates an association between violent behavior and some substances, such as lead, that are toxic to the brain and nervous system.

Although these associations are well established, they are not well understood. The mechanisms by which such physiological factors lead to violence is complicated by the clear evidence that early learning experiences and environmental factors modify the effect of predisposing physiological factors and change neurophysiological functioning. For example, perinatal complications such as birth trauma, early diet, and early childhood trauma can trigger a cascade of events that result in aggressive and violent behavior. Studies show, however, that this downward spiral into violence can be blocked by countervailing environmental factors, such as good parenting. Or it can be accentuated by parental neglect, violent abuse, and poor health care.

Just as some biological factors increase the risk of a child growing up to behave violently, some decrease the risk. Among the biobehavioral factors found to buffer pernicious environmental influences are good learning abilities. We know that juvenile offenders who are quick to learn and easily aroused (e.g., they respond quickly to stimuli of all kinds) are less likely to become habitual criminals in adulthood, for example.

Given this base of knowledge, the following research questions about the biobehavioral basis of violent behavior stand out as deserving more attention:

- What exactly is the role of low serotonin in aggressive and violent behavior? Studies in children and adults have produced conflicting pictures that cannot be explained by existing theories. Yet there is little dispute that serotonin levels are correlated with individual differences in aggression and impulsivity. New technologies in neurophysiology have opened opportunities in this area that should be explored. We need a better understanding of the possibly reciprocal influences of serotonin and aggressive behavior.

- To what extent does the relationship between testosterone and aggression or dominance promote aggression? We know that engaging in aggressive and dominating behaviors can increase testosterone levels; and we know that a higher testosterone level is associated with the likelihood of aggression. But we also know that there is not a simple one-to-one relationship between them. Present knowledge will only become useful in preventing aggression and violence when we learn more about the psychological processes involved and how testosterone levels interact with other factors in a person's life (both males and females).

- Exactly what is the role of "arousability" in the development of aggressive and violent behavior? Both early hyperactivity and early low levels of arousability are clearly correlated with later aggressive, violent, and antisocial behavior. Although several theories have been proposed to explain the correlation, none is completely explanatory. We need more research specifically directed at understanding the mediating psychological influences.

- Exactly what neurotoxins and traumatic brain injuries place a person at risk of becoming violent? What are the physiological and psychological processes through which these injuries or toxins stimulate aggressive and violent behavior? Without this knowledge, intervention becomes problematic.

- What is the role of biological inheritance in the neurophysiological abnormalities associated with increased risk for violent reactions and aggressive behavior? The molecular biology of violence and aggression is poorly understood, particularly as it unfolds across the development of young children. Similarly, we need better understanding of the evolutionary basis for neuro-physiological characteristics that seem to be associated with aggression.

• Which kinds of environments exacerbate the effects of such biological predispositions and which kinds mitigate the effects? In addition to affecting hormones, neurotransmitters, and arousal directly, environmental factors can alter the influence of these biological factors on aggression and violence. We need to know what kind of environments offer the greatest protection for children with abnormal serotonin levels, or with indications of early hyperactivity, or with arousal deficits.

### Socialization Factors

Scientists use the term *socialization* to describe the process by which a child learns the "scripts" for specific social behavior, along with the rules, attitudes, values, and norms that guide interactions with others. Growing children seem to learn as much from observing others as from their own experiences, and what children learn is influenced by their biobehavioral predispositions as well as by their environment.

Some antisocial, aggressive, and violent behaviors may be learned as simple responses to specific situations. A boy becomes frustrated because his sister won't give him a cookie; he hits her and she relents; as a result, he's learned that hitting wins cookies. Other forms of learning are more complex, such as acquiring the complex patterns of behavior that become scripts for how to behave. Suppose a girl listens to her mother plot revenge against a neighbor who slighted her; the girl learns from this example how to retaliate against her own friends. Or what if a boy watches his father get mad because he can't find his car keys and the father releases his frustration by hitting the boy's mother; this model of behavior may become the script the boy follows when he gets angry at his friends.

Substantial evidence shows that how children are socialized during their early years accounts for much of the individual differences in the propensity to act aggressively and violently—not just in childhood but throughout life. This transaction goes both ways: The child's culture, community, neighborhood, peers, family, teachers, economic situation, exposure to mass media—these and myriad other factors influence the child, who affects them in turn.

Research has shown that parents' lack of attention to a child's behavior and inconsistent parental discipline can be major contributors to aggressive behavior. The psychological processes are complex: Extreme punishment is as likely to provoke aggression as inhibit it, for example, and harsh, abusive discipline may undermine the development of self-control as surely as a lack of monitoring and nurturance. Even more important, perhaps, is the failure of many parents to respond positively to their child's nonaggressive efforts to resolve conflict or handle frustration. By ignoring these constructive behaviors, parents inadvertently may teach their children that aggressive acts alone achieve results.

Peers exert influence from an early age, but become more important in the preteen years. As the child enters adolescence, the peer group grows even more powerful and may replace the family as the major influence in socialization. Membership in a peer group that condones antisocial or aggressive behavior is a strong predictor of individual violent behavior. Delinquents associate with each other, and although this inclination to delinquency may bring them together, their togetherness stimulates even greater delinquency.

Certain environmental conditions not only trigger violence, they can also seem to teach aggressive or violent behavior patterns. For example, poverty is associated with both sudden violent outbursts and long-term, habitual aggression. Studies suggest that poverty in itself does not seem to lead to violent behavior. Rather, it is the individual's perceived relative deprivation—the perception of being denied the income, assets, and opportunities available to most other members of society. The stress associated with poverty, combined with the violence endemic in poor neighborhoods, can push children into a corner where violence appears to be a reasonable choice. Poor neighborhoods have higher rates of drug trafficking, more bars and liquor outlets, nonexistent or unsupervised recreational areas for children and teens, dilapidated and overcrowded housing, and many other environmental deficits. Children may come to believe that aggression is normal and acceptable in such a setting. Single mothers living in poverty are often isolated, and these circumstances leave them with few psychological reserves for helping their children learn emotional control. But poor outcomes are by no means universal. Those who escape the negative consequences of such a childhood have attracted particular interest from many behavioral and social scientists trying to understand what features of physiology or psychology protected them. Beliefs and attitudes about aggression also vary by geographic region and cultural and ethnic background, In some groups, the slightest imagined wrong demands a violent response; in others, turning the other cheek is the norm.

Research has also clearly established that children's propensities for aggression are robustly correlated with their exposure to violence in the media. Those who watch more violent movies, videos, and TV are more prone to violence. Unfortunately, young children who are at greatest risk are least likely to have their TV or movie viewing monitored or restricted by their parents. Many of these children are unsupervised and free to watch adult-oriented programs night and day.

Although overwhelming evidence has proven that the mass media play an important role in socializing today's youth, scientists are only beginning to understand how. Long-term exposure to media violence exerts several types of influence: It conveys norms, attitudes, and beliefs justifying aggression and violence; it teaches viewers aggressive scripts for dealing with problems; and it desensitizes viewers to violence, thereby making it more palatable. In short, watching violent movies and television shows year after year and listening to brutal lyrics set to throbbing music can change one's attitudes about antisocial, aggressive behavior. In children it can lead to more aggressive behavior and also can evoke unwarranted fears and defensive actions. Whatever the violent content, movies and television exert powerful influences through visual imagery and dramatic characterizations; video games may have similar effects. These influences create and sustain conceptions about ethnic minorities, women, and other groups that can affect behavior—for good or ill.

Although there are many unanswered questions about the role of early socialization in violent behavior, certain questions stand out at the top of the research agenda:

- Violence flourishes where parental discipline is inadequate, inconsistent, or too harsh. What constitutes appropriate and effective discipline and supervision practices for children of different ages, social settings, and subcultures? When is punishment likely to suppress problem behavior, and when is it likely to promote aggression?

- What are the specific elements of poverty, deprivation, and inequality that promote socialization to violence? Is it the stress of living in poverty and comparative deprivation, the exposure to illegal activity, the lack of available resources? Is it the feeling of helplessness engendered by poverty, the isolation and exclusion from mainstream society, the crowding and other conditions associated with substandard housing?

- High-risk neighborhoods with endemic violence and poverty have different effects on children with apparently similar characteristics. Some are socialized into violence and some are not. We need to understand better what are the protective factors that inoculate children against the detrimental effects of these environments.

- More aggressive, violent children seem to prefer the company of similar children. Why? Are aggressive children more tolerant of other aggressive children? Do aggressive children make their peers more aggressive? How? In general, what is the process through which peers attain so much influence over behavior in middle and later childhood?

- What is the most important process through which long-term exposure to violence in the media promotes violent behavior?

  - Imitation of violent acts in the media?

  - Changes in beliefs and values about violence?

  - Stereotyping groups that are frequent victims of violence, e.g., women and minorities?

  - Emotional desensitization to violence?

### Cognitive Factors

The most lasting effects of early experience seem to be mediated by changes in what might be called the software of the brain. Early socialization interacts with biobehavioral predispositions to mold the mental processes that help a person control behavior—awareness, perception, reasoning, and judgment. Scientists call these cognitive processes.

Research has shown that more aggressive and violent individuals have different ways of processing information and thinking about social situations. They tend to perceive hostility in others when there is no hostility. They tend to be less efficient at thinking of nonviolent ways to solve social disagreements. They tend to be more accepting of aggression and violence in general and think it is acceptable to behave that way.

From their own experience and from watching others around them or in the mass media, children learn patterns of behavior, beliefs about the world, attitudes and values about what is appropriate or required, expectancies about what others may do, and styles of causal attribution. Once such cognitions have crystallized during socialization, they become stubbornly difficult to change.

Cognitive styles not only influence planned behavior, they also affect the likelihood of impulsive aggression. During social interactions one person might strike out without thinking, whereas another, more reflective, person might weigh the consequences of such behavior. Research has shown, however, that even among impulsive individuals, those who are predisposed to perceive hostility in others are more likely to act aggressively. Research has also now shown that, contrary to popular belief, fantasizing about attacking someone makes a real future attack more likely, not less likely. Such fantasies simply serve as cognitive rehearsals for the act. In emotionally charged situations, youth often revert to well-rehearsed, familiar responses, which may turn a conflict into a violent encounter.

Although a culture's tolerance for violence shapes individual attitudes and beliefs, not all members of society are equally affected. Research suggests that children who are less skilled intellectually may be particularly at risk for developing proviolence cognitions. The relationship between aggression and poor intellectual development is a two-way street, however. Committing a violent act often seems to set a vicious circle in motion: Children who act aggressively are more likely to fail in school and flounder socially, and these failures engender frustration that increases the risk of more serious violence.

Within the area of cognitive processes, three major questions stand out as needing further research:

- What is the relative importance of parents, peers, schools, churches, the mass media, and culture in influencing the cognitions (beliefs, biases, scripts, mental processes) about violence among today's children? Why do peers seem to have gained influence, whereas parents seem to have lost it? How can we best intervene to prevent children from acquiring the wrong cognitions or to change their cognitions?

- How do cognitive biases, beliefs, and scripts interact with the experience of a particular moment to cause a person to behave violently? We need more exact understanding of the information processing that goes on in the mind of the person who suddenly acts violently and the one who habitually acts violently. What are the roles of brooding about wrongs and fantasizing about retaliation in such violence? Through what processes have such individuals come to justify what they are doing?

- Is the kind of thinking characteristic of aggressive and violent people related to their early temperament or cognitive abilities? Are there biobehavioral factors that predispose individuals to acquire these characteristic ways of thinking? Or does behaving aggressively and violently start a stream of events that leads to reduced cognitive functioning?

## *Situational Factors*

Social conditions mold children as they grow up, but they also create climates that make violent reactions more or less likely in almost anyone. Often we seek the causes of violence in the person and ignore the contributing effects of the situation.

Almost any aversive situation—continuous loud noise, living in an overcrowded apartment, chronic deprivation, or failure at a job—can provoke aggression and violence in an otherwise tranquil person. A hot spell can kindle it, as can family problems. Alcohol and some drugs have well-documented associations with violent behavior. Stressful life events, such as a death, a move, a change in jobs, or divorce increase the risk for violence. All of these conditions that increase irritability and decrease inhibitions against aggression contribute to the level of violence in our society.

Equally likely to increase violence is anything around us that suggests violence. Fighting in the streets engenders more violence because it "cues" violent thoughts and responses. Guns, especially in the hands of young men, make violent confrontations more deadly when they do occur. Research has shown, however, that just the presence of guns and other weapons also makes violence more likely to occur. The sight of a weapon cues aggressive and violent responses that might not otherwise be considered. Even a picture of a gun or other weapons in a room can increase the likelihood that a youth in that room will behave aggressively.

The family is the setting for much of the violence directed at women, children, the elderly, people with disabilities, and sometimes men. The greatest threat to women and children appears to come from members of their own families or intimate friends, not from strangers. Family violence occurs in all socioeconomic strata, but it may be exacerbated by stress and poverty and it is tolerated in varying degrees by different cultures. Family violence also seems to be more common in families in which the parents had themselves experienced family violence as children.

Crowds can be conducive to mob behavior, and normally peaceable individuals can be lured into acts of violence when they are in a crowd. Studies have shown that being in a mob makes a person feel less personally responsible for his or her behavior. Organized groups or gangs similarly promote violence by diffusing responsibility and inculcating the belief that violence is acceptable or even esteemed. Some groups promote violence in defense of the group as a "prosocial" act. Youth gangs and terrorist organizations promote violence in this way. Even established social institutions, such as police, the military, prisons, mental hospitals, schools, and religious institutions, may inadvertently promote violence by their members through similar psychological processes.

Although scientists now recognize the important role of such situational factors in stimulating aggressive feelings, cuing violent acts, and removing inhibitions about violence, many of the processes are not well enough understood to intervene to reduce violence. In particular, we need more research directed at these questions:

- By what processes do alcohol and drugs provoke violence? Reducing inhibitions may account for some effects, but not all. People who mistakenly think they have consumed alcohol, for example, are more likely to behave violently. What psychological processes account for this phenomenon? To what extent do the effects of such substances depend on beliefs about their effects? To what extent do beliefs about oneself interact with substance use to affect behavior?

- What distinguishes families where violence occurs from those in which it never occurs? Family violence occurs in all socioeconomic and educational strata. What, then, causes it? Do cultural norms for male and female discipline or obedience make it easier to justify violence within some families? Do the social controls associated with more communal living inhibit family violence, or do the frustrations of lack of privacy stimulate family violence? What accounts for the correlation in family violence across generations? Is it simply a reflection of inherited aggressive tendencies, or does it reflect the transmission of specific husband-wife and parent-child dynamics across generations?

- How do poverty and inequality act as immediate stimulants to violence? Is the absolute discomfort produced by deprivation or the psychological alienation of relative deprivation more important in instigating violent acts? Why are some people better able to cope with deprivation than others? Do such persons get more support from their friends and family? How do their coping skills differ, especially in response to stress?

- In order to reduce the prevalence of guns among youth, we need to know more about what firearms mean to people. Why do so many carry guns? How do they justify it to themselves? Do guns give youth a sense of empowerment? Are they imitating the behavior of others they respect? Is it mostly motivated by fear?

- How do gangs that promote violence become established and thrive? What makes them so attractive to urban, minority youth? Do young people join primarily out of fear and need for protection? Do they join to gain a sense of identity? What factors and conditions within the gang make individual youngsters participate in collective acts of violence that they would not commit on their own?

## Designing Effective Treatment and Prevention Programs

Many factors contribute to violence, and these causes need to be better understood if we are to design effective treatment and prevention programs. The research agenda outlined so far would be a significant step in that direction. But we cannot wait for perfect understanding before we try to develop better prevention and treatment methods. Researchers have already made important strides in identifying which treatments are most effective, and we are poised to make further strides. What is needed now is applied research on some critical questions related to the prevention and treatment of violence.

### Treatment Models

Any hope of changing habitual perpetrators of violence depends on developing treatments that are developmentally appropriate, culturally relevant, and cost effective. Equally important is the need for strategies for treating the psychological and social consequences of violence for victims and society.

#### Treating the Habitually Violent

Recent field experiments have demonstrated that some treatments and interventions are effective at reducing habitually aggressive behavior, but little is known about tailoring these treatments to different populations and problems. Techniques that are effective in small experiments often break down when applied in a real-world correctional setting because of practical considerations.

Simply punishing violent offenders, whether juveniles or adults, is not as reasonable as it sounds if the goal is to prevent future violence. The threat of punishment, which serves as a deterrent to some crimes, appears to be less effective with violent behavior. Violence is often the impulsive and unthoughtful response to a provocation, real or imagined. Punishment can actually provoke rather than reduce aggression and violence, particularly in youth. Harsh physical punishment for juveniles can increase violent tendencies by fostering alienation, conditioning hostility and fear, and providing models for imitating violence. Research has shown that the ways aggressive youth think about the punishment and rewards they receive and the speed and certainty with which they are delivered are more important in changing their behavior than the magnitude of the rewards and punishments. Punishment may suppress antisocial behavior briefly, but more lasting behavior modification comes only after alternative ways of coping with social problems are learned. Yet the complex interplay of an individual's thoughts with parental, peer, and societal rewards and punishments is still not well understood.

To improve our success in treating children, adolescents, and adults who have committed violent acts, we need applied research directed at four questions:

- What is the optimal way to combine parental and societal punishments and rewards with other treatments to reduce the risk of subsequent violence? How do differing cultural norms and standards alter the effectiveness of punishments, rewards, and other treatments for different groups? How does the optimal combination of treatments change from early childhood, to adolescence, to young adulthood?

- How effective are programs aimed at changing the ways that violent offenders think about violence (e.g., their attitudes, values, and beliefs) in reducing risk for subsequent violence when combined with appropriate levels of reward and punishment?

- Are programs aimed at changing family interaction patterns and child-rearing practices effective in reducing risk for subsequent violence when combined with appropriate levels of reward and punishment?

- How should treatment programs for aggressive youth under the jurisdiction of juvenile justice systems be organized and coordinated with school and community efforts to minimize the risk of repeated aggressive behavior? How can individual rights be protected at the same time? How should programs be organized and managed outside the juvenile and criminal justice systems to ameliorate the problems of violence?

### Treating the Victims

Violence harms its victims both physically and psychologically. It traumatizes victims, bystanders, and family members alike. It can trigger paralyzing anxiety and fear, long-lasting depression, or deep anger. Some victims become later perpetrators of violence. Although a substantial amount of effort has been devoted to finding the best ways to treat violent offenders, little research has been conducted on the best ways to treat the victims of violence to minimize their psychological problems. Standard treatments for depression and anxiety may be inappropriate in these cases. Programs to treat victims have been shown to be most effective when they are delivered in natural locations (schools, community groups, health care environments) and when they are culturally relevant and age- and sex-specific. Therapies that are more specific to different types of victimization have yet to be developed. Thus, a major goal for applied research is to determine:

- Which types of psychological treatments are most appropriate for victims of different types of violence? What is most appropriate:
  - For women victimized by their husbands or intimate partners?
  - For children who have endured abuse from a parent?
  - For those bullied by peers or gangs in the school and neighborhood?
  - For those who are victims of sexual violence?
  - For the victims of racial or other bias-related violence?
  - For those who seem to be the victims of arbitrary violence?

## Prevention Strategies

Preventing violent behavior before it occurs is obviously preferable to any form of treatment after the fact. A decade of marked growth in prison populations has not reduced violence in American society, particularly among adolescents. It is time to test the promise of well-developed, fully implemented early prevention programs. Advocates of such programs argue that they would decrease the rate of crime and violence for less money than it costs to lock up offenders and keep them confined. It bears repeating, however, that adequate prevention programs can only be constructed on a foundation of knowledge about the causes of violent behavior. Although nowhere near complete, that knowledge base is already sound enough to justify devising and testing prevention strategies for the groups of children at highest risk for adolescent violence and adult crime.

### Comprehensive Prevention Models

Social scientists have learned a great deal about which groups of young people are most likely to commit violent acts, but existing knowledge about the development of violent behavior has not been fully exploited to devise prevention programs for high-risk children and adolescents. Because aggression and violence usually arise from multiple causes, prevention programs directed at only one or two causes are unlikely to succeed. A broad-based ecological approach to prevention is needed.

Childhood aggression can predict adult violence in some individuals. Researchers have learned that a small proportion of children—perhaps 5 or 10 percent—grow up to account for close to 50 percent of all arrests and the majority of all violence. This group of children is a logical target for special prevention planning and prevention research at this time. In childhood they are aggressive, disobedient, and disruptive at home and in school, disliked by peers, neglected by teachers and parents, and likely to fail in school. Later they drop out of school. Unsupervised and susceptible to the pernicious influence of other delinquent youth, they grow up to be antisocial, aggressive, and violent young adults. They are likely to become involved in abusive spousal relationships, and they often abuse their own children, thus transmitting their violent legacy to the next generation. But not every child growing up under these conditions follows this destructive path, and the example of such children has provided valuable insights into how to design prevention programs.

Researchers have shown that targeted interventions can reduce the escalating sequence of aggression and violence in some children. Early help in parenting and home visits from trained outreach workers in early childhood have interrupted this negative sequence for many children. Such help may be particularly important for children of young, poor, single mothers, for as a group, these children have extremely high rates of aggressive behavior. Parent training in behavior management, when consistently received, has been shown to reduce youthful delinquency rates. Other prevention techniques, such as attitude change, anger control, social-skills training, and community action directed at the specific processes involved in violence—i.e., socialization, cognitive, situational, or biobehavioral factors—have shown promise in small-scale tests. Most of these techniques have not been tested adequately in field trials, however, even though some have been implemented at substantial cost. This suggests a top priority:

We need to test whether a theory-based sequencing of biobehavioral, socialization, cognitive, and situational prevention strategies across the prenatal period into early adolescence can produce significantly improved prevention rates.

- *Biobehavioral interventions.* Many neurological deficits or neurotoxins implicated in violent behavior arise from events that could be prevented or treated: Perinatal exposure to alcohol and drugs, prenatal and perinatal injuries, environmental exposure to lead, hormonal abnormalities, child abuse, accidental head injuries. Once the deficits occur, however, attempts to remove or remedy the biological cause may need to be supplemented by active physiological treatment.

- *Socialization.* We need to determine which techniques are most effective in helping parents, teachers, and others to mold appropriate behaviors and thinking in high-risk children. What is the best way to teach young parents how to discipline their children appropriately? How do we best teach children alternative ways of dealing with stress, insults, anger, and family disputes? How do we best counteract the pernicious socializing influence of violence in the mass media? At what age are preventive interventions most effective in altering the course of antisocial socialization in these children?

- *Cognitions, attitudes, and beliefs.* Violent behavior is often most immediately the consequence of attributions, attitudes, beliefs, scripts, and other cognitions that are learned by children. We need to test more carefully a variety of techniques that have been proposed for preventing the formation of these violence-promoting cognitions and for changing them once they are formed. We need to see if early school-based interventions of this type can successfully counteract the influence of poor preschool socialization.

- *Environmental changes.* No matter how much we learn about the socialization process, and no matter how well we learn to change attitudes, beliefs, and other cognitions, we are unlikely to prevent violence unless we can alter the environmental factors in a child's life that promote aggression. Consequently, we need to examine how we can change neighborhoods, schools, and families so that they are less conducive to the development of violent behaviors. What kind of intervention with a child's family would best prevent the violence between family members that has the potential for increasing the child's aggressive tendencies? Almost everyone agrees that eliminating poverty would reduce violence, but other, more achievable social changes could perhaps mitigate the aggression-promoting effects of impoverished environments. What kinds of community actions are most efficacious at diminishing the attractiveness of violent gangs to youth, at reducing the alienation of impoverished youth, and in counteracting the development of a dangerous code of the streets?

We are at the point in our knowledge where the test of such a comprehensive, developmentally oriented preventive intervention is feasible. We also need to test intervention techniques directed at counteracting very specific behaviors that promote violence. Most notably, we need research on how to reduce the prevalence and use of guns by at-risk youth.

The ready availability of guns and other weapons in today's society has intensified the danger inherent in conflict. Some young males have adopted the belief common in violent groups that it is acceptable to react to every perceived or imagined sign of disrespect with aggression. The presence of weapons increases the chances that the conflict will occur in the first place and that it will have lethal consequences once it does occur.

- Research is clearly needed on the best way for communities to keep guns out of the hands of young people. What combination of community social pressure and legal regulation work best? Since no regulation will ever be completely successful, it is equally important to pursue research on how to change attitudes among youth about carrying guns. What combination of family, school, community, and mass media education can best convince people that guns escalate violence more than they protect?

*Bridging Science and Practice*

Few currently funded community violence prevention activities have evolved out of coordinated planning between researchers, practitioners, or community agency directors. As a result, the most up-to-date research findings are rarely translated directly into practice. When they are, it is often after lengthy delay and sometimes without the kind of rigorous evaluation that is the hallmark of good science. Conversely, individuals and agencies responsible for controlling violence day to day typically develop violence prevention strategies that have a weak basis in theory and are never tested rigorously. Their ideas, grounded in practical experience, rarely influence the thinking or the research of social and behavioral scientists. The potential loss to both sides is enormous and wasteful, particularly in the light of the present crisis.

- We need to improve the technology of prevention so that it can be implemented by frontline community service agents without expensive training and supervision. To accomplish this goal, we need to explore how more productive and lasting partnerships can be built between community service agents, community volunteers, schools, researchers, and funding agencies. What kinds of organizational structures and communication channels can best promote these interactions?

- Research is needed on how to implement violence prevention programs that are grounded rigorously in valid theory but are also responsive to the needs of diverse cultural communities and flexible in their application. Which ideas work with what level of effectiveness in which kinds of communities? How can community input be integrated into a prevention program? If achievable, true partnerships between community practitioners, community volunteers, violence researchers, and government agencies would seem to provide the most effective approach for long-term prevention efforts.

## Summary

Violence is a public health problem as perilous as any disease. Although scientists have made significant advances in understanding the causes of violence, these research findings need to be replicated, expanded, and exploited by applying the technology and knowledge that have emerged only recently. True integration of criminological and sociological findings with the results of research in psychology and the neurosciences promises to help us make rapid advances in our understanding of how violence develops. A broad-based research initiative that supports both basic and applied research is needed. Basic research should be aimed at obtaining a better understanding of the causes of violent behavior—the biobehavioral factors, the socialization experiences, the cognitive processes, and the situational factors that promote it. Applied prevention research should be directed at developing the tools to prevent and treat violent behavior within the framework of knowledge on causation provided by the basic research. In the long run the costs of such a program would be small compared to the human and economic losses that our nation suffers because of rampant violence in American society.

# Part Eight

# Additional Help and Information

# Chapter 38

# *Glossary*

This chapter includes definitions excerpted from documents from the National Institutes of Health; U.S. Department of Justice; Office for Victims of Crime, U.S. Department of Justice; U.S. Department of Health and Human Services; National Injury Prevention and Control, Centers for Disease Control and Prevention; National Clearinghouse on Child Abuse and Neglect; and Brazos County Rape Crisis Center; and from the following documents: "Full Faith and Credit for Orders of Protection," the Full Faith and Credit Project of the Pennsylvania Coalition Against Domestic Violence and the U.S. Department of Justice, 1999; *Pathfinder on Domestic Violence in the United States,* Center on Crime, Communities & Culture, 1997; "Are You Being Stalked? Tips for Protection," Privacy Rights, 1997; "Domestic Violence" INFOLINK, National Center for Victims of Crime, 1997; "Child Abuse" INFOLINK, National Center for Victims of Crime, 1997; "Questions and Answers for Immigrant and Refugee Women," Family Violence Prevention Fund, 1996; "The Facts: Battered Women and Economics," National Network to End Domestic Violence Fund, 1997; "Domestic Violence as a Barrier to Women's Economic Self-Sufficiency," Welfare Information Network *Issue Note,* 1999; "Shaken Baby Syndrome," American Humane Association, 1997; "Marital Violence: Batterers," in *Family Violence Across the Lifespan,* eds. Ola W. Barnett, Cindy L. Miller-Perrin, and Robin D. Perrin, Sage Publications, 1997; "Questions and Answers about Memories of Childhood Abuse," American Psychological Association, 1995; "Reducing Violence: A Research Agenda," American Psychological Association, 1996; U.S. Surgeon

General's Report on Mental Health, U.S. Public Health Service, U.S. Department of Health and Human Services, 1999; *Mental Health Disorders Sourcebook*, ed. Karen Bellenir. Second edition. Detroit, MI: Omnigraphics, 2000; *Pregnancy and Birth Sourcebook*, ed. Heather Aldred. Detroit, MI: Omnigraphics, 1997; *Sleep Disorders Sourcebook*, ed. Jenifer Swanson. Detroit, MI: Omnigraphics, 1999.

**Address confidentiality programs:** These programs help victims of stalking secure confidential mailing addresses with a mail-forwarding service that does not reveal the victim's new location. The Address Confidentiality Program, Post Office Box 69, Olympia, Washington 98507-0069, (360) 753-2971, is one such program.

**Adjudicate:** To pronounce or decree by judicial sentence.

**Adult protective services (APS):** Public agencies responsible for both investigating reported cases of elder abuse and for providing victims and their families with treatment and protective services. These agencies are usually located within county departments of social services. Most APS agencies also handle adult abuse cases (where clients are between 18 and 59 years of age).

**Aid to Families with Dependent Children (AFDC):** Federal financial assistance program replaced by the Temporary Assistance for Needy Families program in 1996.

**AIDS:** Acquired immunodeficiency syndrome. A disease characterized by opportunistic infections (e.g., Pneumocystis carinii pneumonia, candidiasis, Kaposi's sarcoma) in immunocompromised persons; caused by the human immunodeficiency virus (HIV) and transmitted by exchange of bodily fluids.

**Alcoholism:** A chronic illness evidenced by compulsive, repeated drinking that injures one's health and social and economic functioning.

**Antisocial disorder:** Antisocial disorder is characterized by long-standing problems, such as a disregard for the rights of others, irresponsibility, and resisting authority.

**Anxiety:** A sense of apprehension and fear often marked by physical symptoms (such as sweating, tension, and increased heart rate). Anxiety and fear are often used to describe the same thing. When the word anxiety is used to discuss a group of mental illnesses (anxiety disorders), it refers to an unpleasant and overriding inner emotional tension that has no apparent identifiable cause. Fear, on the other hand, causes emotional tension due to a specific, external reason. Anxiety disorders include phobias, panic disorder, obsessive-compulsive disorder, and post-traumatic stress syndrome. These disorders are severe enough to interfere with social or occupational functioning.

**Apnea:** Cessation of breathing. Until recently parents whose infants suffered from sleep apnea were advised to "shake gently, then vigorously." Now, parents are specifically advised not to shake babies for sleep apnea.

**Arraignment:** A proceeding in which an individual who is accused of committing a crime is brought into court, told of the charges, and asked to plead guilty or not guilty.

**Assault:** An unlawful physical attack whether aggravated or simple, on a person. It includes attempted assaults with or without a weapon, but excludes rape, attempted rape, and attacks involving theft or attempted theft (classified as robbery). Severity of assaults are classified into two major subcategories:

1) **Simple assault:** An attack without a weapon resulting either in minor injury (that is, bruises, black eyes, cuts, scratches, or swelling) or in undetermined injury requiring less than 2 days of hospitalization. It also includes attempted assault without a weapon and verbal threats of assault.

2) **Aggravated assault:** An attack or attempted attack with a weapon regardless of whether an injury occurred as well as an attack without a weapon when serious injury results. Serious injury includes broken bones, loss of teeth, internal injuries, loss of consciousness, and any injury requiring 2 or more days of hospitalization.

**Batterer intervention programs:** Batterer intervention programs, which seek to educate or rehabilitate known perpetrators of intimate partner violence to be nonviolent, have proliferated since the 1980s, under the auspices of both the criminal justice system and mental health system. The longest established batterer intervention programs include a feminist educational approach and, to varying degrees, incorporate cognitive-behavioral techniques. *See also* **Cognitive-behavioral approach to treating batterers; Family systems approach to treating batterers; Feminist approach to treating batterers; Individual and group psychodynamic therapy for treating batterers; Psychotherapeutic approaches to treating batterers**

**Batterer typologies:** This term refers to specific types of batterers, based on psychological profiles or criminal histories. Although psychological typologies are interesting from a theoretical standpoint, they do not yet offer much assistance to the criminal justice system because of the in-depth assessment needed to identify characteristics and the lack of typology-based interventions available. No consensus on psychological categories for batterers has emerged from the research community.

**Battering:** Dr. Anne H. Flitcraft originally coined the term *woman battering* in the 1970s, describing it as an "identifiable pattern of ongoing, systematic, and escalating abuse that often extends over a lifetime" (Flitcraft, A. H. *Battered Women: An Emergency Room Epidemiology with a Description of a Clinical Syndrome and Critique of Present Therapeutics.* Unpublished doctoral dissertation, Yale University School of Medicine, New Haven, CT, 1977, p. 3). Battering refers to intentionally injuring someone. A wide range of physical and psychological pain is inflicted upon victims by their batterers. Battering is also about control. In addition to overt forms of physical and psychological abuse, the batterer may control the victim's access to the outside world by denying her use of the telephone, money for public transportation, or the simple freedom to leave her home unescorted.

**Battering syndrome:** *Battering syndrome* is also referred to as battered woman syndrome. It is a term used to describe the psychological and emotional impact of repeated victimization by one's partner, which can have farther-reaching and longer-lasting effects on a victim than isolated acts of violence. Women who have been beaten repeatedly over many years and who exhibit the syndrome share two essential characteristics: (1) debilitating fear of physical aggression and (2) unpredictable displays of physical aggression (Ammerman, R. T., & M. Hersen, eds. *Assessment of Family Violence: A Clinical and Legal Sourcebook*, New York: John Wiley & Sons, 1992, pp. 39-40).

The trauma and general medical problems that result from being battered are medically classified as a type of anxiety disorder, or post-traumatic stress disorder, and yield a high incidence of subsequent mental and physical disorders and behavior, such as depression, substance abuse, child abuse, and attempted suicide.

**Borderline personality disorder:** The term *borderline* implies that there is no dominant pattern of deviance, but there are problems with impulsivity, instability of moods, and so forth. *See also* **Personality disorder.**

**Child abuse and neglect:** 1) Any recent act or failure to act on the part of a parent or caretaker which results in death, serious physical or emotional harm, sexual abuse or exploitation; 2) an act or failure to act which presents an imminent risk of serious harm.

**Child abuse, indicated:** "Indicated" means that maltreatment could not be substantiated by a child protective services investigation, but there is reason to believe that the child was maltreated or at risk of maltreatment.

**Child abuse, sexual:** 1) The employment, use, persuasion, inducement, enticement, or coercion of any child to engage in, or assist any other person to engage in, any sexually explicit conduct or simulation of such conduct for the purpose of producing a visual depiction of such conduct; 2) the rape, and in cases of caretaker or inter-familial relationships, statutory rape, molestation, prostitution, or other form of sexual exploitation of children, or incest with children.

**Child abuse, substantiated:** "Substantiated" means that the allegation of maltreatment or the risk of maltreatment was confirmed by a child protective services investigation according to the level of evidence required by state law or policy.

**Child Abuse Prevention and Treatment Act (1974; amended 1996):** Defines what acts are considered physical abuse, neglect, and sexual abuse and provides a foundation for states by identifying a minimum set of acts or behaviors that characterize maltreatment.

The Act also provides financial assistance to child abuse prevention and treatment programs; established a National Center on Child Abuse; and provides resources for research to prevent child abuse.

907

**Child death review teams:** Child death review teams, first initiated in Los Angeles County, Calif., in 1978, now exist in all 50 states and the District of Columbia and are charged with examining the circumstances surrounding certain child deaths known or suspected to be preventable or the result of child abuse or neglect. Child death review teams try to correctly determine when children have died from abuse or neglect, identifying risk factors and systemic problems in hopes of preventing future deaths. Most teams consist of representatives from law enforcement, the prosecutor, child protective services, the medical examiner or coroner's office, public health agencies, and emergency medical personnel and pediatricians.

**Child protective services (CPS):** Public social service organizations, funded by states, with the primary responsibility for receiving and responding to reports of alleged child maltreatment. These are designed to safeguard the child when there is suspicion of abuse, neglect, or abandonment, or where there is no family to take care of the child. Examples of help delivered in the home include financial assistance, vocational training, homemaker services, and day care. If in-home supports are insufficient, the child may be removed from the home on a temporary or permanent basis. The goal is to keep the child with his or her family whenever possible.

**Children's advocacy centers:** These centers allow law enforcement officers, child protection workers, prosecutors, victim advocates, medical professionals, and therapists to coordinate the investigation, prosecution, and treatment of the child victim. More than 350 communities around the country have established or are in the process of developing children's advocacy centers. The Office of Juvenile Justice and Delinquency Prevention in the U.S. Department of Justice provides funds to communities seeking to establish or strengthen children's advocacy centers. The funds are administered by the National Children's Alliance, which maintains a directory of existing centers.

**Clerk of court:** An officer appointed by the court to work with the chief judge in overseeing the court's administration, especially to assist in managing the flow of cases through the court and to maintain court records.

**Cognitive-behavioral approach to treating batterers:** Therapists using a cognitive-behavioral approach apply learning principles to help clients modify behavior identified as problematic by empirically based trait assessments. The cognitive-behavioral approach focuses on the conscious rather than the unconscious and the present rather than the past to help batterers function better by modifying how they think and behave. The approach is compatible with a criminal justice response, simply addressing the violent acts and attempting to change them, without trying to solve larger issues of social inequality or delve into deep-seated psychological problems. Feminists fault the approach for failing to explain why many batterers are not violent in other relationships.

**Cognitive processes:** The mental processes that help a person control behavior—awareness, perception, reasoning, and judgment.

**Cohort:** A group of people being studied in a research project.

**Comorbidity:** This term is used to indicate when a patient suffers from two or more disorders or problematic conditions at once.

**Conduct disorder:** Children or adolescents with conduct disorder behave aggressively by fighting, bullying, intimidating, physically assaulting, sexually coercing, and/or being cruel to people or animals. Common examples of conduct disorder behavior include vandalism with deliberate destruction of property, setting fires or smashing windows, theft, truancy, early tobacco, alcohol, and substance use and abuse, and precocious sexual activity. Girls with a conduct disorder are prone to running away from home and may become involved in prostitution. The behavior interferes with performance at school or work, so that individuals with this disorder rarely perform at the level predicted by their IQ or age. Their relationships with peers and adults are often poor. They have higher injury rates and are prone to school expulsion and problems with the law. Sexually transmitted diseases are common. If they have been removed from home, they may have difficulty staying in an adoptive or foster family or group home, and this may further complicate their development. Rates of depression, suicidal thoughts, suicide attempts, and suicide itself are all higher in children diagnosed with a conduct disorder (Shaffer, D., P. Fisher, M. Dulcan, M. Davies, J. Piacentini, M. Schwab-Stone, B. Lahey, K. Bourdon, P. Jensen, H. Bird, & G. R. D. Canino. (1996). "The Second Version of the NIMH Diagnostic Interview Schedule for Children (DISC–2)." *Journal of the American Academy of Child and Adolescent Psychiatry,* 35, 865–77).

**Conflict Tactics Scales (CTS):** A questionnaire for measuring conflict between people, devised by family violence researcher Murray A. Straus in the late 1970s. The scale asks questions relating to how many times "reasoning and argument," "verbal and symbolic aggression," or "physical aggression" were used during fights over a specified period of time, such as a year. Recently, Straus and colleagues have revised the CTS to also measure "physical assault," "psychological aggression," "negotiation," "injury," and "sexual coercion." The revised CTS is known as the CTS2 (1995).

**Consent order:** An order of protection (*see* **Protection orders**) which is issued against an alleged assailant, usually without a finding (legal conclusion) of abuse, but after the respondent consents or agrees to the entry of the order.

**Conviction:** A judgment of guilt against a criminal defendant.

**Correlation:** An association or linkage of two (or more) events. A correlation simply means that the events are linked in some way. Finding a correlation, for example, between stressful life events and depression would prompt more research on causation. Does stress cause depression? Does depression cause stress? Or are they both caused by an unidentified factor? These would be the questions guiding research.

**Court school programs:** Court school programs are designed to orient the child victim and child witness to the court process and to the role of the witness. These programs are usually facilitated by victim advocates and prosecutors and include a group of children scheduled to testify in the near future. Most programs include role-playing, a courtroom tour, and opportunities to practice answering questions in the courtroom. Court school programs help reduce anxiety in children and normalize what may have been a strange and frightening process. Many programs include a concurrent session for non-offending parents and caretakers to provide information about the court process and how they can support their children.

**CPS.** *See* **Child protective services**

**Crime victim assistance programs:** These programs are located within both state government agencies and private nonprofit or charitable organizations. They provide services including crisis intervention, counseling, emergency shelter, criminal justice advocacy, and emergency transportation.

**Crime victim compensation programs:** These programs, run by the states, reimburse victims of crime occurring within the state (including victims of federal crimes) for crime-related expenses. Crimes include violent crimes such as homicide, rape, drunk driving, domestic violence, and child sexual abuse and neglect. Expenses covered are medical costs, mental health counseling, funeral and burial costs, and lost wages or loss of support.

**Cultural competence:** Help that is sensitive and responsive to cultural differences. Caregivers are aware of the impact of their own culture and possess skills that help them provide services that are culturally appropriate in responding to people's unique cultural differences, such as race and ethnicity, national origin, religion, age, gender, sexual orientation, or physical disability. They adapt their skills to fit a family's values and customs.

**Custody order:** A court order that prohibits a spouse/intimate partner from removing the children of the relationship from the country [or state] in which a custodial parent lives.

**Cycle of violence:**

1) Phrase coined by Lenore Walker to describe a pattern of spousal abuse. The cycle of violence describes interpersonal aggression that intensifies in degree and frequency over time and holds the people involved in an established pattern of behavior. The cycle of violence consists of three phases: 1) Tension building: In this phase, minor incidents of violence may occur along with a buildup of anger. This phase may include verbal put-downs, jealousy, threats, and breaking things and can eventually escalate to the second phase. 2) Acute or battering: In this phase, the major violent outburst occurs. This violence can be seen as the major earthquake. Following the second phase, the couple sometimes enters phase 3. 3) The honeymoon or living respite: In this phase, the batterer is remorseful and afraid of losing his partner. He may promise anything, beg forgiveness, buy gifts, and basically be "the man she fell in love with."

2) Also called the "intergenerational transmission of violence," these terms refer to the possible negative consequences later in life for children who are sexually or physically abused or neglected.

**Date rape drugs.** *See* **Gamma Hydroxybutyrate (GHB)** and **Rohypnol**

**Depression:** A biologically based psychological disorder marked by sadness, inactivity, difficulty with thinking and concentration, significant increase or decrease in appetite and sleep, feelings of dejection and hopelessness, and sometimes suicidal thoughts or actions. When used to describe a mood, depression refers to what may be normal feelings of sadness, despair, and discouragement. More serious depression may be a symptom of a variety of physical and mental disorders, a syndrome of associated symptoms secondary to an underlying disorder or it may itself be a specific mental disorder. The disorder known as major depression is characterized by slowed thinking, decreased purposeful physical activity, sleep and appetite disturbances, low self-esteem, loss of sex drive, and feelings of guilt and hopelessness.

**Dissociation:** An interruption of a person's fundamental aspects of waking consciousness (such as who he is, what his personal history is, etc.). Dissociation means that a memory is not actually lost, but is for some time unavailable for retrieval. That is, it's in memory storage, but cannot for some period of time actually be recalled. Some clinicians believe that severe forms of child sexual abuse are especially conducive to negative disturbances of memory such as dissociation or delayed memory. Many clinicians who work with trauma victims believe that this dissociation is a person's way of sheltering himself or herself from the pain of the memory. Many researchers argue, however, that there is little or no empirical support for such a theory.

**Domestic Violence:** One of the main obstacles to understanding and preventing domestic violence is the lack of a uniform set of definitions. The social service, medical, and legal professions, for example, have differing definitions of what constitutes domestic violence, who the participants are, and what kinds of services they need. Although there are many agencies and fields of study that specialize in domestic violence or various aspects of domestic violence, the definitions that follow have been limited to three of the major service professions.

*Social Service*

The social service field defines domestic violence as the emotional, psychological, economic, or physical abuse, or threat of such abuse between family members or partners, such as spouses, former spouses, parents, children, stepchildren, other persons related by blood, in-laws from a current or previous marriage, persons who live together, persons who are dating or have dated or been engaged, and persons who have disabilities and their caregivers.

*Medicine*

The medical field generally defines domestic violence as physical, psychological, or emotional injuries that are intentionally inflicted by and on family members, including abuse occurring in same-sex relationships. In addition to physical injuries related to partner abuse, child abuse, sexual abuse, and incest, the medical field includes verbal threats, intimidation, forced social isolation, and economic control in its definition of domestic violence.

*Law*

The legal profession distinguishes *family violence,* which is violence against family members (spouses, children, and elders), from *domestic violence,* which is violence against intimate partners (spouse, former spouse, partner, former partner). Unlike the medical field, the legal profession does not recognize economic control as a form of domestic abuse. However, the legal definition recognizes harassment, terrorism, or damage to property as forms of domestic violence.

State laws covering domestic violence-related crimes vary considerably. It may be too much to expect all states to enact the same laws on domestic violence crimes. However, closer scrutiny of the health care and social service professions, together with comprehensive, mandated training in domestic violence-related issues have shown to be effective in improving those professions' response to domestic violence. Closer scrutiny and mandated training for the legal community might also prove effective.

**Dyadic:** Adjective for *dyad,* a term meaning "two," for example, dyadic intimacy involves two people in an intimate relationship.

**Emotional abuse.** *See* **Psychological abuse**

**Epidemiology:** The study of the relationship between various factors that determine the frequency and distribution of diseases in human populations.

**Etiology:** The study of the origins and causes of disease.

**Ex parte order:** An emergency or temporary order issued at the request of the petitioner without first providing notice or a hearing to the respondent.

**Family systems approach to treating batterers:** This approach regards the problem behaviors of individuals as a manifestation of a dysfunctional family, with each family member contributing to the problem. Both partners may contribute to the escalation of conflict, with each striving to dominate the other. In this view, either partner may resort to violence. Intervention involves improving communication and conflict resolution skills, which both partners can develop. It focuses on solving the problem rather than identifying the causes.

Of particular concern to feminist and cognitive-behavioral proponents is the format of couples counseling espoused in the family systems model. They believe it can put the victim at risk if she expresses complaints, prevents a frank exchange between counselor and victim, and is conducive to victim-blaming. For these reasons, couples counseling is expressly prohibited in 20 state standards and guidelines for batterer intervention.

**Family Violence Option (FVO):** An amendment to the Personal Responsibility and Work Opportunity Reconciliation Act (Welfare Reform) of 1996, the Family Violence Option gives states the option to waive work requirements and time limits, and increase services to victims of domestic violence and their families without being penalized financially.

**Felony:** A crime carrying a penalty of more than a year in prison.

**Feminist approach to treating batterers:** The feminist perspective has influenced most batterer intervention programs. Central to the perspective is a gender analysis of power, which holds that domestic violence mirrors the patriarchal organization of society. In this view, violence is one means of maintaining male power in the family. Feminist programs, which attempt to raise consciousness about society's sex-role conditioning and how it constrains people's behavior, present a model of egalitarian relationships based on trust instead of fear.

Support for the feminist analysis comes from the observation that most batterers, when "provoked" by someone more powerful than they, are able to control their anger and avoid resorting to violence. Further support comes from research showing that batterers are less secure in their masculinity than nonbatterers and from studies documenting the sense of entitlement batterers feel in controlling their partners' behavior.

Critics of the feminist perspective claim that it overemphasizes sociocultural factors to the exclusion of traits in the individual, such as growing up abused. In their view, feminist theory predicts that *all* men will be abusive. Other criticisms hold that feminist educational interventions are too confrontational and as a result self-defeating because they alienate batterers, increase their hostility, and make them less likely to enter treatment. Another criticism finds that the education central to the feminist program may not deter violent behavior.

**Flunitrazepam.** *See* **Rohypnol**

**Full Faith and Credit:** A legal term meaning that jurisdictions must honor and enforce protection orders issued by courts in other jurisdictions.

**Gamma Hydroxybutyrate (GHB):** A pharmaceutical drug that acts as a central nervous system depressant  and that has been used as a date rape drug.

**HIV:** Human immunodeficiency virus. The virus occurring in humans that causes a condition that results in a defective immunological mechanism, opportunistic infections, and eventually in the disease process known as AIDS (acquired immunodeficiency syndrome).

**Incidence:** The number of new cases of a condition occurring in a given population during a specified period of time, such as a year.

**Indian Child Welfare Act (ICWA):** A law that applies to custody proceedings in state courts involving foster care placement, termination of parental rights, preadoptive placement, and adoptive placement of Indian children. The ICWA may apply to divorces or custody proceedings where custody of the child(ren) is given to a third party. This law is significant because abusers often threaten to use the ICWA against battered women even though the ICWA does not apply to custody proceedings between the parents of the child(ren).

**Individual and group psychodynamic therapy for treating batterers:** A therapeutic approach that involves techniques that uncover the batterer's unconscious problem with the aim of resolving it consciously. Although a recent study revealed that the approach retained a higher percentage of men in treatment than did a feminist/cognitive-behavioral intervention, critics fault psychodynamic therapy for not explaining what can be done to stop the behavior, allowing the behavior to continue until the underlying problem is solved, and ignoring the cultural acceptability of male dominance.

**Infanticide:** Term increasingly used to define the murdering of children younger than 6 or 12 months by their parents.

**Injunction:** An order of the court prohibiting (or compelling) the performance of a specific act to prevent irreparable damage or injury.

**Intergenerational transmission of violence:** Also called the "cycle of violence," this term refers to the possible negative consequences later in life for children who are sexually or physically abused or neglected.

**Interstate Stalking Punishment and Prevention Act (1996):** This law makes it a federal crime for any stalker to cross state lines to pursue a victim, regardless of whether there is a protection order in effect, they have committed an actual act of violence, or they are a spouse or intimate of the victim.

**Intimates:** Spouses or ex-spouses, boyfriends and girlfriends, or exboyfriends and ex-girlfriends.

**Jacob Wetterling Crimes Against Children and Sexually Violent Offender Registration Act (1994), Megan's Law (1996), and the Pam Lychner Act (1996):** Under these statutes, sex offenders and child molesters must register information about their whereabouts with appropriate state law enforcement agencies for ten years after release from prison and state prison officials must notify local law enforcement when they are released or move. States must notify the public about the release of registered sex offenders when necessary for public safety.

**Jurisdiction (location):**
1) Used as a general name for the geographic areas impacted by the federal law. This includes all 50 states, Indian tribal lands, the District of Columbia, the U.S. Virgin Islands, Puerto Rico, American Samoa, the Northern Mariana Islands, and Guam.

**Issuing Jurisdiction:** Jurisdiction that grants the order of protection.

**Enforcing Jurisdiction:** Jurisdiction that enforces an order of protection issued by another jurisdiction.

2) Used as a legal term to refer to the types of authority that a court may exercise.

**Subject Matter Jurisdiction:** Refers to the authority of a court to hear and determine a particular type of case.

**Personal Jurisdiction:** Refers to the power the court may (or may not) have over the parties involved in a particular case.

**Longitudinal study:** A research study that gathers data on a select group of people over time.

**Meta-analysis:** A meta-analysis is a way of combining results from multiple studies. Its goal is to determine the size and consistency of the "effect" of a particular treatment or other intervention observed across the studies. The statistical technique makes the results of different studies comparable so that an overall "effect size" for the treatment can be identified. A meta-analysis determines if there is consistent evidence of a statistically significant effect of a specified treatment and estimates the size of the effect, according to widely accepted standards for a small, medium, or large effect.

**Misdemeanor:** Usually a petty offense, a less serious crime than a felony, punishable by less than a year of confinement.

**Mutual order:** A single order of protection that includes prohibitions against both the petitioner and respondent. *See also* **Petitioner**; **Protection order**; **Respondent**

**NCIC Protection Order File.** *See* **Protection order registries**

**Neurophysiology:** The branch of physiology that studies the nervous system.

**Neurotransmitter:** A chemical substance released by nerve cell endings to transmit impulses across the space between nerve cells, tissues or organs.

**Neurotoxins:** Substances toxic to the nervous systems, such as lead, thought to place a person at risk of becoming violent.

**No-contact orders.** *See* **Protection order**

**Order of protection.** *See* **Protection order**

**Parental Kidnapping Prevention Act (PKPA):** Federal legislation enacted to ensure that jurisdictions honor and enforce custody orders entered by the courts of other jurisdictions so long as both parties received prior notice and were given a chance to be heard. The PKPA prioritizes home state jurisdiction so other jurisdictions have to defer to orders entered by the jurisdiction where the child lived for the six-month period prior to the filing of the action.

**Patriarchy:** Term used to describe a society or social system dominated by males.

**Pedophilia:** A mental disorder (and a criminal offense) in which an adult engages in sexual activity with a child.

**Perinatal:** Occurring during, or pertaining to, the periods before, during, or after the time of birth, i.e., from the 28th week of gestation through the first seven days after delivery.

**Personality disorder:** A deeply ingrained, inflexible, maladaptive pattern of relating, perceiving and thinking, serious enough to cause distress or impaired functioning. Personality disorders are usually recognizable by adolescence or earlier, continue throughout adulthood and become less obvious in middle or old age. Examples of formally identified personality disorders are antisocial, borderline, compulsive, histrionic, dependent, narcissistic, paranoid, passive-aggressive, schizoid, and schizotypal.

**Petitioner:** The person who presents a petition to the court requesting an order of protection.

**Physical abuse:** The dynamics of an abusive relationship where battering occurs are more complicated than many people realize. Physical abuse in a battering relationship is not just about a husband injuring his wife. S. J. Kaplan points out, in her book *Family Violence: A Clinical and Legal Guide*, that "both men and women are targets of assault during domestic violence" (Kaplan, 1996, p. 142). The abuse may involve one person (the batterer) injuring the victim. But, very often the victim also physically injures the batterer. The victim may retaliate for past abuse, she may defend herself from further violence, or she may simply lose control and strike out at the batterer without provocation.

The victim's abuse generally follows a pattern that begins with occasional slapping or pinching and escalates to more serious abuse, such as burning, punching, or assault with an object or weapon. Battering may also involve sadistic sexual acts ranging from rape to genital mutilation. Repeated violent episodes often lead to the victim's hospitalization and sometimes death.

It is important to note here that, generally speaking, a man's greater average size and strength may mean that a violent act he commits would inflict considerably more pain and injury on a female victim than if the same act were committed by a woman on her male partner.

**Post-traumatic Stress Disorder (PTSD):** PTSD is a psychiatric illness that can develop in response to extreme traumatic stressors, according to DSM-IV, the diagnostic manual published by the American Psychiatric Association. These stressors involve direct personal experience of abuse and violence that may or may not result in the victim's physical injury. A person with PTSD typically has great difficulty reestablishing daily functioning after the traumatic event(s) and exhibits symptoms that continue for more than four weeks after the event(s). Not much is known about the extent to which battered women suffer from posttraumatic stress disorder. However, research over the last 10 years has established a strong correlation between the trauma experienced by battered women and that experienced by prisoners, victims of war, and survivors of concentration camps, mugging, or rape. It is estimated that up to half of all battered women who seek help have diagnosable PTSD. (Houskamp, B. M., and D. W. Foy. "The Assessment of Post-Traumatic Stress Disorder in Battered Women." *Journal of Interpersonal Violence* 6 [1991]: 367-75.) Other psychiatric disorders related to men and women in physically abusive relationships, such as Acute Stress Disorder (ASD), Self-Defeating Personality Disorder, Relationship Disorders, and Intermittent Explosive Disorder, are beginning to receive more serious research attention. For more information on these clinical disorders, see Ammerman, R. T., and M. Hersen, eds. *Assessment of Family Violence: A Clinical and Legal Sourcebook*. New York: John Wiley & Sons, 1992.

**Prevalence:** Refers to the number of cases (i.e., new and existing) of a condition observed at a point in time or during a period of time.

**Probation:** A sentencing alternative to imprisonment in which the court releases convicted defendants under supervision as long as certain conditions are observed.

**Protection order.** Protection, or restraining, orders are court orders "issued for the purpose of preventing violent or threatening acts or harassment against, or contact or communication with, or physical proximity to, another person."

There are several forms of protection orders. Some states have an emergency protection order that a police officer can issue when responding to a domestic violence call. This is usually good until the next business day, and allows the victim time to apply for a more permanent order. Other protection orders last from 30 days to a few years and can be indefinitely renewed. Each jurisdiction and community may differ in the types of protection orders available and the process for application and issuance of orders.

**Protection order, qualifying:** Protection order that meets the following conditions: (i) the protected party must be a spouse, former spouse, present or former cohabitant with the respondent, parent of common child, or a child of the respondent; (ii) the order must have been entered after a hearing of which the respondent had notice and an opportunity to appear; (iii) the order must include a finding that the respondent represents a credible threat to the protected party or must include an express prohibition against harassment, stalking, or the use of force that would reasonably be expected to cause injury.

**Protection order registries:** Many states, tribes, and localities have developed computerized databases that contain records of valid orders of protection issued or registered within the jurisdiction. Some jurisdictions also keep records of expired orders. If a state or tribal registry is *accurate* and *up-to-date*, it can be accessed to verify the existence of a protection order in cases where the victim cannot produce a paper copy or where the paper copy does not appear to be valid. It should be noted that not all states and tribes have centralized databases of protection orders.

In 1997, the FBI established the National Crime Information Center's (NCIC) Protection Order File. Because state and tribal participation is voluntary and NCIC requires certain data elements to list an order, the national registry does not contain orders from all jurisdictions. As such, the NCIC Protection Order File is an imperfect verification tool. *See also* **Protection orders**

**Psychological abuse:** Psychological abuse, also referred to as emotional abuse or nonphysical abuse, is another debilitating form of battering that is sometimes overlooked or downplayed. For example, the FBI's Uniform Crime Reports (UCR) track only the most severe physical forms of spousal violence-homicide and assault. State surveys on crime generally report only the use of physical force (abuse) and not whether this abuse evolves into the battering syndrome. Psychological abuse often accompanies both physical and sexual abuse and can be viewed as functionally equivalent to these forms of abuse (i.e., each function to establish dominance and control of one person over another). The most damaging emotional effects usually result from a combination of these three forms of abuse.

Emerging research confirms that psychological abuse is in itself harmful and can be a powerful predictor of a woman's future psychosocial problems. Ammerman and Hersen have likened the worst psychological abuse to "torture paralleling intentional brainwashing and mistreatment of prisoners of war" (Ammerman, R. T., & M. Hersen, eds. *Assessment of Family Violence: A Clinical and Legal Sourcebook*, New York: John Wiley & Sons, 1992, p. 292).

Psychological abuse involves coercive, regulative, and deceptive mind-controlling techniques that include induced fear or terror through verbal or physical threats; isolation or imprisonment; induced guilt leading to victim self-blame; promotion of powerlessness and helplessness in the victim; exhibition of pathological jealousy; forced secrecy; enforced loyalty; humiliation; and degradation. Other psychologically abusive tactics that increase the batterer's control over his partner include the manipulation of children, rigid gender role expectations, and economic deprivation. (Children can be used in a variety of ways in an abusive relationship. In addition to being subjected to the same physical, psychological, and sexual abuse as a victim, children can also be used as pawns by the abuser. The threat of harm to children, threatened removal of children from the home, exposure of children to abusive acts, and other forms of psychological abuse can involve the use of children.)

Trapped in a cycle of subordination and repeated punishment, the victim develops strategies of response in an attempt to end or control the level of violence directed at her. These strategies include a variety of coping mechanisms, such as staying very quiet in the batterer's presence and/or acquiescing to demands for sex. Other characteristic coping methods include self-blame, rationalization of the violence, and denial or underestimation of the seriousness of the violence.

**Psychopathology:** Term referring to dysfunctional behavioral, cognitive, emotional patterns, or interpersonal relational patterns of individuals, or to the study of same.

**Psychotherapeutic approaches to treating batterers:** These approaches, which focus on the individual, hold that personality disorders or early traumatic life experiences predispose some people to violence. Being physically abusive is seen as symptomatic of an underlying emotional problem, which may be traced to parental abuse, rejection, and failure to meet a child's dependence needs.

From this perspective, two forms of batterer intervention—individual and group psychodynamic therapy and cognitive-behavioral group therapy—have evolved. *See also* **Cognitive-behavioral approach to treating batterers** and **Individual and group psychodynamic therapy**

**Rape:** Sexual intercourse through the use of force or threat of force, including attempts; attempted rape may consist of verbal threats of rape. It includes male as well as female victims.

The definition from the National Crime Victimization Survey (NCVS) interviewer's manual is as follows: "Rape is forced sexual intercourse and includes both psychological coercion as well as physical force. Forced sexual intercourse means vaginal, anal, or oral penetration by the offender(s). This category also includes incidents where the penetration is from a foreign object such as a bottle." *See also* **Sexual assault**

**Recidivism:** Term used to describe the recurrence of criminal or psychologically disturbed behavior.

**Registration/Filing:** Refers to a procedure where an order of protection from one jurisdiction is registered or filed with a clerk of court or law enforcement agency in another jurisdiction. In some jurisdictions, the order may be entered into a local or statewide protective order computer registry. Registration usually creates a public record of the order of protection in the enforcing jurisdiction. *See also* **Protection order registries**

**Respondent:** The person against whom an order of protection is filed.

**Restraining order.** *See* **Protection order**

**Retrospective study:** A method of research study that gathers data about past occurrences.

**Rohypnol:** Brand name for flunitrazepam, a prescription sleeping medicine that has been used as a date rape drug. Common street names for Rohypnol include Roofies, Roachies, La Rocha, the forget pill, and the date rape drug.

**Serotonin:** A neurotransmitter linked to mood regulation. New research has shown that aggressive young adults are likely to have lower levels of serotonin in the brain, although the role of serotonin in childhood aggression has not been sufficiently studied. Yet there is little dispute that serotonin levels are correlated with individual differences in aggression and impulsivity. New technologies in neurophysiology have opened opportunities in this area that should be explored. We need a better understanding of the possibly reciprocal influences of serotonin and aggressive behavior.

**Sex offender registration systems:** Sex offender registration and notification systems are important law enforcement and public safety tools. By informing local authorities of the identities and whereabouts of convicted sex offenders, registration systems aid in the investigation of sex crimes. Likewise, community notification programs enable communities and parents to take common sense measures to protect themselves and their children.

**Sexual abuse:** In an adult partner relationship, sexual abuse includes rape, or otherwise forcing unwanted sexual acts, and talking the partner into doing sexual things which are embarrassing or that feel bad. *See also* **Child abuse, sexual**

**Sexual assault:** A wide range of victimizations, separate from rape or attempted rape. These crimes include attacks or attempted attacks generally involving (unwanted) sexual contact between victim and offender. Sexual assaults may or may not involve force and include such things as grabbing or fondling. Sexual assault also includes verbal threats. Sexual assault occurs when a "person causes the penetration of the anus, vagina, or mouth of another person with a sexual organ or object, without that person's consent OR causes another person to contact or penetrate the mouth, anus, or sexual organ of another person without their consent."

**Shaken baby syndrome:** The medical term used to describe the violent shaking and resulting injuries sustained from shaking an infant.

**Socialization:** The process by which a child learns the "scripts" for specific social behavior, along with the rules, attitudes, values, and norms that guide interactions with others.

**Stalking:** Legal definitions of stalking vary from state to state. Most states define stalking as the willful, malicious, and repeated following and harassing of another person. Some states include in their definition such activities as lying-in-wait, surveillance, nonconsensual communication, telephone harassment, and vandalism. Most states require that the alleged stalker engage in a course of conduct showing that the crime was not an isolated event. Some states specify how many acts (usually two or more) must occur before the conduct can be considered stalking. Most state laws require that the perpetrator, to qualify as a stalker, make a credible threat of violence against the victim; others include in their requirements threats against the victim's immediate family; and still others require only that the alleged stalker's course of conduct constitute an implied threat. The definition of stalking used in the National Violence Against Women Survey is "a course of conduct directed at a specific person that involves repeated visual or physical proximity, nonconsensual communication, or verbal, written or implied threats, or a combination thereof, that would cause a reasonable person fear."

**Stay-away orders.** *See* **Protection orders**

**Subdural hematoma:** A collection of blood in the brain that can be caused by beating or violently shaking a person, causing bleeding under the skull.

**Subdural hemorrhage:** Bleeding that occurs in the brain; it can be caused by beating or violently shaking a person.

**Sudden infant death syndrome (SIDS):** The unexpected death of an apparently healthy baby, usually occurring during sleep, without apparent cause.

**Temporary Aid to Needy Families (TANF):** A fixed block grant to the states for which states must meet certain requirements. The new federal law [passed under the Personal Responsibility and Work Opportunity Reconciliation Act of 1996, known as "Welfare Reform"] provides that one would be eligible to receive assistance for a maximum of 60 months—five years—over one's lifetime. Some states provide even shorter time limits than the federal law.

**Testosterone:** A hormone [that regulates normal growth and development in males]...[which] seems to be correlated with a tendency to dominate others, although recent evidence suggests that a high testosterone level is as much a consequence of dominance as a cause...We know that engaging in aggressive and dominating behaviors can increase testosterone levels; and we know that a higher testosterone level is associated with the likelihood of aggression. But we also know that there is not a simple one-to-one relationship between them.

Present knowledge will only become useful in preventing aggression and violence when we learn more about the psychological processes involved and how testosterone levels interact with other factors in a person's life (both males and females).

**Tort:** A civil wrong or breach of a duty to another person, as outlined by law. A very common tort is negligent operation of a motor vehicle that results in property damage and personal injury in an automobile accident.

**Tribe:** An Indian nation, Indian tribe, or native sovereign nation.

**TPO:** Temporary protective order. *See* **Protection order**

**TRO:** Temporary restraining order. *See* **Protection order**

**Uniform Child Custody Jurisdiction Act (UCCJA):** A uniform law, enacted with few variations by all of the states, which establishes jurisdiction to render custody orders that are enforceable across jurisdictional boundaries. The UCCJA sets forth four possible bases of jurisdiction without giving priority to any one over the others. Because of this, it is still possible for more than one state at a time to establish jurisdiction over the same parties and facts and for courts to render conflicting orders in the same case. The Act is more than 30 years old and is inconsistent with some provisions of subsequently enacted federal law.

**Uniform Child Custody Jurisdiction and Enforcement Act (UCCJEA):** A replacement for the UCCJA currently being considered by the states and already enacted by a few. This Act establishes one jurisdictional base as having priority over the others—the state where the child has lived for the six months prior to the filing of the custody case—and builds in a number of protections for victims of domestic violence not available in the UCCJA. For example, the UCCJEA creates a structure of cooperation among the courts of the competing states so that the victim does not have to return physically to the home state in order to litigate in its courts; more comprehensive emergency jurisdiction in the refuge state; and a greater likelihood that the home state will voluntarily relinquish jurisdiction if it would be unsafe for the victim to litigate there.

**Victim impact statement (VIS):** A statement composed by a crime victim, or with the help of an advocate for the person, indicating the impact of the crime on his or her physical, emotional, and financial well-being. The VIS can then be used in court before the perpetrator is sentenced.

**Violence:** The *American Heritage Dictionary* defines violence as: "(1) physical force exerted for the purpose of violating, damaging, or abusing; (2) the act or an instance of violent action or behavior; (3) intensity or severity, as in natural phenomena; untamed force; (4) abusive or unjust exercise of power; (5) abuse or injury to meaning, content, or intent; (6) vehemence of feeling or expression; fervor."

But in reality, violence is a far more complex issue. No established theory has been able to adequately explain, predict, or prevent violent behavior in our society. In 1993, the National Academy of Sciences concluded that our inability to establish successful violence prevention and intervention programs was due to the lack of a general theory linking the various fields of knowledge regarding violent events and behaviors. Attempts to create a definition free of jargon and bias have proved extraordinarily difficult. The following discussion is an effort to expand upon and supplement our understanding of the meaning of violence.

For further discussion, please see the following texts: Toch, Hans H. *Violent Men: An Inquiry into the Psychology of Violence*. Chicago: Aldine, 1969; Polk, Kenneth. *When Men Kill: Scenarios of Male Violence*. New York: Cambridge University Press, 1994; Stevens, J. E. "Treating Violence as an Epidemic." *Technical Review* (1994): 22-30; and Conway, T. "The Internist's Role in Addressing Violence." *Archives of Internal Medicine* 156 (May 13, 1996): 951-56.

**Violence Against Women Act (VAWA, 1994):** The Violence Against Women Act, enacted as part of the 1994 Crime Act, makes it a crime to cross state lines to continue to abuse a spouse or partner, creates tough new penalties for sex offenders, and prohibits anyone facing a restraining order for domestic abuse from possession of a firearm.

In addition, the Violence Against Women Act provides a substantial commitment of federal resources – more than $1.6 billion over six years—for police, prosecutors, prevention service initiatives in cases involving sexual violence or domestic abuse. Also, the Act requires sexual offenders to pay restitution to their victims, requires states to pay for rape examinations, provides $1.5 million for federal victim-witness counselors and extends rape shield laws to protect crime victims from abusive inquiries into their private conduct. Another section of the crime bill makes an important change in the law to protect women and children from released rapists and other sexual predators—the Jacob Wetterling Act requires that released offenders must be reported to local enforcement authorities. *See also* **Jacob Wetterling Crimes Against Children**

**Wetterling Act.** *See* **Jacob Wetterling Crimes Against Children and Sexually Violent Offender Registration Act**

**Women's shelter (domestic violence shelter):** Women's shelters exist to provide emergency shelter, services, and care to victims of domestic violence and their minor children. Shelters are one of three primary crisis-oriented services on the community level that intervene on behalf of battered women. (The other two crisis-oriented services are rape crisis centers and advocacy.) There are a variety of services that shelters may provide to the victim of domestic abuse and her children. Along with basic provisions of housing, food, and counseling, many shelters offer legal counseling and referrals, social service referrals, transitional housing, child care, and job training. Women's shelters are traditionally nonprofit organizations that are wholly dependent on combinations of government funding, private donations, and the work of volunteers.

For further discussion of women's shelters, please see the following texts: Crowell, N. A., and Burgess, A. W., eds. *Understanding Violence against Women.* Washington, DC: National Academy Press, 1996; and Hughes, G. M. *Shelters for Battered Women: Criteria for Effectiveness.* (Doctoral dissertation, Loma Linda University, 1990). [Photocopy]. Ann Arbor, MI: University Microforms International, 1995.

# Chapter 39

# *Hotlines and Organizations*

This chapter is intended to serve as a starting point in the search for further information. The information in this chapter was compiled from several sources. Contact information was verified in March 2000.

## *National Hotlines*

### Childhelp USA/National Child Abuse Hotline

Along with national 24-hour hotline, provides residential and counseling treatment, educational and advocacy programs.

15757 N. 78th Street
Scottsdale, Arizona 85260
800-4-A-CHILD (800-422-4453), 24 hours
800-2-A-CHILD (800-222-4453), TDD
480-922-8212; fax: 480-922-7061
Web site: http://www.childhelpusa.org/

### National Domestic Violence Hotline

3616 Far West Blvd., Ste. 101-297
Austin, TX 78731-3074
800-799-SAFE (7233), 24 hours
800-787-3224 TTY
Office: 512-453-8117
Fax: 512-453-8541
Web site: http://www.ndvh.org/ndvh5.html
E-mail: ndvh@inetport.com

**National Center for Missing and Exploited Children**
Charles B. Wang International Children's Building
699 Prince Street
Alexandria, Virginia 22314-3175
1-800-THE-LOST (1-800-843-5678), 24 hours
703-274-3900; fax: 703-274-2220
Web site: http://www.missingkids.org/

**800-A-WAY-OUT** (202-0688), for parents considering abducting their children

## State and Local Hotlines for Domestic Violence

(Current as of 4/99, copyright © National Resource Center on Domestic Violence)

Alabama
Hotline: 800-650-6522
Office: 334-832-4842

Arizona
Hotline: 800-782-6400
Office: 602-279-2900

Southern California
Hotline: 888-305-7233
Office: 619-239-0355

Connecticut
Hotline: 888-774-2900
Office: 860-282-7899

Florida
Hotline: 800-500-1119
Office: 850-425-2749

Georgia
Hotline: 800-33-HAVEN (42836)
Office: 770-984-0085

Iowa
Hotline: 800-942-0333
Office: 515-244-8028

Idaho
Hotline: 800-669-3176
Office: 208-384-0419

Indiana
Hotline: 800-332-7385
Office: 317-543-3908

Kansas
Hotline: 888-END-ABUSE (363-22873)
Office: 785-232-9784

Maryland
Hotline: 800-634-3577
Office: 301-352-4574

Michigan
Hotline: 800-996-6228
Office: 517-347-7000

Minnesota
Hotline: 800-289-6177
Office: 651-646-6177

Montana
Hotline: 800-655-7867
Office: 406-443-7794

Nebraska
Hotline: 800-876-6238
Office: 402-476-6256

Nevada
Hotline: 800-500-1556
Office: 775-828-1115

New Hampshire
Hotline: 800-852-3388
Office: 603-224-8893

New Jersey
Hotlines:
800-572-7233;
for battered lesbians 800-224-0211
(evenings/weekends only)
Office: 609-584-8107

New Mexico
Hotline: 800-773-3645
Office: 505-246-9240

New York
Hotlines: English 800-942-6906;
Spanish 800-942-6908
Office: 518-432-4864

North Dakota
Hotline: 800-472-2911
Office: 701-255-6240

Ohio
Hotline: 800-934-9840
Office: 614-784-0023

Rhode Island
Hotline: 800-494-8100
Office: 401-467-9940

South Carolina
Hotline: 800-260-9293
Office: 803-256-2900

South Dakota
Hotline: 800-430-SAFE (7233)
Office: 605-945-0869

Tennessee
Hotline: 800-356-6767
Office: 615-386-9406

Texas
Hotline: 800-799-SAFE (7233)
Office: 800-525-1978

Utah
Hotline: 800-897-5465
Office: 801-538-9886

Vermont
Hotlines:
domestic violence 800-228-7395;
sexual assault 800-489-7273
Office: 802-223-1302

Virginia
Hotline: 800-838-8238
Office: 757-221-0990

Washington
Hotline: 800-562-6025
Office: 360-407-0756

West Virginia
Hotline: 800-352-6513
Office: 304-965-3552

Wyoming
Hotline: 800-990-3877
Office: 307-755-5481

NOTE: In almost all cases, the 800 (or 888) number listed above will only work if called from within the state. In states where there is no crisis hotline listed, victims of domestic violence should be encouraged to call the emergency phone number, which is 911 in most areas. Victims can also call the operator or look under the community or social services pages in their local phone book for the nearest domestic violence program. These programs are usually listed under the headings: abuse, crisis intervention, domestic or family violence and emergency shelters.

## Hotlines to Report Suspected Child Abuse

From the U.S. Department of Health and Human Services, 12-96

Both the reporting party and the child who is allegedly being abused must reside in the same state for the following reporting numbers to be valid. When the reporting party resides in a different state than the child, or for states not listed, please call: Childhelp/IOF Foresters National Abuse Hotline: 1-800-4-A-CHILD (422-4453)

Alabama
Huntsville or Madison County
256-535-4500

Arizona
800-330-1822

Arkansas
800-482-5964

Connecticut
800-842-2288

Delaware
800-292-9582

Florida
800-962-2873

Illinois
800-25-ABUSE (2-2873)
800-358-5117 TDD

Indiana
800-562-2407

Iowa
800-362-2178

Kansas
800-922-5330

Kentucky
800-752-6200

Maine
800-452-1999

Massachusetts
800-792-5200

Michigan
800-942-4357

Mississippi
800-222-8000

Missouri
800-392-3738

Montana
800-332-6100

Nebraska
800-652-1999

Nevada
800-992-5757

New Hampshire
800-894-5533

New Jersey
800-792-8610

New Mexico
800-432-2075

New York
800-342-3720

North Carolina
800-662-7030

Oklahoma
800-522-3511

Oregon
800-854-3508

Pennsylvania
800-932-0313

Rhode Island
800-742-4453

Texas
800-252-5400

Utah
800-678-9399

Virginia
800-552-7096

Washington
800-562-5264

West Virginia
800-352-6513

## *Elder Abuse Reporting Numbers*

From the National Center on Elder Abuse, 2/99

The following numbers are provided to assist you in obtaining help for vulnerable persons who may be in abusive situations. By calling the appropriate state number, you will be connected to the programs which can help; or you will be further assisted to identify the local number for assistance. The numbers marked "DEA" are the numbers to call if the person you are concerned about lives in the community in his/her own home or apartment. The numbers marked "IEA" are the numbers to call if the person you are concerned about lives in an institutional setting such as a nursing home. If the state you want to contact has no number accessible to out-of-state callers, please contact the ELDERCARE LOCATOR at 1-800-677-1116.

Alabama
DEA & IEA: 800-458-7214
Alabama only

Alaska
DEA: 800-478-9996 (Alaska only);
907-269-3666 (out of state)
IEA: 800-730-6393 (Alaska only);
907-269-3666 (out of state)

Arizona
DEA & IEA: 877-767-2385
Arizona only; TDD 877-815-8390

Arkansas
DEA: 800-482-8049
IEA: 800-582-4887
Nationwide

California
DEA: None available
IEA: 800-231-4024
California only; DEA—contact county social services; #s at CA web site: http://dss.cahwnet.gov/getser/cfstable.html

Colorado
DEA: 800-773-1366
IEA: 800-238-1376
Nationwide

Connecticut
DEA: 888-385-4225
IEA: 860-424-5200
Connecticut only

Delaware
DEA & IEA: 800-223-9074
Nationwide

District of Columbia
DEA: 202-727-2345
IEA: 202-434-2140

Florida
DEA & IEA: 800-962-2873
Nationwide

Georgia
DEA: 800-677-1116
IEA: 404-657-5726 or 404-657-4076
800# is Eldercare Locator

Guam
DEA & IEA: 671-475-0268
On weekends, holidays & between
the hours 5pm-8am on weekdays
call 671-646-4455.

Hawaii
DEA & IEA: 808-832-5115 (Oahu)
DEA & IEA: 808-243-5151 (Maui)
DEA & IEA: 808-241-3432 (Kauai)
DEA & IEA: 808-933-8820 (East
  Hawaii)
DEA & IEA: 808-327-6280 (West
  Hawaii)

Idaho
DEA: 208-334-2220
IEA: None available

Illinois
DEA: 800-252-8966
IEA: 800-252-4343
Illinois only; after hours, report
domestic abuse at 800-279-0400

Indiana
DEA & IEA: 800-992-6978
Out of state, call 800-545-7763,
X20135

Iowa
DEA: 800-362-2178
IEA: 515-281-4115
Nationwide; 800# Iowa only

Kansas
DEA: 800-922-5330 (Kansas
only); 785-296-0044 (out of state)
IEA: 800-842-0078 (Kansas only)
Long-Term Care Ombudsman:
877-662-8362 (KS only) or 785-
296-3017 (out of state); Mental

Health and Developmental Disabilities: 800-221-7923

Kentucky
DEA & IEA: 800-752-6200
Kentucky only

Louisiana
DEA & IEA: 800-259-4990
Louisiana only

Maine
DEA & IEA: 800-624-8404
Maine only

Maryland
DEA & IEA: 800-91-PREVENT
(1-800-917-7383)
Maryland only

Massachusetts
DEA: 800-922-2275
IEA: 800-462-5540
Massachusetts only

Michigan
DEA: 800-996-6228
IEA: 800-882-6006
Michigan only

Minnesota
DEA & IEA: 800-333-2433
Nationwide; referral to LINKAGE
and county service

Mississippi
DEA: 800-222-8000
IEA: 800-227-7308

Missouri
DEA & IEA: 800-392-0210
Missouri only

Montana
DEA: 800-332-2272
IEA: None available
Montana only

Nebraska
DEA & IEA: 800-652-1999
Nebraska only

Nevada
DEA & IEA: 800-992-5757
Nationwide; Reno area: 702-784-8090

New Hampshire
DEA: 800-949-0470 (NH only); 603-271-4386 (out of state)
IEA: 800-442-5640 (NH only); 603-271-4396 (out of state)

New Jersey
DEA & IEA: 800-792-8820
New Jersey only

New Mexico
DEA & IEA: 800-797-3260 (NM only); 505-841-6100 (Albuquerque and out of state)

New York
DEA: 800-342-9871
IEA: None available

North Carolina
DEA: & IEA: 800-662-7030
North Carolina only

North Dakota
DEA & IEA: 800-755-8521
North Dakota only

Ohio
DEA: None available
IEA: 800-282-1206
Nationwide

Oklahoma
DEA & IEA: 800-522-3511
Oklahoma only; 24 hours, 7 days

Oregon
DEA & IEA: 800-232-3020
Oregon only

Pennsylvania
DEA: 800-490-8505
IEA: 800-254-5164
Nationwide

Puerto Rico
DEA: 787-725-9788 or 787-721-8225

Rhode Island
DEA & IEA: 401-222-2858 x321

South Carolina
DEA & IEA: 800-868-9095
South Carolina only

South Dakota
DEA & IEA: 605-773-3656
Monday thru Friday 8:00am- 5:00pm

Tennessee
DEA & IEA: 888-277-8366
Nationwide

Texas
DEA: 512-834-3784 (out of state); 800-252-5400 (Texas and contiguous states)

IEA: 512-438-2633 (out of state); 800-458-9858 (Texas and contiguous states)

Utah
DEA and IEA: 801-264-7669 or 800-371-7897
Utah only

Vermont
DEA & IEA: 800-564-1612
Vermont only

Virgin Islands
DEA & IEA: None available

Virginia
DEA & IEA: 888-832-3858 (Virginia only); 804-371-0896 (out of state)
Elder Info. 800-552-3402

Washington
DEA: 800-422-3263
IEA: 800-562-6078
Washington only; Info. 800-422-3263 (nationwide), also http://www.aasa.dshsh.wa.gov

West Virginia
DEA & IEA: 800-352-6513
West Virginia only

Wisconsin
DEA: 608-266-2536 (out of state)
IEA: 800-815-0015 (Wisconsin only)
608-266-8944 (out of state)
Guardianship: 800-488-2596 or 608-224-0660;
Consumer Protection: 800-422-7128

Wyoming
DEA: 307-777-6137
IEA: 307-777-7123
For referrals to local agency.

## *State Victim Assistance (VA) and Compensation (VC) Programs*

Alabama
VA: 334-242-5891
    fax: 334-242-0712
VC: 334-242-4007
    fax: 334-242-4007

Alaska
VA: 907-465-4356
    fax: 907-465-3627
    E-mail: pjandree@psafety.state.ak.us
VC: 907-465-3040
    fax: 907-465-2379
    E-mail: psbrowne@ps.state.ak.us

American Samoa
VA: 011-684-633-5221
   fax: 011-684-633-2269
   E-mail: ascjpa@samoatelco.com

Arizona
VA: 602-223-2480
   fax: 602-223-2943
   Web site: http://www.state.az.us/dps/voca
   E-mail: voca2@dancris.com
VC: 602-542-1928
   fax: 602-542-4852

Arkansas
VA: 501-682-3671
   fax: 501-682-5206
VC: 501-682-1323
   fax: 501-682-5313
   E-mail: gingerb@ag.state.ar.us

California
VA: 916-324-9140
   fax: 916-324-9167
   E-mail: annm@ocjp1.ocjp.ca.gov
VC: 916-323-3432
   fax: 916-327-2933

Colorado
VA: 303-239-5703
   fax: 303-239-4491
   Web site: http://www.state.co.us/gov-dir/cdps/dcj.htm
   E-mail: wwoodwar@safety.state.co.us
VC: 303-239-4402
   fax: 303-239-4491
   same Web site and E-mail address as above

Connecticut
VA: 860-529-3089
   fax: 860-721-0593
   Web site: http://www.state.ct.us
   E-mail: carol.watknis@po.state.ct.us
VC: same as above

Delaware
VA: 302-577-3697
    fax: 302-577-3440
    Web site: http://www.state.de.us/govern/agencies/
    E-mail: copearson@state.de.us
VC: 302-995-8383
    fax: 302-995-8387

District of Columbia
VA: 202-842-8467
    fax: 202-727-1617
VC: 202-879-4216
    fax: 202-879-4230

Florida
VA: 850-414-3300
    fax: 850-487-3013
    Web site: http://legal.firn.edu/
    E-mail: denise-humphrey@oag.state.fl.us
VC: 850-414-3300
    fax: 850-487-1595
    same Web site and E-mail as above

Georgia
VA: 404-559-4949
    fax: 404-559-4960
VC: same as above

Guam
VA: 011-671-475-3406
    fax: 011-671-472-2493
    Web site: http://ns.gov.gu
    E-mail: law@ns.gov.gu
VC: 011-671-475-3406

Hawaii
VA: 808-586-1282
    fax: 808-586-1373
    Web site: http://www.cpja.ag.state.hi.us
    E-mail: lkoga@lava.net

VC: 808-587-1143
   fax: 808-587-1146
   Web site: http://www.cpja.ag.state.hi.us

Idaho
VA: 208-334-5580
   fax: 208-332-7353
   E-mail: heady@dhw.state.id.us
VC: 208-334-6000
   fax: 208-334-6070
   Web site: http://www.state.id.us/iic/indexhtm

Illinois
VA: 312-793-8550
   fax: 312-793-8422
   Web site: http://www.icjia.state.il.us
   E-mail: ckane@icija.state.il.us
VC: 217-782-7101
   fax: 217-524-8968

Indiana
VA: 317-233-3341
   fax: 317-232-4979
   Web site: http://www.ai.org/stateagency/criminaljusticeinstitute
VC: 317-233-3383
   fax: 317-232-4979
   Web site: http://www.ai.org/stateagency/criminaljusticeinstitute

Iowa
VA: 515-281-5044
   fax: 515-281-8199
   E-mail: kbrodie@max.state.id.us
VC: 515-281-5044
   fax: 515-281-8199

Kansas
VA: 913-296-2215
   fax: 913-296-6296
   E-mail: maska@at02po.wpo.state.ks.us
VC: 913-296-2359
   fax: 913-296-0652

Kentucky
VA: 502-564-7554
   fax: 502-564-4840
   E-mail: dlangley@mail.state.ky.us
VC: 502-564-2290
   fax: 502-564-4817

Louisiana
VA: 504-925-1757
   fax: 504-925-1998
VC: 504-925-4437
   fax: 504-925-4998

Maine
VA: 207-287-5060
   fax: 207-626-5555
VC: 207-624-7882
   fax: 207-624-7730
   E-mail: deb.rice@state.me.us

Maryland
VA: 410-767-7477
   fax: 410-333-0256
   Web site: http://www.dhr.state.md.us
VC: 410-764-4214
   fax: 410-764-4182
   Web site: http://www.dhr.state.md.us

Massachusetts
VA: 617-727-5200
   fax: 617-727-6552
VC: 617-727-2200, ext. 2251
   fax: 617-227-1622

Michigan
VA: 517-373-1826
   fax: 517-241-2769
   E-mail: oreillyl@state.mi.us
VC: 517-373-7373
   fax: 517-241-2769
   E-mail: oreillyl@state.mi.us

Minnesota
VA: 612-642-0251
    fax: 612-642-0223
    Web site: http://www.corr.state.mn.us/vsu
    E-mail: etangraf@smtp-co.doc.state.mn.us
VC: 612-282-6267
    fax: 612-282-6269
    Web site: http://www.dps.state.mn.us/crimevic/crimevic.
    E-mail: marie.bibus@state.mn.us

Mississippi
VA: 601-359-7880
    fax: 601-359-7832
    E-mail: psafety@dps.state.ms.us
VC: 601-359-6766
    fax: 601-359-2470
    Web site: http://www.dfa.state.ms.us
    E-mail: morris@novell.dfa.state.ms.us

Missouri
VA: 573-751-4905
    fax: 573-751-5399
    Web site: http://www.dps.state.mo.usdps/diroff/
    E-mail: vscott@mail.state.mo.us
VC: 573-526-6006
    fax: 573-751-4135
    Web site: http://www.dps.state.mo.usdps/diroff/
    E-mail: swright@mail.state.mo.us

Montana
VA: 406-444-3604
    fax: 406-444-4722
VC: 406-444-3653
    fax: 406-444-4722

Nebraska
VA: 402-471-2194
    fax: 402-471-2837
VC: 402-471-2828
    fax: 402-471-2837

Nevada
VA: 702-688-1628
   fax: 702-684-8093
VC: 702-486-2740
   fax: 702-486-2740

New Hampshire
VA: 603-271-1297
   fax: 603-271-2110
   E-mail: gpalmer@counsel.com
VC: 603-271-1284
   fax: 603-271-2110
   E-mail: gpalmer@counsel.com

New Jersey
VA: 609-984-7347
   fax: 609-292-0799
   Web site: http://www.state.nj.us.lps
   E-mail: victimwitness@smtp.lps.state.nj.state
VC: 201-648-2107
   fax: 973-648-7031

New Mexico
VA: 505-841-9432
   fax: 505-841-9437
   Web site: http://www.state.nm.us/cvrc
   E-mail: nmcvr@nm-us.campus.mci.net
VC: same as above

New York
VA: 518-457-1779
   fax: 518-457-1779
   Web site: http://unix2.nysed.gov/ils/cvb1.html
   E-mail: cubdonnelly@uno.com
VC: 518-457-8727
   fax: 518-457-8063
   Web site: http://unix2.nysed.gov/ils/cvb1.html

North Carolina
VA: 919-571-4736
   fax: 919-733-4625
   Web site: http://www.gcc.state.nc.us/victprog.htm

E-mail: barryb@gcc.dcc.state.nc.us
VC: 919-571-7974
    fax: 919-715-4209

North Dakota
VA: 701-328-6195
    fax: 701-328-6651
    E-mail: cc.mail.pcoughli@ranch.state.nd.us
VC: same as above

Northern Mariana Islands
VA: 011-670-664-4450
    fax: 011-670-664-4560
    Web site: http://www.saipan.com/gov/branches/cjpa
    E-mail: jack.cjpa@saipan.com

Ohio
VA: 614-644-5610
    fax: 614-466-5610
    Web site: http://www.ag.ohio.gov/crimevic/cvassist ohio.gov.htm
    E-mail: sharon=boyer%crimevictims%ag.
VC: 614-466-7190
    fax: 614-466-7788

Oklahoma
VA: 405-557-6700
    fax: 405-524-0581
    E-mail: suzanne@telepath.com
VC: same as above

Oregon
VA: 503-378-5348
    fax: 503-378-5738
    Web site: http://www.doj.state.or.us/crime/welcome1.htm
    E-mail: maryellen.johnson@doj.state.or.us
VC: same as above

Palau
VC: 011-680-488-2813 or 011-680-488-2553
    fax: 011-680-488-2553

Pennsylvania
VA: 717-787-2040
   fax: 717-783-7713
   Web site: http://www.pccd.state.pa.us
   E-mail: kunkle@pccd.state.pa.us
VC: 717-787-2040
   fax: 717-783-7713
   Web site: http://www.pccd.state.pa.us
   E-mail: lavery@pccd.state.pa.us

Puerto Rico
VC: 809-723-4949
   fax: 787-721-7280

Rhode Island
VA: 401-277-2620
   fax: 401-222-1294
VC: 401-277-2287
   fax: 401-222-4577

South Carolina
VA: 803-734-1900
   fax: 803-896-8714
   Web site: http://www.state.sc.us/db/office/division.htm
   E-mail: bjn@mailo6.scdps.state.sc.us
VC: 803-737-1930
   fax: 803-734-1708

South Dakota
VA: 605-773-4330
   fax: 605-773-6834
   Web site: http://www.sstate.sd.us/state/executive/social/ada/domestic/
   E-mail: susans@dss.sd.us
VC: 605-773-6317
   fax: 605-773-6834
   Web site: http://www.sstate.sd.us/state/executive/social/ada/domestic/
   E-mail: annh@dss.state.sd.us

Tennessee
VA: 615-313-4764
   fax: 615-532-9956
   Web site: http://www.state.tn.us/humanserv

VC: 615-741-2734
  fax: 615-532-4979
  Web site: http://www.treasury.state.tn.us
  E-mail: sclayton@mail.state.tn.us

Texas
VA: 512-463-1936 or 512-463-1944
  fax: 512-475-2440
  Web site: http://www.governor.state.tx.us
VC: 512-936-1200
  fax: 512-320-8270

Utah
VA: 801-533-4000
  fax: 801-533-4127
VC: same as above

Vermont
VA: 802-241-1255
  fax: 802-241-1253
VC: same as above

Virginia
 VA: 804-786-4000
  fax: 804-371-8981
  Web site: http://www.state.va.us/~dcjs/dcjs.htm
  E-mail: mpatterson.dcjs@state.va.us
VC: 804-367-8686
  fax: 804-367-9740

Virgin Islands
VA: 809-774-6400
  fax: 809-774-6400
  E-mail: hsmollett@aol.com
VC: 809-774-0930
  fax: 340-774-3466

Washington
VA: 360-586-0253
  fax: 360-902-7903
  E-mail: hsus300@dshs.wa.gov

VC: 360-902-5355
    fax: 360-902-5333
    Web site: http://www.wa.gov/lni
    E-mail: nnan235@lni.wa.gov

West Virginia
VA: 304-558-8814
    fax: 304-558-0391
    Web site: http://www.wv-cj-hs.com
    E-mail: wvcjhs@citynet.net
VC: 304-347-4850
    fax: 304-347-4851

Wisconsin
VA: 608-266-6470
    fax: 608-264-6368
    Web site: http://doj.state.wi.us/cvs
    E-mail: derenes@doj.state.wi.us
VC: 608-264-9497
    fax: 608-264-6368
    Web site: http://doj.state.wi.us/cvs
    E-mail: derenes@doj.state.wi.us

Wyoming
VA: 307-635-4050
    fax: 307-777-6869
    E-mail: sbagdo@missc.state.wy.us
VC: same as above

For Additional Information Contact:
    The Office For Victims of Crime
    State Compensation and Assistance Division
    810 Seventh Street NW
    Washington, D.C. 20531
    202-307-5983; Fax: 202-514-6383
    Web site: http://www.ojp.usdoj.gov/ovc

## Service and Information Organizations

### Government Agencies

#### *Family Violence*

**National Center for Injury Prevention and Control**
Division of Violence Prevention
Family and Intimate Violence Prevention Team
Centers for Disease Control and Prevention
Mailstop K60
4770 Buford Highway N.E.
Atlanta, GA 30341-3724
Phone: 770-488-4410
Fax: 770-488-1011
Web site: http://www.cdc.gov/ncipc/dvp/fivpt/fivpt.htm
E-mail: FIVPINFO@cdc.gov

**National Women's Health Information Center**
1-800-994-WOMAN (1-800-994-9662)
TDD: 1-888-220-5446; weekdays 9 a.m. to 6 p.m. (excluding federal holidays)
Web site: http://www.4woman.org/
E-mail: 4woman@soza.com

**Office for Victims of Crime**
U.S. Department of Justice
   Funds victim assistance and compensation programs throughout the U.S., advocates for the fair treatment of crime victims, provides training programs, and publishes and distributes materials.
810 Seventh St., N.W.
Washington, DC 20530
202-307-5983
Web site: http://www.ojp.usdoj.gov/ovc/
Resource Center
800-627-6872
Web site: http://www.ncjrs.org
E-mail: askncjrs@ncjrs.org

**PAVNET Online**
 A "virtual library" of information about violence and youth-at-risk, representing data from seven different federal agencies.
 Phone: 301-504-5462
 Web site: http://www.pavnet.org/
 E-mail: jgladst@nalusda.gov

*Spousal and Partner Abuse*

**National Criminal Justice Reference Service**
 U.S. Department of Justice
 Provides research and information.
 P.O. Box 6000
 Rockville, MD 20849-6000
 800-851-3420
 Web site: http://www.ncjrs.org
 E-mail: askncjrs@ncjrs.org

**Office of Minority and Women's Health** (Bureau of Primary Health Care, U.S. Department of Health and Human Services)
 Provides information, training, and technical assistance, and promotes policies and programs.
 4350 East-West Highway, 3rd Floor
 Bethesda, MD 20814
 301-594-4490; fax: 301-594-0089
 Web site: http://www.bphc.hrsa.dhhs.gov/omwh/omwh.htm
 E-mail: feedback@hrsa.dhhs.gov

**Office of Women's Health**
 Provides information on women's health concerns, including domestic violence.
 Centers for Disease Control and Prevention
 1600 Clifton Rd., MS: D-51
 Atlanta, GA 30033
 404-639-7230; fax: 404-639-7331
 Web site: http://www.cdc.gov/od/owh/whhome.htm

*Child Abuse*

**National Clearinghouse on Child Abuse and Neglect Information**
(Children's Bureau, Administration for Children and Families, Department of Health and Human Services)
Provides information, publishes materials.
330 C St., S.W.
Washington, DC 20447
800-394-3366; 703-385-7565
BBS: 800-877-8800
Fax: 703-385-3206
Web site: http://www.calib.com/nccanch
E-mail: nccanch@calib.com

*Elder Abuse*

**National Institute on Aging**
Information Center
P.O. Box 8057
Gaithersburg, MD 20898-8057
800-222-2225
800-222-4225 TTY
Web site: http://www.nih.gov/nia/
E-mail: niainfo@access.digex.net

*National Organizations (Non-Government)*

*Family Violence*

**American Bar Association Commission on Domestic Violence**
740 15th Street, NW, 9th Floor
Washington, DC 20005-1022
Web site: http://www.abanet.org/domviol/home.html
E-mail: abacdv@abanet.org

**American College of Emergency Physicians (ACEP)**
Provides informational resources for physicians specializing in emergency room treatment and advocacy on behalf of victims of family violence.
1111 19th Street NW, Suite 650
Washington, DC 20036-3603
800-320-0610; 202-728-0610
Fax: 202-728-0617
Web site: http://www.acep.org/

**Center for the Prevention of Sexual and Domestic Violence**
936 N 34th Street, Suite 200
Seattle, WA 98103
206-634-1903; fax: 206-634-0115
Web site: http://www.cpsdv.org
E-mail: cpsdv@cpsdv.org

**Family Violence and Sexual Assault Institute**
Provides information, services, and referrals
7120 Herman Jared Drive
Fort Worth, TX 76180
817-485-2244; fax: 817-485-0660
Web site: http://www.fvsai.org
E-mail: dwforkids@earthlink.net

**Family Violence and Sexual Assault Institute**
Provides information, services, and referrals
6160 Cornerstone Court East
San Diego, CA 92121
858-623-2777, ext. 406; fax: 858-646-0761
Web site: http://www.fvsai.org
E-mail: fvsai@mail.cspp.edu

**Family Violence Prevention Fund**
Provides newsletters, training materials
383 Rhode Island St., Ste. 304
San Francisco, CA 94103-5133
800-313-1310
415-252-8900; fax: 415-252-8991
Web site: http://www.fvpf.org/
E-mail: fund@fvpf.org

## Good Samaritan Homeless Center for Women and Children
Provides emergency shelter, food, clothing, and support in major U.S. cities.
Spiritual Gift Ministries, Inc.
1117 Perimeter Center West, Suite 500E
Atlanta, GA 30338
24-hour hotline: 1-888-824-9802
770-399-8810
Web site: http://www.helpforwomen.org/gsmain.htm
E-mail: jesusn98@trusted.net

## Jewish Women International
Provides educational resources, referrals, and advocacy.
Web site: http://www.jewishwomen.org/
E-mail: jwiinfo@jewishwomen.org

## Muslims Against Family Violence
Provides referrals and support services.
Web site: http://www.mpac.org/mafv/

## National Coalition for the Homeless
Network providing information, technical assistance, and policy advocacy; publishes newsletter, *Safety Network*.
1012 14th St., N.W., #600
Washington, DC 20005-3410
202-737-6444
Fax: 202-737-6445
Web site: http://nch.ari.net/
E-mail: nch@ari.net

## National Organization for Victim Assistance
Provides victim assistance and legal advocacy, support and development to victim and witness assistance providers, criminal justice professionals, researchers, and survivors committed to victims' rights.
1757 Park Rd., N.W.
Washington, DC 20010
800-TRY-NOVA (879-6682)
202-232-6682; fax: 202-462-2255
Web site: http://www.try-nova.org
E-mail: nova@try-nova.org

**National Resource Center on Violence to People and Animals**
American Humane Association
    Provides information and resources.
63 Inverness Drive East
Englewood, CO 80112-5117
800-227-4645; 303-792-9900; fax: 303-792-5333
Web site: http://www.americanhumane.org/
E-mail: LINK@americanhumane.org

**National Center for Victims of Crime**
    Provides assistance and referrals to victims of crime, distributes
    information, performs research and training, develops policy.
2111 Wilson Blvd., Suite 300
Arlington, VA 22201
800-FYI-CALL (394-3255)
1-800-211-7996 TTY/TDD
703-276-2880
Fax: 703-276-2889
Web site: http://www.ncvc.org
E-mail: mailto:webmaster@nvc.org

**Nicole Brown Charitable Foundation**
    Provides grants for shelters and educational initiatives.
Web site: http://www.nbcf.org/lobby.htm
E-mail: abusenomor@fea.net

**Office for Victims of Crime Resource Center**
    Provides information and resources.
Box 6000
Rockville, MD 20850
800-627-NVRC (6872)
Web site: http://www.ojp.usdoj.gov/ovc

**Rape, Abuse and Incest National Network (RAINN)**
    Provides national hotline, support, and referrals for survivors of
    sexual abuse.
635-B Pennsylvania Ave., S.E.
Washington, DC 20003
800-656-HOPE (4673), 24 hours
Fax: 202-544-3556
Web site: http://www.rainn.org/
E-mail: rainnmail@aol.com

**Resource Center on Domestic Violence, Child Protection and Custody**
Operated by the Family Violence Project of the National Council of Juvenile and Family Court Judges, offers technical assistance, information, legal research to judges, court workers, advocates, lawyers, child protection workers, law enforcement, and other professionals, and publishes newsletter, *Synergy*.
800-527-3223

*Spousal and Partner Abuse*

**Asian Domestic Violence Resources**
Provides referrals for services for Asian women around the country.
Family Culture
P.O. Box 239
Southborough, MA 01772-0239
508-881-7156
Web site: http://www.asianfamily.com/domestic_violence_resources.htm
E-Mail: info@familyculture.com

**Battered Women's Justice Center**
Provides legal information about domestic violence.
Pace University School of Law
White Plains, NY
Web site: http://orion.law.pace.edu/bwjc/bwjcmai4.htm

**Battered Women's Justice Project**
Part of the Domestic Violence Resource Network, provides information and training on civil and criminal justice issues related to domestic violence.
4032 Chicago Ave. S.
Minneapolis, MN 55407
800-903-0111
612-824-8768 TTY
Fax: 612-824-8965

**Domestic Abuse Intervention Project**
Provides information and training programs.
Minnesota Program Development, Inc.
206 W. Fourth St.
Duluth, MN 55806
218-722-2781; fax: 218-722-0779

## Jewish Women International

Provides education and advocacy.
202-857-1300
Web site: http://www.jewishwomen.org/AWAKEN.htm
E-mail: jwiinfo@jewishwomen.org

## Minnesota Center Against Violence and Abuse (MINCAVA)

Clearinghouse of material on violence of all kinds.
School of Social Work, University of Minnesota
105 Peters Hall, 1404 Gortner Avenue
St. Paul, Minnesota 55108-6142
612-624-0721; fax: 612-625-4288
Toll free in Minnesota: 800-646-2282
Web site: http://www.mincava.umn.edu/index.asp
Email: mincava@umn.edu

## National Clearinghouse for the Defense of Battered Women

Legal advice, technical assistance, expert witnesses, and referrals
to local advocates.
125 South Ninth St., Ste. 302
Philadelphia, PA 19107
215-351-0010

## National Clearinghouse on Marital and Date Rape/Women's History Library

2325 Oak St.
Berkeley, CA 94708
Web site: http://members.aol.com/ncmdr/index.html

## National Coalition Against Domestic Violence

Provides information, training, policy development, and newsletter, *The Voice.*
P.O. Box 18749
Denver, CO 80218
303-839-1852; fax: 303-831-9251
Web site: http://www.ncadv.org
E-mail: ncadv2@sprynet.com

**National Coalition for Low-Income Housing**
1012 14th St. N.W., Suite 610
Washington, DC 20005
202-662-1530; fax: 202-393-1973
Web site: http://www.nlihc.org
E-mail: info@nlihc.org

**National Domestic Violence Resource Network**
A network of four resource centers of domestic violence: National
Resource Center on Domestic Violence, Battered Women's Justice
Project, Health Resource Center on Domestic Violence, and Re-
source Center on Domestic Violence: Child Protection and Custody
(see separate listings).
800-537-2238
800-553-2508 TTY
Fax: 717-545-9456
Web site: http://www.pcadv.org

**National Health Resource Center on Domestic Violence**
Part of the Family Violence Prevention Fund, provides information
and training on domestic violence for the health care community.
383 Rhode Island St., Ste. 304
San Francisco, CA 94103-5133
888-Rx-ABUSE (792-2873)
415-252-8900; fax: 415-252-8991
Web site: http://www.fvpf.org/health/index.html
E-mail: fund@fvpf.org

**National Network on Behalf of Battered Immigrant Women**
Web site: http://www.fvpf.org/immigration/national_network.html

**National Organization for Women Legal Defense and Education
Fund**
Provides legal information regarding domestic abuse, incest, and
sexual abuse.
395 Hudson St.
New York, NY 10014
212-925-6635; fax: 212-226-1066
Web site: http://www.nowldef.org/
E-mail: ademarco@nowldef.org

## National Resource Center on Domestic Violence

Part of the Domestic Violence Resource Network, provides information, training, and technical assistance to service providers; publishers newsletter, *The Link.*
6400 Flank Dr., Ste. 1300
Harrisburg, PA 17112
800-537-2238; 800-553-2508 TTY
717-545-6400; fax: 717-545-9456

## Northwest Network of Bisexual, Trans & Lesbian Survivors of Abuse

(formerly Advocates for Abused and Battered Lesbians)
Provides counseling, support, legal advocacy, community education, and training in Puget Sound area.
P.O. Box 22869
Seattle, WA 98122
206-568-7777
206-517-9670 (TTY MSG)
Web site: http://www.aabl.org/
E-mail: info@aabl.org

## Resource Center on Domestic Violence: Child Protection and Custody

Part of the Domestic Violence Resource Network, provides information on domestic violence and child protection and custody.
P.O. Box 8970
Reno, NV 89507
800-527-3223; fax: 702-784-6160

## SAWNET

Online resources and contact information for South Asian and Asian women in the U.S. and Canada
Web site: http://www.umiacs.umd.edu/users/sawweb/sawnet/violence.html

## Young Women's Christian Association (YWCA)

Provides shelter and other services.
Empire State Building
350 Fifth Ave., Suite 301
New York, NY 10118
212-273-7800; fax: 212-465-2281
Web site: http://www.ywca.org/html/B4b2.asp
E-mail: jchestnutt@ywca.org

*Child Abuse*

## American Humane Association
Children's Division
> Provides information, support programs, advocacy, training, and other services; conducts research.

63 Inverness Dr. E.
Englewood, CO 80112-5117
800-227-4645
303-792-9900; fax: 303-792-5333
Web site: www.amerhumane.org
E-mail: children@amerhumane.org

## Childhelp USA
> Provides counseling, education, advocacy, referrals, residential treatment in various locations around the country, as well as operates the National Child Abuse Hotline, 1-800-4-A-CHILD.

15757 N. 78th Street
Scottsdale, Arizona 85260
480-922-8212
Web site: http://www.childhelpusa.org/

## Child Welfare League of America
> Provides information, training resources, and referrals; proposes policy.

440 First St., N.W., 3rd Floor
Washington, DC 20001
202-638-2952; fax: 202-638-4004
Web site: http://www.cwla.org/

## Kempe National Center for the Prevention and Treatment of Child Abuse and Neglect
> Provides resources, conducts research.

1825 Marion Street
Denver, CO 80218
303-864-5252; fax: 303-864-5302
Web site: http://www.kempecenter.org/
E-mail: Kempe@KempeCenter.org

**National Center for Missing and Exploited Children**
Resource center on abduction and sexual exploitation of children; provides hotline, networks with law enforcement, child protective services, victim advocacy organizations, medical professionals, legislators, attorneys, and judges.
Charles B. Wang International Children's Building
699 Prince Street
Alexandria, VA 22314-3175
703-274-3900; fax: 703-274-2220
1-800-THE-LOST (1-800-843-5678), 24 hours
Web site: http://www.missingkids.org/

**National Children's Advocacy Center**
Provides prevention, intervention, and treatment services to physically and sexually abused children.
200 Westside Square, Ste. 700
Huntsville, AL 35801
256-533-0531; fax: 256-534-6883
Web site: http://www.ncac-hsv.org/
E-mail: webmaster@ncac-hsv.org

**National Children's Alliance**
(formerly the National Network of Children's Advocacy Centers)
Provides training, technical assistance, and networking opportunities to communities developing children's advocacy centers for abused children.
1319 F Street, N.W., Ste. 1001
Washington, DC 20004
800-239-9950 or 202-639-0597
Web site: http://www. nncac.org
E-mail: info@nncac.org

**Parents Anonymous**[sm]
Provides support groups for parents.
675 W. Foothill Blvd., Suite 220
Claremont, CA 91711
909-621-6184; fax: 909-625-6304
Web site: http://www.parentsanonymous-natl.org/
E-mail: parentsanon@msn.com

**Prevent Child Abuse America** (formerly National Committee to Prevent Child Abuse)
Offers information, including videos, volunteer networks, technical assistance, and prevention programs.
200 S. Michigan Ave., 17th Floor
Chicago, IL 60604-2404
312-663-3520; fax: 312-939-8962
Web site: http://www.preventchildabuse.org/
E-mail: mailbox@preventchildabuse.org

**Red Flag Green Flag Resources**
Develops and sells abuse awareness materials for children as well as treatment materials.
Rape and Abuse Crisis Center
P.O. Box 2984
Fargo, ND 58108-2984
800-627-3675; fax: 888-237-5332
Web site: http://www.redflaggreenflag.com/
E-mail: rfgf@netcenter.net

**Resource Center on Child Custody and Child Protection**
Information and legal research on child protection and custody issues related to domestic violence.
National Council on Juvenile and Family Court Judges
P.O. Box 8970
Reno, NV 89507
775-784-6012; fax: 775-784-6628
Web site: http://www.ncjfcj.unr.edu
E-mail: admin@ncjfcj.unr.edu

**SBS Prevention Plus**
Provides information on shaken baby syndrome and child abuse prevention.
649 Main St.
Groveport, OH 43125
800-858-5222; fax: 614-836-8359
Web site: http://www.sbsplus.org
E-mail: sbspp@aol.com

**Survivors of Incest Anonymous (SIA)**
Offers twelve-step recovery program.
P.O. Box 21817
Baltimore, MD 21222-6187
310-282-3400

**VOICES** (Victims Of Incest Can Emerge Survivors) in Action, Inc.
Provides referrals, newsletters, annual conference, and networking support groups.
P.O. Box 148309
Chicago, IL 60614
800-7-VOICE-8; 800-786-4238
773-327-1500; fax: 773-327-4590
Web site: http://www.voices-action.org/
E-mail: voices@voices-action.org

*Elder Abuse*

**American Association of Retired Persons** (AARP)
Criminal Justice Services
Provides information and resources.
601 E St., N.W.
Washington, DC 20049
202-434-2222
Web site: http://www.aarp.org/ontheissues/issueelderab.html

**Eldercare Locator**
Referrals to elder caregivers.
Administration of Aging
800-677-1116

**National Center on Elder Abuse (NCEA)**
Develops and distributes information, training, research, and publishes *NCEA Newsletter*.
1225 I Street, N.W., Suite 725
Washington, DC 20005
202-898-2586; fax: 202-898-2583
Web site: http://www.gwjapan.com/NCEA
E-mail: NCEA@nasua.org

**National Committee for Prevention of Elder Abuse (NCPEA)**
Provides referrals, promotes research, advocacy, public awareness, and publishes *Journal of Elder Abuse & Neglect.*
c/o Institute on Aging
UMass Memorial Health Care
119 Belmont St.
Worcester, MA 01605
508-793-6166
Web site: http://www.preventelderabuse.org

## State and Local Organizations and Services

The resources listed below do not comprise a complete list of organizations in each state. For more referrals, contact the domestic violence coalition for your state.

**Alabama**

Alabama Coalition Against Domestic Violence
P.O. Box 4762
Montgomery, AL 36101
334-832-4842; fax: 334-832-4803

**Alaska**

Alaska Network on Domestic Violence and Sexual Assault
130 Seward St., Rm. 209
Juneau, AK 99801
907-586-3650; fax: 907-463-4493

**Arizona**

Arizona Coalition Against Domestic Violence
100 W. Camelback Rd., Ste. 109
Phoenix, AZ 85013
602-279-2900; fax: 602-279-2980
E-mail: acdav@goodnet.com

Arizona Humane Society
Provides various programs, including shelter for pets of women seeking shelter from abuse and Saddle Up, a program for troubled youth.
9226 N. 13th Ave.
Phoenix, AZ 85021
602-870-1999; fax: 602-395-3862
Web site: http://www.azhumane.org

**Arkansas**

Arkansas Coalition Against Domestic Violence
#1 Sheriff Lane, Ste. C
North Little Rock, AR 72114
501-399-9486 or 501-812-0571
Fax: 501-371-0450 or 501-371-0450
E-mail: ssigmon@arkansas.net

**California**

California Alliance Against Domestic Violence
619 13th St., Ste. I
Modesto, CA 95354
209-524-1888; fax: 209-524-0616

Community United Against Violence
    Provides services to battered gay men, addresses hate violence via
    speaker program, and distributes information.
973 Market St., #500
San Francisco, CA 94103
Hotline: 415-333-HELP, 24 hours
Fax: 415-777-5565
Web site: http://www.cuav.org/
E-mail: cuav@xq.com

Domestic Violence Project of Santa Clara County
    Provides information and resources.
Web site: http://www.growing.com/nonviolent/
E-mail: dvteam@growing.com

Haven Hills
   Provides shelter and kosher facilities in San Fernando Valley, California area
Office: 818-887-7481
Crisis Line: 818-887-6589 (24 hours a day)

Jewish Family Service of Los Angeles
Family Violence Project
   Provides counseling and education.
6851 Lennox Ave.
Van Nuys, CA 91405
818-505-0900, 24 hours
818-623-0300, NISHMA, Orthodox counseling program
Web site: http://www.jfsla.org

Muslims Against Family Violence
   Offers information, community education, referrals, and support services in the Bay Area.
San Francisco, CA
Web site: http://www.mpac.org/mafv/

Shelter Against Violent Environments (SAVE)
   Provides shelter, support services, counseling, children's programs; offers speakers, police training program; serving Fremont, Newark, Union City, Hayward, and San Leandro, in northern California.
P.O. Box 8238
Fremont, CA 94537
Hotline: 510-794-6055, 24 hours
510-574-2250; fax: 510-574-2252
Web site: http://www.infolane.com/save/
E-mail: dvshelter@aol.com

Support Network for Battered Women
   Provides crisis hotline, counseling, legal assistance, shelter, child care, information, and community education; serves Santa Clara County.
444 Castro Street, Suite 305
Mountain View, CA 94041
24-hour crisis line (English and Spanish): 1-800-572-278200
Office: 650-940-7850; TDD: 650-940-7857; fax: 650-940-1037
Web site: http://www.snbw.org/frmain.htm
E-mail: snbw@snbw.org

## Colorado

CHAI: Community Help and Abuse Information
P.O. Box 102316
Denver, CO 80250
303-836-1818

Colorado Coalition Against Domestic Violence
Provides community education, training, advocacy, and support to
service programs.
P.O. Box 18902
Denver, CO 80218
Toll-free: 888-778-7091
303-831-9632; fax: 303-832-7067

Crossroads Safehouse
    Provides shelter, counseling, support groups, children's programs,
    domestic abuse response team, and outreach education for Larimer
    County.
P.O. Box 993
Fort Collins, CO 80522
970-482-3502
Web site: http://www.fortnet.org/crossroads/

## Connecticut

Connecticut Coalition Against Domestic Violence
135 Broad St.
Hartford, CT 06105
860-524-5890; fax: 860-249-1408

## Delaware

Delaware Coalition Against Domestic Violence
P.O. Box 847
Wilmington, DE 19899
302-658-2958; fax: 302-658-5049
24-Hour Bilingual Line: 888-LAC-C571 (888-522-2571)
New Castle: 302-762-6110
Kent & Sussex: 302-422-8058

## District of Columbia

Ayuda
   Provides support and legal services to immigrant and refugee domestic violence victims, training, and policy development.
1736 Columbia Rd., N.W.
Washington, DC 20009
202-387-4848; fax: 202-387-0324
Web site: http://www.incacorp.com/ayuda
E-mail: cllayuda@erols.com (domestic violence)
immayuda@erols.com (refugee assistance)

D.C. Coalition Against Domestic Violence
513 U Street NW
Washington, DC 20001
202-783-5332; fax: 202-387-5684

## Florida

Child Abuse Prevention Project
   Offers parenting assistance programs in north central Florida.
Department of Pediatrics
College of Medicine
University of Florida
1701 SW 16th Ave., Room 2193
Gainesville, FL 32608
352-334-1330
Web site: http://www.med.ufl.edu:80/peds/capp/

Florida Coalition Against Domestic Violence
308 East Park Ave.
Tallahassee, FL 323081
Hotline: 800-500-1119
850-425-2749; fax: 850-425-3091

Northaid Victim Center
   Provides counseling and other services to victims of violent crime in the Miami area.
305-758-2545

Refuge House
    Provides shelter, counseling, injunction assistance, and rape crisis services for Franklin, Gadsden, Jefferson, Leon, Liberty, Madison, Taylor, and Wakulla counties.
P.O. Box 4356d
Tallahassee, FL 32315
Hotline: 904-681-2111, 24 hours
904-922-6062

## Georgia

Child Abuse Prevention Program Clearinghouse of Georgia
Georgia Southern University
    Distributes information on child abuse prevention programs.
P.O. Box 8099
Statesboro, GA 30460-8099
912-681-5060; fax: 912-681-0703

Georgia Advocates for Battered Women and Children
250 George Ave., S.E., Ste. 308
Atlanta, GA 30312
404-524-3847; fax: 404-524-5959

Georgia Council on Child Abuse
1375 Peachtree St., N.E., Suite 200
Atlanta, GA 30309
800-532-3208 (statewide)
404-870-6565; fax: 404-870-6541
Web site: http://www.gcca.org

## Hawaii

Hawaii State Coalition Against Domestic Violence
98-939 Moanalua Rd.
Aiea, HI 96701-5012
808-486-5072; fax: 808-486-5169

Hawaii State Committee on Family Violence
808-486-5072

## Idaho

Idaho Coalition Against Sexual and Domestic Violence
815 Park Blvd., Ste. 140
Boise, ID 83712
Toll-Free: 888-384-0419
208-384-0419; fax: 208-331-0687
E-mail: domvio@micron.net

## Illinois

Illinois Coalition Against Domestic Violence
801-South 11<sup>th</sup> Street
Springfield, IL 62703
217-789-2830; fax: 217-789-1939
E-Mail: ilcadv@springnet1.com

SHALVA (Shelter, Advice, and Legal Aid for Victims of Abuse)
    Serves metropolitan Chicago.
1610 Highland, Box 1610
Chicago, IL 60660
312-583-HOPE (4673)

## Indiana

Indiana Coalition Against Domestic Violence
2511 E. 46th St., Ste. N-3
Indianapolis, IN 46205
Hotline: 800-332-7385
317-543-3908; fax: 317-568-4045

Middle Way House, Inc.
    Provides shelter, for Monroe, Martin, Morgan, Owen, Greene, and
    Lawrence counties.
Hotline: 812-336-0846, 24 hours

# Iowa

Iowa Coalition Against Domestic Violence
2603 Bell Avenue, Ste. 100
Des Moines, IA 50321
Hotline: 800-942-0333
515-244-8028; fax: 515-244-7417

## Kansas

Kansas Coalition Against Sexual and Domestic Violence
820 S.E. Quincy, Ste. 600
Topeka, KS 66612
Toll-Free: 888-END-ABUSE
785-232-9784; fax: 785-232-9937

## Kentucky

Kentucky Domestic Violence Association
P.O. Box 356
Frankfort, KY 40602
502-875-4132; fax: 502-875-4268
Web site: http://www.kdva.org

## Louisiana

Louisiana Coalition Against Domestic Violence
P.O. Box 77308
Baton Rouge, LA 70879-7308
225-752-1296; fax: 225-751-8927

## Maine

Maine Coalition to End Domestic Violence
128 Main St.
Bangor, ME 04401
207-941-1194; fax: 207-941-2327

**Maryland**

Maryland Network Against Domestic Violence
6911 Laurel Bowie Road, Suite 309
Bowie, MD 20715
Hotline: 800-MD-HELPS (634-3577)
301-352-4574; fax: 301-809-0422

**Massachusetts**

Jewish Domestic Violence Coalition of Greater Boston
    Provides information, referrals, education.
126 High St.
Boston, MA 02110
617-457-8888; fax: 617-988-6246
E-mail: JewishDV@aol.com

Gay Men's Domestic Violence Program
PMB 131
955 Mass Ave.
Cambridge, MA 02139
617-354-6056
Crisis Line: 800-832-1901
Web site: http://www.gmdvp.org
E-mail: gmdvp@juno.com

Massachusetts Coalition of Battered Women's Service Groups/Jane
Doe Safety Fund
    Network of 32 battered women's programs, provides referrals, in-
    formation, and community education, and develops policy.
14 Beacon St., Ste. 507
Boston, MA 02108
617-248-0922; fax: 617-248-0902
Web site: http://www.besafe.org/

**Michigan**

Batterer Intervention Services Coalition
    Conducts networking, community education, program development.
4925 Packard Rd.
Ann Arbor, MI 48108-1521
313-971-9781, ext. 427
Fax: 313-971-2730
Web site: http://comnet.org/bisc/
E-mail: adacss@aol.com

Domestic Violence Project, Inc./SAFE House
    Provides shelter, counseling, support groups, on-call services, legal
    advocacy and referrals, children's services, referrals for batterers,
    training, community education, and legislative work.
P.O. Box 7052
Ann Arbor, MI 48107
Hotline: 734-995-5444, 24 hours
734-973-0242; fax: 734-973-7817
E-mail: dvpsh@aol.com

Jewish Family Service
24123 Greenfield Rd.
Southfield, MI 48237
313-559-1500

Michigan Coalition Against Domestic Violence
P.O. Box 16009
Lansing, MI 48901
517-484-2924; fax: 517-372-0024
Web site: http://members.aol.com/aardvarc1/dv/michdv.htm

**Minnesota**

Central Minnesota Task Force on Battered Women
  Provides shelter, crisis intervention, referrals, support groups, advocacy, children's programs, training, rural outreach and community education for Stearns, Benton, Sherbourne, Wright, Mille Lacs, Isanti, Kanabec, Chisago, and Pine counties.
Hotline: 800-950-2203, 24 hours, TDD accessible, or
320-253-6900
Web site: http://www.annamaries.org/
E-mail: information@annamaries.org

Domestic Abuse Project
  Provides counseling, children's program, professional training, legal advocacy; conducts research.
204 W. Franklin Ave.
Minneapolis, MN 55404
612-874-7063; fax: 612-874-8445
Web site: http://www.mndap.org/
E-mail: dap@mndap.org

Jewish Family and Children's Service
Minneapolis
612-546-0616

Minnesota Coalition for Battered Women
450 N. Syndicate St., Ste. 122
St. Paul, MN 55104
Metro-Area Hotline: 651-646-0994
651-646-6177, TDD accessible; fax: 651-646-1527
E-mail: mcbw@pclink.com

Rape and Abuse Crisis Center of Fargo-Moorhead, Inc.
  Provides crisis intervention, shelter, support groups, legal, medical and social services advocacy, community education, court-watch program, and publishes Red Flag Green Flag® resources.
P.O. Box 2984
Fargo, ND 58108
Hotline: 800-344-7273 24 hours
701-293-7273; fax: 701-293-9424
Web site: http://www.redflaggreenflag.com
E-mail: racc@netcenter.net

Women's Rural Advocacy Programs
  Provides shelter and services for southwest Minnesota
Hotline: 800-796-2244 or 507-831-2244, 24 hours (Cottonwood office)
Web site: http://www.LetsWRAP.com/

## Mississippi

Mississippi State Coalition Against Domestic Violence
P.O. Box 4703
Jackson, MS 39296-4703
Hotline: 800-898-3234
601-981-9196; fax: 601-981-2501
E-mail: mcadv@misnet.com

## Missouri

Missouri Coalition Against Domestic Violence
415 E. McCarty Street
Jefferson City, MO 65101
573-634-4161; fax: 573-636-3728

## Montana

Montana Coalition Against Domestic Violence
P.O. Box 633
Helena, MT 59624
406-443-7794; fax: 406-449-8193

## Nebraska

Nebraska Domestic Violence and Sexual Assault Coalition
825 M Street, Suite 404
Lincoln, NE 68508-2253
Hotline: 800-876-6238
402-476-6256; fax: 402-476-6806

## Nevada

Nevada Network Against Domestic Violence
100 West Grove, Suite 315
Reno, NV 89509
Hotline: 800-500-1556
775-828-1115; fax: 775-828-9991

## New Hampshire

New Hampshire Coalition Against Domestic and Sexual Violence
    Network of 14 programs in the state providing referrals to service
    programs, information, speakers, and training.
P.O. Box 353
Concord, NH 03302-0353
Hotline: 800-852-3388 (in New Hampshire)
Helpline: 603-225-9000 (outside of New Hampshire)
603-224-8893; fax: 603-228-6096
Web site: http://www.nhvbc.com/nhwomen/services.htm

## New Jersey

Association of Jewish Family and Children's Agencies
3084 State Highway 27, Suite 1
Kendall Park, NJ 08824
800-634-7346

Manavi: An Organization for South Asian Women
P.O. Box 2131
Union, NJ 07083-2131
908-687-2662; fax: 908-687-1868
E-mail: manavi@worldnet.att.net

New Jersey Coalition for Battered Women
2620 Whitehorse/Hamilton Square Rd.
Trenton, NJ 08690
Hotline for battered lesbians: 800-224-0211 (in NJ only)
609-584-8107; fax: 609-584-9750
TTY: 609-584-0027 (9am-5pm, then into message service)

**New Mexico**

New Mexico State Coalition Against Domestic Violence
P.O. Box 25266
Albuquerque, NM 87125
Hotline: 800-773-3645 (in NM only)
505-246-9240; fax: 505-246-9434
E-mail: nmcadv@nmcadv.org

**New York**

Jewish Child Care Association of New York
    Provides counseling for abused children and their families.
575 Lexington Ave.
New York, NY 10022
212-371-1313

The New York City Gay & Lesbian Anti-Violence Project
    Provides counseling, support groups, information, and resources.
240 West 35th Street
New York, NY 10001
212-714-1184; 212-714-1141, 24 hours
212-714-1134 TTY
Web site: http://www.avp.org
E-mail: webmaster@avp.org

New York State Coalition Against Domestic Violence
79 Central Ave.
Albany, NY 12206
Hotline: 800-942-6906
518-432-4864; fax: 518-432-4864

OHEL: Children's Home and Family Services
    Includes Safe Haven shelter program.
4510 16t Avenue
Brooklyn, New York 11204
Toll-Free: 800-603-6435
718-851-6400; fax: 718-851-2772
Web site: http://www.ohelfamily.org
E-mail: response@OhelFamily.org

Sanctuary for Families
    Provides shelter, support, and other services.
P.O. Box 1406
Wall Street Station
New York, NY 10258
212-582-2091; fax: 212-349-6810

The Transition Center
    Provides shelter and kosher facilities.
P.O. Box 629
Far Rockaway, NY 11691
718-520-8045

Victim Services
    Provides shelter, counseling, court advocacy, emergency day care,
    and information.
2 Lafayette St.
New York, NY 10007
800-621-HOPE (4673), 24 hours
800-810-7444 TDD
212-577-7700; fax: 212-385-0331
212-233-3456 TDD
Domestic Violence Shelter Tour and Information online: http://
www.dvsheltertour.org/

**North Carolina**

North Carolina Coalition Against Domestic Violence
301 W. Main Street
Durham, NC 27701
919-956-9124; fax: 919-682-1449

**North Dakota**

North Dakota Council on Abused Women's Services
State Networking Office
418 E. Rosser Ave., Ste. 320
Bismarck, ND 58501
Hotline: 800-472-2911 (in ND only)
701-255-6240; fax: 701-255-1904

Rape Abuse and Crisis Center of Fargo-Moorhead
    Provides shelter, counseling and other assistance to victims in the
    eastern Dakotas and western Minnesota; also publishes *Red Flag
    Green Flag* materials.
P.O. Box 2984
Fargo, ND 58108
800-627-3675 24 hours
701-293-7273; fax: 701-293-9424
Web site: http://www.redflaggreenflag.com/html/racc.html
E-mail: racc@netcenter.net

## Ohio

Action Ohio Coalition for Battered Women
614-221-1255

Jewish Family Service Association
Project Chai: Family Violence Program
    Provides counseling, shelter, education.
24075 Commerce Park Rd.
Beachwood, OH 44118
216-691-7233, 24 hours
216-292-3999; fax: 216-292-6313

Ohio Domestic Violence Network
4041 N. High St., Ste. 400
Columbus, OH 43214
Hotline: 800-934-9840
614-784-0023; fax: 614-784-0033

Sounding Board Counseling Center
Domestic Violence Project
    Provides online information, consultation, discussions, and listing
    of domestic violence centers.
P.O. Box 91137
Columbus, OH 43209
Domestic Violence Information Line: 800-829-1122 (for Ohio, Kentucky,
and West Virginia)
614-231-1164; fax: 614-338-8059
Web site: http://www.sboard.org/
E-mail: SBCC@sboard.org

**Oklahoma**

Oklahoma Coalition on Domestic Violence and Sexual Assault
2525 NW Expressway, Suite 208
Oklahoma City, OK 73116
Hotline: 800-522-9054
405-848-1815; fax: 405-848-3469

**Oregon**

Greenhill Humane Society Domestic Violence Assistance Program:
Protecting Women and Their Pets
    Provides shelter for pets of women seeking shelter from abuse.
88530 Greenhill Road
Eugene, OR 97402
541-689-1503; fax: 541-689-5261
Web site: http://www.green-hill.org
E-mail: information@green-hill.org

Mid-Valley Women's Crisis Service
    Provides shelter, support group, children's programs, community
    education for Marion and Polk counties; offers on-line lethality as-
    sessment. English and Spanish.
795 Winter St. N.E.
P.O. Box 851
Salem, OR 97308
Hotlines: 399-7722, 24 hours; 399-7722 TTY, 24 hours
Web site: http://www.mvwcs.com
E-mail: mvwcs@mvwcs.com

Oregon Coalition Against Domestic and Sexual Violence
520 N.W. Davis, Ste. 310
Portland, OR 97204
Toll-Free: 800-622-3782
503-223-7411; fax: 503-223-7490

Raphael House of Portland
  Provides shelter, low-income housing program, counseling, and community education.
2057 N.W. Overton
Portland, OR 97209
Hotline: 503-222-6222, 24 hours
503-222-6507; fax: 503-222-4754
Web site: http://www.raphaelhouse.com/
E-mail: develop@raphaelhouse.com

## Pennsylvania

Domestic Abuse Counseling Center
  Provides counseling for batterers and community education; collaborates with social service, criminal justice, victim-advocacy, and health organizations.
411 Boggs Ave.
Pittsburgh, PA 15211
412-431-4999
Web site: http://www.dacc.net/
E-mail: info@dacc.net

Jewish Family and Children's Service
Philadelphia
215-545-3290

Pennsylvania Coalition Against Domestic Violence
6400 Flank Dr., Ste. 1300
Harrisburg, PA 17112-2778
Hotline: 800-932-4632
717-545-6400; fax: 717-545-9456

## Puerto Rico

Comision Para Los Asuntos De La Mujer
787-722-2907

**Rhode Island**

Rhode Island Coalition Against Domestic Violence
422 Post Rd., Ste. 202
Warwick, RI 02888
Hotline: 800-494-8100
401-467-9940; fax: 401-467-9943

**South Carolina**

National Crime Victims Research and Treatment Center
    Provides education, clinical services, policy development; conducts
    research.
Department of Psychiatry and Behavioral Sciences
Medical University of South Carolina
171 Ashley Ave.
Charleston, SC 29425-0742
843-792-2945
Fax: 843-792-2300
Web site: http://www.musc.edu

Sistercare, Inc.
    Provides shelters, counseling, crisis hotline, legal advocacy, and
    community education for Richland, Lexington, Fairfield, Newberry,
    and Kershaw counties.
P.O. Box 1029
Columbia, SC 29202-1029
803-765-9428, 24 hours
1-800-637-7607, crisis line for outside Columbia area
803-926-0505
Web site: http://www.midnet.sc.edu/sister/%21sisterc.htm

South Carolina Coalition Against Domestic Violence and Sexual Assault
P.O. Box 7776
Columbia, SC 29202-7776
Hotline: 800-260-9293
803-256-2900; fax: 803-256-1030

## South Dakota

Native American Women's Health Education Resource Center
Provides shelter and services.
P.O. Box 572
Lake Andes, SD 57356-0572
605-487-7072; fax: 605-487-7964

South Dakota Coalition Against Domestic Violence and Sexual Assault
P.O. Box 141
Pierre, SD 57401
Hotline: 800-572-9196
605-945-0869; fax: 605-945-0870

## Tennessee

Center for Children in Crisis
Provides treatment for children who have been abused or neglected.
Le Bonheur Children's Medical Center
Memphis, TN 38103
Web site: http://www.lebonheur.org/services/childrencrisis.html
E-mail: herrona@lebonheur.org

Metro Nashville Police Department
Domestic Violence Section
Provides information and assistance to battered women, including
safety plans.
615-880-3000, 8 a.m.-10 p.m.; 615-862-8600, after 10 p.m.
Web site: http://www.telalink.net/~police/abuse/index.html
E-mail: melissa@police.nashville.org

Tennessee Task Force Against Domestic Violence
P.O. Box 120972
Nashville, TN 37212
Hotline: 800-356-6767
615-386-9406; fax: 615-383-2967
Web site: http://nashville.citysearch.com/E/V/NASTN/0002/55/27/

**Texas**

Brazos County Rape Crisis Center, Inc.
Provides information, services for victims, advocacy, and online anonymous, confidential counseling service.
Bryan, TX
24-hour hotline: 800-922-7273 (Texas)
409-268-7273
Web site: http://rapecrisis/txcyber.com/
E-mail: bcrcc@txcyber.com

National Council of Jewish Women
Aid to Victims of Domestic Abuse
Provides counseling and legal information for battered women.
5009 Caroline St.
Houston, TX 77004
713-520-8620
Web site: http://www.ncjw.org

SPCA of Texas
Safe Haven Educational Outreach Program for Kids
Provides programs for children from abusive families and foster care for pets of women seeking shelter from abuse.
362 S. Industrial Blvd.
Dallas, TX 75207
214-651-9611; fax: 214-651-9244
E-mail: kconover@spca.org (Kim Conover)

Texas Council on Family Violence
P.O. Box 161810
Austin, TX 78716
Toll-Free: 800-525-1978
512-794-1133; fax: 512-794-1199

Texas Department of Human Services
Family Violence Program
Provides shelter, counseling, referrals, information, transportation, employment services, and assistance obtaining medical care.
701 W. 51st St.
Austin, TX 78751
512-438-4800
Web site: http://www.dhs.state.tx.us

## Utah

Utah Domestic Violence Advisory Council
120 North 200 West
Salt Lake City, UT 84145
Hotline: 800-897-LINK (5465)
801-538-4100; fax: 801-538-3993
Web site: http://www.hsdcfs.state.ut.us/DomViol.htm

## Vermont

Vermont Network Against Domestic Violence and Sexual Assault
P.O. Box 405
Montpelier, VT 05601
802-223-1302; fax: 802-223-6943
E-mail: vnadvsa@sover.net

## Virginia

Virginians Against Domestic Violence
2850 Sandy Bay Rd., Ste. 101
Williamsburg, VA 23185
Hotline: 800-838-VADV (8238)
804-221-0990; fax: 804-229-1553

## Virgin Islands

Women's Coalition of St. Croix
809-773-9272

Women's Resource Center
809-776-3966

## Washington

Center for the Prevention of Sexual and Domestic Violence
1914 N. 34th St., Suite 105
Seattle, WA 98103
206-634-1903

Spokane County Domestic Violence Consortium
  Provides information, community education, training, and referrals.
Web site: http://www.domesticviolence.net/
E-mail: scdvc@ior.com

Washington State Coalition Against Domestic Violence
8645 Martin Way NE, Suite 103
Lacy, WA 98516
360-407-0756; fax: 360-407-0761
TTY: 360-407-0767
E-mail: wscadv@cco.net

Washington State Domestic Violence Hotline and Crisis Support Network
  Provides crisis support, referrals, and information in English and
  Spanish.
800-435-7276, 24-hour hotline for Washington state in English and
Spanish
Web site: http://www.domestic-violence.org/
E-mail: csn@willapabay.org

**West Virginia**

West Virginia Coalition Against Domestic Violence
P.O. Box 85
181B Main St.
Sutton, WV 26601-0085
304-765-2250; fax: 304-765-5071

**Wisconsin**

Wisconsin Coalition Against Domestic Violence
1400 E. Washington Ave., Ste. 232
Madison, WI 53703
608-255-0539; fax: 608-255-3560

**Wyoming**

Wyoming Coalition Against Domestic Violence and Sexual Assault
P.O. Box 236
Laramie, WY 82073
Hotline: 800-990-3877
307-755-5481; fax: 307-775-5482

### *Batterers Programs*

**California**

ManAlive Marin County
345 Johnstone Dr.
San Rafael, CA 94903
415-552-1361

Oakland Men's Project
1203 Preservation Park Way, Ste. 200
Oakland, CA 94612-1201
510-835-2433

**Georgia**

Men Stopping Violence Inc.
1025 DeKalb Ave., #25
Atlanta, GA 30307
404-688-1376
Web site: http://www.menstoppingviolence.org

**Massachusetts**

Emerge: Counseling and Education to End Male Violence
2380 Massachusetts Ave., Suite 101
Cambridge, MA 02140
617-422-1550
Web site: http://www.emergedv.com
E-mail: info@emergedv.com

**Minnesota**

Domestic Abuse Intervention Project
206 W. Fourth St.
Duluth, MN 55806
218-722-2781; fax: 218-722-0779

Domestic Abuse Project
204 W. Franklin Ave.
Minneapolis, MN 55404
612-874-7063

Wilder Men's Domestic Abuse Program
650 Marshall Ave.
St. Paul, MN 55104
612-221-0048

## Missouri

RAVEN: Rape And Violence End Now
7314 Manchester, 2nd Floor
St. Louis, MO 63143
314-645-2075 or 314-645-2493
Web site: http://members.tripod.com/~raventeaches/

## New York

VCS Batterer's Intervention Project
P.O. Box 674
New York, NY 10956
914-634-5729

## *Research Organizations*

American Professional Society on the Abuse of Children (APSAC)
    Performs research, networking, publishing, and advocacy.
Web site: http://www.apsac.org/

Asian Institute on Domestic Violence
    Research, networking, advocacy.
415-954-9961
Web site: http://www.apiahf.org/institute.html
E-mail: penserga@apiahf.org

Center on Crime, Communities & Culture
888 Seventh Ave., 9th Fl.
New York, NY 10106
212-887-0135
Fax: 212-245-3429
Web site: http://www.soros.org/crime/
E-mail: cccc@sorosny.org

Center for the Study and Prevention of Violence
University of Colorado at Boulder
Institute of Behavioral Science
Campus Box 442
Boulder, CO 80309-0442
303-492-1032; fax: 303-443-3297
Web site: http://www.colorado.edu
E-mail: cspv@colorado.edu

Center for Women Policy Studies
    Offers publications on violence against women.
1211 Connecticut Avenue, N.W., Ste. 312
Washington, DC 20036
202-872-1770; fax: 202-296-8962
Web site: http://www.centerwomenpolicy.org/wisewomen.html

Child Abuse Prevention Network
Family Life Development Center
Cornell University
Ithaca, NY
Web site: http://child.cornell.edu/

Clearinghouse on Abuse and Neglect of the Elderly
    Provides bibliographies, printed materials, and referrals.
College of Human Resources
University of Delaware
Newark, DE 19716
302-831-2394

Family Research Laboratory
126 Horton Social Science Center
University of New Hampshire
Durham, NH 03824-1888
603-862-1888; fax: 603-862-1122
Web site: http://www.unh.edu/frl/frlbroch.htm
E-mail: mas2@christa.unh.edu

Family Violence Research Program
University of Rhode Island
Social Science Research Center Bldg
Kingston, RI 02881
401-874-7782; fax: 401-874-5562

Institute on Domestic Violence in the African American Community
    Scholarly community engaged in research, training, and advocacy.
Web site: http://www.dvinstitute.org/

Institute on Violence and Destructive Behavior
University of Oregon
Web site: http://interact.uoregon.edu/ivdb/htmls/hist.html

Institute for Women's Policy Research
1707 L Street, N.W., Suite 750
Washington, DC 20036
202-785-5100; fax: 202-833-4362
Web site: http://www.iwpr.org/
E-mail: iwpr@iwpr.org

Mid-Atlantic Addiction Training Institute
Indiana University of Pennsylvania
724-357-4405; fax: 724-357-3944
Web site: http://www.iup.edu/maati/

National Center on Child Fatality Review
Inter-Agency Council on Child Abuse and Neglect
Web site: http://www.ican-ncfr.org/
E-mail: jlangsta@co.la.ca.us

National Crime Victims Research and Treatment Center
Medical University of South Carolina
165 Cannon Street, P.O. Box 250852
Charleston, SC 29325-0742
843-792-2945; fax: 843-792-3388
Web site: http://www.musc.edu/cvc/

Stony Brook State University of New York
Marital and Family Research Laboratory
Web site: http://www.psy.sunysb.edu/marital/

### Community Action Organizations

Center for the Prevention of Sexual and Domestic Violence
Offers educational resources, seminars, training to clergy on domestic violence and sexual abuse; publishes newsletter, Working Together.
936 N. 34th, Ste. 200
Seattle, WA 98103
206-634-1903
Fax: 206-634-0115
Web site: http://www.cpsdv.org
E-mail: cpsdv@cpsdv.org

The Clothesline Project
700 Ravinia
Orland Park, IL 60462
708-460-9749; Fax: 708-460-0570
Web site: http://clothesline.org

Hermanas Unidas/Sisters United
c/o Ayuda
1736 Columbia Rd., N.W.
Washington, DC 20009
202-387-4848; fax: 202-387-0324

Silent Witness National Initiative
7 Sheridan Ave. S.
Minneapolis, MN 55405
612-377-6629
Fax: 612-374-3956
Web site: http://www.silentwitness.net
E-mail: info@silentwitness.net

# Chapter 40

# *Bibliography*

This bibliography of books, journals and web sites is organized according to the following categories: Historical Background and Social and Political Dimensions; Family Violence; Spouse and Partner Abuse; Dating Violence; Stalking; Child Abuse; Sibling Abuse; Parent Abuse; and Elder Abuse. The resources listed were selected from recommended reading lists produced by several domestic violence organizations and from material reviewed by the editor. They range from classic works on the subject from the fields of psychology and sociology to self-help books. Some books and journals may be available at your local library. Others may be obtained from the publishing organizations. For information on how to contact these organizations, see Chapter 38, Hotlines and Organizations.

## *Historical Background and Social and Political Dimensions*

### *Books*

Ashby, Leroy. *Endangered Children: Dependency, Neglect, and Abuse in American History*. New York: Twayne, 1997.

Barnes, Patricia G. *Domestic Violence: From a Private Matter to a Federal Offense*. New York: Garland, 1998.

Berrick, Jill Duerr, and Neil Gilbert. *With the Best of Intentions: The Child Sexual Abuse Prevention Movement.* New York: Guilford, 1991.

Carll, Elizabeth K. *Violence in Our Lives: Impact on Workplace, Home, and Community.* Boston: Allyn & Bacon, 1998.

Costin, Lela B., Howard Jacob Karger, and David Stoesz. *The Politics of Child Abuse in America.* New York: Oxford University Press, 1996.

Daniels, Christine, and Michael V. Kennedy. *Over the Threshold: Intimate Violence in Early America.* New York: Routledge, 1999.

De Rivera, Joseph, and Theodore R. Sarbin, eds. *Believed-In Imaginings: The Narrative Construction of Reality.* Washington, D.C.: American Psychological Association, 1998. (Memory, Trauma, Dissociation, and Hypnosis series.)

Dorne, Clifford K. *Child Maltreatment: A Primer in History, Public Policy, and Research.* Guilderland, N.Y.: Harrow & Heston, 1997.

Fineman, Martha Albertson, and Roxanne Mykitiuk, eds. *The Public Nature of Private Violence: The Discovery of Domestic Abuse.* New York: Routledge, 1994.

Gagne, Patricia. *Battered Women's Justice: The Movement for Clemency and the Politics of Self-Defense.* New York: Twayne, 1998.

Gordon, Linda. *Heroes of Their Own Lives: The Politics and History of Family Violence: Boston: 1880-1960.* New York: Viking, 1988.

Greven, Philip. *Spare the Child: The Religious Roots of Punishment and the Psychological Impact of Physical Abuse.* New York: Vintage Books, 1992.

Hampton, Robert L., Pamela Jenkins, and Thomas P. Gullotta, eds. *Preventing Violence in America* (Issues in Children's and Families' Lives, Vol. 4). Thousand Oaks, Calif.: Sage, 1996.

Howe, Mark L. *The Fate of Early Memories: Developmental Science and the Retention of Childhood Experiences.* Washington, D.C.: American Psychological Association, 2000.

Koppelman, Susan, ed. *Women in the Trees: U.S. Women's Short Stories about Battering and Resistance, 1839-1994.* Boston: Beacon Press, 1996.

*Legal Interventions in Family Violence: Research Findings and Policy Implications.* Washington, D.C.: U.S. Department of Justice, Office of Justice Programs, National Institute of Justice, 1998.

Lindsey, Duncan. *The Welfare of Children*. New York: Oxford University Press, 1994.

Linsky, Arnold S., Ronet Bachman, and Murray A. Straus. *Stress, Culture, and Aggression in the United States*. New Haven: Yale University Press, 1995.

Loseke, Donileen R. *The Battered Woman and Shelters: The Social Construction of Wife Abuse*. Albany, N.Y.: State University of New York Press, 1992.

Pecora, Peter J., James K. Whittaker, Anthony N. Maluccio, with Richard P. Barth and Robert D. Plotnick. *The Child Welfare Challenge: Policy, Practice, and Research*. New York: Aldine de Gruyter, 1992.

Peled, Einat, Peter G. Jaffe, and Jeffrey L. Edleson, eds. *Ending the Cycle of Violence: Community Responses to Children of Battered Women*. Thousand Oaks, Calif.: Sage, 1994.

Peterson Del Mar, David. *What Trouble I Have Seen: A History of Violence Against Wives*. Cambridge, Mass.: Harvard University Press, 1998.

Pleck, Elizabeth. *Domestic Tyranny: The Making of American Social Policy Against Family Violence from Colonial Times to the Present*. New York: Oxford University Press, 1987.

Ptacek, James. *Battered Women in the Courtroom: The Power of Judicial Responses*. Boston: Northeastern University Press, 1999.

Reiss, Albert J., and Jeffrey A. Roth, eds. *Understanding and Preventing Violence*. Sixth edition. Washington, D.C.: National Academy Press, 1996.

Schechter, Susan. *Women and Male Violence: The Visions and Struggles of the Battered Women's Movement*. Boston: South End Press, 1982.

Shelman, Eric A., and Stephen Lazoritz. *Out of the Darkness: The Story of Mary Ellen Wilson*. Mission Viejo, Calif.: Dolphin Moon Publishing, 1999.

Websdale, Neil. *Rural Women Battering and the Justice System: An Ethnography*. Thousand Oaks, Calif.: Sage, 1997.

Wexler, Richard. *Wounded Innocents: The Real Victims of the War Against Child Abuse*. Revised edition. Buffalo, N.Y.: Prometheus Books, 1995.

## *Family Violence*

### *Books*

*Action Plan to Prevent Family and Intimate Partner Violence: National Family and Intimate Partner Violence Prevention Initiative/Health Resources and Services Administration*. [Rockville, Md.]: Office of Minority Health, [1998?].

Ascione, Frank R., and Phil Arkow, eds. *Child Abuse, Domestic Violence, and Animal Abuse: Linking the Circles of Compassion for Prevention and Intervention*. West Lafayette, Ind.: Purdue University Press, 1999.

Bachman, Ronet. *Death and Violence on the Reservation: Homicide, Suicide and Family Violence in American Indian Populations*. Westport, Conn.: Auburn House, 1992.

Barnett, Ola, W., Cindy L. Miller-Perrin, and Robin D. Perrin. *Family Violence Across the Lifespan: An Introduction*. Thousand Oaks, Calif.: Sage, 1997.

Browne, Kevin, and Martin Herbert. *Preventing Family Violence*. Chichester, England; New York: Wiley, 1997.

Chalk, Rosemary R., and Patricia A. King, eds. *Violence in Families: Assessing Prevention and Treatment Programs*. Washington, D.C.: National Academy Press, 1998.

Ewing, Charles Patrick. *Fatal Families: The Dynamics of Intrafamilial Homicide*. Thousand Oaks, Calif.: Sage, 1997.

Gelles, Richard J. *Intimate Violence in Families*. 3rd ed. Thousand Oaks, Calif.: Sage, 1997.

Gelles, Richard J., and Donileen R. Loseke, eds. *Current Controversies on Family Violence*. Newbury Park, Calif.: Sage, 1993.

Goetting, Ann. *Homicide in Families and Other Special Populations*. New York: Springer, 1995.

Hampton, Robert L., ed. *Black Family Violence: Current Research and Theory*. Lexington, Mass.: Lexington Books, 1991.

Hampton, Robert L., ed. *Family Violence: Prevention and Treatment.* 2nd edition. Thousand Oaks, Calif.: Sage, 1999.

Herman, Judith Lewis. *Trauma and Recovery.* Revised edition. New York: BasicBooks, 1997.

Kaufman Kantor, Glenda, and Jana L. Jasinski, eds. *Out of the Darkness: Contemporary Perspectives on Family Violence.* Thousand Oaks, Calif.: Sage, 1997.

Kaufmann, M. "Animal Abuse, Domestic Violence, and Childhood Cruelty to Animals." In Aubrey H. Fine, ed. *Handbook on Animal-Assisted Therapy: Theoretical Foundations and Guidelines for Practice.* San Diego, Calif.: Academic Press, 1999.

Leehan, James. *Pastoral Care for Survivors of Family Abuse.* Louisville, Ky.: Westminster/John Knox Press, 1989.

Potter-Efron, Ronald T., and Patricia S. Potter-Efron, eds. *Aggression, Family Violence, and Chemical Dependency.* New York: Haworth Press, 1996.

Snow, Robert L. *Family Abuse: Tough Solutions to Stop the Violence.* New York: Plenum Press, 1997.

Steinmetz, Suzanne K. *The Cycle of Violence: Assertive, Aggressive, and Abusive Family Interaction.* New York: Praeger, 1977.

Straus, Murray A., and Richard J. Gelles. *Physical Violence in American Families: Risk Factors and Adaptations to Violence in 8,145 Families.* New Brunswick, N.J.: Transaction, 1990.

Straus, Murray A., Richard J. Gelles, and Suzanne K. Steinmetz. *Behind Closed Doors: Violence in the American Family.* Garden City, N.Y.: Anchor Press/Doubleday, 1980.

Straus, Murray, and Suzanne Steinmetz, eds. *Violence in the Family.* Toronto, Ontario, Canada: Dodd, Mead, 1975.

Viano, E., ed. *Intimate Violence: Interdisciplinary Perspectives.* Bristol, Pa.: Hemisphere, 1992.

Wiehe, Vernon R. *Understanding Family Violence: Treating and Preventing Partner, Child, Sibling, and Elder Abuse.* Thousand Oaks, Calif.: Sage, 1998.

## *Journals*

*Family Violence & Sexual Assault Bulletin*. 1985–. Family Violence and Sexual Assault Institute, Tyler, Tex. (Formerly *Family Violence Bulletin*.)

*Journal of Comparative Family Studies*. 1970–. Calgary, Alberta, Canada.

*Journal of Emotional Abuse*. 1998–. Haworth Maltreatment & Trauma Press, Binghamton, N.Y.

*Journal of Family Violence*. 1986–. Plenum Press, New York

*Journal of Interpersonal Violence*. 1986–. Sage Publications, Beverly Hills, Calif.

*Journal of Marriage and the Family*. 1964–. National Council on Family Relations, Menasha, Wis.

## *Web Sites*

Minnesota Center Against Violence and Abuse (MINCAVA) clearinghouse on partner abuse, violence against women, child abuse, dating violence, and more. http://www.mincava.umn.edu/

## Spouse and Partner Abuse

### *Books*

Ackerman, Robert J. *Before It's Too Late: Help for Women in Controlling or Abusive Relationships*. Deerfield Beach, Fla.: Health Communications, 1995.

Adams, Carol J. *Woman-Battering* (Creative Pastoral Care and Counseling Series). Minneapolis, Minn.: Fortress Press, 1997.

Agtuca, Jacqueline R. *A Community Secret: For the Filipina in an Abusive Relationship*. Seattle, Wash.: Seal Press, 1994.

Anderson, Vera. *A Woman Like You: The Face of Domestic Violence*. Interviews and photographs. Seattle, Wash.: Seal Press, 1997.

Bergen, Raquel Kennedy, ed. *Issues in Intimate Violence*. Thousand Oaks, Calif.: Sage, 1998.

Betancourt, Marian. *What to Do When Love Turns Violent: A Practical Resource for Women in Abusive Relationships*. New York: Harperperennial Library, 1997.

Brandwein, Ruth A., ed. *Battered Women, Children, and Welfare Reform: The Ties That Bind*. Thousand Oaks, Calif.: Sage, 1999.

Brown, Louis, Francois Dubau, and Merritt McKeon. *Stop Domestic Violence: An Action Plan for Saving Lives*. New York: St. Martin's Press, 1997.

Browne, Angela. *When Battered Women Kill*. New York: Free Press, 1987.

Busch, Amy Lou. *Finding Their Voices: Listening to Battered Women Who've Killed*. Commack, N.Y.: Kroshka Books, 1999.

Buzawa, E. S., and C. G. Buzawa. *Do Arrests and Restraining Orders Work?* Thousand Oaks, Calif.: Sage, 1996.

Cardarelli, Albert P., ed. *Violence Between Intimate Partners: Patterns, Causes, and Effects*. Boston: Allyn & Bacon, 1997.

Carrillo, Ricardo, and Jerry Tello, eds. *Family Violence and Men of Color: Healing the Wounded Male Spirit*. New York: Springer, 1998.

Celani, David P. *The Illusion of Love: Why the Battered Woman Returns to Her Abuser*. New York: Columbia University Press, 1994.

Clarke, Rita-Lou. *Pastoral Care of Battered Women*. Philadelphia, Pa.: Westminster Press, 1986.

Cook, Philip W. *Abused Men: The Hidden Side of Domestic Violence*. Westport, Conn.: Praeger, 1997.

Crowell, Nancy A., and Ann W. Burgess, eds. *Understanding Violence Against Women*. Washington, D.C.: National Academy Press, 1996.

Davis, Angela Y. *Violence Against Women and the Ongoing Challenge to Racism*. Lantham, N.Y.: Kitchen Table: Women of Color Press, 1987.

Davis, Richard L. *Domestic Violence: Facts and Fallacies*. Westport, Conn.: Praeger, 1998.

Doane, Sharon. *New Beginnings: A Creative Writing Guide for Women Who Have Left Abusive Partnerships*. Seattle, Wash.: Seal Press, 1996.

Dobash, R. Emerson, and Russell P. Dobash. *Violence Against Wives*. New York: Free Press, 1983.

———. *Women, Violence and Social Change*. New York: Routledge, 1992.

*Domestic Violence: National Directory of Professional Services.* New York: Center on Crime, Communities, and Culture, 1999. Online at http://www.soros.org/crime/index.html.

Domestic Violence Shelter Tour and Information, by Victim Services, New York, online at http:// ww.dvsheltertour.org/

Dutton, Donald G. *The Abusive Personality: Violence and Control in Intimate Relationships.* New York: Guilford, 1998.

Dutton, Donald G., and Susan K. Golant. *The Batterer: A Psychological Profile.* New York: Basic Books, 1995.

Engel, Beverly. *The Emotionally Abused Woman: Overcoming Destructive Patterns and Reclaiming Yourself.* New York: Fawcett Books, 1992.

Enns, Greg, and Jan Black. *It's Not Okay Anymore: Your Personal Guide to Ending Abuse, Taking Charge, and Loving Yourself.* Oakland, Calif.: New Harbinger Publications, 1997.

Evans, Patricia. *The Verbally Abusive Relationship: How to Recognize It and How to Respond.* Holbrook, Mass.: Bob Adams, 1992.

Ewing, Charles Patrick. *Fatal Families: The Dynamics of Intrafamilial Homicide.* Thousand Oaks, Calif.: Sage, 1997.

Finkelhor, David, and Kersti Yllö. *License to Rape: Sexual Abuse of Wives.* New York: Free Press, 1985.

Fortune, Marie M. *Keeping the Faith: Questions and Answers for the Abused Woman.* San Francisco, Calif.: HarperSanFrancisco, 1987.

Gartner, Richard B. *Betrayed as Boys: Psychodynamic Treatment of Sexually Abused Men.* New York: Guilford, 1999.

Gelles, Richard J., and Murray Straus. *Intimate Violence: The Causes and Consequences of Abuse in the American Family.* New York: Touchstone, 1989.

———. *Physical Violence in American Families.* New Brunswick, N.J.: Transaction, 1990.

Goetting, Ann. *Getting Out: Life Stories of Women Who Left Abusive Men.* New York: Columbia University Press, 1999.

———. *Homicide in Families and Other Special Populations.* New York: Springer, 1995.

Gondolf, Edward W. *Man Against Woman: What Every Woman Should Know About Violent Men.* Bradenton, Fla.: Human Services Initiative; Blue Ridge Summit, Pa.: Tab Books, 1989.

Gondolf, Edward W. *Men Who Batter: An Integrated Approach for Stopping Wife Abuse*. Holmes Beach, Fla.: Learning Publications, 1985.

Groetsch, Michael. *He Promised He'd Stop*. Brookfield, Wis.: Crisis Prevention Institute, 1997.

Hamberger, Kevin L., and Claire Renzetti, eds. *Domestic Partner Abuse*. New York: Springer, 1996.

Hart, Barbara J. *Safety for Women: Monitoring Batterers' Programs*. Harrisburg, Pa.: Pennsylvania Coalition Against Domestic Violence, 1988. [717-545-6400]

Heise, L., M. Ellsberg, and M. Gottemoeller. *Ending Violence Against Women. Population Reports* Series L, No. 11. Baltimore, Md.: Johns Hopkins University School of Public Health, Population Information Program, December 1999. Online at http://www.jhuccp.org/pr/l11edsum.stm#top

Horton, Anne L., and Judith A. Williamson, eds. *Abuse and Religion: When Praying Isn't Enough*. Lexington, Mass.: Lexington Books, 1988.

Island, David, and Patrick Letellier. *Men Who Beat the Men Who Love Them: Battered Gay Men and Domestic Violence*. New York: Haworth Press, 1991.

Jacobson, Neil S., and John M. Gottman. *When Men Batter Women: New Insights into Ending Abusive Relationships*. New York: Simon & Schuster, 1998.

Jasinski, Jana L., and Linda M. Williams, eds. *Partner Violence: A Comprehensive Review of 20 Years of Research*. Thousand Oaks, Calif.: Sage, 1998.

Jewish Women International. *Resource Guide for Rabbis on Domestic Violence*. Washington, D.C.: Jewish Women International, 1996.

Jones, Ann. *Next Time She'll Be Dead: Battering and How to Stop It*. New York: Beacon Press, 1993.

Jones, Ann, and Susan Schechter. *When Love Goes Wrong: What to Do When You Can't Do Anything Right*. New York: HarperCollins, 1993.

Jones, Kathleen. *Living between Danger and Love: The Limits of Choice*. New Brunswick, N.J.: Rutgers University Press, 2000.

Kashani, Javad H., and Wesley D. Allan. *The Impact of Family Violence on Children and Adolescents*. Thousand Oaks, Calif.: Sage, 1998.

Kirkwood, Catherine. *Leaving Abusive Partners: From the Scars of Survival to the Wisdom for Change*. Thousand Oaks, Calif.: Sage, 1993.

Klein, Ethel, et al. *Ending Domestic Violence: Changing Public Perceptions/Halting the Epidemic*. Thousand Oaks, Calif.: Sage, 1997.

Koss, Mary P., Lisa A. Goodman, and Angela Browne. *No Safe Haven: Male Violence Against Women at Home, at Work, and in the Community*. Washington, D.C.: American Psychological Association, 1994.

Leventhal, Beth, and Sandra E. Lundy, eds. *Same-Sex Domestic Violence: Strategies for Change*. Thousand Oaks, Calif.: Sage, 1999.

Lissette, Andrea, and Richard Kraus. *Free Yourself from an Abusive Relationship: Seven Steps to Taking Back Your Life*. Alameda, Calif.: Hunter House, 1999.

Lobel, Kerry, ed. *Naming the Violence: Speaking Out about Lesbian Battering*. Seattle, Wash.: Seal Press, 1986.

McKenzie, V. Michael. *Domestic Violence in America*. Lawrenceville, Va.: Brunswick, 1995.

Martin, Del. *Battered Wives*. Revised edition. San Francisco, Calif.: Volcano Press, 1989.

Mercier, Peter J., and Judith D. Mercier, eds. *Battle Cries on the Home Front: Violence in the Military Family*. Springfield, Ill.: Charles C. Thomas, 2000.

Miedzian, Myriam. *Boys Will Be Boys: Breaking the Link Between Masculinity and Violence*. New York: Doubleday, 1991.

Miller, Mary Susan. *No Visible Wounds: Identifying Nonphysical Abuse of Women by Their Men*. Chicago: Contemporary Books, 1995.

Murphy-Milano, Susan. *Defending Our Lives: Getting Away from Domestic Violence and Staying Safe*. New York: Anchor Books, 1996.

Muslim Women's League. "An Islamic Perspective on Violence Against Women," March 1995. Online at http://www.mwlusa.org/pub_violence.shtml

Nason-Clark, Nancy. *The Battered Wife: How Christians Confront Family Violence*. Louisville, Ky.: Westminster/John Knox Press, 1997.

Nelson, Noelle. *Dangerous Relationships: How to Stop Domestic Violence Before It Stops You*. New York: Insight Books, 1997.

NiCarthy, Ginny. *The Ones Who Got Away: Women Who Left Abusive Partners*. Seattle, Wash.: Seal Press, 1987.

NiCarthy, Ginny, and Sue Davidson. *You Can Be Free: An Easy-to-Read Handbook for Abused Women*. Seattle, Wash.: Seal Press, 1997.

Paymar, Michael. *Violent No More: Helping Men End Domestic Abuse*. Alameda, Calif.: Hunter House, 1993.

Radomsky, Nellie A. *Lost Voices: Women, Chronic Pain, and Abuse*. Binghamton, N.Y.: Harrington Park Press, 1995.

Renzetti, Claire M. *Violent Betrayal: Partner Abuse in Lesbian Relationships*. Newbury Park, Calif.: Sage, 1992.

Renzetti, Claire M., and Charles Harvey Miley, eds. *Violence in Gay and Lesbian Domestic Partnerships*. New York: Haworth Press, 1996.

Richie, Beth. *Compelled to Crime: The Gender Entrapment of Battered, Black Women*. New York: Routledge, 1996.

Richie, Beth. *Understanding Family Violence with U.S. Refugee Communities: A Training Manual*. Washington, D.C.: Refugee Women in Development Staff, 1988. [202-628-9600]

Robertson, Robert. *Confessions of an Abusive Husband: A How-To Book for "Abuse-Free" Living for Everyone*. Lake Oswego, Ore.: Heritage Park, 1992.

Russell, Diana E. H. *Rape in Marriage*. Revised edition. Bloomington, Ind.: Indiana University Press, 1990.

Scarf, Mimi. *Battered Jewish Wives: Case Studies in the Response to Rage*. Lewiston, N.Y.: Edwin Mellen Press, 1988.

Sev'Er, Aysan, ed. *A Cross-Cultural Exploration of Wife Abuse: Problems and Prospects*. Lewiston, N.Y.: Edwin Mellen Press, 1997.

Sipe, Beth, and Evelyn J. Hall. *I Am Not Your Victim: Anatomy of Domestic Violence*. Thousand Oaks, Calif.: Sage, 1996.

Song, Young I. *Battered Women in Korean Immigrant Families: The Silent Scream*. New York: Garland, 1996.

Sonkin, Daniel Jay, and Michael Durphy. *Learning to Live Without Violence: A Handbook for Men*. Updated edition. San Francisco, Calif.: Volcano Press, 1997.

Stacey, William A., Lonnie R. Hazlewood, and Anson Shupe. *The Violent Couple*. Westport, Conn.: Praeger, 1994.

Stark, Evan, and Anne Flitcraft. *Women at Risk: Domestic Violence and Women's Health*. Thousand Oaks, Calif.: Sage, 1996.

Statman, Jan Berliner. *The Battered Woman's Survival Guide*. Dallas, Tex.: Taylor, 1995.

Stith, Sandra M., and Murray A. Straus, eds. *Understanding Partner Violence: Prevalence, Causes, Consequences, and Solutions*. Minneapolis, Minn.: National Council on Family Relations, 1995.

Walker, Lenore E. *The Battered Woman*. New York: Harper & Row, 1979.

———. *The Battered Woman Syndrome*. New York: Springer, 1984.

Weiss, Elaine. *Surviving Domestic Violence: Voices of Women Who Broke Free*. Salt Lake City, Utah: Agreka Books, 2000.

White, Evelyn C. *Chain Chain Change: For Black Women in Abusive Relationships*. Expanded 2nd ed. Seattle, Wash.: Seal Press ; [Emeryville, Calif.] : Distributed to the trade by Publishers Group West, 1995.

Williams, O. J. *Are Partner Abuse Programs Prepared to Work with African American Men Who Batter?* (monograph) Minneapolis, Minn.: University of Minnesota School of Social Work, 1993.

Wilson, K. J. *When Violence Begins at Home: A Comprehensive Guide to Understanding and Ending Domestic Abuse*. Alameda, Calif.: Hunter House, 1997.

Yl025 Yllö, Kersti, and Michele Bograd. *Feminist Perspectives on Wife Abuse*. Newbury Park, Calif.: Sage, 1988.

Zambrano, Myrna M. *Mejor Sola Que Mal Acompañada: For the Latina in an Abusive Relationship*. Seattle, Wash.: Seal Press, 1985. [English and Spanish.]

## Journals

*Journal of Comparative Family Studies*. 1970–. Calgary, Alberta, Canada.

*Journal of Emotional Abuse*. 1998–. Haworth Maltreatment & Trauma Press, Binghamton, N.Y.

*Journal of Family Violence*. 1986–. Plenum Press, New York.

*Journal of Interpersonal Violence*. 1986–. Sage Publications, Beverly Hills, Calif.

*Journal of Marriage and the Family*. 1964–. National Council on Family Relations, Menasha, Wis.

*Violence and Victims*. 1986–. Springer Publishing, New York.

### Web Sites

The Jewish Domestic Abuse and Agunah Problem Web Page, http://users.aol.com/Agunah/

The Safety Zone Provides information and links on domestic violence, http://www.serve.com/zone/

Violence Against Women Office, U.S. Department of Justice, Office of Justice Programs. Includes Domestic Violence Awareness Manual, 1997, http://www.usdoj.gov/vawo/domestic.htm

Violence Against Women Online Resources, U.S. Department of Justice, Office of Justice Programs, http://www.vaw.umn.edu/

## *Dating Violence*

### Books

Chaiet, Donna. *Staying Safe on Dates*. New York: Rosen Publishing Group, 1995.

Levy, Barrie. *Dating Violence: Young Women in Danger*. Seattle, Wash.: Seal Press, 1998.

———. *In Love and in Danger: A Teen's Guide to Breaking Free of Abusive Relationships*. Second edition. Seattle, Wash.: Seal Press, 1998.

———. *Skills for Violence-Free Relationships: Curriculum for Young People Ages 13-18*. Santa Monica, Calif.: Southern California Coalition on Battered Women, 1984. [213-578-1442]

Levy, Barrie, and Patricia O. Giggans. *What Parents Need to Know about Dating Violence: Learning the Facts and Helping Your Teen*. Seattle, Wash.: Seal Press, 1995.

Lloyd, Sally A., and Beth C. Emery. *The Dark Side of Courtship: Physical and Sexual Aggression*. Thousand Oaks, Calif.: Sage, 1999.

Wiehe, Vernon R., and Ann L. Richards. *Intimate Betrayal: Understanding and Responding to the Trauma of Acquaintance Rape.* Thousand Oaks, Calif.: Sage, 1995.

Wolfe, David A., Christine Wekerle, and Katreena Scott. *Alternatives to Violence: Empowering Youth to Develop Healthy Relationships.* Thousand Oaks, Calif.: Sage, 1996.

### Web Sites

Minnesota Center Against Violence and Abuse (MINCAVA) clearinghouse: http://www.mincava.umn.edu/dateviol.asp

## Stalking

### Books

De Becker, Gavin. *The Gift of Fear: Survival Signals that Protect Us from Violence.* Boston, Mass.: Little Brown & Company, 1997.

Lardner, Jr., George. *The Stalking of Kristin: A Father Investigates the Murder of His Daughter.* New York: Onyx, 1995.

Orion, Doreen R. *I Know You Really Love Me: A Psychiatrist's Journal of Erotomania, Stalking, and Obsessive Love.* New York: Macmillan, 1997.

Snow, Robert L. *Stopping a Stalker: A Cop's Guide to Making the System Work for You.* New York: Plenum Press, 1998.

### Journals

Irene Hanson Frieze, Keith Davis, Roland D. Maiuro, eds. Special issue of *Violence and Victims.* "Stalking and Obsessive Behaviors in Everyday Life: Assessments of Victims and Perpetrators." 15, 1 (Spring 2000).

### Web Sites

Minnesota Center Against Violence and Abuse (MINCAVA) clearinghouse: http://www.mincava.umn.edu/stalkin.asp

## Child Abuse

### Books

Adams, Caren, and Jennifer Fay. *Helping Your Child Recover from Sexual Abuse.* Seattle, Wash.: University of Washington Press, 1992.

Ammerman, R. T., and M. Hersen, eds. *Children at Risk: An Evaluation of Factors Contributing to Child Abuse and Neglect.* New York: Plenum Press, 1990.

Bannister, Anne. *The Healing Drama: Psychodrama and Dramatherapy with Abused Children.* London; New York: Free Association Books, 1997.

Bartholet, Elizabeth. *Nobody's Children: Abuse and Neglect, Foster Drift, and the Adoption Alternative.* Boston: Beacon Press, 1999.

Besharov, Douglas J. *Recognizing Child Abuse: A Guide for the Concerned.* New York: Free Press, 1990.

Bifulco, Antonia, and Patricia Moran. *Wednesday's Child: Research into Women's Experience of Neglect and Abuse in Childhood and Adult Depression.* London; New York: Routledge, 1998.

Butler, Sandra. *Conspiracy of Silence: The Trauma of Incest.* San Francisco, Calif.: Volcano Press, 1985.

Cross, Merry. *Proud Child, Safer Child: A Handbook for Parents and Carers of Disabled Children.* Women's Press Ltd., 1999.

Davis, Diane. *Something Is Wrong at My House: A Book for Children about Domestic Violence.* Seattle, Wash.: Parenting Press, 1985.

DeMause, Lloyd, ed. *History of Childhood: The Untold Story of Child Abuse.* New York: P. Bedrick Books, 1988.

Fontana, Vincent J. *Save the Family, Save the Child: What We Can Do to Help Children at Risk.* New York: Dutton, 1991.

Fontes, Lisa Aronson, ed. *Sexual Abuse in Nine North American Cultures: Treatment and Prevention.* Thousand Oaks, Calif.: Sage, 1995.

Forward, Susan, and Craig Buck. *Betrayal of Innocence: Incest and Its Devastation.* Rev. ed. New York: Penguin, 1988.

Frehsee, Detlev, Wiebke Horn, and Kai-D. Bussmann, eds. *Family Violence Against Children: A Challenge for Society.* Berlin; New York: Walter de Gruyter, 1996.

Garbarino, James. *Lost Boys: Why Our Sons Turn Violent and How We Can Save Them*. New York: Free Press, 1999.

Gelles, Richard J. *The Book of David: How Preserving Families Can Cost Children's Lives*. New York: BasicBooks, 1996.

Gil, Eliana. *Outgrowing the Pain: A Book for and about Adults Abused as Children*. New York: Dell, 1988. (Also available in Spanish: *Superando el dolor: un libro para y acerca de adultos víctimas de abuso en la niñez*. Walnut Creek, Calif.: Lauch Press, 1990.)

Gil, Eliana. *Outgrowing the Pain Together: A Book for Spouses and Partners of Adults Abused as Children*. New York: Dell, 1992.

Gordon, Sol, and Judith Gordon. *A Better Safe Than Sorry Book: A Family Guide for Sexual Assault Prevention*. Buffalo, N.Y.: Prometheus Books, 1992. For children.

Graber, Ken. *Ghosts in the Bedroom: A Guide for Partners of Incest Survivors*. Deerfield Beach, Fla.: Health Communications, 1991.

Grossman, Frances Kaplan, Alexandra B. Cook, Selin S. Kepkep, and Karestan C. Koenen, eds. *With the Phoenix Rising: Lessons from Ten Resilient Women Who Overcame the Trauma of Childhood Sexual Abuse*. San Francisco, Calif.: Jossey-Bass, 1999.

Hagans, Kathryn B., and Joyce Case. *When Your Child Has Been Molested: A Parent's Guide to Healing and Recovery*. San Francisco, Calif.: Jossey-Bass, 1998.

Heide, Kathleen M. *Why Kids Kill Parents: Child Abuse and Adolescent Homicide*. Columbus, Ohio: Ohio State University Press, 1992.

Helfer, Mary Edna, Ruth S. Kempe, and Richard D. Krugman, eds. *The Battered Child*. 5th edition. Chicago: University of Chicago Press, 1999.

Helfner, Ray E., and C. Henry Kempe, eds. *Child Abuse and Neglect: The Family and the Community*. Preface by Walter F. Mondale. Cambridge, Mass.: Ballinger, 1976.

Holden, George W., Robert A. Geffner, and Ernest N. Jouriles, eds. *Children Exposed to Marital Violence: Theory, Research, and Applied Issues*. Washington, D.C.: American Psychological Association, 1998.

Hyman, Irwin A. *The Case Against Spanking: How to Discipline Your Child without Hitting*. San Francisco, Calif.: Jossey-Bass, 1997.

Johnson, Toni Cavanagh. *Sexual, Physical, and Emotional Abuse in Out-of-Home Care: Prevention Skills for At-Risk Children*. New York: Haworth Maltreatment and Trauma Press, 1997.

Karr-Morse, Robin, and Meredith S. Wiley. *Ghosts from the Nursery: Tracing the Roots of Violence*. New York: Atlantic Monthly Press, 1999.

Kehoe, Patricia. *Something Happened and I'm Scared to Tell: A Book for Young Victims of Abuse*. Seattle, Wash.: Parenting Press, 1987.

Kempe, Ruth S., and C. Henry Kempe. *Child Abuse*. Cambridge, Mass.: Harvard University Press, 1978.

Kempe, Ruth S., and C. Henry Kempe. *The Common Secret: Sexual Abuse of Children and Adults*. New York: W. H. Freeman, 1984.

Kleven, Sandy. *The Right Touch: A Read-Aloud Story to Help Prevent Child Sexual Abuse*. Bellevue, Wash.: Illumination Arts, 1998.

Krupinski, Eve, and Donna Weikel. *Death from Child Abuse—No One Heard*. Winter Park, Fla.: Currier-Davis, 1986.

Lee, Sharice A. *The Survivor's Guide: A Guide for Teenage Girls Who Are Survivors of Sexual Abuse*. Thousand Oaks, Calif.: Sage, 1995.

Lew, Mike. *Victims No Longer: Men Recovering from Incest and Other Sexual Child Abuse*. New York: Perennial Library, 1990.

Lynch, Eleanor W., and Marci J. Hanson. *Developing Cross-Cultural Competence: A Guide for Working with Young Children and Their Families*. 2nd edition. Baltimore, Md.: Paul H. Brookes Publishing, 1998.

Malchiodi, Cathy A. *Breaking the Silence: Art Therapy with Children from Violent Homes*. 2nd edition revised and expanded. Bristol, Pa.: Brunner/Mazel, 1997.

Mather, Cynthia L., and Kristina E. Debye. *How Long Does It Hurt?: A Guide to Recovering from Incest and Sexual Abuse for Teenagers, Their Friends, and Their Families*. San Francisco, Calif.: Jossey-Bass, 1994.

Matthews, Rosita, and Sherry Richmond. *What Will Happen Next: A Child Care Manual for Children from Domestic Violent Families*. Windsor, Ontario, Canada: Hiatus House, 1985.

Miller-Perrin, Cindy L., and Robin D. Perrin. *Child Maltreatment: An Introduction*. Thousand Oaks, Calif.: Sage, 1999.

Money, John. *The Kaspar Hauser Syndrome of "Psychosocial Dwarfism": Deficient Statural, Intellectual, and Social Growth Induced by Child Abuse.* Buffalo, N.Y.: Prometheus, 1992.

Morey, Ann-Janine. *What Happened to Christopher: An American Family's Story of Shaken Baby Syndrome.* Carbondale, Ill.: Southern Illinois University Press, 1998.

Myers, John E. B. *A Mother's Nightmare—Incest: A Practical Legal Guide for Parents and Professionals.* Thousand Oaks, Calif.: Sage, 1997.

National Data Archive on Child Abuse and Neglect (project of the Family Life Development Center, College of Human Ecology, Cornell University), http://www.ndacan.cornell.edu/

*National Directory of Children, Youth and Families Services.* Englewood, Colo.: Prevent Child Abuse America, annual.

Parnell, Teresa F., and Deborah O. Day, eds. *Munchausen by Proxy Syndrome: Misunderstood Child Abuse.* Thousand Oaks, Calif.: Sage, 1997.

Rhodes, Ginger, and Richard Rhodes. *Trying to Get Some Dignity: Stories of Triumph over Childhood Abuse.* New York: William Morrow & Company, 1996.

Rosencrans, Bobbie. *The Last Secret: Daughters Sexually Abused by Mothers.* Brandon, Vt.: Safer Society Press, 1997.

Roy, Ranjan. *Childhood Abuse and Chronic Pain: A Curious Relationship?* Toronto: University of Toronto Press, 1998.

Rubin, Lillian. *The Transcendent Child: Tales of Triumph over the Past.* New York: HarperCollins, 1997.

Schwartz, Mark F., and Leigh Cohn, eds. *Sexual Abuse and Eating Disorders.* New York: Brunner/Mazel, 1996.

Shengold, Leonard. *Soul Murder: The Effects of Child Abuse and Deprivation.* New Haven, Conn.: Yale University Press, 1989.

———. *Soul Murder Revisited: Thoughts about Therapy, Hate, Love, and Memory.* New Haven, Conn.: Yale University Press, 1999.

Smith, Selwyn M. *The Battered Child Syndrome.* London, England: Butterworth, 1975.

Sonkin, Daniel Jay. *Wounded Boys Heroic Men: A Man's Guide to Recovering from Child Abuse.* Holbrook, Mass.: Adams Media, 1998.

Straus, Murray A. *Beating the Devil out of Them: Corporal Punishment by Parents.* San Francisco, Calif.: Jossey-Bass/Lexington, 1994.

Trickett, Penelope K., and Cynthia J. Schellenbach, ed. *Violence Against Children in the Family and the Community.* Washington, D.C.: American Psychological Association, 1998.

Waldfogel, Jane. *The Future of Child Protection: How to Break the Cycle of Abuse and Neglect.* Cambridge, Mass.: Harvard University Press, 1998.

Welsh, Lesley A., Francis X. Archambault, and Mark-David Janus. *Running for Their Lives: Physical and Sexual Abuse of Runaway Adolescents.* New York: Garland, 1995.

Wilczynski, Ania. *Child Homicide.* London, England: Greenwich Medical Media, 1997.

Wilson, Melba. *Crossing the Boundary: Black Women Survive Incest.* Seattle, Wash.: Seal Press, 1994.

Wisechild, Louise M. *The Mother I Carry: A Memoir of Healing from Emotional Abuse.* Seattle, Wash.: Seal Press, 1993.

Wyckoff, Jerry, and Barbara C. Unell. *Discipline without Shouting or Spanking: Practical Solutions to the Most Common Preschool Behavior Problems.* New York: Simon & Schuster, 1985.

## *Journals*

*American Journal of Orthopsychiatry.* 1930–. Journal of the American Orthopsychiatric Association, New York.

*APSAC Advisor.* 1988–. American Professional Society on the Abuse of Children, Chicago, Ill.

*Child Abuse & Neglect.* 1977–. Publication of the International Society for Prevention of Child Abuse and Neglect. Oxford; New York: Pergamon Press.

*Child Abuse Review.* 1985–. Journal of the British Association for the Study and Prevention of Child Abuse and Neglect, Croydon, England.

*Child Maltreatment: The Journal of the American Professional Society on the Abuse of Children.* 1996–. Thousand Oaks, Calif.: Sage.

*Child Welfare Review.* 1998–. Internet journal at http://www.childwelfare.com/kids/news.htm; E-mail: dlindsey@ucla.edu or info@childwelfare.com. Edited by Duncan Lindsey, School of Public Policy and Social Research, University of California at Los Angeles.

*Family Violence & Sexual Assault Bulletin.* 1985–. Family Violence and Sexual Assault Institute, Tyler, Tex. (Formerly *Family Violence Bulletin.*)

*Future of Children.* 1991–. Published by the David and Lucile Packard Foundation, Los Altos, Calif. Special issue on Domestic Violence and Children 9, 3 (Winter 1999).

*Journal of Emotional Abuse.* 1998–. Haworth Maltreatment & Trauma Press, Binghamton, N.Y.

*Journal of Family Violence.* 1986–. Plenum Press, New York.

*Journal of Interpersonal Violence.* 1986–. Sage Publications, Beverly Hills, Calif.

*Protecting Children.* 1984–. Journal of the Children's Division of the American Humane Association, Englewood, Colo. (special issues on the link between child abuse and animal abuse, volume 13 [1997] and volume 15 [1999]).

### Web Sites

Minnesota Center Against Violence and Abuse (MINCAVA) clearinghouse: http://www.mincava.umn.edu/ca.asp

## Sibling Abuse

### Books

Caffaro, John V., and Allison Conn-Caffaro. *Sibling Abuse Trauma : Assessment and Intervention Strategies for Children, Families, and Adults.* New York: Haworth Maltreatment and Trauma Press, 1998.

Wiehe, Vernon R. *The Brother/Sister Hurt: Recognizing the Effects of Sibling Abuse.* Brandon, Vt.: Safer Society Press, 1996.

———. *Sibling Abuse: Hidden Physical, Emotional, and Sexual Trauma.* 2nd edition. Thousand Oaks, Calif.: Sage, 1997.

Wiehe, Vernon R., and Teresa Herring. *Perilous Rivalry: When Siblings Become Abusive.* Lexington, Mass.: Lexington Books, 1991.

## Parent Abuse

### Books

Mones, Paul. *When a Child Kills: Abused Children Who Kill Their Parents*. New York: Pocket Books, 1991.

### Articles

Agnew, R., and S. Huguley. "Adolescent Violence towards Parents." *Journal of Marriage and the Family* 51 (1989): 699–711.

Cornell, C. P., and R. J. Gelles. "Adolescent to Parent Violence." *Urban Social Change Review* 15 (1982): 8–14.

Harbin, H., and D. Madden. "Battered Parents: A New Syndrome." *American Journal of Psychiatry* 136 (1979): 1288–91.

## Elder Abuse

### Books

Aitken, Lynda, and Gabriele Griffin. *Gender Issues in Elder Abuse*. Thousand Oaks, Calif.: Sage, 1996.

Brownell, Patricia J. *Family Crimes Against the Elderly: Elderly Abuse and the Criminal Justice System*. New York: Garland, 1998.

Kosberg, Jordan I., and Juanita L. Garcia, eds. *Elder Abuse: International and Cross-Cultural Perspectives*. New York: Haworth Press, 1995.

Mastrocola-Morris, Elaine. *Woman Abuse: The Relationship between Wife Assault and Elder Abuse*. [Ottawa, Canada]: Family Violence Prevention Division, National Clearinghouse on Family Violence, Health and Welfare Canada, 1989.

Pillemer, Karl A., and Rosalie S. Wolf. *Elder Abuse*. Dover, Mass.: Auburn House, 1993.

Quinn, Mary Joy, and Susan K. Tomita. *Elder Abuse and Neglect: Causes, Diagnosis, and Intervention Strategies*. New York: Springer, 1986.

Tatara, Toshio, ed. *Understanding Elder Abuse in Minority Populations*. Philadelphia, Pa.: Brunner/Mazel, 1998.

U.S. Congress. Senate. Special Committee on Aging. *Society's Secret Shame: Elder Abuse and Family Violence*. Washington, D.C.: Government Printing Office, 1995.

## *Journals*

*Journal of Elder Abuse & Neglect*. 1989–. Journal of the National Committee for the Prevention of Elder Abuse. Binghamton, N.Y.: Haworth Press.

*Journal of Family Violence*. 1986–. Plenum Press, New York.

*NCEA Newsletter.* Newsletter from the National Center on Elder Abuse, available online at http://www.gwjapan.com/NCEA/newsletter/index.html

## *Web Sites*

American Association of Retired Persons: http://www.aarp.org/

Minnesota Center Against Violence and Abuse (MINCAVA) clearinghouse: http://www.mincava.umn.edu/elderv.asp

National Center on Elder Abuse: http://www.gwjapan.com/NCEA/

# Index

# *Index*

1015

# Health Reference Series

## COMPLETE CATALOG

## AIDS Sourcebook, 1st Edition

Basic Information about AIDS and HIV Infection, Featuring Historical and Statistical Data, Current Research, Prevention, and Other Special Topics of Interest for Persons Living with AIDS

Along with Source Listings for Further Assistance

Edited by Karen Bellenir and Peter D. Dresser. 831 pages. 1995. 0-7808-0031-1. $78.

"One strength of this book is its practical emphasis. The intended audience is the lay reader ... useful as an educational tool for health care providers who work with AIDS patients. Recommended for public libraries as well as hospital or academic libraries that collect consumer materials."
— Bulletin of the Medical Library Association, Jan '96

"This is the most comprehensive volume of its kind on an important medical topic. Highly recommended for all libraries."         — Reference Book Review, '96

"Very useful reference for all libraries."
— Choice, Association of College and Research Libraries, Oct '95

"There is a wealth of information here that can provide much educational assistance. It is a must book for all libraries and should be on the desk of each and every congressional leader. Highly recommended."
— AIDS Book Review Journal, Aug '95

"Recommended for most collections."
— Library Journal, Jul '95

## AIDS Sourcebook, 2nd Edition

Basic Consumer Health Information about Acquired Immune Deficiency Syndrome (AIDS) and Human Immunodeficiency Virus (HIV) Infection, Featuring Updated Statistical Data, Reports on Recent Research and Prevention Initiatives, and Other Special Topics of Interest for Persons Living with AIDS, Including New Antiretroviral Treatment Options, Strategies for Combating Opportunistic Infections, Information about Clinical Trials, and More

Along with a Glossary of Important Terms and Resource Listings for Further Help and Information

Edited by Karen Bellenir. 751 pages. 1999. 0-7808-0225-X. $78.

"Highly recommended."
— American Reference Books Annual, 2000

"Excellent sourcebook. This continues to be a highly recommended book. There is no other book that provides as much information as this book provides."
— AIDS Book Review Journal, Dec-Jan 2000

"Recommended reference source."
— Booklist, American Library Association, Dec '99

"A solid text for college-level health libraries."
— The Bookwatch, Aug '99

Cited in Reference Sources for Small and Medium-Sized Libraries, American Library Association, 1999

## Alcoholism Sourcebook

Basic Consumer Health Information about the Physical and Mental Consequences of Alcohol Abuse, Including Liver Disease, Pancreatitis, Wernicke-Korsakoff Syndrome (Alcoholic Dementia), Fetal Alcohol Syndrome, Heart Disease, Kidney Disorders, Gastrointestinal Problems, and Immune System Compromise and Featuring Facts about Addiction, Detoxification, Alcohol Withdrawal, Recovery, and the Maintenance of Sobriety

Along with a Glossary and Directories of Resources for Further Help and Information

Edited by Karen Bellenir. 635 pages. 2000. 0-7808-0325-6. $78.

**SEE ALSO** Drug Abuse Sourcebook, Substance Abuse Sourcebook

## Allergies Sourcebook

Basic Information about Major Forms and Mechanisms of Common Allergic Reactions, Sensitivities, and Intolerances, Including Anaphylaxis, Asthma, Hives and Other Dermatologic Symptoms, Rhinitis, and Sinusitis

Along with Their Usual Triggers Like Animal Fur, Chemicals, Drugs, Dust, Foods, Insects, Latex, Pollen, and Poison Ivy, Oak, and Sumac; Plus Information on Prevention, Identification, and Treatment

Edited by Allan R. Cook. 611 pages. 1997. 0-7808-0036-2. $78.

## Alternative Medicine Sourcebook

Basic Consumer Health Information about Alternatives to Conventional Medicine, Including Acupressure, Acupuncture, Aromatherapy, Ayurveda, Bioelectromagnetics, Environmental Medicine, Essence Therapy, Food and Nutrition Therapy, Herbal Therapy, Homeopathy, Imaging, Massage, Naturopathy, Reflexology, Relaxation and Meditation, Sound Therapy, Vitamin and Mineral Therapy, and Yoga, and More

Edited by Allan R. Cook. 737 pages. 1999. 0-7808-0200-4. $78.

"Recommended reference source."
— Booklist, American Library Association, Feb '00

# Alzheimer's, Stroke & 29 Other Neurological Disorders Sourcebook, 1st Edition

*Basic Information for the Layperson on 31 Diseases or Disorders Affecting the Brain and Nervous System, First Describing the Illness, Then Listing Symptoms, Diagnostic Methods, and Treatment Options, and Including Statistics on Incidences and Causes*

Edited by Frank E. Bair. 579 pages. 1993. 1-55888-748-2. $78.

*SEE ALSO* Brain Disorders Sourcebook

■

# Alzheimer's Disease Sourcebook, 2nd Edition

*Basic Consumer Health Information about Alzheimer's Disease, Related Disorders, and Other Dementias, Including Multi-Infarct Dementia, AIDS-Related Dementia, Alcoholic Dementia, Huntington's Disease, Delirium, and Confusional States*

*Along with Reports Detailing Current Research Efforts in Prevention and Treatment, Long-Term Care Issues, and Listings of Sources for Additional Help and Information*

Edited by Karen Bellenir. 524 pages. 1999. 0-7808-0223-3. $78.

# Arthritis Sourcebook

*Basic Consumer Health Information about Specific Forms of Arthritis and Related Disorders, Including Rheumatoid Arthritis, Osteoarthritis, Gout, Polymyalgia Rheumatica, Psoriatic Arthritis, Spondyloarthropathies, Juvenile Rheumatoid Arthritis, and Juvenile Ankylosing Spondylitis*

*Along with Information about Medical, Surgical, and Alternative Treatment Options, and Including Strategies for Coping with Pain, Fatigue, and Stress*

Edited by Allan R. Cook. 550 pages. 1998. 0-7808-0201-2. $78.

■

# Asthma Sourcebook

*Basic Consumer Health Information about Asthma, Including Symptoms, Traditional and Nontraditional Remedies, Treatment Advances, Quality-of-Life Aids, Medical Research Updates, and the Role of Allergies, Exercise, Age, the Environment, and Genetics in the Development of Asthma*

*Along with Statistical Data, a Glossary, and Directories of Support Groups, and Other Resources for Further Information*

Edited by Annemarie S. Muth. 628 pages. 2000. 0-7808-0381-7. $78.

■

# Back & Neck Disorders Sourcebook

*Basic Information about Disorders and Injuries of the Spinal Cord and Vertebrae, Including Facts on Chiropractic Treatment, Surgical Interventions, Paralysis, and Rehabilitation*

*Along with Advice for Preventing Back Trouble*

Edited by Karen Bellenir. 548 pages. 1997. 0-7808-0202-0. $78.

■

# Blood & Circulatory Disorders Sourcebook

*Basic Information about Blood and Its Components, Anemias, Leukemias, Bleeding Disorders, and Circulatory Disorders, Including Aplastic Anemia, Thalassemia, Sickle-Cell Disease, Hemochromatosis, Hemophilia, Von Willebrand Disease, and Vascular Diseases*

*Along with a Special Section on Blood Transfusions and Blood Supply Safety, a Glossary, and Source Listings for Further Help and Information*

Edited by Karen Bellenir and Linda M. Shin. 554 pages. 1998. 0-7808-0203-9. $78.

# Brain Disorders Sourcebook

*Basic Consumer Health Information about Strokes, Epilepsy, Amyotrophic Lateral Sclerosis (ALS/Lou Gehrig's Disease), Parkinson's Disease, Brain Tumors, Cerebral Palsy, Headache, Tourette Syndrome, and More*

*Along with Statistical Data, Treatment and Rehabilitation Options, Coping Strategies, Reports on Current Research Initiatives, a Glossary, and Resource Listings for Additional Help and Information*

Edited by Karen Bellenir. 481 pages. 1999. 0-7808-0229-2. $78.

"Belongs on the shelves of any library with a consumer health collection." —*E-Streams, Mar '00*

"Recommended reference source."
—*Booklist, American Library Association, Oct '99*

**SEE ALSO** *Alzheimer's, Stroke & 29 Other Neurological Disorders Sourcebook, 1st Edition*

# Breast Cancer Sourcebook

*Basic Consumer Health Information about Breast Cancer, Including Diagnostic Methods, Treatment Options, Alternative Therapies, Help and Self-Help Information, Related Health Concerns, Statistical and Demographic Data, and Facts for Men with Breast Cancer*

*Along with Reports on Current Research Initiatives, a Glossary of Related Medical Terms, and a Directory of Sources for Further Help and Information*

Edited by Edward J. Prucha. 600 pages. 2001. 0-7808-0244-6. $78.

**SEE ALSO** *Cancer Sourcebook for Women, 1st and 2nd Editions, Women's Health Concerns Sourcebook*

# Burns Sourcebook

*Basic Consumer Health Information about Various Types of Burns and Scalds, Including Flame, Heat, Cold, Electrical, Chemical, and Sun Burns*

*Along with Information on Short-Term and Long-Term Treatments, Tissue Reconstruction, Plastic Surgery, Prevention Suggestions, and First Aid*

Edited by Allan R. Cook. 604 pages. 1999. 0-7808-0204-7. $78.

"This key reference guide is an invaluable addition to all health care and public libraries in confronting this ongoing health issue."
—*American Reference Books Annual, 2000*

"This is an exceptional addition to the series and is highly recommended for all consumer health collections, hospital libraries, and academic medical centers." —*E-Streams, Mar '00*

"Recommended reference source."
—*Booklist, American Library Association, Dec '99*

**SEE ALSO** *Skin Disorders Sourcebook*

# Cancer Sourcebook, 1st Edition

*Basic Information on Cancer Types, Symptoms, Diagnostic Methods, and Treatments, Including Statistics on Cancer Occurrences Worldwide and the Risks Associated with Known Carcinogens and Activities*

Edited by Frank E. Bair. 932 pages. 1990. 1-55888-888-8. $78.

Cited in *Reference Sources for Small and Medium-Sized Libraries, American Library Association, 1999*

"Written in nontechnical language. Useful for patients, their families, medical professionals, and librarians."
—*Guide to Reference Books, 1996*

"Designed with the non-medical professional in mind. Libraries and medical facilities interested in patient education should certainly consider adding the *Cancer Sourcebook* to their holdings. This compact collection of reliable information . . . is an invaluable tool for helping patients and patients' families and friends to take the first steps in coping with the many difficulties of cancer."
—*Medical Reference Services Quarterly, Winter '91*

"Specifically created for the nontechnical reader . . . an important resource for the general reader trying to understand the complexities of cancer."
—*American Reference Books Annual, 1991*

"This publication's nontechnical nature and very comprehensive format make it useful for both the general public and undergraduate students."
—*Choice, Association of College and Research Libraries, Oct '90*

# New Cancer Sourcebook, 2nd Edition

*Basic Information about Major Forms and Stages of Cancer, Featuring Facts about Primary and Secondary Tumors of the Respiratory, Nervous, Lymphatic, Circulatory, Skeletal, and Gastrointestinal Systems, and Specific Organs; Statistical and Demographic Data; Treatment Options; and Strategies for Coping*

Edited by Allan R. Cook. 1,313 pages. 1996. 0-7808-0041-9. $78.

"An excellent resource for patients with newly diagnosed cancer and their families. The dialogue is simple, direct, and comprehensive. Highly recommended for patients and families to aid in their understanding of cancer and its treatment."
—*Booklist Health Sciences Supplement, American Library Association, Oct '97*

## Cancer Sourcebook, 3rd Edition

*Basic Consumer Health Information about Major Forms and Stages of Cancer, Featuring Facts about Primary and Secondary Tumors of the Respiratory, Nervous, Lymphatic, Circulatory, Skeletal, and Gastrointestinal Systems, and Specific Organs*

*Along with Statistical and Demographic Data, Treatment Options, Strategies for Coping, a Glossary, and a Directory of Sources for Additional Help and Information*

Edited by Edward J. Prucha. 1,069 pages. 2000. 0-7808-0227-6. $78.

## Cancer Sourcebook for Women, 1st Edition

*Basic Information about Specific Forms of Cancer That Affect Women, Featuring Facts about Breast Cancer, Cervical Cancer, Ovarian Cancer, Cancer of the Uterus and Uterine Sarcoma, Cancer of the Vagina, and Cancer of the Vulva; Statistical and Demographic Data; Treatments, Self-Help Management Suggestions, and Current Research Initiatives*

Edited by Allan R. Cook and Peter D. Dresser. 524 pages. 1996. 0-7808-0076-1. $78.

***SEE ALSO*** *Breast Cancer Sourcebook, Women's Health Concerns Sourcebook*

## Cancer Sourcebook for Women, 2nd Edition

*Basic Consumer Health Information about Specific Forms of Cancer That Affect Women, Including Cervical Cancer, Ovarian Cancer, Endometrial Cancer, Uterine Sarcoma, Vaginal Cancer, Vulvar Cancer, and Gestational Trophoblastic Tumor; and Featuring Statistical Information, Facts about Tests and Treatments, a Glossary of Cancer Terms, and an Extensive List of Additional Resources*

Edited by Edward J. Prucha. 600 pages. 2001. 0-7808-0226-8. $78.

***SEE ALSO*** *Breast Cancer Sourcebook, Women's Health Concerns Sourcebook*

## Cardiovascular Diseases & Disorders Sourcebook, 1st Edition

*Basic Information about Cardiovascular Diseases and Disorders, Featuring Facts about the Cardiovascular System, Demographic and Statistical Data, Descriptions of Pharmacological and Surgical Interventions, Lifestyle Modifications, and a Special Section Focusing on Heart Disorders in Children*

Edited by Karen Bellenir and Peter D. Dresser. 683 pages. 1995. 0-7808-0032-X. $78.

***SEE ALSO*** *Healthy Heart Sourcebook for Women, Heart Diseases & Disorders Sourcebook, 2nd Edition*

## Caregiving Sourcebook

*Basic Consumer Health Information for Caregivers, Including a Profile of Caregivers, Caregiving Responsibilities, Tips for Specific Conditions, Care Environments, and the Effects of Caregiving*

*Along with Legal Issues, Financial Concerns, Future Planning, a Glossary, and a Listing of Additional Resources*

Edited by Joyce Brennfleck Shannon. 550 pages. 2001. 0-7808-0331-0. $78.

## Colds, Flu & Other Common Ailments Sourcebook

*Basic Consumer Health Information about Common Ailments and Injuries, Including Colds, Coughs, the Flu, Sinus Problems, Headaches, Fever, Nausea and Vomiting, Menstrual Cramps, Diarrhea, Constipation, Hemorrhoids, Back Pain, Dandruff, Dry and Itchy Skin, Cuts, Scrapes, Sprains, Bruises, and More*

*Along with Information about Prevention, Self-Care, Choosing a Doctor, Over-the-Counter Medications, Folk Remedies, and Alternative Therapies, and Including a Glossary of Important Terms and a Directory of Resources for Further Help and Information*

Edited by Chad T. Kimball. 600 pages. 2001. 0-7808-0435-X. $78.

■

## Communication Disorders Sourcebook

*Basic Information about Deafness and Hearing Loss, Speech and Language Disorders, Voice Disorders, Balance and Vestibular Disorders, and Disorders of Smell, Taste, and Touch*

Edited by Linda M. Ross. 533 pages. 1996. 0-7808-0077-X. $78.

"This is skillfully edited and is a welcome resource for the layperson. It should be found in every public and medical library." — *Booklist Health Sciences Supplement, American Library Association, Oct '97*

■

## Congenital Disorders Sourcebook

*Basic Information about Disorders Acquired during Gestation, Including Spina Bifida, Hydrocephalus, Cerebral Palsy, Heart Defects, Craniofacial Abnormalities, Fetal Alcohol Syndrome, and More*

*Along with Current Treatment Options and Statistical Data*

Edited by Karen Bellenir. 607 pages. 1997. 0-7808-0205-5. $78.

"Recommended reference source."
— *Booklist, American Library Association, Oct '97*

***SEE ALSO*** *Pregnancy & Birth Sourcebook*

■

## Consumer Issues in Health Care Sourcebook

*Basic Information about Health Care Fundamentals and Related Consumer Issues, Including Exams and Screening Tests, Physician Specialties, Choosing a Doctor, Using Prescription and Over-the-Counter Medications Safely, Avoiding Health Scams, Managing Common Health Risks in the Home, Care Options for Chronically or Terminally Ill Patients, and a List of Resources for Obtaining Help and Further Information*

Edited by Karen Bellenir. 618 pages. 1998. 0-7808-0221-7. $78.

"Both public and academic libraries will want to have a copy in their collection for readers who are interested in self-education on health issues."
— *American Reference Books Annual, 2000*

"The editor has researched the literature from government agencies and others, saving readers the time and effort of having to do the research themselves. Recommended for public libraries."
— *Reference and User Services Quarterly, American Library Association, Spring '99*

"Recommended reference source."
— *Booklist, American Library Association, Dec '98*

■

## Contagious & Non-Contagious Infectious Diseases Sourcebook

*Basic Information about Contagious Diseases like Measles, Polio, Hepatitis B, and Infectious Mononucleosis, and Non-Contagious Infectious Diseases like Tetanus and Toxic Shock Syndrome, and Diseases Occurring as Secondary Infections Such as Shingles and Reye Syndrome*

*Along with Vaccination, Prevention, and Treatment Information, and a Section Describing Emerging Infectious Disease Threats*

Edited by Karen Bellenir and Peter D. Dresser. 566 pages. 1996. 0-7808-0075-3. $78.

■

## Death & Dying Sourcebook

*Basic Consumer Health Information for the Layperson about End-of-Life Care and Related Ethical and Legal Issues, Including Chief Causes of Death, Autopsies, Pain Management for the Terminally Ill, Life Support Systems, Insurance, Euthanasia, Assisted Suicide, Hospice Programs, Living Wills, Funeral Planning, Counseling, Mourning, Organ Donation, and Physician Training*

*Along with Statistical Data, a Glossary, and Listings of Sources for Further Help and Information*

Edited by Annemarie S. Muth. 641 pages. 1999. 0-7808-0230-6. $78.

"This book is a definite must for all those involved in end-of-life care." — *Doody's Review Service, 2000*

■

## Diabetes Sourcebook, 1st Edition

*Basic Information about Insulin-Dependent and Non-insulin-Dependent Diabetes Mellitus, Gestational Diabetes, and Diabetic Complications, Symptoms, Treatment, and Research Results, Including Statistics on Prevalence, Morbidity, and Mortality*

*Along with Source Listings for Further Help and Information*

Edited by Karen Bellenir and Peter D. Dresser. 827 pages. 1994. 1-55888-751-2. $78.

". . . very informative and understandable for the layperson without being simplistic. It provides a comprehensive overview for laypersons who want a general understanding of the disease or who want to focus on various aspects of the disease."
— Bulletin of the Medical Library Association, Jan '96

■

## Diabetes Sourcebook, 2nd Edition

Basic Consumer Health Information about Type 1 Diabetes (Insulin-Dependent or Juvenile-Onset Diabetes), Type 2 (Noninsulin-Dependent or Adult-Onset Diabetes), Gestational Diabetes, and Related Disorders, Including Diabetes Prevalence Data, Management Issues, the Role of Diet and Exercise in Controlling Diabetes, Insulin and Other Diabetes Medicines, and Complications of Diabetes Such as Eye Diseases, Periodontal Disease, Amputation, and End-Stage Renal Disease

Along with Reports on Current Research Initiatives, a Glossary, and Resource Listings for Further Help and Information

Edited by Karen Bellenir. 688 pages. 1998. 0-7808-0224-1. $78.

"This comprehensive book is an excellent addition for high school, academic, medical, and public libraries. This volume is highly recommended."
— American Reference Books Annual, 2000

"An invaluable reference." — Library Journal, May '00

Selected as one of the 250 "Best Health Sciences Books of 1999." — Doody's Rating Service, Mar-Apr 2000

"Recommended reference source."
— Booklist, American Library Association, Feb '99

". . . provides reliable mainstream medical information . . . belongs on the shelves of any library with a consumer health collection." — E-Streams, Sep '99

"Provides useful information for the general public."
— Healthlines, University of Michigan Health Management Research Center, Sep/Oct '99

■

## Diet & Nutrition Sourcebook, 1st Edition

Basic Information about Nutrition, Including the Dietary Guidelines for Americans, the Food Guide Pyramid, and Their Applications in Daily Diet, Nutritional Advice for Specific Age Groups, Current Nutritional Issues and Controversies, the New Food Label and How to Use It to Promote Healthy Eating, and Recent Developments in Nutritional Research

Edited by Dan R. Harris. 662 pages. 1996. 0-7808-0084-2. $78.

"Useful reference as a food and nutrition sourcebook for the general consumer." — Booklist Health Sciences Supplement, American Library Association, Oct '97

"Recommended for public libraries and medical libraries that receive general information requests on nutrition. It is readable and will appeal to those interested in learning more about healthy dietary practices."
— Medical Reference Services Quarterly, Fall '97

"An abundance of medical and social statistics is translated into readable information geared toward the general reader." — Bookwatch, Mar '97

"With dozens of questionable diet books on the market, it is so refreshing to find a reliable and factual reference book. Recommended to aspiring professionals, librarians, and others seeking and giving reliable dietary advice. An excellent compilation." — Choice, Association of College and Research Libraries, Feb '97

SEE ALSO Digestive Diseases & Disorders Sourcebook, Gastrointestinal Diseases & Disorders Sourcebook

■

## Diet & Nutrition Sourcebook, 2nd Edition

Basic Consumer Health Information about Dietary Guidelines, Recommended Daily Intake Values, Vitamins, Minerals, Fiber, Fat, Weight Control, Dietary Supplements, and Food Additives

Along with Special Sections on Nutrition Needs throughout Life and Nutrition for People with Such Specific Medical Concerns as Allergies, High Blood Cholesterol, Hypertension, Diabetes, Celiac Disease, Seizure Disorders, Phenylketonuria (PKU), Cancer, and Eating Disorders, and Including Reports on Current Nutrition Research and Source Listings for Additional Help and Information

Edited by Karen Bellenir. 650 pages. 1999. 0-7808-0228-4. $78.

"This reference document should be in any public library, but it would be a very good guide for beginning students in the health sciences. If the other books in this publisher's series are as good as this, they should all be in the health sciences collections."
— American Reference Books Annual, 2000

"Recommended reference source."
— Booklist, American Library Association, Dec '99

SEE ALSO Digestive Diseases & Disorders Sourcebook, Gastrointestinal Diseases & Disorders Sourcebook

■

## Digestive Diseases & Disorders Sourcebook

Basic Consumer Health Information about Diseases and Disorders that Impact the Upper and Lower Digestive System, Including Celiac Disease, Constipation, Crohn's Disease, Cyclic Vomiting Syndrome, Diarrhea, Diverticulosis and Diverticulitis, Gallstones, Heartburn, Hemorrhoids, Hernias, Indigestion (Dyspepsia), Irritable Bowel Syndrome, Lactose Intolerance, Ulcers, and More

Along with Information about Medications and Other Treatments, Tips for Maintaining a Healthy Digestive

*Tract, a Glossary, and Directory of Digestive Diseases Organizations*

Edited by Karen Bellenir. 335 pages. 1999. 0-7808-0327-2. $48.

**"Recommended reference source."**
*—Booklist, American Library Association, May '00*

**SEE ALSO** *Diet & Nutrition Sourcebook, 1st and 2nd Editions, Gastrointestinal Diseases & Disorders Sourcebook*

# Disabilities Sourcebook

*Basic Consumer Health Information about Physical and Psychiatric Disabilities, Including Descriptions of Major Causes of Disability, Assistive and Adaptive Aids, Workplace Issues, and Accessibility Concerns*

*Along with Information about the Americans with Disabilities Act, a Glossary, and Resources for Additional Help and Information*

Edited by Dawn D. Matthews. 616 pages. 2000. 0-7808-0389-2. $78.

**"Recommended reference source."**
*—Booklist, American Library Association, Jul '00*

**"An involving, invaluable handbook."**
*—The Bookwatch, May '00*

# Domestic Violence & Child Abuse Sourcebook

*Basic Consumer Health Information about Spousal/ Partner, Child, Sibling, Parent, and Elder Abuse, Covering Physical, Emotional, and Sexual Abuse, Teen Dating Violence, and Stalking; Includes Information about Hotlines, Safe Houses, Safety Plans, and Other Resources for Support and Assistance, Community Initiatives, and Reports on Current Directions in Research and Treatment*

*Along with a Glossary, Sources for Further Reading, and Governmental and Non-Governmental Organizations Contact Information*

Edited by Helene Henderson. 1,064 pages. 2000. 0-7808-0235-7. $78.

# Drug Abuse Sourcebook

*Basic Consumer Health Information about Illicit Substances of Abuse and the Diversion of Prescription Medications, Including Depressants, Hallucinogens, Inhalants, Marijuana, Narcotics, Stimulants, and Anabolic Steroids*

*Along with Facts about Related Health Risks, Treatment Issues, and Substance Abuse Prevention Programs, a Glossary of Terms, Statistical Data, and Directories of Hotline Services, Self-Help Groups, and Organizations Able to Provide Further Information*

Edited by Karen Bellenir. 629 pages. 2000. 0-7808-0242-X. $78.

**SEE ALSO** *Alcoholism Sourcebook, Substance Abuse Sourcebook*

# Ear, Nose & Throat Disorders Sourcebook

*Basic Information about Disorders of the Ears, Nose, Sinus Cavities, Pharynx, and Larynx, Including Ear Infections, Tinnitus, Vestibular Disorders, Allergic and Non-Allergic Rhinitis, Sore Throats, Tonsillitis, and Cancers That Affect the Ears, Nose, Sinuses, and Throat*

*Along with Reports on Current Research Initiatives, a Glossary of Related Medical Terms, and a Directory of Sources for Further Help and Information*

Edited by Karen Bellenir and Linda M. Shin. 576 pages. 1998. 0-7808-0206-3. $78.

**"Overall, this sourcebook is helpful for the consumer seeking information on ENT issues. It is recommended for public libraries."**
*—American Reference Books Annual, 1999*

**"Recommended reference source."**
*—Booklist, American Library Association, Dec '98*

# Endocrine & Metabolic Disorders Sourcebook

*Basic Information for the Layperson about Pancreatic and Insulin-Related Disorders Such as Pancreatitis, Diabetes, and Hypoglycemia; Adrenal Gland Disorders Such as Cushing's Syndrome, Addison's Disease, and Congenital Adrenal Hyperplasia; Pituitary Gland Disorders Such as Growth Hormone Deficiency, Acromegaly, and Pituitary Tumors; Thyroid Disorders Such as Hypothyroidism, Graves' Disease, Hashimoto's Disease, and Goiter; Hyperparathyroidism; and Other Diseases and Syndromes of Hormone Imbalance or Metabolic Dysfunction*

*Along with Reports on Current Research Initiatives*

Edited by Linda M. Shin. 574 pages. 1998. 0-7808-0207-1. $78.

**"Omnigraphics has produced another needed resource for health information consumers."**
*—American Reference Books Annual, 2000*

**"Recommended reference source."**
*— Booklist, American Library Association, Dec '98*

# Environmentally Induced Disorders Sourcebook

*Basic Information about Diseases and Syndromes Linked to Exposure to Pollutants and Other Substances in Outdoor and Indoor Environments Such as Lead, Asbestos, Formaldehyde, Mercury, Emissions, Noise, and More*

Edited by Allan R. Cook. 620 pages. 1997. 0-7808-0083-4. $78.

**"Recommended reference source."**
*— Booklist, American Library Association, Sep '98*

## Ethnic Diseases Sourcebook

*Basic Consumer Health Information for Ethnic and Racial Minority Groups in the United States, Including General Health Indicators and Behaviors, Ethnic Diseases, Genetic Testing, the Impact of Chronic Diseases, Women's Health, Mental Health Issues, and Preventive Health Care Services*

*Along with a Glossary and a Listing of Additional Resources*

Edited by Joyce Brennfleck Shannon. 600 pages. 2001. 0-7808-0336-1. $78.

## Family Planning Sourcebook

*Basic Consumer Health Information about Planning for Pregacy and Contraception, Including Traditional Methods, Barrier Methods, Hormonal Methods, Permanent Methods, Future Methods, Emergency Contraception, and Birth Control Choices for Women at Each Stage of Life*

*Along with Statistics, a Glossary, and Sources of Additional Information*

Edited by Amy Marcaccio Keyzer. 600 pages. 2001. 0-7808-0379-5. $78.

*SEE ALSO Pregnancy & Birth Sourcebook*

## Fitness & Exercise Sourcebook, 1st Edition

*Basic Information on Fitness and Exercise, Including Fitness Activities for Specific Age Groups, Exercise for People with Specific Medical Conditions, How to Begin a Fitness Program in Running, Walking, Swimming, Cycling, and Other Athletic Activities, and Recent Research in Fitness and Exercise*

Edited by Dan R. Harris. 663 pages. 1996. 0-7808-0186-5. $78.

## Fitness & Exercise Sourcebook, 2nd Edition

*Basic Consumer Health Information about the Fundamentals of Fitness and Exercise, Including How to Begin and Maintain a Fitness Program, Fitness as a Lifestyle, the Link between Fitness and Diet, Advice for Specific Groups of People, Exercise as It Relates to Specific Medical Conditions, and Recent Research in Fitness and Exercise*

*Along with a Glossary of Important Terms and Resources for Additional Help and Information*

Edited by Kristen M. Gledhill. 600 pages. 2001. 0-7808-0334-5. $78.

## Food & Animal Borne Diseases Sourcebook

*Basic Information about Diseases That Can Be Spread to Humans through the Ingestion of Contaminated Food or Water or by Contact with Infected Animals and Insects, Such as Botulism, E. Coli, Hepatitis A, Trichinosis, Lyme Disease, and Rabies*

*Along with Information Regarding Prevention and Treatment Methods, and Including a Special Section for International Travelers Describing Diseases Such as Cholera, Malaria, Travelers' Diarrhea, and Yellow Fever, and Offering Recommendations for Avoiding Illness*

Edited by Karen Bellenir and Peter D. Dresser. 535 pages. 1995. 0-7808-0033-8. $78.

## Food Safety Sourcebook

*Basic Consumer Health Information about the Safe Handling of Meat, Poultry, Seafood, Eggs, Fruit Juices, and Other Food Items, and Facts about Pesticides, Drinking Water, Food Safety Overseas, and the Onset, Duration, and Symptoms of Foodborne Illnesses, Including Types of Pathogenic Bacteria, Parasitic Protozoa, Worms, Viruses, and Natural Toxins*

*Along with the Role of the Consumer, the Food Handler, and the Government in Food Safety; a Glossary, and Resources for Additional Help and Information*

Edited by Dawn D. Matthews. 339 pages. 1999. 0-7808-0326-4. $48.

SEE ALSO Diet & Nutrition Sourcebook, 1st and 2nd Editions, Digestive Diseases & Disorders Sourcebook

# Forensic Medicine Sourcebook

Basic Consumer Information for the Layperson about Forensic Medicine, Including Crime Scene Investigation, Evidence Collection and Analysis, Expert Testimony, Computer-Aided Criminal Identification, Digital Imaging in the Courtroom, DNA Profiling, Accident Reconstruction, Autopsies, Ballistics, Drugs and Explosives Detection, Latent Fingerprints, Product Tampering, and Questioned Document Examination

Along with Statistical Data, a Glossary of Forensics Terminology, and Listings of Sources for Further Help and Information

Edited by Annemarie S. Muth. 574 pages. 1999. 0-7808-0232-2. $78.

# Gastrointestinal Diseases & Disorders Sourcebook

Basic Information about Gastroesophageal Reflux Disease (Heartburn), Ulcers, Diverticulosis, Irritable Bowel Syndrome, Crohn's Disease, Ulcerative Colitis, Diarrhea, Constipation, Lactose Intolerance, Hemorrhoids, Hepatitis, Cirrhosis, and Other Digestive Problems, Featuring Statistics, Descriptions of Symptoms, and Current Treatment Methods of Interest for Persons Living with Upper and Lower Gastrointestinal Maladies

Edited by Linda M. Ross. 413 pages. 1996. 0-7808-0078-8. $78.

# Genetic Disorders Sourcebook, 1st Edition

Basic Information about Heritable Diseases and Disorders Such as Down Syndrome, PKU, Hemophilia, Von Willebrand Disease, Gaucher Disease, Tay-Sachs Disease, and Sickle-Cell Disease, Along with Information about Genetic Screening, Gene Therapy, Home Care, and Including Source Listings for Further Help and Information on More Than 300 Disorders

Edited by Karen Bellenir. 642 pages. 1996. 0-7808-0034-6. $78.

# Genetic Disorders Sourcebook, 2nd Edition

Basic Consumer Health Information about Hereditary Diseases and Disorders, Including Cystic Fibrosis, Down Syndrome, Hemophilia, Huntington's Disease, Sickle Cell Anemia, and More; Facts about Genes, Gene Research and Therapy, Genetic Screening, Ethics of Gene Testing, Genetic Counseling, and Advice on Coping and Caring

Along with a Glossary of Genetic Terminology and a Resource List for Help, Support, and Further Information

Edited by Kathy Massimini. 650 pages. 2000. 0-7808-0241-1. $78.

# Head Trauma Sourcebook

Basic Information for the Layperson about Open-Head and Closed-Head Injuries, Treatment Advances, Recovery, and Rehabilitation

Along with Reports on Current Research Initiatives

Edited by Karen Bellenir. 414 pages. 1997. 0-7808-0208-X. $78.

# Health Insurance Sourcebook

Basic Information about Managed Care Organizations, Traditional Fee-for-Service Insurance, Insurance Portability and Pre-Existing Conditions Clauses, Medicare, Medicaid, Social Security, and Military Health Care

Along with Information about Insurance Fraud

Edited by Wendy Wilcox. 530 pages. 1997. 0-7808-0222-5. $78.

"Particularly useful because it brings much of this information together in one volume. This book will be a handy reference source in the health sciences library, hospital library, college and university library, and medium to large public library."
— *Medical Reference Services Quarterly, Fall '98*

**Awarded "Books of the Year Award"**
— *American Journal of Nursing, 1997*

"The layout of the book is particularly helpful as it provides easy access to reference material. A most useful addition to the vast amount of information about health insurance. The use of data from U.S. government agencies is most commendable. Useful in a library or learning center for healthcare professional students."
— *Doody's Health Sciences Book Reviews, Nov '97*

---

# Healthy Aging Sourcebook

Basic Consumer Health Information about Maintaining Health through the Aging Process, Including Advice on Nutrition, Exercise, and Sleep, Help in Making Decisions about Midlife Issues and Retirement, and Guidance Concerning Practical and Informed Choices in Health Consumerism

Along with Data Concerning the Theories of Aging, Different Experiences in Aging by Minority Groups, and Facts about Aging Now and Aging in the Future; and Featuring a Glossary, a Guide to Consumer Help, Additional Suggested Reading, and Practical Resource Directory

Edited by Jenifer Swanson. 536 pages. 1999. 0-7808-0390-6. $78.

"Recommended reference source."
— *Booklist, American Library Association, Feb '00*

*SEE ALSO* Physical & Mental Issues in Aging Sourcebook

---

# Healthy Heart Sourcebook for Women

Basic Consumer Health Information about Cardiac Issues Specific to Women, Including Facts about Major Risk Factors and Prevention, Treatment and Control Strategies, and Important Dietary Issues

Along with a Special Section Regarding the Pros and Cons of Hormone Replacement Therapy and Its Impact on Heart Health, and Additional Help, Including Recipes, a Glossary, and a Directory of Resources

Edited by Dawn D. Matthews. 336 pages. 2000. 0-7808-0329-9. $48.

*SEE ALSO* Cardiovascular Diseases & Disorders Sourcebook, 1st Edition, Heart Diseases & Disorders Sourcebook, 2nd Edition, Women's Health Concerns Sourcebook

---

# Heart Diseases & Disorders Sourcebook, 2nd Edition

Basic Consumer Health Information about Heart Attacks, Angina, Rhythm Disorders, Heart Failure, Valve Disease, Congenital Heart Disorders, and More, Including Descriptions of Surgical Procedures and Other Interventions, Medications, Cardiac Rehabilitation, Risk Identification, and Prevention Tips

Along with Statistical Data, Reports on Current Research Initiatives, a Glossary of Cardiovascular Terms, and Resource Directory

Edited by Karen Bellenir. 612 pages. 2000. 0-7808-0238-1. $78.

*SEE ALSO* Cardiovascular Diseases & Disorders Sourcebook, 1st Edition, Healthy Heart Sourcebook for Women

---

# Immune System Disorders Sourcebook

Basic Information about Lupus, Multiple Sclerosis, Guillain-Barré Syndrome, Chronic Granulomatous Disease, and More

Along with Statistical and Demographic Data and Reports on Current Research Initiatives

Edited by Allan R. Cook. 608 pages. 1997. 0-7808-0209-8. $78.

---

# Infant & Toddler Health Sourcebook

Basic Consumer Health Information about the Physical and Mental Development of Newborns, Infants, and Toddlers, Including Neonatal Concerns, Nutrition Recommendations, Immunization Schedules, Common Pediatric Disorders, Assessments and Milestones, Safety Tips, and Advice for Parents and Other Caregivers

Along with a Glossary of Terms and Resource Listings for Additional Help

Edited by Jenifer Swanson. 585 pages. 2000. 0-7808-0246-2. $78.

---

# Kidney & Urinary Tract Diseases & Disorders Sourcebook

Basic Information about Kidney Stones, Urinary Incontinence, Bladder Disease, End Stage Renal Disease, Dialysis, and More

Along with Statistical and Demographic Data and Reports on Current Research Initiatives

Edited by Linda M. Ross. 602 pages. 1997. 0-7808-0079-6. $78.

# Learning Disabilities Sourcebook

*Basic Information about Disorders Such as Dyslexia, Visual and Auditory Processing Deficits, Attention Deficit/Hyperactivity Disorder, and Autism*

*Along with Statistical and Demographic Data, Reports on Current Research Initiatives, an Explanation of the Assessment Process, and a Special Section for Adults with Learning Disabilities*

Edited by Linda M. Shin. 579 pages. 1998. 0-7808-0210-1. $78.

**Named "Oustanding Reference Book of 1999."**
— *New York Public Library, Feb 2000*

**"An excellent candidate for inclusion in a public library reference section. It's a great source of information. Teachers will also find the book useful. Definitely worth reading."**
— *Journal of Adolescent & Adult Literacy, Feb 2000*

**"Readable . . . provides a solid base of information regarding successful techniques used with individuals who have learning disabilities, as well as practical suggestions for educators and family members. Clear language, concise descriptions, and pertinent information for contacting multiple resources add to the strength of this book as a useful tool."**
— *Choice, Association of College and Research Libraries, Feb '99*

**"Recommended reference source."**
— *Booklist, American Library Association, Sep '98*

**"This is a useful resource for libraries and for those who don't have the time to identify and locate the individual publications."**
— *Disability Resources Monthly, Sep '98*

■

# Liver Disorders Sourcebook

*Basic Consumer Health Information about the Liver and How It Works; Liver Diseases, Including Cancer, Cirrhosis, Hepatitis, and Toxic and Drug Related Diseases; Tips for Maintaining a Healthy Liver; Laboratory Tests, Radiology Tests, and Facts about Liver Transplantation*

*Along with a Section on Support Groups, a Glossary, and Resource Listings*

Edited by Joyce Brennfleck Shannon. 591 pages. 2000. 0-7808-0383-3. $78.

**"Recommended reference source."**
— *Booklist, American Library Association, Jun '00*

■

# Medical Tests Sourcebook

*Basic Consumer Health Information about Medical Tests, Including Periodic Health Exams, General Screening Tests, Tests You Can Do at Home, Findings of the U.S. Preventive Services Task Force, X-ray and Radiology Tests, Electrical Tests, Tests of Blood and Other Body Fluids and Tissues, Scope Tests, Lung Tests, Genetic Tests, Pregnancy Tests, Newborn Screening Tests, Sexually Transmitted Disease Tests, and Computer Aided Diagnoses*

*Along with a Section on Paying for Medical Tests, a Glossary, and Resource Listings*

Edited by Joyce Brennfleck Shannon. 691 pages. 1999. 0-7808-0243-8. $78.

**"A valuable reference guide."**
— *American Reference Books Annual, 2000*

**"Recommended for hospital and health sciences libraries with consumer health collections."**
— *E-Streams, Mar '00*

**"This is an overall excellent reference with a wealth of general knowledge that may aid those who are reluctant to get vital tests performed."**
— *Today's Librarian, Jan 2000*

■

# Men's Health Concerns Sourcebook

*Basic Information about Health Issues That Affect Men, Featuring Facts about the Top Causes of Death in Men, Including Heart Disease, Stroke, Cancers, Prostate Disorders, Chronic Obstructive Pulmonary Disease, Pneumonia and Influenza, Human Immunodeficiency Virus and Acquired Immune Deficiency Syndrome, Diabetes Mellitus, Stress, Suicide, Accidents and Homicides; and Facts about Common Concerns for Men, Including Impotence, Contraception, Circumcision, Sleep Disorders, Snoring, Hair Loss, Diet, Nutrition, Exercise, Kidney and Urological Disorders, and Backaches*

Edited by Allan R. Cook. 738 pages. 1998. 0-7808-0212-8. $78.

**"This comprehensive resource and the series are highly recommended."**
— *American Reference Books Annual, 2000*

**"Recommended reference source."**
— *Booklist, American Library Association, Dec '98*

■

# Mental Health Disorders Sourcebook, 1st Edition

*Basic Information about Schizophrenia, Depression, Bipolar Disorder, Panic Disorder, Obsessive-Compulsive Disorder, Phobias and Other Anxiety Disorders, Paranoia and Other Personality Disorders, Eating Disorders, and Sleep Disorders*

*Along with Information about Treatment and Therapies*

Edited by Karen Bellenir. 548 pages. 1995. 0-7808-0040-0. $78.

**"This is an excellent new book . . . written in easy-to-understand language."** — *Booklist Health Sciences Supplement, American Library Association, Oct '97*

**". . . useful for public and academic libraries and consumer health collections."**
— *Medical Reference Services Quarterly, Spring '97*

**"The great strengths of the book are its readability and its inclusion of places to find more information. Especially recommended."** — *Reference Quarterly, American Library Association, Winter '96*

1059

## Mental Health Disorders Sourcebook, 2nd Edition

*Basic Consumer Health Information about Anxiety Disorders, Depression and Other Mood Disorders, Eating Disorders, Personality Disorders, Schizophrenia, and More, Including Disease Descriptions, Treatment Options, and Reports on Current Research Initiatives*

*Along with Statistical Data, Tips for Maintaining Mental Health, a Glossary, and Directory of Sources for Additional Help and Information*

Edited by Karen Bellenir. 605 pages. 2000. 0-7808-0240-3. $78.

## Mental Retardation Sourcebook

*Basic Consumer Health Information about Mental Retardation and Its Causes, Including Down Syndrome, Fetal Alcohol Syndrome, Fragile X Syndrome, Genetic Conditions, Injury, and Environmental Sources*

*Along with Preventive Strategies, Parenting Issues, Educational Implications, Health Care Needs, Employment and Economic Matters, Legal Issues, a Glossary, and a Resource Listing for Additional Help and Information*

Edited by Joyce Brennfleck Shannon. 642 pages. 2000. 0-7808-0377-9. $78.

"From preventing retardation to parenting and family challenges, this covers health, social and legal issues and will prove an invaluable overview."
— *Reviewer's Bookwatch, Jul '00*

## Obesity Sourcebook

*Basic Consumer Health Information about Diseases and Other Problems Associated with Obesity, and Including Facts about Risk Factors, Prevention Issues, and Management Approaches*

*Along with Statistical and Demographic Data, Information about Special Populations, Research Updates, a Glossary, and Source Listings for Further Help and Information*

Edited by Wilma Caldwell and Chad T. Kimball. 400 pages. 2001. 0-7808-0333-7. $48.

## Ophthalmic Disorders Sourcebook

*Basic Information about Glaucoma, Cataracts, Macular Degeneration, Strabismus, Refractive Disorders, and More*

*Along with Statistical and Demographic Data and Reports on Current Research Initiatives*

Edited by Linda M. Ross. 631 pages. 1996. 0-7808-0081-8. $78.

## Oral Health Sourcebook

*Basic Information about Diseases and Conditions Affecting Oral Health, Including Cavities, Gum Disease, Dry Mouth, Oral Cancers, Fever Blisters, Canker Sores, Oral Thrush, Bad Breath, Temporomandibular Disorders, and other Craniofacial Syndromes*

*Along with Statistical Data on the Oral Health of Americans, Oral Hygiene, Emergency First Aid, Information on Treatment Procedures and Methods of Replacing Lost Teeth*

Edited by Allan R. Cook. 558 pages. 1997. 0-7808-0082-6. $78.

"Unique source which will fill a gap in dental sources for patients and the lay public. A valuable reference tool even in a library with thousands of books on dentistry. Comprehensive, clear, inexpensive, and easy to read and use. It fills an enormous gap in the health care literature." — *Reference and User Services Quarterly, American Library Association, Summer '98*

"Recommended reference source."
— *Booklist, American Library Association, Dec '97*

## Osteoporosis Sourcebook

*Basic Consumer Health Information about Primary and Secondary Osteoporosis, Juvenile Osteoporosis, Related Conditions, and Other Such Bone Disorders as Fibrous Dysplasia, Myeloma, Osteogenesis Imperfecta, Osteopetrosis, and Paget's Disease*

*Along with Information about Risk Factors, Treatments, Traditional and Non-Traditional Pain Management, and Including a Glossary and Resource Directory*

Edited by Allan R. Cook. 600 pages. 2001. 0-7808-0239-X. $78.

*SEE ALSO Women's Health Concerns Sourcebook*

## Pain Sourcebook

*Basic Information about Specific Forms of Acute and Chronic Pain, Including Headaches, Back Pain, Muscular Pain, Neuralgia, Surgical Pain, and Cancer Pain*

*Along with Pain Relief Options Such as Analgesics, Narcotics, Nerve Blocks, Transcutaneous Nerve Stimulation, and Alternative Forms of Pain Control, Including Biofeedback, Imaging, Behavior Modification, and Relaxation Techniques*

Edited by Allan R. Cook. 667 pages. 1997. 0-7808-0213-6. $78.

"The text is readable, easily understood, and well indexed. This excellent volume belongs in all patient education libraries, consumer health sections of public libraries, and many personal collections."
— *American Reference Books Annual, 1999*

"A beneficial reference." — *Booklist Health Sciences Supplement, American Library Association, Oct '98*

"The information is basic in terms of scholarship and is appropriate for general readers. Written in journalistic style . . . intended for non-professionals. Quite thorough in its coverage of different pain conditions and summarizes the latest clinical information regarding pain treatment." — *Choice, Association of College and Research Libraries, Jun '98*

"Recommended reference source."
— *Booklist, American Library Association, Mar '98*

## Pediatric Cancer Sourcebook

*Basic Consumer Health Information about Leukemias, Brain Tumors, Sarcomas, Lymphomas, and Other Cancers in Infants, Children, and Adolescents, Including Descriptions of Cancers, Treatments, and Coping Strategies*

*Along with Suggestions for Parents, Caregivers, and Concerned Relatives, a Glossary of Cancer Terms, and Resource Listings*

Edited by Edward J. Prucha. 587 pages. 1999. 0-7808-0245-4. $78.

"A valuable addition to all libraries specializing in health services and many public libraries."
— *American Reference Books Annual, 2000*

"Recommended reference source."
— *Booklist, American Library Association, Feb '00*

"An excellent source of information. Recommended for public, hospital, and health science libraries with consumer health collections." — *E-Stream, Jun '00*

## Physical & Mental Issues in Aging Sourcebook

*Basic Consumer Health Information on Physical and Mental Disorders Associated with the Aging Process, Including Concerns about Cardiovascular Disease, Pulmonary Disease, Oral Health, Digestive Disorders, Musculoskeletal and Skin Disorders, Metabolic Changes, Sexual and Reproductive Issues, and Changes in Vision, Hearing, and Other Senses*

*Along with Data about Longevity and Causes of Death, Information on Acute and Chronic Pain, Descriptions of Mental Concerns, a Glossary of Terms, and Resource Listings for Additional Help*

Edited by Jenifer Swanson. 660 pages. 1999. 0-7808-0233-0. $78.

"Recommended for public libraries."
— *American Reference Books Annual, 2000*

"This is a treasure of health information for the layperson." — *Choice Health Sciences Supplement, Association of College & Research Libraries, May 2000*

"Recommended reference source."
— *Booklist, American Library Association, Oct '99*

**SEE ALSO** *Healthy Aging Sourcebook*

## Podiatry Sourcebook

*Basic Consumer Health Information about Foot Conditions, Diseases, and Injuries, Including Bunions, Corns, Calluses, Athlete's Foot, Plantar Warts, Hammertoes and Clawtoes, Club Foot, Heel Pain, Gout, and More*

*Along with Facts about Foot Care, Disease Prevention, Foot Safety, Choosing a Foot Care Specialist, a Glossary of Terms, and Resource Listings for Additional Information*

Edited by M. Lisa Weatherford. 600 pages. 2001. 0-7808-0215-2. $78.

## Pregnancy & Birth Sourcebook

*Basic Information about Planning for Pregnancy, Maternal Health, Fetal Growth and Development, Labor and Delivery, Postpartum and Perinatal Care, Pregnancy in Mothers with Special Concerns, and Disorders of Pregnancy, Including Genetic Counseling, Nutrition and Exercise, Obstetrical Tests, Pregnancy Discomfort, Multiple Births, Cesarean Sections, Medical Testing of Newborns, Breastfeeding, Gestational Diabetes, and Ectopic Pregnancy*

Edited by Heather E. Aldred. 737 pages. 1997. 0-7808-0216-0. $78.

"A well-organized handbook. Recommended."
— *Choice, Association of College and Research Libraries, Apr '98*

"Reecommended reference source."
— *Booklist, American Library Association, Mar '98*

"Recommended for public libraries."
— *American Reference Books Annual, 1998*

**SEE ALSO** *Congenital Disorders Sourcebook, Family Planning Sourcebook*

## Public Health Sourcebook

*Basic Information about Government Health Agencies, Including National Health Statistics and Trends, Healthy People 2000 Program Goals and Objectives, the Centers for Disease Control and Prevention, the Food and Drug Administration, and the National Institutes of Health*

*Along with Full Contact Information for Each Agency*

Edited by Wendy Wilcox. 698 pages. 1998. 0-7808-0220-9. $78.

"Recommended reference source."
— *Booklist, American Library Association, Sep '98*

"This consumer guide provides welcome assistance in navigating the maze of federal health agencies and their data on public health concerns."
— *SciTech Book News, Sep '98*

## Reconstructive & Cosmetic Surgery Sourcebook

*Basic Consumer Health Information on Cosmetic and Reconstructive Plastic Surgery, Including Statistical Information about Different Surgical Procedures, Things to Consider Prior to Surgery, Plastic Surgery Techniques and Tools, Emotional and Psychological Considerations, and Procedure-Specific Information*

*Along with a Glossary of Terms and a Listing of Resources for Additional Help and Information*

Edited by M. Lisa Weatherford. 400 pages. 2001. 0-7808-0214-4. $48.

■

## Rehabilitation Sourcebook

*Basic Consumer Health Information about Rehabilitation for People Recovering from Heart Surgery, Spinal Cord Injury, Stroke, Orthopedic Impairments, Amputation, Pulmonary Impairments, Traumatic Injury, and More, Including Physical Therapy, Occupational Therapy, Speech/ Language Therapy, Massage Therapy, Dance Therapy, Art Therapy, and Recreational Therapy*

*Along with Information on Assistive and Adaptive Devices, a Glossary, and Resources for Additional Help and Information*

Edited by Dawn D. Matthews. 531 pages. 1999. 0-7808-0236-5. $78.

**"Recommended reference source."**
   *—Booklist, American Library Association, May '00*

■

## Respiratory Diseases & Disorders Sourcebook

*Basic Information about Respiratory Diseases and Disorders, Including Asthma, Cystic Fibrosis, Pneumonia, the Common Cold, Influenza, and Others, Featuring Facts about the Respiratory System, Statistical and Demographic Data, Treatments, Self-Help Management Suggestions, and Current Research Initiatives*

Edited by Allan R. Cook and Peter D. Dresser. 771 pages. 1995. 0-7808-0037-0. $78.

**"Designed for the layperson and for patients and their families coping with respiratory illness. . . . an extensive array of information on diagnosis, treatment, management, and prevention of respiratory illnesses for the general reader."**          *— Choice, Association of College and Research Libraries, Jun '96*

**"A highly recommended text for all collections. It is a comforting reminder of the power of knowledge that good books carry between their covers."**
   *—Academic Library Book Review, Spring '96*

**"A comprehensive collection of authoritative information presented in a nontechnical, humanitarian style for patients, families, and caregivers."**
   *—Association of Operating Room Nurses, Sep/Oct '95*

## Sexually Transmitted Diseases Sourcebook

*Basic Information about Herpes, Chlamydia, Gonorrhea, Hepatitis, Nongonoccocal Urethritis, Pelvic Inflammatory Disease, Syphilis, AIDS, and More*

*Along with Current Data on Treatments and Preventions*

Edited by Linda M. Ross. 550 pages. 1997. 0-7808-0217-9. $78.

■

## Sexually Transmitted Diseases Sourcebook, 2nd Edition

*Basic Consumer Health Information about Sexually Transmitted Diseases, Including Information on the Diagnosis and Treatment of Chlamydia, Gonorrhea, Hepatitis, Herpes, HIV, Mononucleosis, Syphilis, and Others*

*Along with Information on Prevention, Such as Condom Use, Vaccines, and STD Education; And Featuring a Section on Issues Related to Youth and Adolescents, a Glossary, and Resources for Additional Help and Information*

Edited by Dawn D. Matthews. 600 pages. 2000. 0-7808-0249-7. $78.

■

## Skin Disorders Sourcebook

*Basic Information about Common Skin and Scalp Conditions Caused by Aging, Allergies, Immune Reactions, Sun Exposure, Infectious Organisms, Parasites, Cosmetics, and Skin Traumas, Including Abrasions, Cuts, and Pressure Sores*

*Along with Information on Prevention and Treatment*

Edited by Allan R. Cook. 647 pages. 1997. 0-7808-0080-X. $78.

**". . . comprehensive, easily read reference book."**
   *—Doody's Health Sciences Book Reviews, Oct '97*

***SEE ALSO** Burns Sourcebook*

■

## Sleep Disorders Sourcebook

*Basic Consumer Health Information about Sleep and Its Disorders, Including Insomnia, Sleepwalking, Sleep Apnea, Restless Leg Syndrome, and Narcolepsy*

*Along with Data about Shiftwork and Its Effects, Information on the Societal Costs of Sleep Deprivation, Descriptions of Treatment Options, a Glossary of Terms, and Resource Listings for Additional Help*

Edited by Jenifer Swanson. 439 pages. 1998. 0-7808-0234-9. $78.

**"This text will complement any home or medical library. It is user-friendly and ideal for the adult reader."**
   *—American Reference Books Annual, 2000*

**"Recommended reference source."**
   *—Booklist, American Library Association, Feb '99*

"A useful resource that provides accurate, relevant, and accessible information on sleep to the general public. Health care providers who deal with sleep disorders patients may also find it helpful in being prepared to answer some of the questions patients ask."
— *Respiratory Care, Jul '99*

## Sports Injuries Sourcebook

*Basic Consumer Health Information about Common Sports Injuries, Prevention of Injury in Specific Sports, Tips for Training, and Rehabilitation from Injury*

*Along with Information about Special Concerns for Children, Young Girls in Athletic Training Programs, Senior Athletes, and Women Athletes, and a Directory of Resources for Further Help and Information*

Edited by Heather E. Aldred. 624 pages. 1999. 0-7808-0218-7. $78.

"Public libraries and undergraduate academic libraries will find this book useful for its nontechnical language." — *American Reference Books Annual, 2000*

"While this easy-to-read book is recommended for all libraries, it should prove to be especially useful for public, high school, and academic libraries; certainly it should be on the bookshelf of every school gymnasium." — *E-Streams, Mar '00*

## Substance Abuse Sourcebook

*Basic Health-Related Information about the Abuse of Legal and Illegal Substances Such as Alcohol, Tobacco, Prescription Drugs, Marijuana, Cocaine, and Heroin; and Including Facts about Substance Abuse Prevention Strategies, Intervention Methods, Treatment and Recovery Programs, and a Section Addressing the Special Problems Related to Substance Abuse during Pregnancy*

Edited by Karen Bellenir. 573 pages. 1996. 0-7808-0038-9. $78.

"A valuable addition to any health reference section. Highly recommended." — *The Book Report, Mar/Apr '97*

". . . a comprehensive collection of substance abuse information that's both highly readable and compact. Families and caregivers of substance abusers will find the information enlightening and helpful, while teachers, social workers and journalists should benefit from the concise format. Recommended." — *Drug Abuse Update, Winter '96/'97*

***SEE ALSO*** *Alcoholism Sourcebook, Drug Abuse Sourcebook*

## Traveler's Health Sourcebook

*Basic Consumer Health Information for Travelers, Including Physical and Medical Preparations, Transportation Health and Safety, Essential Information about Food and Water, Sun Exposure, Insect and Snake*

*Bites, Camping and Wilderness Medicine, and Travel with Physical or Medical Disabilities*

*Along with International Travel Tips, Vaccination Recommendations, Geographical Health Issues, Disease Risks, a Glossary, and a Listing of Additional Resources*

Edited by Joyce Brennfleck Shannon. 613 pages. 2000. 0-7808-0384-1. $78.

## Women's Health Concerns Sourcebook

*Basic Information about Health Issues That Affect Women, Featuring Facts about Menstruation and Other Gynecological Concerns, Including Endometriosis, Fibroids, Menopause, and Vaginitis; Reproductive Concerns, Including Birth Control, Infertility, and Abortion; and Facts about Additional Physical, Emotional, and Mental Health Concerns Prevalent among Women Such as Osteoporosis, Urinary Tract Disorders, Eating Disorders, and Depression*

*Along with Tips for Maintaining a Healthy Lifestyle*

Edited by Heather E. Aldred. 567 pages. 1997. 0-7808-0219-5. $78.

"Handy compilation. There is an impressive range of diseases, devices, disorders, procedures, and other physical and emotional issues covered . . . well organized, illustrated, and indexed." — *Choice, Association of College and Research Libraries, Jan '98*

***SEE ALSO*** *Breast Cancer Sourcebook, Cancer Sourcebook for Women, 1st and 2nd Editions, Healthy Heart Sourcebook for Women, Osteoporosis Sourcebook*

## Workplace Health & Safety Sourcebook

*Basic Consumer Health Information about Workplace Health and Safety, Including the Effect of Workplace Hazards on the Lungs, Skin, Heart, Ears, Eyes, Brain, Reproductive Organs, Musculoskeletal System, and Other Organs and Body Parts*

*Along with Information about Occupational Cancer, Personal Protective Equipment, Toxic and Hazardous Chemicals, Child Labor, Stress, and Workplace Violence*

Edited by Chad T. Kimball. 626 pages. 2000. 0-7808-0231-4. $78.

## Worldwide Health Sourcebook

*Basic Information about Global Health Issues, Including Malnutrition, Reproductive Health, Disease Dispersion and Prevention, Emerging Diseases, Risky Health Behaviors, and the Leading Causes of Death*

*Along with Global Health Concerns for Children, Women, and the Elderly, Mental Health Issues, Re-*

*search and Technology Advancements, and Economic, Environmental, and Political Health Implications, a Glossary, and a Resource Listing for Additional Help and Information*

Edited by Joyce Brennfleck Shannon. 500 pages. 2001. 0-7808-0330-2. $78.

■

# Health Reference Series Cumulative Index 1999

*A Comprehensive Index to the Individual Volumes of the Health Reference Series, Including a Subject Index, Name Index, Organization Index, and Publication Index;*

*Along with a Master List of Acronyms and Abbreviations*

Edited by Edward J. Prucha, Anne Holmes, and Robert Rudnick. 990 pages. 2000. 0-7808-0382-5. $78.